Microeconomics

THEORY / APPLICATIONS

Shorter Sixth Edition

Companion volumes prepared by

E D W I N   M A N S F I E L D

———————————

Microeconomic Problems:
Case Studies and Exercises for Review
Sixth Edition

Microeconomics: Selected Readings
Fifth Edition

EDWIN MANSFIELD

UNIVERSITY OF PENNSYLVANIA

Microeconomics

THEORY/APPLICATIONS

Shorter Sixth Edition

W · W · NORTON & COMPANY

NEW YORK · LONDON

The text of this book is composed in photocomposition Century Schoolbook, with
display type set in Meridien Medium and Prisma. Composition by New England
Typographic Service, Inc. Manufacturing by The Maple-Vail Book Group. Page
makeup by Ben Gamit. Book design by Marjorie J. Flock. Cover photography
courtesy J. Fennell, Bruce Coleman, Inc.

TO DIXIE

*who once again asked that this dedication be
as short as possible*

Library of Congress Cataloging-in-Publication Data
Mansfield, Edwin.

    Microeconomics: theory and applications.
    Bibliography: p.
    Includes index.
    1. Microeconomics.   I. Title.
HB172.M36 1988   338.5   87–22131

ISBN 0-393-95637-7

W. W. Norton & Company, Inc., 500 Fifth Avenue, New York, N.Y. 10110
W. W. Norton & Company Ltd., 37 Great Russell Street, London WC1B 3NU

1 2 3 4 5 6 7 8 9 0

Contents

PART 2

Consumer Behavior and Market Demand

PART 3

The Firm: Its Technology and Costs

P A R T   4

Market Structure, Price, and Output

PART 5

Markets for Inputs

PART 6

Welfare Economics and General Equilibrium Analysis

Preface / *Shorter Sixth Edition*

This is an abridged version of the sixth edition of my text *Microeconomics: Theory and Applications*. Specialized topics such as linear programming, benefit-cost analysis, intertemporal choice, decision-making under risk and uncertainty, and technological change have been eliminated. Also deleted are more advanced materials and footnotes which contain mathematical derivations. This shorter version is intended for use in courses where these materials are not needed. The emphasis is on clear and interesting exposition of the essentials of microeconomics.

Microeconomics is a dynamic field with an expanding core of basic theory and a growing range of applications. In a textbook, as in the classroom, it is important that there be a proper balance between classic and more modern approaches and ideas. My top priority in this edition has been to expand the coverage of relatively new theoretical models and concepts, as well as to make sure that the applications and examples continue to deal fully with the problems of today.

The chapters on monopolistic competition (Chapter 10) and oligopoly (Chapter 11) have been completely rewritten. In Chapter 10, major new sections have been added on advertising, including (1) a detailed treatment of the Dorfman-Steiner rule for optimal advertising expenditures, and (2) a discussion of the social value of advertising. Less emphasis is put on the Chamberlin model and its frailties, although this model is still treated fully. I believe that this new chapter has a more modern and less historical character than its predecessor.

In Chapter 11, entirely new sections have been added on (1) entry deterrence (from a game theoretic viewpoint), (2) the Prisoner's Dilemma, (3) Nash equilibria, (4) repeated Prisoner's Dilemma and "tit for tat," and (5) contestable markets. The material on cost-plus pricing has been expanded and sharpened, and has been moved to a chapter appendix. Much more emphasis has been put on modern game theory, although the treatment continues to be designed for students with a modest mathematical background. As in Chapter 10, the revision is designed to modernize the treatment without making it any more difficult.

A major effort has also been made to update the examples and to add new studies indicating how microeconomics can illuminate the pressing problems facing the American economy in the late 1980s and early 1990s. More emphasis is placed on relatively new industries like robots, computers, aircraft, and biotechnology. For example, there is a new boxed example on robotics in Chapter 11.

A large amount of fresh empirical material has been added, ranging from the replacement of Alcoa by De Beers in Chapter 9 to the substitution of the following six new boxed examples for old ones: (1) The 1983 Increase in the Cigarette Tax: How Much Was Passed On to Consumers? (2) The Demand for Cigarettes in the United States, (3) Analyzing New York's Shortage of Rental Housing, (4) Speculation and the Coffee Market, (5) Entry and Exit in the Beer Industry, and (6) The Brave New World of Robotics.

In Part Five, there is a new cross-chapter case, "Sex Discrimination and Comparable Worth," an interesting and timely example. (The material on the negative income tax, which it replaces, has been transferred to a long end-of-chapter problem.) Also, each of the cross-chapter cases has been moved to the end of its part of the book, and about a half-dozen analytical questions have been added to each one. The answers to these questions are provided at the end of the book. In my opinion, these questions are a valuable addition because they force the student to think more carefully about the cases and to play a more active role in their analysis.

Finally, a glossary of terms has been added. This new feature should enable students to thread their way more efficiently and easily through the minefields of economic terminology. Also, a number of new end-of-chapter exercises have been added, and a variety of small changes have been inserted to make the discussion more current. Each sentence has been gone over with an eye toward improvement.

As with the previous editions, a workbook and reader accompany the text. *Microeconomic Problems: Case Studies and Exercises for Review*, sixth edition, has been revised, making it more effective in guiding students toward an understanding of the theories comprising and underlying microeconomics. In particular, new problems and questions have been added in each chapter that test students' skills in applying microeconomic theory to real-world situations. *Microeconomic Problems* now contains about 1,100 questions and problems, together with their solutions.

Microeconomics: Selected Readings, fifth edition, includes papers on topics such as the demand for lemons, market signaling, laboratory experimentation in economics, recent antitrust cases, predatory behavior, and the economic implications of robots, among many others. In my opinion, this reader continues to be broader and more varied than other books of readings at the intermediate level.

An *Instructor's Manual* is available for the text. In addition to teaching suggestions for each chapter, it includes a test bank of multiple-choice questions and problem sets which not only reflects the decision-making emphasis of the text, but also develops theory as a set of principles that yields insights into everyday problems. Paul Sommers and William Gunther, the authors of the *Instructor's Manual,* have created a freshly varied diet of teaching materials for this new edition, and this is the place to record my thanks to them.

Test questions also are available to instructors on floppy disks for use with a personal computer. Information on obtaining these disks can be obtained from the publisher.

Since it would be impossible to list all of the many instructors and reviewers who have contributed in important ways to this and the previous editions, I must be content with thanking only a sample: Allan Braff, University of New Hampshire; Stephen R. Brenner, Grinnell College; Byron Brown, Michigan State University; Eleanor Brown, Pomona College; Neil Bruce, Queen's University; James Cairns, Royal Military College of Canada; Joseph Cammarosano, Fordham University; Alvin Cohen, Lehigh University; Marshall Colberg, Florida State University; Avinash Dixit, Princeton University; James Dolan, Regis College; Robert Dorfman, Harvard University; Catherine Eckel, Virginia Polytechnic Institute; Allan Feldman, Brown University; Alan Fisher, California State University at Fullerton; J. Fred Giertz, Miami University; Ellen Goldstein, California State University at Fullerton; Warren Gramm, Washington State University; William Gunther, University of Alabama; Kanji Haitani, State University of New York, Fredonia; Richard Harmstone, Pennsylvania State University; William Holohan, University of Wisconsin at Milwaukee; Jonathan Kesselman, University of British Columbia; Charles Knoeber, North Carolina State University; Steven Kohlhagen, University of California, Berkeley; Shou-Eng Koo, Indiana University and Purdue University; John Laitner, University of Michigan; Richard Levin, Yale University; J. Patrick Lewis, Otterbein College; C. Richard Long, Georgia State University; Paul Malatesta, Colgate University; M. R. Metzger, George Washington University; Edwin Mills, Princeton University; Hajime

Miyazaki, Stanford University; David Molina, North Texas State University; John Murphy, Canisius College; Richard Musgrave, Harvard University; K. R. Nair, West Virginia Wesleyan College; John Neufeld, University of North Carolina; Mancur Olson, University of Maryland; John Palmer, University of Western Ontario; R. D. Peterson, Colorado State University; Charles Plourde, York University; Robert Pollak, University of Pennsylvania; Richard Porter, University of Michigan; Charles Ratliff, Davidson College; Thomas Riddell, Bucknell University; Ray Roberts, Jr., Furman University; Anthony Romeo, University of Connecticut; Robert E. Rosenman, Washington State University; Anthony Rufolo, Federal Reserve Bank of Philadelphia; Sol S. Shalit, University of Wisconsin at Milwaukee; Barry Siegel, University of Oregon; N. J. Simler, University of Minnesota; A. Michael Spence, Harvard University; James Stephenson, Iowa State University; Daniel Sullivan, Northwestern University; Richard Sylla, North Carolina State University; W. James Truitt, Baylor University; Gordon Tullock, Virginia Polytechnic Institute; Hal Varian, University of Michigan; David Vrooman, St. Lawrence University; Donal Walker, Indiana University of Pennsylvania; Joan Werner, University of Michigan; A. R. Whitaker, U.S. Naval Academy; Bronislaw Wojtun, Lemoyne-Owen College; Gary Yohe, Wesleyan University; and Richard Zeckhauser, Harvard University. Further, I would like to thank W. Drake McFeely of Norton for doing a fine job with the publishing end of the work. And special thanks go to my wife, who again helped in countless ways.

E. M.

Philadelphia, 1988

Introduction

1

The Nature of Microeconomics

INTRODUCTION

Derek Bok, Harvard's president, once said that, "If you think education is expensive, try ignorance." To be ignorant of economics is particularly expensive, since economics helps us to understand the nature and organization of our society, the arguments underlying many of the great public issues of the day, and the operation and behavior of business firms and other economic decision-making units. To perform effectively and responsibly as a citizen, an administrator, a worker, or a consumer, one needs to know some economics.

Precisely what does economics deal with? According to one standard definition, economics is concerned with the way in which resources are allocated among alternative uses to satisfy human wants. It is customary to divide economics into two parts: microeconomics and macro-economics. *Microeconomics* deals with the economic behavior of individual units such as consumers, firms, and resource owners; while macroeconomics deals with the behavior of economic aggregates such as gross national product and the level of employment.

Micro-economics

This book is concerned with microeconomics. A general definition of microeconomics fraught with vague words like *resources* and *human wants* is unlikely to communicate the power of microeconomic theory or its usefulness in solving major problems in the real world. So we begin our discussion by giving four examples of the kinds of problems that microeconomics can help to solve. (Each of these examples is considered in detail in subsequent chapters.) Although these four examples cover only a small sample of the questions to which microeconomics is relevant, they give you a reasonable first impression of the nature of microeconomics and its relevance to the real world.

OPTIMAL PRODUCTION DECISIONS

Business firms are constantly faced with the problem of choosing among alternative ways of manufacturing their products. Consider a manufacturer of personal computers. Suppose that the number of personal computers that this firm can produce per week is limited by the capacity of its manufacturing equipment and the amount of skilled labor it has available to carry out the work. The firm is considering the use of three manufacturing processes: processes 1, 2, and 3. Suppose that the firm knows that the profit per computer made with each of the processes is as shown in Table 1.1.

Table 1.1 CHARACTERISTICS OF THREE PROCESSES FOR MANUFACTURING PERSONAL COMPUTERS

	Process 1	Process 2	Process 3
Profit per computer (dollars)	100	90	110
Hours of skilled labor required per computer	40	50	35
Machine-hours of manufacturing equipment required per computer	30.0	25.0	52.5

For instance, each computer made with process 1 yields a profit of $100. Suppose that the number of hours of skilled labor and the number of machine-hours of manufacturing equipment required to make a computer with each process is as shown in Table 1.1. For example, process 1 requires the use of 30 machine-hours of manufacturing equipment and 40 hours of skilled labor per computer.

Under these circumstances, if 60,000 machine-hours per week is the maximum capacity of the manufacturing equipment and 80,000 hours per week is the maximum amount of skilled labor that the firm can hire, which processes should the firm use? And how many computers should be made using each process? This is an example of one type of problem that microeconomics is designed to solve. It is a problem faced by an individual firm that is trying to maximize its profit or attain some other set of objectives of its owners and managers. Microeconomics serves as the basis for, and is helpful in promoting an understanding of, the powerful modern tools of managerial decision-making that help to solve such problems.

These analytical tools are as applicable in Tokyo or Singapore as in New York or Toronto, and woe to the firm that ignores or misapplies them in this era of intense international competition. Gone are the days when firms in a handful of nations in North America and Europe were the only ones that used them in a sophisticated way. Now the Japanese and others set the standard with regard to production decisions of this sort in industries like steel and consumer electronics. Besides being useful throughout the world, these analytical tools are applicable to government as well as business. The techniques introduced in recent decades in many government agencies to promote better decision-making are fundamentally applications of microeconomics.[1]

PRICING POLICY

Most firms are also faced with the problem of pricing their products. For example, suppose that a firm is the sole producer of a product and that it can sell this product in California and Arizona, but that the law prohibits the product from being carried from one state to the other. The amount of the product that the firm can sell at various prices in California is shown in Table 1.2. Similarly, the amount of the product that the firm can sell at various prices in Arizona is also shown in Table 1.2. Since the product cannot be carried from one state to another, the firm is able to set different prices for the product in the two states. If it costs the firm $1.00 to produce each ton of product, what price should the firm charge in each state if it wants to maximize its profits?

Table 1.2 RELATIONSHIP BETWEEN PRICE AND QUANTITY SOLD IN ARIZONA AND CALIFORNIA

Arizona		California	
Price per ton in Arizona (dollars)	*Quantity sold in Arizona* (tons)	*Price per ton in California* (dollars)	*Quantity sold in California* (tons)
1.00	1,000	1.00	1,500
1.10	900	1.10	1,400
1.20	800	1.20	1,300
1.30	700	1.30	1,200
1.40	600	1.40	1,100
1.50	500	1.50	1,000
1.60	400	1.60	900

1. For the answer to the kind of problem posed in this section, see Chapter 7.

This kind of problem faces many, many firms. Since many goods and services cannot be resold, it is often possible for the producer of such goods or services to sell them at different prices to different groups of consumers. For example, an operation to cure a particular type of cancer may be $5,000 for a rich person and $1,000 for a poor person. In these cases—as well as in the simpler and more straightforward case where a firm's product can be sold only at a single price—it is important that the firm know how to set price to achieve its objectives. Microeconomics provides a basis for analyzing and solving such problems. When a management consultant is hired to help solve a problem of this sort, his or her recommendations, if sound, will rely heavily on the application of well-established principles of microeconomics.[2]

As in the case of the previous example, this problem may seem quite simple to solve, at least to some readers, and they may wonder why special techniques are required to solve such easy problems. The reason is that the problems that occur in real life often involve more variables and are more complicated than those presented in these two sections. The examples given here were constructed to illustrate the type of problems with which microeconomics attempts to deal, and for this purpose, it is best to strip the problem to the simplest essentials. But it would be very misleading to conclude that because trial-and-error methods—and patience—can produce a solution to these examples, such methods—and perhaps a little more patience—can also produce a solution to most real problems. Microeconomics attempts to provide techniques to help solve problems of this sort when trial-and-error and other such methods are not adequate.

OPTIMAL ALLOCATION OF A SOCIETY'S RESOURCES

In the previous two sections we were concerned with problems facing individual business firms. Although such problems are important and interesting, they are by no means the only type dealt with by microeconomics. On the contrary, much of microeconomics is concerned with problems that face us all as citizens. Together we must somehow decide how we want to organize the production and marketing of goods and services in our country. We must also decide how these goods and services are to be distributed among the people. Some of the subtlest and most significant applications of microeconomics are in this area.

In recent years, there has been a great deal of talk concerning the restructuring of various aspects of the economy. Some people charge that many basic American industries like steel and automobiles are unable to compete with their foreign rivals, and that fundamental changes should be made in govern-

---

2. For a description of the way in which a pricing problem like that described in this section can be solved, see Chapter 9.

ment policy concerning taxes, education, foreign trade, and a host of other topics influencing the competitiveness of American firms in world markets. Suppose that we ask the following basic question: If we could restructure the entire economic system and if we agreed that the goal was to make anyone better off (in terms of his or her own tastes) as long as this did not make someone else worse off (in terms of the latter's tastes), what sort of changes would we be justified in making? More specifically, suppose that we could take resources away from some sectors of the economy and provide them to other sectors, or that we could prohibit consumers from consuming certain goods, or that we could prohibit firms from laying off workers or charging certain prices. What actions of this sort (if any) would we be justified in taking?

Students sometimes complain that they are not confronted with significant or relevant questions. Surely such complaints cannot be lodged legitimately against this question! Having said this, it is important to add that microeconomics has progressed far enough to be able to provide at least partial answers to this kind of question, which is fortunate since the value of a field lies more in its power to answer questions than in the audacity with which it poses them. Nonetheless, one should not be encouraged to believe that microeconomics is the key that by itself will unlock the answers to the great social problems of the day. Microeconomics provides a way of thinking about many of these problems that is valuable, as indicated perhaps by the formidable number of economists appointed by both Democratic and Republican administrations to positions of great responsibility. But microeconomics, although valuable, is only one of many disciplines that have important roles to play in this area.[3]

PUBLIC POLICY CONCERNING MARKET STRUCTURE

Another problem that faces us all as citizens is the way that industries are structured. Suppose for simplicity that all industries sell to a large number of independent buyers, none of which is in a position to influence the price of the product. Suppose that we have three choices: to allow each industry to be taken over by a single firm, to allow each industry to become dominated by a few firms (but prevent a single firm from taking over), or to make sure that each industry is composed of a large number of independent firms. Which choice should we make?

This is a very important problem—and one that continues to be the center of considerable controversy. In the United States, the antitrust laws are designed to promote competition and to control monopoly. For example, the Sherman Act of 1890, the first major federal legislation directed against monopoly, outlaws conspiracies or combinations in restraint of trade and forbids

---

3. For a discussion of the problem described in this section, see Chapter 14.

the monopolizing of trade or commerce. This seems to indicate that we as a nation have decided not to allow industries to be taken over by a single firm. But is this policy justified? To what extent has it been outmoded by developments in the years that have elapsed since the passage of the Sherman Act?

According to some prominent observers, a policy designed to insure that each industry be composed of a large number of independent firms would be a mistake. They claim that very large firms are required in many industries to insure efficiency and promote progress. How can their arguments be evaluated? What criteria can be used to judge the relative advantages of alternative ways that industries can be structured? In various discussions, one often hears of the advantages of a competitive system in which industries are composed of many small firms. In what sense can such a system be shown to be optimal? Is it always optimal, or just under certain special conditions?

This problem is of the utmost importance, since it concerns the basic framework within which the nation's business activity is carried out. It is one of the most fundamental questions of public policy. Compared with the production and pricing problems of individual firms, it—like the problem in the previous section—is certainly more difficult to formulate and to solve, if for no other reason than that it is harder to decide what benefits the entire country than it is to decide what benefits a particular firm. By the same token, this problem is much broader than the problems of the individual firms discussed above. Whereas our interest there was to find policies that would benefit a particular firm, our interest here is to find policies that will benefit the nation as a whole.

This is another example of a problem that microeconomics is aimed at helping to solve. Although it is not possible to solve this problem in as neat or as simple a fashion as one might solve a less complicated problem, it is possible to throw considerable light on the issues involved—and microeconomists have labored for generations to see to it that problems of this sort are analyzed as dispassionately and as scientifically as possible. Moreover, the results have been put to use in the world of action as well as in the world of speculation and study. The lawyer who argues an antitrust case, and the judge who decides one, must both rely on and use the principles of microeconomics.[4]

MICROECONOMICS: PROBLEM-SOLVING AND SCIENCE

The previous four sections have provided some examples of problems that microeconomics can help solve. These examples are useful in indicating the relevance of microeconomics but they may be misleading if they suggest that microeconomics is wholly a bag of techniques to solve practical problems. On the contrary, *microeconomics, like any branch of the natural or social sciences, is*

---

4. For discussion of the problem described in this section, see Chapters 8–11, and 14.

concerned with the explanation and prediction of observed phenomena regardless of whether these explanations or predictions have any immediate applications to practical problems. As indicated in the previous sections, it has turned out that many parts of microeconomics have been relevant and useful in solving practical problems, but this does not mean that all of microeconomics *has* found an application of this sort or that all of microeconomics *should* find an application of this sort.

For example, one of the principal objectives of microeconomics is to answer questions like the following: What determines the price of various commodities? (Why is lobster more expensive than chicken?) What determines the amount that a worker makes? (Why are dentists paid more than cab drivers?) What determines the way that a consumer allocates his or her income among various commodities? (How will an increase in the price of butter affect the amount of margarine purchased by Mrs. Simon?) What determines how much of a particular commodity will be produced? (What accounts for the woeful decrease in the number of cigar-store Indians produced?) What determines the number and size of firms in a particular industry? (Why are there so many producers of corn and so few producers of computers?)

None of these questions is, as it stands, in the form of a practical problem. Yet to understand the world about us and to perform effectively as a citizen, administrator, or worker, it is obvious that one must have at least a minimal understanding of the answers to these questions. The situation is something like that of mathematics. Although pure mathematics is not concerned with the solution of particular problems, it has turned out that various branches of mathematics are of great value in solving practical problems. And a minimal knowledge of mathematics is extremely important as a basis for understanding the world around us and for further professional and technical training.

HUMAN WANTS AND RESOURCES

At the beginning of this chapter, we gave a very brief definition of economics which must now be expanded and explained. It will be recalled that we said that economics focuses on the way in which resources are allocated among alternative uses to satisfy human wants. This is a perfectly satisfactory definition, but it does not mean much unless we define what is meant by *human wants* and by *resources*. What do these terms mean?

Human wants are the things, services, goods, and circumstances that people desire. Wants vary greatly among individuals and over time for the same individual. Some people like sports, others like books; some want to travel, others want to putter in the yard. An individual's desire for a particular good during a particular period of time is not infinite, but in the aggregate human wants seem to be insatiable. Besides the basic desires for food, shelter, and clothing, which must be fulfilled to some extent if

Human wants

the human organism is to maintain its existence, wants arise from cultural factors. For example, society, often helped along by advertising and other devices to modify tastes, promotes certain images of the "full, rich life," which frequently entail the possession and consumption of certain types of automobiles, houses, appliances, and other goods and services.

Resources are the things or services used to produce goods which can be used to satisfy wants. Economic resources are scarce, while free resources, such as air, are so abundant that they can be obtained without charge. The test of whether a resource is an economic resource or a free resource is price: Economic resources command a nonzero price but free resources do not. In a world where all resources were free, there would be no economic problem since all wants could be satisfied.

Resources

An economic resource that is used in the production of a particular good is called an input. Thus, in the example in Table 1.1, the inputs in the manufacture of personal computers were skilled labor and manufacturing equipment. Economic resources have alternative uses. A particular resource generally can be used in the production of many types of goods. For example, the skilled labor used by the computer manufacturer could be used by many other kinds of firms and in many other kinds of work. Of course, as resources become more specialized, there generally are fewer alternative jobs for them—but there are still some. Even the equipment used to make the computers can probably be adapted for somewhat different uses.

Economic resources are of a variety of types. In the nineteenth century it was customary for economists to classify economic resources into three categories: land, labor, and capital. In recent years this sort of classification has tended to go out of style in part because each category contains such an enormous variety of resources. Nevertheless, it is worthwhile defining each of these general types of resources. Land is a shorthand expression for natural resources. Labor is human effort, both physical and mental. Capital includes equipment, buildings, inventories, raw materials, and other nonhuman producible resources that contribute to the production, marketing, and distribution of goods and services. Note that the economist's definition of capital is different from that of the man in the street who employs the word to mean money. For example, a man with a hot dog stand who has $200 in his pocket may say that he has $200 in capital; but his definition is different from that of the economist who would include in the man's capital the value of his stand, the value of his equipment, the value of his inventory of hot dogs and mustard, and the value of other nonlabor resources (other than land) that he uses.

TECHNOLOGY

Another term that must be defined at this point is *technology*. Technology is society's pool of knowledge regarding the industrial and agricultural arts.

Technology

Technology consists of knowledge used in industry and agriculture concerning the principles of physical and social phenomena (such as the laws of motion and the properties of fluids), knowledge regarding the application of these principles to production (such as the application of various aspects of genetic theory to the breeding of new plants), and knowledge regarding the day-to-day operation of production (such as the rules of thumb of the skilled craftsman). Note that technology is different from the techniques in use, since not all that is known is likely to be in use. Also, technology is different from pure science, although the distinction is not very precise. Pure science is directed toward understanding, whereas technology is directed toward use.

The important thing about technology is that it sets limits on the amount and types of goods that can be derived from a given amount of resources. Put differently, it sets limits on the extent to which human wants can be satisfied by a given amount of resources. For instance, consider the computer manufacturers cited above. With the existing technology, the only three processes that are available require the input combinations shown in Table 1.1. Given the existing technology, Table 1.1 shows that there is no way to produce a computer using only 10 hours of skilled labor and 10 machine-hours of manufacturing equipment. This is beyond the current state of the art. Engineers and craftsmen do not yet know how to accomplish this. It is obvious that this limitation of existing knowledge results in a corresponding limitation on how much the firm can produce with its 80,000 hours of skilled labor and its 60,000 machine-hours of manufacturing equipment. When, and if, technology advances to the point where it is possible to produce a computer with 10 hours of skilled labor and 10 machine-hours of manufacturing equipment, the firm will be able to produce more with its existing amount of skilled labor and equipment. More will then be produced with the existing resources.

THE TASKS PERFORMED BY AN ECONOMIC SYSTEM

Economics, of course, deals with the functioning of economic systems—just as, for example, biology deals with the functioning of biological systems. Perhaps the best way to define the economic system is to describe what it does. A society's economic system must allocate its resources among competing uses, combine and process these resources in such a way as to produce goods and services, determine the amount of various goods and services that will be produced, distribute these goods and services among the society's members, and determine what provision is to be made for the future growth of the society's per capita income. Put in a single sentence, these tasks do not seem quite as awesome as in fact they are. To do justice to each of these tasks, a fuller explanation is needed.

First, the economic system must allocate its resources among competing uses and combine and process these resources to produce the desired level and composition of output. Suppose that the desired level and composition of output is known. There usually are many ways of producing a commodity, and it is not easy to decide which way is best. For example, a plant can use different types and quantities of equipment, different amounts and qualities of raw materials, different amounts and qualities of labor, different locations, different means of transporting and distributing its product, and different ways of informing potential customers of the product's existence. Of the many combinations of resources that could be used, which should be used? Or looking at the problem from a somewhat different point of view, there is an enormous quantity and variety of resources in any society: How should each of these resources be used?

Even if some smart Philadelphia lawyer, or some other type of philosopher-king, could tell us which combination of resources is best for the production of each good, this would not be a complete solution to the problem. We would also have to find a way to insure that this combination would in fact be used. The difficulty of solving this aspect of the problem should not be underestimated. Even in highly disciplined organizations like armies, it is not unusual for a general's plan of action to be executed improperly or distorted considerably.

Second, an economic system must determine the level and composition of output. To what extent should society's resources be used to produce weapons systems? To what extent should they be used to rebuild old cities? To what extent should they be used to produce cotton and wool cloth? To what extent should they be used to produce artificial fibers like nylon? To what extent should they be used to produce dresses? To what extent should they be used to produce Levis? What is the proper combination of goods—weapons systems, rebuilt cities, natural fibers, artificial fibers, dresses, Levis, and so on—that should be produced? The enormous complexity of this question, as well as its importance, should be obvious. If you feel a bit overwhelmed by it, this is precisely the message we wish to convey.

Third, the economic system must also determine how the goods and services that are produced are distributed among the members of society. How much of each type of good and service is each person to receive? This is a subject that has generated, and continues to generate, heated controversy. Some people are in favor of a relatively egalitarian society where the amount received by one family varies little from that received by another family of the same size. Other people favor a less egalitarian society where the amount that a family or person receives varies a great deal. Few people favor a thoroughly egalitarian society, if for no other reason than that some differences in income are required to stimulate workers to do certain types of work.

Fourth, another task of an economic system is to provide for whatever rate of growth of per capita income the society desires and can achieve. The goal of economic growth is a relatively new one; most past societies have had economies that were unprogressive. Regardless of its newness, however, it has come to be regarded as an extremely important task, particularly in the less-developed countries of Africa, Asia, and South America. There is very strong pressure in these countries for changes in technology, the adoption of superior techniques, increases in the stock of capital resources, and better and more extensive education and training of the labor force. These are viewed as some of the major ways to promote the growth of per capita income. In the industrialized nations, the goal of rapid economic growth has become more controversial in recent years. This has been due in part to the fact that some observers have questioned the extent to which economic growth is worth its costs in social dislocation, pollution, and so forth. But there is no indication that most industrialized nations have lost interest in further economic growth.

OUR MIXED CAPITALIST SYSTEM

The previous section described the four basic functions that any economic system must perform. How does our economic system in the United States perform each of these functions? Let's begin with the determination of the level and composition of output in the society. How is this decided? In a substantially free-enterprise economy, such as ours, consumers choose the amount of each good that they want, and producers act in accord with these decisions. The importance that consumers attach to a good is indicated by the price they are willing to pay for it.

However, consumer sovereignty does not extend to all areas of our society. For example, with regard to the consumption of commodities like drugs, society imposes limits on the decisions of individuals. Moreover, some goods cannot be bought and sold in the marketplace, or even if they can be, it would be inefficient to do so. Such goods, called public goods, will not be provided in the right amounts by private industry, so the government tends to intervene. Examples of public goods are national defense and a healthful environment. Decisions regarding the provision of these goods tend to be made in the political arena.

Going back to the first function described in the previous section, how does our economic system allocate its resources among competing uses, and how does it process these resources to obtain the desired level and composition of output? Basically, the *price system* does the job by indicating

Price system   the desires of workers and the relative value of various types of materials and equipment as well as the desires of consumers. For example, if computer programmers are scarce relative to the uses for them, their price in the labor market—their wage—will be bid up and they will tend to be used only in the places where they are most productive. The forces that push firms in the direction of actually carrying out the proper decisions take the form principally of profits or losses. Profits are the carrot, and losses are the stick which are used to eliminate the less efficient and the less alert firms and to increase the more efficient and the more alert.

Although decentralized decision-making based on the price system is used to organize production in most areas of our economy, there are notable exceptions. For example, in the acquisition of new weapons by the Department of Defense, the price system, in anything like its customary form, has not been applied. Instead, the government has exercised control over sellers through the auditing of costs and through the intimate involvement of its agents in the managerial and operating structure of the sellers. Moreover, there is extensive government ownership of the seller's facilities; the government decides what weapons are to be created through its program decisions; and it often decides how they are to be created and produced.

Turning to the next function, how does our economic system determine how much in the way of goods and services each member of the society is to receive? In general, the income of individuals depends largely on the quantities of resources of various kinds that they own and the prices they get for them. For example, if a person both works and rents out houses he or she owns, the person's total income is the number of hours worked per year multiplied by his or her hourly wage rate plus the number of houses owned times the annual rental per house. Thus the distribution of income depends on the way that resource ownership is distributed. Some individuals own higher-priced labor resources than others, because of greater intelligence or superior training. Some individuals own a much greater amount of capital and land than others. However, this is only part of the story. The government modifies the resulting distribution of income by imposing progressive income taxes and by welfare programs such as aid to dependent children. In this way, an attempt is made to reduce income differentials somewhat.

Finally, how does our economic system determine our nation's rate of growth of per capita income? A nation's rate of growth of per capita income depends on the rate of growth of its resources and the rate of increase of the efficiency with which they are used. In our economy, the rate at which labor and capital resources are increased is motivated, at least in part, through the price system. Higher wages for more highly skilled work are an incentive for an individual to undergo further training and education. Capital accumulation occurs in response to expectations of profit. Increases in efficiency, due in considerable measure to the advance of technology, are also stimulated by the price system, but it must be recognized that the government plays an extremely significant role in supporting research and development. In areas like defense, space, atomic energy, and many aspects of agriculture and medicine, the government plays a dominant role in research and development.

THE PRICE SYSTEM AND MICROECONOMICS

From the discussion in the previous section it is clear that the price system plays a major role in the way our economy goes about performing the four principal functions that any economic system must perform. It is not the only means by which our economy goes about performing these tasks, but its role is very important. A person who wants to understand the way in which our economic system functions must therefore have at least a basic knowledge of how the price system works. Microeconomics—or at least a major part of it—is often called price theory because so much of it is concerned so directly with the workings of the price system.

At this point, we are in a position to bring together various strands of the preceding discussion in order to describe more fully the nature and purpose of microeconomics. Economics, it will be recalled, deals with the way in which scarce resources are allocated among alternative uses to satisfy human wants. Microeconomics is the branch of economics that is concerned with the economic behavior of individual consumers, firms, and resource owners, not with the aggregate changes of the economy. As pointed out in the previous paragraph, one of the principal purposes of microeconomics is to provide an understanding of the workings and effects of the price system, which plays an important role in the way our economy functions.

In the course of providing such an understanding, microeconomics helps to answer questions like: What determines the price of various commodities? What determines the amount that a worker makes? What determines the way that a consumer allocates his or her income among various commodities? What determines how much of a particular commodity will be produced? What determines the number and size of firms in a particular industry? Moreover, in the course of investigating these and related questions, microeconomics has shed considerable light on the kinds of problems discussed at the beginning of this chapter: How should a firm choose among alternative manufacturing processes if it wants to maximize its profits? What sort of pricing policy should it adopt? What kinds of social changes can be made if it is agreed that the goal is to make anyone better off if it does not make someone else worse off? What are the advantages and disadvantages of various ways in which industries might be organized?

MODEL-BUILDING AND THE ROLE OF MODELS

Before concluding this introductory chapter, it is important that we describe briefly the basic methodology used in microeconomics to answer the kinds of questions cited above. This methodology is much the same as that used in any

other type of scientific analysis. The basic procedure is the formulation of
models. A *model* is composed of a number of assumptions from which conclusions—or predictions—are deduced. For example, suppose

Model

that we want to formulate a model of the solar system. We might
represent each of the planets by a point in space, and we might
make the assumption that each would change position in accord with certain
mathematical equations. Based on this model, we might predict when an
eclipse would occur.

To be useful, a model must in general simplify and abstract from the real
situation. Although the assumptions that are made obviously must bear some
relationship to the type of situation to which the model is applicable (since
randomly chosen assumptions are unlikely, for example, to predict eclipses
very well), it is very important to understand that the assumptions need not be
exact replicas of reality. Thus, in the example above, the fact that planets are
in fact not points makes little or no difference. Moreover, even if the equations
representing their movements are somewhat in error, this may make little difference since, despite these errors, the model may predict well enough to be
useful. In both the natural and social sciences, models based on simplified and
idealized circumstances have found many, many uses. Also, some assumptions
may refer to things that are not directly measurable, like utility in economic
theory. The fact that they are not directly measurable does not mean that they
are useless: Their usefulness depends on whether or not they result in models
that are more powerful and accurate.

There are a number of important reasons why economists, like other scientists, use models. One is that the real world is so complex that it is necessary
to simplify and abstract if any progress is to be made. Another is that a simple
model may be the cheapest way of obtaining needed information. Of course, although the use of models is well accepted throughout the various branches of
the scientific community, this does not mean that all models are good or useful. A model may be so over-simplified and distorted that it is utterly useless.
The trick is to construct a model in such a way that irrelevant and unimportant considerations and variables are neglected, but the important factors—
those that have an important effect on the phenomena the model is designed
to predict—are included.

THE EVALUATION OF A MODEL

The purpose of a model is to make predictions concerning phenomena in the
real world, and in many respects the most important test of a model is how well
it predicts these phenomena. In this sense, a model that predicts the price of
lamb within plus or minus 1 cent a pound is better than a model that predicts
the price of lamb within plus or minus 2 cents a pound. Of course, this does not
mean that a model is useless if it cannot predict very accurately. Under some

circumstances, one does not need a very accurate prediction. For some purposes, it is sufficient that a model's predictions be accurate to within a mile; for other purposes, its predictions must be accurate to within a gnat's whisker. Also, for some purposes, a model's predictions must describe various aspects and dimensions of reality; for other purposes, only one aspect or dimension is important.

A model's predictions are derived by applying the rules of logic to the assumptions. For example, in the model of the solar system described above, we see at what point in time an eclipse will occur according to the model by making computations based on the model's assumptions and employing the rules of logic. One elementary test of a model's predictions is whether or not they really do flow logically from the model's assumptions. Sometimes errors of logic and computation creep in to mar a prediction. More fundamentally, another test of a model is whether its assumptions are logically consistent, one with another. Sometimes the natural or social scientist, in building a model, makes assumptions that are not really compatible.

Another important consideration in judging a model is the range of phenomena to which it applies. In any science, there is a great and understandable attempt to formulate models that are as general as possible. A model that can predict the behavior of any consumer in the economy is more valuable than one that can predict only the behavior of Mary Smith. Hence the economist is much more interested in a model that is relevant to many consumers in the economy than in one that is relevant to only one consumer. However, the more general a model is meant to be, the more difficult it is to attain a given degree of accuracy. It is relatively easy to construct empirically valid models with little or no generality. For example, if one wanted to go to the trouble of studying a particular person's eating habits, it is likely that one could formulate a model that would predict his or her choice of breakfast food cereals pretty well. But it would be much more difficult to find a model that would be equally accurate in predicting the choice of any type of food by any consumer in the economy. If a theory is to be general, it must ignore many details (and sometimes some variables that are considerably more important than details); the result is that its predictions are likely to fall short—perhaps considerably short—of a high degree of accuracy.

It is important to add another point that is frequently misunderstood: If one is interested in predicting the outcome of a particular event, one will be forced to use the model that predicts best, even if this model does not predict very well. The choice is not between a model and no model; it is between one type of model and another. After all, if one must make a forecast, one will use the most accurate device available to make such a forecast. And any such device is a model of some sort. Consequently, when economists make simplifying assumptions and derive conclusions that are only approximately true, it is somewhat beside the point to complain that the assumptions are simpler than reality or that the predictions are not always accurate. All of this may be true, but if the predictions are better than those obtained on the basis of other models, this model must be used until something better comes along. Thus, if a model can predict the price of lamb to within plus or minus 1 cent a pound and no other model can do better, this model will be used even if those interested in predicting the price of lamb bewail the model's limitations and wish it could be improved.

The basic point can perhaps be illustrated by the story of the man whose weakness was games of chance and whose wife told him one day that the local casino was dishonest and asked him to stop visiting it. He replied "It's a darned shame and I'd like to stop going . . . but it's the only game in town." Similarly, if a model is the best that is available, it will—and should—be used until a better model appears.

At this point, a final word should be added concerning the microeconomic models discussed in subsequent chapters. No claim is made that these models are sufficiently accurate or powerful to solve all—or most—of the problems that face firms, governments, or others. Some of these models have been used to predict reasonably well; others have not been nearly so successful. Still others have not really been tested, and no one knows how well they would predict. Moreover, no claim is made that the models discussed in subsequent chapters are the last word on the subject. Undoubtedly they will be improved. All that we do claim is that, according to a consensus of the economics profession, they are the best models we have. Like the local casino they may have their imperfections (although dishonesty is not among them), but they are the best in town.

SUMMARY

1. Economics deals with the way in which resources are allocated among alternative uses to satisfy human wants. Economic activity is directed toward the satisfaction of human wants. Resources are the things and services used to produce goods that can satisfy wants. Economic resources are scarce and have a nonzero price; free resources are not scarce and can be obtained free of charge.

2. Technology is society's pool of knowledge regarding the industrial and agricultural arts. It sets limits on the amount and types of goods and services that can be derived from a given set of resources.

3. Any economic system must accomplish four tasks: It must allocate resources, determine the composition of output, distribute the product, and provide for growth. In our society, individual consumers have great power in determining the composition of output; the prices they are willing to pay for a good indicate how much importance they attach to it. The price system also is

an important determinant of how resources are allocated and how the product is distributed.

4. Government also plays a very important role in these tasks. In some areas, the composition of output and the allocation of resources are determined by political decisions. Moreover, the government modifies the distribution of income, and it plays an important role in stimulating and maintaining growth.

5. The methodology used by economists is much the same as that used in any other type of scientific analysis; the basic procedure is the formulation of models.

6. Economic theory is divided into two parts: microeconomics and macroeconomics. Microeconomics is concerned with the economic behavior of individual economic units like consumers, firms, and resource owners.

7. One of the most important purposes of microeconomics is to provide an understanding of the working and effects of the price system. In the course of providing such an understanding, microeconomics helps to answer many practical problems of businesses and governments and throws important light on many fundamental issues that confront responsible citizens and elected representatives.

QUESTIONS/PROBLEMS

1) Cigarette bootleggers take cigarettes from states with low cigarette taxes and sell them in states with high cigarette taxes. Such smuggling results in a loss in tax revenue to the latter states. The Advisory Commission on Intergovernmental Relations estimated that this loss in 1979 and 1975 was as follows:

Loss from cigarette-tax evasion

	1975	1979
	(millions of dollars)	
All states	337	280
Florida	36	43

(a) If you had to construct a model to predict the amount of cigarettes bootlegged, what factors would you include? (b) Based on the above figures, do you think that Florida's cigarette-tax rate is lower than that of neighboring states? Why or why not? (c) Between 1975 and 1979, Florida changed its tax on a pack of cigarettes by 3 cents per pack. Do you think that it increased or decreased the tax? Why? (d) Could the change in the total loss from cigarette-tax evasion have been due in part to the great increase in the price of gasoline in the late 1970s? Why or why not?

2) In 1985, President Ronald Reagan's Commission on Industrial Competitiveness concluded: "Perhaps the most glaring deficiency in America's technological capabilities has been our failure to devote enough attention to manufacturing or 'process' technology. It does us little good to design state-of-the-art products, if within a short time our foreign competitors can manufacture them more cheaply." How can one tell whether too little attention is being devoted to manufacturing technology? What factors might induce firms to devote too little attention to it?

3) On most questions of policy one can find disagreements among economists. Thus, the economic advisers of Republican presidents have tended to have views somewhat different from those of Democratic presidents. Does this prove that economics is not a science?

4) According to the principle of Occam's razor, if two models predict equally well, the one that is less complicated should be chosen. Do you agree? How can you tell how complicated a model is?

5) If a certain proposition holds true for a part of a system, must it hold true for the whole system? For example, suppose that a farmer will benefit from producing a larger crop. Does it follow that all farmers will benefit from producing a larger crop? Explain.

6) The median salary of teachers of economics has generally been higher than that of teachers of physics, chemistry, mathematics, or biology. Is this a powerful argument that ecomomics is a science? Why or why not?

7) In evaluating the accuracy of their statements, should you distinguish between (1) economists' descriptive statements, propositions, and predictions about the world, and (2) their statements about what policies should be adopted? Explain.

8) One purpose of microeconomics is to determine how we can achieve an optimal allocation of resources. Describe some of the problems involved in defining an "optimal" allocation. Do you think that there is an optimal allocation of resources in the United States at present? Why or why not?

9) What considerations must be taken into account in judging or evaluating a model?

10) Suppose that you were given the task of constructing a model to predict IBM Corporation's total sales next year. How would you go about it? What variables would you include?

Demand and Supply

INTRODUCTION

Since so much of microeconomics is concerned with the workings of the price system, it is important to understand the mechanism at the center of that system: the market. We begin by discussing the basic concepts of demand and supply, as well as the price elasticity of demand and the price elasticity of supply. Then we describe briefly how price is determined. Finally, we show how our results can be used to throw important light on some major present-day policy issues. This chapter provides a brief, initial look at these central concepts, not an exhaustive treatment. In later chapters, each of these topics will be discussed in much more detail.[1]

MARKETS

Because this chapter is concerned with the behavior of markets, it is necessary to describe at the outset what we mean by a market. This is not quite as straightforward as it may seem, since most markets are not well defined in a

---

1. Readers familiar with these concepts can use this chapter for review, or go directly to Chapter 3 without loss of continuity.

geographical or physical sense. (For example, the New York Stock Exchange is an atypical market in the sense that it is located principally in a particular building.) What is a *market?* A good working definition is that it **Market** is a group of firms and individuals in touch with each other in order to buy or sell some good. Of course, not every person in a market has to be in contact with every other person in the market; a person or firm is part of a market even if in contact with only a subset of the other persons or firms in the market.

Markets vary enormously in their size, arrangements, and procedures. For some household goods, all of the consumers west of the Rocky Mountains may be members of the same market. For other goods, like Picasso paintings, only a few collectors, dealers, and museums scattered around the world are members of the market. Basically, however, all markets consist primarily of buyers and sellers, although third parties like brokers and agents may be present as well. In most markets, the sellers suggest the price, but this is not always the case. In this chapter, we assume that a market contains many small buyers and sellers so that none of them individually exerts a significant influence on the price.[2] We will relax that assumption in later chapters.

THE DEMAND SIDE OF THE MARKET

The Market Demand Curve

According to Thomas Carlyle, the famous nineteenth-century historian and essayist, "it is easy to train an economist; teach a parrot to say Demand and Supply." Although he may have exaggerated the susceptibility of parrots to an economics education, Carlyle certainly was right about the central role played by demand and supply in economics. The market for every good has a demand side and a supply side. The demand side can be represented by a *market demand schedule,* a table which shows the quantity of the good that would be purchased at each price. (The price of the good is, of course, the amount of money that must be paid for a unit of it.) For example, suppose that the market demand schedule for coal is as shown in Table 2.1.[3] According to this table, 665 million tons of coal will be demanded per year if its price is $36 per ton, 670 million tons of coal will be demanded if its price is $35 per ton, and so on. An-

---

2. More accurately, we generally assume in this chapter that markets are perfectly competitive. A perfectly competitive market exists when no buyer or seller can influence price, output is homogeneous, resources are mobile, and knowledge is perfect. A fuller definition of a perfectly competitive market is given in Chapter 8.

3. These figures are hypothetical, but adequate for present purposes. In subsequent chapters, we shall provide data describing the actual relationship between the price and quantity demanded of various goods. At this point, the emphasis is on the concept of a market demand schedule, not on the detailed accuracy of these figures.

Table
2.1

MARKET DEMAND SCHEDULE FOR COAL, 1988

Price per ton (dollars)	Quantity demanded per year (millions of tons)
36	665
35	670
34	680
33	690
32	700
31	710
30	730

Market demand curve

other way of presenting the data in Table 2.1 is by a *market demand curve,* which is a plot of the market demand schedule on a graph. The vertical axis of the graph measures the price per unit of the good, and the horizontal axis measures the quantity of the good demanded per unit of time. Figure 2.1 shows the market demand curve for coal, based on the figures in Table 2.1.

Two things should be noted concerning Figure 2.1. First, the market demand curve for coal *slopes downward to the right.* In other words, the quantity of coal demanded increases as the price falls. This is true of the demand curve

Fig.
2.1

MARKET DEMAND CURVE FOR COAL, 1988 / *The market demand curve for coal shows the quantity of coal that would be purchased at each price.*

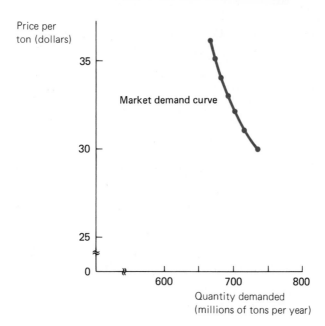

for most goods: They almost always slope downward to the right. In subsequent chapters, we shall learn why this is not always the case, but these reasons need not concern us at present. Second, the market demand curve in Figure 2.1 pertains to a *particular period of time:* 1988. It is important to recognize that any demand curve pertains to some period of time, and that its shape and position depend on the length and other characteristics of this period. For example, if we were to estimate the market demand curve for coal for the first week in 1988, it would be a different curve than the one in Figure 2.1, which pertains to the whole year. The difference arises partly because consumers can adapt their purchases more fully to changes in the price of coal in a year than in a week.

Besides the length of the time period, what other factors determine the position and shape of the market demand curve for a good? One important factor is the *tastes of consumers.* If consumers show an increasing preference for a product, the demand curve will shift to the right: That is, at each price, consumers will desire to buy more than previously. On the other hand, if consumers show a decreasing preference for a product, the demand curve will shift to the left, since, at each price, consumers will desire to buy less than previously. For example, let's turn from coal to the case of electricity. If consumers become more energy-conscious, and begin to take more pride in cutting back on the unnecessary use of electricity, the demand curve for electricity may shift to the left, as shown in Figure 2.2. The greater the shift in preferences, the larger the shift in the demand curve.

Another factor that influences the position and shape of a good's market demand curve is *the level of consumer incomes.* For some types of products, the

Fig. 2.2 EFFECT OF INCREASED ENERGY-CONSCIOUSNESS ON MARKET DEMAND CURVE FOR ELECTRICITY / *If people take pride in reducing the unnecessary use of electricity, the demand curve for electricity may shift to the left.*

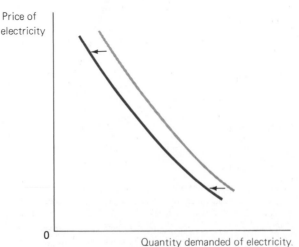

Fig.
2.3

EFFECT OF INCREASE IN PER CAPITA INCOME ON MARKET DEMAND CURVE
FOR ELECTRICITY / *An increase in per capita income would shift the
demand curve for electricity to the right.*

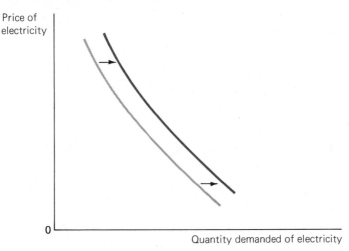

demand curve shifts to the right if per capita income increases; whereas for
other types of commodities, the demand curve shifts to the left if per capita income rises. In subsequent chapters, we shall analyze why some goods fall into
one category and other goods fall into the other, but, at present, this need not
concern us. All that is important here is that changes in per capita income affect the demand curve. In the case of electricity, all the available studies indicate that an increase in per capita income would shift the demand curve to the
right, as shown in Figure 2.3.

Still another factor that influences the position and shape of a good's
market demand curve is the *level of other prices.* For example, since natural gas
can be substituted to some extent for electricity, the quantity of electricity demanded depends on the price of natural gas. If the price of gas is high, more
electricity will be demanded than if the price of gas is low, because people and
firms will be stimulated to substitute electricity for the high-priced gas. Thus,
as shown in Figure 2.4, increases in the price of gas will shift the market demand curve for electricity to the right (and decreases in the price of gas will
shift it to the left).[4]

---

4. Let the quantity demanded of a good per unit of time equal Q_D. In general,

$$Q_D = f(P, T, I, R, N)$$

where P is the price of the good, T stands for the tastes of consumers, I is the level of consumer income, R is the price of related goods, and N is the number of consumers in the market. The demand curve shows the relationship between Q_D and P when the other variables
are held constant. In general, changes in the values at which these other variables are held
constant will affect the relationship between Q_D and P, which is another way of saying that
these other variables will generally influence the position and shape of the market demand
curve.

Fig. EFFECT OF INCREASE IN THE PRICE OF NATURAL GAS ON MARKET DEMAND
2.4 CURVE FOR ELECTRICITY / *An increase in the price of natural gas will shift
the demand curve for electricity to the right.*

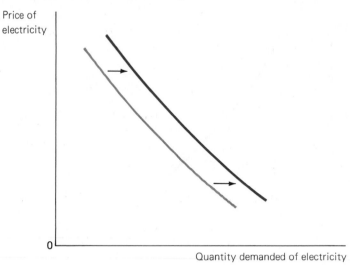

The Price Elasticity of Demand

The shape of a good's market demand curve varies from one good to another and from one market to another. In particular, market demand curves
vary in the sensitivity of quantity demanded to price. For some goods, a small
change in price results in a large change in quantity demanded;
Price elasticity   for other goods, a large change in price results in a small change
of demand   in quantity demanded. To gauge the sensitivity, or responsiveness, of the quantity demanded to changes in price, economists
use a measure called the *price elasticity of demand.* The price elasticity of demand is defined to be *the percentage change in quantity demanded resulting
from a 1 percent change in price.*[5]

For example, suppose that a 1 percent reduction in the price of electricity
results in a 1.2 percent increase in the quantity demanded in the United
States. If so, the price elasticity of demand for electricity is 1.2. Convention

---

5. For readers with a knowledge of calculus, it is worth noting that, if Q_D is the quantity demanded and P is the price, a more precise definition of the price elasticity of demand is

$$\eta = \frac{-dQ_D}{dP} \cdot \frac{P}{Q_D} .$$

Much more will be said about the measurement, effects, and determinants of the price elasticity of demand in Chapter 5.

dictates that we give the elasticity a positive sign despite the fact that the change in price is negative and the change in quantity demanded is positive. Clearly, the price elasticity of demand will generally vary from one point to another on a demand curve. For example, the price elasticity of demand may be higher when the price of electricity is high than when it is low. Similarly, the price elasticity of demand will vary from market to market. For example, Japan may have a different price elasticity of demand for electricity than does the United States. (More is said about the demand curve for electricity in Problem 1 in Chapter 5.)

Alfred Marshall, the great English economist who lived about seventy years ago, was one of the first economists to give a clear formulation of the concept of the price elasticity of demand. It is a very important concept and one that will be used repeatedly throughout this book. One thing to note at the outset is that the price elasticity of demand is expressed in terms of *relative* changes in price and quantity demanded, not *absolute* changes in price and quantity demanded. This is because absolute changes are difficult to interpret. For example, suppose that a price goes up by a dime. This is a lot for a subway ride but little for a house. Similarly, it is a lot for a bottle of beer but little for a fifty-gallon keg. A frequent error is to confuse the price elasticity of demand with the slope of the demand curve. They are by no means the same thing.[6]

Suppose that we have a market demand schedule showing the quantity of a commodity demanded in the market at various prices. How can we estimate the price elasticity of market demand? Let ΔP be a change in the price of the good and ΔQ_D be the resulting change in its quantity demanded. If ΔP is very small, we can compute the *point elasticity of demand:*

Point elasticity

$$\eta = -\frac{\Delta Q_D}{Q_D} \div \frac{\Delta P}{P}. \qquad [2.1]$$

For example, consider Table 2.2 where data are given for very small increments in the price of a commodity. If we want to estimate the price elasticity of

Table 2.2 QUANTITY DEMANDED AT VARIOUS PRICES (SMALL INCREMENTS IN PRICE)

Price (cents per unit of commodity)	*Quantity demanded per unit of time* (units of commodity)
99.95	40,002
100.00	40,000
100.05	39,998

---

6. The slope of the demand curve is dP/dQ_D. A glance at footnote 5 will show that this slope is not equal to the price elasticity of demand. Sometimes the price elasticity of demand is also confused with dQ_D/dP. This too is an error since they are by no means the same thing.

demand when the price is between 99.95 cents and $1, we obtain the following result:

$$\eta = -\frac{40{,}002 - 40{,}000}{40{,}000} \div \frac{99.95 - 100}{100} = .1.$$

Note that we used $1 as P and 40,000 as Q_D. We could have used 99.95 cents as P and 40,002 as Q_D, but it would have made no real difference to the answer. (Try it and see.)

Table QUANTITY DEMANDED AT VARIOUS PRICES (LARGE INCREMENTS IN PRICE)
2.3

Price (dollars per unit of commodity)	Quantity demanded per unit of time (units of commodity)
3	40
4	20
5	3

However, if we have data concerning only large changes in price (that is, if ΔP and ΔQ_D are large), the answer may vary considerably depending on which value of P and Q_D is used in Equation 2.1. For example, take the case in Table 2.3. Suppose that we want to estimate the price elasticity of demand in the price range between $4 and $5. Then, depending on which value of P and Q_D is used, the answer will be

Arc elasticity

$$\eta = -\frac{20 - 3}{3} \div \frac{4 - 5}{5} = 28.33$$

$$\eta = -\frac{3 - 20}{20} \div \frac{5 - 4}{4} = 3.40.$$

The difference between these two results is enormous. In a case of this sort, it is advisable to compute the *arc elasticity of demand,* which uses the average value of P and Q_D:

$$\eta = -\frac{\Delta Q_D}{(Q_{D1} + Q_{D2})/2} \div \frac{\Delta P}{(P_1 + P_2)/2}$$

$$= -\frac{\Delta Q_D (P_1 + P_2)}{\Delta P (Q_{D1} + Q_{D2})} \qquad [2.2]$$

where P_1 and Q_{D1} are the first values of price and quantity demanded, and P_2 and Q_{D2} are the second set. Thus, in Table 2.3,

$$\eta = -\frac{20 - 3}{(20 + 3)/2} \div \frac{4 - 5}{(4 + 5)/2} = 6.65.$$

This is the way economists get around this difficulty.

Price Elasticity and Total Expenditure

Elastic vs. inelastic

The demand for a commodity is said to be *price elastic* if the elasticity of demand exceeds 1. The demand for a commodity is said to be *price inelastic* if the elasticity of demand is less than 1. And the demand for a commodity is said to be of *unitary elasticity* if the price elasticity of demand is equal to 1. Many important decisions hinge on the price elasticity of demand for a commodity. One reason why this is so is that the price elasticity of demand determines whether a given change in price will increase or decrease the amount of money spent on a commodity—often a matter of basic importance to firms and government agencies.

To illustrate, suppose that the demand for a commodity is elastic, that is, the price elasticity of demand exceeds 1. In this situation, if the price is reduced, the percentage increase in the quantity consumed is greater than the percentage reduction in price. (That this is the case follows from the definition of the price elasticity of demand.) Consequently, a price *reduction* must lead to an *increase* in the expenditure on the product, and a price *increase* must lead to a *decrease* in the expenditure on the product.

On the other hand, suppose that the demand for a commodity is inelastic, that is, the price elasticity of demand is less than 1. In this situation, if the price is reduced, the percentage increase in the quantity consumed is less than the percentage reduction in price. (This follows from the definition of the price elasticity.) Thus a price *reduction* must lead to a *decrease* in the expenditure on the product, and a price *increase* must lead to an *increase* in the consumer's expenditure on the product. Finally, if the demand for a product is of unitary elasticity, price increases or decreases do not affect the expenditure on the product.

THE SUPPLY SIDE OF THE MARKET

The Market Supply Curve

Market supply curve

Each market has a supply side as well as a demand side. The supply side can be represented by a *market supply schedule,* a table which shows the quantity of the good that would be supplied at various prices. For example, suppose that the market supply schedule for coal is shown in Table 2.4.[7] Then 600 million tons of coal will be supplied if its price is $30 per ton, 650 million tons of coal will be supplied if its price is $31 per ton, and so on. Another way of presenting the data in Table 2.4 is by a *market supply curve,* which is a plot of the market supply schedule on a graph. The vertical axis of the graph measures the price

---

7. These figures are hypothetical, but adequate for present purposes. In subsequent chapters, we shall provide data describing the actual relationship between the price and quantity supplied

Table   MARKET SUPPLY SCHEDULE FOR COAL, 1988
2.4

Price per ton (dollars)	Quantity supplied per year (millions of tons)
30	600
31	650
32	700
33	750
34	775
35	800
36	825

per unit of the good, and the horizontal axis measures the quantity of the good supplied per unit of time. Figure 2.5 shows the market supply curve for coal, based on the figures in Table 2.4.[8]

Two things should be noted concerning Figure 2.5. First, the market supply curve for coal *slopes upward to the right.* In other words, the quantity of coal supplied increases as the price increases. This is because increases in its price give the makers of coal a greater incentive to produce it and offer it for sale. Empirical studies indicate that the market supply curves for a great many commodities share this characteristic of sloping upward to the right. In subsequent chapters, we will analyze in detail the factors responsible for the shape of a particular good's market supply curve. Second, the market supply curve in Figure 2.5 pertains to a *particular period of time:* 1988. Any supply curve pertains to some period of time, and its shape and position depend on the length and other characteristics of this period. For example, if we were to estimate the market supply curve for coal for the first week in 1988, it would be a different curve than the one in Figure 2.5, which pertains to the whole year. In part, the difference arises because coal producers can adapt their output rate more fully to changes in coal's price in a year than in a week.

Besides the length of the time period, what other factors determine the position and shape of the market supply curve for a good? One important factor is *technological change.* Recall that technology was defined in Chapter 1 as society's pool of knowledge concerning the industrial arts. As technology progresses, it becomes possible to produce commodities more cheaply, so that firms often are willing to supply a given amount at a lower price than formerly. Thus technological change often causes the supply curve to shift to the right. For example, this certainly has occurred in the case of coal, as indicated in Figure 2.6. There have been many important technological changes in coal pro-

---

of various goods. At this point, the emphasis is on the concept of a market supply schedule, not on the detailed accuracy of these figures.

8. Note once more that we assume that the market for coal is perfectly competitive. (See footnote 2.) This simplification is adopted throughout this chapter. In subsequent chapters we relax the assumption that markets are perfectly competitive.

Fig. MARKET SUPPLY CURVE FOR COAL, 1988 / *The market supply curve for*
2.5 *coal shows the quantity of coal that would be supplied at each price.*

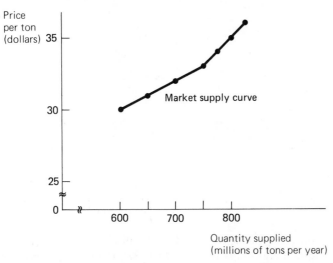

duction in the past fifty years, including the invention and improvement of
continuous mining machinery, trackless mobile loaders, and shuttle cars.

   Another factor that influences the position and shape of a good's market
supply curve is the *level of input prices.* The supply curve for a commodity is
affected by the prices of the resources (labor, capital, and land) used to produce
it. Decreases in the prices of these inputs make it possible to produce commodities more cheaply, so that firms may be willing to supply a given amount at a
lower price than they formerly would. Thus decreases in the price of inputs
may cause the supply curve to shift to the right. On the other hand, increases

Fig. EFFECT OF TECHNOLOGICAL CHANGE ON THE MARKET SUPPLY CURVE FOR
2.6 COAL / *Improvements in technology shift the supply curve to the right.*

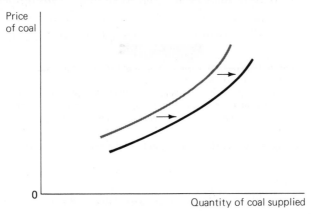

Fig. EFFECT OF INCREASE IN WAGES OF COAL MINERS ON MARKET SUPPLY
2.7 CURVE FOR COAL / *Increases in wage rates shift the supply curve to the left.*

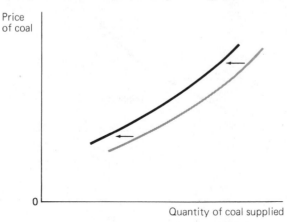

in the price of inputs may cause it to shift to the left. For example, if the wage rates of coal miners increase (as they did in 1987), the supply curve for coal may shift to the left, as shown in Figure 2.7.[9]

The Price Elasticity of Supply

Like market demand curves, market supply curves vary in shape. In particular, they vary with respect to the sensitivity of quantity supplied to price. For some goods, a small change in price results in a large change in quantity supplied; for other goods, a large change in price results in a small change in quantity supplied. To gauge the sensitivity of the quantity sup-

Price elasticity plied to changes in price, economists use a measure called the
of supply *price elasticity of supply,* which is defined to be *the percentage change in quantity supplied resulting from a 1 percent change in price.*[10] Thus, if a 1 percent increase in the price of natural gas results in a 0.5

---

9. Let the quantity supplied of a good per unit of time equal Q_s. In general,

$$Q_s = g(P, M, V)$$

where P is the price of the good, M is the level of input prices, and V stands for the level of technology. The supply curve shows the relationship between Q_s and P when the other variables are held constant. In general, changes in the values at which these other variables are held constant will affect the relationship between Q_s and P, which is another way of saying that these other variables will generally influence the position and shape of the market supply curve.

10. More accurately, if Q_s is the quantity supplied and P is the price, the price elasticity of supply is

$$\eta_s = \frac{dQ_s}{dP} \cdot \frac{P}{Q_s}.$$

More will be said about the measurement of the price elasticity of supply in Chapter 8.

percent increase in the quantity supplied, the price elasticity of supply of natural gas is 0.5.

Clearly, the price elasticity of supply is analogous to the price elasticity of demand. Like the latter, it is expressed in terms of relative, not absolute, changes in price and quantity, and it should not be confused with the slope of the supply curve. Its value is likely to vary from one point to another on a supply curve. For example, the price elasticity of supply of natural gas may be higher when the price is low than when it is high. In general, the price elasticity of supply would be expected to increase with the length of the period to which the supply curve pertains. Why? Because, as noted in the previous section, manufacturers of the good will be able to adapt their output rates more fully to changes in its price if the period is long rather than short.

If we have a market supply schedule showing the quantity of a commodity supplied at various prices, we can readily estimate the price elasticity of supply. Let ΔP be the change in the price of the good and ΔQ_s be the resulting change in its quantity supplied. If ΔP is very small, we can compute the *point elasticity of supply*:

$$\eta_s = \frac{\Delta Q_s}{Q_s} \div \frac{\Delta P}{P}. \qquad [2.3]$$

If ΔP is not so small, we can compute the *arc elasticity of supply* by using the average value of Q_s and P in Equation 2.3. These calculations are similar to (but not exactly the same as[11]) those required to compute the price elasticity of demand. To illustrate them, take the case in Table 2.4. Suppose that we want to compute the price elasticity of supply between \$30 and \$31. The arc elasticity of supply is

$$\eta_s = \frac{\Delta Q_s}{(Q_{S1} + Q_{S2})/2} \div \frac{\Delta P}{(P_1 + P_2)/2}$$

$$= \frac{650 - 600}{(650 + 600)/2} \div \frac{31 - 30}{(31 + 30)/2}$$

$$= 2.44.$$

---

11. In calculating the price elasticity of demand, we multiply the relative change in quantity demanded resulting from a 1 percent change in price by -1, so that the result will be a positive number. In calculating the price elasticity of supply, we do *not* have to multiply the relative change in quantity supplied resulting from a 1 percent change in price by -1, because it already is positive in the typical case. This is because, as we have already stressed, supply curves generally slope *upward* to the right, whereas demand curves generally slope *downward* to the right.

DETERMINANTS OF PRICE

The Equilibrium Price

Recall from the previous chapter that prices in a free-enterprise economy are important determinants of what is produced, how it is produced, who receives it, and how rapidly per capita income grows. It behooves us, therefore, to look carefully at how prices themselves are determined in a free-enterprise economy. As a first step toward describing this process, we must define the equilibrium price of a good. At various points in this book, you will encounter the concept of an equilibrium, which is very important in economics, as in many other scientific fields.

An equilibrium *is a situation where there is no tendency for change;* in other words, it is a situation that can persist. Thus *an equilibrium price is a price that can be maintained.* Any price that is not an equilibrium *Equilibrium*   price cannot be maintained for long, since there are basic forces at work to stimulate a change in price. The best way to understand what we mean by an equilibrium price is to take a particular case, such as the market for coal. Let's put both the demand curve for coal (in Figure 2.1) and the supply curve for coal (in Figure 2.5) together in the same diagram. The result, shown in Figure 2.8, will help us determine the equilibrium price of coal.

Fig. 2.8   Equilibrium Price and Quantity of Coal, 1988 / *The equilibrium price is $32 per ton; the equilibrium quantity is 700 million tons per year.*

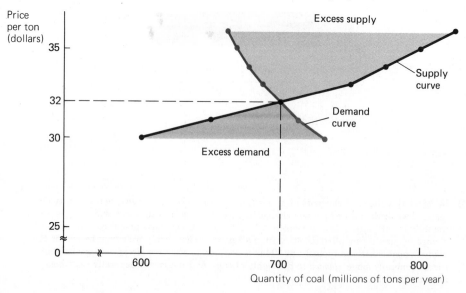

We begin by seeing what would happen if various prices were established in the market. For example, if the price were $34 a ton, the demand curve indicates that 680 million tons of coal would be demanded, while the supply curve indicates that 775 million tons would be supplied. Thus, if the price were $34 a ton, there would be a mismatch between the quantity supplied and the quantity demanded per year, since the rate at which coal is supplied would be greater than the rate at which it is demanded. Specifically, as shown in Figure 2.8, there would be an *excess supply* of 95 million tons. Under these circumstances, some of the coal supplied by producers could not be sold, and as inventories of coal built up, suppliers would tend to cut their prices in order to get rid of unwanted inventories. Thus a price of $34 per ton would not be maintained for long—and for this reason, $34 per ton is not an equilibrium price.

If the price were $30 per ton, on the other hand, the demand curve indicates that 730 million tons of coal would be demanded, while the supply curve indicates that 600 million tons would be supplied. Again we find a mismatch between the quantity supplied and the quantity demanded per year, since the rate at which coal is supplied would be less than the rate at which it is demanded. Specifically, as shown in Figure 2.8, there would be an *excess demand* of 130 million tons. Under these circumstances, some of the consumers who want coal at this price would have to be turned away empty-handed. There would be a shortage. And given this shortage, suppliers would find it profitable to increase the price, and competition among buyers would bid the price up. Thus a price of $30 per ton could not be maintained for long—so $30 per ton is not an equilibrium price.

The equilibrium price must be the price where the quantity demanded equals the quantity supplied. Obviously this is the only price at which there is no mismatch between the quantity demanded and the quantity supplied; and consequently the only price that can be maintained for long. In Figure 2.8, the price at which the quantity supplied equals the quantity demanded is $32 per ton, the price where the demand curve intersects the supply curve. Thus $32 per ton is the equilibrium price of coal under the circumstances visualized in Figure 2.8, and 700 million tons is the equilibrium quantity.[12]

The Actual Price

What we set out to explain was the actual price, not the equilibrium price —since the actual price is all that is observed in the real world. In general, economists simply assume that the actual price will approximate the equilibrium price, which seems reasonable enough, since the basic forces at work tend

---

12. If $P = D(Q)$ is the demand curve and $P = S(Q)$ is the supply curve, we have two equations in two unknowns— price (P) and quantity (Q). To determine the equilibrium price, we can solve these equations simultaneously for P and Q.

to push the actual price toward the equilibrium price. Thus, if the demand and supply curves remain fairly stable for a time, the actual price should move toward the equilibrium price.

To see that this is the case, consider the market for coal, as described by Figure 2.8. What if the price somehow is set at $34 per ton? As we saw in the previous section, there is downward pressure on the price of coal under these conditions. Suppose the price, responding to this pressure, falls to $33. Comparing the quantity demanded with the quantity supplied at $33, we find that there is still downward pressure on price, since the quantity supplied exceeds the quantity demanded at $33. The price, responding to this pressure, may fall to $32.50, but comparing the quantity demanded with the quantity supplied at this price, we find that there is still a downward pressure on price, since the quantity supplied exceeds the quantity demanded at $32.50.

So long as the actual price exceeds the equilibrium price, there will be a downward pressure on price. Similarly, so long as the actual price is less than the equilibrium price, there will be an upward pressure on price. Thus there is always a tendency for the actual price to move toward the equilibrium price. But it should not be assumed that this movement is always rapid. Sometimes it takes a long time for the actual price to get close to the equilibrium price. Sometimes the actual price never gets to the equilibrium price because by the time it gets close, the equilibrium price changes. All that safely can be said is that the actual price will move toward the equilibrium price. But of course this information is of great value, both theoretically and practically. For many purposes, all that is required is a prediction of whether the price will move up or down.

Effects on Price of Shifts in the Demand Curve

We have already seen that demand curves shift in response to changes in tastes, income, and prices of other products. Any supply-and-demand diagram like Figure 2.8 is essentially a snapshot of the situation during a particular period of time. The results in Figure 2.8 are limited to a particular period because the demand and supply curves in the figure pertain only to that period. What happens to the equilibrium price of a product (which we shall call good X) when its demand curve changes?

Suppose that consumer tastes shift in favor of good X, causing the demand curve for good X to shift to the right. This state of affairs is shown in Figure 2.9, where the demand curve shifts from D to D_1. It is not hard to see the effect on the equilibrium price of good X. When D is the demand curve, the equilibrium price is OP. But when the demand curve shifts to D_1, a shortage of (OQ_2-OQ) develops at this price. That is, the quantity demanded exceeds the quantity supplied at this price by (OQ_2-OQ). Consequently, suppliers raise their prices. After some testing of market reactions and trial-and-error ad-

Fig. 2.9 EFFECTS OF SHIFTS IN DEMAND CURVE ON EQUILIBRIUM PRICE / *A rightward shift of the demand curve tends to increase price; a leftward shift tends to reduce price.*

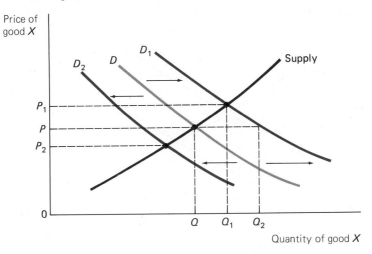

justments, the price will tend to settle at OP_1, the new equilibrium price, and quantity will tend to settle at OQ_1.

On the other hand, suppose that consumer demand for good X falls off, perhaps because of a great drop in the price of a product that is an effective substitute for good X. The demand for good X now shifts to the left. Specifically, as shown in Figure 2.9, it shifts from D to D_2. What will be the effect on the equilibrium price of good X? Clearly, the new equilibrium price will be OP_2, where the new demand curve intersects the supply curve.

To illustrate the usefulness of this model, consider the market for fish. In 1966, the Roman Catholic Church abolished the requirement that no meat be consumed on Fridays, with the result that the demand curve for fish shifted markedly to the left. What happened to the price of fish? In accord with our model, it fell substantially in areas like New England where there is a large Catholic population. Specifically, the price of flounder, haddock, cod, and perch fell about 10 to 20 percent in New England.[13]

In general, a shift to the right in the demand curve results in an increase in the equilibrium price, and a shift to the left in the demand curve results in a decrease in the equilibrium price. This is the lesson of Figure 2.9. Of course, this conclusion depends on the assumption that the supply curve slopes upward to the right, but, as we noted in a previous section, this is generally the case.

---

13. F. W. Bell, "The Pope and the Price of Fish," *American Economic Review*, December 1968.

Fig.   EFFECTS OF SHIFTS IN SUPPLY CURVE ON EQUILIBRIUM PRICE / *A rightward*
2.10   *shift of the supply curve tends to reduce price; a leftward shift tends to*
        increase price.

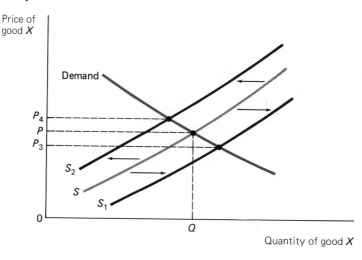

Effects on Price of Shifts in the Supply Curve

Supply curves, like demand curves, shift over time. What happens to the equilibrium price of a good when its supply curve shifts? Suppose that, because of technological advances, producers of good X are willing and able to supply more of good X at a given price than they used to. Specifically, suppose that the supply curve shifts from S to S_1 in Figure 2.10. What will be the effect on the equilibrium price? Clearly, it will fall from OP (where the S supply curve intersects the demand curve) to OP_3 (where the S_1 supply curve intersects the demand curve). On the other hand, suppose that input prices rise, with the result that the supply curve shifts from S to S_2 in Figure 2.10. Clearly, the equilibrium price will increase from OP (where the S supply curve intersects the demand curve) to OP_4 (where the S_2 supply curve intersects the demand curve).

Lovers of coffee were shown in late 1985 and early 1986 what a shift to the left in the supply curve of a commodity will do. A severe drought in southern Brazil wreaked havoc with the coffee crop, cutting Brazilian annual output from about 33 to 13 million bags. The result of this big shift to the left in the supply curve for coffee was just what our theory would predict: a big jump in coffee prices. For example, coffee sold for over $2.30 per pound in January 1986, compared to about $1.45 per pound before the drought.

In general, a shift to the right in the supply curve results in a decrease in the equilibrium price, and a shift to the left in the supply curve results in an increase in the equilibrium price. Of course, this conclusion depends on the assumption that the demand curve slopes downward to the right, but, as we noted in a previous section, this is generally the case.

Example 2.1

MEDICARE, MEDICAID, AND THE PRICE OF MEDICAL CARE

In 1965, the federal government enacted Medicare (a subsidy for medical care received by the aged) and Medicaid (a subsidy for medical care received by the poor). For simplicity, assume that these programs specify that the government pays all of the medical costs of the aged and the poor. Suppose that the demand curve for medical care by the aged and the poor and the demand curve for medical care by other people are as shown below. (a) What was the market demand curve for medical care prior to the enactment of Medicare and Medicaid? (b) What was the market demand curve for medical care after the enactment of Medicare and Medicaid? (c) What was the effect of Medicare and Medicaid on the price of medical care?

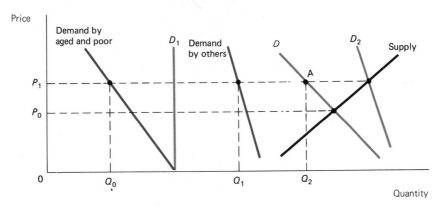

SOLUTION

(a) The market demand curve for medical care shows the total amount of medical care demanded at each price. To obtain the total amount of medical care demanded at a particular price, we must add the amount demanded by the poor and the aged to the amount demanded by others at that price. For example, if the price is OP_1, the amount demanded by the poor and aged is OQ_0, the amount demanded by other people is OQ_1, and the total amount demanded is OQ_2 (which equals $OQ_0 + OQ_1$). Thus, A is the point on the market demand curve corresponding to a price of OP_1. Points on the market demand curve corresponding to other prices can be determined in the same way. Connecting these points, we find that the market demand curve is D. (b) After the enactment of Medicare and Medicaid, the poor and the aged demanded the amount of medical care that they wanted at a zero price. They could obtain all the medical care they wanted free of charge, regardless of the true price. Thus the amount they demanded is shown by a vertical line, D_1. Adding their demand for medical care to that of other people, the result is D_2, the new market demand curve for medical care. (c) The price increased. Before Medicare and Medicaid, the equilibrium price was OP_0, where the market demand curve (D) intersected the market supply curve. After Medicare and Medicaid, the equilibrium price was OP_1, where the new market demand curve (D_2) intersected the market supply curve. In fact, during 1966–70, the price of medical care rose about 9 percentage points more than consumer prices generally.*

* For further discussion, see Karen Davis, *National Health Insurance: Benefits, Costs, and Consequences* (Washington, D.C.: Brookings, 1975).

Fig.   EFFECT OF EXCISE TAX ON PRICE AND OUTPUT OF CIGARETTES / *A 20 cent*
2.11   *excise tax shifts the supply curve upward by 20 cents, and increases the*
        equilibrium price from $1.20 to $1.30 per pack.

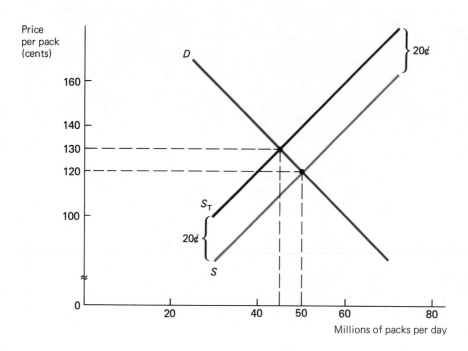

Analyzing the Effects of an Excise Tax

To illustrate how basic demand-and-supply models can be used to throw light
on the effects of various public-policy measures, we discuss in this section the
effects on price of an excise tax. Suppose that such a tax is imposed on a particular good, say cigarettes.[14] In Figure 2.11, we show the demand and supply
curves, *D* and *S*, for cigarettes before the imposition of the tax. Obviously, the
equilibrium price of a pack of cigarettes is $1.20, and the equilibrium quantity
is 50 million packs. If a tax of 20 cents is imposed on each pack produced, what
is the effect on the price of each pack? Or to see it from the smoker's perspective, how much of the tax is passed on to the consumer in the form of a higher
price?

Since the tax is collected from the sellers, the supply curve is shifted upward by the amount of the tax. In Figure 2.11, the posttax supply curve is S_T.
For example, if the pretax price had to be $1.00 a pack to induce sellers to sup-

---

14. For simplicity, we assume here that the market for cigarettes is perfectly competitive. In later
    chapters, we shall present models that pertain to cases where there are relatively few pro-
    ducers.

ply 40 million packs of cigarettes, the posttax price would have to be 20 cents higher—or $1.20 a pack—to induce the same supply. Similarly, if the pretax price had to be $1.20 a pack to induce sellers to supply 50 million packs of cigarettes, the posttax price would have to be 20 cents higher—or $1.40 a pack—to induce the same supply. The reason why the sellers require 20 cents more per pack to supply the pretax amount is that they must pay the 20 cents per pack to the government. Thus to wind up with the same amount as before (after paying the tax), they require the extra 20 cents per pack.

Figure 2.11 shows that, after the tax is imposed, the equilibrium price of cigarettes is $1.30, an increase of 10 cents over its pretax level. Consequently, in this case, half of the tax is passed on to consumers, who pay 10 cents more for cigarettes. And half of the tax is swallowed by the sellers, who receive (after they pay the tax) 10 cents per pack less for cigarettes. But it is not always true that sellers pass half of the tax on to consumers and absorb the rest themselves. On the contrary, in some cases, consumers may bear almost all of the tax (and sellers may bear practically none of it), while in other cases consumers may bear almost none of the tax (and sellers may bear practically all of it). The result will depend on how sensitive the quantity demanded and the quantity supplied are to the price of the good.

In particular, holding the supply curve constant, the less sensitive the quantity demanded is to the price of the good, the bigger the portion of the tax that is shifted to consumers. To illustrate this, consider panel A of Figure 2.12, which shows the effect of a 20 cents per pack tax on cigarettes in two markets, one where the quantity demanded (D_1) is much more sensitive to price than in the other case (D_2). Before the tax, the equilibrium price is OP_0, regardless of whether D_1 or D_2 is the demand curve. After the tax, the equilibrium price is OP_1 if the demand curve is D_1, or OP_2 if the demand curve is D_2. Clearly, the increase in the price to the consumer is greater if the quantity demanded is less sensitive to price (D_2) than if it is more sensitive (D_1).

Also, holding the demand curve constant, the less sensitive the quantity supplied is to the price of the good, the bigger the portion of the tax that is absorbed by producers. To illustrate this, consider panel B of Figure 2.12, which shows the effect of a 20 cents per pack tax on cigarettes in two markets, one where the quantity supplied (S_1) is much more sensitive to price than in the other case (S_2). Before the tax, the equilibrium price is OP_3, regardless of whether S_1 or S_2 is the pretax supply curve. After the tax, the equilibrium price is OP_4, if the (pretax) supply curve is S_2, or OP_5 if the (pretax) supply curve is S_1. Clearly, the increase in price to the consumer is greater if the quantity supplied is more sensitive to price (S_1) than if it is less sensitive (S_2).[15]

15. If government intervention is warranted to reduce cigarette smoking, one way of effecting such a reduction is by taxing cigarettes according to their tar and nicotine content. For an interesting discussion of such a tax, see J. Harris, "Taxing Tar and Nicotine," *American Economic Review*, June 1980.

Fig. EFFECT OF EXCISE TAX ON PRICE OF CIGARETTES, UNDER ALTERNATIVE
2.12 ASSUMPTIONS CONCERNING SENSITIVITY OF QUANTITY DEMANDED AND
QUANTITY SUPPLIED TO PRICE / *The tax results in a larger increase in price
if the quantity demanded is less sensitive to price than if it is more
sensitive, and if the quantity supplied is more sensitive to price than if it
is less sensitive.*

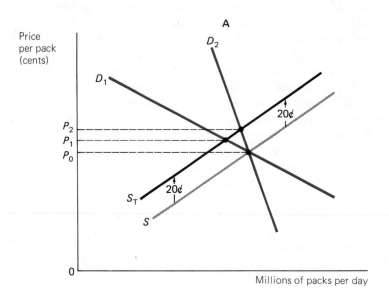

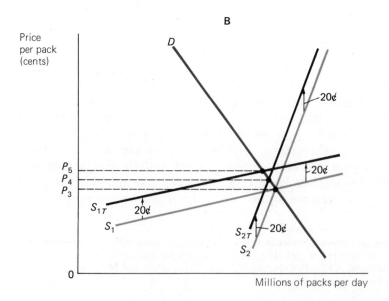

PRICE FLOORS AND CEILINGS

As a further illustration of how the simple models taken up in this chapter can help to illuminate public-policy issues, consider the case of price floors or price ceilings. As is well known, governments often intervene in markets to prop up the price of a particular good or to see to it that its price does not exceed a certain level. At this point we will sketch only roughly the effects of such price floors or price ceilings. More details on this subject will be added in later chapters.

The effects of a price floor are shown in Figure 2.13. As is evident, the equilibrium price of the good is OP. Nonetheless, because the government feels that this price is not equitable, it sets a minimum price of OP_m. At this minimum price, the quantity supplied (OQ_S) exceeds the quantity demanded (OQ_D), and the government is faced with the problem of disposing of the surplus or of limiting production so that the quantity supplied is no more than OQ_D. One important area where price floors have been adopted in the United States has been agriculture. For major farm commodities like wheat and corn, there long have been minimum prices established by the government. As our model predicts, a major problem stemming from these price floors has been the disposal and limitation of farm surpluses.[16]

Fig. 2.13 EFFECT OF A PRICE FLOOR / *If the government sets a minimum price of* OP_m, *the quantity supplied exceeds the quantity demanded, and there is the problem of disposing of the surplus.*

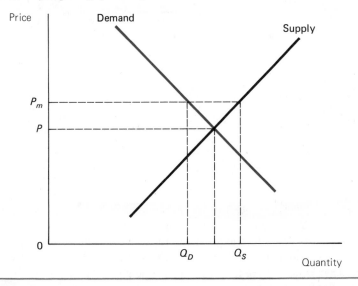

16. In Chapters 8 and 14, we discuss these agricultural price floors and their effects in much more detail.

Example 2.2

THE 1983 INCREASE IN THE CIGARETTE TAX: HOW MUCH WAS PASSED ON TO CONSUMERS?

On January 1, 1983, federal taxes on cigarettes doubled from 8 to 16 cents a pack. (a) If, as some economists believe, the supply curve for cigarettes is horizontal, how much of this federal tax increase was passed on to consumers? (b) According to MIT's Jeffrey Harris, the price of cigarettes rose about 28 cents a pack between August 1982 and 1986. Was this price increase due entirely to the tax hike? If not, what other factors might account for it?

SOLUTION

(a) Under the assumptions made above, all of it was passed on to consumers. If the supply curve is horizontal, and if the tax per pack equals 8 cents, the supply curve is as shown in the graph below. If the tax increases from 8 cents to 16 cents per pack, the supply curve is 8 cents higher than when the tax equaled 8 cents. Thus, as indicated in the graph, the price goes up from OP_1 to OP_2, an increase of 8 cents per pack. (b) Based on the assumption in part (a), one would expect the tax hike to increase the price of cigarettes by 8 cents, not 28 cents a pack. However, this market is not perfectly competitive. According to Harris, the cigarette manufacturers, wanting to diversify into other lines of business, felt that the "time had finally come to exercise market power and take profits." Much more will be said in Chapters 9–11 about pricing in markets that are not perfectly competitive.*

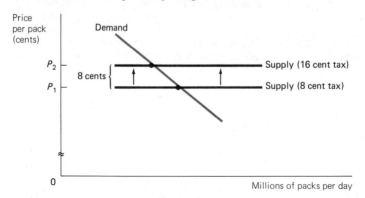

*J. Harris, "Who Should Profit From Cigarettes?," *New York Times,* March 15, 1987.

The effects of a price ceiling are shown in Figure 2.14. Although the equilibrium price is OP, the government sets a maximum price of OP_n, because it does not want the price of the good to rise to its equilibrium level. At this maximum price, the quantity demanded (OQ_D) exceeds the quantity supplied (OQ_S); in other words, there is a shortage of the good. To allocate the limited supply among the many buyers who want to purchase the good, the government may resort to some form of rationing. For example, in World War II

Fig. 2.14 EFFECTS OF A PRICE CEILING / *If the government sets a ceiling price of* OP_n, *the quantity demanded exceeds the quantity supplied, and there is a shortage of the good.*

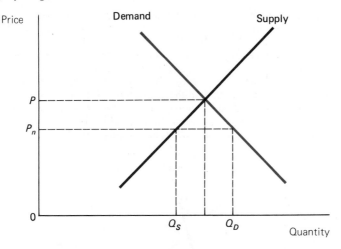

when price controls were in effect, families were issued ration coupons which determined how much they could buy of various commodities. Frequently, *black markets* develop under these circumstances, where the good is sold illegally at a price higher than the legal maximum. As our model predicts, a major problem stemming from price ceilings has been the resolution of the shortages that ensue.

Rent Control in New York City: Illustration of a Price Ceiling

Price floors and ceilings can and do affect our everyday lives. Since 1943, New York City has had a system of rent control which imposes ceilings on rents. The purpose is, of course, to establish a rent (that is, the price of using an apartment for a month) that is below the equilibrium level. One important justification that proponents of rent control give for such price ceilings is that they help the poor. In the short run, rent control is likely to transfer income from landlords to tenants.

But as time goes on, rent control can have some very undesirable effects. As shown in Figure 2.14, a price ceiling results in a shortage. That is, the quantity demanded of apartments will exceed the quantity supplied. According to some observers, New York City has a shortage of about $3 billion worth of new rental housing despite a loss in population of about 1 million people in the 1970s and the nation's largest government-assisted middle-income and low-rent public housing programs. In 1986, the *New York Times* reported that some people have had to look for a year or more to obtain an apartment.

Because the quantity demanded exceeds the quantity supplied, the avail-

Example 2.3

THE BATTLE OVER NATURAL GAS PRICING

One of the bloodiest economic battles in Congress in the late 1970s was over the government-imposed ceiling on the price of natural gas (in interstate commerce). This ceiling came about as a result of the 1954 Supreme Court decision that the Federal Energy Regulatory Commission (then the Federal Power Commission) should regulate the price of natural gas. In 1977 and 1978, there was a struggle between those who favored continuation of the price ceiling and those who opposed it. This struggle was waged with vigor, if not ferocity, since billions of dollars were at stake. In late 1978 legislation was passed which called for deregulation of the price of new gas.

(a) The basic argument of the opponents of the price ceiling was that it was below the equilibrium price, as shown below. (*OP* is the ceiling price.) What is the likely ef-

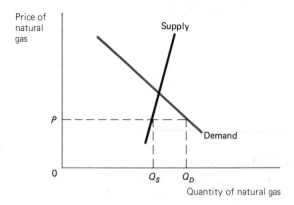

fect? (b) If the price ceiling was below the equilibrium price, what advantages would result from allowing the price of natural gas to rise? (c) Many who favored continuation of the price ceiling argued that the supply curve for natural gas has a very low price elasticity. Why was this regarded as relevant? (d) Many observers also questioned whether the market for natural gas was competitive. Why was this regarded as important?

SOLUTION

(a) If the price is below its equilibrium level, there is a shortage of natural gas. In this case, OQ_D is demanded and only OQ_S is supplied. (b) In the words of President Gerald Ford's Council of Economic Advisers, "Deregulation of the price of new natural gas ... would redirect supplies toward their most valuable uses, [and] increase incentives to enlarge future supplies ..."* (c) If the price elasticity of supply is low, increases in price would not elicit much additional supply. Thus, it was argued that such price increases would mean a transfer of billions of dollars from consumers to gas producers—but little additional supply of gas. (d) Unless the market is competitive, the supply-and-demand analysis shown in the figure above is really not appropriate. Instead, models of the sort taken up in Part IV should be used.†

* *Economic Report of the President* (Washington, D.C.: U.S. Government Printing Office, 1976), p. 24.

† For further discussion, see J. Griffin and H. Steele, *Energy Economics and Policy*, 2d ed. (New York: Academic Press, 1985).

able apartments have to be rationed by some device other than price. This, of course, may allow landlords to engage in many forms of subtle and not-so-subtle discrimination in choosing tenants. Also, landlords will have an incentive to accept side payments or bribes from those looking for housing. They will curtail maintenance of their properties in many cases; because there is a shortage, renters are willing to accept poorer service and do more things for themselves. To the extent possible, landlords may try to subdivide apartments, since the ceiling on the rents from the subdivisions may exceed that of the original apartment. In all these ways, landlords may try to adjust to, and to some extent evade, the price ceilings.

In New York, according to estimates made by the RAND Corporation, rent increases have fallen far short of cost increases because of the rent-control laws. For housing units built before 1943, the average increase in rents was about 2 percent per year, whereas the average increase in landlords' costs was about 6 percent per year. Thus, it is not surprising that more new housing has not been built, and that existing housing often has been poorly maintained.

In April 1987, the *New York Times* said that "New York's housing market is filled with anomalies and distortions that tend to turn reality on its head. There is a crushing demand for housing, yet developers do not build anything affordable by any part of the population but the upper middle class."[17] Most economists certainly would agree that the continuation of a price ceiling is not a policy that is likely to resolve a serious shortage. But our purpose here is not to decide whether the opponents of rent controls are right or wrong; instead, it is to indicate the central role played by the microeconomic concepts discussed in this chapter in understanding the issue. Even though this chapter deals only with the basic concepts of demand and supply, the results are of importance in illuminating this and many other major policy issues.

SUMMARY

1. The market demand curve for a good almost always slopes downward to the right; that is, the quantity demanded increases as the price falls. The position and shape of the market demand curve for a good depend on the tastes of consumers, the level of consumer incomes, the prices of other goods, and the length of the time period to which the demand curve pertains.

2. The price elasticity of demand, defined as the percentage change in the quantity demanded resulting from a 1 percent change in price, is a measure of the responsiveness of quantity demanded to changes in price. The price elasticity of demand will generally vary from one point to another on a demand

---

17. "State to Compare Rents with Incomes," *New York Times,* April 19, 1987.

curve. Estimated price elasticities are of two types: point elasticities and arc elasticities.

3. The market supply curve for a good generally slopes upward to the right; that is, the quantity supplied increases as the price rises. The position and shape of the market supply curve for a good depends on the state of technology, input prices, and the length of the time interval to which the supply curve pertains.

4. The price elasticity of supply, defined as the percentage change in the quantity supplied resulting from a 1 percent change in price, is a measure of the responsiveness of quantity supplied to changes in price. The price elasticity of supply will generally vary from one point to another on a supply curve.

5. An equilibrium price is a price that can be maintained. In a competitive market, it is the price where the quantity demanded equals the quantity supplied. In other words, it is the price where the demand curve intersects the supply curve. If the actual price exceeds the equilibrium price, there will be an excess supply of the good, and the actual price will tend to fall. If the actual price is less than the equilibrium price, there will be an excess demand for the good, and the actual price will tend to rise.

6. In general, a shift to the right in the demand curve results in an increase in the equilibrium price, and a shift to the left in the demand curve results in a decrease in the equilibrium price. In general, a shift to the right in the supply curve results in a decrease in the equilibrium price, and a shift to the left in the supply curve results in an increase in the equilibrium price.

7. Demand-and-supply analysis can be used to throw light on the effect of an excise tax. Since the tax is collected from the sellers, the supply curve of the good on which the tax is imposed is shifted upward by the amount of the tax. How much the price of the good is increased by the tax depends on how sensitive the quantity demanded and quantity supplied are to changes in the price of the good.

8. Models of this type can also be used to analyze the effects of price floors and price ceilings imposed by the government. Price floors tend to result in surpluses, and price ceilings tend to result in shortages.

QUESTIONS / PROBLEMS

1) There is a considerable amount of air travel between Los Angeles and New York City; it is one of the most intensively traveled routes in the country. According to P. Verleger, the price elasticity of demand for air travel between Los Angeles and New York City is about 0.67. (a) Suppose that an economic consultant says that the demand curve for air travel between Los Angeles and New York City is as shown below.

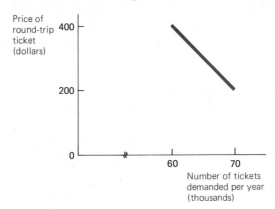

Is this graph in accord with Verleger's finding? Why or why not? (b) Suppose that the airlines double the price of a ticket between Los Angeles and New York City. Will this price increase affect the demand curve for air travel between these two cities? If so, in what way? (c) Suppose that a severe recession occurs. Will this affect the demand curve for air travel between these two cities? If so, in what way? (d) Because of the marked increase in the price of jet fuel (and other things), the cost of providing air transportation between Los Angeles and New York City has risen appreciably in recent decades. Does such a cost increase affect the demand curve for air travel between these two cities? If so, in what way?

2) The market supply curve for good Y is a straight line through the origin. Does the price elasticity of supply vary with good Y's price? What is good Y's price elasticity of supply?

3) Suppose that the number of bicycles demanded in the United States at various prices is as follows:

Price of a bicycle (dollars)	Quantity demanded per year (millions of bicycles)
80	20
100	18
120	16

Draw three points on the demand curve for bicycles. Calculate the arc price elasticity of demand when (a) the price is between $80 and $100, and (b) the price is between $100 and $120.

4) Suppose that the relationship between the quantity of bicycles supplied per year in the United States and the price per bicycle is as follows:

Price of a bicycle	*Quantity supplied per year*
(dollars)	*(millions of bicycles)*
60	14
80	16
100	18
120	19

Draw four points on the supply curve for bicycles, and estimate the price elasticity of supply when the price is between $80 and $100.

5) Based on the data presented in Questions 3 and 4, what is the equilibrium price of a bicycle in the United States? If the price is $80, will there be an excess demand? An excess supply? If the price is $120, will there be an excess demand? An excess supply?

6) Suppose that an excise tax of $40 is imposed on each bicycle. What will be the posttax equilibrium price of a bicycle? What will be the posttax equilibrium quantity? How does it compare with the pretax equilibrium quantity?

7) After the government imposes the tax in Question 6, it decides to set a price ceiling of $100 on the price of a bicycle. Will there be a surplus of bicycles? A shortage? If so, how big a surplus or shortage?

8) According to Richard Titmuss of the London School of Economics, no Englishman pays even a shilling for all the blood his physicians prescribe for him, and no blood donor is paid for his blood. Yet blood is more readily available for patients there than in the United States where we pay for the donation of blood. What hypotheses can be advanced to account for this?

9) Suppose that the demand curve for cantaloupes is

$$P = 120 - 3\,Q_D$$

where P is the price per pound (in cents) of a cantaloupe and Q_D is the quantity demanded per year (in millions of pounds). Suppose that the supply curve for cantaloupes is

$$P = 5Q_S$$

where Q_S is the quantity supplied per year (in millions of pounds). What is the equilibrium price per pound of a cantaloupe? What is the equilibrium quantity of cantaloupes produced?

10) Indicate whether each of the following will shift the demand curve for cantaloupes to the left, to the right, or have no effect on it: (a) a report by the U.S. Surgeon-General that cantaloupes cause cancer; (b) a 10 percent increase in the price of honeydew melons; (c) a 20 percent increase in per capita income; (d) a 10 percent increase in the wages of workers producing cantaloupes.

11) Suppose that the government puts a price floor of 80 cents per pound on cantaloupes. How big will be the resulting surplus of cantaloupes, based on the data in Question 9? What measures can the government adopt to cut down on this surplus?

12) In July 1986, there was a major drought in the southeastern United States. As a result, beef prices fell 5 percent. Why? (Hint: The drought reduced hay and feed production, and farmers moved their cattle much earlier to slaughterhouses.)

Consumer Behavior and Market Demand

The Tastes and Preferences
of the Consumer

INTRODUCTION

Microeconomics is the branch of economics that deals with the behavior of individual decision-making units, one of the most important of which is the consumer. For many purposes the consumer is not an individual but a household; the decisions regarding the purchase of a house or car, for example, often are household rather than individual decisions. In other cases, however, the individual person is the consumer, as, for example, when he or she buys a meal at a restaurant. Regardless of the precise way in which the consumer is defined, there are millions of consumers in the United States—and they spend a great deal of money. In recent years, the American consumer has spent over $2 trillion per year on final goods and services. About 70 percent of the final goods and services produced by the American economy go directly to consumers. Moreover, the importance of consumers is not a purely American phenomenon. For example, in our neighbor to the north, Canada, about two-thirds of the final goods and services produced by the Canadian economy go directly to consumers. Similar figures could be cited for many other countries.

In this chapter we present a simple model to represent the consumer's tastes and to help predict how much of various commodities he or she will buy. Besides being of interest for its own sake, this model is a first step toward analyzing the forces underlying the market demand curve, the importance of which was stressed in the previous chapter. Some of the major concepts that are introduced in this model are utility, indifference curves, the marginal rate of substitution, and the budget line. Finally, we show how this body of theory has been applied to help solve very important practical problems of budget allocation by government agencies.

THE NATURE OF THE CONSUMER'S PREFERENCES

Our purpose in this chapter is to present a simple model of consumer behavior that will enable us to predict how much of a particular commodity—hot dogs, paint, housing—a consumer buys during a particular period of time. Clearly, one of the most important determinants of a consumer's behavior is his or her tastes or preferences. After all, some consumers like Charles Dickens while others like comic books; some like Richard Wagner and others like the Rolling Stones. And it is obvious that these differences in tastes result in quite different decisions by consumers as to what commodities they buy. In this section we present three basic assumptions that the economist makes about the nature of the consumer's tastes.

To begin with, suppose that the consumer is confronted with any two market baskets, each containing various quantities of commodities. For example, one market basket might contain 1 ticket to a football game and 3 chocolate bars, while the other might contain 4 bottles of soda and a bus ticket. The first assumption that the economist makes is that consumers can decide whether they prefer the first market basket to the second, whether they prefer the second to the first, or whether they are indifferent between them.[1] This certainly seems to be a plausible assumption.

Second, we assume that the consumer's preferences are transitive. For example, if a man prefers Budweiser to Miller and Miller to Coors, he must also prefer Budweiser to Coors. Otherwise his preferences would not be transitive, which would mean that his preferences would be contradictory or inconsistent. Similarly, if he is indifferent between mince pie and pumpkin pie and between pumpkin pie and apple pie, he must also be indifferent between mince pie and apple pie. His tastes may be judged to be shallow or deep, lofty or mean, selfish or generous: This makes no difference to the theory. But his preferences must be transitive. Although not all consumers may exhibit preferences

---

1. One way of telling whether the consumer prefers one market basket to another is to set equivalent prices for them and ask which one the consumer wants.

that are transitive, this assumption certainly seems to be a plausible basis for a model of consumer behavior.

Third, we assume that the consumer always prefers more of a commodity to less. For example, if one market basket (a very big one) contains 15 harmonicas and 2 gallons of gasoline, whereas another market basket (also big) contains 15 harmonicas and 1 gallon of gasoline, we assume that the first market basket, which unambiguously contains more commodities, is preferred. Also, we assume that, by adding a certain amount of harmonicas to the second market basket, we can make it equally desirable in the eyes of the consumer to the first market basket; that is, we can make the consumer indifferent between them. These assumptions, like the previous two, seem quite plausible.

Utility

To understand the theory of consumer behavior, it is essential to understand the concept of utility. In the next five sections of this chapter, we assume that utility is measurable, like a person's height or weight. Then, in the rest of this chapter, we relax this simplifying assumption. To focus on the important factors at work here, let's assume that there are only two goods, food and medicine. This is an innocuous assumption, since the results we shall obtain can be generalized to include cases where any number of goods exists. For simplicity, food is measured in pounds, and medicine is measured in ounces.

Consider consumers making choices concerning how much of each good to buy. Undoubtedly, they regard certain market baskets—that is, certain combinations of food and medicine (the only commodities)—to be more desirable than others. For example, a consumer certainly would regard 2 pounds of food and 1 ounce of medicine to be more desirable than 1 pound of food and 1 ounce of medicine. For simplicity, suppose that it is possible to measure the amount of satisfaction that the consumer gets from each market *Total utility* basket by its utility. A utility *is a number that represents the level of satisfaction that the consumer derives from a particular market basket.* For example, the utility attached to the market basket containing 2 pounds of food and 1 ounce of medicine may be 13 utils, and the utility attached to the market basket containing 1 pound of food and 1 ounce of medicine may be 8 utils. (A util is the traditional unit in which utility is expressed.)

It is important to distinguish between total utility and marginal utility. The total utility of a market basket is the number described in the previous paragraph, whereas *the* marginal utility *measures the additional* *Marginal* *satisfaction derived from an additional unit of a commodity (when* *utility* *the levels of consumption of all other commodities are held constant).* To see how marginal utility is obtained, let's take a close look at Table 3.1. The total utility the consumer derives from the consumption of various amounts of food is given in the middle column of this table. (For

Table CONSUMER'S TOTAL AND MARGINAL UTILITY FROM CONSUMING VARIOUS
3.1   AMOUNTS OF FOOD PER DAY

Pounds of food	Total utility	Marginal utility*
0	0	—
1	4	4(= 4 − 0)
2	9	5(= 9 − 4)
3	13	4(= 13 − 9)
4	16	3(= 16 − 13)
5	18	2(= 18 − 16)

* These figures pertain to the interval between the indicated
number of pounds of food and one pound less than the indicated number. This table assumes that no medicine is consumed.

simplicity, we assume for the moment that only food is consumed.) The marginal utility, shown in the right-hand column, is the extra utility derived from
each amount of food over and above the utility derived from 1 less pound of
food. Thus it equals the difference between the total utility of a certain amount
of food and the total utility of 1 less pound of food.

For example, as shown in Table 3.1, the *total* utility of 3 pounds of food is
13 utils, which is a measure of the total amount of satisfaction that the consumer gets from this much food. In contrast, the *marginal* utility of 3 pounds of
food is the extra utility obtained from the third pound of food—that is, the
total utility of 3 pounds of food less the total utility of 2 pounds of food. Specifically, as shown in Table 3.1, it is 4 utils. Similarly, the *total* utility of 2 pounds
of food is 9 utils, which is a measure of the total amount of satisfaction that the
consumer gets from this much food. In contrast, the *marginal* utility of 2
pounds of food is the extra utility from the second pound of food—that is, the
total utility of 2 pounds of food less the total utility of 1 pound of food. Specifically, as shown in Table 3.1, it is 5 utils.

The Law of Diminishing Marginal Utility

It seems reasonable to believe that, as a person consumes more and more
of a particular commodity, there is, beyond some point, a decline in the extra
satisfaction derived from the last unit of the commodity consumed. For example, if a person consumes 2 pounds of food in a particular period of time, it may
be just what the doctor ordered. If he or she consumes 3 pounds of food in the
same period of time, the third pound of food is likely to yield less satisfaction
than the second. If he or she consumes 4 pounds of food in the same period of
time, the fourth pound of food is likely to yield less satisfaction than the third.
And so on.

Fig. DIMINISHING MARGINAL UTILITY / *If more than* OB *units of the commodity*
3.1 *are consumed, marginal utility declines.*

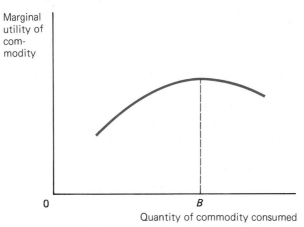

This assumption or hypothesis is often called the law of diminishing marginal utility. This law states that, *as a person consumes more and more of a given commodity (the consumption of other commodities being held constant), the marginal utility of the commodity eventually will tend to decline.* In other words, it states that the relationship between the marginal utility of a commodity and the amount consumed will be as shown in Figure 3.1. Beyond some point (*OB* in Figure 3.1), the marginal utility declines as the amount consumed increases. Finally, note that the figures concerning the consumer in Table 3.1 are in accord with this law. Once the consumption of food exceeds 2 pounds, the marginal utility of food declines.

THE RATIONAL CONSUMER

Assume for the moment that it is possible to measure the utility a consumer attaches to each market basket. If so, these measurements are a complete representation of his or her tastes and preferences. From them we can tell at a glance which market baskets the consumer would prefer over other market baskets. If the utility attached to the first market basket is higher than the second, he or she will prefer the first over the second market basket. If the utility attached to the first market basket is lower than the second, he or she will prefer the second over the first market basket. If the utility attached to the first market basket equals the second, he or she will be indifferent between the two market baskets.

Given the consumer's tastes, we assume that he or she is rational, in the

Utility maximi-
zation

sense that he or she tries to *maximize utility.* This assumption is so general and so reasonable that most people would accept it as a good approximation to reality. Of course, this is not to deny that some acts are irrational. However, by and large, people's actions seem to be such that they promote, not frustrate, the achievement of their goals. Even the ascetic, although his actions may seem irrational at first glance, can be regarded as attempting to maximize utility, if we recognize the very peculiar nature of his tastes.

Going a step further, we note that, although the consumer may attempt to maximize utility, he or she may not succeed in doing so because of miscalculation or for other reasons. The problem of maximizing utility may not be as simple as it looks. For example, how many people know how much their cars really cost them? It is not that they do not know how to do the arithmetic; more important is the fact that what should or should not be regarded as a cost in a particular situation is not always straightforward. More will be said on this score in subsequent chapters. For the moment, all we want to point out is that consumers may not be able to achieve the maximization of utility, at least right away.

However, if the consumer is allowed some time to adapt and to learn, it seems likely that he or she will eventually find the market basket that maximizes his or her utility. Let us define the consumer's equilibrium behavior as a course of action that will not be changed by him or her in favor of some other course of action, if the consumer's money income, tastes, and the prices he or she faces remain the same. Then the consumer's equilibrium behavior will be to choose the market basket that maximizes his or her utility. And eventually one would expect the consumer to come very close to acting in accord with his or her equilibrium behavior.

To maximize utility, the consumer must take account of factors other than his or her own tastes. Account must be taken of the *prices* of various commodities and the level of the consumer's *money income,* since both of these factors limit, or constrain, the nature and size of the market basket that he or she can buy. The consumer's money income is the amount of money that he or she can spend per unit of time.[2] If a consumer had an infinite money income, there would be no need to worry that certain market baskets might be too expensive to purchase. The consumer could simply buy the market basket he or she liked best. But no one has an unlimited money income. Even the Rockefellers and Mellons cannot buy the market basket they like best, since this would mean the expenditure of more than even they have. For us poorer folk, the problem is much more difficult still, since our incomes are much smaller. What we can buy is much more severely constrained by our incomes.

---

2. To the extent that the consumer can borrow, the amount he or she can borrow can, for some purposes, also be included as income, since it increases the amount the consumer can spend during the period.

Besides his or her money income, the consumer must also take account of the prices of all relevant commodities. The price of a commodity is the amount of money that the consumer must pay for a unit of the commodity. The higher prices are, the fewer units of a commodity can be bought with a given money income. For example, an income of $20,000 went a lot further when movies were 50 cents and sodas were 5 cents a bottle than it does now when movies are often $5 and sodas are 60 cents or more a can.

The Equilibrium Market Basket

What is the optimal market basket, the one that maximizes utility subject to these constraints? It is the one where *the consumer's income is allocated among commodities so that, for every commodity purchased, the marginal utility of the commodity is proportional to its price.* Thus, in the case of the consumer whose choices are limited to food and medicine, the optimal market basket is the one where

$$\frac{MU_F}{P_F} = \frac{MU_M}{P_M} \qquad\qquad [3.1]$$

where MU_F is the marginal utility of food, MU_M is the marginal utility of medicine, P_F is the price of a pound of food, and P_M is the price of an ounce of medicine.

To understand why the rule in Equation 3.1 is correct, it is convenient to begin by pointing out that $MU_F \div P_F$ is the marginal utility of the *last dollar's worth* of food and that $MU_M \div P_M$ is the marginal utility of the *last dollar's worth* of medicine. To see why this is so, take the case of food. Since MU_F is the extra utility of the *last pound* of food bought, and since P_F is the price of this *last pound,* the extra utility of the *last dollar's worth* of food must be $MU_F \div P_F$. For example, if the last pound of food results in an extra utility of 4 utils and this pound costs $2, then the extra utility from the last dollar's worth of food must be 4 ÷ 2, or 2 utils. In other words, the marginal utility of the last dollar's worth of food is 2 utils.

Since $MU_F \div P_F$ is the marginal utility of the last dollar's worth of food and $MU_M \div P_M$ is the marginal utility of the last dollar's worth of medicine, what Equation 3.1 really says is that *the rational consumer will choose a market basket where the marginal utility of the last dollar spent on all commodities purchased is the same.* To see why this must be so, consider the numerical example in Table 3.2, which shows the marginal utility the consumer derives from various amounts of food and medicine. Rather than measuring food and medicine in physical units, we measure them in Table 3.2 in terms of the amount of money spent on them.

Given the information in Table 3.2, how much of each commodity should the consumer buy if his or her money income is only $4 (a ridiculous assumption but one that will help to make our point)? Clearly, the first dollar the

Table CONSUMER'S MARGINAL UTILITY FROM CONSUMING VARIOUS AMOUNTS OF
3.2   FOOD AND MEDICINE PER DAY

Dollars worth of each commodity	Food	Medicine
1	9	4
2	7	3
3	4	2
4	3	1
5	2	0

consumer spends should be on food since it will yield him or her a marginal utility of 9. The second dollar he or she spends should also be on food since a second dollar's worth of food has a marginal utility of 7. (Thus the total utility derived from the $2 of expenditure is $9 + 7 = 16$.[3]) The marginal utility of the third dollar is 4 if it is spent on more food—and 4 too if it is spent on medicine. Suppose that he or she chooses more food. (The total utility derived from the $3 of expenditure is $9 + 7 + 4 = 20$.) What about the final dollar? Its marginal utility is 3 if it is spent on more food and 4 if it is spent on medicine; thus he or she will spend it on medicine. (The total utility derived from all $4 of expenditure is then $9 + 7 + 4 + 4 = 24$.)

Clearly, the consumer, if rational, will allocate $3 of his or her income to food and $1 to medicine. This is the equilibrium market basket, the market basket that maximizes consumer satisfaction. The important thing to note is that this market basket demonstrates the principle set forth at the beginning of this section. As shown in Table 3.2, the marginal utility derived from the last dollar spent on food is equal to the marginal utility derived from the last dollar spent on medicine. (Both are 4.) Thus this market basket has the characteristic described above: The marginal utility of the last dollar spent on all commodities purchased is the same. In the next section, we show that this will always be the case for market baskets that maximize the consumer's utility. If it were not true, the consumer could obtain a higher level of utility by changing the composition of his or her market basket.

The Budget Allocation Rule: Further Proof

In the previous section, we stated the proposition that the consumer, to maximize utility, will choose a market basket where the marginal utility of the

---

3. Since the marginal utility is the extra utility obtained from each dollar spent, the total utility from the total expenditure must be the sum of the marginal utilities of the individual dollars of expenditure.

last dollar spent on all commodities purchased is the same. In this section, we show that, if this budget allocation rule is not followed, the consumer cannot be maximizing utility. This is offered as further proof of the proposition in the previous section. For simplicity, we continue to assume that the consumer buys only two commodities, food and medicine.

Suppose that the marginal utility of the last dollar spent on food is 3 utils whereas the marginal utility of the last dollar spent on medicine is 2 utils. Clearly, the consumer is not maximizing utility, because spending $1 more on food will increase total utility by 3 utils,[4] and spending $1 less on medicine will reduce total utility by 2 utils. Thus the transfer of $1 of expenditure from medicine to food will increase total utility by 1 util. More generally, a transfer of expenditure from medicine to food will always increase a consumer's utility so long as the marginal utility of the last dollar spent on food exceeds the marginal utility of the last dollar spent on medicine. Thus *the consumer will not be maximizing utility if the marginal utility of the last dollar spent on food exceeds the marginal utility of the last dollar spent on medicine.*

Suppose that the situation is reversed, with the marginal utility of the last dollar spent on food being 2 utils and the marginal utility of the last dollar spent on medicine being 3 utils. Clearly, the consumer is not maximizing utility, because spending $1 more on medicine will increase total utility by 3 utils,[5] and spending $1 less on food will reduce total utility by 2 utils. Thus the transfer of $1 of expenditure from food to medicine will result in a net increase of utility of 1 util. More generally, a transfer of expenditure from food to medicine will always increase total utility so long as the marginal utility of the last dollar spent on medicine exceeds the marginal utility of the last dollar spent on food. Thus *the consumer will not be maximizing utility if the marginal utility of the last dollar spent on medicine exceeds the marginal utility of the last dollar spent on food.*

In the previous paragraph, we showed that the consumer will *not* be maximizing utility if the marginal utility of the last dollar spent on food is *less than* the marginal utility of the last dollar spent on medicine. In the paragraph before last, we showed that the consumer will *not* be maximizing utility if the marginal utility of the last dollar spent on food *exceeds* the marginal utility of the last dollar spent on medicine. Consequently, it follows that the consumer will be maximizing utility only when the marginal utility of the last dollar spent on food equals the marginal utility of the last dollar spent on medicine. This is what we set out to prove.

---

4. We assume here that the extra utility from an *extra* dollar spent on food equals the extra utility from the *last* dollar spent on food. This is an innocuous assumption.

5. We assume here that the extra utility from an *extra* dollar spent on medicine equals the extra utility from the *last* dollar spent on medicine. This, like the assumption in footnote 4, is innocuous.

CARDINAL AND ORDINAL UTILITY

In previous sections, we assumed that utility is measurable, like weight or height. In this regard, we followed the example of such great nineteenth-century economists as William Stanley Jevons of England, Karl Menger of Austria, and Léon Walras of France. In their view, utility was measurable in a *cardinal* sense, which means that the difference between two measurements is itself numerically significant. For example, if I weigh 185 pounds and you weigh 170 pounds, the difference between these measurements has numerical significance: It says that I weigh 15 pounds more than you do. Moreover, if the difference between Ed McMahon's and Johnny Carson's weights is 60 pounds, it follows that the difference between my weight and yours is less than the difference between Ed McMahon's weight and Johnny Carson's. According to most nineteenth-century economists, utility was measurable in the same sense.

Cardinal utility

In contrast, most twentieth-century economists, following the lead of E. Slutsky, Vilfredo Pareto, Sir John Hicks, and other great figures of the more recent past, assume that utility is measurable in an *ordinal* sense, which means that a consumer can only *rank* various market baskets with regard to the satisfaction they give him or her.[6] For example, you may be able to say with assurance that you prefer two tickets to the Super Bowl to two tickets to the San Francisco Opera, but you may not be able to say how many more utils of satisfaction you get from the former than the latter. For an ordinal measurement of utility, this is adequate, since all that is needed is a ranking. If the consumer prefers market basket 1 to market basket 2, and market basket 2 to market basket 3, the utility of market basket 1 must be higher than the utility of market basket 2, and the utility of market basket 2 must be higher than the utility of market basket 3. But any set of numbers conforming to these requirements is an adequate measure of utility in an ordinal sense. For example, the utility of market baskets 1, 2, and 3 may be 50, 40, and 30, or 10, 9, 8. Both are adequate utility measures, since all that counts is that the utility of market basket 1 be higher than that of market basket 2, which in turn should be higher than that of market basket 3.

Ordinal utility

The modern assumption that utility is ordinally measurable is less restrictive than the older assumption that utility is cardinally measurable. That is, we need not assume that a consumer can answer questions like: How many extra utils of satisfaction will you get from a second helping of mashed potatoes? Indeed, the concept of marginal utility loses much of its meaning if util-

---

6. For example, see J. Hicks, *Value and Capital* (New York: Oxford University Press, 1946); H. Hotelling, "Demand Functions with Limited Budgets," *Econometrica,* 1935; and P. Samuelson, *Foundations of Economic Analysis* (Cambridge, Mass.: Harvard University Press, 1947).

ity is ordinally measurable, since, as noted above, differences in ordinal utilities are arbitrary. For example, if the consumer prefers two helpings of mashed potatoes to one helping, ordinal utility is higher for two helpings than one, but how much higher is arbitrary. Why? Because, to be a proper ordinal utility measure, all that is required is that market baskets giving equal satisfaction to the consumer must receive the same utility and that market baskets he or she prefers must receive higher utilities than those that are not preferred. No particular significance attaches to the scale that is used or to the size of the difference between the utilities attached to two market baskets.

The fact that modern economists generally assume that utility is ordinally, not cardinally, measurable does not mean that results based on the assumption of cardinal utility are wrong. If the consumer is able to characterize his or her preferences by attaching a cardinal utility to each market basket, these results are correct—and should be used. But what if the consumer cannot characterize his or her preferences in this way? In that case, a different kind of model of consumer behavior is required. The rest of this chapter provides such a model. This model, based on the assumption that utility is ordinally measurable, is the leading one at present. There is no contradiction between these two models. The model presented in previous sections (which assumes the existence of cardinal utilities) can be regarded as a special case of the one to be presented below (which assumes ordinal utilities). If utility is cardinally measurable, both models yield the same results.

INDIFFERENCE CURVES

Assuming utility is only ordinally measurable, we can represent the consumer's tastes or preferences by a set of indifference curves. *An* indifference curve *is the locus of points representing market baskets among which the consumer is indifferent.* For example, suppose we confine our atten-

Indifference
curve

tion to the ten market baskets in Table 3.3, in which the first market basket contains 1 pound of meat and 4 pounds of potatoes, the second market basket contains 1 pound of meat and 6 pounds of potatoes, and so on. Suppose the consumer is asked to choose between various pairs of these market baskets and that he or she is indifferent between some of these market baskets. For example, the consumer may not care whether he or she consumes 4 pounds of meat plus 2 pounds of potatoes or 2 pounds of meat plus 3 pounds of potatoes. Suppose that we enlarge the number of market baskets (containing various quantities of meat and potatoes) under consideration, so that we include all market baskets in which from 1 to 8 pounds of meat are combined with from 1 to 8 pounds of potatoes. Then suppose we plot each of the market baskets on a diagram like Figure 3.2 and that *curve* A *is the set of points representing market baskets among which the*

Table ALTERNATIVE MARKET BASKETS
3.3

Market basket	Meat (pounds)	Potatoes (pounds)
	(per unit of time)	
1	1	4
2	1	6
3	2	3
4	2	4
5	3	2
6	3	3
7	4	1
8	4	2
9	5	0
10	5	1

consumer is indifferent. For example, this curve includes all of the market baskets that the consumer regards as being equivalent (in terms of his or her satisfaction) to 4 pounds of meat plus 2 pounds of potatoes.

Curve *A* is an *indifference curve.* Of course there are many such indifference curves, each pertaining to a different level of satisfaction. For example, indifference curve *B* in Figure 3.2 represents a higher level of utility than indifference curve *A,* since it includes market baskets with more of both meat and potatoes than the market baskets represented by indifference curve *A.* One can visualize a series of indifference curves—one showing all market bas-

Fig. INDIFFERENCE CURVES / *The consumer is indifferent among the market*
3.2 *baskets represented by points on indifference curve* A. *Market baskets represented by points on indifference curve* B *are preferred over those represented by points on indifference curve* A.

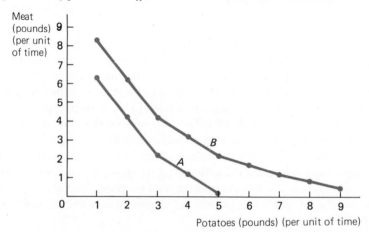

kets that are equivalent (in the eyes—or belly—of the consumer) to 1 pound of
potatoes and 2 pounds of meat, one showing all market baskets that are equivalent to 2 pounds of potatoes and 2 pounds of meat, and so on. The resulting
series of indifference curves is called an indifference map.

A consumer's indifference map lies at the heart of the theory of consumer
behavior, since such a map provides a representation of the consumer's tastes.
To illustrate how a consumer's indifference map mirrors his or her tastes, consider the various indifference maps in Figure 3.3. Consumer A's indifference
curves are relatively steep, whereas consumer B's indifference curves are relatively flat. What does this mean? Apparently consumer A needs several extra
units of good Y to compensate for the loss of a single unit of good X. Thus, in
this sense, good Y is less important (relative to good X) to consumer A than to
consumer B.

What about consumers C and D in Figure 3.3? Apparently consumer C

Fig.   INDIFFERENCE MAPS OF VARIOUS CONSUMERS / *The shape of a consumer's*
3.3   *indifference curves may vary greatly, depending on his or her tastes.*
       However, consumer D's positively sloped indifference curves are ruled out
       by the assumption that the consumer prefers more of a commodity to less.

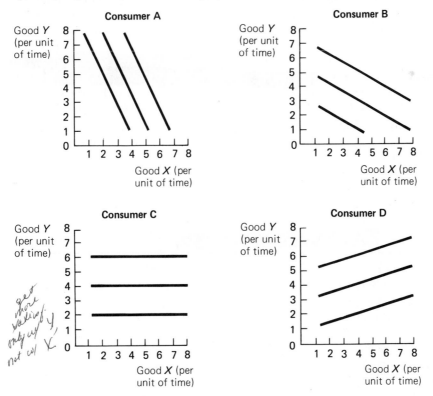

regards good X as useless, since he does not care whether he has more or less of it. Consumer D seems to regard good X as a nuisance, since she is willing to reduce the amount of good Y she consumes in order to get rid of some good X. But situations of this sort are ruled out by the assumption (discussed on p. 51) that the consumer prefers more of a commodity to less. This does not mean that some things are not a nuisance. It means only that in the case of consumer D we would define a commodity as the lack of good X, not the consumption of good X. Using this simple, legitimate trick, we no longer violate this assumption, since more of all commodities is now preferred to less.

Characteristics of Indifference Curves

All indifference curves have certain characteristics that should be noted. First, given the fact (noted in the last section) that every commodity is defined so that more of it is preferred to less, it follows that indifference curves must have a negative slope. If more of both commodities is desirable, and if one market basket has more of good Y, it must have less of good X than another market basket if the two market baskets are to be equivalent in the eyes of the consumer. If the two market baskets are equivalent, and if one market basket contains more of both commodities—which would be the case if an indifference curve had a positive slope—it would mean that one or the other of the commodities is not defined so that more of it is preferred to less.

Second, given the fact that every commodity is defined so that more of it is preferred to less, it also follows that indifference curves that are higher in graphs like Figure 3.2 represent greater levels of consumer satisfaction than indifference curves that are lower. For example, curve B in Figure 3.2 is preferred to curve A. Why? Because the higher curve, curve B, includes market baskets with as much of one good and more of the other (or as much of the second good and more of the first) than the lower curve, curve A. This is what we mean when we say that a curve is higher or lower. Put differently, the utility attached to all market baskets on a higher indifference curve is greater than the utility attached to all market baskets on a lower indifference curve. However, the difference between these utilities is arbitrary if utility is only ordinally measurable.

Third, indifference curves cannot intersect. To prove this statement, let's show that a contradiction arises if two indifference curves were to intersect. For example, take the case of two intersecting indifference curves in Figure 3.4. On indifference curve A, market basket 1 is equivalent to market basket 2. On indifference curve B, market basket 1 is equivalent to market basket 3. Hence, if the indifference curves intersect, market basket 2 must be equivalent to market basket 3. But this cannot be, since market basket 3 contains more of both commodities than market basket 2, and commodities are defined so that more of them is preferred to less. If the consumer's tastes are transitive, as we assume in this model, there cannot be an intersection of indifference curves.

Fig.
3.4 INTERSECTING INDIFFERENCE CURVES: A CONTRADICTION OF THE
ASSUMPTIONS / *If indifference curves* A *and* B *were to intersect, the consumer would be indifferent between market baskets 2 and 3, which is impossible since market basket 3 contains more of both commodities than market basket 2.*

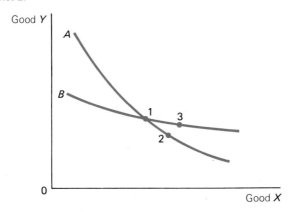

The Marginal Rate of Substitution

In the section before last, we pointed out that consumers differ in the importance that they attach to an extra unit of a particular good. Of course, this is hardly news. For example, it is well known that an alcoholic will sometimes trade a valuable item like a watch for an extra drink of whiskey, whereas the president of the Temperance Union will not give a cent for an extra (presumably the first) dose of Demon Rum. However, news or not, it is useful to have a measure of the relative importance attached by the consumer to the acquisition of another unit of a particular good. The measure that economists have devised is called the *marginal rate of substitution,* a term indicative of the economist's talent for elegant and graceful phrase-making.

The *marginal rate of substitution* is defined as the number of units of good Y that must be given up if the consumer, after receiving an extra unit of good X, is to maintain a constant level of satisfaction. For exam-

Marginal rate of substitution ple, in Figure 3.5, the consumer can give up $(OY_2 - OY_1)$ units of good Y to receive $(OX_2 - OX_1)$ extra units of good X, and this trade will leave him or her no better or no worse off. Thus the marginal rate of substitution of good X for good Y is $(OY_2 - OY_1)/(OX_2 - OX_1)$. This is the number of units of good Y that must be given up— per unit of good X received—to maintain a constant level of satisfaction.

More precisely, the marginal rate of substitution is equal to -1 times the slope of the indifference curve. Thus the marginal rate of substitution of good X for good Y is higher for consumer A (whose indifference curve on p. 61 is steeper) than for consumer B (whose indifference curve is flatter). In general, the marginal rate of substitution will vary from point to point on a given in-

Fig. 3.5   THE MARGINAL RATE OF SUBSTITUTION / *The marginal rate of substitution of good* X *for good* Y *is* $(OY_2 - OY_1)/(OX_2 - OX_1)$, *which is the number of units of good* Y *that must be given up—per unit of good* X *received—to maintain a constant level of satisfaction.*

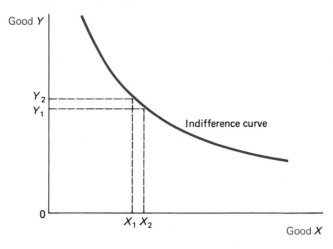

Example 3.1

THE EXPERIMENTAL DETERMINATION OF INDIFFERENCE CURVES

K. MacCrimmon and M. Toda published an experimental study in which they asked a group of college students to choose among market baskets containing various amounts of money and pens. One of the students said she was indifferent among market baskets *A* to *E* below. MacCrimmon and Toda also asked the students to choose among market baskets containing various quantities of money and French pastries (to be eaten on the spot). The same student said she was indifferent among market baskets *F* to *J* below.

Market basket	Number of pens	Amount of money (dollars)	Market basket	Number of French pastries	Amount of money (dollars)
A	0	20.00	*F*	0	6.00
B	50	17.50	*G*	3	5.50
C	100	15.00	*H*	6	5.00
D	130	14.00	*I*	8	6.00
E	160	13.00	*J*	10	7.00

(a) Draw the student's indifference curve for money and pens. (Assume that the points given in the table can be connected with straight lines.) (b) Draw her indifference curve for money and French pastries. (c) Do these indifference curves represent the same level of utility? (d) Are French pastries always a good? (e) If the French pastries could be taken home and eaten later, would the indifference curve for money and French pastries be the same as that given above?

difference curve, since the indifference curve's slope will vary from point to point. For example, on indifference curve *A* (or curve *B*) in Figure 3.2, the marginal rate of substitution of potatoes for meat gets smaller as the consumer has more potatoes and less meat.

In the economist's model of consumer behavior it is generally assumed that indifference curves have the sort of shape exhibited by curves *A* and *B* in Figure 3.2. More specifically, it is assumed that they show that the more the consumer has of a particular good, the less will be the marginal rate of substitution of this good for any other good. Put somewhat crudely, this amounts to assuming that the more the consumer has of a particular good,

Convexity   the less important to him or her (relative to other goods) is an extra unit of this good. In mathematical terms, this assumption means that indifference curves are *convex*. In other words, an indifference curve lies above its tangent, as illustrated in panel A of Figure 3.6. This contrasts with the case presented in panel B of Figure 3.6 where the indifference curve is not convex.[7]

---

7. The assumption of convexity may not always hold, but a discussion of cases where it fails belongs in a more advanced book.

SOLUTION

(a) and (b) The indifference curves are shown below.

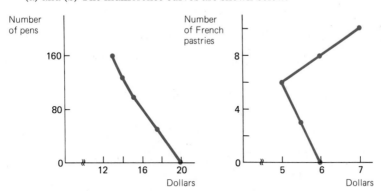

(c) No, since one indifference curve includes market basket *A*, which contains $20 alone, while the other indifference curve includes market basket *F*, which contains $6 alone. So long as more money is preferred to less, the former indifference curve must represent a higher level of utility than the latter. (d) No. For more than 6 French pastries, the indifference curve is upward sloped to the right because the student was willing to consume more French pastries only if she received more money. (e) No. The student would probably have not required more money to make her willing to consume more than 6 French pastries, if she did not have to eat them on the spot.*

* For further discussion, see K. MacCrimmon and M. Toda, "The Experimental Determination of Indifference Curves," *Review of Economic Studies,* October 1969.

Fig.   INDIFFERENCE CURVES: CONVEXITY / *The economist's model of consumer*
3.6   *behavior assumes that indifference curves are convex, as shown in panel A.*
        In other words, it is assumed that an indifference curve lies above its
        tangent.

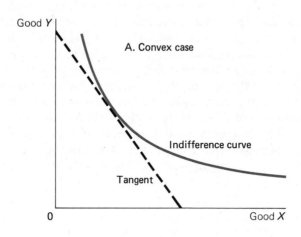

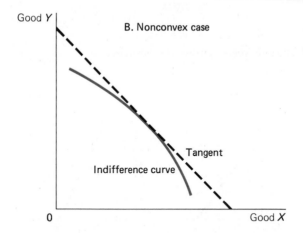

THE BUDGET LINE

Earlier in this chapter, we presented a rule indicating which market basket the
rational consumer would purchase, given that utility was cardinally measurable. Now we must do the same thing, under the assumption that utility is ordinally measurable. To begin with, we must show how the consumer's money
income and the level of commodity prices influence the nature and size of the
market baskets available to the consumer. It simplifies matters without dis-

torting the essentials of the situation if we assume that there are only two commodities that the consumer can buy, good X and good Y. Since the consumer must spend all of his or her money income on one or the other of these two commodities,[8] it is evident that

$$Q_x P_x + Q_y P_y = I \qquad\qquad [3.2]$$

where Q_x is the amount the consumer buys of good X, Q_y is the amount the consumer buys of good Y, P_x is the price of good X, P_y is the price of good Y, and I is the consumer's money income. For example, if the price of good X is \$1 a unit and the price of good Y is \$2 a unit and the consumer's income is \$100, it must be true that $Q_x + 2Q_y = 100$. Note that we assume that the consumer takes prices as given. This, of course, is generally quite realistic.

It is possible to plot the combinations of quantities of goods X and Y that the consumer can buy on the same sort of graph as the indifference map. Solving Equation 3.2 for Q_y, we have

$$Q_y = \frac{1}{P_y} I - \frac{P_x}{P_y} Q_x. \qquad\qquad [3.3]$$

Equation 3.3, which is a straight line, is plotted in Figure 3.7. The first term on the right-hand side of Equation 3.3 is the intercept of the line on the vertical

Fig. 3.7   THE BUDGET LINE / *The budget line shows all of the combinations of quantities of goods* X *and* Y *that the consumer can buy. The slope of the budget line equals* $-P_x \div P_y$.

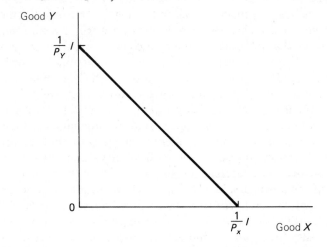

8. Of course, the consumer can also save some of his or her income, but, from the point of view of this model, savings can be viewed as a commodity like any other. Thus, with this amendment, Equation 3.2 can easily encompass saving.

Fig.   EFFECT OF CHANGE IN INCOME ON THE BUDGET LINE / *Increases in money*
3.8   *income increase the intercept of the budget line, but do not affect its slope.*

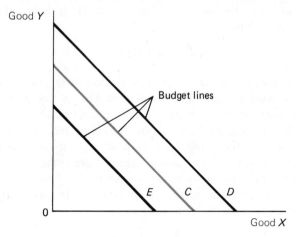

axis: It is the amount of good *Y* that could be bought by the consumer if he or
she spent all of his or her income on good *Y*. The slope of the line is equal to the
negative of the price ratio, P_x/P_y.

The straight line in Equation 3.3 is called the *budget line*. It shows all of
the combinations of quantities of good *X* and good *Y* that the consumer can
buy. In subsequent sections, we shall be interested in the effects

Budget line   of changes in product prices and money income on consumer behavior. These changes are reflected by changes in the budget line.
Equation 3.3 shows that increases in money income increase the intercept of
the budget line, but leave unaffected the slope of the budget line. For example,
Figure 3.8 shows the effect of an increase in income, with *C* the original budget
line and *D* the budget line after the increase in income. Conversely, decreases
in income lower the intercept of the budget line. In Figure 3.8, *E* is the budget
line after a decrease in income, with *C* once again the original budget line.

Equation 3.3 also shows what happens to the budget line if the price of
good *X* changes. Increases in P_x increase the absolute value of the slope of the
budget line; decreases in P_x decrease the absolute value of the slope. The vertical intercept of the line is unaffected. Figure 3.9 shows the effect of changes
in P_x on the budget line. Suppose that the original budget line is *F*. If P_x increases, the budget line becomes *G*. If P_x decreases, the budget line becomes *H*.
Intuitively, it is easy to see why an increase (decrease) in the price of good *X*
results in the budget line's cutting the *X* axis at a point closer to (farther from)
the origin. The point where the budget line cuts the *X* axis equals the maximum number of units of good *X* that the consumer can buy with his or her
fixed money income, and this number obviously is inversely related to the
price of good *X*.

Fig.
3.9

EFFECT OF CHANGE IN PRICE OF GOOD X on Budget Line / *If the original budget line is F, an increase in the price of good* X *changes the budget line to* G; *a decrease in the price of good* X *changes it to* H.

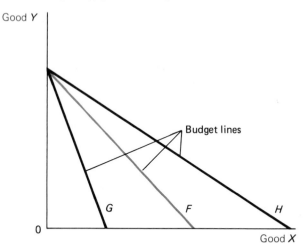

THE EQUILIBRIUM OF THE CONSUMER

At the beginning of the previous section, we said that we would show which market basket the rational consumer will purchase, if utility is ordinal. To do this, we must answer the question, What market basket will maximize the consumer's utility? Figure 3.10 brings together the consumer's indifference map and his or her budget line. All of the relevant information needed to answer this question is contained in Figure 3.10. *The indifference map shows what the consumer's preferences are.* For example, any market basket on indifference curve 3 is preferred to any on indifference curve 2; and any market basket on indifference curve 2 is preferred to any on indifference curve 1. The consumer would like to choose a market basket on the highest possible indifference curve. This is the way to maximize his or her utility.

But not all market baskets are within reach. *The budget line shows what the consumer can do.* He or she can choose any market basket such as *U, V,* or *W* on the budget line, but he or she cannot obtain a market basket like *T* which is above the budget line. (Of course, the consumer can also buy any market basket below the budget line, but any such market basket lies on a lower indifference curve than a market basket on the budget line.) Since this is the case, *the market basket that will maximize the consumer's utility is the one on the budget line that is on his or her highest indifference curve*—which is *V* in Figure 3.10. It can readily be seen that this market basket is at a point where the budget line is tangent to an indifference curve. This market basket, *V,* is the one that the rational consumer would, according to our model, be predicted to buy in equilibrium.

Example 3.2

THE FOOD-STAMP PROGRAM

In 1985 the food-stamp program in the United States included about 19 million individuals, and cost about $11 billion. Suppose that if a family is eligible for food stamps, it pays $80 per month to obtain $150 worth of food. (a) If the family's cash income is $250 and it is not eligible for food stamps, draw its budget line on a graph where the quantity of food consumed per month is measured along the horizontal axis and the quantity of nonfood items consumed per month is measured along the vertical axis. (b) Draw the family's budget line on this graph if it is eligible for food stamps. (c) Show that if the family were given $70 in cash (rather than in food), it might achieve a higher level of satisfaction.

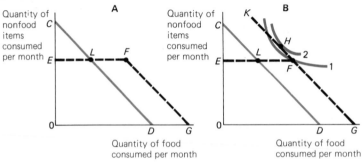

SOLUTION

(a) Without food stamps, the family's budget line is CD in panel A. In this panel, OC is the quantity of nonfood items the family can obtain with its entire income ($250) and OD is the quantity of food it can obtain with it. (b) With food stamps, the family's budget line is $CLFG$ in panel A. EC is the quantity of nonfood items the family can buy with $80. If the family buys food stamps, OE is the maximum quantity of nonfood items it can obtain once it pays for the food stamps. EF is the $150 worth of food it receives with the food stamps, and DG ($= LF$) is the $70 worth of food that it can obtain with food stamps that it couldn't otherwise obtain, when the quantity of nonfood items is held constant. If the quantity of nonfood items consumed by the family exceeds OE, it does not have enough money left for food to buy food stamps, so the budget line is the same as without food stamps. (That is, it is CL.) If the quantity of nonfood items consumed by the family does not exceed OE, it can buy food stamps, and consume an extra amount of food equal to DG, so the budget line is FG. (c) If the family were given $70 in cash (rather than in food), its budget line would be GK in panel B. Because its money income increases by $70, the budget line is higher, but parallel to, the old budget line, CD. With this budget line, the family can reach point H on indifference curve 2, whereas with budget line $CLFG$, the best it can do is reach point F on indifference curve 1. Since indifference curve 2 is higher than indifference curve 1, the family achieves a higher level of satisfaction if it receives the cash rather than the food. Of course, not all families have indifference curves of this sort; some have indifference curves such that they achieve as high a level of satisfaction with the food as with the cash. This is the case for families with indifference curves tangent to the budget line between F and G.*

---

* For further discussion, see K. Clarkson, "Welfare Benefits of the Food Stamp Program," *Southern Economic Journal*, July 1976; and M. MacDonald, *Food, Stamps, and Income Maintenance* (New York: Academic Press, 1977).

Fig. EQUILIBRIUM OF THE CONSUMER / *The market basket that will maximize*
3.10 *the consumer's utility is* V, *the one on the budget line that is on his or her*
highest indifference curve.

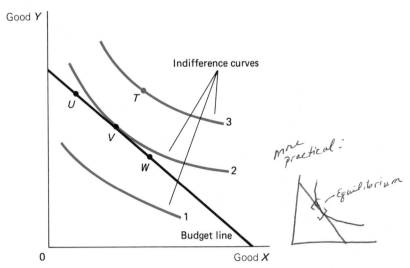

Budget Allocation by a Government Agency: An Application

In Chapter 1 we said that microeconomics has turned out to be useful in helping to solve many important practical problems; yet in this chapter we have provided no evidence so far to support that statement. The material provided in previous sections of the present chapter must be understood if the reader is to understand the theory of consumer behavior. But it is by no means obvious how it would enable anyone to solve any kind of a practical problem. Appearances, however, can be deceiving. The kind of analysis discussed in this chapter can be useful in many contexts. The purpose of this section is to show how the model described in previous sections has been used to solve problems of budget allocation by government agencies.

For concreteness' sake, let's consider a particular agency, the Department of Transportation. And let's consider the decision that it (and Congress) must make with regard to the allocation of funds between urban highways and urban mass transit (buses and rail lines), both of which can be used to meet the transportation needs of our urban population. Suppose that the Department of Transportation has $2 billion to spend on urban highways and/or mass transit. How should it allocate this sum between them? In other words, how much should it spend on highways, and how much should it spend on mass transit? This is an important decision, one that involves huge sums of money and the time, comfort, and convenience of many people.

What in the world has this problem got to do with the theory of consumer

Example 3.3

WARTIME RATIONING AND CONSUMER CHOICE

In major wars, the United States and other countries often have turned to rationing. For example, during World War II, the Office of Price Administration was created with the authority to enforce rationing of meats, butter, fats, cheese, canned milk, canned fish, and canned fruits, among other things. Each family received a certain income of ration points that it could spend per unit of time, and each good had a price in terms of ration points as well as dollars. (a) Under this set of circumstances, were a family's decisions subject to more than one budget line? (b) If a family was sufficiently poor, was only one of the budget lines relevant? (c) If both budget lines were relevant, at what point on which budget line would the family choose to be?

SOLUTION

(a) Yes. There really were two budget lines, one for point income, the other for money income. Given the prices of goods X and Y in terms of points, the combinations of quantities of goods X and Y that the family's *point* income could buy are shown by line AB in the graph below. Given the money prices of goods X and Y, the

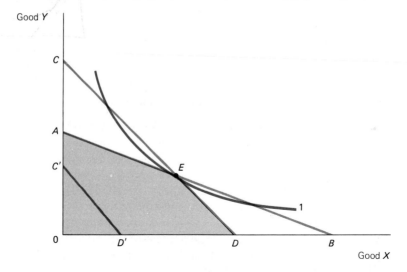

combinations of quantities of goods X and Y that the family's *money* income could buy are shown by line CD. Since the family had to have *both* enough points and enough money to buy a particular market basket, only those combinations of quantities of goods X and Y along AED (or in the shaded area) could be bought. (b) Yes. Decreases in income push the budget line downward and to the left, as shown in Figure 3.8. At a sufficiently low money income, the budget line based on money income would be totally below and inside AB. For example, it might be $C'D'$. Such a budget line is the only relevant budget line since any combination of quantities of goods X and Y that the family has money enough to buy will require less points than the family has. (c) The family would choose that attainable point which is on its highest indifference curve. For example, if AB and CD are the relevant budget lines, the set of attainable points is AED (and the shaded area); and if indifference curve 1 is the highest attainable indifference curve, the family would choose point E.

preferences we discussed in previous sections of this chapter? Strange as it may seem, economists have used the theory discussed above to help solve this kind of problem. The way in which they have dealt with the problem is instructive in many respects, one being that it illustrates how simple models can be adapted to throw light on very complicated problems.

In effect, the economists have said, "Let's view the Department of Transportation as a consumer. Let's regard highways and mass transit as two goods that the department can buy, with each good having a price and the total amount that can be spent on them both being fixed. Assuming that the department is interested in maximizing the effectiveness of the'nation's transportation system, let's use as indifference curves for the department the combinations of extra miles of highway and of extra miles of mass transit that will result in a certain expected addition to the nation's total transportation capability. Clearly, the bigger the expected addition to this capability, the higher the indifference curve. Then let's find the point on the budget line (which can be derived from the price of a mile of highway, the price of a mile of mass transit, and the total budget to be allocated) that lies on the highest indifference curve. This point will indicate the optimal allocation of the budget."

To actually attack the problem in this way, the first step, of course, is to determine various "indifference curves" of the "consumer," the Department of Transportation. Figure 3.11 shows what they might look like. As in Figure 3.5, each indifference curve slopes downward, since highways can be substi-

Fig. 3.11   ALLOCATION OF TRANSPORTATION BUDGET BETWEEN URBAN HIGHWAYS AND MASS TRANSIT / *The Department of Transportation should fund the construction of 120 miles of mass transit and 160 miles of urban highways.*

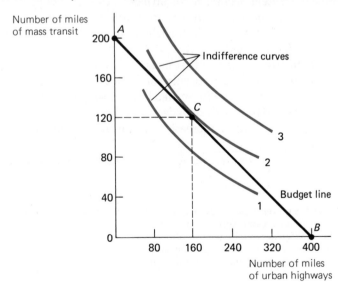

tuted for mass transit, and vice versa. Moreover, they are likely to be convex. What exactly does each of these indifference curves mean? Consider indifference curve 1. Each point on this indifference curve represents a combination of highways and mass transit that results in the same addition to transportation capability, that is, the same expected addition to our ability to transport people quickly and safely. The Department of Transportation is viewed as being interested in maximizing the nation's transportation capability. In other words, transportation capability (measured in this way) is a measure of this consumer's "utility." Thus the consumer is indifferent among all of the points on curve 1. And the consumer clearly prefers indifference curve 2 to indifference curve 1, because points on indifference curve 2 result in more transportation capability than those on indifference curve 1.

Having constructed the indifference curves, the next step is to construct the appropriate budget line. If the Department of Transportation has $2 billion to spend, if each mile of mass transit costs $10 million, and if each mile of highway costs $5 million, the budget line is *AB* in Figure 3.11. Based on our discussion on pp. 66–68, this should be clear enough. Given this budget line and the indifference map, the problem boils down to finding the point on the budget line that lies on the highest indifference curve. A careful inspection of Figure 3.11 shows that this optimal point is point *C*, where the Department of Transportation funds the construction of 120 miles of mass transit and 160 miles of urban highways.

In recent years, economic analysis of this kind has played an important role in policy-making in many government agencies. In practice, of course, the measurement of "transportation capability" or "social worth" often presents extremely difficult problems, with the result that it is not possible to draw curves like 1, 2, and 3 with great accuracy. Nevertheless, this does not mean that this type of analysis is not useful. On the contrary, it has proved very useful, since it provides a correct way of thinking about the problem. It focuses attention on the relevant factors, and puts them in their proper place.[9]

This example also illustrates the fact that most aspects of microeconomics are concerned with means to achieve specified ends, not with the choice of ends. Thus economists in this case were interested in increasing the transportation capability to be obtained from a given budget. But they took as given the hypothesis that it was a good thing to increase transportation capability. In other words, they took as given the fact that the "utility" of the "consumer" should be increased. In certain circumstances, this hypothesis could perhaps

---

9. It should be emphasized, however, that the particular example presented in this section is highly simplified. For one thing, costs incurred by parties other than the federal government are ignored. Also, the indifference curves may not always have the shape shown in Figure 3.11. Further, miles of highway or mass transit are rather crude units of measurement. Nonetheless, despite these and other limitations, this example communicates the spirit of this sort of analysis.

be wrong. For example, suppose that the department wants to maximize its power and influence in the federal government, or to maximize the political fortunes of its top officials, rather than the nation's transportation capability. The same techniques could be used; all that would be required is a reinterpretation of the indifference curves.[10] Of course, this does not mean that it is not valuable to have techniques like those discussed here. They are obviously of great value. What it does mean is that one cannot expect them to do more than they are designed to do. They cannot tell us what our goals or ends should be.

SUMMARY

1. We assume that, when confronted with two market baskets, a consumer can say which one is preferred, or whether he or she is indifferent between them. Also, we assume that the consumer's tastes are transitive and that a commodity is defined in such a way that more is preferred to less.

2. Utility is a number that indexes the level of satisfaction derived from a particular market basket. Market baskets with higher utilities are preferred over market baskets with lower utilities. The consumer is assumed to be rational in the sense that he or she tries to maximize utility.

3. If he or she maximizes utility, the consumer's income is allocated among commodities so that, for every commodity he or she buys, the marginal utility of the commodity is proportional to its price. In other words, the marginal utility of the last dollar spent on each commodity is made equal for all commodities.

4. An indifference curve is the locus of points representing market baskets among which the consumer is indifferent. A consumer's tastes can be represented by a set of indifference curves. An indifference curve must have a negative slope, and two indifference curves cannot intersect. Market baskets on higher indifference curves have higher utilities than those on lower indifference curves.

5. The slope of an indifference curve (multipled by −1) is called the marginal rate of substitution. The marginal rate of substitution shows approximately how many units of one good must be given up if the consumer, after receiving an extra unit of another good, is to maintain a constant level of satisfaction.

---

10. Under these circumstances, each indifference curve would show the combinations of highways and mass transit that result in the same level of power for the department or the same level of political fortunes for the department's top officials.

6. The budget line indicates all of the combinations of quantities of goods—all of the market baskets—that the consumers can buy, given his or her money income and the level of each price. In equilibrium, we would expect the consumer to attain the highest level of satisfaction that is compatible with the budget line, which means that the consumer will choose the market basket on the budget line that is on the highest indifference curve. This market basket is at a point where the budget line is tangent to an indifference curve.

7. The model of consumer behavior presented in this chapter has been used to solve problems of budget allocation by government agencies. To illustrate its use in this way, we took up a case study involving expenditures on urban transportation.

QUESTIONS/PROBLEMS

1) Suppose that James Gray spends his entire income on goods X and Y. The marginal utility of each good (shown below) is independent of the amount consumed of the other good. The price of X is $100 and the price of Y is $500.

Number of units of good consumed	Mr. Gray's marginal utility (utils)	
	Good X	Good Y
1	20	50
2	18	45
3	16	40
4	13	35
5	10	30
6	6	25
7	4	20
8	2	15

If Mr. Gray has an income of $1,000 per month, how many units of each good should he purchase?

2) Draw Mr. Gray's budget line from the data in the previous question. At what point does it cut the axis along which the quantity of good Y is measured?

3) In the diagram on p. 77, we show one of Ellen White's indifference curves and her budget line. If the price of good A is $50, what is Ms. White's income? What is the equation for her budget line? What is the slope of the budget line? What is the price of good B? What is her marginal rate of substitution in equilibrium?

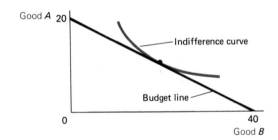

4) "A survey shows that most people prefer Cadillacs to Chevrolets." What exactly does this mean? If this is true, why do more people drive Chevrolets than Cadillacs?

5) One of Ms. Jones's indifference curves includes the following market baskets. Each of these market baskets gives her equal satisfaction.

Market basket	Meat (pounds)	Potatoes (pounds)
1	2	8
2	3	7
3	4	6
4	5	5
5	6	4
6	7	3
7	8	2
8	9	1

In her case, what is the marginal rate of substitution of potatoes for meat? How does the marginal rate of substitution vary as she consumes more meat and less potatoes? Is this realistic?

6) "As a society becomes increasingly affluent, wants are increasingly created by the process by which they are satisfied." Do you agree? Why or why not? Assuming that this is true, what would be the implications of this proposition for the theory of consumer behavior?

7) Martin Cole purchases 100 loaves of bread per year when the price is $1 per loaf. The price increases to $1.50. To offset the harm to Martin, his father gives him $50 a year. Will Martin be better or worse off after the price increase plus the gift than he was before? Will his consumption of bread increase or decrease?

8) "Whether or not utility is some kind of glow or warmth, or happiness, is here irrelevant; all that counts is that we can assign numbers to entities or conditions which a person can strive to realize." Comment on this statement. Do you agree with it? Why or why not?

9) Suppose that consumers in San Francisco pay twice as much for apples as for pears, whereas consumers in Los Angeles pay 50 percent more for apples than for pears. If consumers in both cities maximize utility, will the marginal rate of substitution of pears for apples be the same in San Francisco as in Los Angeles? If not, in which city will it be higher?

10) A consumer is willing to trade one pound of steak for three pounds of hamburger. He currently is purchasing as much steak as hamburger per month. The price of steak is twice that of hamburger. Should he increase his consumption of hamburger and reduce his consumption of steak? Or should he reduce his consumption of hamburger and increase his consumption of steak?

Consumer Behavior and Individual Demand

THE EQUILIBRIUM OF THE CONSUMER: REVIEW AND ANOTHER VIEWPOINT

In this chapter, we proceed further with the development of a model of consumer behavior. Building on the results of the previous chapter, we show how the consumer responds to changes in his or her money income and to changes in the prices of commodities. In addition, we present some illustrations of how this theory has been applied to help solve important problems of public policy. Specifically, we describe how it has been applied to the evaluation of the effects of sugar import quotas.

To begin with, it is useful to review briefly the conditions under which the consumer is in equilibrium. However, rather than merely parrot what has already been said in the previous chapter, we look at these conditions from a somewhat different point of view. We said in the previous chapter that the consumer's equilibrium market basket is at a point where the budget line is tangent to an indifference curve: This is the market basket that maximizes the consumer's utility. Since the slope of the indifference curve equals −1 times the marginal rate of substitution of good X for good Y (see p. 63) and since the slope of the budget line is $-P_x/P_y$ (see p. 68), it follows that the rational consumer will choose in equilibrium to allocate his or her income between good X and good Y so that the marginal rate of substitution of good X for good Y equals P_x/P_y.

This is a famous result—and a very useful one that should be understood fully. It is easier to agree that it is true than it is to see what it really means and why it is true. Perhaps the best way to understand this result is to define once again the marginal rate of substitution: The marginal rate of substitution is the rate at which the consumer is *willing* to substitute good X for good Y, holding his or her total level of satisfaction constant. Thus, if the marginal rate of substitution is 3, the consumer is willing to give up three units of good Y in order to get one more unit of good X.

On the other hand, the price ratio, P_x/P_y, is the rate at which the consumer is *able* to substitute good X for good Y. Thus, if P_x/P_y is two, he or she *must* give up two units of good Y to get one more unit of good X. What the result described in this section is really saying is: The rate at which the consumer is willing to substitute good X for good Y (holding satisfaction constant) must equal the rate at which he or she is able to substitute good X for good Y. Otherwise it is always possible to find another market basket that will increase the consumer's satisfaction. And this means, of course, that the present market basket is not the equilibrium one that maximizes consumer satisfaction.

To see that this must be the case, suppose that the consumer has chosen a market basket in which the marginal rate of substitution of good X for good Y is 3. Suppose that the ratio, P_x/P_y, is 2. If this is the case, the consumer can trade two units of good Y for an extra unit of good X in the market, since the price ratio is 2. But this extra unit of good X is worth three units of good Y to the consumer, since the marginal rate of substitution is 3. Consequently, he or she can increase satisfaction by trading good Y for good X—and this will continue to be the case as long as the marginal rate of substitution exceeds the price ratio. Conversely, if the marginal rate of substitution is less than the price ratio, the consumer can increase satisfaction by trading good X for good Y. Only when the marginal rate of substitution equals the price ratio does the consumer's market basket maximize his or her utility.

EFFECTS OF CHANGES IN CONSUMER MONEY INCOME

With this review in mind, let us turn to new territory and consider the effect of changes in money income on the amounts of good X and good Y purchased by the consumer. For example, suppose that the consumer is a student and that the amount of money he earns and receives from home increases from \$5,000 to \$7,000 a year. What effect will this have on his purchases? How much of the extra money will he spend on books? On entertainment? On clothes? On food?

In the previous chapter, we saw that an increase in money income results in an increase in the intercept of the budget line, but leaves unaffected the slope of the budget line (as long as the prices of commodities remain constant). Similarly, a decrease in money income results in a decrease in the intercept of the budget line, but leaves unaffected the slope of the budget line (as long as the prices of commodities remain constant). To determine the effect of a change in money income on the market basket chosen by the consumer, one can compare the equilibrium position based on the budget line corresponding to the old level of money income with the equilibrium position based on the budget line corresponding to the new level of money income.

For example, suppose that the budget line corresponding to the old level of income—$5,000 in the case of the student—is A in Figure 4.1. Given the consumer's indifference map, the market basket that maximizes his utility is comprised of Oa units of good X and Ob units of good Y, if his income is at the old level. Now suppose that his income rises—to $7,000 in the case of the student—and that the new budget line is B in Figure 4.1. With these new conditions, the market basket that maximizes his utility is comprised of Oc units of good X and Od units of good Y.

Clearly, the way in which an increase in money income influences a consumer's purchases depends on his tastes. In other words, the nature of the market basket chosen at the old income, the nature of the market basket chosen at the new income, and consequently the nature of the difference between these two market baskets is influenced by the shape of the consumer's indifference curves. Also, the way in which an increase in money income influences a consumer's purchases depends on the price ratio, P_x/P_y. Of course, this price ratio is held constant when we analyze the effects of changes in money income on consumer behavior, but the level at which the price ratio is held constant will influence the results.

Income-Consumption and Engel Curves

Holding commodity prices constant, we find that each level of money income results in an equilibrium market basket for the consumer. That is, corresponding to each level of money income is an equilibrium market basket for a particular consumer. For example, the equilibrium market baskets corresponding to three income levels are represented by points U, V, and W in Figure 4.1. If we connect all of the points representing equilibrium market baskets corresponding to all possible levels of money income, the resulting curve is called the *income-consumption curve*. Figure 4.1 shows such a curve.

Income-consumption curve

The income-consumption curve can be used to derive Engel curves, which

EFFECTS OF CHANGES IN MONEY INCOME ON CONSUMER EQUILIBRIUM / *The*
4.1 *income-consumption curve connects points (like U, V, and W) representing*
equilibrium market baskets corresponding to all possible levels of
money income.

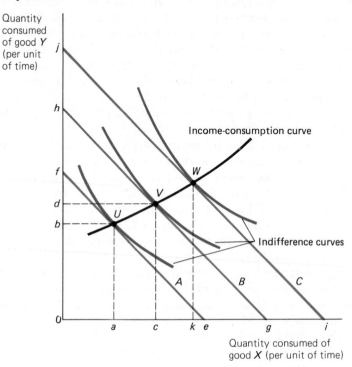

are important for studies of family expenditure patterns. An *Engel curve* is the
relationship between the equilibrium quantity purchased of a
Engel curve   good and the level of income.[1] Ernst Engel was a nineteenth-
century German statistician who did pioneering work related to
such curves; economists have named them after him.

It is easy to see how an Engel curve can be derived from the income-consumption curve. Take the case in Figure 4.1 as an example. When money income equals P_x times Oe (or P_y times Of, since they are equal), the
income-consumption curve shows that the consumer buys Oa units of good X.
When money income equals P_x times Og (or P_y times Oh), the income-consumption curve shows that the consumer buys Oc units of good X. When

---

1. Often an Engel curve is defined to be the relationship between the consumer's *expenditure* on a
commodity and his or her money income. But since the commodity prices are held constant,
the consumer's expenditure on the product is proportional to the number of units of the commodity that he or she consumes. So it makes no real difference for present purposes whether
we use expenditure or quantity demanded of the commodity as the relevant variable.

Fig. THE ENGEL CURVE FOR GOOD X / *An Engel curve is the relationship*
4.2 *between the equilibrium quantity purchased of a good and the level of*
income.

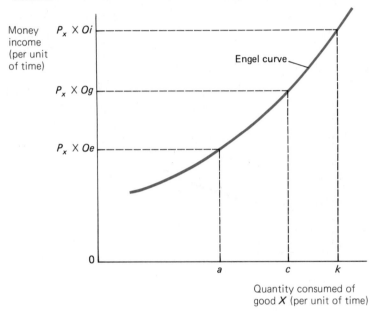

money income is P_x times Oi (or P_y times Oj), the income-consumption curve
shows that the consumer buys Ok units of good X. These are three points on
the Engel curve for good X for this consumer. Each of these points shows the
equilibrium amount of good X that he or she purchases at a certain level of
money income. As more and more points are included, all of the points on the
Engel curve for good X for this consumer are traced out. The result is shown in
Figure 4.2.

Of course, the shape of a consumer's Engel curve for a particular good will
depend on the nature of the good, the nature of the consumer's tastes, and the
level at which commodity prices are held constant. For example, Engel curves
with quite different shapes are shown in panels A and B of Figure 4.3. According to the Engel curve in panel A, the quantity consumed of the good increases
with income, but at a *decreasing* rate. According to the Engel curve in panel B
the quantity consumed of the good increases with income, but at an *increasing*
rate. A comparison of panel A with panel B shows that a change in income from
Ou to Ov does not have as great an effect on consumption of the good in panel B
as on consumption of the good in panel A.

In general, one would expect that Engel curves for goods like salt and
shoelaces would show that the consumption of these commodities does not
change very much in response to changes in income. For example, only a

Fig.   ENGEL CURVES: VARIOUS SHAPES / *In panel A, the quantity consumed of*
4.3   *the good increases with income, but at a* decreasing *rate. In panel B, the
quantity consumed of the good increases with income, but at an* increasing
rate.

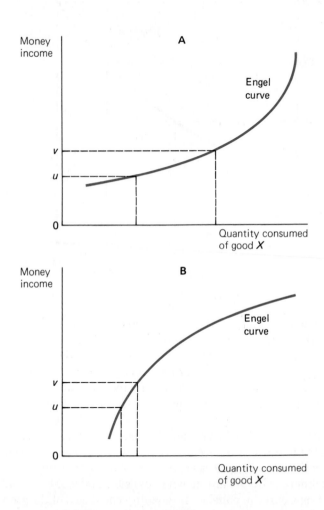

rather unusual type of person would respond to a large increase in income by
gorging himself or herself with salt and shoelaces—singly or in combination.
On the other hand, goods like caviar and filet mignon might be expected to
have Engel curves showing that their consumption increases considerably
with increases in income. In general, this is probably so. But one should be
careful about such generalizations. For example, if the consumer were a vege-
tarian, this would not hold true for filet mignon.

EFFECTS OF CHANGES IN COMMODITY PRICE

In the previous two sections we have been concerned with the effect of changes in money income on the market basket that, in equilibrium, will be chosen by the consumer. Another important question is: Holding the consumer's money income constant, what will be the effect of a change in the price of a certain commodity on the amount of this commodity that the consumer will purchase? For example, take the case of the college student mentioned in the section before last. Suppose that his income remains constant at $5,000 and that the prices of all commodities other than food are held constant. Suppose that the price of food is allowed to vary and that we watch how the quantity of food that he consumes (per unit of time) varies in response to changes in the price of food. What sort of relationship exists between the price of food and the quantity of food that he consumes (per unit of time)?

This case is unnecessarily specific. Let's pose the question more generally. Let's assume that there are only two commodities, good X and good Y. Suppose that the price of good Y and the money income of the consumer are held constant, but the price of good X is allowed to vary from one level to another. Suppose that the budget line corresponding to the original price of good X is B in Figure 4.4. If the price of good X is increased and the new budget line

Fig.   EFFECTS OF CHANGES IN PRICE OF GOOD X ON CONSUMER EQUILIBRIUM /
4.4   *The price-consumption curve connects points (like R, S, and T)*
representing equilibrium market baskets corresponding to all possible
levels of the price of good X.

is C, the new equilibrium market basket for the consumer will be T, rather than the original equilibrium market basket of S. (In the previous chapter, we saw that an increase in the price of good X increases the absolute value of the slope of the budget line but does not affect the vertical intercept of the line.) Thus the increase in the price of good X will result in the consumer's buying Ou units of good X and Ov units of good Y, rather than the original market basket composed of Or units of good X and Os units of good Y.

Corresponding to each price of good X is an equilibrium market basket that can be determined in this way. The curve that connects the various equilibrium points is called the *price-consumption curve*. Figure 4.4

Price-consumption curve
shows the price-consumption curve for this consumer, given the level of his or her money income and the price of good Y. One reason why the price-consumption curve is of interest is that it can be used to derive the consumer's individual demand curve for the commodity in question. The individual demand curve shows how much of a given commodity the consumer would purchase (per unit of time) at various prices of the commodity, holding constant the consumer's money income, his or her tastes, and the prices of other commodities. The individual demand curve is one of the central concepts in the theory of consumer behavior.

How can the individual demand curve be derived from the price-consumption curve? To illustrate the procedure, consider the case in Figure 4.4. When the price of good X is I/Oa (where I is the money income of the consumer), the price-consumption curve shows that the consumer buys Ou units of good X.[2] When the price of good X is I/Ob, the price-consumption curve shows that the consumer buys Or units of good X. When the price of good X is I/Oc, the price-consumption curve shows that the consumer buys Ow units of good X. These are three points on the individual demand curve. By deriving more and more points in this way, one can obtain the entire individual demand curve for good X. The result, curve D, is shown in Figure 4.5.

The Individual Demand Curve: Location and Shape

The location and shape of an individual demand curve will depend on the level of money income and the level at which the prices of other goods are held constant, as well as on the nature of the commodity and the tastes of the consumer. For example, suppose that we consider the demand curve for good X of the consumer represented in Figure 4.5. If his or her income were to be held constant at a level higher than I, a different demand curve would result. Rather than D it might be E in Figure 4.5. Also, if the price of good Y were higher than that assumed in Figure 4.4, a different demand curve would result.

---

2. From Figure 4.4, we know that the price of good X must be I/Oa when the budget line is C because, if the consumer devotes all of his or her money income, I, to good X, he or she can get Oa units of good X.

Example 4.1

MEDICAL INSURANCE AND THE DEMAND FOR MEDICAL CARE

Many employees receive medical insurance as a fringe benefit from their employers. Since employees have not had to pay income taxes on this fringe benefit, some economists, such as Martin Feldstein (former chairman of President Reagan's Council of Economic Advisers), argue that too much medical insurance has been provided by employers, and that the resulting economic waste runs into the billions of dollars.

(a) Why would an employee (who pays 30 cents in taxes for every extra dollar earned) prefer an additional dollar of nontaxed medical insurance rather than another dollar of wages, even if the dollar's worth of insurance is worth only 80 or 90 cents to him or her? (b) Why are employers led to provide medical insurance which is worth less to their employees than it costs? (c) If less medical insurance were provided tax free, what would be the effect on the price paid by an employee for medical care? (d) Suppose that an employee's demand curve for medical care is as shown below. If the cost of a patient-day of care is OP_0, but if (because of the insurance) the employee pays a price of only OP_2, will the employee demand some medical care that is worth less to him or her than it costs?

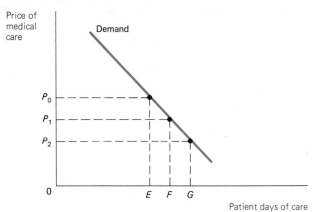

SOLUTION

(a) Another dollar of wages, if the tax rate is 30 percent, is worth 70 cents. Thus, even if a dollar's worth of medical insurance is worth only 80 or 90 cents, it is worth more than an extra dollar of wages. (b) Employers are competing among themselves to obtain and keep good workers. If workers prefer a dollar's worth of medical insurance to an extra dollar's worth of wages, employers will act accordingly. (c) If less medical insurance were provided tax free, this employee would have to pay more of the full costs of medical care. In other words, the price to him or her of medical care would increase. (d) Yes. The maximum amount that the employee would pay for an extra unit of medical care can be determined from the demand curve. For example, the maximum amount that the employee would pay for the OF^{th} day of care is OP_1. (Why? Because if the price were any higher than OP_1, the employee would demand less than OF days of care.) If the employee pays a price of only OP_2, he or she demands OG days of care. But the maximum amount that the employee would pay exceeds the cost (OP_0) only for the first OE days of care. (This is obvious because the demand curve lies above OP_0 only for quantities demanded that are less than OE.) For the remaining EG days of care, the maximum amount that the employee would pay is less than the cost.*

* For further discussion, see Martin Feldstein, "The Welfare Loss of Excess Health Insurance," *Journal of Political Economy,* March 1973.

Fig.
4.5 INDIVIDUAL DEMAND CURVE FOR GOOD *X* / *The individual demand curve
shows how much good* X *the consumer would purchase at various prices of
good* X. *The location of the individual demand curve (such as* D, E, *or* F*)
depends on the consumer's income and tastes, as well as on the prices of
other goods.*

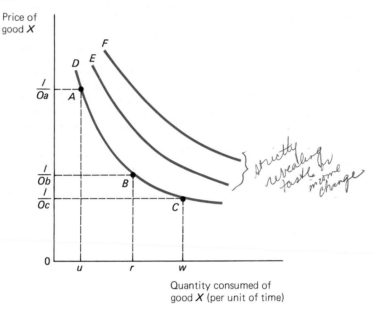

Rather than *D*, it might be *F* in Figure 4.5. An important point to remember
about a demand curve is that it is always drawn with certain assumptions
about the level of the consumer's money income and the level of other prices in
mind. In general it is only valid if these assumptions are correct.

It is important to differentiate between shifts in a consumer's demand
curve for a particular commodity and changes in the amount of the commodity
that he or she consumes. As we have seen, a consumer's demand curve may
shift because of changes in his or her income or tastes, as well as because of
changes in the prices of other goods. Such shifts in the consumer's demand
curve are likely to result in changes in the amount of the commodity that he or
she consumes, but they are not the only reason for such changes. In addition,
changes in the price of the good will result in changes in the amount of the
commodity that he or she consumes. We must be careful to distinguish between cases where the demand curve remains the same and changes in the
consumption of the commodity occur because of changes in the commodity's
price, and those cases where the demand curve shifts. The movement from
point *A* to point *B* in Figure 4.5 is an example of the former; the shift of the
demand curve from *D* to *E* is an example of the latter.

SUBSTITUTION AND INCOME EFFECTS

When the price of a good changes, the consumer is affected in two ways: First, he or she attains a different level of satisfaction, and second, he or she is likely to substitute now cheaper goods for more expensive goods. The total effect of a price change is illustrated in Figure 4.6. The original price ratio is given by the slope of the budget line A. Given this price ratio, the consumer chooses point U on indifference curve 1, and consumes Ox_1 units of good X. Now suppose that the price of good X is increased and B is the new budget line. Given the new price ratio, the consumer chooses point V on indifference curve 2, and consumes Ox_2 units of good X. The total effect of the price change on the quantity demanded of good X is a reduction of $Ox_1 - Ox_2$ units.

The total effect of this—or any—price change can be divided conceptually into two parts: the substitution effect and the income effect. First, consider the substitution effect. In Figure 4.6, when the price of good X increases, it is clear that a decrease occurs in the consumer's level of satisfaction: He or

Fig. 4.6   SUBSTITUTION AND INCOME EFFECTS FOR A NORMAL GOOD / *If the price of good* X *increases (and the budget line shifts from* A *to* B*), the total effect of this price change on the quantity demanded of good* X *is a reduction of* $Ox_1 - Ox_2$ *units. This total effect can be divided into two parts: the substitution effect (a reduction of the quantity consumed from* Ox_1 *to* Ox_3 *units) and the income effect (a reduction of the quantity consumed from* Ox_3 *to* Ox_2 *units).*

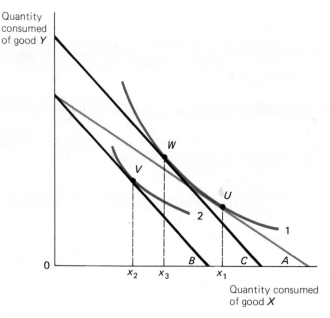

she winds up on indifference curve 2 rather than indifference curve 1. Suppose that, when the price goes up, we could increase the consumer's money income by an amount sufficient to keep him or her on the old indifference curve. If this could be done, it would mean that the budget line would be parallel to the budget line B, but that it would be tangent to indifference curve
Substitution effect
1. This hypothetical budget line is labeled C in Figure 4.6. The *substitution effect* is defined to be the movement from the original equilibrium point U to the imaginary equilibrium point W, which corresponds to the hypothetical budget line C. The substitution effect is the reduction of the quantity consumed from Ox_1 to Ox_3 units of good X. Put differently, it is the change in quantity demanded of good X resulting from a price change when the level of satisfaction is held constant.

Next, consider the income effect. The movement from the imaginary equilibrium point W to the actual new equilibrium point V is the income effect. This movement does not involve any change in prices; the price ratio is the same in budget line C as in budget line B. It is due to a change in total satisfaction; such a change is a movement from one indifference curve to another. If we define the consumer's real income as his or her level of satisfaction (or
Income effect
utility), the *income effect* is the change in quantity demanded of good X due entirely to a change in real income, *all prices being held constant*. In Figure 4.6, it is the reduction from Ox_3 to Ox_2 units. The total effect of a change in price is obviously the sum of the income effect and the substitution effect.

Normal and Inferior Goods

The substitution effect is always negative. That is, if the price of good X increases and real income is held constant, there will always be a decrease in the consumption of good X; and if the price of good X decreases and real income is held constant, there will always be an increase in the consumption of good X. This result follows from the fact that indifference curves have a negative slope (see Chapter 3). However, the income effect is not predictable from the theory alone. In most cases, one would expect that increases in real income will result in increases in consumption of a good and that decreases in real income will result in decreases in consumption of a good. This is the case for so-called *normal goods*. But not all goods are normal. Some goods
Normal vs. inferior goods
are called *inferior goods* because the income effect is the opposite (of that of a normal good) for them. An illustration of an inferior good is given in Figure 4.7, where real income is assumed to increase from indifference curve 1 to indifference curve 2. Prices are assumed to be the same before and after the increase in real income; the original budget line is A and the subsequent budget line is B. Figure 4.7 shows that, because of

Fig.   An Inferior Good / *With an increase in real income, the consumer*
4.7   *reduces his or her consumption of good* X *from* OX_2 *to* OX_3 *units. For this*
       consumer, good X *is an inferior good.*

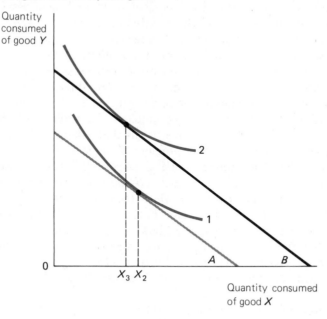

the shapes of the indifference curves, the consumer purchases $(OX_2 - OX_3)$
fewer units of good X after the increase in real income than he originally did.

Ordinarily, the substitution effect of a price change is strong enough to
offset an inferior good's income effect, with the consequence that the quantity
demanded of a good is inversely related to its price. However, it is possible for
an inferior good to have an income effect that is so strong that it
offsets the substitution effect, with the result that the quantity
demanded is directly related to the price, at least over some range
of variation of price. A case of this sort is known as *Giffen's paradox.* For Giffen's paradox to occur, a good must be an inferior good, but not all
inferior goods exhibit Giffen's paradox.

***Giffen's
paradox***

Oleomargarine is likely to be an inferior good for many consumers. Increases in real income are likely to lead to a substitution of butter for oleomargarine. Many other examples of inferior goods could be put forth, although, as
stated above, inferior goods are in the minority. Giffen's paradox is a much,
much rarer phenomenon. In the rest of this book, we shall assume that goods
do not exhibit Giffen's paradox. That is, all demand curves are assumed to
have a negative slope.

CONSUMER'S SURPLUS

Previous sections have presented a model of how consumers respond to changes in price and money income. But no attempt has been made to indicate how this model can be used to help solve practical problems. In the balance of this chapter, we discuss some applications of this model. Let's start with the very simple case where a consumer receives an additional amount of some good. For example, suppose that the consumer receives three pounds of sugar from a kindly (and not particularly calorie-conscious) neighbor. How much is this sugar worth to the consumer? This example, while trivial and homely in the extreme, will enable us to derive some results that will be used in the next section to throw light on an important problem of public policy.

To determine how much the additional three pounds of sugar are worth to this consumer, the proper question to ask is: What is the maximum amount that he or she would be willing to pay for the extra sugar? The consumer's demand curve for sugar provides the answer to this question. Suppose that the consumer's demand curve for sugar is as shown in the left-hand panel of Figure 4.8, and that he or she is presently consuming no sugar. For simplicity, suppose that sugar can only be purchased in units of a pound; in other words, fractions of a pound cannot be purchased. (This assumption will be relaxed later.)

The maximum amount that the consumer will pay for the first pound of sugar is 60 cents. As shown by the demand curve in the left-hand panel of Figure 4.8, the consumer would not buy any sugar at all if the price were above 60 cents per pound, but at a price of 60 cents he or she will buy one pound. The maximum amount that the consumer will pay for the second pound of sugar is 45 cents. As shown in Figure 4.8, the price must be lowered to 45 cents to induce the consumer to buy a second pound. Finally, the maximum amount that the consumer will pay for the third pound of sugar is 30 cents. As shown in Figure 4.8, the price must be lowered to 30 cents to induce the consumer to buy a third pound.

Adding up the maximum amounts that the consumer would pay for each pound of sugar, we find that the total maximum amount that he or she would be willing to pay for all three additional pounds of sugar is $60 + 45 + 30 = 135$ cents. The important thing to note is that this total maximum amount equals the area under the demand curve from zero to three pounds of sugar. In other words, it equals the shaded area in the left-hand panel of Figure 4.8. To see this, note that this shaded area equals the sum of three rectangles shown in this panel. The area of the tallest shaded rectangle equals 60 cents; the area of the next tallest rectangle equals 45 cents; and the area of the shortest rectangle equals 30 cents; thus, the total shaded area equals $60 + 45 + 30 = 135$ cents.

Having determined the value of the additional three pounds of sugar to the consumer, let's suppose that he or she no longer receives sugar from a

Fig.
4.8
CONSUMER'S SURPLUS FROM THREE POUNDS OF SUGAR / *Whereas the consumer would be willing to pay up to 135 cents (the shaded area in the left-hand panel) for three extra pounds of sugar, he or she only has to pay 90 cents (the shaded area in the middle panel) for them. Thus, the consumer's surplus—the net benefit to the consumer—is 135 − 90 = 45 cents (the shaded area in the right-hand panel).*

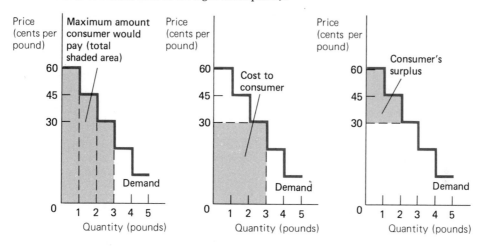

kindly neighbor. Instead, the consumer must pay 30 cents per pound for sugar. At this price, the consumer's demand curve in Figure 4.8 shows that he or she will buy three pounds of sugar, and pay 3 × 30 = 90 cents for them. Since the total cost of the three pounds of sugar equals the price per pound (30 cents) times the quantity purchased (three pounds), it equals the shaded area in the middle panel of Figure 4.8. (This shaded area is a rectangle with length equal to the price per pound and width equal to the quantity purchased.)

Whereas the three pounds of sugar are worth 135 cents to the consumer, he or she only has to pay 90 cents for them. The difference between what the consumer would be willing to pay (135 cents) and what the consumer actually has to pay (90 cents) is called *consumer's surplus.* Consumer's surplus is a measure of the net benefit received by the consumer. Since the consumer receives sugar worth 135 cents (to him or her) for 90 cents, he or she receives a net benefit of 45 cents. Geometrically, consumer's surplus can be represented by the shaded area in the right-hand panel of Figure 4.8. To see why this is the case, note that, to obtain consumer's surplus, we must deduct the shaded area in the middle panel (which equals the cost of the sugar) from the shaded area in the left-hand panel (which equals the maximum amount the consumer would pay for the sugar). The result is, of course, the shaded area in the right-hand panel.

Finally, we must relax the assumption that sugar can only be purchased in units of a pound. If fractions of a pound can be purchased, the demand curve is a smooth line, as in Figure 4.9 (rather than a series of steps, as in Figure 4.8).

Consumer's surplus

Fig.
4.9 CONSUMER'S SURPLUS: CASE WHERE FRACTIONS OF A POUND CAN BE
PURCHASED / *Consumer's surplus equals the area of triangle* PAB.

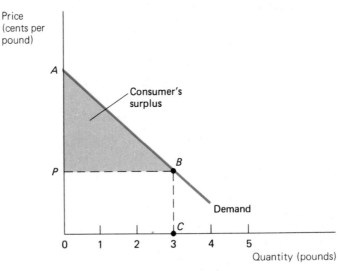

But regardless of whether the demand curve is smooth or a series of steps, the maximum amount that the consumer will pay for the three pounds of sugar is the area under the demand curve from zero to three pounds of sugar. In Figure 4.9, this area equals *OABC*. Since the price of a pound of sugar is *OP* in Figure 4.9, the amount that the consumer actually pays for the three pounds of sugar is equal to the area of rectangle *OPBC*. Since consumer's surplus equals the maximum amount that the consumer would pay (area *OABC*) minus the amount he or she actually pays (area *OPBC*), the shaded area in Figure 4.9 equals consumer's surplus.

Consumer's Surplus and Restrictions on Sugar Imports

The concept of consumer's surplus is of practical importance. To illustrate how it has been used, let's consider American restrictions on sugar imports, a subject that has stimulated plenty of controversy. Because their costs are relatively high, American sugar producers find it difficult to compete with Central American and other foreign producers. To protect the American sugar industry from foreign competition, the U.S. government has imposed restrictions on how much foreign-produced sugar can be imported into the United States. (In 1987, only about 1 million tons could be imported.) One of the major questions concerning such restrictions is: How much of a loss do they impose on U.S. consumers?

To see how the theory introduced in the previous section can be of use in dealing with this question, suppose that, in the absence of government restric-

Fig.
4.10
REDUCTION IN CONSUMER'S SURPLUS DUE TO AN INCREASE IN THE PRICE OF
SUGAR / *If the price of sugar increases from* OP$_0$ *to* OP$_1$, *there will be a*
reduction in consumer's surplus equal to area P$_0$P$_1$LM.

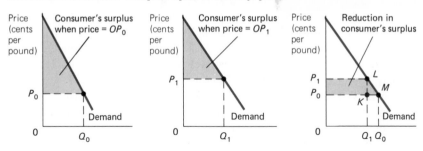

tions on sugar imports, the price of sugar in the United States would be OP_0 in Figure 4.10. Based on the consumer's demand curve in the left-hand panel of this graph, the consumer would purchase OQ_0 pounds of sugar per year, the total cost of the sugar being $OP_0 \times OQ_0$. However, this total cost is an underestimate of what the sugar is really worth to the consumer. As stressed in the previous section, the consumer receives a consumer's surplus equal to the shaded area in the left-hand panel of Figure 4.10.

If the government imposes restrictions on sugar imports into the United States, the price of sugar will rise (because the import restrictions push the supply curve for sugar upward and to the left). Suppose that the price goes up to OP_1, as shown in the middle panel of Figure 4.10. Because of the higher price, the consumer will purchase somewhat less sugar (OQ_1 rather than OQ_0 pounds per year). The total amount spent on sugar will increase from $OP_0 \times OQ_0$ to $OP_1 \times OQ_1$. More important, the price increase results in a reduction in consumer's surplus. If price equals OP_1, the consumer's surplus equals the shaded area in the middle panel of Figure 4.10. Thus, the increase in price from OP_0 to OP_1 results in a reduction in consumer's surplus equal to the shaded area in the right-hand panel of Figure 4.10. (Clearly, this shaded area equals the shaded area in the left-hand panel minus that in the middle panel.) As shown there, the loss in consumer's surplus equals the area to the left of the demand curve from the original price to the increased price.[3]

The loss to the consumer from the price increase can be measured by the shaded area in the right-hand panel of Figure 4.10. To understand more clearly why this measure is a sensible one, note that this shaded area is composed of two parts: rectangle P_0P_1LK and triangle KLM. The first part (rectangle P_0P_1LK) shows the extra amount that the consumer has to pay for the amount of sugar he or she consumes (after the price increase). Clearly, this extra

---

3. The shaded area in the right-hand panel of Figure 4.10 also measures the *gain* in consumer's surplus if price is *lowered* from OP_1 to OP_0. Based on our discussion in this and the previous section, the reader should be able to demonstrate that this is true.

amount equals $(OP_1 - OP_0)OQ_1$, and is equal to the area of rectangle P_0P_1LK. The second part (triangle KLM) shows the net loss to the consumer because he or she consumes less sugar (OQ_1 rather than OQ_0 pounds) due to the higher price. As we saw in the previous section, the value to the consumer of the forgone ($OQ_0 - OQ_1$) pounds of sugar (that is, the maximum amount that he or she would pay for them) is equal to area Q_1LMQ_0. If we subtract area Q_1KMQ_0, which equals the amount that the consumer would have had to pay for these ($OQ_0 - OQ_1$) pounds, the net loss to the consumer is triangle KLM.

Ilse Mintz, in a study published by the American Enterprise Institute, applied this technique to estimate the loss to consumers due to the restrictions on sugar imports.[4] According to her estimates, the demand curve for sugar in the United States was as shown in Figure 4.11. The restrictions raised the price of sugar by 2.57 cents, as shown in Figure 4.11. Without the restrictions, U.S. consumers would have purchased 23.2 billion pounds of sugar; with them, they purchased 22.4 billion pounds. As indicated in the right-hand panel of Figure 4.10, the reduction in consumer's surplus due to the price increase equals the area to the left of the demand curve from the original price to the

Fig. 4.11   REDUCTION IN CONSUMER'S SURPLUS DUE TO RESTRICTIONS ON SUGAR IMPORTS / *Because of restrictions on sugar imports, the price of sugar was increased by 2.57 cents per pound. The reduction in consumer's surplus equaled $586 million per year, the shaded area in the graph.*

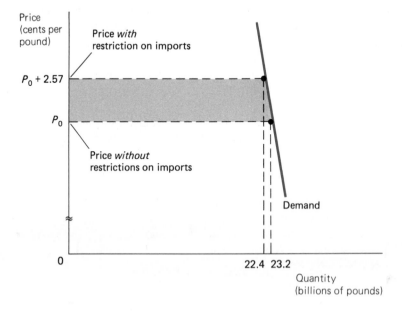

4. I. Mintz, *U.S. Import Quotas, Costs and Consequences* (Washington, D.C.: American Enterprise Institute, February 1973).

increased price. This area, which is shaded in Figure 4.11, equals ½(2.57 cents) (22.4 billion pounds + 23.2 billion pounds) = $586 million per year.

Thus Mintz's results indicated that American consumers were worse off by about $586 million per year because of restrictions on sugar imports. Subsequent studies, based on the same technique, have borne out her conclusion that these restrictions have imposed considerable losses on American consumers.[5] It is not our intention to take up the pros and cons of such restrictions at this point. (Much more will be said on this score in the cross-chapter case dealing with steel import quotas at the end of Part 6.) For present purposes, all that we want to do is illustrate how the concept of consumer's surplus has been used to shed light on important questions of public policy.

Consumer's Surplus and Indifference Curves

One further point needs to be made concerning the concept of consumer's surplus. When we use this concept, we assume that the consumer's indifference curves are of a particular type.[6] Suppose that we plot the consumer's indifference curves in Figure 4.12, in which the amount of sugar consumed per day is one good and the amount of money that the consumer can spend on all goods other than sugar is the other good. Admittedly, the latter is a peculiar sort of good, but there is nothing to prevent us from defining a good in this way. In weighing every purchase, the consumer must decide whether to give up money he or she can spend on things other than sugar (the good on the horizontal axis). Since the good on the vertical axis is money, its price is always 1. For example, it takes a quarter to buy a quarter. The introduction of this kind of good is a useful trick that we will adopt elsewhere in this book.

When we use the concept of consumer's surplus, we assume that the indifference curves (1, 2, and 3, as well as others not shown in Figure 4.12) are parallel; that is, the vertical distance between any two indifference curves is the same regardless of where along the horizontal axis one measures this distance. This is a very restrictive assumption, but according to some economists it may be a reasonable approximation for commodities, like sugar, on which the consumer spends only a small amount of his or her income.[7]

---

5. For example, see M. Morkre and D. Tarr, *Staff Report on Effects of Restrictions on U.S. Imports,* Federal Trade Commission, June 1980. According to the 1987 Annual Report of the Council of Economic Advisers, the import quota is imposed to maintain price supports for sugar at three to four times the world price. See *Economic Report of the President* (Washington, D.C.: Government Printing Office, 1987).

6. Also, there are problems, described in Chapter 14, involved in comparing and combining the results for different consumers. Much more will be said on this score in Chapter 14.

7. Basically, the assumption underlying the analysis is that the marginal utility of income is constant. If this is the case, the indifference curves in Figure 4.12 will be parallel. This assumption is stringent, indeed. See P. Samuelson, *Foundations of Economic Analysis* (Cambridge, Mass.: Harvard University Press, 1947), pp. 189–202; and J. Hicks, *Value and Capital* (New York: Oxford University Press, 1946), pp. 38–41.

Fig.
4.12

SPECIAL ASSUMPTION UNDERLYING CALCULATIONS OF CONSUMER'S
SURPLUS / *Strictly speaking, when we measure consumer's surplus as we
did in Figures 4.8–4.11, we assume that the indifference curves (like 1, 2,
and 3) are parallel. However, if this is not the case, this measurement
procedure may still be a good approximation.*

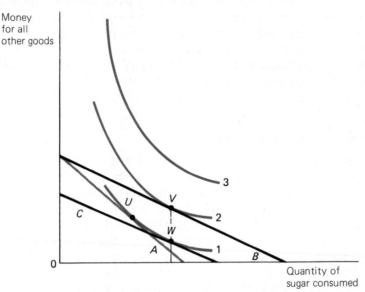

What does it mean when we assume that the indifference curves in Figure
4.12 are parallel? If they are parallel, their slopes must be equal at a given point
along the horizontal axis. This means that, if a change occurs in the price of
sugar, the income effect (on the consumption of sugar) of the price change is
zero. To see this, suppose that the price of sugar decreases so that the consumer's equilibrium point shifts from *U* to *V*. The income effect of this price
decrease can be measured by inserting a budget line, *C*, which has the slope of
the new budget line, *B*, but which is tangent to the old indifference curve, 1. If
this fictitious budget line were the real one, the equilibrium point would be *W*.
The income effect is the movement along the horizontal axis from *W* to *V*,
which is clearly equal to zero.

Unless this assumption (that the indifference curves are parallel) is valid,
the technique used to measure consumer's surplus in Figures 4.8 and 4.9—and
to measure the reduction in consumer's surplus in Figures 4.10 and 4.11—is
only an approximation. Fortunately, however, for many applications, it can be
shown that the approximation is good enough for practical purposes.[8]

---

8. R. Willig, "Consumer Surplus Without Apology," *American Economic Review*, September
1976.

Example 4.2

NEW YORK CITY'S WATER CRISIS

On January 7, 1986, Mayor Koch of New York City proposed that water meters be installed in all buildings in the city. This was not a new idea. When New York City experienced a water crisis a number of years ago (because the average rate of use of water exceeded the yield of the water system), the mayor's Committee on Management Survey recommended the use of universal metering. Many consumers paid only a flat fee for water and were not metered. With metering, consumers would be charged 2 cents per hundred gallons of water. The cost of installing and operating the meters was estimated to be about $50 per million gallons of water saved per day. But this was only part of the cost of metering, since it did not include the loss to consumers arising from the fact that they would be led to consume less water. To make a fair comparison of the cost of metering with the cost of other ways of meeting the crisis, it was obvious that such losses should be taken into account.

(a) If a consumer's demand curve for water was approximately linear, as shown below, how large was the monetary value of his or her loss due to the consumption of less water? (b) How much was the monetary value of such losses per million gallons of water saved? (c) Including such losses as well as the cost of installing and operating the meters, what was the total cost of each million gallons of water saved by metering? (d) The cost of providing water with a new dam was estimated to be about $1,000 per million gallons per day. Was building a new dam (which in fact was done) the right solution?

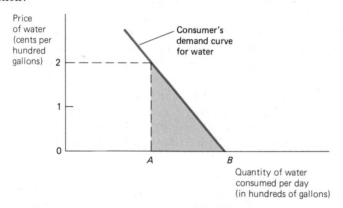

SOLUTION

(a) Without metering, the consumer would consume OB hundreds of gallons of water per day (since the price of an extra hundred gallons was zero). With metering, the consumer would consume OA hundreds of gallons of water per day (since the price of an extra hundred gallons was 2 cents). The consumer would be willing to pay an amount equal to the shaded area under the demand curve for the $(OB - OA)$ hundreds of gallons per day that he or she forgoes because of metering. Since the demand curve is assumed to be linear, this area equals ½ × (2 cents) × the quantity of water saved per day (in hundreds of gallons). In other words, it equals 1 cent per hundred gallons saved per day. (b) Since 1 cent per hundred gallons is equivalent to $100 per million gallons, the monetary value of such losses was $100 per million gallons saved. (c) $100 + $50 = $150. (d) It appears that metering would have been cheaper than building the dam. (However, it should be recognized that this kind of analysis is subject to limitations described on p. 98 and in Chapter 14.)*

*For further discussion of this case, see J. Hirschleifer, J. Milliman, and J. DeHaven, *Water Supply* (Chicago: University of Chicago Press, 1960).

INFORMATION AND SEARCH ACTIVITY BY CONSUMERS

Finally, we must recognize that our model of consumer behavior assumes that the consumer knows the minimum price that he or she must pay for each commodity. The consumer, however, frequently does not have such information. For example, if a person is shopping for a new car, he or she does not know which auto dealer will sell a particular model at the lowest price. In fact, studies show that a particular model of Chevrolet may sell for several hundred dollars more at one dealer than at another. But unless the consumer shops around, there is no way to determine which dealer will quote the lowest price, or what the lowest price is.

The reasons for such price dispersion are not difficult to find. Because of changes in market conditions (described in subsequent chapters), some firms find it profitable to change their prices. Since it takes time for other firms to find out about the price changes and to react to them, temporary price disparities occur. Also, some buyers (and sellers) are inexperienced and/or uninformed, with the result that they are willing to pay (or charge) prices that are out of line with current market conditions. Clearly, the greater the amount of instability in market conditions and the greater the amount of ignorance among buyers and sellers, the greater the amount of price dispersion.

How much search activity will the rational consumer carry out? In other words, how much shopping around will the consumer do? The answer depends on the cost of search, among other things. For example, if it is very costly to determine the price charged by a seller, the consumer will contact fewer sellers than if it is cheap to do so. The cost of search will be influenced by the geographical size of the market and whether the consumer must contact a seller in person to obtain a price quotation. Obviously, the cost of obtaining each quotation tends to be higher if the sellers are far apart and if the consumer must contact them personally.

The optimal amount of search activity also depends on the expected gains to the consumer from search. In general, one would expect that, the larger the fraction of the consumer's income that is spent on a particular commodity, the greater the prospective gains to the consumer from search, and thus the greater the amount of search carried out. Consequently, one might expect consumers to shop around more for major items like cars and houses than for minor items like candy and shoelaces.[9]

---

9. For a pioneering analysis of this topic, see G. Stigler, "The Economics of Information," *Journal of Political Economy*, June 1961. In recent years, a considerable amount of interesting and important work has been carried out in this area by G. Stigler, J. Marschak, J. Hirshleifer, L. Telser, and others. See A. M. Spence, "Job Market Signaling," reprinted in E. Mansfield, *Microeconomics: Selected Readings*, 5th ed., for an analysis of the role of information in labor markets. Also, see the papers by J. Stiglitz, S. Salop, S. Grossman, J. Green, G. Butters, R. Wilson, and others in the "Symposium on Information," *Review of Economic Studies*, October 1977.

SUMMARY

1. Another way of expressing the conditions for consumer equilibrium is as follows: The rational consumer will choose in equilibrium to allocate his or her income between good X and good Y in such a way that the marginal rate of substitution of good X for good Y equals the ratio of the price of good X to the price of good Y.

2. If we hold commodity prices constant, each level of money income results in an equilibrium market basket for the consumer, and the curve that connects the points representing all of these equilibrium market baskets is called the income-consumption curve. The income-consumption curve can be used to derive the Engel curve, which is the relationship between the equilibrium amount of a good purchased by a consumer and the level of the consumer's money income. Engel curves play an important role in family expenditure studies.

3. Holding constant the consumer's money income as well as the prices of other goods, we can determine the relationship between the price of a good and the amount of this good that a consumer will consume. This relationship is called the consumer's individual demand curve for the good in question. The individual demand curve, one of the central concepts in the theory of consumer behavior, can be derived from the price-consumption curve, which includes all of the equilibrium market baskets corresponding to various prices of the good.

4. The location and shape of an individual demand curve will depend on the level of money income and the level at which the prices of other goods are held constant, as well as on the nature of the good and the tastes of the consumer. It is important to differentiate between shifts in a consumer's demand curve for a particular commodity and changes in the amount of the commodity that he or she consumes.

5. The total effect of a price change on the quantity demanded can be divided into two parts: the substitution effect and the income effect. The substitution effect is the change in quantity demanded of a good resulting from a price change when the level of satisfaction, or real income, is held constant. The income effect shows the effect of the change in real income that is due to the price change. The substitution effect is always negative. The income effect is not predictable from the theory alone: Its sign is different for normal goods than for inferior goods.

6. An illustration of how this model of consumer behavior has been used to help solve practical problems is provided by the study of the effects of sugar

import quotas. An important question in this case was: How can one estimate the monetary value of the loss to consumers arising from the fact that import quotas raise the price of sugar and lower sugar consumption? If certain assumptions are made, this question can be answered, at least approximately, based on the concept of consumer's surplus.

▬▬▬▬▬ QUESTIONS/PROBLEMS ▬▬▬▬▬

1) (a) As shown below, the price-consumption curve for good X is upward sloping, when good Y is the money spent by the consumer on goods other than good X. Prove that the consumer's demand curve for good X is price inelastic. (Hint: Recall from Chapter 2 that, if the demand for a good is price inelastic, a decrease in its price results in a decrease in the amount spent on it.)

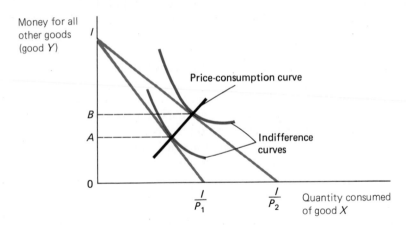

(b) Prove that, if this price-consumption curve were downward sloping, the consumer's demand curve for good X would be price elastic.

2) In late 1985, New York City's Department of Consumer Affairs published the results of an eleven-month study of prescription drug prices charged by ninety-two pharmacies in New York. The survey reported that thirty tablets of Dyazide (prescribed for high blood pressure) cost $16.95 at one pharmacy and $6.95 at another pharmacy about three miles away. What factors may be responsible for this discrepancy? Will it persist over time? According to a spokesman for the department, "in low-income areas with no competition, they can charge pretty high prices, and there is no pressure to bring those prices down."[10] Why is there no such pressure?

3) Lewis and Clark Lake is a large reservoir in South Dakota created on the Missouri River by the Gavins Point Dam. It is located in an area where there are few natural bodies of water, and it has become very popular as a recreational area. Suppose that 10,000 families are potential users of the lake for recreational purposes and that each family's demand curve for recreational trips to the lake is as follows:

---

10. *New York Times*, December 28, 1985, p. 48.

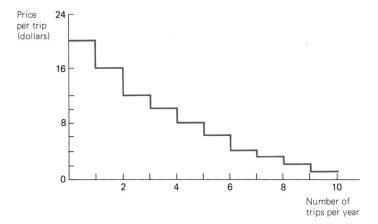

(a) If an ordinance were passed which limited each family to no more than 5 trips per year to the lake, what is the loss (in money terms) to each family? (b) If an ordinance were passed which allowed a family to use the lake for recreational purposes only if it purchased a permit for $75 a year, would it be worthwhile for each family to buy the permit, if it could not use the lake without the permit (and it could use the lake as much as it liked with one)? (c) Suppose that we consider two goods: trips to the lake and money that can be spent on things other than trips to the lake. In answering questions (a) and (b), what assumption are you making regarding each family's indifference curves concerning these two goods?

4) In the previous question, how much is the consumer's surplus from each family's utilization of the lake if there is a charge of $8 for each trip to the lake?

5) Suppose that all consumers pay 25 cents for a telephone call and 25 cents for a newspaper (and that all consumers purchase some of both goods). (a) If all consumers are maximizing utility, is it possible to determine each consumer's marginal rate of substitution of telephone calls for newspapers? (b) Suppose that a local economist applies for a grant to estimate this marginal rate of substitution; his proposed procedure is to ask a sample of consumers. Can you suggest a simpler procedure? (c) Based on these facts alone, can you estimate this marginal rate of substitution? If so, what is it?

6) A representative of the dairy industry asserts that, as income increases, the proportion of income spent on food tends to rise. (a) Do you think this proposition is true? Why or why not? (b) Indicate the general shape of the Engel curve for food, based on this proposition.

7) According to some observers, the typical Irish peasant in the nineteenth century was so poor he spent almost all his income for potatoes. When the price of potatoes fell, he could get the same amount of nutrition for a smaller expenditure on potatoes, so some of his income was diverted to vegetables and meat. Since the latter also provided calories, he could even reduce his consumption of potatoes under these circumstances. If this is true, were potatoes (a) a normal good? (b) an inferior good? (c) a good exhibiting Giffen's paradox?

8) Suppose that a 1 percent increase in the price of pork chops results in Ms. Smith's buying 3 percent fewer pork chops per week. What is the price elasticity of

demand for pork chops on the part of Ms. Smith? Is her demand for pork chops price elastic or price inelastic? Will an increase in the price of pork chops result in an increase, or a decrease, in the total amount of money that she spends on pork chops?

9) Suppose Ms. Smith's utility function can be described by $U = Q_c Q_p$, where U is her utility, Q_c is the number of pounds of corn she consumes, and Q_p is the number of pounds of potatoes she consumes. Suppose that the total amount of money she can spend on these two commodities is $100 and the price of corn is $1 per pound. How many potatoes will she buy if potatoes are 50 cents per pound?

Market Demand

INTRODUCTION

The previous chapter was concerned with the determinants of the quantity of a good demanded by an individual consumer. For many purposes, it is not so much the quantity demanded by a particular consumer that counts; instead it is the quantity demanded by all the consumers in a market. For example, the auto industry is much more concerned with the quantity of cars that will be demanded by the entire national market than with the quantity of cars that you or I will purchase next year. Economists, too, when confronted with many problems, are much more interested in the quantity of a good demanded in a market than in the quantity of a good demanded by a particular individual. For example, as we saw in Chapter 2, it is the market demand curve, not the individual demand curve, that (together with the market supply curve) determines the equilibrium price of a good.

In this chapter we are concerned with market demand. After showing how the market demand curve is related to the demand curves of the individual consumers in the market, we discuss some major determinants of the price elasticity of market demand. Then we take up the effects of two other factors, besides the good's price, on the quantity of the good that is demanded in the market—aggregate money income and the prices of other commodities. Next, we look at market demand from the seller's side of the market, placing emphasis on the concept of marginal revenue and the differences between the demand curve for the industry and the demand curve for the firm. Finally, we discuss the measurement of market demand curves, and we describe two cases where such measurements were used to help guide public and private decision-makers.

DERIVATION OF THE MARKET DEMAND CURVE

In Chapter 4, we showed how an individual demand curve can be derived from a consumer's indifference map. This demand curve is of course the relationship between the quantity of the good demanded by the consumer (per unit of time) and the good's price, when the money income of the consumer and the prices of other goods are held constant. The shape and level of the individual demand curve obviously depend on the consumer's tastes, as reflected in his or her indifference map. They also depend on the level of the consumer's money income and the level of the prices of other goods.

Market demand curve

The *market demand curve* for a commodity is simply the *horizontal* summation of the individual demand curves of all the consumers in the market. Put differently, to find the market quantity demanded at each price, we add up the individual quantities demanded at that price. For example, Table 5.1 shows the individual demand schedules[1] for four consumers. If these four consumers comprise the entire

Table 5.1 INDIVIDUAL AND MARKET DEMAND SCHEDULES

Price (cents per unit of the commodity)	Quantity demanded (per unit of time)				Quantity demanded in market (per unit of time)
	Individual A	Individual B	Individual C	Individual D	
	(units of the commodity)				
1	50	40	30	20	140
2	40	30	25	19	114
3	30	20	18	18	86
4	25	15	13	17	70
5	20	14	13	16	63
6	15	13	11	15	54
7	10	12	9	14	45
8	8	11	7	13	39
9	6	10	5	12	33
10	5	9	3	11	28

1. Recall from Chapter 2 that a demand schedule is a table showing the quantity demanded at various prices.

Fig. INDIVIDUAL AND MARKET DEMAND CURVES / *The market demand curve is*
5.1 *the horizontal summation of the individual demand curves.*

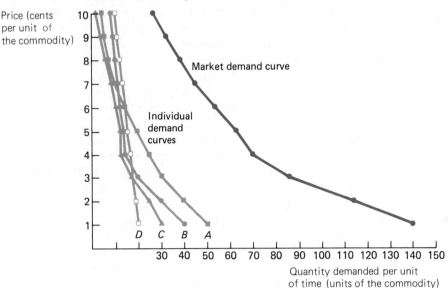

market, the market demand schedule is given in the last column of Table 5.1. Figure 5.1 shows the individual demand curves based on these same data, as well as the resulting market demand curve.

The market demand curve for a commodity is one of the most important concepts in microeconomics. The market demand curve shows how much of the commodity will be purchased (per unit of time) by the consumers in the market at each possible price (given that the level of money income of the consumers and the prices of other commodities are held constant). Information regarding the market demand curve is of the utmost importance to producers of the commodity. Obviously, they need to know how much can be sold at various prices. The market demand curve is also of great importance to economists because, as pointed out in Chapter 2, it plays an important role in determining the price of the commodity.

PRICE ELASTICITY: MEASUREMENT, EFFECTS, AND DETERMINANTS

Graphical Measurement of the Price Elasticity of Demand

At each point on the market demand curve, the price elasticity of demand, defined as the percentage change in the quantity demanded resulting from a 1 percent change in price, gauges the sensitivity of the quantity demanded to changes in price. Chapter 2 pointed out the significance of the price elasticity of demand. In the next two sections of this chapter, we go further in discussing its measurement and determinants. To begin with, let's consider how it can be measured. In Chapter 2, we described how one can compute the price elasticity of demand from a table showing the quantity demanded at each of a number of prices. But suppose that we are given a demand curve, such as that shown in Figure 5.1. Is there any way to make a rough estimate of the price elasticity at a given point on this demand curve by means of visual inspection of the demand curve? The answer is yes; the following method is applicable to problems of this sort.

Suppose that the problem is to estimate the price elasticity of demand at point A on the demand curve in Figure 5.2. The first step is to construct the tangent to the demand curve at point A; this tangent is labeled CAD. If the price falls from OP_1 to OP_2, the resulting change in the quantity demanded can be approximated by Q_1Q_2. This approximation should be reasonably good if the change in price is small or if the demand curve is close to linear. Thus the elasticity at point A can be approximated by

$$\frac{Q_1Q_2}{OQ_1} \div \frac{P_2P_1}{OP_1} = \frac{Q_1Q_2}{P_2P_1} \cdot \frac{OP_1}{OQ_1}.$$

Fig. 5.2   GRAPHICAL MEASUREMENT OF PRICE ELASTICITY / *The price elasticity of demand equals* AD ÷ CA.

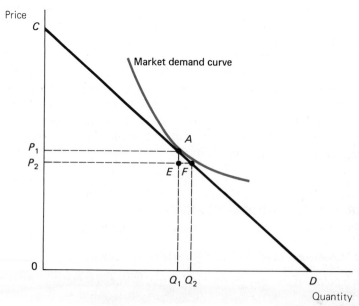

Fig.   GRAPHICAL MEASUREMENT OF PRICE ELASTICITY: LINEAR DEMAND CURVE /
5.3   *The price elasticity of demand exceeds 1 if price is greater than* OP, *and is
less than 1 if price is less than* OP.

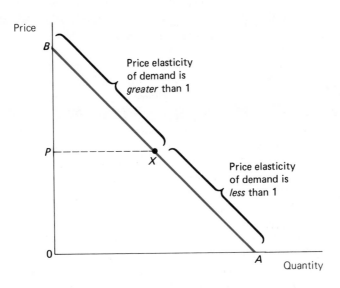

It is obvious that $Q_1Q_2 \div P_2P_1 = EF \div EA$. Also, since AEF and AQ_1D are similar right triangles, $EF \div EA = Q_1D \div Q_1A = Q_1D \div OP_1$. Thus, the price elasticity of demand (denoted by η) equals

$$\eta = \frac{Q_1D}{OP_1} \cdot \frac{OP_1}{OQ_1} = \frac{Q_1D}{OQ_1},$$

and since $Q_1D \div OQ_1 = AD \div CA$,

$$\eta = AD \div CA. \qquad [5.1]$$

Let us apply this result to the case of a linear demand curve, such as BA in Figure 5.3. It is obvious from inspection of this figure that the price elasticity of demand exceeds 1 at prices exceeding OP, that the price elasticity of demand is less than 1 at prices under OP, and that there is unitary price elasticity of demand at a price of OP. To prove that there is unitary elasticity of demand at a price of OP, we need only note that $XA = BX$. To prove that the elasticity of demand is greater than 1 at prices above OP, choose any price above OP and find the point corresponding to this price on the demand curve; it is clear that the distance from this point to A is greater than the distance from this point to B. To prove that the elasticity of demand is less than 1 at prices under OP, choose any price below OP and find the point corresponding to this price on the demand curve; it is clear that the distance from this point to A is less than the distance from this point to B.

Determinants of the Price Elasticity of Demand

In previous sections we have stressed the importance of the price elasticity of demand, but nothing has been said about the determinants of the price elasticity of demand. What determines whether the demand for a commodity is price elastic or price inelastic in a certain price range? Why does the price elasticity of demand for one commodity equal 3.0 and the price elasticity of demand for another commodity equal 1.5? This is a very important question, and the one to which we turn our attention in this section.

First, and foremost, the price elasticity of demand for a commodity depends on the number and closeness of the *substitutes* that are available. If a commodity has many close substitutes, its demand is likely to be price elastic. If increases occur in the price of the product, a large proportion of its buyers will turn to the close substitutes that are available; if decreases occur in its price, a great many buyers of substitutes will switch to this product.

The role of substitutes

Of course, the extent to which a commodity has close substitutes depends on how narrowly it is defined. In general, one would expect that, as the definition of the product becomes narrower and more specific, the product has more close substitutes and its demand becomes more price elastic. Thus the demand for a particular brand of cigarettes is likely to be more price elastic than the overall demand for cigarettes and the demand for cigarettes is likely to be more price elastic than the demand for tobacco products as a whole. If a commodity is defined so that it has perfect substitutes, its price elasticity of demand is infinite. Thus, if the cotton produced by Farmer Jones is exactly the same as the cotton produced by other farmers and if he increases his price slightly (to a point above the market level), his sales would be reduced to nothing.

Second, it is sometimes asserted that the price elasticity of demand for a commodity is likely to depend on the importance of the commodity in consumers' budgets. For example, the demand for commodities like thumbtacks, pepper, and salt may be quite inelastic. The typical consumer spends only a very small fraction of his income on such goods. On the other hand, for commodities that bulk larger in the typical consumer's budget, like major appliances, the elasticity of demand may tend to be higher. Consumers may be more conscious of, and influenced by, price changes in the case of goods that require larger outlays. However, although a tendency of this sort is sometimes hypothesized, there is no guarantee that it exists. As some economists have pointed out, the link between a commodity's price elasticity of demand and its importance in consumer's budgets may in fact be much weaker than is implied by this hypothesis.

Third, the price elasticity of demand for a commodity is likely to depend on the length of the period to which the demand curve pertains. (Every market demand curve—like every individual demand curve—pertains, of course, to a certain time interval.) In general, demand is likely to be more elastic, or less

Example 5.1

GOVERNMENT POLICY-MAKING IN THE 1973 FUEL CRISIS

Top government policy-makers confronted a now-famous energy crisis at the end of 1973 when the Arab oil-producing countries announced a cutback of exports of oil to the United States. The first official estimates were that American consumers would have to reduce their consumption of gasoline by 20 or 30 percent. William E. Simon, the newly appointed federal "energy czar," stated repeatedly that he wanted to avoid rationing gasoline, if possible. So did other government officials, on the grounds that rationing would lead to black markets and create a large bureaucracy.

(a) How could gasoline consumption be cut by 20 or 30 percent without rationing? (b) Many economists pointed out to Simon and other government policy-makers that the short-term demand for gasoline is quite inelastic. Among the estimates of the price elasticity of demand for gasoline that were presented were the following:

Source of estimate*	Estimate
Hendrik Houthakker, Harvard University	0.3
Phillip Verleger, Data Resources, Inc.	0.3
Alan Greenspan, Townsend-Greenspan and Co.	0.4
U.S. Department of Transportation	0.2

If the arc elasticity of demand for gasoline equaled 0.3, how big a price increase was required to cut consumption by 25 percent? (c) Was rationing avoided? If so, how was the problem solved?

SOLUTION

(a) By increasing the price of gasoline. This, of course, is what would happen in a free market. (b) Increases in price of about 182 percent would be required. To see this, let Q_{D2} be the quantity demanded after the increase in price (from P_1 to P_2), Q_{D1} be the quantity demanded before the increase in price, η be the price elasticity of demand, $\Delta P = P_2 - P_1$, and $\Delta Q_D = Q_{D2} - Q_{D1}$. It follows from Equation 2.2 that $- \Delta Q_D (P_1 + P_2) \div \Delta P(Q_{D1} + Q_{D2}) = \eta$. If consumption is to be cut by 25 percent, Q_{D2} equals $0.75Q_{D1}$, and $\Delta Q_D = -.25Q_{D1}$. Thus $.25Q_{D1}(P_1 + P_2) \div 1.75Q_{D1}\Delta P = \eta$, or

$$\frac{\Delta P}{P_1 + P_2} = \frac{.25}{1.75\eta} = \frac{1}{7\eta}.$$

Consequently, if $\eta = 0.3$,

$$\frac{\Delta P}{P_1 + P_2} = \frac{1}{7 \times .3} = \frac{1}{2.1} = 0.476,$$

and (since $\Delta P = P_2 - P_1$),

$$\frac{P_2 - P_1}{P_1 + P_2} = 0.476.$$

Solving † for P_2 in terms of P_1,

$$P_2 = 2.82\,P_1.$$

That is, the price must increase by 182 percent. (c) Fortunately, subsequent analysis indicated that gasoline consumption did not have to be cut so severely, and it was possible to avoid both rationing and the enormous price increase set forth in the answer to (b). However, there were substantial price increases.

---

* For details, see *Business Week,* December 15, 1973, p. 23.

† Since $\dfrac{P_2 - P_1}{P_1 + P_2} = 0.476$, it follows that $P_2 - P_1 = 0.476\,(P_1 + P_2)$, which means that

$$0.524P_2 = 1.476P_1, \text{ or } P_2 = 2.82P_1.$$

inelastic, over a long period of time than over a short period of time. The longer the period of time, the easier it is for consumers and business firms to substitute one good for another. If, for example, the price of natural gas should decline relative to other fuels, the consumption of natural gas in the week after the price decline would probably increase very little. But over a period of several years, people would have an opportunity to take account of the price decline in choosing the type of fuel to be used in new houses and renovated old houses. In the longer period of several years, the price decline would have a greater effect on the consumption of natural gas than in the shorter period of one week.

THE INCOME ELASTICITY OF DEMAND

Up to this point, we have been concerned solely with the effect of price on the quantity of the commodity demanded in the market. Yet price is not the only factor that influences the quantity demanded in the market. Another important factor is the level of money income among the consumers in the market. For example, if consumers have plenty of money to spend, the quantity demanded of beef is likely to be greater than if they are poverty-stricken. Or if incomes in a pàrticular community are high, the quantity demanded of caviar is likely to be greater than if incomes are low.

Income elastic-
ity of demand

For an individual consumer, we saw in Chapter 4 that the relationship between money income (per period of time) and the amount consumed of a particular commodity (per period of time) can be represented by an Engel curve. Recall that this curve is based on the condition that the prices of all commodities remain constant. At any point on the Engel curve, one can characterize the sensitivity of the amount consumed to changes in the consumer's money income by the *income elasticity of demand,* which is defined as

$$\eta_I = \frac{\Delta Q}{Q} \div \frac{\Delta I}{I} \qquad [5.2]$$

where ΔQ is the change in quantity consumed that results from a small change in the consumer's money income ΔI, Q is the original quantity consumed, and I is the original money income of the consumer.[2]

Some goods have positive income elasticities, indicating that increases in the consumer's money income result in increases in the amount of the good

---

2. More precisely, the income elasticity of demand is

$$\frac{dQ}{dI} \div \frac{Q}{I}.$$

The text definition is the same except that finite differences are substituted for derivatives.

consumed. For example, one would generally expect steak and caviar to have positive income elasticities. Other goods have negative income elasticities, indicating that increases in the consumer's money income result in decreases in the amount of the good consumed. For example, margarine and poor grades of vegetables and other types of food might have negative income elasticities.[3] However, one must be careful to point out that the income elasticity of demand for a good is likely to vary considerably, depending on the level of the consumer's money income. Thus, in some ranges of income, the income elasticity may be positive; in other ranges of income, it may be negative.

The concept of income elasticity of demand can be applied to an entire market as well as to a single consumer, the only change in Equation 5.2 being that we must interpret Q as the total quantity demanded in the market, I as the aggregate money income of all consumers in the market, and ΔQ and ΔI as the changes in total quantity demanded and in aggregate money income. As in the case of the individual consumer, it is assumed that the prices of all commodities are held constant. Figure 5.4 shows a variety of possible relationships between the total quantity demanded in the market and the aggregate money income of the consumers. Curve A shows a case in which the income elasticity is greater than 1, which means that a 1 percent increase in money income results in more than a 1 percent increase in the total quantity demanded. Curve B shows a case in which the income elasticity is less than 1, which means that a

Fig. 5.4   VARIOUS TYPES OF RELATIONSHIPS BETWEEN QUANTITY DEMANDED AND AGGREGATE INCOME / *The quantity demanded of a good may be related in a variety of quite different ways to aggregate income.*

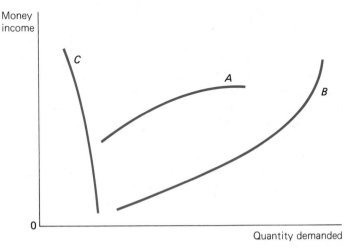

3. The similarity between goods with a negative income elasticity and inferior goods should be obvious.

1 percent increase in money income results in less than a 1 percent increase in the total quantity demanded. Case *C* shows a case in which the income elasticity is negative, indicating that increases in aggregate money income result in decreases in the total quantity demanded.[4]

There are, of course, enormous differences among goods with respect to their income elasticity of demand. No refined statistical surveys are needed to tell us that the income elasticity of demand for high-quality food and clothes is generally higher than the income elasticity of demand for salt and Kleenex. Luxury items are generally assumed to have high income elasticities of demand. Indeed, one way to define *luxuries* and *necessities* is to say that luxuries are goods with high income elasticities of demand, and necessities are goods with low income elasticities of demand.

Luxuries and necessities

An empirical law of consumption, *Engel's law,* was developed in the nineteenth century by Ernst Engel (whose work was noted in Chapter 4). Based on data concerning the budgets and expenditures of a large number of families, Engel found that the income elasticity of demand for food was quite low. He concluded from this result that the proportion of its income spent on food by a nation (or a family) was a good index of its welfare, with the better-off nations spending a smaller proportion on food than the poorer ones. This generalization is crude, but still serviceable within limits.[5]

Engel's law

CROSS ELASTICITIES OF DEMAND

In previous sections we have discussed the effects of two factors—the price of the commodity and the level of aggregate money income—on the quantity of the commodity demanded in the market. These two factors are not the only important ones; another important factor is the price of other commodities. Holding constant the commodity's own price (as well as the level of money incomes) and allowing the price of another commodity to vary, there may be important effects on the quantity demanded in the market for the commodity in question. By observing these effects, we can classify pairs of commodities as *substitutes* or *complements,* and we can measure how close the relationship (either substitute or complementary) is.

---

4. Of course, the quantity demanded may be influenced by the distribution of money income among consumers as well as the aggregate money income. We assume that the income distribution is held constant.

5. For an excellent study of Engel's law, see H. Houthakker, "An International Comparison of Household Expenditures Patterns," *Econometrica,* October 1957.

Consider two commodities, good X and good Y. Suppose that good Y's price goes up. What is the effect on the quantity of good X that is bought (per unit of time)? The *cross elasticity of demand* is defined as

Cross elasticity of demand

$$\eta_{xy} = \frac{\Delta Q_x}{Q_x} \div \frac{\Delta P_y}{P_y} \qquad [5.3]$$

where ΔP_y is the change in the price of good Y, P_y is the original price of good Y, ΔQ_x is the resulting change in the quantity demanded of good X, and Q_x is the original quantity demanded of good X. Thus the cross elasticity of demand is the relative change in the quantity of good X resulting from a 1 percent change in the price of good Y.[6]

Whether goods X and Y are classified as *substitutes* or *complements* depends on whether the cross elasticity of demand is positive or negative. For example, an increase in the price of lamb, when the price of pork remains constant, will tend to increase the quantity of pork demanded; thus η_{xy} is positive, and lamb and pork are classified as substitutes. On the other hand, an increase in the price of fishing licenses may tend to decrease the purchase of fishing poles, when the price of fishing poles remains constant; thus η_{xy} is negative, and fishing licenses and fishing poles are classified as complements. Figure 5.5 shows the relationship between the consumption of good X and the price of good Y, given that they are substitutes or complements.

Substitutes and complements

The cross elasticity of demand looks at the change in quantity demanded that results from a change in price *without* compensating for the change in the level of real income. This is the only feasible procedure because we seldom have data concerning the indifference maps of individual consumers. Moreover, we are generally interested in the relationship between commodities in the whole market rather than the relationship for a particular consumer.[7]

Finally, one other point should be noted. Whether goods X and Y are

---

6. More precisely the cross elasticity of demand is

$$\frac{dQ_x}{dP_y} \div \frac{Q_x}{P_y}.$$

The definition in the text is the same except that finite differences are substituted for derivatives.

    In subsequent discussions of marginal revenue, marginal product, marginal cost, and other such terms, we shall use finite differences and not bother to repeat each time the alternate definition based on the use of derivatives (since the alternative definition is obvious in each case).

7. For a single individual, goods can be classified as substitutes or complements more accurately on the basis of his or her utility function. Good Y is a substitute (complement) for good X if the marginal rate of substitution of good Y for money is reduced (increased) when good X is substituted for money in such a way as to leave the consumer no better or worse off than before. See J. Hicks, *Value and Capital* (New York: Oxford University Press, 1946), p. 44.

Fig.   RELATIONSHIP BETWEEN CONSUMPTION OF GOOD *X* AND PRICE OF GOOD *Y*,
5.5   GIVEN THAT THEY ARE SUBSTITUTES OR COMPLEMENTS / *If goods* X *and* Y
        are substitutes, the quantity demanded of X *is directly related to the price
        of good* Y. *If they are complements, the relationship is inverse.*

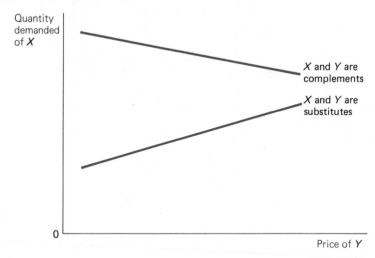

substitutes or complements can be determined by looking at the relative
change in the quantity demanded of good *X* divided by the relative change in
the price of good *Y*, that is, η_{xy}. It can also be determined by looking at the relative change in the quantity demanded of good *Y* divided by the relative change
in the price of good *X*, η_{yx}. However, it should not be expected that the two
elasticities will have the same numerical value. For example, goods *X* and *Y*
may be substitutes, but the consumption of good *X* may be more sensitive to
changes in the price of good *Y* than the consumption of good *Y* is to changes in
the price of good *X*.

THE SELLERS' SIDE OF THE MARKET AND
MARGINAL REVENUE

Up to this point, we have looked at the subject of demand chiefly from the
point of view of consumers. But, as we have already noted, the expenditures of
the consumers are the receipts of the sellers. In the next three sections, we look
at demand from the other side of the market—the seller's side. We begin by
defining marginal revenue. Then, in the following section, we show how marginal revenue can be estimated from the demand curve. Next we discuss the
differences between the demand curve for the industry and the demand curve
for the firm. Finally, we discuss the relationship between marginal revenue
and the price elasticity of demand. These results are of great importance and
they form a bridge to the theory of the firm, which is presented in succeeding
chapters.

The sellers of a commodity are interested, of course, in the total amount of money spent by consumers on the commodity. This amount is called *total revenue* by economists. From the market demand curve, one can easily determine the total revenue of the sellers at each price, since total revenue is, by definition, price times quantity. Thus,

Total revenue

Example 5.2

THE DEMAND FOR CIGARETTES IN THE UNITED STATES

E. Lewit and D. Coate estimated the price elasticity of demand for cigarettes among adults to be about 0.42 and the income elasticity to be about 0.08. (a) Among adults in a Texas community, holding other factors constant, there is the following relationship between their aggregate money income and the amount of cigarettes they consume:

Aggregate income (millions of dollars)	Quantity of cigarettes consumed
100	1,000
110	1,001
121	1,002

Is this evidence consistent with the results presented by Lewit and Coate? (b) Does your answer to question (a) depend on the units in which the quantity of cigarettes consumed is measured in the table above? (c) During 1967 to 1970, the Federal Communications Commission required that one anti-smoking television commercial be aired for every four pro-smoking advertisements, under the Fairness Doctrine. What effect did this have on the demand curve for cigarettes? (d) Would you expect changes in price to have as much effect on how many cigarettes existing smokers consume as on whether or not people begin to smoke?

SOLUTION

(a) Based on the data in the table, a 10 percent increase in income seems to result in about 0.1 percent increase in cigarette consumption. Thus, the income elasticity seems to be about 0.01, not 0.08, as reported by Lewit and Coate. This discrepancy could be due to the fact that smokers in this community regard cigarettes as more of a necessity than do all Americans. (b) No. Regardless of what the units may be, the income elasticity is the same—namely, about 0.1, as pointed out in the answer to question (a). (c) It shifted the demand curve to the left. According to a 1986 study, demand was 5.9 percent lower during the Fairness Doctrine period than would otherwise have been expected. (d) No. Studies indicate that higher prices reduce cigarette demand more by affecting the decision to smoke or not, rather than by causing existing smokers to cut significantly the amount of cigarettes they smoke.*

* For further discussion, see R. Porter, "The Impact of Government Policy on the U.S. Cigarette Industry," in P. Ippolito and D. Scheffman (eds.), *Empirical Approaches to Consumer Protection Economics* (Washington, D.C.: Federal Trade Commission, 1986); and E. Lewit and D. Coate, "The Potential for Using Excise Taxes to Reduce Smoking," *Journal of Health Economics,* 1982.

Table QUANTITY DEMANDED, TOTAL REVENUE, AND MARGINAL REVENUE
5.2

Price (dollars per unit of the commodity)	Quantity demanded (units of the commodity)	Total revenue (dollars)	Marginal revenue (dollars per unit of the commodity)
13	0	0	
12	1	12	12
11	2	22	10
10	3	30	8
9	4	36	6
8	5	40	4
7	6	42	2
6	7	42	0
5	8	40	−2
4	9	36	−4
3	10	30	−6

in Table 5.2, total revenue is $36 at a price of $9. The value of total revenue at various prices is shown in the third column of Table 5.2.

Economists and firms are also concerned with *marginal revenue,* which is defined as the addition to total revenue attributable to the addition of 1 unit to sales. Thus, if $R(q)$ is total revenue when q units are sold and $R(q-1)$ is total revenue when $(q-1)$ units are sold, the marginal revenue between q units and $(q-1)$ units is $R(q) - R(q-1)$. This is illustrated in Table 5.2. For example, when only 1 unit is sold, it is possible to charge a price of $12 and the total revenue is $12. The marginal revenue between 1 unit of output and zero units of output is total revenue at one unit of output minus total revenue at zero units of output. Since the latter is zero, the marginal revenue between 1 unit of output and zero units of output is $12.

Marginal revenue

It is evident from Table 5.2 that total revenue from a given number of units of output—say n units—is equal to the sum of marginal revenue between zero and 1 units of output, marginal revenue between 1 and 2 units of output, marginal revenue between 2 and 3 units of output, and so on up to marginal revenue between $(n-1)$ and n units of output. For example, total revenue for 2 units of output is $22, which equals the sum of marginal revenue between zero and 1 units of output ($12) and marginal revenue between 1 and 2 units of output ($10). It is easy to prove that this will always be true. By the definition of marginal revenue, the sum of the marginal revenue between zero and 1 units of output, 1 and 2 units of output, and so on up to $(n-1)$ and n units of output is

$$[R(1) - R(0)] + [R(2) - R(1)] + [R(3) - R(2)] + \cdots + [R(n) - R(n-1)].$$

Since $R(1), R(2), \cdots, R(n-1)$ appear with both positive and negative signs, they cancel out; and since $R(0) = 0$, this sum must equal $R(n)$.

The *marginal revenue curve* shows marginal revenue at various levels of output of a commodity. For example, panel A of Figure 5.6 shows the marginal revenue curve for the situation in Table 5.2. Note that the marginal revenue curve lies above zero when total revenue is increasing, that it lies below zero when total revenue is decreasing, and that it equals zero when total revenue is at a maximum. For example, in panel A of Figure 5.6, the marginal revenue curve is zero between 6 and 7 units of output, and inspection of Table 5.2 confirms that they are the output levels where total revenue is maximized. Also, marginal revenue is shown to be positive for output levels of less than 6 units and negative for output levels of greater than 7 units; inspection of Table 5.2 confirms that total revenue is increasing up to 6 units of output and is decreasing beyond 7 units of output.

The marginal revenue curve consists of a number of "steps" when the demand curve is defined for only a relatively few points. For example, this is the case in panel A of Figure 5.6. However, as the demand curve is defined for more and more points, the "teeth" of the saw-toothed marginal revenue curve become finer and finer. For example, they are finer in panel B than in panel A. Finally, when the demand curve is continuous, as in panel C, the marginal revenue curve becomes continuous, too.

Fig. 5.6   DEMAND CURVE AND MARGINAL REVENUE CURVE / *As the demand curve is defined for more and more points, the "teeth" of the saw-toothed marginal revenue curve become finer and finer. When the demand curve is continuous, so is the marginal revenue curve.*

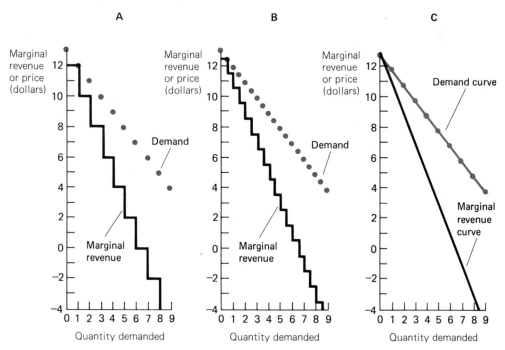

Determination of the Marginal Revenue Curve

Presented with a table like Table 5.2, it is no problem to calculate marginal revenue. But often one is given a demand curve, like DD' in Figure 5.7. How does one go about determining the marginal revenue curve in this case? To begin with, we assume that the demand curve is linear. The results in panel c of Figure 5.6 suggest quite correctly that, if the demand curve is a straight line, the marginal revenue curve will be a straight line, too. Also, they suggest that the marginal revenue curve and the demand curve start out at the same point on the vertical axis. Since the marginal revenue curve is a straight line that intersects the vertical axis at D, we need to determine only one additional point on this curve to identify the entire curve, since two points determine a straight line.

Consider any output level, OQ, in Figure 5.7. What is the marginal revenue at this point? The total revenue at this point is OP times OQ, which is the area of the quadrangle $OPBQ$. The total revenue at this point must also equal the sum of all the marginal revenues up to this point, which is the area $ODAQ$. Thus the unknown A (which is what we are trying to determine) must be such that the area of $OPBQ$ equals the area of $ODAQ$. These two areas have in common the area $OPCAQ$. Deducting this common area, it follows that A must

Fig. 5.7   GRAPHICAL ESTIMATION OF THE MARGINAL REVENUE CURVE: THE CASE IN WHICH THE DEMAND CURVE IS LINEAR / *The marginal revenue curve can be constructed by drawing a line from point D to point A.*

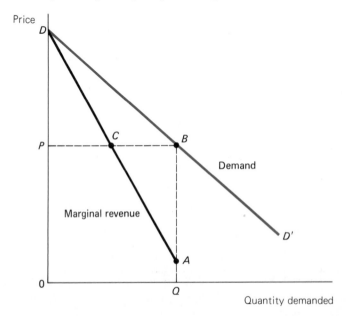

be such that the triangle CBA equals the area of the triangle DPC. But these two triangles are similar, since angle PCD equals angle BCA, and angle DPC equals angle CBA (both being $90°$). Thus, if they have the same area, these triangles must be congruent, and PD must equal AB. Consequently, one can find the unknown point A on the marginal revenue curve by dropping a perpendicular from B to the x axis and a perpendicular from B to the y axis, and by marking off a distance of PD from B on the perpendicular QB. Given the determination of A, the entire marginal revenue curve can be constructed by drawing a straight line through D and A.

Another method that is sometimes used is as follows: First, drop a perpendicular from B to the x axis and from B to the y axis. Second, find the midpoint of the perpendicular to the y axis. Call this midpoint C. (In fact, in Figure 5.7, it will accord with C.) Finally, draw a line through D and C. This line is also the marginal revenue curve. Naturally, this method amounts to the same thing as the method described in the previous paragraph, and the results are precisely the same.

Thus far, we have assumed that the demand curve is linear. Fortunately, our procedure needs to be changed only slightly even if the demand curve is not linear. To illustrate, consider the demand curve shown in Figure 5.8. To

Fig. 5.8 GRAPHICAL ESTIMATION OF THE MARGINAL REVENUE CURVE: THE CASE IN WHICH THE DEMAND CURVE IS NONLINEAR / *Two points on the marginal revenue curve are* A_1 *and* A_2.

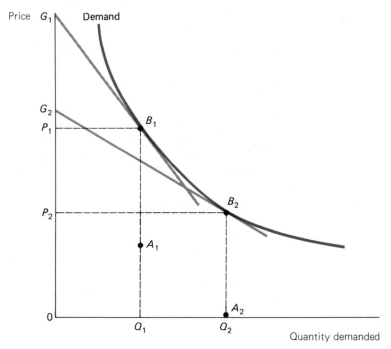

derive the marginal revenue curve, we begin by finding the marginal revenue of quantity OQ_1. First, drop perpendiculars from B_1 to both axes. Second, form the tangent to the demand curve at B_1 and extend it to intersect the price axis at G_1. Third, to find marginal revenue at OQ_1, deduct an amount equal to P_1G_1 from Q_1B_1, the result being Q_1A_1 which indicates that point A_1 is on the marginal revenue curve. Having found the point on the marginal revenue curve at quantity OQ_1, we can do the same for OQ_2 (the resulting point on the marginal revenue curve is A_2), and so forth. Connecting the resulting points, we can approximate the true marginal revenue curve.

INDUSTRY AND FIRM DEMAND CURVES

Throughout this chapter we have been concerned with the market demand curve for a commodity. It is important to distinguish between the market demand curve for a commodity and the market demand curve for the output of a single firm producing the commodity. Of course, if only one firm produces the commodity (in which case the industry in question is a *monopoly*) there is no difference between these demand curves. But if there is more than one firm producing the commodity, as is usually the case, the demand curve for the output of each firm will generally be quite different from the demand curve for the commodity. In particular, the firm's demand curve will generally be more price elastic than that facing the industry as a whole, since the products of other firms are close substitutes for the products of any one firm.

A perfectly competitive firm's demand curve

Suppose that there are a great many sellers of the product in question, say 50,000 sellers of the same size, and that the conditions in the industry are close to *perfectly competitive*. (In perfect competition, the number of firms is large and their products are homogeneous, and for simplicity it is assumed that the firms have full knowledge of the market. Much more will be said about perfect competition in subsequent chapters.) In a case of this sort, if any one firm were to triple its output and sales, the total industry output would increase by only .004 percent. Since this change in total output is too small to have any noticeable effect on the price of the commodity, each seller can act as if variations in its own output will have no real effect on market price. Put differently, it appears to each firm that it can sell all it wants—within the range that is within its capabilities—without influencing the price. Thus the demand curve facing the individual firm in perfect competition is *horizontal*.

The firm in a perfectly competitive market can increase its sales rate without shading its price to get the extra business. Its demand curve, shown in Figure 5.9, is infinitely elastic: A very small decrease in price would result in an indefinitely large increase in the quantity it could sell, and a very small increase in price would result in its selling nothing. Moreover, since price re-

Fig.
5.9
DEMAND CURVE FOR THE OUTPUT OF A FIRM IN A PERFECTLY COMPETITIVE
INDUSTRY / *For a firm in a perfectly competitive industry, the demand
curve is horizontal.*

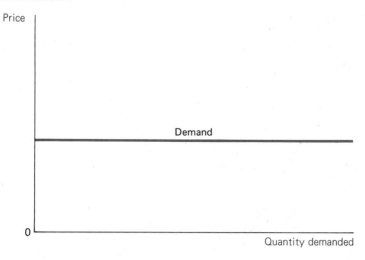

mains constant, each additional unit sold increases total revenue by the
amount of the price, the consequence being that price and marginal revenue
are always equal. Thus, in the case of perfect competition, the demand curve
facing a particular firm and the marginal revenue curve facing that firm are
one and the same.

In a situation where the industry is not perfectly competitive, the demand
curve for the output of a particular firm will not be horizontal, but it is likely to
be more elastic than the demand curve for the commodity. If competition is
not perfect, marginal revenue will not equal price, as it does in perfect competition. Instead, it will be less than price because demand is less than infinitely
elastic. (As we shall see in the next section, there is a simple relationship between marginal revenue and the price elasticity of demand.)

MARGINAL REVENUE AND THE ELASTICITY OF DEMAND

Before turning to the measurement of market demand curves, one additional
theoretical result should be presented, since it is of widespread use. This result
states that there is the following relationship between the elasticity of demand
at a certain output level and marginal revenue at that output level:

$$MR = P\left[1 - \frac{1}{\eta}\right] \qquad [5.4]$$

Fig.   Relationship between Marginal Revenue and Price Elasticity of
5.10   Demand / *Using this diagram, we show that marginal revenue*

$$= price\left(1 - \frac{1}{\eta}\right).$$

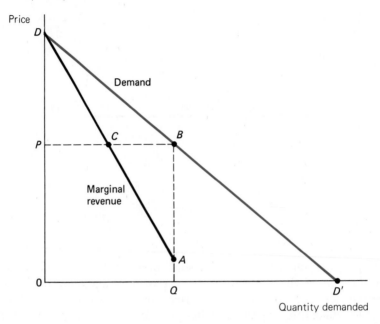

where MR is marginal revenue, P is price, and η is the price elasticity of demand. To prove that this is true, consider Figure 5.10. For simplicity, we assume that the demand curve, DD', is linear, but the result holds for any shape
of demand curve. Consider point B on DD'. Using the method described on pp.
120–22, we find that QA is the marginal revenue at B. Using the method described on p. 109, the elasticity of demand at B is $BD' \div DB$. Since
$PD \div PB = QB \div QD'$ and $AB = PD$, we know that

$$AB = PB\left[\frac{QB}{QD'}\right] = QB\left[\frac{PB}{QD'}\right].$$

Since

$$QA = QB - AB,$$

$$QA = QB - QB\left[\frac{PB}{QD'}\right]$$

$$= QB\left[1 - \frac{PB}{QD'}\right].$$

Since QA is marginal revenue, QB is price, and $PB \div QD' = OQ \div QD' = DB \div BD' = 1/\eta$, Equation 5.4 follows.

MEASUREMENT OF DEMAND CURVES

The market demand curve plays a very important role in microeconomics, and there have been literally hundreds of published studies—and many more unpublished ones—that attempt to measure the market demand curves for particular commodities. This section describes briefly various ways in which such empirical studies have been carried out. The following two sections provide examples of the ways in which the results of such studies have been used to help solve important practical problems.

One technique that is frequently used to estimate the demand curve for a particular commodity is the direct market experiment. The idea is to vary the price of the product while attempting to keep other market conditions fairly stable (or to take changes in other market conditions into account). For example, the Parker Pen Company conducted an experiment some years ago to determine the price elasticity of demand for its product, Quink. They raised the price from 15 cents to 25 cents in four cities and found that demand was quite inelastic. Also, in some stores, the old package selling at 15 cents was put next to a package marked "New Quink, 25 cents"; the results also indicated that demand was quite inelastic. Attempts were also made to estimate the cross elasticity of demand with other brands.

Another technique that is sometimes employed is to interview consumers and administer questionnaires concerning their buying habits, motives, and intentions. Unfortunately, the direct approach of simply asking people how much they would buy of a particular commodity at particular prices does not seem to work very well in most cases. The snap judgments of consumers in response to such a hypothetical question do not seem to be very accurate. However, more subtle approaches can be of value. For example, interviews indicated that most buyers of a certain baby food selected it on their doctor's recommendation, and that most of them knew very little about prices or substitutes. This information, together with other data, led the manufacturer to the conclusion that the price elasticity of demand was quite low.

Still another very popular technique is the use of statistical methods to extract information from data regarding sales, prices, incomes, and other variables in the past. Basically, what is involved is a comparison of various points in time or various sectors of the market; the point of this comparison is to see what effect the observed variation in price, income, and other relevant variables, had on the quantity demanded. For example, to estimate the price elasticity of demand, one might plot the quantity demanded in 1988 versus the 1988 price, the quantity demanded in 1987 versus the 1987 price, and so on. If the results were as shown by the points in Figure 5.11, one might construct a curve like D as an estimate of the demand curve.

Fig.   ILLUSTRATION OF IDENTIFICATION PROBLEM / *The estimated demand curve*
5.11   D *is a hybrid that resembles none of the true demand curves* (D$_1$, . . . , D$_6$).

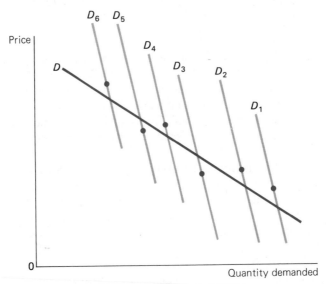

Although this example provides some understanding of the type of analysis that is involved, it makes the naïve assumption that the demand curve has remained constant over the period. Suppose that the 1988 demand curve was D_1, that the 1987 demand curve was D_2, and so on. Then the estimated demand curve D is a hybrid that resembles none of the true demand curves. Sophisticated econometric techniques have been developed for dealing with this so-called *identification problem*. Econometric techniques have also been devised to measure at the same time the effect of money income and the prices of other commodities on the quantity demanded; thus estimates can be made of the relationship between a commodity's price and the quantity demanded, when these other factors are held constant. However, even an elementary description of these econometric techniques lies outside the scope of this book.[8]

Each of the approaches to the measurement of demand curves has its disadvantages. Direct experimentation can be expensive or risky because customers may be lost and profits cut by the experiment. Also, since they are seldom really controlled experiments and since they are often of relatively brief duration and the number of observations is small, experiments often cannot produce all of the information that is needed. Interviews and questionnaires suffer from a great many disadvantages, some of which are noted above. So do consumer clinics where consumers are placed in simulated mar-

---

8. For a description of these techniques, see J. Johnston, *Econometric Methods,* 3d ed. (New York: McGraw-Hill, 1984).

Example 5.3

ANIMAL EXPERIMENTS AND THE THEORY OF DEMAND

Experimental psychologists like B. F. Skinner have long studied the behavior of rats and other animals. During the early 1980s, some microeconomists began to carry out similar sorts of research. In one well-known experiment, white rats were put in cages containing levers to activate dipper cups. When its lever was pushed down by a rat, one dipper cup provided a certain amount of collins mix; the other provided a certain amount of root beer. A rat was allotted a fixed "income" of so many pushes per day on the levers, and the experimental economists established the "price" per unit of collins mix and root beer as the number of pushes the rat had to "spend" to procure a unit.

(a) One rat was given an income of 300 pushes per day, and both liquids were priced at 20 pushes per day, with the result that the rat drank about 11 units of root beer and about 4 units of collins mix per day. Then the experimenters increased the price of root beer to 40 pushes and reduced the price of collins mix to 10 pushes, while adjusting the rat's income so that it could purchase its old "market basket" if it wanted. Did this mean that the rat's budget line was unchanged? (b) After the changes in prices and income described in part (a), the rat changed its "market basket" to 17 units of collins mix and 8 units of root beer per day. Was this in accord with the theory of consumer behavior? (c) In another experiment, a rat was able to obtain either standard laboratory food or water by pushing down the levers. No alternative food or liquid was available. Based on the rat's behavior when the "prices" of food and water were varied, its price elasticity of demand for food was 0.20. Why is this price elasticity so low? (d) In the same experiment, the cross elasticities of demand were

Cross elasticity of demand

Commodity	(percentage change in quantity demanded of this good due to a 1 percent change in the price of the other good)
Food	− 0.55
Water	− 0.32

Why are the cross elasticities of demand negative?

SOLUTION

(a) No. The slope of the budget line is −1 times the price ratio. When both liquids were priced at 20 pushes per day, the slope was −1. After the price changes, the ratio of the price of root beer to the price of collins mix was 4; thus, the slope was −4. Since its slope changed, it is obvious that the budget line must have changed. (b) Yes. Since root beer became more expensive relative to collins mix, one would expect anyone (rat or human being) to reduce the consumption of root beer and to increase the consumption of collins mix. (c) Goods that have few good substitutes tend to have low price elasticities of demand. There obviously are few, if any, good substitutes for food. (d) Food and water are complements because there are physiological limits on the amount that animals can increase their food consumption without increasing their intake of fluids.*

*For further discussion, see J. Kagel, R. Battalio, H. Rachlin, and L. Green, "Demand Curves for Animal Consumers," *Quarterly Journal of Economics,* February 1981; and J. Kagel, R. Battalio, H. Rachlin, L. Green, R. Basmann, and W. Klemm, "Experimental Studies of Consumer Demand Behavior," *Economic Inquiry,* March 1975.

ket conditions and changes in their behavior are observed as the conditions of the experiment are changed; consumer clinics are expensive and they cannot avoid the distortion due to the consumers' realizing that they are in an experimental situation.[9]

The difficulties involved in the application of statistical and econometric techniques are also very considerable. Unreliable and biased results can be obtained if important variables are unwittingly (or wittingly) omitted from the analysis. If some of the variables influencing the quantity demanded are highly correlated among themselves, it may not be possible to obtain reliable estimates of the separate effects of each of them. Also, the demand function is likely to be only one of a number of equations that connect the relevant variables, and it may be difficult to unscramble these equations adequately from the available statistics.

There are no easy remedies for these problems. Nevertheless, these problems, although sometimes formidable, are not insolvable. Many interesting and important studies have been made of the demand curves for particular commodities. And many interesting estimates have been made of the price

Table 5.3 ESTIMATED PRICE ELASTICITY OF DEMAND FOR SELECTED COMMODITIES, UNITED STATES

Commodity	Price elasticity	Commodity	Price elasticity
Electricity	1.20	Potatoes	0.31
Beef	0.92	Oats	0.56
Women's hats	3.00	Barley	0.39
Sugar	0.31	Buckwheat	0.99
Corn	0.49	Haddock	2.20
Cotton	0.12	Tires	1.20
Wheat	0.08	Movies	3.70

SOURCE: H. Schultz, *Theory and Measurement of Demand*, (Chicago: University of Chicago Press, 1938); M. Spencer and L. Siegelman, *Managerial Economics* (Homewood, Ill.: Irwin, 1959); F. Bell, "The Pope and the Price of Fish," *American Economic Review*, December 1968; L. Taylor, "The Demand for Electricity: A Survey," *Bell Journal of Economics*, Spring 1975; and H. Houthakker and L. Taylor, *Consumer Demand in the United States* (Cambridge, Mass.: Harvard, 1970).

elasticity, the income elasticity, and the cross elasticity of demand of various commodities. For example, Table 5.3 shows the results of Henry Schultz's pioneering study of the price elasticity of various farm products, as well as selected results from other studies. Table 5.4 shows various cross elasticities of

9. W. Baumol, "The Empirical Determination of Demand Relationships," reprinted in E. Mansfield, *Microeconomics: Selected Readings*, 5th ed. (New York: Norton, 1985).

Table   ESTIMATED CROSS ELASTICITIES OF DEMAND FOR SELECTED COMMODITIES
5.4

Commodity	Cross elasticity with respect to price of:	Cross elasticity
Beef	Pork	+0.28
Butter	Margarine	+0.67
Margarine	Butter	+0.81
Pork	Beef	+0.14
Electricity	Natural gas	+0.20
Natural gas	Fuel oil	+0.44

SOURCE: H. Wold, *Demand Analysis* (New York: Wiley, 1953); R. Halvorsen, "Energy Substitution in U.S. Manufacturing," *Review of Economics and Statistics,* November 1977.

demand estimated by Herman Wold, in his well-known study, and others. Table 5.5 shows the income elasticity of demand for selected commodities, as estimated by Wold and others. The reader should study these tables carefully.

Table   ESTIMATED INCOME ELASTICITY OF DEMAND FOR SELECTED COMMODITIES
5.5

Commodity	Income elasticity	Commodity	Income elasticity
Butter	0.42	Meat	0.35
Cheese	0.34	Milk and cream	0.07
Cream	0.56	Restaurant	
Eggs	0.37	consumption	1.48
Fruits and berries	0.70	Tobacco	1.02
Flour	−0.36	Haddock	0.46
Electricity	0.20	Dentists' services	1.41
Liquor	1.00	Furniture	1.48
Margarine	−0.20	Books	1.44

SOURCE: H. Wold, p. 265; F. Bell; H. Houthakker and L. Taylor; and L. Taylor.

APPLICATIONS

Free Public Transit

The concepts of price elasticity, income elasticity, and cross elasticity of demand have many practical uses. For example, consider the proposals that have been made to provide free public transit service in our metropolitan areas. Proponents of free public transit point out that there is considerable concern in our cities over traffic congestion, and they argue that, if public transit were free, many commuters would use public transit rather than their cars, thus alleviating traffic problems, decreasing air pollution, and reducing the demand for parking facilities.

Whether or not public transit should be free is an important and complex issue of public policy. To evaluate this proposal, decision-makers have to consider a host of questions, including how the public transit agencies would be financed in the absence of fares. Two of the most fundamental questions are: To what extent would free transit fares increase the use of public transit? To what extent would it reduce the use of automobiles in the city? Clearly, these questions must be answered if one is to forecast the consequences of free public transit.

Faced with these questions, the U.S. Department of Transportation asked a team of economists at Charles River Associates to study them.[10] With respect to the effect of free fares on the use of public transit, the economists pointed out that the answer depends on the price elasticity of demand for public transit service. If this price elasticity is high, the reduction of the price of public transit from its current level to zero will result in a considerable increase in the number of trips made on public transit. On the other hand, if it is very low, such a price reduction would result in little increase in the number of such trips. In fact, according to estimates made by the economists, this price elasticity is about 0.17. Thus, free transit fares would result in about a 40 percent increase in the number of trips made on public transit.[11]

With respect to the effects of free public transit on the use of automobiles in the city, the economists pointed out that the answer depends on the cross elasticity of demand for auto travel (in the city) with respect to transit fares. This cross elasticity is positive because auto travel and public transit are substitutes. If this cross elasticity is high, the reduction of transit fares to zero will result in a considerable drop in the use of autos in the city. On the other hand, if this cross elasticity is low, such a fare reduction would have little effect on the number of auto trips in the city. In fact, according to the economists' estimates, the value of this cross elasticity is such that free transit would reduce auto trips in the city by only about 7 percent.[12]

These results have been of use to federal, local, and other officials, as well as to other groups, in their treatment of this important issue. Based on these results, it appears that free transit would not stimulate huge increases in transit usage, and "that it will be very difficult to divert auto travelers to tran-

---

10. T. Domencich and G. Kraft, *Free Transit* (Lexington, Mass.: Heath, 1970).

11. To obtain this figure, note that it follows from Equation 2.2 that, if P_2 equals zero (and thus if $\Delta P = P_2 - P_1 = -P_1$), η equals $\Delta Q_D \div (Q_{D1} + Q_{D2}) = (Q_{D2}/Q_{D1} - 1) \div (1 + Q_{D2}/Q_{D1})$. Thus $Q_{D2}/Q_{D1} = (1 + \eta) \div (1 - \eta)$. Since η is approximately 0.17, Q_{D2}/Q_{D1} is approximately $(1 + .17) \div (1 - .17) = 1.41$.

The elasticity figure used here pertains to work travel. For a more complete discussion, see ibid.

12. Ibid., p. 102.

sit by lowering fares. . . . "[13] While these facts alone cannot resolve the issue, they certainly are of great relevance. Without question, the concepts of the price elasticity and cross elasticity of demand have played an important role in illuminating this major policy issue.

Pricing at Columbia Records

The concepts discussed in this chapter are obviously of fundamental importance in the formulation of business policy, as well as public policy. To illustrate the use of the concept of price elasticity by business, let's go back several decades and consider a famous case involving Columbia Records. In 1938, the Columbia Broadcasting Company purchased the American Record Company and changed its name to Columbia Records. When the new company began operations, classical records were sold by the industry at about $1.50, semiclassical and well-established popular records were sold at $0.75, and popular records were sold at $0.35. Among classical records, a sale of 5,000 was considered good; although extremely popular releases might reach a sales volume of 50,000, some records might not sell more than 200.

In November 1938, a New York newspaper began a promotion scheme whereby it offered classical albums to its readers at prices averaging about $0.50 a record. The results were very impressive; more than 50,000 records of a single symphony were sold in a few weeks. Observing this fact, and the enthusiastic reception of the radio broadcasts of symphonic and operatic performances, the executives of the Columbia Broadcasting System concluded that there was a very good opportunity to increase the market for classical records by price reductions. However, during the first couple of years, the new company maintained the high level of prices on classical records while it improved the mechanical quality of its records and the skill and reputation of the artists it recorded.

Before instituting a price reduction, Columbia obviously had to estimate more precisely what the effect of a price reduction would be on its revenues and costs. The answers to these questions clearly depended upon the price elasticity of demand for classical records, as well as on the way in which the firm's costs varied with the quantity of records it produced (a subject that is discussed at length in Chapter 7). Edward Wallerstein, president of Columbia Records, began by trying to estimate the public's reaction to lower prices. He asked a number of dealers to keep detailed records of their customary sales and then for one month to offer all people who entered their stores regular classical and semiclassical records at two-thirds of list price. These dealers found that the unannounced price reduction of $33\frac{1}{3}$ percent more than doubled the number of records sold. Thus the apparent price elasticity of demand, based on this crude experiment, was well above 1. This evidence, in addition to the other

---

13. Ibid., p. 98.

indications, convinced Wallerstein that Columbia should go further in analyzing the pros and cons of a price reduction of substantial magnitude.

Based on the estimated price elasticity of demand, it was possible to estimate the effect of a price cut on the firm's total revenue. In addition, a close examination was made of the firm's cost structure to determine the effect of a price cut on the firm's total costs. Since many costs were fixed, total costs would not increase in proportion to the increased volume resulting from the price cut. After considerable study, it was decided to reduce the price of 10-inch classical records from about $1.25 to $0.75 and to reduce the price of 12-inch classical records from about $1.75 to $1.00. Presumably a price reduction of this extent was chosen because it was felt to be the most profitable one. The response was overwhelming. Other firms followed Columbia's lead. To the surprise of much of the industry, total expenditure on classical records rose greatly.

SUMMARY

1. The market demand curve for a commodity is simply the horizontal summation of the individual demand curves of all the consumers in the market. Since individual demand curves almost always slope downward to the right, it follows that market demand curves will do so, too.

2. The price elasticity of demand for a commodity depends on the number and closeness of substitutes that are available. If a commodity has many close substitutes, its demand is likely to be elastic. Of course, the extent to which a commodity has close substitutes depends on how narrowly it is defined. Graphical techniques are available to estimate the elasticity at a given point.

3. The income elasticity of demand is the percentage change in quantity demanded resulting from a 1 percent change in money income. Commodities differ greatly in their income elasticities. Goods that people regard as luxuries are generally assumed to have high income elasticities of demand. Indeed, one way to define luxuries and necessities is to say that luxuries are goods with high income elasticities of demand, and necessities are goods with low income elasticities of demand.

4. The cross elasticity of demand is the relative change in the quantity demanded of good X divided by the relative change in the price of good Y. Whether commodities are classified as substitutes or complements depends on whether the cross elasticity is positive or negative.

5. Marginal revenue is the addition to total revenue attributable to the addition of the last unit to sales. Obviously, total revenue from n units of output is equal to the sum of marginal revenue in the intervals between zero and 1 unit of output, 1 and 2 units of output, and so on up to $(n-1)$ to n units of output.

6. The marginal revenue curve shows marginal revenue at various levels of output of the commodity. Graphical techniques are available to estimate the marginal revenue curve from the demand curve.

7. It is important to distinguish between the market demand curve for a commodity and the market demand curve for the output of a single firm producing the commodity. In a perfectly competitive industry, the firm's demand curve will be horizontal. If the industry contains more than one firm but is not perfectly competitive, the firm's demand curve will not be horizontal, but it is likely to be more price elastic than the demand curve for the commodity.

8. One technique used to estimate the market demand curve is direct market experimentation. Another technique is to interview consumers and administer questionnaires concerning their habits, motives, and intentions. Still another technique is the use of statistical and econometric techniques to extract information from data regarding sales, prices, incomes, and other variables in the past.

9. Each of these approaches has its disadvantages, and there is no easy remedy to the estimation problem. Nevertheless, the difficulties generally are not insurmountable. Many interesting and important estimates have been made of the demand curves for various goods.

QUESTIONS/PROBLEMS

1) D. Chapman, T. Tyrell, and T. Mount estimated that the long-run price elasticity of demand for electricity by all U.S. residential consumers is 1.2, that the income elasticity of demand for electricity by such consumers is 0.2, and that the cross elasticity of demand for electricity with respect to the price of natural gas is 0.2. (a) If the price of electricity is expected to rise by 1 percent in the long run, by how much would the price of natural gas have to change to offset the effect of this increase in electricity's price on the quantity of electricity consumed? (b) Among residential consumers in a Chicago suburb, holding other factors constant, there was the following relationship between their aggregate money income and the amount of electricity they consumed:

Aggregate income (millions of dollars)	Quantity of electricity consumed
100	300
110	303
121	306

Is this evidence consistent with the results presented by Chapman, Tyrell, and Mount? If not, what factors might account for the discrepancy? (c) Would you expect the income elasticity of demand and the cross elasticity of demand to be higher or lower in the short run than in the long run? Why?

2) A business analyst says that the demand curve for videocassette recorders has shifted to the right, and that at the same time the price elasticity of demand for videocassette recorders has increased from 3 to 4. Is this possible? Can the new demand curve be entirely above and to the right of the old demand curve, if the new price elasticity is 4 whereas the old price elasticity was 3?

3) The steel industry has long maintained that the demand for steel is price inelastic. According to a well-known study by T. Yntema, the price elasticity of demand for steel is no more than 0.4. (a) Are there any major substitutes for steel? If so, what are some of them? (b) Some years ago the chief executive officer of Bethlehem Steel testified before a Senate committee that the price elasticity of demand for steel was much less than 1. If so, can we deduce that the demand for Bethlehem's steel is price inelastic? (c) If the demand for Bethlehem's steel is inelastic at the price it is charging, is it maximizing its profits? (d) Is the cross elasticity of demand between Bethlehem's steel and imported Japanese steel positive or negative? Why?

4) The cross elasticity of demand can be used to determine which products belong to the same market. For example, in the famous cellophane case, the U.S. Department of Justice brought suit against the Du Pont Company for having monopolized the sale of cellophane. In its defense, Du Pont claimed that cellophane had many close substitutes, such as aluminum foil, waxed paper, and polyethylene. Can you guess how Du Pont used cross elasticities of demand in this case? (Incidentally, the Supreme Court accepted Du Pont's argument in its landmark decision handed down in 1953.)

5) Suppose that a consumer considers Geritol of supreme importance and that he spends all of his income on Geritol. To this consumer, what is the price elasticity of demand for Geritol? What is the income elasticity of demand for Geritol? What is the cross elasticity of demand between Geritol and any other good?

6) In the aluminum industry, is the demand curve for the output of each firm horizontal? (Why or why not?) Is it less elastic than the demand curve for aluminum as a whole? (Why or why not?) Is the price of aluminum less than, equal to, or greater than marginal revenue?

7) Which of the following are likely to have a positive cross elasticity of demand: (a) automobiles and oil, (b) wood tennis rackets and metal tennis rackets, (c) gin and tonic, (d) fishing poles and fishing licenses, (e) a Harvard education and a Stanford education.

8) The demand for refined sugar in the United States has declined greatly since 1975, due in part to reports that it causes tooth decay and reduces the nutri-

tional value of the diet or leads to obesity. Given that per capita consumption of refined sugar has declined, can we be sure that the price elasticity of demand for refined sugar is (a) less than 1, (b) greater than 1, (c) greater than zero?

9) Suppose the mayor of New York asked you to advise him concerning the proper fare that should be charged by the New York City subway. In what way might information concerning the price elasticity of demand be useful?

10) According to the Senate Subcommittee on Antitrust and Monopoly, the income elasticity of demand for automobiles in the United States is between 2.5 and 3.9. What does this mean? If incomes rise by 5 percent, what effect will this have on the quantity of autos demanded? How might this fact be used by General Motors?

11) Suppose you are a trustee of a major university. At a meeting of the board of trustees, one university official argues that the demand for places at this university is completely inelastic. As evidence, he cites the fact that, although the university has doubled its tuition in the last decade, there has been no appreciable decrease in the number of students enrolled. Do you agree? Comment on his argument.

12) According to William Baumol, "Some mail-order houses have employed systematic programs in which a few experimental pages were bound inconspicuously into the catalogues distributed to customers within restricted geographical regions, thus permitting observation of the effects of price, product, or even catalogue display variations." Comment on the accuracy of this technique. What might be some of the problems in estimating a product's price elasticity of demand in this way? What techniques might be better than this one?

13) Show that, if the Engel curve for a good is a straight line through the origin, the income elasticity of demand for the good is 1.

NATIONAL DENTAL INSURANCE AND THE
DEMAND FOR DENTAL CARE

Many countries, such as Sweden and the United Kingdom, have national health insurance covering dental services. In the United States, there have been proposals for such dental insurance. A number of questions arise concerning the effects of these proposed insurance schemes, two of the most important being (1) How much more dental care would be demanded if these plans were implemented? (2) How much would such plans cost?

To answer these questions, it is essential that we have information concerning the shape and position of the demand curve for dental services. Basically, what dental insurance does is to reduce the price to the consumer. To find out how much dental care will be demanded under such an insurance plan, we must use the demand curve for dental services to forecast the quantity demanded at the reduced price. If, for example, such insurance pays for the full cost of dental care, we would want to determine the quantity demanded at a zero price. If such insurance pays for 75 percent of the cost of dental care, we would want to determine the quantity demanded at 25 percent of the real price.

In a recent study, a team of economists at the RAND Corporation estimated the demand curve for dental services, and used it to forecast the effects of such dental insurance.[1] As shown in Figure 1, three separate demand curves were estimated, one for adult males, one for adult females, and one for children. The results indicate that the quantity demanded of dental care would more than double if people pay 25 percent or less of the full price. For children, the quantity demanded more than triples if dental services are free.

To see the situation more clearly, the RAND economists also estimated the price and income elasticities of demand for dental care among various segments of the population. For example, Table 1 shows the price and income elasticities among whites with an income level of $15,000. It is apparent that the price elasticity of demand for children is much greater than among adult males or adult females. This is entirely consistent with the finding (in the previous paragraph) that a reduction in the price of dental services would have more effect on the quantity demanded for children than for adults.

---

1. W. Manning and C. Phelps, "The Demand for Dental Care," *Bell Journal of Economics,* Autumn 1979.

Fig. 1 DEMAND CURVES FOR DENTAL CARE, ADULT MALES, ADULT FEMALES, AND CHILDREN, UNITED STATES / *The quantity demanded of dental care would more than double if people pay 25 percent or less of the full price.*

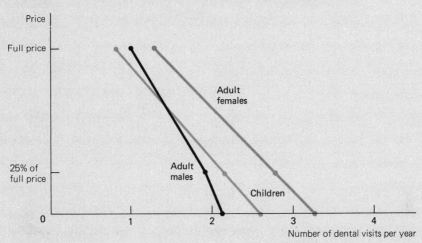

Going into more detail, price and income elasticities were also estimated for four primary dental services: (1) cleanings, (2) fillings, (3) extractions, (4) examinations. As shown in Table 2, the demand for cleanings, fillings, and extractions among children is quite sensitive to price, the price elasticity of demand being about 1 or more. Note that these results pertain to all consumers, not just those at an income level of $15,000 (as in Table 1).

Table 1 PRICE AND INCOME ELASTICITIES OF DEMAND FOR DENTAL CARE, CONSUMERS WITH ANNUAL INCOME OF $15,000, UNITED STATES

	Price elasticity	Income elasticity
Adult males	0.70	0.82
Adult females	1.05	0.81
Children	1.81	1.05

SOURCE: Manning and Phelps, "The Demand."

In general, the income elasticities in Table 2 are positive, which would be expected. Holding prices constant, one would expect that the quantity demanded of a particular dental service would increase with the consumer's income. More surprising perhaps is the size of the income elasticities, which often are substantial. For example, a 1 percent increase in income seems to be associated with about a 0.8 percent increase in cleanings and about a 0.6 percent increase in examinations. But the income elasticity is not positive for all

Table PRICE AND INCOME ELASTICITIES OF DEMAND FOR PRIMARY DENTAL
2   SERVICES, UNITED STATES

	Cleanings	Fillings	Extractions	Examinations
Price elasticity				
Adult males	0.79	0.58	0.21	0.56
Adult females	0.14	0.73	1.51	0.03
Children	1.34	0.95	0.97	0.59
Income elasticity				
Adult males	0.76	0.54	−0.13	0.64
Adult females	0.80	0.88	−0.08	0.73
Children	0.74	0.28	0.47	0.51

SOURCE: Manning and Phelps, "The Demand."

services. Extractions seem to be "poor people's dentistry," at least for adults.
As incomes rise, fewer extractions occur among adults, perhaps because of
more preventive care and other (presumably superior) ways of dealing with the
consumer's dental problems.

Based on these and other findings, the RAND economists came to the following two conclusions. First, because the price elasticity of demand for dental
care is substantial, persons with full dental insurance would demand two or
three times as much dental care as uninsured persons. If a large proportion of
the U.S. population were provided with such insurance, it would be impossible
to meet such an increase in demand with the current number of dentists and at
current dental prices. It is quite likely that consumers would have to wait considerable periods of time for dental care.

Second, because national expenditures on dental services in the United
States would more than double under such a plan, many proposals provide for
insurance coverage of dental care of children only. If insurance covered 75
percent of the real price of dental care (for bills exceeding $150) for children
aged 13 or under, the quantity demanded of dental services would rise by at
least 11 percent, due to the very substantial price elasticity of demand among
children (or, more accurately, among parents for children). Thus some economists suggest that any such plan, if adopted, should be phased in slowly and
gradually (as in Sweden in 1974) so that the supply of dental services can adjust to increases in demand.

ANALYTICAL QUESTIONS

1) The price elasticity of demand for dental care by consumers with an annual
income of $25,000 was found to be .77 (adult males), 1.40 (adult females), and 2.81
(children). Comparing these results with those in Table 1, does it appear that higher-

income people are influenced less than those with lower incomes by the price of dental care? Some people argue that "the rich can ignore prices." Does this seem to be the case here?

2) If insurance were offered which paid for 75 percent of the cost of dental care, does it appear (based on the figures in the previous question and Table 1) that the amount of dental care demanded by higher-income people would increase more than the amount demanded by those with lower incomes? Why or why not?

3) Based on the results in Table 1, would a reduction in the price of dental care increase the amount of money spent on dental care by adult males? By adult females?

4) The income elasticity of demand for orthodontia for children is 1.24. (Orthodontia is the correction of abnormally aligned or positioned teeth.) Why is it higher than the income elasticities for the other services for children in Table 2?

The Firm: Its Technology and Costs

The Firm and Its Technology

THE ASSUMPTION OF PROFIT MAXIMIZATION

Both the IBM Corporation and the Ford Foundation have assets that run into the billions of dollars. Both are large, powerful organizations, but only one of them is a firm. What is a firm? Put briefly, it is a unit that produces a good or service for sale. In contrast to not-for-profit institutions like the Ford Foundation, firms attempt to make a profit. There are literally millions of firms in the United States: Some are proprietorships (owned by a single person), some partnerships (owned by two or more people), and some corporations (which are fictitious legal persons). About six-sevenths of the goods and services produced in the United States are produced by firms; the rest are provided by government and not-for-profit institutions. It is obvious that an economy like ours revolves around the activities of firms.

As a first approximation, economists generally assume that firms attempt to maximize profits. However, the economist's definition of profits does not coincide with the accountant's. The economist does not assume that the firm attempts to maximize the current, short-run profits measured by the accoun-

Economic profit

tant. Instead he or she assumes that the firm will attempt to maximize the sum of profits over a long period of time, these profits being properly discounted to the present. Also, when the economist speaks of profits, he or she means profit after taking account of the capital and labor provided by the owners. More will be said on this score in the next chapter.

Although the assumption of profit maximization serves as a reasonable first approximation, it has obvious limitations. For one thing, the making of profits generally requires time and energy, and if the owners of the firm are the managers as well, they may decide that it is preferable to sacrifice profits for leisure. (Profit-maximizers in Miami Beach and the Virgin Islands encourage this type of thinking.) In a case of this sort, it is more accurate to assume that the owner-manager, like the consumer, is maximizing utility, since utility is a function of his or her profits and the amount of leisure he or she enjoys. Using the kind of analysis described in Chapter 3, we can determine how much money the owner-manager will give up for leisure (see Example 6.1).

It should also be noted that, in an uncertain world, the concept of maximum profit is not clearly defined. Since any particular course of action will not result in a unique, certain level of profit, but in a variety of possible levels of profit, each with a certain probability of occurrence, it makes no sense to speak about the maximization of profits. However, if the firm is able, explicitly or implicitly, to attach a probability to each level of profit that could result from each course of action, it is meaningful to assume that the firm attempts to maximize expected profits.[1] For simplicity, we shall assume in the following pages that the firm has full knowledge of the relevant variables, and that there is no uncertainty.

Observers of the modern corporation often state that profits are not the sole objective of these firms. Industry spokesmen often claim that the following objectives are also of importance: achieving better social conditions in the firm's community, increasing (or at least maintaining) its market share, creating an image as a good employer and a useful part of the community, and so forth. For example, oil firms often stress their concern over the environment and over the reduction of wasteful uses of fuel. Besides the question of how seriously one should take such self-proclaimed goals, the important question is how distinct these goals are from the goal of profit maximization. To the extent that many of these goals are simply means to achieve profits *in the long run*, there may be less inaccuracy in the profit maximization assumption than might appear at first glance.

In recent years economists have begun to experiment with models of the

---

1. Expected profit is defined as the long-term average value of profit—the sum of the various possible levels of profit, after each level is weighted by the probability of its occurrence. The firm may be interested in the variance, as well as the expected value of profits, in which case it will maximize some function of both the expected value and the variance.

firm that do not assume profit maximization. A brief introduction to such models is contained in the appendix to this chapter. Although these models are useful for certain purposes, profit maximization remains the standard assumption of microeconomcs. In large part, this is because it is a close enough approximation for many of the most important purposes of microeconomics.

Example 6.1

UTILITY MAXIMIZATION BY THE ENTREPRENEUR

In a famous article, Tibor Scitovsky suggested that the entrepreneur (that is, the owner-manager of the firm) maximizes utility, which is a function of the firm's profits and the amount of leisure the entrepreneur enjoys. Suppose that a particular entrepreneur's indifference curves between profit and leisure are as shown in the graph below. Also, suppose that the amount of work that the entrepreneur must do is proportional to his or her firm's output. If this is the case, the relationship between leisure and profit is given by the curved line *ABCD*.

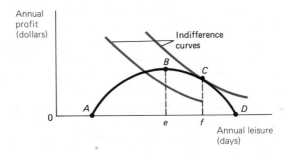

(a) Why does the relationship between leisure and profit have the shape indicated by *ABCD*? (b) Will the entrepreneur maximize profit? (c) If the entrepreneur's indifference curves were horizontal lines, would he or she maximize profit?

SOLUTION

(a) Up to some point, increases in the firm's output result in increases in profit; beyond this point, they result in decreases in profit. Thus, since the entrepreneur's days of work are assumed to be proportional to the firm's output, up to some point, increases in the number of days he or she works result in increases in profit; beyond this point, they result in decreases in profit. Finally, since the entrepreneur's number of days of leisure equals the total time during the year minus his or her number of days of work, it follows that, up to some point, increases in his or her number of days of leisure are associated with increases in profit; beyond that point (indicated by *e* in the graph), they are associated with decreases in profit. (b) No. He or she maximizes utility by choosing point *C,* where there are *Of* days of leisure, and profit is below the maximum that could be achieved. (c) Yes. He or she would choose point *B,* where profits are a maximum.*

* For further discussion, see T. Scitovsky, "A Note on Profit Maximization and Its Implications," *Review of Economic Studies,* Winter 1943.

For example, even some of the proponents of alternative models admit that profit maximization may be a suitable assumption in models designed to show how the price system functions.

In addition economists are interested in the theory of the profit-maximizing firm because it provides rules of behavior for firms that do want to maximize profits. The theory of the profit-maximizing firm suggests how a firm should operate if it wants to make as such money as possible. Even if a firm does not want to maximize profit, the theory can be useful. For example, it can show how much the firm is losing by taking certain courses of action. In recent years the theory of the profit-maximizing firm has been studied more and more for the sake of determining rules of business behavior.

TECHNOLOGY AND INPUTS

One of the fundamental determinants of a firm's behavior is the state of technology. Whether a firm produces textiles or locomotives, whether a firm is big or small, whether a firm is run by a genius or a moron (or even your brother-in-law), the firm cannot do more than is permitted by existing technology. Technology, as we defined it in Chapter 1, is the sum total of society's pool of knowledge concerning the industrial and agricultural arts. Although this definition is accurate, it is not very useful in indicating how we can represent the state of technology in a model of the firm. The purpose of the rest of this chapter is to show how economists represent the state of technology.

To begin with, an *input* is defined as anything that a firm uses in its production process. Most firms require a wide variety of inputs. For example, some of the inputs in the iron and steel industry are iron ore, coal, oxygen, skilled labor of various types, the services of blast furnaces, open hearths, electric furnaces, and rolling mills, as well as the services of the people managing the companies. To give a more humble example, the inputs in the production and sale of hot dogs by a street vendor are the hot dogs, the rolls, the stove, the truck, and the services of the vendor.

In representing and analyzing production processes, we assume that all inputs can be divided into two categories: fixed inputs and variable inputs. A

Fixed input

fixed input is an input whose quantity cannot be changed during the period of time under consideration. This period will vary from problem to problem. Of course, the amount of most inputs can be varied to some extent, no matter how brief the time interval. But for some inputs, the cost of quick variation in their amount is so large as to make such variation impractical. For simplicity, we regard these inputs as being fixed. The firm's plant and equipment are examples of inputs that often are included in this category.

On the other hand, a *variable input* is an input whose quantity can be changed during the relevant period. For example, the number of workers hired

Variable input

to perform a job like construction can often be increased or decreased on short notice. The amount of raw material used in the production of a commodity like dresses can often be increased or decreased by using up or building up the firm's inventories. The amount of water used in the production of a service like a car wash can sometimes be varied within limits simply by turning the relevant knobs.

THE SHORT RUN AND THE LONG RUN

Short run vs. long run

Whether or not an input is regarded as variable or fixed depends on the length of the period under consideration. The longer the period, the more inputs are variable, not fixed. Although the length of the relevant period varies from problem to problem, economists have found it useful to focus special attention on two time periods: the short run and the long run. The *short run* is defined to be that period of time in which some of the firm's inputs are fixed. More specifically, since the firm's plant and equipment are among the most difficult inputs to change quickly, the short run is generally understood to mean the length of time during which the firm's plant and equipment are fixed. On the other hand, the *long run* is that period of time in which all inputs are variable. In the long run, the firm can make a complete adjustment to any change in its environment.

In both the short run and the long run, a firm's productive processes ordinarily permit substantial variation in the proportions in which inputs are used. In the long run, there can be no question but that input proportions can be varied considerably. For example, an automobile die can be made on conventional machine tools with more labor and less expensive equipment, or it can be made on numerically controlled machine tools with less labor and more expensive equipment. Similarly, an airplane can be almost handmade or it can be made using much equipment and relatively little labor. In the short run, there are also considerable opportunities for changes in input proportions. For one thing, the ratio between fixed and variable inputs can vary greatly.

Production processes with fixed, not variable, proportions are ones where there is one, and only one, ratio of inputs that can be used. For example, to produce a certain product, 2 hours of labor must be combined with a certain amount of capital. Consequently, if output is increased or decreased, the quantity of all inputs must be varied in proportion to output. There seem to be very few cases where all inputs must be combined in fixed proportions. However, there are cases where the amount of a *certain* input can be varied only within narrow limits. For example, a particular drug may have to contain a certain amount of aspirin per ounce of the drug. Thus it is not unusual for some inputs to be required in relatively fixed proportions but it is very unusual for this to be the case for all, or most, inputs.

THE PRODUCTION FUNCTION

Production function

For any commodity, the *production function* is the relationship between the quantities of various inputs used per period of time and the maximum quantity of the commodity that can be produced per period of time. More specifically, the production function is a table, a graph, or an equation showing the maximum output rate that can be achieved from any specified set of usage rates of inputs. The production function summarizes the characteristics of existing technology at a given point in time; it shows the technological constraints that the firm must reckon with.

To illustrate the production function, consider the simplest case—when there is one fixed input and one variable input. Suppose that the fixed input is the service of an acre of land, the variable input is labor (in units per year), and the output is corn (in bushels). Suppose that a scientifically inclined farmer decides to find out what the effect on annual output will be if he or she applies various numbers of units of labor during the year to the acre of land. (The farmer can vary the number of units of labor by hiring fewer or more laborers.) If he or she obtains the results in Table 6.1, then these results might be re-

Table 6.1   OUTPUT OF CORN WHEN VARIOUS AMOUNTS OF LABOR ARE APPLIED TO AN ACRE OF LAND

Amount of labor (units per year)	Output of corn (bushels per year)
1	6
2	13.5
3	21
4	28
5	34
6	38
7	38
8	37

garded as the production function in this situation. Alternatively, the curve in Figure 6.1, which presents exactly the same results, might be regarded as the production function.

Average and marginal products

The production function is an important starting point for the analysis of the firm's technology: It gives us the maximum *total output* that can be realized by using each combination of quantities of inputs. But there is more that we need to know about the production process. In particular, two other important concepts are the average product and the marginal product of an input. The *average product* of an input is total product (that is, total output) divided by the

Fig.   RELATIONSHIP BETWEEN TOTAL OUTPUT AND AMOUNT OF LABOR USED ON
6.1   ONE ACRE OF LAND / *The production function shows the relationship*
        between output (in this case, bushels of corn) and input (in this case, units
        of labor).

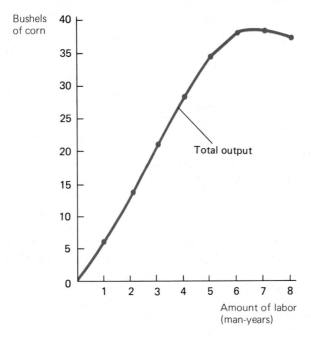

amount of the input used to produce this amount of output. The *marginal*
product of an input is the addition to total output due to the addition of the last
unit of the input, when the amounts of other inputs used are held constant.

   To illustrate these concepts, let us go back to the farmer in Table 6.1. On
the basis of the production function shown in this table, we can compute the
average product and marginal product of labor. Both the average product and
the marginal product of labor will vary, of course, depending on how much
labor is used. If $Q(L)$ is the total output rate when L units of labor are used per
year, the average product of labor when L units of labor are used per year is
$Q(L)/L$. And the marginal product of labor when between L and $(L-1)$ units
of labor are used per year is

$$[Q(L) - Q(L-1)].$$

Thus the average product of labor is 6 bushels of corn per unit of labor when 1
unit of labor is used, and the marginal product of labor is 7.5 bushels of corn
per unit of labor when between 1 and 2 units of labor are used. The results for
other levels of utilization of labor are shown in Table 6.2.

Table
6.2

AVERAGE AND MARGINAL PRODUCTS OF LABOR

Amount of labor	Total output	Average product of labor	Marginal product of labor*
0	0	—	—
1	6.0	6.00	6.0
2	13.5	6.75	7.5
3	21.0	7.00	7.5
4	28.0	7.00	7.0
5	34.0	6.80	6.0
6	38.0	6.30	4.0
7	38.0	5.40	0.0
8	37.0	4.60	−1.0

* These figures pertain to the interval between the indicated amount of labor and one unit less than the indicated amount of labor.

Panel A of Figure 6.2 shows the average product curve for labor. The numbers are taken from Table 6.2. As is typically the case for production processes, the average product of labor (which is the only variable input in this case) rises, reaches a maximum, and then falls. Panel B of Figure 6.2 shows the

Fig.
6.2

AVERAGE AND MARGINAL PRODUCT CURVES FOR LABOR / *Marginal product exceeds average product when the latter is increasing, and is less than average product when the latter is decreasing.*

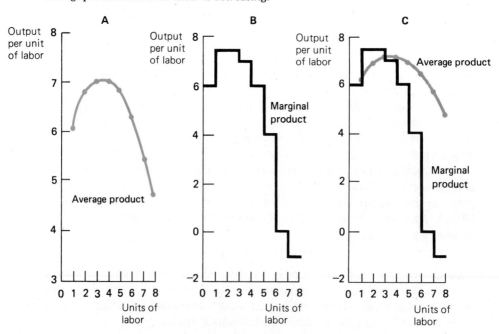

Fig.
6.3

TOTAL, AVERAGE, AND MARGINAL PRODUCT CURVES FOR LABOR, WITH ONE
AND TWO ACRES OF LAND / *An increase in the amount of land results in a
shift in the total, average, and marginal product curves for labor. (Note
that only part of each of these curves is shown; the region where average
or marginal product is increasing is omitted.)*

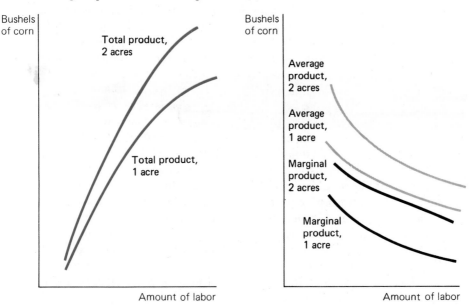

marginal product curve for labor. (These numbers also are taken from Table
6.2.) The marginal product of labor also rises, reaches a maximum, and then
falls. This, too, is typical of many production processes.[2] Finally, panel c of
Figure 6.2 shows both the average product curve and the marginal product
curve for labor. As is always the case, marginal product exceeds average product when the latter is increasing, equals average product when the latter
reaches a maximum, and is less than average product when the latter is decreasing. This is simply a matter of arithmetic: If the addition to a total is
greater (less) than the average, the average is bound to increase (decrease).

Tables 6.1 and 6.2 are constructed on the assumption that land, the fixed
input, is equal to one acre. Suppose that we could increase the amount of land
to two acres. What effect would this have on the total, average, and marginal
products of labor? Generally, over the relevant range of production, an increase in the fixed input will result in an increase in all of them. For example,
the result might be like that shown in Figure 6.3.

---

2. Sometimes, however, an input's marginal product decreases throughout the entire range of its
utilization.

THE LAW OF DIMINISHING MARGINAL RETURNS AND THE GEOMETRY OF AVERAGE AND MARGINAL PRODUCT CURVES

Previous sections have defined the production function and the average and marginal products of an input. We are now in a position to discuss one of the most famous laws of microeconomics—the law of diminishing marginal returns. The law of diminishing marginal returns, like the Scriptures, is often quoted and frequently misinterpreted. Put very briefly, this law states that *if equal increments of an input are added, the quantities of other inputs held constant, the resulting increments of product will decrease beyond some point; that is, the marginal product of the input will diminish.* This law is illustrated by Table 6.2; beyond 3 units of labor, the marginal product of labor decreases.

Several things should be noted concerning this law. First, the law of diminishing marginal returns is an empirical generalization, not a deduction from physical or biological laws. In fact, it seems to hold for most production functions in the real world. Second, it is assumed that technology remains fixed. The law of diminishing marginal returns cannot predict the effect of an additional unit of input when technology is allowed to change. Third, it is assumed that there is at least one input whose quantity is being held constant. The law of diminishing marginal returns does not apply to cases where there is a proportional increase in all inputs. Fourth, it must be possible, of course, to vary the proportions in which the various inputs are used.

If there is a fixed input and only one variable input, the typical form of the relationship between the amount of the variable input and the total output is given by OT in Figure 6.4.[3] Given such a graph, how can we determine the average product and the marginal product of the variable input? To make the analysis more concrete, suppose that Figure 6.4 refers to another farm like the one in Table 6.1, that the output is corn, and that the variable input is labor. First, consider the average product of the variable input, labor. Since average product equals total product divided by the amount of variable input, the average product of any amount of variable input, OA, equals $AB(=OC)$ divided by OA. And AB/OA is obviously the slope of the line, OB, which joins the origin and the point on the total product curve corresponding to this amount of variable input. Thus the slope of the line joining the origin and the relevant point on the total product curve is equal to the average product of the variable input, labor.

Second, consider the marginal product of the variable input, labor. Given the total product curve in Figure 6.5 (which is the same as that in Figure 6.4),

---

3. In Figure 6.4, we assume that the amount of the variable input is varied continuously, with the result that the total product, the average product, and the marginal product curves are continuous.

Fig.
6.4
MEASUREMENT OF THE AVERAGE PRODUCT / *When OA units of the variable input are used, the average product of the variable input equals the slope of the line OB.*

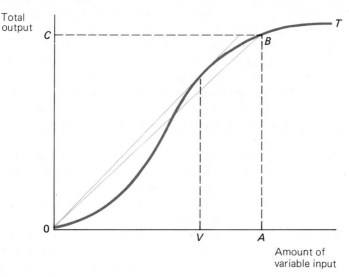

Fig.
6.5
MEASUREMENT OF MARGINAL PRODUCT / *The marginal product of the variable input equals the slope of line NN' when OG units of variable input are used.*

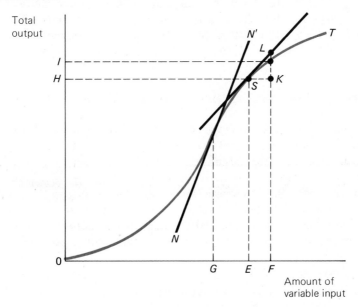

how can we determine the marginal product? If the amount of variable input increases from OE to OF, total output increases from OH to OI. Clearly, as the increment in the amount of variable input becomes smaller and smaller, the extra product divided by the extra variable input, HI/EF, approaches the slope of the total product curve at S. (Even if the increment is EF, the approximation is not too bad: The slope of the total product curve is $KL/SK = KL/EF$, which is fairly close to HI/EF.) Thus, since the slope of a curve at any point equals the slope of its tangent at that point, we can determine the marginal product of any amount of variable input by drawing the tangent to the total product curve at that amount of variable input and measuring its slope. For example, the slope of NN' is the marginal product of variable input when OG units of variable input are used.

Using these results, it is possible to prove a number of interesting results concerning the average product curve (the curve showing the relationship between average product and the amount of variable input used) and the marginal product curve (the curve showing the relationship between marginal product and the amount of variable input used). To begin with, in Figure 6.4, since a line joining the origin and a point on the total product curve is bound to be steepest (that is, has the maximum slope) when the line is tangent to the total product curve, it follows that the average product must be a maximum if OV units of variable input are used. Moreover, since the tangent to the total product curve is exactly the same as the line joining the origin and the total product curve when OV units of the variable input are used, the slope of the tangent must equal the slope of this line, and marginal product must equal average product. Thus *marginal product must equal average product when the latter is a maximum.*[4] Also, since the marginal product is a maximum at OG (Figure 6.5), where the slope of the tangent to the total product curve is greatest, and since OG is less than OV, it follows that *the maximum marginal product occurs at a lower level of variable input than the maximum average product.*

THE PRODUCTION FUNCTION: TWO VARIABLE INPUTS

In the previous sections, we were concerned with the case in which there is only one variable input. In the next four sections, we take up the more general case in which there are two variable inputs. These variable inputs can be thought of as working with one or more fixed inputs, or they may be thought of as the only two inputs (in which case the situation is the long run). In either case, it is easy to extend the results to as many inputs as one likes. This section takes up the production function, and the next two sections are concerned with its representation through a system of geometric constructs called isoquants.

---

4. Of course this is precisely the same result as that stated on p. 149.

Table HYPOTHETICAL PRODUCTION FUNCTION FOR CORN, TWO VARIABLE INPUTS
6.3

Amount of labor (units)	Number of acres			
	1	2	3	4
	(bushels of corn produced per year)			
1	5	11	18	24
2	14	30	50	72
3	22	60	80	99
4	29	80	115	125
5	34	84	140	145

If we increase the number of variable inputs from one to two, the production function becomes slightly more complicated, but it is still the relationship between various combinations of inputs and the maximum amount of output that can be obtained from them. Really, the only change is that the output is a function of two variables rather than one. For example, suppose in our agricultural example that we allow both land and labor to vary; the results might be given by Table 6.3. This is the production function in tabular form. Note that we can obtain the marginal product of each input by holding the other input constant. For example, the marginal product of land when 4 units of labor are used and when between 1 and 2 acres of land are used is 51 bushels per acre; the marginal product of labor when 2 acres are used and when between 3 and 4 units of labor are used is 20 bushels per unit. Similarly, the average product of either land or labor can be computed simply by dividing the total output by the amount of either land or labor that is used.

Another way to present the production function is by a surface, like that in Figure 6.6. The production surface is $OAQB$.[5] The height of a point on this surface denotes the quantity of output. Dropping a perpendicular down from a point on the production surface to the "floor" and seeing how far the resulting point is from the labor and land axes indicates how much of each input is required to produce this much output. For example, to produce $U'U$ units of output requires OB_1 ($= A_1U'$) units of labor and OA_1 ($= B_1U'$) acres of land. Conversely, one can take any amounts of land and labor, say OA_2 acres of land and OB_2 units of labor, and find out how much output they will produce by measuring the height of the production surface at D', the point where labor input is OB_2 and land input is OA_2. According to Figure 6.6, the answer equals $D'D$.

Note that this hypothetical production function illustrates the fact that a given amount of output can be produced in quite different ways. For example, in Table 6.3, 80 bushels of corn can be produced with either 4 units of labor and

---

5. Note that this surface is not meant to represent the numerical values in Table 6.3 but is a general representation of how a production surface of this sort is likely to appear.

Fig.   PRODUCTION FUNCTION, TWO VARIABLE INPUTS / *The production surface,*
6.6   OAQB, *shows the amount of total output that can be obtained from
           various combinations of quantities of land and labor.*

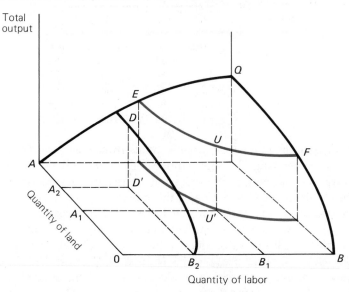

2 acres of land or with 3 units of labor and 3 acres of land. (Moreover, the production function does not include many of the different ways in which a given
output can be produced because it includes only efficient combinations of
inputs.)[6] Generally there is a variety of ways to produce a given output and a
variety of efficient input combinations; thus it is possible for the firm to substitute one input for another in producing a specified amount of output.

ISOQUANTS

An *isoquant* is a curve showing all possible (efficient) combinations of inputs
that are capable of producing a certain quantity of output. Given the production function, one can readily derive the isoquant pertaining to

Isoquant   any level of output. For example, in Figure 6.6, suppose that we
want to find the isoquant corresponding to an output of $U'U$. All
that we need to do is to cut the production surface at the height of $U'U$ parallel

---

6. For example, if 2 units of labor and 3 units of capital can produce 1 unit of output, this combination of inputs and output will not be included in the production function if it is also possible to produce 1 unit of output with 2 units of labor and 2 units of capital. The former input
combination is clearly inefficient, since it is possible to obtain the result with the same
amount of labor and less capital.

Fig.
6.7 ISOQUANTS / *These three isoquants show the various combinations of*
capital and labor that can produce 50, 100, and 150 units of output.

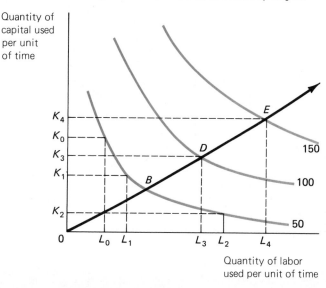

to the base plane, the result being *EUF*, and to drop perpendiculars from *EUF*
to the base. Clearly, this results in a curve that includes all efficient combinations of land and labor that can produce *U'U* bushels of corn.

A number of isoquants, each pertaining to a different output rate, is
shown in Figure 6.7. The two axes measure the quantities of inputs that are
used. In contrast to the previous diagrams, we assume that labor and capital
—not labor and land—are the relevant inputs in this case. The curves show
the various combinations of inputs that can produce 50, 100, and 150 units of
output. For example, consider the isoquant pertaining to 50 units of output per
period of time. According to this isoquant, it is possible to attain this output
rate if OL_0 units of labor and OK_0 units of capital are used per period of time.
Alternatively, this output rate can be attained if OL_1 units of labor and OK_1
units of capital—or OL_2 units of labor and OK_2 units of capital—are used per
period of time.

A ray is a line that starts from some point and goes off into space. A ray
from the origin, such as *OBDE*, describes all input combinations where the
capital-labor ratio is constant, with the slope of the ray being equal to the
constant capital-labor ratio. For example, at points *D* and *E*, 100 and 150 units
of output are produced with a capital-labor ratio of $OK_3/OL_3 = OK_4/OL_4$.
Moving out from the origin along any ray, such as *OBDE*, we see that various
output levels can be produced with the same ratio of one input to another. Of
course, the absolute amount of each input increases as we move out to higher
and higher output levels, but the ratio of one input to the other remains con-

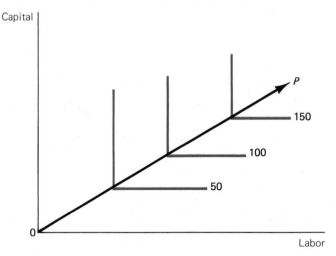

stant. It is important to understand the difference between such a ray and an isoquant; an isoquant pertains to a fixed, not a changing, output rate and a changing, not a fixed, ratio of inputs.

An isoquant plays much the same kind of role in production theory that an indifference curve plays in demand theory. An indifference curve shows the various combinations of two commodities that provide equal satisfaction to the consumer; an isoquant shows the various combinations of two inputs that result in an equal output for the firm. It is obvious that, like indifference curves, two isoquants cannot intersect. If an intersection were to occur, it would mean that two different output rates are the maximum obtainable from a given combination of resources; this is obviously absurd.

Isoquants can be used to illustrate the case in which inputs must be used in fixed proportions. Figure 6.8 shows a case of this sort; the necessary ratio of capital to labor is the slope of the ray OP. The isoquants are right angles, indicating that, if one input is increased (beyond the amount needed to complement the other input) while the other input is held constant, there is no increase in the output rate. In other words, the marginal product of either input is zero if the other input is held constant.

The Economic Region of Production

In some cases, isoquants may have positively sloped segments, or bend back upon themselves, as shown in Figure 6.9. Above OA and below OB, the slope of the isoquants is positive, which implies that increases in both capital and labor are required to maintain a certain output rate. If this is the case, the marginal product of one or the other input must be negative. Above OA, the

Fig. THE ECONOMIC REGION OF PRODUCTION / *No profit-maximizing firm will*
6.9 *operate at a point outside the ridge lines,* OA *and* OB.

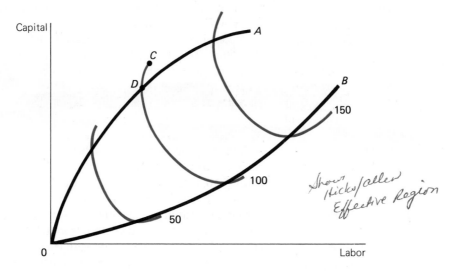

marginal product of capital is negative; thus output will increase if less capital is used, while the amount of labor is held constant. Below *OB,* the marginal product of labor is negative; thus output will increase if less labor is used, while the amount of capital is held constant. The lines *OA* and *OB* are called *ridge lines.*

Clearly, no profit-maximizing firm will operate at a point outside the ridge lines, since it can produce the same output with less of both inputs, which must be cheaper. To illustrate this, consider point *C* in Figure 6.9. Because this is a point where the isoquant is positively sloped—and thus outside the ridge lines—it requires a greater amount of both labor and capital than some other point (for example, point *D*) on the same isoquant. Since both capital and labor have positive prices, it must be cheaper to operate at point *D* than at point *C*. In general, it is always possible to find a cheaper way to produce a given quantity of output than to operate at a point outside the ridge lines. Thus the zone between the ridge lines is often called the *economic region of production.* For example, in Figure 6.9, the economic region of production is the zone between *OA* and *OB*. No rational firm will venture outside this region.

Substitution among Inputs

From both a practical and a theoretical point of view, it is important to study the rate at which one input must be substituted for another to maintain a constant output rate. Consider the isoquant, *Z,* in Figure 6.10. The relevant output rate can be produced with OL_0 units of labor and OK_0 units of capital.

However, if the amount of labor is increased to OL_1, the same output rate can be attained with less capital: OK_1 units rather than OK_0. Thus, in the relevant range, the rate at which labor can be substituted for capital is $-(OK_0 - OK_1)/(OL_0 - OL_1) = BA/BC$; the minus sign is added to make the result a positive number. If we consider a very small increase in labor (OL_1 being very close to OL_0), BA/BC equals -1 times the slope of the tangent, G, to the isoquant at A, which is called the *marginal rate of technical substitution*. It measures, for small changes in labor, the change in capital required per unit change in labor. The reader will note that, as its name indicates, it is analogous to the marginal rate of substitution in demand theory. (Economists, having found an elegant and felicitous phrase like the marginal rate of substitution, did not want to abandon it for anything cumbersome.)

Marginal rate of technical substitution

Using the diagram in Figure 6.10, it is easy to demonstrate that the marginal rate of technical substitution of labor for capital is equal to the ratio of the marginal product of labor to the marginal product of capital. Suppose that labor input is held at the OL_0 level, while capital is increased from OK_1 to OK_0. Output would increase from the level (say Q_1) corresponding to isoquant W to the level (say Q_0) corresponding to isoquant Z. The marginal product of capital is $(Q_0 - Q_1) \div (OK_0 - OK_1) = (Q_0 - Q_1) \div BA$. On the other hand, suppose that capital is held at OK_1, while labor is increased from OL_0 to OL_1. The marginal product of labor is $(Q_0 - Q_1) \div (OL_1 - OL_0) = (Q_0 - Q_1) \div BC$. Thus the ratio of the marginal product of labor to the marginal product of capital equals $BA \div BC$, which (in the limit for small changes in the amount of labor) equals the marginal rate of technical substitution.

Fig. 6.10   THE MARGINAL RATE OF TECHNICAL SUBSTITUTION / *The marginal rate of technical substitution equals minus one times the slope of the tangent,* G, *to the isoquant.*

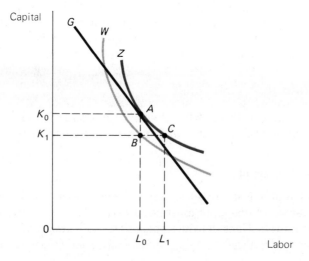

Example 6.2

MILK PRODUCTION

Based on data obtained by the U.S. Department of Agriculture, 8,500 pounds of milk can be produced during a specified time period by a cow fed the following combinations of quantities of hay and grain:

Quantity of hay (pounds)	Quantity of grain (pounds)
5,000	6,154
5,500	5,454
6,000	4,892
6,500	4,423
7,000	4,029
7,500	3,694

(a) Plot these data as an isoquant. (b) Calculate the marginal rate of technical substitution at all points along this isoquant. (c) Is this isoquant convex? (d) If the price of a pound of hay equals the price of a pound of grain, should a cow be fed 5,000 pounds of hay and 6,154 pounds of grain?

SOLUTION

(a) The isoquant is as follows:

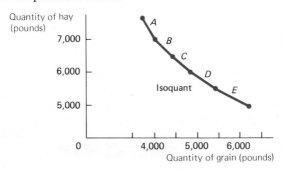

(b) For each segment $(A, B, \ldots, E)$ of the isoquant, the marginal rate of technical substitution is as follows:

Segment	Marginal rate of technical substitution
A	$-(7,500 - 7,000) \div (3,694 - 4,029) = 1.49$
B	$-(7,000 - 6,500) \div (4,029 - 4,423) = 1.27$
C	$-(6,500 - 6,000) \div (4,423 - 4,892) = 1.07$
D	$-(6,000 - 5,500) \div (4,892 - 5,454) = 0.89$
E	$-(5,500 - 5,000) \div (5,454 - 6,154) = 0.71$

(c) Yes, since the marginal rate of technical substitution falls as more grain is substituted for hay. (d) No, because other combinations of quantities of hay and grain are cheaper. If P equals the price of a pound of either hay or grain, the cost of 5,000 pounds of hay and 6,154 pounds of grain is $11,154P$. In contrast, the cost of 6,000 pounds of hay and 4,892 pounds of grain is $10,892P$, which is lower.*

*For further discussion, see E. Heady's classic work, *Economics of Agricultural Production and Resource Use* (New York: Prentice-Hall, 1952).

It is also easy to show that the marginal rate of technical substitution of labor for capital tends to decrease as an increasing amount of labor is substituted for capital. As labor is substituted for capital, the marginal product of labor tends to fall. Increases in labor, holding capital constant, result in a decrease in the marginal product of labor in the economic region of production. When capital is decreased, even more of a decrease occurs in the marginal product of labor, since a decrease in capital results in a downward shift in the marginal product curve for labor. At the same time, the marginal product of capital rises (for the same kinds of reasons) as more labor is substituted for capital. Thus, since the marginal rate of technical substitution equals the marginal product of labor (which is falling) divided by the marginal product of capital (which is rising), it must be falling as labor is substituted for capital.

Since the marginal rate of technical substitution falls as labor is substituted for capital, it follows that isoquants must be convex. (See p. 65.) Because the marginal rate of technical substitution equals −1 times the slope of the isoquant and because the marginal rate of technical substitution falls as we move to the right along an isoquant, the absolute value of the slope of the isoquant must be getting smaller as we move to the right along an isoquant. But if the absolute value of the slope is getting smaller as we move to the right, the isoquant must be convex.

THE LONG RUN AND RETURNS TO SCALE

Previous sections have shown how a firm's technology can be represented by a production function and have described the characteristics of production functions (and of related concepts like the marginal and average product) that seem to hold in general for production processes. However, one important characteristic of production functions has not been described: how output responds in the long run to changes in the *scale* of the firm. In other words, suppose that we consider a long-run situation in which all inputs are variable, and suppose that the firm increases the amount of all inputs by the same proportion. What will happen to output? This is an important question, the answer to which (as we shall see in subsequent chapters) helps to determine whether firms of certain sizes can survive in the industry.

To repeat, what will happen to output under the assumed conditions?

Increasing, decreasing, and constant returns to scale

Clearly, there are three possibilities: First, output may increase by a larger proportion than each of the inputs. For example, a doubling of all inputs may lead to more than a doubling of output. This is the case of *increasing returns to scale*. Second, output may increase by a smaller proportion than each of the inputs. For example, a doubling of all inputs may lead to less than a doubling of output. This is the case of *decreasing returns to scale*. Third, output may increase by exactly the same proportion as the inputs. For example, a doubling of all inputs may lead to a doubling of output. This is the case of *constant returns to scale.*

At first glance it may seem that production functions must necessarily exhibit constant returns to scale. After all, if two factories are built with the same plant and the same types of workers, it would seem obvious that twice as much output will result. Unfortunately (or fortunately, depending on your point of view), it is not as simple as that. For instance, if a firm doubles its scale, it may be able to use techniques that could not be used at the smaller scale. Thus, although one could double a firm's size by simply building two small factories, this may be inefficient. One large factory may be more efficient than two smaller factories of the same total capacity because it is large enough to use certain techniques that the smaller factories cannot use.

Another reason for increasing returns to scale stems from certain geometrical relations. For example, since the volume of a box that is $4 \times 4 \times 4$ feet is 64 times as great as the volume of a box that is $1 \times 1 \times 1$ foot, the former box can carry 64 times as much as the latter box. But since the area of the six sides of the $4 \times 4 \times 4$-foot box is 96 square feet and the area of the six sides of the $1 \times 1 \times 1$-foot box is 6 square feet, the former box only requires 16 times as much wood as the latter. Greater specialization also can result in increasing returns to scale: As more men and machines are used, it is possible to subdivide tasks and allow various inputs to specialize. Also, economies of scale may arise because of probabilistic considerations: For example, because the aggregate behavior of a bigger number of customers tends to be more stable, a firm's inventory may not have to increase in proportion to its sales.

Decreasing returns to scale can also occur; the most frequently cited reason is the difficulty of coordinating a large enterprise. It can be difficult even in a small firm to obtain the information required to make important decisions; in a large firm, the difficulties tend to be greater. It can be difficult even in a small firm to be certain that management's wishes are being carried out; in a larger firm these difficulties too tend to be greater. Although the advantages of a large organization seem to have captured the public fancy, there are often very great disadvantages. For example, in certain kinds of research and development, there is evidence that large engineering teams tend to be less effective than smaller ones and that large firms tend to be less effective than small ones.

Diagrams like those in Figure 6.11 can be used to analyze and describe the situation in a particular firm. Panel A describes a case in which there are constant returns to scale. Examination of the isoquants for outputs of 50, 100, and 150 units shows that they intersect any ray from the origin, like *OA,* at equal distances. (That is, $OD = DC = CB$.) In other words, twice as much of both inputs are needed to produce 100 units of output than to produce 50 units of output, and three times as much of both inputs are needed to produce 150 units of output than to produce 50 units of output. Panel B describes a case in which there are increasing returns to scale. In this case, successive isoquants, as one moves out from the origin, become closer and closer together. For example,

Fig. Constant, Increasing, and Decreasing Returns to Scale / *Panel A*
6.11 *shows constant returns to scale, panel B shows increasing returns to scale,*
and panel C shows decreasing returns to scale.

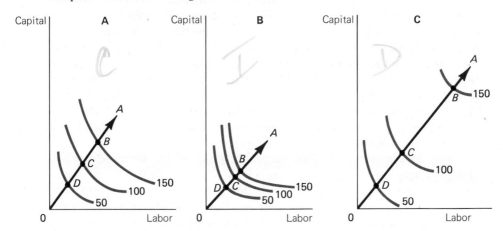

$OD > DC > CB$. Panel c describes a case in which there are decreasing returns to scale. In this case, successive isoquants become farther and farther apart as we move out from the origin. For example, $OD < DC < CB$.

Whether or not there are constant, increasing, or decreasing returns to scale in a particular situation is an empirical question that must be settled case by case. There is no simple, all-encompassing answer.[7] In some industries the available evidence may indicate that increasing returns are present over a certain range of output. In other industries, decreasing or constant returns may be present. In the next section, we turn to a discussion of empirical studies.

MEASUREMENT OF PRODUCTION FUNCTIONS

Economists and statisticians have devoted a great deal of time and effort, particularly in the past forty years, to the measurement of production functions. Three methods have been used in most of these studies. The first method is based on the statistical analysis of time-series data concerning the amount of various inputs used in various periods in the past and the amount of output produced in each period. For example, one might obtain data concerning the amount of labor, the amount of capital, and the amount of various raw materials used in the aluminum industry during each year from 1948 to 1988. On the basis of such data and information concerning the annual output of alumi-

---

7. Also, it is important to note that the answer is likely to depend on the level of output that is considered. There may be increasing returns to scale at small output levels and constant or decreasing returns to scale at larger output levels.

num during 1948 to 1988, one might estimate the relationship between the amounts of the inputs and the resulting output.

The second method is based on the statistical analysis of cross-section data concerning the amount of various inputs used and output produced in various firms or sectors of the industry at a given point in time. For example, one might obtain data concerning the amount of labor, the amount of capital, and the amount of various raw materials used in various firms in the aluminum industry in 1988. On the basis of such data and information concerning the 1988 output of each firm, one might estimate the relationship between the amounts of the inputs and the resulting output.

The third method is based on technical information supplied by the engineer or the agricultural scientist. This information is collected by experiment or from experience with the day-to-day workings of the technical process. There are considerable advantages to be gained from approaching the measurement of the production function from this angle because the range of applicability of the data is known, and, unlike time-series and cross-section studies, we are not restricted to the narrow range of actual observations. However, there are also some difficult problems in this approach, which are discussed in the following paragraphs.

All three approaches are handicapped by the fact that the data may not always represent technically efficient combinations of inputs and output. For example, because of errors or constraints, the amount of inputs used by the aluminum industry in 1988 may not have been the minimum required to produce the 1988 output of the aluminum industry. Since the production function theoretically includes only efficient input combinations, a case of this sort should be excluded, if our measurements are to be pristine pure. In practice, however, such cases are not always excluded (or recognized) and the resulting estimate of the production function is in error for this reason.

Another important problem is the measurement of capital input. The principal difficulty stems from the fact that the stock of capital is composed of various types and ages of machines, buildings, and inventories. Combining them into a single measure—or a few measures—is a formidable problem. In addition, errors can arise in the first two techniques because various data points, which are assumed to be on the same production function, are in fact on different ones. Moreover, biases can occur because of identification problems somewhat similar to those discussed on pp. 125–26.

With regard to the third method, it is difficult to combine the results for the processes for which engineers have data into an overall plant or firm production function. Since engineering data generally pertain to only a part of the firm's activities, this is often a very hard job. For example, engineering data tell us little or nothing about the firm's marketing or financial activities. Moreover, engineering data are generally available for only parts of the firm's fabricating activities.

Despite these difficulties, estimates of production functions have proved

**Table ESTIMATES OF α_1, α_2, AND α_3 FOR SELECTED INDUSTRIES
6.4**

Industry	*Country*	α_1	α_2	α_3	$\alpha_1+\alpha_2+\alpha_3$
Gas	France	.83	.10	—	0.93
Railroads	United States	.89	.12	.28	1.29
Coal	United Kingdom	.79	.29	—	1.08
Food	United States	.72	.35	—	1.07
Metals and machinery	United States	.71	.26	—	0.97
Communications	Soviet Union	.80	.38	—	1.18
Cotton	India	.92	.12	—	1.04
Jute	India	.84	.14	—	0.98
Sugar	India	.59	.33	—	0.92
Coal	India	.71	.44	—	1.15
Paper	India	.64	.45	—	1.09
Chemicals	India	.80	.37	—	1.17
Electricity	India	.20	.67	—	0.87
Food*	United States	.63	.44	—	1.07
Paper*	United States	.62	.37	—	0.98
Telephone	Canada	.70	.41	—	1.11
Chemicals†	United States	.54	.38	.11	1.03
Aircraft†	United States	.79	.18	.04	1.01

* The figure for α_1 is the sum of the figures given for production workers and nonproduction workers.

† In these cases, M is cumulated past expenditure on research and development, not the quantity of raw materials, and K is the quantity of capital services.

SOURCE: A. A. Walters, "Production and Cost Functions," *Econometrica*, January 1963; J. Moroney, "Cobb-Douglas Production Functions and Returns to Scale in U.S. Manufacturing," *Western Economic Journal*, 1967; A. Dobell, L. Taylor, L. Waverman, T. Liu, and M. Copeland, "Communications in Canada," *Bell Journal of Economics and Management Science*, 1972; J. P. Lewis, "Postwar Economic Growth and Productivity in the Soviet Communications Industry," *Bell Journal of Economics and Management Sciences*, Autumn 1975; and Z. Griliches, "Returns to Research and Development Expenditures in the Private Sector," in J. Kendrick and B. Vaccara, *New Developments in Productivity Measurement and Analysis* (Chicago: National Bureau of Economic Research, 1980).

of considerable interest and value. Many of these estimates have been based on the assumption that the production function is a so-called Cobb-Douglas function, which is

$$Q = AL^{\alpha_1}K^{\alpha_2}M^{\alpha_3} \qquad [6.1]$$

where Q is the output rate; L is the quantity of labor; K is the quantity of capital; and M is the quantity of raw materials; and A, α_1, α_2, and α_3 are parameters that vary from case to case. Ordinarily it is assumed that the value of each α is less than 1, which assures that the marginal product of each input (which equals its α times its average product) decreases with increases in its utilization. Increasing returns to scale occur if $\alpha_1 + \alpha_2 + \alpha_3 > 1$; decreasing returns to scale occur if $\alpha_1 + \alpha_2 + \alpha_3 < 1$.

Table 6.4 shows the estimates of α_1, α_2, and α_3 for a number of industries in the United States and abroad. They provide interesting information concerning production relations in these industries. To see more clearly the implications of these results, note that α_1 is the percentage increase in output resulting from a 1 percent increase in labor, holding the quantities of the other inputs constant. For example, in the Canadian telephone industry in about 1972, a 1 percent increase in labor would have resulted in a 0.70 percent increase in output. Similarly, α_2 is the percentage increase in output resulting from a 1 percent increase in capital, holding the quantities of other inputs constant.

The results also cast light on returns to scale. In 6 of the 18 cases, there seem to be decreasing returns; in 12 of the 18 cases there seem to be increasing returns to scale. Finally, it is possible to construct isoquants from the results in Table 6.4. For example, Figure 6.12 shows some isoquants for the French gas industry. Note that these isoquants (A, B, and C) are similar in shape to the hypothetical isoquants introduced earlier in this chapter.[8]

Fig. 6.12 ISOQUANTS FOR FRENCH GAS INDUSTRY / *These estimates of actual isoquants for the French gas industry are similar in shape to what microeconomic theory predicts.*

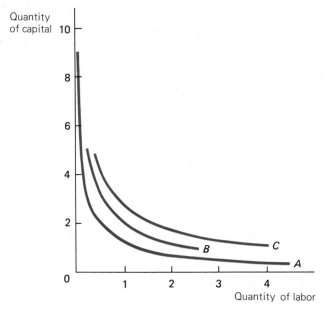

8. For further discussion, see M. Brown, *The Theory and Empirical Analysis of Production* (New York: National Bureau of Economic Research, 1967). There has also been much use made of the transcendental logarithmic production function described in L. Christenson, D. Jorgenson, and L. Lau, "Conjugate Duality and the Transcendental Logarithmic Production Function," *Econometrica*, July 1971.

SUMMARY

1. As a first approximation, economists generally assume that firms attempt to maximize profits. In recent years, there have been a number of attempts to experiment with alternative assumptions concerning the goals of the firm; most of these alternative assumptions stem from a more detailed view of the firm's organization. Although these theories are useful for some purposes, profit maximization remains the standard assumption in economics, because it is a close enough approximation for many important purposes and because it provides rules of behavior for firms that do want to make as much money as possible.

2. The production function is used by economists to represent the technology available to the firm. For any commodity, the production function is the relationship between the quantities of various inputs used per period of time and the maximum quantity of the commodity produced per period of time.

3. In analyzing production processes, we generally assume that all inputs can be divided into two categories: fixed and variable. In the short run, the firm's plant and equipment are fixed; in the long run, all inputs are variable. Both in the short run and in the long run, a firm's production processes ordinarily permit substantial variation in input proportions.

4. The law of diminishing marginal returns states that as equal increments of one input are added, the quantities of other inputs held constant, the resulting increments of product will decrease beyond some point; that is, the marginal product of the input will diminish.

5. An input's marginal product must equal its average product when the latter is a maximum. The maximum marginal product occurs at a lower level of variable input than the maximum average product.

6. An isoquant is a curve that shows all possible combinations of inputs that are capable of producing a certain quantity of output. We can construct ridge lines so that all points where the isoquants are positively sloped lie outside the ridge lines. No rational firm will operate outside the ridge lines because the marginal product of one or the other input is negative in this region.

7. If the firm increases all inputs by the same proportion and output increases by more (less) than this proportion, there are increasing (decreasing) returns to scale. Whether or not there are constant, increasing, or decreasing returns to scale is an empirical question that must be settled case by case.

8. Economists and statisticians have devoted a great deal of time and effort to the measurement of production functions. Three methods have been used in most of these studies: statistical analysis based on time series of inputs and output, statistical analysis based on cross-section data, and analysis based on engineering data. Although there are a great many difficulties in existing measurement techniques, estimates of production functions have proved of considerable interest and value.

APPENDIX / Organization of the Firm and Alternative Models of Firm Behavior

In recent years, there have been a number of attempts to experiment with models of the firm based on assumptions other than profit maximization. Most of these alternative models are tied to a more detailed look at the organization of the firm and its divisions. Until recently, economists have proceeded on the basis of extremely simple assumptions regarding the organization of the firm. Traditionally, they have posited the existence in each firm of an entrepreneur who exercises control over the firm's activities. The entrepreneur decides whether the firm should continue its existence (or be founded in the first place); he or she sets the price or decides what price to accept; and he or she decides whether output and capacity should be increased or decreased. The entrepreneur is the locus of decision-making in the firm. This concept of the organization of the firm is not unrealistic in many cases. In the United States, millions of small businessmen satisfy, more or less, the definition of the entrepreneur. For example, in a small tool-and-die shop, there is typically a single owner-manager who makes practically all of the major decisions.

However, in large corporations, the concept of the entrepreneur seems strained, since in most cases there is no single entrepreneur and it is difficult to know exactly where, how, and by whom decisions are made. Rather than a single entrepreneur, there are large numbers of people in middle management, as well as the top brass occupying key management positions, all of whom participate in varying degrees in the formulation of company policy. Various groups within the firm develop their own party lines, and intrafirm politics is an important part of the process determining company policy. For example, if a firm is composed of two divisions (each making a different product), each division may fight to maintain and expand its share of the firm's budget, and each may try to put the other in a subordinate position. Whereas in a small firm it may be fairly accurate to regard the goals of the firm as being the goals of the entrepreneur, in the large corporation the decision on the goals of the firm is in a real sense a matter of politics.

It has been suggested by Herbert Simon[9] (1978 Nobel laureate in eco-

---

9. For example, see H. Simon, "Theories of Decision-Making in Economic and Behavioral Science," reprinted in E. Mansfield, *Microeconomics: Selected Readings*, 5th ed.

nomics) and others that the firm *"satisfices"* rather than maximizes profit. That is, business firms aim at a satisfactory rate of profit rather than the maximum figure. A firm's aspiration level is the boundary be-

Satisficing   tween unsatisfactory and satisfactory outcomes. The firm aban-
dons the attempt to maximize profits because the calculations required are too complicated and the available data are too poor. Instead the firm tries to attain certain minimal standards of performance.

This theory would, of course, be incomplete if it did not specify how the firm's aspiration level will change, the aspiration level being a certain goal like "our profit for this year should be $2,000,000." According to some economists, if the environment facing the firm is relatively constant, the aspiration level will tend to be slightly higher than the firm's performance. If performance is improving, the aspiration level will tend to lag behind actual performance; and if performance is decreasing, the aspiration level will tend to be above actual performance. Of course, if the aspiration level is close to the maximum profit, there is little difference between the results obtained by assuming profit maximization and those obtained using satisficing.

An interesting feature of this theory is that it focuses attention on internal slack in the firm, a concept that has no place in traditional theory. One implication of the traditional assumption that firms maximize profits is that they produce whatever volumes of output they choose at minimum cost. Although this may be a reasonable first approximation, it seems likely that there is a certain amount of slack in most firms, in the sense that costs are not pushed down to the minimum. This slack acts as a cushion when the firm is submitted to pressures from the outside and from within. For example, if profits are reduced by a fall in demand, the firm is sometimes able to recoup part of the losses by eliminating slack, that is, by lowering its costs. However, this slack is usually not created to provide stability; instead it arises in part from the bargaining process within the firm.[10]

Simon's satisficing model is not the only alternative to the assumption of profit maximization. It has also been suggested that, when differences arise between profit maximization and the interests of the management group, executives are likely to follow policies favoring their own interests.[11] Important in this regard is the separation of ownership from control in the large corporation in the United States. The owners of the firm—the stockholders—usually have little detailed knowledge of the firm's operations. Even if the board of di-

---

10. See R. Cyert and J. March, *A Behavioral Theory of the Firm* (Englewood Cliffs, N.J.: Prentice-Hall, 1963), and other works of these authors for a discussion of the topics included in the last few paragraphs. Also, see H. Leibenstein, "Allocative Efficiency vs. X-Efficiency," reprinted in E. Mansfield, *Microeconomics: Selected Readings,* 5th ed.

11. See R. Marris, *The Economic Theory of "Managerial" Capitalism* (New York: Free Press, 1964); and R. Marris and D. Mueller, "The Corporation, Competition, and the Invisible Hand," reprinted in E. Mansfield, *Microeconomics: Selected Readings,* 5th ed.

rectors is made up largely of people other than top management, top management usually has a great deal of freedom as long as it seems to be performing reasonably well. Under these circumstances, one might suppose that the behavior of the firm often will be dictated in part by the interests of the management group, the result being larger salaries, more perquisites, and a bigger staff than otherwise would be the case.

Oliver Williamson has constructed a model incorporating these factors. The managers of the firm are viewed as maximizers of utility, and their utility is assumed to depend on their own salaries, perquisites, and number of subordinates, as well as on the profit of the firm.[12] Williamson has also studied the hierarchical structure of firms, and the ways they are organized.[13] Two key prototypical organizational structures are the functionally specialized firm (organized into departments, each undertaking a particular function like production, finance, and marketing) and the multidivisional firm (organized into divisions assigned different tasks, producing entirely different products, or serving different markets). During recent decades, there has been a tendency for more firms to adopt the multidivisional structure.

Still another alternative to the assumption of profit maximization has been proposed by William Baumol,[14] who suggests that firms attempt to maximize total sales, rather than profits. However, profits are not ignored in Baumol's scheme; it is assumed that there is a certain minimum level of profits that the firm attempts to attain. Thus the firm can wind up in one of two types of equilibrium: one where the profit constraint bars the firm from *maximizing sales,* and one where it does not. According to Baumol, sales represent a measure of management's success, especially since many observers focus attention on a firm's share of the market as an indicator of its performance. Also, according to Baumol, there is a closer correlation between the salaries of the executives and the company's sales than between their salaries and profits.

Sales maximization

Although each of these theories is useful for certain purposes and under certain conditions, profit maximization remains the standard assumption in microeconomics. In part, this is because it is a close enough approximation for many important purposes; in part, it is because some of these alternative theories require more in the way of data than does the simpler theory of profit maximization. Even some of the proponents of these alternative theories admit that profit maximization is an adequate assumption for a wide range of

---

12. O. Williamson, *The Economics of Discretionary Behavior* (Englewood Cliffs, N.J.: Prentice-Hall, 1964).

13. O. Williamson, *Markets and Hierarchies: Analysis and Antitrust Implications* (New York: Free Press, 1975); and *Corporate Control and Business Behavior* (Englewood Cliffs, N.J.: Prentice-Hall, 1970).

14. See W. Baumol, *Business Behavior, Value and Growth,* 2d ed. (New York: Macmillan, 1959).

important purposes. Also as we have noted before, the theory of the profit-maximizing firm is of great interest because it provides rules of rational behavior for firms that do want to maximize profits.

═══════════ QUESTIONS/PROBLEMS ═══════════

1) Fill in the blanks in the following table:

Number of units of variable input	Total output (number of units)	Marginal product* of variable input	Average product of variable input
3	—	Unknown	30
4	—	20	—
5	130	—	—
6	—	5	—
7	—	—	$19\frac{1}{2}$

* These figures pertain to the interval between the indicated amount of the variable input and one unit less than the indicated amount of the variable input.

2) In Question 1, does the production function exhibit diminishing marginal returns? If so, at what number of units of variable input do diminishing marginal returns begin to set in? Can you tell on the basis of the table in Question 1?

3) As the quantity of a variable input increases, explain why the point where *marginal* product begins to decline is encountered before the point where *average* product begins to decline. Explain, too, why the point where *average* product begins to decline is encountered before the point where *total* product begins to decline.

4) Suppose that a good is produced with two inputs, labor and capital, and that the production function is

$$Q = 10 \sqrt{L} \sqrt{K}$$

where Q is the quantity of output, L is the quantity of labor, and K is the quantity of capital. Does this production function exhibit increasing returns to scale? Decreasing returns to scale? Constant returns to scale? Explain.

5) Econometric studies of the cotton industry in India indicate that the Cobb-Douglas production function can be applied, and that the exponent of labor is .92 and the exponent of capital is .12. Suppose that both capital and labor were increased by 1 percent. By what percent would output increase?

6) According to Herbert Simon, "Models of satisficing behavior are richer than models of maximizing behavior, because they treat not only of equilibrium but of the method of reaching it as well." Comment on this statement. Do you agree? Why or why not?

7) (Advanced) Suppose you are assured by the owner of an aircraft factory that his plant is subject to constant returns to scale, with labor and capital the only inputs. He claims that output per worker in his plant is a function of capital per worker only. Is he right?

8) Laserex, a manufacturer of lasers, reports that the marginal product of labor is 10 units of output per hour of labor and that the marginal rate of technical substitution of labor for capital is 5. What is the marginal product of capital?

9) The following graph shows the combinations of grain and protein that must be used to produce 150 pounds of pork. Curve A assumes that no Aureomycin is added, while curve B assumes that some of it is added.

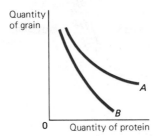

(a) If Aureomycin can be obtained free, should pork producers add it? (b) Does the addition of Aureomycin affect the marginal rate of technical substitution? If so, how?

10) Suppose that an entrepreneur's utility depends on the size of his or her firm (as measured by its output) and its profits. In particular, the indifference curves are as follows:

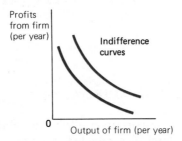

(a) Will the entrepreneur maximize profit? (b) If not, will he or she produce more or less than the profit-maximizing output? (c) Draw a graph to indicate the point he or she will choose. (Hint: Reread Example 6.1.)

Optimal Input Combinations
and Cost Functions

DECISIONS REGARDING INPUT COMBINATIONS

In the previous chapter we were concerned with the motivation of the firm and the way in which the technology available to the firm can be represented. We decided to assume, as a first approximation, that firms attempt to maximize profit. We also decided that the technology available to the firm can be represented by a production function, which conforms to certain rules like the law of diminishing marginal returns. These decisions take us part way—but only part way—toward a model of the firm. The next step is to determine how a profit-maximizing firm will combine inputs to produce a given quantity of output. That is the purpose of this chapter.

　　To be specific, suppose that a producer of electronic computers decides for some reason to produce 100,000 computers next year. Suppose that, in accord with the conclusions of the previous chapter, we assume that the firm is an out-and-out profit-maximizer, and that we are given its production function, derived largely through engineering studies and statistical analysis. On the basis of this information, can we predict what combination of inputs the firm will use to produce 100,000 computers next year and how much it will cost to produce this amount? Or putting the problem somewhat differently, suppose that we are hired by the firm to help with this decision. Can we tell the firm what combination of inputs it *should* use and how much it *should* cost to produce this amount?

In this chapter, we begin by determining which combination of inputs a firm will choose if it minimizes the cost of producing a given amount of output. Then we discuss the nature of costs—what is meant by a cost and how various concepts of cost differ from one another. Finally, we show how the short-run and long-run cost functions of the firm can be derived theoretically, and we provide a brief discussion of the measurement of cost functions.

THE OPTIMAL COMBINATION OF INPUTS

For the sake of generality, let's consider a firm of any sort, not just the computer firm noted previously. If the firm maximizes profit, it will minimize the cost of producing a given output or maximize the output derived from a given level of cost.[1] This seems obvious. Suppose that the firm is a perfect competitor in the input markets, which means that it takes input prices as given. (The case in which the firm can influence input prices is taken up in Chapter 13.) Suppose that there are two inputs, capital and labor, that are variable in the relevant time period. What combination of capital and labor should the firm choose if it wants to maximize the quantity of output derived from the given level of cost?

As a first step toward answering this question, let's determine the various combinations of inputs that the firm can obtain for a given expenditure. For example, if capital and labor are the inputs and the price of labor is P_L per unit and the price of capital is P_K per unit, the input combinations that can be obtained for a total outlay of R are such that

$$P_L L + P_K K = R \qquad [7.1]$$

where L is the amount of the labor input and K is the amount of the capital input. Given P_L, P_K, and R, it follows that

$$K = \frac{R}{P_K} - \frac{P_L}{P_K} L. \qquad [7.2]$$

Thus the various combinations of capital and labor that can be purchased, given P_L, P_K, and R, can be represented by a straight line like that shown in Figure 7.1. (Capital is plotted on the vertical axis, labor is plotted on the horizontal.) This line, which has an intercept on the vertical axis equal to R/P_K and a slope of $-P_L/P_K$, is called an *iso-*

Isocost curve

cost curve.

---

1. The conditions for minimizing the cost of producing a given output are the same as those for maximizing the output from a given cost. This is shown in the present section. Thus we can view the firm's problem in either way.

Fig.
7.1   Isocost Curve / *The isocost curve shows the combinations of inputs that
can be obtained for a total outlay of* R.

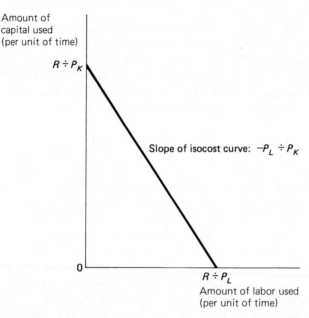

If we superimpose the relevant isocost curve on the firm's isoquant map,
we can readily determine graphically which combination of inputs will maximize the output for the given expenditure. Obviously, the firm should pick that
point on the isocost curve that is on the highest isoquant, for example, P in
Figure 7.2. This clearly is a point where the isocost curve is tangent to the isoquant. Thus, since the slope of the isocost curve is the negative of P_L/P_K and
the slope of the isoquant is the negative of the marginal rate of technical substitution, it follows that the optimal combination of inputs must be such that
the ratio of input prices, P_L/P_K, equals the marginal rate of technical substitution. And since it will be recalled that the marginal rate of technical substitution of labor for capital is MP_L/MP_K, it follows that the optimal
combination of inputs is one where $MP_L/MP_K = P_L/P_K$. Or put differently,
the firm should choose an input combination where $MP_L/P_L = MP_K/P_K$.

In general, the firm will maximize output by distributing its expenditures
among various inputs in such a way that the marginal product of a dollar's
worth of any one input is equal to the marginal product of a dollar's worth of
any other input used. Thus the firm will choose an input combination such
that

$$\frac{MP_a}{P_a} = \frac{MP_b}{P_b} = \cdots = \frac{MP_m}{P_m}$$ [7.3]

Fig. **MAXIMIZATION OF OUTPUT FOR GIVEN COST** / *To maximize output for a*
7.2 *given cost, the firm should choose the input combination at point* P.

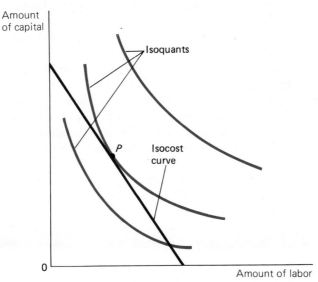

where MP_a, $MP_b, \cdots MP_m$ are the marginal product of inputs a, $b, \cdots m$, and P_a, $P_b, \cdots P_m$ are the prices of inputs a, $b, \cdots m$.

Returning to the case where labor and capital are the only two inputs, suppose that a firm decides to spend $200 on these inputs and that the price of labor is $10 per unit and the price of capital is $20 per unit. Table 7.1 shows the

Table **MARGINAL PRODUCTS OF CAPITAL AND LABOR**
7.1

Amount of input used		Marginal product*	
Labor	Capital	Labor	Capital
2	9	20	4
4	8	18	6
6	7	16	8
8	6	14	10
10	5	12	12
12	4	10	14
14	3	8	16
16	2	6	18
18	1	4	20

* The marginal products are defined for the interval between the indicated amount of labor or capital and one unit (capital) or two units (labor) less than this amount.

marginal product of each input when various combinations of inputs (the total cost of each combination being $200) are used. What combination is best? According to Equation 7.3, the marginal product of capital should be set at twice the marginal product of labor, since the price of a unit of capital is twice the price of a unit of labor. This occurs at 14 units of labor and 3 units of capital; thus this is the optimal combination.

To prove that this allocation of cost ($140 to labor and $60 to capital) is optimal, suppose that we shift $20 from labor to capital (with the result that $120 is devoted to labor and $80 to capital). Since the marginal product of the extra unit of capital that is gained is 14 units of output and the marginal product of the 2 units of labor given up is 2 times 8 units of product,[2] this change will reduce output by 2 units. Similarly, the transfer of $20 from capital to labor will reduce output.

A graph similar to Figure 7.2 can be used to determine the input combination that will minimize the cost of producing a given output. Moving along the isoquant corresponding to the stipulated output level, we must find that point on the isoquant that lies on the lowest isocost curve, for example, W in Figure 7.3. Input combinations on isocost curves like C_0 that lie below W are cheaper

Fig. 7.3   MINIMIZATION OF COST FOR GIVEN OUTPUT / *To minimize the cost of producing the amount of output corresponding to this isoquant, the firm should choose the input combination at point* W.

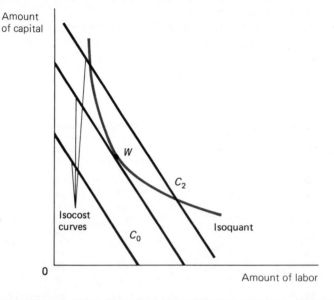

2. The marginal product of labor between 12 and 14 units of labor is 8 units of output per unit of labor. The marginal product of capital between 3 and 4 units of capital is 14 units of output per unit of capital.

than W, but they cannot produce the desired output. Input combinations on isocost curves like C_2 that lie above W will produce the desired output but at a higher cost than W. It is obvious that the optimal point, W, is a point where the isocost curve is tangent to the isoquant. Thus, to minimize the cost of producing a given output or to maximize the output from a given cost outlay, the firm must equate the marginal rate of technical substitution and the input-price ratio.

Note that this tells us how to solve the problem posed at the beginning of the chapter—the problem of the computer firm that decides for some reason to produce 100,000 computers next year and wants to know what combination of inputs to use. All that we need to do is to estimate the isoquant that pertains to an output by the firm of 100,000 computers per year. (If we are given the firm's production function, this is simple enough.) Then using data concerning the prices of the inputs, we can draw isocost curves, as in Figure 7.3, and determine the point, like W, where the isoquant is tangent to an isocost curve. This point represents the optimal combination of inputs.

THE PRODUCTION OF CORN: AN APPLICATION

To show how the theory presented in previous sections can be applied to help improve decision-making, this section describes how Earl Heady, a prominent agricultural economist, helped to determine the optimal combination of fertilizers in the production of Iowa corn.[3] He carried out experiments to determine the effect of various quantities of nitrogen (N) and phosphate (P) on corn yield per acre (Y), and found that

$$Y = -5.682 - .316N - .417P$$
$$+ 6.3512 \sqrt{N} + 8.5155 \sqrt{P} + .3410 \sqrt{PN} \qquad [7.4]$$

where P and N are measured in pounds per acre and Y is measured in bushels per acre. This equation is, of course, a production function: It shows the amount of output (Y) that can be derived from various amounts of the inputs (N and P). Various isoquants are shown in Figure 7.4.

What is the least-cost combination of nitrogen and phosphate fertilizers? This is an important question, both to farm managers and to the general public. Corn is a very large and valuable crop, and it is important that it be produced as economically as possible. To solve this problem, Heady used the result we derived in the previous section; he said that the optimal N and P must be such that the ratio of the marginal product of nitrogen to its price must equal the ratio of the marginal product of phosphate to its price. At the

---

3. See E. Heady, "An Econometric Investigation of the Technology of Agricultural Production Functions," *Econometrica*, April 1957.

Fig. 7.4   CORN ISOQUANTS FROM EQUATION 7.4 / *These estimates of actual isoquants for Iowa corn have been used to help farm managers and others.*

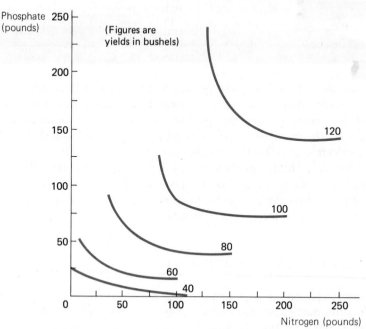

time of the experiment, the price of nitrogen was 18 cents per pound and the price of phosphate was 12 cents per pound. From Equation 7.4 it follows that

$$MP_N = -.316 + 3.1756 \ \sqrt{\frac{1}{N}} + .1705 \ \sqrt{\frac{P}{N}} \qquad [7.5]$$

$$MP_P = -.417 + 4.2578 \ \sqrt{\frac{1}{P}} + .1705 \ \sqrt{\frac{N}{P}} \qquad [7.6]$$

where MP_N is the marginal product of nitrogen and MP_P is the marginal product of phosphate.

Suppose that a farm manager is thinking of spending $30 per acre on fertilizers and that he wants to know how this expenditure should be allocated between nitrogen and phosphate. Following Equation 7.3, the optimal N and P must be such that

$$\frac{1}{18} \left\{ -.316 + 3.1756 \ \sqrt{\frac{1}{N}} + .1705 \ \sqrt{\frac{P}{N}} \right\}$$

$$= \frac{1}{12} \left\{ -.417 + 4.2578 \ \sqrt{\frac{1}{P}} + .1705 \ \sqrt{\frac{N}{P}} \right\},$$

and since he is going to spend $30,

$$18N + 12P = 3,000.$$

Solving these two equations simultaneously, Heady's results indicate that the optimal input combination is about 91 pounds of nitrogen per acre and about 113.5 pounds of phosphate per acre. Of course, the figure of $30 was chosen arbitrarily but regardless of the total expenditure that is chosen, this method will provide the optimal allocation.

THE NATURE OF COSTS

The costs incurred by a firm are often thought to include only the money outlays the firm must make to obtain the use of resources. However, the firm's money outlays are only part of the cost picture. In many cases, economists are interested in the social costs of production, the costs to society when its resources are employed to make a given commodity. Since economic resources are, by definition, limited, when resources are used to produce a certain product, less can be produced of some other product that can be made with those resources. For example, aluminum can be used to produce airplanes, cooking utensils, outdoor furniture, and cans, among other things. Thus, when aluminum is used in the making of airplanes, some value of alternative products is given up.

According to the economist's definition, the *cost* of producing a certain product is the value of the other products that the resources used in its production could have produced instead. For example, the cost of pro-

Alternative cost, or opportunity cost

ducing airplanes is the value of the goods and services that could be obtained from the manpower, equipment, and materials used currently in aircraft production. The costs of inputs to a firm are their values in their most valuable alternative uses. These costs, together with the firm's production function (which indicates how much of each input is required to produce various amounts of the product), determine the cost of producing the product. This is called the *alternative cost doctrine* or the *opportunity cost doctrine*.

It is important to note that the alternative cost of an input may not equal its *historical cost,* which is defined to be the amount the firm actually paid for it. For example, if some gullible soul buys the Brooklyn Bridge

Historical cost

for $1,000, this does not mean that its value, either to the buyer or to society, is $1,000. Similarly, if a firm invests $1 million in a piece of equipment that is quickly outmoded and is too inefficient relative to new equipment to be worth operating, its value is clearly not $1 million. Although conventional accounting rules place great emphasis on historical costs, the economist—and the sophisticated accountant and businessman—stress that historical costs should not be accepted uncritically.

Example 7.1

RICE MILLING IN INDONESIA

Indonesia recently had a study performed by a team of American engineers to determine what sorts of facilities it should adopt for the milling of rice. Four types of facilities were evaluated: (1) husker-polishers, (2) integrated rice mill, (3) bulk satellite, (4) bulk terminal. In its initial report, the team recommended that Indonesia devote the bulk of its funds to the last three types. Soon after this report was submitted, C. Peter Timmer, a Harvard economist, constructed an isoquant for milling rice (corresponding to the relevant quantity of rice to be produced), the inputs being labor and capital.

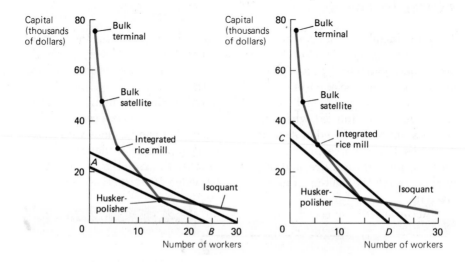

Of course, the alternative cost of an input depends on the use for which the cost is being determined. For example, the cost of a pound of aluminum to transportation uses is the amount the aluminum is worth in nontransportation uses; the cost of a pound of aluminum to the aircraft industry is the amount the aluminum is worth to other transportation industries as well as in nontransportation uses; and the cost of a pound of aluminum to Boeing is the amount the aluminum is worth to other aircraft manufacturers as well as in all nonaircraft uses. If all aluminum were homogeneous in all relevant respects, all three of these alternative costs would tend to be the same, because aluminum would be transferred from low-value uses to high-value uses until the yields in all uses were the same. However, if aluminum is not homogeneous, it is not necessary that these alternative costs be equal.

The alternative uses of a resource will often be different in the long run than in the short run. For example, in the short run, a plumber generally cannot enter fields requiring specialized skills unrelated to plumbing. But given

This isoquant is shown in both of the panels on p. 180. The point on the isoquant corresponding to each type of facilities is indicated. For example, the bulk terminal requires about $78,000 in capital inputs and about one worker to produce this amount of output.

(a) If the isocost curves were straight lines parallel to AB (as in the left-hand panel of the figure), what type of facility was optimal? (b) If the isocost curves were straight lines parallel to CD (as in the right-hand panel of the figure), what type of facility was optimal? (c) Timmer was not sure what the ratio of the price of labor to the price of capital would be, but he was reasonably sure that it would be between that underlying isocost curve AB and that underlying isocost curve CD. If this is true, can we be reasonably certain of what type of facility was optimal? (d) Was the set of isocost curves that was parallel to AB based on a higher or a lower ratio of the price of labor to the price of capital than that underlying isocost curve CD? (e) The engineering team recommended the use of bulk terminals and bulk satellites because they were necessary to *modernize* (their term) Indonesian rice marketing. Is this a persuasive argument?

SOLUTION

(a) Husker-polishers, since the point on the isoquant corresponding to this type of facility was on the lowest isocost curve (this curve being AB). (b) Husker-polishers, since the point on the isoquant corresponding to this type of facility was on the lowest isocost curve (this curve being CD). (c) Yes. Husker-polishers will be optimal. (d) It was based on a lower ratio. We know that this is true because the slope of AB is closer to zero than the slope of CD. (AB is closer to being horizontal than CD.) As pointed out previously, the slope of an isocost curve equals $- P_L \div P_K$. Thus, if AB's slope is closer to zero than CD's, it must be based on a lower ratio of P_L to P_K. (e) No. Policymakers generally are interested in minimizing the cost of producing a given output, not obtaining the most modern type of equipment (for its own sake).*

* See C. P. Timmer, J. Thomas, L. Wells, and D. Morawetz, *The Choice of Technology in Developing Countries* (Cambridge, Mass.: Harvard University Press, 1975).

time he or she can acquire other skills and become a programmer or a machinist. In the long run, alternatives tend to be greater and more varied than in the short run. Frequently, the alternative cost of an input is underestimated because people look only at its alternative uses in the short run.

The Enforcement of the Laws: An Application

Many of the concepts of microeconomics are useful for the formulation of public policy, as well as for business decision-making. To illustrate this point, let's consider how the concept of alternative costs can be used to shed light on the optimal enforcement of the laws. The question here is: What proportion of the people who commit crimes of a certain kind should society try to apprehend and convict? Your first reaction may be that they all should be caught and convicted; but, if so, it is easy to show that you ought to reconsider.

To answer this question properly, let's begin by looking at how the costs

Fig.
7.5 THE OPTIMAL LEVEL OF LAW ENFORCEMENT / *Taking account of both the costs to society from crime and the costs of apprehending and convicting criminals, the optimal value of the probability of apprehension and conviction of a criminal is 0.6.*

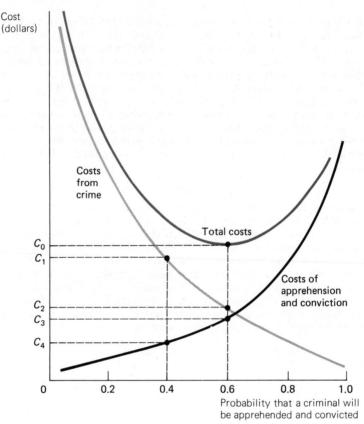

to society from crime depend on the level of law enforcement. Clearly, the damage to the victims will tend to increase as the laws are enforced more leniently because people will be encouraged to engage in criminal activities. In other words, as the chance of getting caught decreases, more people will be willing to take the chance, with the result that criminal activity will increase, and the damage to crime victims will increase. Thus, as shown in Figure 7.5, the costs to society from crime will increase if society permits a decrease in the probability that a criminal will be apprehended and convicted. For example, in Figure 7.5, these costs will be OC_1 if the probability is 0.4, but OC_2 if the probability is 0.6.

Looking only at the costs to society from crime, it appears that the optimal level of this probability is 1.00; that is, that the optimal policy is to catch and convict all criminals. But this ignores another important type of cost—the cost to society of apprehending and convicting criminals. After all, the services of policemen, detectives, prosecutors, judges, and wardens, as well as other resources used to apprehend and convict criminals, are not free. On the contrary, these resources all have alternative costs—since they can be used in other activities. For example, the policeman who tries to nail a purse snatcher could be working in industry or in some other part of government.[4]

How do the social costs of apprehending and convicting criminals depend on the level of law enforcement? Clearly, they go up as the laws are enforced more stringently because more people and nonhuman resources are required to ferret out and convict criminals. Thus, as shown in Figure 7.5, the costs to society of apprehending and convicting criminals will increase with increases in the probability that a criminal will be apprehended and convicted. For example, these costs will be OC_4 if the probability is 0.4, but OC_3 if it is 0.6.

Recognizing that both of these costs must be taken into account, it is clear that the optimal level of law enforcement is at the point where the sum of both costs is a minimum. Thus, under the circumstances shown in Figure 7.5, the optimal value of the probability of apprehension and conviction is 0.6. To increase it beyond 0.6 would not be socially desirable because the extra cost of apprehension and conviction would exceed the resulting reduction in the cost to society from crime. Among others, Gary Becker, George Stigler, and Simon Rottenberg have carried out a number of illuminating studies of the economics of crime and punishment. Of course, economics is only one of many disciplines that have a role to play here. But as illustrated by Figure 7.5, relatively simple microeconomic concepts can throw a great deal of light on many fundamental questions in this area.[5]

SOCIAL VERSUS PRIVATE COSTS AND EXPLICIT VERSUS IMPLICIT COSTS

The social costs of producing a given commodity do not always equal the private costs, which are defined to be the costs to the individual producer. For example, a steel plant may discharge waste products into a river located near the plant. To the plant, the cost of disposing of the wastes is simply the amount paid to pump the wastes to the river. However, if the river becomes polluted

---

4. Even the conscription of juries results in social costs, since the jurors could be performing other services. According to one estimate, this cost was over $200 million in 1962. See D. Martin, "The Economics of Jury Conscription," *Journal of Political Economy,* July 1972.

5. See G. Becker, "Crime and Punishment: An Economic Approach," *Journal of Political Economy,* March 1968; S. Rottenberg, "The Clandestine Distribution of Heroin, Its Discovery and Suppression," *Journal of Political Economy,* January 1968; and G. Stigler, "The Optimum Enforcement of Laws," *Journal of Political Economy,* May 1970.

Note that the kind of model utilized in this section will be discussed further and in more detail when we discuss environmental pollution in Chapter 14.

and if its recreational uses are destroyed and the water becomes unfit for drinking, additional costs are incurred by other people. Differences of this sort between private and social costs occur frequently; in Chapter 14 we shall see that such differences may call for remedial public-policy measures.

Turning to the private costs of production, it is important to recognize that there are two types of costs, both of which are generally important. The first type is explicit costs, which are the ordinary expenses that accountants include as the firm's expenses. They are the firm's payroll, payments for raw materials, and so on. The second type is implicit costs, which include the costs of resources owned and used by the firm's owner. The second type of costs is often omitted in calculating the costs of the firm.

Implicit costs arise because the alternative cost doctrine must be applied to the firm as well as to society as a whole. Consider Martin Moran, the proprietor of a firm who invests his own labor and capital in the business. These inputs should be valued at the amount he would have received if he had used these inputs in another way. For example, if he could have received a salary of $50,000 if he worked for someone else, and if he could have received dividends of $10,000 if he invested his money in someone else's firm, he should value his labor and his capital at these rates. It is important that these implicit costs be included in a firm's total costs. Their exclusion can result in serious error.

THE PROPER COMPARISON OF ALTERNATIVES

It is also important to note that, in making decisions, costs incurred in the past often are irrelevant. Suppose that you are going to make a trip and that you want to determine whether it will be cheaper to drive your car or to go by bus. What costs should be included if you drive your car? Since the only *extra* costs that will be incurred will be the gas and oil (and a certain amount of wear and tear on tires, engine, etc.), they are the only costs that should be included. Costs incurred in the past, such as the original price of the car, and costs that will be the same regardless of whether you make the trip by car or bus, such as your auto insurance, should not be included. On the other hand, if you are thinking about buying a car to make this and many other trips, these costs should be included.[6]

As an illustration, consider the case of Continental Air Lines, which deliberately runs extra flights that do no more than return a little more than their out-of-pocket costs. Suppose that Continental is faced with the decision of whether or not to run an extra flight between city X and city Y. Suppose that the fully allocated costs—the out-of-pocket costs plus a certain percent of overhead, depreciation, insurance, and other such costs—is $4,500 for the

6. This example is worked out in more detail in the paper by E. Grant and W. Ireson in E. Mansfield, *Managerial Economics and Operations Research* 5th ed. (New York: Norton, 1987).

flight. Suppose that the out-of-pocket costs—the actual sum that C
has to disburse to run the flight—are $2,000 and the expected re
the flight is $3,100. In a case of this sort, Continental will run the f₁₁
the correct decision, since the flight will add $1,100 to profit. It will increa
revenue by $3,100 and costs by $2,000. Overhead, depreciation, and insurance
would be the same whether the flight is run or not. In this decision, the correct
concept of cost is out-of-pocket, not fully allocated costs. Fully allocated costs
are irrelevant and misleading here. The importance of this way of looking at
costs cannot be overemphasized.[7]

COST FUNCTIONS IN THE SHORT RUN

At the beginning of this chapter, we showed how the profit-maximizing firm
will choose the combination of inputs to produce any given level of output.
(Recall that this input combination is the one that minimizes the firm's cost of
producing this level of output.) Given this optimal input combination, it is a
simple matter to determine the profit-maximizing firm's cost of producing any
level of output, since this cost is the sum of the amount of each input used by
the firm multiplied by the price of the input. Given the firm's cost of producing
each level of output, we can define the firm's *cost functions,* which play a very
important role in the theory of the firm. A firm's cost functions show various
relationships between its costs and its output rate. The firm's production
function and the prices it pays for inputs determine the firm's cost functions.
Since the production function can pertain to the short run or the long run, it
follows that the cost functions can also pertain to the short run or the long run.
In the next four sections, we discuss the short-run cost functions; then we turn
to the long-run cost functions.

The short run is a time period so brief that the firm cannot change the
quantity of some of its inputs. As the length of the time period increases, the
quantities of more and more inputs become variable. Any time interval between one where the quantity of no input is variable and one where the quantity of all inputs is variable could reasonably be called the short run. However,
as we pointed out in Chapter 6, we use a more restrictive definition: We say
that the short run is the time period so brief that the firm cannot vary the
quantities of plant and equipment. These are the firm's *fixed inputs,* and they
determine the firm's *scale of plant.* Inputs like labor, which the firm can vary in
quantity in the short run, are the firm's *variable inputs.*

---

7. See "Airline Takes the Marginal Route," *Business Week,* April 20, 1963.

   It is very important in applied work to recognize what are the relevant alternatives and
   their effects. In this connection, it may be worthwhile to cite the case of Maurice Chevalier,
   who, when asked how it felt to have reached his advanced age, is said to have replied, "Fine,
   relative to the alternative."

Table **FIXED, VARIABLE, AND TOTAL COSTS**
7.2

Units of output	Total fixed cost (dollars)	Total variable cost (dollars)	Total cost (dollars)
0	1,000	0	1,000
1	1,000	50	1,050
2	1,000	90	1,090
3	1,000	140	1,140
4	1,000	196	1,196
5	1,000	255	1,255
6	1,000	325	1,325
7	1,000	400	1,400
8	1,000	480	1,480
9	1,000	570	1,570
10	1,000	670	1,670
11	1,000	780	1,780
12	1,000	1,080	2,080

The amount of calendar time corresponding to the short run will be longer in some industries than in others. In industries where the amount of fixed inputs is small and relatively easily modified, the short run may be very short. For example, this may be the case in cotton textiles. On the other hand, in other industries the short run may be measured in years. For example, in the steel industry, it takes a long time to expand a firm's basic productive capacity.

Three concepts of total cost in the short run are important: total fixed cost, total variable cost, and total cost. *Total fixed costs* are the total obligations per period of time incurred by the firm for fixed inputs.

Total fixed costs

Since the quantity of the fixed inputs is fixed (by definition), the total fixed cost will be the same regardless of the firm's output rate. Examples of fixed costs are depreciation of buildings and equipment and property taxes. In Table 7.2, the firm's total fixed costs are assumed to be $1,000; the firm's total fixed cost function is shown graphically in Figure 7.6A.

Total variable costs are the total costs incurred by the firm for variable inputs. They increase as the firm's output rate increases, since larger output rates require larger variable input rates, which mean higher variable costs. For example, the larger the product of a cotton mill,

Total variable costs

the larger the quantity of cotton that must be used, and the higher the total cost of the cotton. A hypothetical total variable cost schedule is shown in Table 7.2; Figure 7.6B shows the corresponding total variable cost function. Up to a certain output rate (2 units of output), total variable costs are shown to increase at a decreasing rate; beyond that output

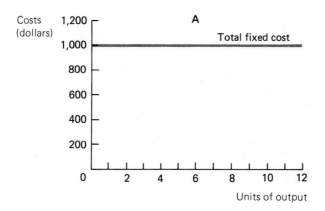

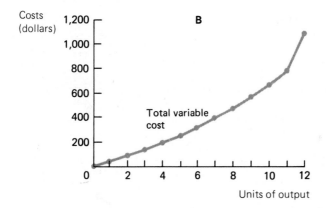

level, total variable costs increase at an increasing rate. *This latter characteristic of the total variable cost function follows from the law of diminishing marginal returns.* At small levels of output, increases in the variable inputs may
result in increases in their productivity, with the result that total variable costs
increase with output, but at a decreasing rate. More will be said on this score in
the next section.

     Finally, *total costs* are the sum of total fixed costs and total variable costs.
To derive the total cost column in Table 7.2, add total fixed cost and total variable cost at each output. The corresponding total cost function is
Total costs   shown in Figure 7.7. The total cost function and the total variable cost function have the same shape, since they differ by only
a constant amount. All of the total cost functions are shown together in Figure
7.8.

**Fig.
7.7**   TOTAL COSTS / *Because total variable costs increase with output, so do
total costs.*

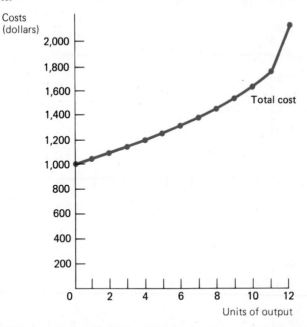

**Fig.
7.8**   FIXED, VARIABLE, AND TOTAL COSTS / *The total cost function and the total
variable cost function have the same shape, since they differ by only a
constant amount, which is total fixed cost.*

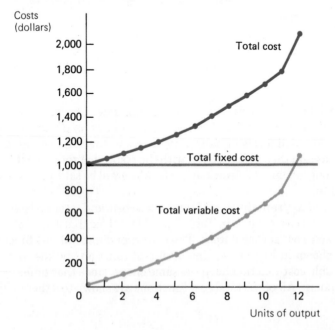

Table AVERAGE AND MARGINAL COSTS
7.3

Units of output	Average fixed cost (dollars)	Average variable cost (dollars)	Average total cost (dollars)	Marginal cost* (dollars)
1	1,000.00 (= 1,000 ÷ 1)	50.00 (= 50 ÷ 1)	1,050.00 (= 1,050 ÷ 1)	50 (= 1,050 − 1,000)
2	500.00 (= 1,000 ÷ 2)	45.00 (= 90 ÷ 2)	545.00 (= 1,090 ÷ 2)	40 (= 1,090 − 1,050)
3	333.33 (= 1,000 ÷ 3)	46.67 (= 140 ÷ 3)	380.00 (= 1,140 ÷ 3)	50 (= 1,140 − 1,090)
4	250.00 (= 1,000 ÷ 4)	49.00 (= 196 ÷ 4)	299.00 (= 1,196 ÷ 4)	56 (= 1,196 − 1,140)
5	200.00 (= 1,000 ÷ 5)	51.00 (= 255 ÷ 5)	251.00 (= 1,255 ÷ 5)	59 (= 1,255 − 1,196)
6	166.67 (= 1,000 ÷ 6)	54.17 (= 325 ÷ 6)	220.83 (= 1,325 ÷ 6)	70 (= 1,325 − 1,255)
7	142.86 (= 1,000 ÷ 7)	57.14 (= 400 ÷ 7)	200.00 (= 1,400 ÷ 7)	75 (= 1,400 − 1,325)
8	125.00 (= 1,000 ÷ 8)	60.00 (= 480 ÷ 8)	185.00 (= 1,480 ÷ 8)	80 (= 1,480 − 1,400)
9	111.11 (= 1,000 ÷ 9)	63.33 (= 570 ÷ 9)	174.44 (= 1,570 ÷ 9)	90 (= 1,570 − 1,480)
10	100.00 (= 1,000 ÷ 10)	67.00 (= 670 ÷ 10)	167.00 (= 1,670 ÷ 10)	100 (= 1,670 − 1,570)
11	90.91 (= 1,000 ÷ 11)	70.91 (= 780 ÷ 11)	161.82 (= 1,780 ÷ 11)	110 (= 1,780 − 1,670)
12	83.33 (= 1,000 ÷ 12)	90.00 (= 1,080 ÷ 12)	173.33 (= 2,080 ÷ 12)	300 (= 2,080 − 1,780)

* Note that marginal cost pertains to the interval between the indicated output level and one unit less than this output level.

Average and Marginal Costs

The total cost functions are of great importance, but it is possible to get a better understanding of the behavior of cost by looking at the average cost functions and the marginal cost function as well. There are three average cost functions, corresponding to the three total cost functions. The *average fixed cost* is total fixed cost divided by output. Table 7.3 and Figure 7.9 show the average fixed cost function in the example given in the previous section. The average fixed cost declines with increases in output; mathematically, the average fixed cost function is a rectangular hyperbola.

Average fixed cost

The *average variable cost* is total variable cost divided by output. For the example in the previous section, the average variable cost function is shown in Table 7.3 and Figure 7.10. At first, increases in output result in decreases in average variable cost, but beyond a point, they result in higher average variable cost. The results of the theory of production in Chapter 6 lead us to expect this curvature of the average variable cost function. If AVC is the average variable cost, TVC is the total variable cost, Q is the quantity of output, V is the quantity of the variable input, and P is the price of the variable input, it is obvious that

Average variable cost

$$AVC = \frac{TVC}{Q} = P\frac{V}{Q}.$$

Thus, since Q/V is the average product of the variable input (AVP),

$$AVC = P\frac{1}{AVP}. \qquad [7.7]$$

**Fig.
7.9**   AVERAGE FIXED COST / *Average fixed cost declines with increases in
output, since it equals total fixed cost divided by output.*

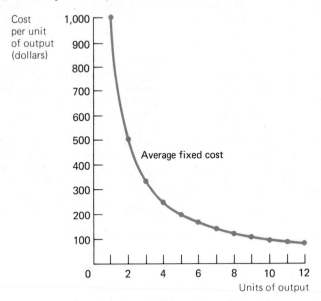

Consequently, since *AVP* generally rises and then falls with increases in output (see Figure 6.2, p. 148) and since *P* is constant, *AVC* must decrease and then rise with increases in output. The fact that the shape of the average vari-

**Fig.
7.10**   AVERAGE VARIABLE COST / *Because the average product of the variable
input generally rises and then falls with increases in output, average
variable cost decreases and then rises with increases in output.*

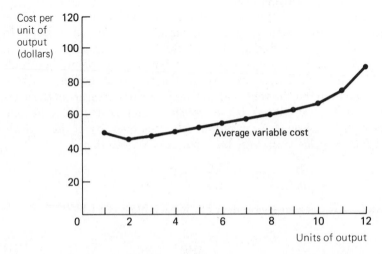

Fig.   AVERAGE TOTAL COST / *Average total cost equals average fixed cost plus*
7.11   *average variable cost. It falls and then rises with increases in output.*

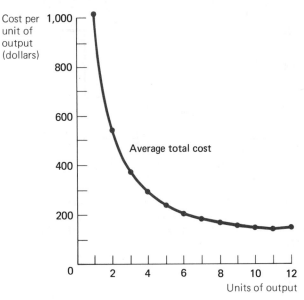

able cost curve follows in this way from the characteristics of the production
function is important and should be fully understood.

The *average total cost* is total cost divided by output. For the example in
the previous section, the average total cost function is shown in Table 7.3 and
Figure 7.11. The average total cost equals the sum of average
Average   fixed cost and average variable cost, which helps to explain the
total cost   shape of the average total cost function. For those levels of output where both average fixed cost and average variable cost decrease, average total cost must decrease too. However, average total cost
achieves its minimum after average variable cost, because the increases in
average variable cost are for a time more than offset by decreases in average
fixed cost. (All of the average cost curves are shown in Figure 7.13.)

The *marginal cost* is the addition to total cost resulting from the addition
of the last unit of output. That is, if $C(Q)$ is the total cost of producing Q units
of output, the marginal cost between Q and $(Q-1)$ units of out-
Marginal cost   put is $C(Q) - C(Q-1)$. For the example in the previous section,
the marginal cost function is shown in Table 7.3 and Figure 7.12.
At low output levels, marginal cost may decrease (as it does in Figure 7.12)
with increases in output, but after reaching a minimum, it increases with further increases in output. The reason for this behavior is found in the law of diminishing marginal returns. If ΔTVC is the change in total variable costs
resulting from a change in output of ΔQ and if ΔTFC is the change in total

Fig.
7.12

MARGINAL COST / *Because of the law of diminishing marginal returns, marginal cost, after reaching a minimum, rises with further increases in output.*

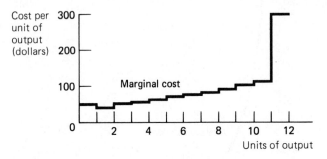

Fig.
7.13

AVERAGE AND MARGINAL COST CURVES / *Average total cost achieves its minimum at a higher output rate than average variable cost, because the increases in average variable cost are up to a point more than offset by decreases in average fixed cost.*

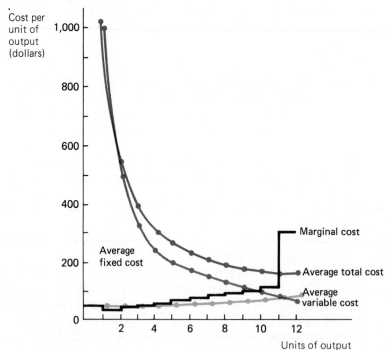

fixed costs resulting from a change in output of ΔQ, marginal cost equals

$$\frac{\Delta TVC + \Delta TFC}{\Delta Q}.$$

But since ΔTFC is zero (fixed costs being fixed), marginal cost equals

$$\frac{\Delta TVC}{\Delta Q}.$$

Moreover, if the price of the variable input is taken as given by the firm, $\Delta TVC = P(\Delta V)$, where ΔV is the change in the quantity of the variable input resulting from the increase of ΔQ in output. Thus the marginal cost equals

$$MC = P\frac{\Delta V}{\Delta Q} = P\frac{1}{MP} \qquad [7.8]$$

where MP is the marginal product of the variable input. Since MP generally increases, attains a maximum, and declines with increases in output (see Figure 6.2, p. 148), marginal cost normally decreases, attains a minimum, and then increases. The fact that the shape of the marginal cost function depends in this way on the law of diminishing marginal returns is important and should be fully understood.

Geometry of Average and Marginal Cost Functions

Given the total cost function, we frequently want to derive the average and marginal cost functions. The purpose of this section is to show how this can be done graphically. The procedures are quite similar to those used in Chapter 6 to derive average and marginal product curves. Figure 7.14 shows how the average cost function can be derived from the total cost function,

Fig. 7.14   CONSTRUCTION OF THE AVERAGE COST FUNCTION / *The average cost at output OQ$_0$ is OU, which is the slope of OR. The average cost at output OQ$_1$ is OW, which is the slope of OS.*

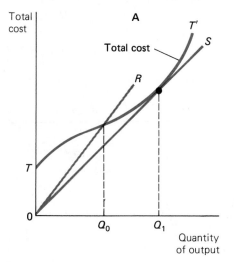
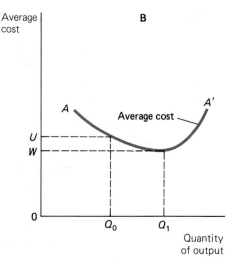

OTT', which is shown in panel A. (Note that, when we refer to average cost, we mean average *total* cost.) The average cost at any output level is given by the slope of the ray from the origin to the relevant point on the total cost function. For example, the average cost at an output OQ_0 is the slope of OR. We plot this slope, which equals OU, against OQ_0 in panel B. For each output, we plot in panel B the slope of the ray (from the origin to the relevant point on the total cost function) against the output, which results in AA', the average cost function. Beginning with a very small output, it is clear from Figure 7.14 that increases in output result in decreases in average cost, since the slope of such rays decreases with increases in output. However, it is also clear that average cost reaches a minimum at OQ_1, since beyond OQ_1 the slope of these rays increases with increases in output.

Figure 7.15 illustrates the derivation of the marginal cost function. As output increases from OQ_2 to OQ_3, total cost (OTT' in panel A) increases from OC_2 to OC_3. Thus the extra cost per unit of output is

$$\frac{OC_3 - OC_2}{OQ_3 - OQ_2} = \frac{BA}{CB}.$$

If we increase OQ_2 until the distance between OQ_2 and OQ_3 is extremely small, the slope of the tangent (UU') at A becomes a very good estimate of BA/CB. In the limit, for changes in output in a very small neighborhood around OQ_3, the

Fig. 7.15   CONSTRUCTION OF THE MARGINAL COST FUNCTION / *The marginal cost at output* OQ$_3$ *is the slope of the tangent,* UU'. *When average cost is a minimum (at output* OQ$_1$), *marginal cost equals average cost (=* OW).

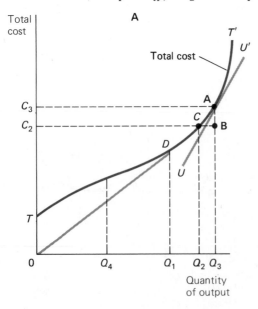

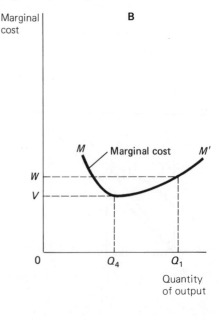

slope of the tangent to the total cost function at OQ_3 is marginal cost. In panel B, MM' shows the slope of the tangent to the total cost curve at each output; this is the marginal cost function. It is evident from Figure 7.15 that, at small output rates, marginal cost decreases with increases in output, since the slope of the tangent to the total cost function decreases with increases in output. However, it is also evident that marginal cost reaches a minimum, OV, at OQ_4

Example 7.2

SHORT-RUN COSTS OF A BOEING 747

The Boeing 747 is an airplane that carries many of the world's travelers. According to data provided by Boeing to a Senate committee in 1975, the cost (in cents) per passenger-mile of operating such an airplane on a flight of 1,200 and 2,500 miles with 250, 300, and 350 passengers aboard was as follows:

Number of passengers	*Number of miles*	
	1,200	*2,500*
	(cents per passenger-mile)	
250	4.3	3.4
300	3.8	3.0
350	3.5	2.7

(a) If the number of passengers is between 250 and 300, what is the marginal cost of carrying an extra passenger on a 1,200 mile flight? (b) If the number of passengers is 300 and if the flight is between 1,200 and 2,500 miles, what is the marginal cost of flying an additional mile? (c) In 1975, the economy fare for a 2,500-mile flight was $156.60. If a Boeing 747 carried 300 passengers on such a flight, would it cover its operating costs? (d) Do you think that the above table can be applied to 1988? Why or why not?

SOLUTION

(a) If 250 passengers were carried, total operating costs were $1,200 \times 250 \times 4.3$ cents, or $12,900. If 300 passengers were carried, total operating costs were $1,200 \times 300 \times 3.8$ cents, or $13,680. Thus, since 50 extra passengers cost an extra $13,680 - $12,900, or $780, one extra passenger costs (approximately) an extra $780 \div 50$, or $15.60. (b) For a 1,200-mile flight, total operating costs were $1,200 \times 300 \times 3.8$ cents, or $13,680. For a 2,500-mile flight, total operating costs were $2,500 \times 300 \times 3.0$ cents, or $22,500. Since 1,300 extra miles cost an extra $22,500 - $13,680, or $8,820, one extra mile cost (approximately) an extra $8,820 \div 1,300$, or $6.78. (c) Yes. The total operating cost per passenger equaled $2,500 \times 3.0$ cents, or $75, which is less than $156.60. (d) No. Input prices are different in 1988 than in 1975. For example, fuel prices increased greatly in the late 1970s. Also, wage rates of airline personnel are different in 1988 than in 1975.*

* See S. Breyer, *Regulation and Its Reform* (Cambridge, Mass.: Harvard University Press, 1982); and U.S. Senate Committee on the Judiciary, *Civil Aeronautics Board Practices and Procedures,* 1975. Note that these data pertain only to an airplane's operating costs.

and increases thereafter, since the slope of the tangent to the total cost function is a minimum at OQ_4 and increases thereafter.

It should also be noted that when average cost is a minimum (at output OQ_1), the slope of the ray OD equals the slope of the tangent to the total cost function, since OD *is* the tangent to the total cost function. Thus, since average cost equals the slope of the ray OD and marginal cost equals the slope of the tangent to the total cost function, it follows that *average cost must equal marginal cost at the output level where average cost is a minimum.* In Figures 7.14 and 7.15, both equal OW.

The Break-Even Chart: An Application

A standard tool used by economists to help solve certain kinds of managerial problems is the break-even chart, which is an important practical application of cost functions. Typically, a break-even chart assumes that the firm's average variable costs are constant in the relevant output range. Thus the firm's total cost function is assumed to be a straight line, as shown in Figure 7.16. In Figure 7.16, we assume that the firm's fixed costs are $300 per month and that its variable costs are $1 per unit of output per month. Since average variable cost is constant, the extra cost of an extra unit—marginal cost—must be constant, too, and equal to average variable cost.

To construct a break-even chart, the firm's total revenue curve must be plotted on the same chart with its total cost function. It is generally assumed that the price the firm receives for its product will not be affected by the amount it sells, with the result that total revenue is proportional to output and the total revenue curve is a straight line through the origin. Figure 7.16 shows the total revenue curve, assuming that the price of the product will be $1.50 per unit. The break-even chart, which combines the total cost function and the total revenue curve, shows the monthly profit or loss resulting from each sales level. For example, Figure 7.16 shows that, if the firm sells 300 units per month, it will make a loss of $150 per month. The chart also shows the break-even point, the output level that must be reached if the firm is to avoid losses; in Figure 7.16, the break-even point is 600 units of output per month.

In recent years, break-even charts have been used extensively by company executives, government agencies, and other groups. Under the proper circumstances, break-even charts can produce useful projections of the effect of the output rate on costs, receipts, and profits. For example, a firm may use a break-even chart to determine the effect of a projected decline in sales on profits. Or it may use it to determine how many units of a particular product it must sell in order to break even. However, break-even charts must be used with caution, since the assumptions underlying them may be inappropriate. If the product price is highly variable or costs are difficult to predict, the estimated total cost function and the estimated total revenue curve may be subject to considerable error.

Fig. **BREAK-EVEN CHART** / *The break-even point, the output level that must be*
7.16 *reached if the firm is to avoid losses, is 600 units of output per month.*

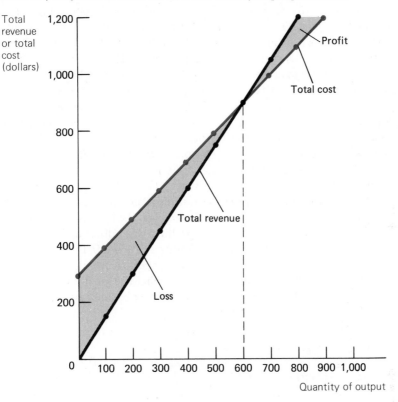

Although the total cost function generally is assumed to be a straight line in break-even charts, this assumption can easily be dropped and a curvilinear total cost function can be used instead. However, for fairly small changes in output, a linear approximation is probably good enough in many cases. As we shall see (later in this chapter), empirical studies suggest that the total cost function is often close to linear, as long as the firm is not operating at capacity.[8]

COST FUNCTIONS IN THE LONG RUN

In the long run, the firm can build any scale or type of plant that it wants. All inputs are variable; the firm can alter the amounts of land, buildings, equip-

---

8. Note, however, that the results of some of these studies have been subjected to criticism of various sorts. See p. 207.

ment, and other inputs per period of time. There are no fixed cost functions (total or average) in the long run, since no inputs are fixed. A useful way to look at the long run is to consider it a *planning horizon.* While operating in the short run, the firm must continually be planning ahead and deciding its strategy in the long run. Its decisions concerning the long run determine the sort of short-run position the firm will occupy in the future. For example, before a firm makes the decision to add a new type of product to its line, the firm is in a long-run situation, since it can choose among a wide variety of types and sizes of equipment to produce the new product. But once the investment is made, the firm is confronted with a short-run situation, since the type and size of equipment is, to a considerable extent, frozen.

Suppose that it is possible for a firm to construct only three alternative scales of plant; the short-run average cost function for each scale of plant is represented by $S_1 S_1'$, $S_2 S_2'$, and $S_3 S_3'$, in Figure 7.17. In the long run, the firm can build (or convert to) any one of these possible scales of plant. Which scale is most profitable? Obviously, the answer depends on the long-run output rate to be produced, since the firm will want to produce this output at a minimum average cost. For example, if the anticipated output rate is OQ, the firm should choose the smallest plant, since it will produce OQ units of output per period of time at a cost per unit, OC, which is smaller than what the medium-sized plant (its cost per unit being OB) or the large plant (its cost per unit being OA) can

Fig. 7.17   SHORT-RUN AVERAGE COST FUNCTIONS FOR VARIOUS SCALES OF PLANT / *The long-run average cost function is the solid portion of the short-run average cost functions,* $S_1 DES_3'$.

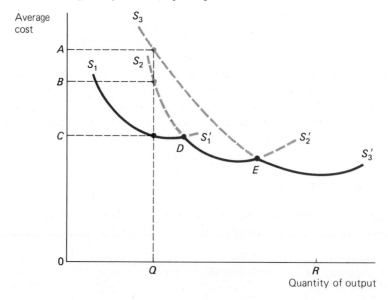

Fig.
7.18 LONG-RUN AVERAGE COST FUNCTION / *The long-run average cost function, which shows the minimum long-run cost per unit of producing each output level, is the envelope of the short-run functions.*

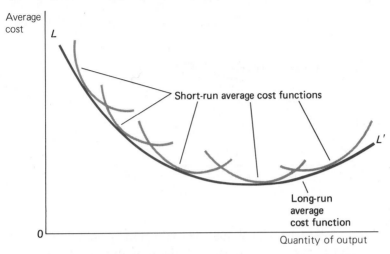

do. However, if the anticipated output rate is *OR*, the firm should choose the largest plant.

The *long-run average cost function* shows the minimum cost per unit of producing each output level when any desired scale of plant can be built. In
Long-run average cost function Figure 7.17, the long-run average cost function is the solid portion of the short-run average cost functions, S_1DES_3'. The broken-line segments of the short-run functions are not included because they are not the lowest average costs, as is evident from the figure.

At this point, we must abandon the simplifying assumption that there are only three alternative scales of plant. In fact, there are a great many alternative scales, with the result that the firm is confronted with a host of short-run average cost functions, as shown in Figure 7.18. The minimum cost per unit of producing each output level is given by the long-run average cost function, *LL'*. The long-run average cost function is tangent to each of the short-run average cost functions at the output where the plant corresponding to the short-run average cost function is optimal. Mathematically, the long-run average cost function is the envelope of the short-run functions.

Note, however, that the long-run average cost function (*LL'*) is not tangent to the short-run functions at their minimum points, unless the *LL'* curve is horizontal. When the *LL'* curve is decreasing, it is tangent to the short-run functions to the left of their minimum points. When the *LL'* curve is increasing, it is tangent to the short-run functions to the right of their minimum points. A famous mistake was made by the well-known Princeton economist,

Fig.
7.19   LONG-RUN TOTAL COST FUNCTION / *The long-run total cost of a given
output equals the long-run average cost (given in Figure 7.18) times output.*

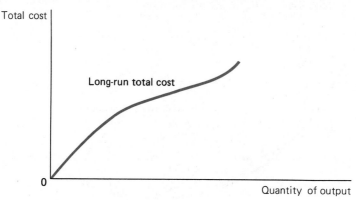

Jacob Viner, in his pathbreaking 1931 article regarding cost functions. He
tried to get the *LL'* curve to be tangent to the short-run functions at their
minimum points. As noted above, this in general cannot be done.

In terms of least-cost input combinations, the long-run average cost
function can be interpreted in the following way: For any specified output, the
total cost—and the average cost—is the smallest in the long run when all
inputs (not just those that were variable in the short run) are combined in such
a way that the marginal product of a dollar's worth of one input equals the
marginal product of a dollar's worth of any other input used. Only if the firm
uses the least-cost combination of all inputs to produce each level of output
can the levels of cost shown by the long-run average cost function be reached.

Given the long-run average cost of producing a given output, it is easy to
derive the long-run total cost of the output, since the latter is simply the product of long-run average cost and output. Figure 7.19 shows the
relationship between long-run total cost and output; this relationship is called the *long-run total cost function*. Given the long-
run total cost function, it is easy to derive the *long-run marginal
cost function*, which shows the relationship between output and
the cost resulting from the production of the last unit of output, if
the firm has plenty of time to make the optimal changes in the
quantities of all inputs used. Of course, long-run marginal cost
must be less than long-run average cost when the latter is decreasing, equal to
long-run average cost when the latter is a minimum, and greater than long-run
average cost when the latter is increasing. It can also be shown that, when the
firm has built the optimal scale of plant for producing a given level of output,
long-run marginal cost and short-run marginal cost will be equal at that output.

**Long-run total
cost function**

**Long-run
marginal cost
function**

Fig. THE EXPANSION PATH / *The expansion path indicates how, as output*
7.20 *changes from 50 to 100 to 150 units (but input prices remain fixed), the*
quantity that is used of each input changes.

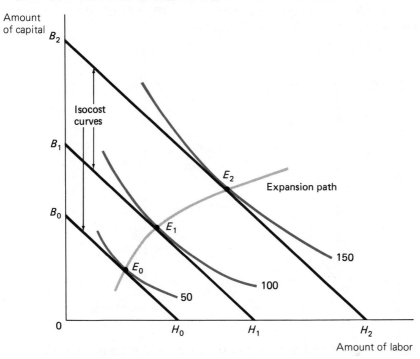

The Expansion Path and Long-Run Total Costs

At this point, it is also worthwhile to show how a firm's long-run total cost function can be derived from its isoquants. Figure 7.20 shows a firm's isoquants corresponding to output levels of 50, 100, and 150. The least-cost combination of inputs to produce 50 units of output is represented by point E_0, where the isoquant is tangent to the relevant isocost curve. Similarly, the least-cost combination of inputs to produce 100 units of output is represented by point E_1, and the least-cost combination of inputs to produce 150 units of output is represented by point E_2. These tangency points (E_0, E_1, *Expansion path* E_2), as well as those representing the least-cost combinations of inputs to produce other quantities of output, lie along a curve known as the *expansion path*, shown in Figure 7.20. The expansion path indicates how, as the output rate changes (but input prices remain fixed), the quantity of each input changes.

If capital and labor are the only inputs, it is a simple matter to derive the

Fig.
7.21   DERIVATION OF LONG-RUN TOTAL COST FUNCTION / *The total cost of input combinations* E_0, E_1, *and* E_2 *in Figure 7.20 is* $OH_0 \times P_L$, $OH_1 \times P_L$, *and* $OH_2 \times P_L$, *respectively. Thus the minimum cost of producing 50 units is* $OH_0 \times P_L$, *the minimum cost of producing 100 units is* $OH_1 \times P_L$, *and the minimum cost of producing 150 units is* $OH_2 \times P_L$.

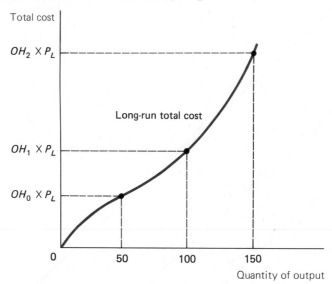

long-run total cost function from the expansion path. Each point on the expansion path represents the least-cost combination of inputs to produce a certain output in the long run (since neither input is fixed). Consider point E_0, which corresponds to an output of 50 units. The total cost of the combination of inputs represented by E_0 is OH_0 times P_L, the price of a unit of labor. Why? Because point E_0 is on isocost curve B_0H_0, which means that the input combination at point E_0 costs the same as that at point H_0. And the cost of the input combination at point H_0 equals OH_0 times P_L.

Consequently, to obtain one point on the long-run total cost function, we plot OH_0 times P_L against 50 units of output, as shown in Figure 7.21. To obtain a second such point, consider point E_1 on the expansion path, which corresponds to an output of 100 units. Using the same reasoning as in the previous paragraph, the total cost of the combination of inputs represented by E_1 is OH_1 times P_L. Thus the minimum cost of producing 100 units of output in the long run is OH_1 times P_L, which means that the point on the long-run total cost function corresponding to an output of 100 units is OH_1 times P_L. Consequently, OH_1 times P_L is plotted against 100 units of output in Figure 7.21. Repeating this procedure for each of a number of different output levels, we obtain the long-run total cost function shown in Figure 7.21.

The Shape of the Long-Run Average Cost Function

The long-run average cost function in Figure 7.18 is drawn with much the same sort of shape as the short-run average cost function. Both decrease with increases in output up to a certain point, reach a minimum, and increase with further increases in output. However, the factors responsible for this shape are not the same in the two cases. In the case of the short-run average cost function, the theory of diminishing marginal returns is operating behind the scenes. The short-run average cost function turns upward because decreases in average fixed costs are eventually counterbalanced by increases in average variable costs due to decreases in the average product of the variable input. However, the law of diminishing marginal returns is not responsible for the shape of the long-run average cost function, since there are no fixed inputs in the long run.

The shape of the long-run average cost function is determined in part by economies and diseconomies of scale. As pointed out in Chapter 6, increases in scale often result in important economies, at least up to some point. Because larger scale permits the introduction of different kinds of techniques, because larger productive units are more efficient, and because larger plants permit greater specialization and division of labor, the long-run average cost function declines, up to some point, with increases in output. Of course, the range of output over which the average cost function declines varies from industry to industry. (Moreover, in a given industry, this range varies over a period of time, particularly in response to changes in technology.)

Why does the long-run average cost function turn upward? The answer that is generally given is that, beyond a point, increases in scale result in inefficiencies in management. More and more responsibility and power must be given by top management to lower-level employees. Coordination becomes more difficult, red tape increases, and flexibility is reduced. It is not easy to determine just when these diseconomies of scale begin to offset the economies of scale already cited. In many industries, the available empirical studies seem to indicate that after an initial decline, long-run average cost is constant over a considerable range of output. The situation is like that shown in Figure 7.22. Eventually, however, one would expect the long-run average cost function to rise.

It is important to note that the shape of the long-run average cost function is of great significance from the viewpoint of public policy. If the long-run average cost function decreases markedly up to a level of output that corresponds to all, or practically all, that the market demands of the commodity, it makes little sense to force competition in this industry, since costs would be higher if the output were divided among a number of firms than if it were produced by only one firm. In this case, the industry is a natural monopoly, and government agencies like the Federal Energy Regulatory Commission and the

Fig. Apparent Shape of Many Long-Run Average Cost Functions / *In*
7.22 *many industries, after an initial decline, long-run average cost seems to be*
constant over a considerable range of output.

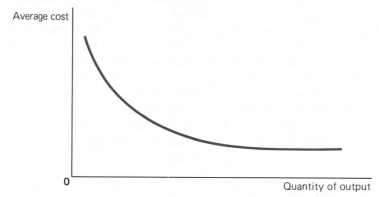

Federal Communications Commission, rather than competition, often are relied on to regulate the industry's performance. (This will be discussed further
in Chapter 9.)

MEASUREMENT OF COST FUNCTIONS

Economists have made a great many studies to estimate cost functions—or
cost curves, as they are often called—in particular firms and industries. Typically, these studies have been based on the statistical analysis of historical
data regarding cost and output. Some studies have relied primarily on time-
series data, in which the output level of a firm is related to its costs. For example, Figure 7.23 plots the output level of a hypothetical firm against its costs in
various years in the past. Other studies have relied primarily on cross-section
data, in which the output levels of various firms at a given point in time are
related to their costs. For example, Figure 7.24 plots the 1988 output of eight
firms in a given industry against their 1988 costs. Using data of this sort, as
well as engineering data, economists have attempted to estimate the relationship between cost and output.

There are a number of important difficulties in estimating cost functions
in this way. First, accounting data, which are generally the only cost data
available, suffer from a number of deficiencies, when used for this purpose.
The time period used for accounting purposes generally is longer than the
economist's short run. The depreciation of an asset over a period of time is
determined largely by the tax laws rather than economic criteria. Many inputs
are valued at historical, rather than alternative, cost. Moreover, accountants
often use arbitrary allocations of overhead and joint costs.

Second, engineering data also suffer from important limitations. Engi-

Fig.   RELATIONSHIP BETWEEN TOTAL COST AND OUTPUT: TIME SERIES FOR A
7.23   GIVEN FIRM / *Each year's level of total cost is plotted against the firm's
output level during the year. Ordinarily, such a relationship is only a very
crude approximation to the firm's total cost function.*

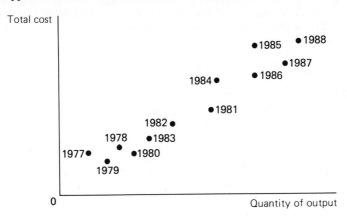

Fig.   RELATIONSHIP BETWEEN TOTAL COST AND OUTPUT: CROSS SECTION / *Each
7.24   firm's level of cost during 1988 is plotted against the firm's output level
during that year. Such a relationship generally is only a very rough
approximation to the relevant cost function.*

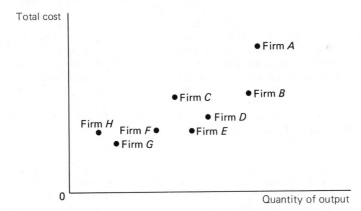

neering data, like cost accounting data, relate to processes within the firm.
One difficulty in using them to estimate cost functions for an entire firm is
that the costs of various processes may affect one another and may not be ad-
ditive. Also, there is the inevitable arbitrariness involved in allocating costs
that are jointly attached to the production of more than one commodity in
multiproduct firms.

Third, an important criticism of cross-section studies is that they are
subject to the so-called regression fallacy. It is often argued that the output

Example 7.3

LONG-RUN COSTS AT IBM

The IBM Corporation is the leading manufacturer of electronic computers in the world. Based on its internal memoranda, IBM's long-run total cost of producing various quantities of its Pisces (370/168) machines was as shown below.

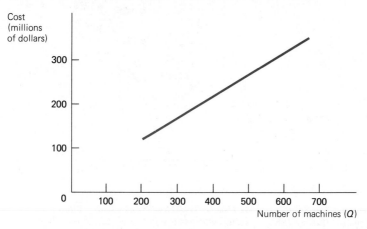

For output levels in the relevant range, the equation for this total cost function is
$$C = 28{,}303{,}800 + 460{,}800Q$$
where C is total cost (in dollars) and Q is the number of machines.

    (a) If the entire market for this type of machine is 1,000 machines, and if all firms have the same long-run total cost function, to what extent would a firm with 50 percent of the market have a cost advantage over a firm with 20 percent of the market? (b) What is the long-run marginal cost of producing such a machine? Does marginal cost depend on output? (c) Do there appear to be economies of scale? (d) The data presented above are forecasts of costs based largely on engineering data, not an historical record of actual costs. Why would IBM make such forecasts? What factors might result in errors in these forecasts?

SOLUTION

    (a) If Q equals 500, average cost equals $[28{,}303{,}800 + 460{,}800(500)] \div 500 = \$517{,}408$. If Q equals 200, average cost equals $[28{,}303{,}800 + 460{,}800(200)] \div 200 = \$602{,}319$. Thus, a firm with 50 percent of the market has an average cost that is about 14 percent below that of a firm with 20 percent of the market. (b) \$460,800. (It is clear from the above equation that, if Q increases by 1, C increases by \$460,800). In the output range covered by the data (about 200 to 700 units, according to the graph above), marginal cost does not vary. (c) Yes. Since long-run average cost equals $460{,}800 + 28{,}303{,}800/Q$, long-run average cost declines with increases in Q. (d) Since profits equal revenues minus costs, such forecasts are very useful in estimating the profits (or losses) that will accrue to the firm if it sells various quantities of output. However, such forecasts can be in error if input prices (such as wage rates) differ from the assumptions on which the forecasts are based, or if the productivity of inputs differs from what is expected.[*]

---

[*] See G. Brock, *The U.S. Computer Industry* (Cambridge, Mass.: Ballinger, 1975); and IBM, "Poughkeepsie SDD Cost Estimating," *Telex v. IBM,* Plaintiff's Exhibit 213.

produced and sold by the firm is only partly under the control of the firm and that actual and expected output will differ. When firms are classified by actual output, firms with very high output levels are likely to be producing at an unusually high level, and firms with very low output levels are likely to be producing at an unusually low level. Since firms producing at an unusually high level of output are likely to be producing at lower unit costs than firms producing at an unusually low level of output, cross-section studies are likely to be biased, the observed cost of producing various output levels being different from the minimum cost of producing these output levels.

Despite these and other problems, estimates of cost functions have proved of considerable use, both to economists interested in promoting better managerial decisions and to economists interested in testing and extending economic theory. From the latter point of view, one of the most interesting conclusions of the empirical studies is that the long-run average cost function in most industries seems to be L-shaped (as in Figure 7.22), not U-shaped. That is, there is no evidence that it turns upward, rather than remaining horizontal, at high output levels (in the range of observed data). A summary of the results of some of the major studies carried out in recent years is presented in Tables 7.4 and 7.5. The reader should study these tables carefully, since they summarize a great many interesting results.

Another interesting conclusion of the empirical studies is that marginal cost in the short run tends to be constant in the relevant output range. As shown in Tables 7.4 and 7.5, this is a frequent result of these studies. This result seems to be at variance with the theory presented earlier (pp. 191–93), which says that marginal cost curves should be U-shaped. To explain this variance, critics have asserted that the empirical studies are biased toward constant marginal cost by the nature of accounting data and the statistical methods used. Another reason why marginal costs appear constant is that the data used in these studies often do not cover periods when the firm was operating at the peak of its capacity. Although marginal costs may well be relatively constant over a wide range, it is inconceivable that they do not eventually increase with increases in output.

An illustration of the sort of empirical work that has been done in this area is Joel Dean's pioneering study of the short-run cost functions in a hosiery mill. This study, published in 1941, was one of the first attempts by an economist to measure a firm's cost function. Dean found that the total cost function was linear within the range of observation, marginal cost being constant. His estimate of the total cost function is shown in Figure 7.25.[9]

Another illustration of studies of this kind is Martin Feldstein's study of cost functions in British hospitals, Among other things, he found that the long-run average cost function "is a shallow U-shaped curve with a minimum

9. See J. Dean, "Statistical Cost Functions of a Hosiery Mill," *Studies in Business Administration* 14 (no. 3), University of Chicago Press, 1941. See also A. A. Walters, "Production and Cost Functions," *Econometrica*, January 1963.

Table
7.4
RESULTS OF STUDIES OF COST FUNCTIONS: GENERAL INDUSTRY STUDIES*

Author	Industry	Type	Period	Result
Bain	Manufacturing	Q	L	Small economies of scale of multiplant firms.
Eiteman and Guthrie	Manufacturing	Q	S	MC below AC at all outputs below "capacity."
Hall and Hitch	Manufacturing	Q	S	Majority have MC decreasing.
Lester	Manufacturing	Q	S	Decreasing average variable cost to capacity.
Moore	Manufacturing	E	L	Economies of scale generally.
T.N.E.C. Monograph 13	Various industries	CS	L	Small- or medium-size plants usually have lowest costs. Blair draws different conclusions.
Alpert	Metal	E	L	Economies of scale to 80,000 pounds/month; then constant returns.
Johnston	Multiple product	TS	S	"Direct" cost is linearly related to output. MC is constant.
Dean	Leather belts	TS	S	Significantly increasing MC rejected by Dean.
Dean	Hosiery	TS	S	MC constant. SRAC "failed to rise."
Dean and James	Shoe stores	CS	L	LRAC is U-shaped (interpreted as not due to diseconomies of scale).
Holton	Retailing (Puerto Rico)	E	L	LRAC is L-shaped. But Holton argues that inputs of management may be undervalued at high outputs.
Ezekiel and Wylie	Steel	TS	S	MC declining, but large sampling errors.
Yntema	Steel	TS	S	MC constant.
Ehrke	Cement	TS	S	Ehrke interprets as constant MC. Apel argues that MC is increasing.
Nordin	Light plant	TS	S	MC is increasing.
Gupta	29 manufacturing industries (India)	CS	L	LRAC is L-shaped in 18 industries, U-shaped in 5, and linear in the rest.
Jansson and Schneerson	Shipping	CS	L	Economies of scale in hauling, but not in handling.
Norman	Cement	CS,E	L	Substantial economies of scale.

* The following abbreviations are used: MC = marginal cost, AC = average cost, SRAC = short-run average cost, LRAC = long-run average cost, S = short run, and L = long run, Q = questionnaire, E = engineering data, CS = cross section, and TS = time series.

SOURCE: A. A. Walters, "Production and Cost Functions," *Econometrica,* January 1963; V. Gupta, "Cost Functions, Concentration, and Barriers to Entry in 29 Manufacturing Industries in India," *Journal of Industrial Economics,* 1968; J. Jansson and D. Schneerson, "Economies of Scale of General Cargo Ships," *Review of Economics and Statistics,* May 1978; and G. Norman, "Economies of Scale in the Cement Industry," *Journal of Industrial Economics,* June 1979.

Table RESULTS OF STUDIES OF COST FUNCTIONS: PUBLIC UTILITIES
7.5

Author	Industry	Type*	Result†
Lomax	Gas (U.K.)	CS	LRAC of production declines (no analysis of distribution)
Gribbin	Gas (U.K.)	CS	LRAC of production declines (no analysis of distribution)
Lomax	Electricity (U.K.)	CS	LRAC of production declines (no analysis of distribution)
Johnston	Electricity (U.K.)	CS	LRAC of production declines (no analysis of distribution)
Johnston	Electricity (U.K.)	TS	SRAC falls, then flattens tending toward constant MC up to capacity.
McNulty	Electricity (U.S.A.)	CS	Average costs of administration are constant.
Nerlove	Electricity (U.S.A.)	CS	LRAC excluding transmission costs declines, then shows signs of increasing.
Johnston	Coal (U.K.)	CS	Wide dispersion of costs per ton.
Johnston	Road passenger transport (U.K.)	CS	LRAC either falling or constant.
Johnston	Life assurance	CS	LRAC declines.
Dhrymes and Kurz	Electricity (U.S.A.)	CS, TS	Substantial economies of scale.
Eads, Nerlove, and Raduchel	Airlines (U.S.A.)	CS, TS	No evidence of substantial economies of scale.
Knapp	Sewage purification (U.K.)	CS	Significant economies of scale up to 10 million gallons daily.
Stevens	Refuse collection (U.S.A.)	CS	Considerable economies of scale in cities up to 20,000 population.
Railways			
Borts	U.S.A.	CS	LRAC increasing in East, decreasing in South and West.
Broster	U.K.	TS	Operating cost per unit of output falls.
Mansfield and Wein	U.S.A.	TS	MC is constant.
Griliches	U.S.A.	CS	No significant economies of scale to an indiscriminate expansion of traffic.

* CS means cross-section; TS means time series.

† LRAC means long-run average cost; SRAC means short-run average cost; MC means marginal cost.

SOURCE: A. A. Walters, "Production and Cost Functions," *Econometrica,* January 1963; P. Dhrymes and M. Kurz, "Technology and Scale in Electricity Generation," *Econometrica,* July 1964; G. Eads, M. Nerlove, and W. Raduchel, "A Long-Run Cost Function for the Local Service Airline Industry," *Review of Economics and Statistics,* August 1969; Z. Griliches, "Railroad Cost Analysis," *Bell Journal of Economics and Management Science,* 1972; M. Knapp, "Economies of Scale in Sewage Purification and Disposal," *Journal of Industrial Economics,* December 1978; and B. Stevens, "Scale, Market Structure, and the Cost of Refuse Collection," *Review of Economics and Statistics,* August 1978.

Fig. TOTAL COST CURVE: HOSIERY MILL (MONTHLY COSTS) / *According to a*
7.25 *very early, classic study, the total cost function for a hosiery mill was as*
shown here.

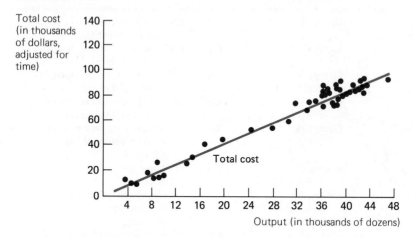

Output (in thousands of dozens)

at the current average size (310 beds), [which indicates] . . . that the medium
size hospital of 300 to 500 beds is at least as efficient at providing general ward
care as are larger hospitals."[10] Figure 7.26 shows the average cost function he
estimated. His study illustrates the fact that microeconomic concepts are use-

Fig. LONG-RUN AVERAGE COST FUNCTION: BRITISH HOSPITALS / *Based on this*
7.26 *estimated long-run cost function, hospitals of about 300 to 500 beds have*
lower long-run average costs than larger hospitals.

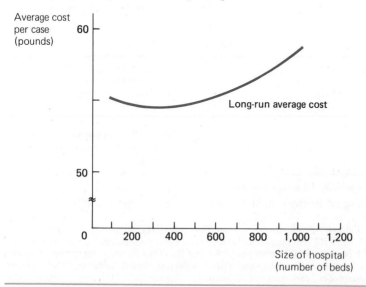

Size of hospital
(number of beds)

10. M. Feldstein, *Economic Analysis for Health Service Efficiency* (Chicago: Markham, 1968),
    p. 86.

ful for nonprofit (and government) organizations as well as for firms. In recent years, a considerable amount of research has been carried out concerning the economics of health. More will be said about this topic in Chapter 12, where we shall analyze important aspects of the labor market for nurses.

SUMMARY

1. To minimize the cost of producing a given output, a firm must combine inputs so that the marginal product of a dollar's worth of any one input is equal to the marginal product of a dollar's worth of any other input used. The optimal combination of inputs can be determined graphically by superimposing the relevant isocost curves on the firm's isoquant map, and by determining the point at which the relevant isoquant touches the lowest isocost curve.

2. The cost of producing a certain product is the value of the other products that the resources used in its production could have produced instead. This is the alternative cost doctrine. The alternative cost of an input may not be equal to its historical cost, and it is likely to be smaller in the short run than in the long run. (Opportunity cost is another name for alternative cost.)

3. The social costs of producing a given commodity do not always equal the private costs, as in the case of a steel mill that discharges wastes into a river. In making decisions, costs incurred in the past and costs that are the same for all alternative courses of action are irrelevant.

4. A cost function is a relation between a firm's costs and its output rate. The firm's production function and the prices it pays for inputs determine a firm's cost function.

5. Three concepts of total cost are important in the short run: total fixed costs, total variable costs, and total costs. The average fixed costs, average variable costs, average costs, and marginal costs are also important.

6. The short-run average cost function decreases at first, but eventually it turns up because of the law of diminishing marginal returns. Similarly, the marginal cost curve eventually turns up for the same reason.

7. A useful way to look at the long run is to view it as a planning horizon. Economies and diseconomies of scale affect the shape of the long-run average cost function. Because of economies of scale, the long-run average cost curve is likely to decrease, up to some point, with increases in output. As output becomes greater and greater, it is often stated that diseconomies of scale will result, with the consequence that the long-run average cost curve will turn

upward. The shape of the long-run average cost curve in a particular industry is of great importance from the viewpoint of public policy.

8. Economists have made a great many studies to estimate the cost functions of particular firms and industries. Typically, these studies have been based on historical data regarding cost and output, although accounting data, which are generally the only cost data available, suffer from a number of deficiencies when used for this purpose.

9. One of the most interesting conclusions of these studies is that the long-run average cost curve often seems to be L-shaped. However, the evidence is limited. Another interesting conclusion is that the short-run marginal cost function often seems to be horizontal, not U-shaped. But this may be due in considerable part to the limited range of the observations.

QUESTIONS/PROBLEMS

1) In October 1986, about nine months after the crash of the space shuttle *Challenger,* the Congressional Budget Office published a study indicating that the marginal cost of a 1989 flight by a space shuttle would be about $48 million. (a) What kinds of expenses are included in this figure? (b) Should the entire cost of the shuttle be included? Why or why not? (c) According to the study, the "Challenger accident will increase the marginal cost of shuttle operations. . ."[11] Why is this likely?

2) According to the National Academy of Engineering, the long-run average total cost of producing an aircraft increases by about 35 percent if 350, rather than 700, of the aircraft are produced. Since the end of World War II, the number of prime free-world manufacturers of large commercial air transports has decreased from 22 to 5.[12] Are these two facts related? If so, how?

3) Fill in the blanks in the table below.

Output	Total cost (dollars)	Total fixed cost (dollars)	Total variable cost (dollars)	Average fixed cost (dollars)	Average variable cost (dollars)
0	50	—	—	—	—
1	70	—	—	—	—
2	100	—	—	—	—
3	120	—	—	—	—
4	135	—	—	—	—
5	150	—	—	—	—
6	160	—	—	—	—
7	165	—	—	—	—

11. Congressional Budget Office, *Setting Space Transportation Policy for the 1990s* (Washington, D.C.: U.S. Government Printing Office, 1986), p. 25.

12. National Academy of Engineering, *The Competitive Status of the U.S. Civil Aviation Manufacturing Industry* (Washington, D.C.: National Academy Press, 1985).

Suppose that the price of an important input increased greatly, with the result that each of the figures concerning total cost rose by 50 percent. What effect would this have on the value of marginal cost?

4) As we saw in Example 6.2, 8,500 pounds of milk can be produced by a cow fed the following combinations of quantities of hay and grain:

Quantity of hay (pounds)	Quantity of grain (pounds)
5,000	6,154
5,500	5,454
6,000	4,892
6,500	4,423
7,000	4,029
7,500	3,694

(a) If the price of a pound of hay equals one-half the price of a pound of grain (which equals P), what is the cost of each combination? What is the minimum-cost combination (of those shown above)? (b) Plot the isocost curves and the isoquant. Use this graph to determine the minimum-cost combination. Compare your results with those obtained in part (a).

5) Economist T. Yntema estimated the short-run total cost function of the United States Steel Corporation (now USX Corporation) in the 1930s to be as follows:

$$C = 182.1 + 55.73Q$$

where C is total annual cost (in millions of dollars) and Q is millions of tons of steel produced. (a) What was U.S. Steel's fixed cost? (b) If U.S. Steel produced 10 million tons of steel, what was its average variable cost? (c) What was U.S. Steel's marginal cost? (d) Do you think that this equation provided a faithful representation of U.S. Steel's short-run total cost function, regardless of the value of Q? (e) If you needed to estimate U.S. Steel's current marginal cost, would you use this equation? (f) In recent years, there have been charges that Japanese steel makers have been "dumping" steel in the United States—that is, selling here below cost. Can this equation be used to tell whether this is so?

6) According to Frederick Moore, "The '.6 rule' derived by engineers is a rough method of measuring increases in capital cost as capacity is expanded. Briefly stated the rule says that the increase in cost is given by the increase in capacity raised to the .6 power." Give some reasons why this rule holds for tanks, columns, compressors and similar types of equipment. (Hint: Capacity of a container is related to volume, whereas cost is related to surface area.)

7) The graph on p. 214 shows the average total cost of producing a ton of ammonia using the partial oxidation process and the steam reforming process, with plants of various sizes (as measured by daily capacities). In particular, curve C pertains to the partial oxidation process when naptha is used as a raw material, curve D pertains to the steam reforming process when naptha is used as a raw material, and curve E pertains to the steam reforming process when natural gas is used as a raw material.

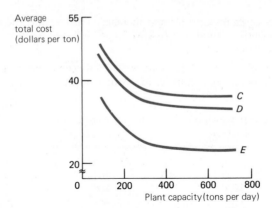

(a) Can the short-run cost function for ammonia be derived from this graph? (b) This graph assumes that naptha costs $0.008 per pound and natural gas costs $0.20 per mcf; if this assumption is true, which process should be used? (c) Does this graph suggest that there are economies of scale in ammonia production? (d) The graph above pertains to conditions in the early 1960s. In the late 1960s, a new process for producing ammonia was introduced. Using this new process, a plant with a capacity of 1,400 tons per day had an average cost of about $16 per ton. Did the long-run cost function for the production of ammonia shift between the early and late 1960s?

8) A plant producing a component of the space shuttle can produce any number of these components (up to 100 per week) at a total cost of $100, but it cannot produce more than 100 per week, regardless of how much its costs are. Graph its marginal cost curve. Indicate why few (if any) plants in the real world have a marginal cost curve of this sort.

9) Suppose that you are a consultant to a firm that publishes books. Suppose that the firm is about to publish a book that will sell for $10 a copy. The fixed costs of publishing the book are $5,000; the variable cost is $5 a copy. What is the break-even point for this book?

10) Suppose that a semiconductor plant's production function is $Q = 5LK$, where Q is its output rate, L is the amount of labor it uses per period of time, and K is the amount of capital it uses per period of time. Suppose that the price of labor is $1 a unit and the price of capital is $2 a unit. The firm's vice-president for manufacturing hires you to figure out what combination of inputs the plant should use to produce 20 units of output per period. What advice would you give?

OPTIMAL LOT SIZE AND JAPANESE MANUFACTURING METHODS

In recent years, American firms have been trying to learn about, and in some cases catch up with, the manufacturing techniques used by the Japanese. One of the hallmarks of Japanese manufacturers is that products are made in small batches or lots, whereas in the United States they are made in relatively large batches or lots. There are many advantages in small lot sizes. Less inventories must be held. Also, there may be less scrap and better quality of workmanship. If a worker makes a single part and passes it to the next worker immediately (rather than making a large batch of the parts and then passing them on all at once), the first worker will be informed very soon if the next worker finds it defective. Thus, the causes of defects tend to be nipped in the bud, and the production of large lots containing many defective items is avoided.

Why do American firms produce relatively large lot sizes? To answer this question, we must discuss the factors determining the most economical lot size. Suppose that a firm needs to produce 100,000 identical parts of a particular type per year. For example, a manufacturer of outboard motors may have to produce 100,000 parts of a particular type, since each of its outboard motors requires such a part. Each time that the firm begins to produce this type of part, it incurs a setup cost of S dollars. For example, the outboard motor manufacturer may have to devote considerable labor time to setting up the equipment that produces this part.

The advantage of producing large lots is that this cuts the total setup costs incurred during the year. If the firm were to produce its annual requirement of 100,000 parts in one huge lot, it would only have to set up the equipment once, the result being that its total setup costs for the year would be S dollars. If it produced its annual requirement of 100,000 parts in two lots (each of 50,000), it would have to set up the equipment twice, the result being that the total setup costs for the year would be $2S$ dollars. The relationship between the size of a lot and the annual total setup costs is shown in Figure 1.

The disadvantage of producing large lots is that they result in large inventories that are expensive to maintain and finance. If, for example, the firm produces all 100,000 of the parts in one huge lot at the beginning of the year, its inventory equals 100,000 parts at the beginning of the year and zero parts at the end of the year. Its average inventory is 50,000 parts, as shown in the left-hand panel of Figure 2. On the other hand, if the firm produces the annual requirement of 100,000 parts in two lots (each of 50,000 units), its inventory

Fig. RELATIONSHIP BETWEEN THE SIZE OF LOT AND THE ANNUAL SETUP
1 COST / *The larger the lot size, the lower the annual setup costs.*

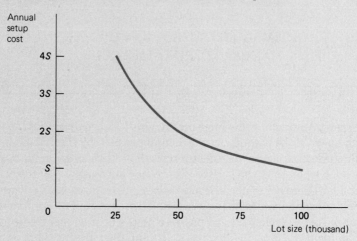

equals 50,000 parts at the beginning of the year and zero parts at the end of six
months; then after the second lot is produced, its inventory jumps back up to
50,000 parts, after which it declines once again to zero parts at the end of the
year. Thus its average inventory is 25,000 parts, as shown in the right-hand
panel of Figure 2.

Assuming that the annual cost of holding inventory is proportional to the
average inventory, the relationship between the size of a lot and the annual

Fig. SIZE OF INVENTORY DURING THE YEAR, GIVEN THAT LOT SIZE EQUALS
2 100,000 AND 50,000 / *Average inventory is 50,000 parts if the lot size
equals 100,000, and 25,000 parts if the lot size equals 50,000.*

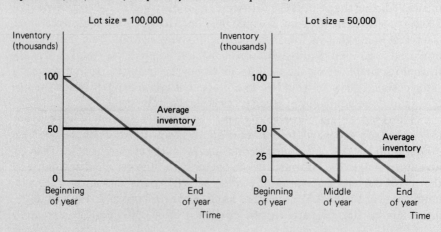

Fig. 3   RELATIONSHIP BETWEEN SIZE OF LOT AND TOTAL ANNUAL COSTS / *Total cost is the sum of the cost of carrying inventory and the setup cost. Thus the "Total cost" curve is the vertical sum of the "Cost of carrying inventory" curve and the "Setup cost" curve. For example, if the lot size is 70,711, annual setup cost equals OA, annual inventory cost equals OB, and annual total cost equals OA + OB = OE.*

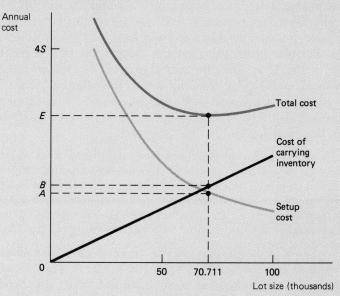

cost of holding inventory is shown in Figure 3. Adding the annual setup costs for each lot size (taken from Figure 1 and reproduced in Figure 3) to the inventory costs, we obtain the total annual cost for each lot size. Under the conditions shown in Figure 3, the optimal lot size is 70,711, where the total annual costs are a minimum.[1]

---

1. In general, total annual setup costs equal SQ/L, where S is the cost per setup, Q is the total annual requirement of the relevant part, and L is the number of identical parts of this sort produced in a lot. Since $L/2$ is the average inventory, the annual cost of holding inventory equals $bL/2$, where b is the annual cost of holding each identical part of this sort in inventory for a year. Adding the annual setup costs and the annual costs of holding inventory, we obtain the following expression for the total annual costs:

$$C = bL/2 + SQ/L.$$

To minimize total annual costs, we set

$$\frac{dC}{dL} = \frac{b}{2} - SQ/L^2 = 0.$$

Solving for L, we find that, to minimize total annual costs, L should equal

$$\sqrt{\frac{2SQ}{b}}.$$

(cont.)

The value of the optimal lot size depends on the cost of setting up the equipment each time. If this cost is high, the optimal lot size tends to be large; if it is small, the optimal lot size tends to be small. This fact is shown in Figure 4. In the upper panel, the cost of each setup is large, which means that the curve showing the annual setup costs is higher than in the lower panel where the cost of each setup is small. Consequently, the optimal lot size, OL, is bigger in the case shown in the upper panel than in the case shown in the lower panel.

At this point, it is easy to understand why American firms produce larger lot sizes than Japanese firms. The Japanese, using ingenuity and determination, have succeeded in lowering the cost of each setup. In other words, the Japanese have managed to get themselves into the situation shown in the lower panel of Figure 4, whereas American firms tend to be in the situation shown in the top panel. The importance of this factor has been pointed out in the following way by Robert Hall:

When the Japanese explain in detail how they achieved their big increases in productivity, the biggest "war stories" from the plant floor involve hard-fought battles to reduce setup times on a piece of equipment which at first was regarded as an insurmountable obstacle. Accounts of these battles detail changing the design of bolts, and the fit of pieces together on the machine. They describe the building of special tools to speed changeover, and practice sessions to learn how to perform changeovers quickly.[2]

To illustrate more specifically how the Japanese have gone about this, consider Toyota, a major auto producer. In 1971, it took Toyota's workers about an hour to set up the 800-ton presses used in forming auto hoods and fenders. After five years of intensive effort, the setup time was reduced to 12 minutes (as contrasted with about 6 hours in the United States), and the aim was to reduce it to under 10 minutes. To accomplish this, "The press was modified to allow the old dies to quickly slide out of the press onto a waiting table while new dies are pushed in from the other side. The workers performing the changeover 'dry ran' the procedure so that it worked like kicking the extra point after a touchdown in football."[3]

Recognizing the importance of this factor, American firms have been exploring the possibility of making similar reductions in setup costs. Because the Japanese industrial climate differs in many respects from that in the United

---

In the particular case in Figure 3, Q equals 100,000 and b equals $S \div 25,000$. Thus, to minimize total annual costs, L should equal $\sqrt{2S(100,000) \div (S/25,000)} = \sqrt{5 \text{ billion}} = 70,711$. In other words, the optimal lot size is 70,711, which means that 70,711 identical parts of this sort should be produced in each lot. (Of course, there is no reason for the number of setups per year to be an integer number. For example, one could have 5 setups during each two-year period, or 2½ setups per year.)

2. See R. Schonberger, *Japanese Manufacturing Techniques* (New York: Free Press, 1982) p. 20.

3. Ibid., p. 21.

Fig.   EFFECT OF COST PER SETUP ON OPTIMAL LOT SIZE / *If the cost per setup is*
4   *relatively high (as in panel A), the optimal lot size tends to be relatively large.*

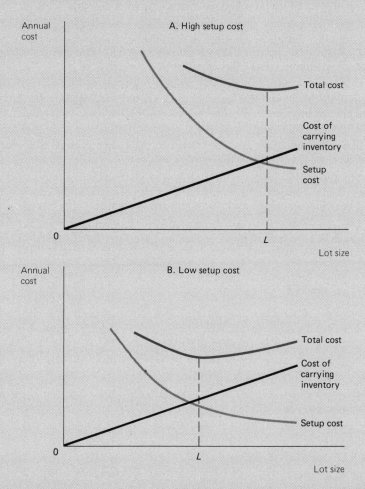

States, it would be simplistic to think that what works in Japan will necessarily work in the United States. But there can be no doubt about the American interest in Japanese manufacturing techniques.[4]

<hr>

━━━━━━━━━━━━ ANALYTICAL QUESTIONS ━━━━━━━━━━━━

1) When Toyota reduced the time required to set up its presses, did it change its production function? If so, how?

<hr>

4. See ibid, and R. Hayes, "Why Japanese Factories Work," in A. Kantrow (ed.), *Survival Strategies for American Industry* (New York: Wiley, 1983).

2) If the manufacturer of outboard motors incurs a setup cost of $100,000 each time that it begins to produce a particular type of part, how much are its total setup costs per year if it produces 50,000 parts of this type each year and if the lot size is 10,000?

3) Under the conditions described in the previous question, what is the average level of inventory for this part? Why is it likely that the cost to the firm of carrying this inventory will increase as the inventory gets bigger?

4) Under the conditions described in Question 2, if the annual cost to the firm of holding each identical part of this sort in the inventory is $2, what is the total annual cost of holding inventory? What is the sum of the annual setup cost and the annual cost of holding inventory?

5) Under the conditions described in Questions 2 and 4, is the firm producing the optimal lot size? If not, what is the optimal lot size?

6) The firm's managers ask you to estimate how sensitive the firm's total cost (of setup and holding inventory) is to variations in the lot size from its optimal level. Why is this question important, and how would you answer it?

7) A government official asks you whether American firms should invest whatever resources are required to reduce their setup costs to the Japanese level. How would you answer this question?

Market Structure, Price, and Output

Price and Output under Perfect Competition

MARKET STRUCTURE: AN INTRODUCTION

Previous chapters have provided models of the behavior of consumers and firms. In Chapters 8 to 11 we turn to the analysis of markets; our principal purpose is to explain the behavior of price and output. We will be concerned with questions of the following sort: What determines the price of a product? What determines how much of a product is produced? How are resources allocated among alternative uses? These are some of the most basic—and most important—questions in economics. In Chapter 2, we provided some preliminary answers to these questions. In Chapters 8 to 11, we discuss them in much more detail.

To begin with, we must distinguish between various types of markets. Economists have found it useful to classify markets into four general types: perfect competition, monopoly, monopolistic competition, and oligopoly. This classification is based largely on the number of firms in the industry that supplies the product. In perfect competition and monopolistic competition, there are many sellers, each of which produces only a small part of the industry's output. In monopoly, on the other hand, the industry consists of only a single firm. Oligopoly is an intermediate case where there are few sellers.

In this chapter we investigate how price and output are determined in perfectly competitive markets. Monopoly, monopolistic competition, and oligopoly are taken up in subsequent chapters. The analysis in this chapter brings together, and builds on, the topics discussed in previous chapters. In Chapter 2, we emphasized the important role played by the market demand and market supply curves. In Chapter 5, we used the tools devised in Chapters 3 and 4 to show how a product's market demand curve can be derived. In the present chapter, we use the tools devised in Chapters 6 and 7 to show how a product's market supply curve can be derived. Then we discuss in detail the way in which the demand and supply sides of the market interact to determine the equilibrium price and output of the firm and the industry in the market period, the short run, and the long run.

PERFECT COMPETITION

What do economists mean by perfect competition? When first exposed to this concept, students sometimes find it difficult to grasp because it is quite different from the concept of competition used by their relatives and friends in the business world. When businessmen speak of a highly competitive market, they generally mean a market where each firm is keenly aware of its rivalry with a few others and where advertising, packaging, styling, and other competitive weapons are used to attract business away from them. In contrast, the basic feature of the economist's definition of perfect competition is its impersonality. Because there are so many firms in the industry, no firm views another as a competitor, any more than one small wheat farmer views another small wheat farmer as a competitor.

More specifically, *perfect competition* is defined by four conditions. First, perfect competition requires that the product of any one seller be the same as the product of any other seller. This is an important condition

Perfect competition

because it makes sure that buyers do not care whether they purchase the product from one seller or another, as long as the price is the same. Note that the *product* may be defined by a great deal more than the physical characteristics of the good. Although the various English pubs may serve the same beer, their products may not be identical because the atmosphere may be friendlier in one place than another, the location may be better, and so forth.

Second, perfect competition requires each participant in the market, whether buyer or seller, to be so small, in relation to the entire market, that he or she cannot affect the product's price. No buyer can be large enough to wangle a better price from the sellers than some other buyer. No seller can be large enough to influence the price by altering his or her output rate. Of course, if all producers act together, changes in output will certainly affect price, but any producer acting alone cannot do so. It will be recalled from Chapter 5 that this means that the firm's demand curve is horizontal.

Third, perfect competition requires that all resources be completely mobile. In other words, each resource must be able to enter or leave the market, and switch from one use to another, very readily.[1] More specifically, it means that labor must be able to move from region to region and from job to job; it means that raw materials must not be monopolized; and it means that new firms can enter and leave an industry. Needless to say, this condition is often not fulfilled in a world where considerable retraining is required to allow a worker to move from one job to another and where patents, large investment requirements, and economies of scale make difficult the entry of new firms.

Fourth, perfect competition requires that consumers, firms, and resource owners have perfect knowledge of the relevant economic and technological data. Consumers must be aware of all prices. Laborers and owners of capital must be aware of how much their resources will bring in all possible uses. Firms must know the prices of all inputs and the characteristics of all relevant technologies. Moreover, in its purest sense, perfect competition requires that all of these economic decision-making units have an accurate knowledge of the future together with the past and present.

Having described these four requirements, it is obvious that no industry is perfectly competitive. Some agricultural markets may be reasonably close, since the first three requirements are frequently met; but even they do not meet all of the requirements.[2] Nevertheless, this does not mean that the study of the behavior of perfectly competitive markets is useless. Recall from Chapter 1 that a model may be quite useful even though some of its assumptions are unrealistic. The conclusions derived from the model of perfect competition have proved very useful in explaining and predicting behavior in the real world. They have permitted a reasonably accurate view of resource allocation in important segments of our economy.

PRICE DETERMINATION IN THE MARKET PERIOD

Besides the short run and the long run, discussed in previous chapters, there is also the market period during which the supply of a good is fixed. For example, retailers may have only a certain number of Rolling Stones records in stock, and it may take a certain period of time before they can obtain more from the

---

1. Of course, this does not mean that such movements of resources do not take time. In the short run, many resources cannot be transferred from one use to another.

2. Some agricultural markets in which the conditions would otherwise be reasonably close to perfect competition are heavily affected by government programs. See pp. 246–53.

Fig.
8.1
PRICE DETERMINATION IN THE MARKET PERIOD / *The equilibrium price is*
OP_0, OP_1, *or* OP_2, *depending on whether the demand curve is* D, D_1, *or* D_2.

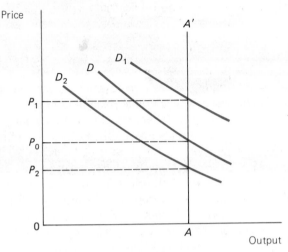

producers. Or the quantity of an agricultural commodity may be fixed for some
time after a harvest. Also, in some cases, the quantity of a certain commodity
may be fixed for a long period of time. For example, the quantity of Renoir
paintings cannot be augmented—although forgers sometimes try.

Whereas the quantity of output is variable in the short and long runs, it is
fixed in the *market period,* the consequence being that the *supply curve,* the
curve that shows the quantity of output supplied at each price, is a vertical
straight line. For example, in Figure 8.1, the quantity available for sale is *OA,*
and the market supply curve is *AA'.* Since each seller has a fixed supply that it
sells for the market-established price, the behavior of the sellers is perfectly
straightforward: They simply sell what they have for as much as they can get.[3]

Equilibrium is achieved, of course, at that price which clears the market
by equating the amount demanded with the amount supplied. At a lower price,
buyers will want more of the commodity than exists in the market; at a higher
price they will want less of the commodity than exists in the market. In Figure
8.1, if the market demand curve is *D,* the equilibrium price is OP_0. If the demand curve were higher (like D_1) the equilibrium price would be higher (like
OP_1). If the demand curve were lower (like D_2), the equilibrium price would be
lower (like OP_2). But the quantity would be the same, since it is fixed. Consequently, in the market period, quantity is set by supply alone and (given supply) price is set by demand alone.

---

3. Of course, the sellers themselves may be among those who can use and want the good, the result being that their demand is included in the market demand curve. If this is the case, it
may turn out that they sell some of the good to themselves; that is, they keep it.

The role played by prices as rationing devices is particularly obvious in the market period, where this is the major function of price. When the market equilibrium price is reached, the available supply has been rationed, without resort to fights among consumers or government intervention. Those consumers who can and will pay the price have the commodity—and there are just enough such consumers to exhaust the available supply.

PRICE DETERMINATION IN THE SHORT RUN

The Output of the Firm

Having dealt with the determination of price and output in the market period, we proceed to the case of price and output determination in the short run. The first question we take up is: How much output will the firm produce in the short run? In the short run, the firm can expand or contract its output rate by increasing or decreasing the rate at which it employs variable inputs. For simplicity, assume that the firm cannot affect the price of its product and that it can sell any amount of its product that it wants at this price (that is, it is a perfectly competitive firm). Also, assume, as in previous chapters, that the firm maximizes its profits. To illustrate the firm's situation, consider the example in Table 8.1. The market price is $10 a unit, and the firm can produce as

Table COST AND REVENUE OF A FIRM: PRICES TAKEN AS GIVEN BY THE FIRM
8.1

Output per period	Price (dollars)	Total revenue (dollars)	Total fixed cost (dollars)	Total variable cost (dollars)	Total cost (dollars)	Total profit (dollars)
0	10	0	12	0	12	−12
1	10	10	12	2	14	− 4
2	10	20	12	3	15	5
3	10	30	12	5	17	13
4	10	40	12	8	20	20
5	10	50	12	13	25	25
6	10	60	12	23	35	25
7	10	70	12	38	50	20
8	10	80	12	69	81	− 1

much as it chooses. Thus the firm's total revenue at various output rates is given in column 3 of Table 8.1. The firm's total fixed cost, total variable cost, and total cost are given in columns 4, 5, and 6 of Table 8.1. Finally, the last column shows the firm's total profit, the difference between total revenue and total cost, at various output rates.

Fig.
8.2

RELATIONSHIP BETWEEN TOTAL COST AND TOTAL REVENUE: PRICES TAKEN
AS GIVEN BY THE FIRM / *The output rate that will maximize the firm's
profits is either 5 or 6 units per time period. At either of these output
rates, profit (total revenue minus total cost) equals $25.*

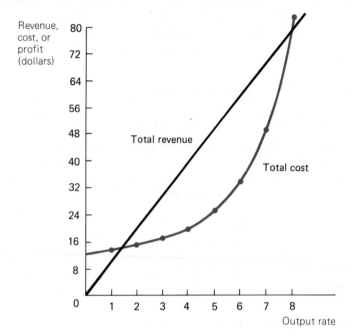

Figure 8.2 provides a graphical description of the relationship between
total revenue and total cost, on the one hand, and output, on the other. Of
course, the vertical distance between the total revenue curve and the total cost
curve is the profit at the corresponding output rate. (Note once again that cost
curves are another name for cost functions. Both terms are in common use.)
Below 2 units of output and above 7 units of output, this distance is negative.
Since the firm can sell either large or small volumes of output at the same price
per unit, the total revenue curve will be a straight line through the origin. This
is always the case when the firm takes the price as given. The total cost curve
has the kind of shape we would expect, on the basis of Chapter 7, of a short-run
total cost curve.

Based on an examination of either Table 8.1 or Figure 8.2, the output rate
that will maximize the firm's profits is either 5 or 6 units per time period.
These are the output rates where the profit figure in the last column of Table
8.1 is the largest and where the vertical distance between the total revenue and
total cost curves in Figure 8.2 is the greatest.

For many purposes it is convenient to present the marginal revenue and
marginal cost curves, as well as the total revenue and total cost curves. Table
8.2 shows marginal revenue and marginal cost at each output rate. These fig-

Table   MARGINAL REVENUE AND MARGINAL COST: PRICES
8.2   TAKEN AS GIVEN BY THE FIRM

Output per period	Marginal revenue (dollars)	Marginal cost* (dollars)
1	10	2
2	10	1
3	10	2
4	10	3
5	10	5
6	10	10
7	10	15
8	10	31

* This is the marginal cost between the indicated output level and one unit less than this output level.

ures were derived in the way shown in Chapters 5 and 7. Figure 8.3 shows the resulting marginal revenue and marginal cost curves. Since the firm takes the price as given, marginal revenue equals price, since the change in total revenue resulting from a 1-unit change in sales necessarily equals the price.

Fig.   MARGINAL REVENUE AND MARGINAL COST: PRICES TAKEN AS GIVEN BY THE
8.3   FIRM / *When output is at the profit-maximizing level of 5 or 6 units, price equals marginal cost.*

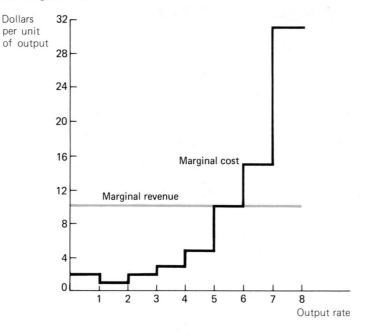

The important thing to note is that the maximum profit is achieved at the output rate where price (= marginal revenue) equals marginal cost. Both the figures in Table 8.2 and the curves in Figure 8.3 indicate that price equals marginal cost at an output rate between 5 and 6 units, which we know from Table 8.1 or Figure 8.2 to be the profit-maximizing output. Is this merely a chance occurrence, or will it usually be true that price will equal marginal cost at the profit-maximizing output rate?

Price Equals Marginal Cost

The fact that price equals marginal cost at the optimal output rate is not merely a chance occurrence; it will usually be true if the firm takes as given the price of the product. To prove that this is the case, consider Figure 8.4, which shows a typical short-run marginal cost curve. Suppose that the price is OP_0. At any output rate (after perhaps an irrelevant range in which marginal cost is falling) less than OX, price exceeds marginal cost; thus increases in output will increase profit since they will add more to total revenues than to total costs. At any output rate above OX, price is less than marginal cost; thus decreases in output will increase profits, since they will reduce total cost more than total revenue. Since increases in output up to OX result in increases in profit and further increases in output result in decreases in profit, OX must be the profit-maximizing output.

Even if the firm is doing the best it can, it may not be able to earn a profit.

Fig. 8.4   SHORT-RUN AVERAGE AND MARGINAL COST CURVES / *If price is* OP_0, *the firm will produce an output of* OX; *if price is* OP_2, *it will produce an output of* OY; *and if price is less than* OP_3, *it will produce nothing.*

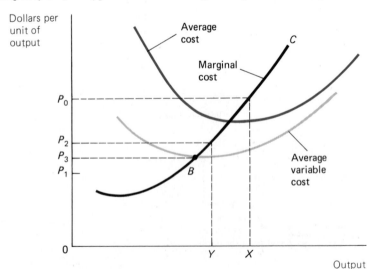

For example, if the price is OP_2 in Figure 8.4, short-run average costs exceed the price at all possible outputs. Since the short run is too short to allow the firm to alter the scale of its plant, it cannot liquidate its plant in the short run. All that the firm can do is to produce at a loss or discontinue production. The firm's decision will depend on whether the price of the product will cover average variable costs. If there exists an output rate where price exceeds average variable costs, it will pay the firm to produce, even though price does not cover average total costs. If there does not exist an output rate where price exceeds average variable costs, the firm is better off to produce nothing at all. Thus, if the average variable cost curve is as shown in Figure 8.4, the firm will produce if the price is OP_2, but not if it is OP_1.

The reasoning behind this conclusion is as follows: If the firm produces nothing, it must still pay its fixed costs. Consequently, if the loss resulting from production is less than the firm's fixed costs, it is more profitable (in the sense that losses are smaller) to produce than not to produce. On a per unit basis, this means that it is better to produce than to discontinue production if the loss per unit of production is less than average fixed costs, that is, if $ATC - P < AFC$, where ATC is average total costs, P is price, and AFC is average fixed cost. But this will be so if $ATC < AFC + P$, since P has merely been added to both sides of the inequality. Subtracting AFC from both sides, this will be so if $ATC - AFC < P$. But $ATC - AFC$ is average variable costs, which means that we have proved what we set out to prove: that it is better to produce than to discontinue production if price exceeds average variable costs.

Thus if the firm maximizes profit or minimizes losses, it sets its output rate so that short-run marginal cost equals price. But this rule, like most others, has an exception: If the market price is too low to cover the firm's average variable costs at any conceivable output rate, the firm will minimize losses by discontinuing production.

Finally, it is a simple matter to derive the firm's short-run supply curve. Suppose that the firm's short-run cost curves are those in Figure 8.4. If the price of the product is below OP_3, the firm will produce nothing, because there is no output level where price exceeds average variable cost. If the price of the product exceeds OP_3, the firm will set its output rate at the point at which price equals marginal cost. This is the output rate that maximizes profit. Thus, if the price is OP_0, the firm will produce OX; if the price is OP_2, the firm will produce OY, and so forth. The resulting supply curve is that shown in Figure 8.5 as OP_3BC. Given the way it was constructed, this curve is exactly the same as the firm's short-run marginal cost curve for prices above OP_3; at or below OP_3, the supply curve coincides with the price axis.

Short-Run Supply Curve of the Industry

The price of the industry's product in the short run was given to us in the previous section. What we want to do is to see how it is determined. This price

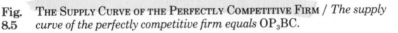

Fig.
8.5

THE SUPPLY CURVE OF THE PERFECTLY COMPETITIVE FIRM / *The supply curve of the perfectly competitive firm equals* OP_3BC.

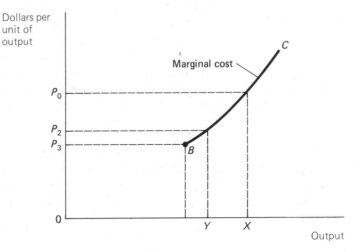

is influenced both by the consumers that demand the good and the firms that supply it. The determinants of the industry demand curve (that is, the market demand curve) have been discussed in previous chapters, particularly in Chapter 5. In this section, we discuss the determinants of the short-run industry supply curve, and in the next section, we combine the demand and supply curves to determine the industry's price and output in the short run.

As a rough approximation, the industry's short-run supply curve can be regarded as the horizontal summation of the short-run supply curves of all of the firms in the industry. For example, if there were three firms in the industry and if their supply curves were OSS_1S_1', OSS_2S_2', and OSS_3S_3' in Figure 8.6, the industry's supply curve would be $OSS'S''$, since $OSS'S''$ shows the amounts of the product that all of the firms together would supply at various prices. Of course, if there were only three firms, the industry would not be perfectly competitive, but we can ignore this inconsistency. The point of Figure 8.6 is to illustrate the fact that the industry supply curve is the horizontal summation of the firm supply curves, at least under one important assumption.

The assumption underlying this construction of the short-run industry supply curve is that supplies of inputs to the industry as a whole are perfectly elastic. In other words, it is assumed that increases or decreases in output by all firms simultaneously do not affect input prices. This is a strong assumption. Although changes in the output of one firm alone often cannot affect input prices, the simultaneous expansion or contraction of output by all firms may well alter input prices, with the result that the individual firm's cost curves—and supply curve—will shift. For example, an expansion of the whole

Fig.   HORIZONTAL SUMMATION OF SHORT-RUN SUPPLY CURVES OF FIRMS / *If*
8.6   *increases or decreases in output by all firms simultaneously do not affect*
           input prices, the industry supply curve is OSS′S″, *the horizontal*
           summation of the firms' supply curves.

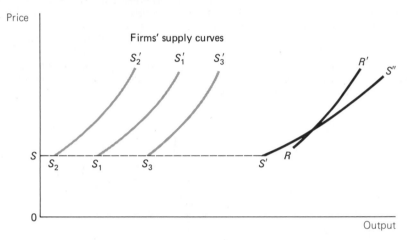

industry may bid up the price of certain inputs, with the result that the cost
curves of the individual firms will be pushed upward.[4]

If contrary to the assumption underlying Figure 8.6, input prices are influenced in this way by expansion of the industry, what will be the effect on the
short-run industry supply curve? It will make the short-run industry supply
curve less elastic than *OSS′S″*. In the relevant price range, the curve might be
more like *RR′*. To see this, note that expansion of the industry causes the
short-run average cost curve and the short-run marginal cost curve to move
upward, because of the resulting increase in input prices. But if the marginal
cost curve moves upward, price will equal marginal cost at a lower output than
would have been the case if the marginal cost curve had not moved.

In summary, the shape of the short-run supply curve is determined by the
number of firms in the industry, the size of the plant and other factors determining the shape of the marginal cost curve of each firm, and the effect of
changes in industry output on input prices.

Short-Run Equilibrium Price and Output for the Industry

As we know from Chapter 2, the short-run equilibrium price level is the
price at which the quantity demanded and the quantity supplied of the product
in the short run are equal. For example, if the demand curve is *D* and the sup-

---

4. More will be said about the effect of industry output on individual cost curves in subsequent
   sections of this chapter.

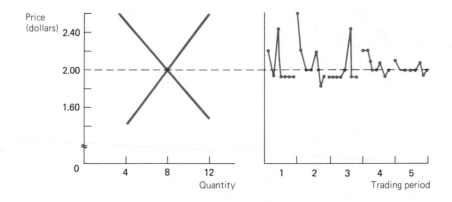
ply curve is as shown in Figure 8.7, the equilibrium price is *OP* and the equilibrium industry output is *OQ*, this point being the intersection of the demand and supply curves. Once enough time has elapsed for firms to adjust their utilization of the variable inputs, the price will tend to equal this equilibrium level, aside from the effects of certain factors that will be discussed on pp. 243–45. If the price is above this equilibrium level, the quantity supplied will tend to exceed the quantity demanded, with the result that the price will tend to fall. If the price is below this equilibrium level, the quantity demanded will tend to exceed the quantity supplied, with the result that the price will tend to rise. There is no tendency for the price to move in one direction or the other if and only if it is at the equilibrium level.

At the equilibrium price, price will equal marginal cost for all firms that choose to produce, rather than shut down their plants. Price may be above or below average total cost, since there is no necessity that profits be zero or that fixed costs be covered in the short run. An increase in demand will increase equilibrium price and output in the short run. For example, suppose that demand shifts from *D* to *E* in Figure 8.7. The shift in the demand curve will cause a shortage at the old price, *OP,* with the result that the price will eventually be pushed up to OP_1. At the same time, each firm will adjust its output rate up-

In one of Smith's experiments, an auction occurred in which public bids or offers were made to buy or sell units of the good in question. There were five trading periods. Each participant was free to accept whatever terms he or she chose. The market demand and supply curves were as shown in the left-hand panel on p. 232. The right-hand panel shows the price of every sale in the order in which it occurred.

(a) In this experiment, did the actual price converge on the competitive equilibrium price? (b) How many trading periods were required before the actual prices all were within about 10 percent of the competitive equilibrium price? (c) Did this experiment incorporate all of the characteristics of perfect competition? (d) Did this experiment prove that actual price always converges on the competitive equilibrium price?

SOLUTION

(a) Yes. The competitive equilibrium price is $2, and it is clear from the right-hand panel of the graph that the actual price tended to converge on it as time went on. (b) By the fourth trading period, all of the actual prices at which sales were made were within about 10 percent of $2, the competitive equilibrium price. (c) No. According to the customary definition, a perfectly competitive market contains a great many buyers and sellers, whereas only a few existed in this experiment. It is noteworthy that the competitive equilibrium price is a good approximation to the outcome of this auction even though the number of buyers and sellers is not very large. (d) No. The results of experiments vary depending on the number of buyers and sellers and the way the market is organized. For example, if there is only one seller, the price tends to depart from the competitive equilibrium price. (More will be said on this score in Chapter 9.)*

* For further discussion, see C. Plott, "Theories of Industrial Organization and Explorations of Experimental Market Behavior", reprinted in E. Mansfield, *Microeconomics: Selected Readings,* 5th ed.; and V. Smith, A. Williams, W. K. Bratton, and M. Vannoni, "Competitive Market Institutions: Double Auctions vs. Sealed Bid-Offer Auctions," *American Economic Review,* March 1982.

Fig. 8.7   DETERMINATION OF PRICE AND OUTPUT IN THE SHORT RUN / *If the demand curve shifts from* D *to* E, *the price will eventually rise to* OP_1, *and each firm (that produces) will adjust its output rate upward so its marginal cost equals the higher price.*

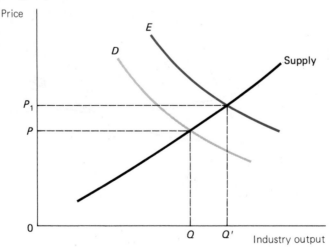

ward so that its marginal cost will equal the higher price, with the result that industry output will grow to OQ'.

PRICE DETERMINATION IN THE LONG RUN

The Long-Run Adjustment Process

In the long run, the firm can change its plant size. This means that established firms may leave an industry if the industry has below-average profits, or that new firms may enter an industry if the industry has above-average profits. The next two sections are concerned with the long-run equilibrium of a perfectly competitive industry. We begin in this section by describing the adjustment process for an established firm.

Suppose that the firm has a plant with short-run average and marginal cost curves of A_0A_0' and M_0M_0', shown in Figure 8.8. Suppose that the price of the product is OP. With its existing plant the firm makes a small profit on each unit of output. However, in the long run, the firm is not limited to this plant. The firm could build a plant corresponding to any of the short-run cost curves in Figure 8.8. For example, it could build a medium-sized plant corresponding to the short-run cost curves of A_1A_1' and M_1M_1', or it could build a large plant corresponding to the short-run cost curves of A_2A_2' and M_2M_2'. What will the

Fig.   INITIAL CHANGE OF PLANT SIZE IN THE LONG RUN / *To maximize profit in*
8.8   *the long run, the firm will choose an output level* (OQ_2) *and plant size so*
that the long-run marginal cost is equal to price (OP) *at the point where*
the short-run marginal cost $(M_2 M_2')$ *of the plant is equal to price.*

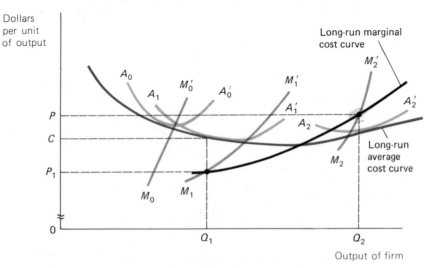

firm do in the long run? If it attempts to maximize profit it will choose to build
the plant corresponding to short-run cost curves of A_2A_2' and M_2M_2'. The maximum attainable profit under the postulated circumstances will be earned by
using this plant and by producing OQ_2 units of output per period of time.

In general, maximum profit will be obtained by producing at an output
rate and with a plant such that the *long-run marginal cost is equal to price at the
point where the short-run marginal cost of the plant is equal to price.* This, of
course, is true at the output of OQ_2 units and with the plant corresponding to
short-run cost curves A_2A_2' and M_2M_2' in Figure 8.8. The plant will be chosen so
that long-run marginal cost equals price, since this clearly is a condition for
profit maximization in the long run. To maximize profit, the firm will operate
this plant at the point where short-run marginal cost equals price. Thus the
equality of long-run marginal cost, short-run marginal cost, and price follows
from the assumption of profit maximization.

If all firms in the industry except this one had plants of optimal size, the
expansion of this one firm would have no significant influence on price. Consequently, since OP is greater than the average cost of producing OQ_2 units, all
firms would be earning a profit. Recall from Chapter 7 that costs, as reckoned
by economists (but not accountants), include the returns that could be gotten
from the most lucrative alternative use of the firm's resources. Consequently,
an *economic profit* means that the firm is making more than it could make with
its resources in other industries. Of course, the existence of above-average
profits in this industry attracts new entrants; when these new firms enter the
industry, the adjustment process must go on.

The arrival of new entrants shifts the industry supply curve to the right.
That is, more will be supplied at a given price than before. For example, suppose that the industry supply curve shifts from S to S_1 in Figure 8.9, with the
result that the price drops from OP to OP_1 and industry output increases from
OQ to OQ_3. Although total industry output increases (because of the new entrants), the output of each of the firms is smaller. Given that the price is now
OP_1 the optimal output of each firm is OQ_1, rather than OQ_2 (see Figure 8.8).
And the optimal plant is the one corresponding to the short-run cost curves,
A_1A_1' and M_1M_1'. Firms that have built plants corresponding to the short-run
cost curves A_2A_2' and M_2M_2' will lose a great deal of money. But even those
firms that have plants of optimal size (corresponding to the short-run curves
A_1A_1' and M_1M_1') will lose P_1C dollars per unit.

This does not mean that firms with plants of optimal size are not maximizing profits. On the contrary, it is evident from Figure 8.8 that, with the
price at OP_1, long-run marginal cost equals short-run marginal cost equals
price when the firm produces OQ_1 units of output with the plant corresponding
to the short-run cost curves, A_1A_1' and M_1M_1'. Thus this is the profit-maximizing solution for the firm. The trouble is that, even if the firm does the best it
can, it cannot make an economic profit. The result will be an out-migration of
firms from the industry. Since the returns that could be obtained from the

EFFECTS OF ENTRY OF NEW FIRMS / *Because of the entry of firms, the*
industry supply curve shifts to the right, and equilibrium price falls from
OP *to* OP$_1$.

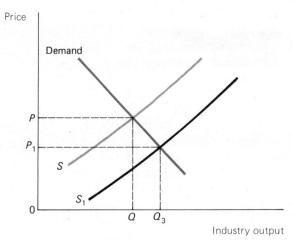

firm's resources are greater in other industries, entrepreneurs will transfer
these resources to other industries. In this way, the adjustment process will go
on, since the exit of firms will shift the industry's supply curve to the left.

Long-Run Equilibrium of the Firm

When and where will this adjustment process end? Eventually, enough
firms will leave the industry so that economic losses are eliminated, but profits
are avoided, too. At this point the remaining firms will be in equilibrium. In
other words, the long-run equilibrium position of the firm is at the point at
which its long-run average total costs equal price. If price is in excess of average total costs for any firm, economic profits are being earned and new firms
will enter the industry. If price is less than average total costs for any firm, that
firm will eventually leave the industry.

Going a step further, we can show that price must be equal to the *lowest
value* of long-run average total costs. In other words, firms must be producing
at the minimum point on their long-run average cost curves. The reason for
this is as follows: To maximize their profits, firms must operate where price
equals long-run marginal cost. Also, we have just seen that they must operate
where price equals long-run average cost. But if both of these conditions are
satisfied, it follows that long-run marginal cost must equal long-run average
cost. And we know from Chapter 7 that long-run marginal cost is equal to
long-run average cost only at the point at which long-run average cost is a
minimum. Thus this must be the equilibrium position of the firm.

This equilibrium position is illustrated in Figure 8.10. When all adjust-

Fig.   LONG-RUN EQUILIBRIUM OF A PERFECTLY COMPETITIVE FIRM / *In*
8.10   *long-run equilibrium, the firm produces an output of* OV, *and*
         price = marginal cost (both long-run and short-run) = average cost
         (both long-run and short-run).

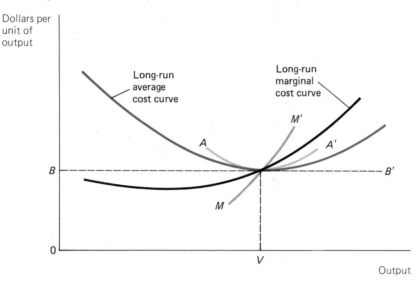

ments are made, price equals *OB*. Since the demand curve is horizontal, the
marginal revenue curve is the same as the demand curve, both being *BB'*. The
equilibrium output of the firm is *OV*, and its plant corresponds to short-run
average and marginal cost curves, *AA'* and *MM'*. At this output and with this
plant, long-run marginal cost equals short-run marginal cost equals price:
This insures that the firm is maximizing profit. Also, long-run average cost
equals short-run average cost equals price. This insures that economic profits
are zero. Since the long-run marginal cost and long-run average cost must be
equal, the equilibrium point is at the bottom of the long-run average cost
curve.

    Since price must be the same for all firms in the industry, this implies that
the minimum of the long-run average cost curve must be the same for all firms.
However, this is not as unrealistic as it appears at first glance. Firms that appear to have lower costs than others in the industry often have unusually good
resources or particularly able managements. The owners of superior resources
(including management ability) can obtain a higher price for them if they are
put to alternative uses than more ordinary resources. Consequently, the alternative costs, or implicit costs, of one's using superior resources are higher than
those of using ordinary resources. If this is taken into account, and if these superior resources are costed properly, the firms with apparently lower costs
have no lower costs at all.

Fig.
8.11
LONG-RUN EQUILIBRIUM: CONSTANT-COST INDUSTRY / *A constant-cost
industry has a horizontal long-run supply curve, as shown in panel B. If
demand shifts upward from* D *to* D$_1$, *the resulting increase in price (to
OP$_1$) results in the entry of firms, which shifts the supply curve to the right
(to* S$_1$), *thus pushing the price back to its original level (OP).*

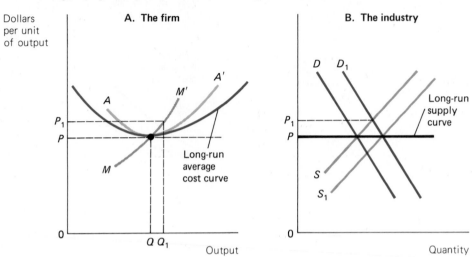

Constant-Cost Industries

In the previous two sections, it was assumed implicitly that the industry
exhibited constant costs, which means that expansion of the industry does not
result in an increase in input prices. Figure 8.11 shows long-run equilibrium
under conditions of constant cost. The left-hand panel shows the short- and
long-run cost curves of a typical firm in the industry. The right-hand panel
shows the demand and supply curves in the market as a whole, *D* being the
original demand curve and *S* being the original short-run supply curve. It is
assumed that the industry is in long-run equilibrium, with the result that the
price line is tangent to the long-run (and short-run) average cost curve at its
minimum point. (*OP* is the price.)

Assume now that the demand curve shifts to *D$_1$*. In the short run, with the
number of firms fixed, the price of the product will rise from *OP* to *OP$_1$*; each
firm will expand output from *OQ* to *OQ$_1$*; and each firm will be making economic profits since *OP$_1$* exceeds the short-run average costs of the firm at *OQ$_1$*.
The consequence is that firms will enter the industry and shift the supply
curve to the right. In the case of a constant-cost industry, the entrance of the
new firms does not affect the costs of the existing firms. The inputs used by
this industry are used by many other industries as well, and the appearance of
the new firms in this industry does not bid up the price of inputs and conse-

quently raise the costs of existing firms. Neither does the appearance of the new firms lower the costs of existing firms.

Consequently, *a constant-cost industry has a horizontal long-run supply curve.* Since output can be increased by increasing the number of firms producing OQ units at an average cost of OP, the long-run supply

Constant-cost industry

curve is horizontal at OP. So long as the industry remains in a state of constant costs, its output can be increased indefinitely. If price exceeds OP, firms would enter the industry; if price were less than OP, firms would leave the industry. Thus long-run equilibrium can only occur in this industry when price is OP. And industry output can be expanded or contracted, in accord with demand conditions, without altering this long-run equilibrium price.

Increasing- and Decreasing-Cost Industries

An increasing-cost industry is shown in Figure 8.12. The original conditions are the same as in Figure 8.11, D being the original demand curve, S being the original supply curve, OP being the equilibrium price, and the long-run and short-run average cost curves of each firm being LL' and AA' in the left panel. As in Figure 8.11, the original position is one of long-run equilibrium, since the price line is tangent to the average cost curves at their minima.

Fig. 8.12 LONG-RUN EQUILIBRIUM: INCREASING-COST INDUSTRY / *An increasing-cost industry has a positively sloped long-run supply curve, as shown in panel B. After long-run equilibrium is achieved, increases in output require increases in the price of the product.*

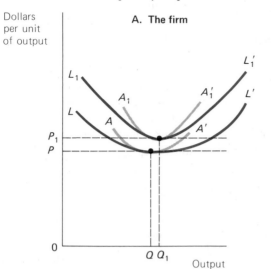
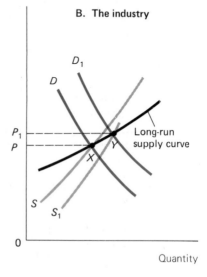

Now suppose that the demand curve shifts to D_1, with the result that the price of the product increases and firms earn economic profits, thus attracting new entrants. More and more inputs are required by the industry, and in an increasing-cost industry, the price of inputs increases with the amount used by the industry. Consequently, the cost of inputs increases for the established firms as well as the new entrants and the average cost curves are pushed up to L_1L_1' and A_1A_1'.

If the marginal cost curve of each firm is shifted to the left by the increase in input prices, the industry supply curve will also tend to shift to the left. However, this tendency is more than counterbalanced by the effects of the increase in the number of firms, which shifts the industry supply curve to the right. The latter effect must more than offset the former effect because otherwise there would be no expansion in total industry output. (No new resources would have been attracted to the industry.) The process of adjustment must go on until a new point of long-run equilibrium is reached. In Figure 8.12, this point is where the price of the product is OP_1 and each firm produces OQ_1 units;[5] the new short-run supply curve is S_1.

An increasing-cost industry *has a positively sloped long-run supply curve.* That is, after long-run equilibrium is achieved, increases in output require increases in the price of the product. For example, points X and Y

Increasing-cost industry

in Figure 8.12 are both on the long-run supply curve for this industry. The difference between constant-cost and increasing-cost industries is as follows: In constant-cost industries, new firms enter in response to an increase in demand until price returns to its original level; whereas in increasing-cost industries, new firms enter until the minimum point on the long-run cost curve has increased to the point where it equals the new price.[6]

A decreasing-cost industry is shown in Figure 8.13. Once again, we begin with an industry in long-run equilibrium, the demand curve being D, the short-run supply curve being S, price being OP, and the long-run and short-run average cost curves of each firm being LL' and AA'. As before, we postulate an increase in demand to D_1, the result being economic profit for established firms and the entry of new firms. However, in the case of a decreasing-cost industry, the expansion of the industry results in a decrease in the costs of the established firms. Thus the new long-run equilibrium is at a price of OP_1, the equilibrium output of each firm being OQ_1, and the new long-run and short-run average cost curves being $L_1L'_1$ and $A_1A'_1$.

---

5. We cannot be sure that OQ_1 exceeds OQ, as shown in Figure 8.12. It is possible for OQ_1 to be less than or equal to OQ.

6. This is only one way in which equilibrium can be achieved in increasing-cost industries. It is also possible that the increase in input prices (due to the expansion of industry output) raises average cost more than the increase in demand raises average revenue. Thus, firms may experience losses, some may leave the industry, and the remaining firms may produce at a larger scale.

Fig.
8.13

LONG-RUN EQUILIBRIUM: DECREASING-COST INDUSTRY / *A decreasing-cost industry has a negatively sloped long-run supply curve, as shown in panel* B. *After long-run equilibrium is achieved, increases in output are accompanied by decreases in price.*

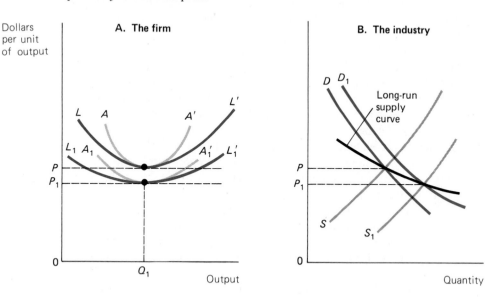

A decreasing-cost industry *has a negatively sloped long-run supply curve.* That is, after long-run equilibrium is reached, increases in output are accompanied by decreases in price. *External economies,* which are cost **Decreasing-cost** reductions that occur when the industry expands, may be respon-**industry** sible for the existence of decreasing-cost industries. An example of an external economy is an improvement in transportation that is due to the expansion of an industry and that reduces the costs of each firm in the industry. If there are important external economies, an industry may be subject to decreasing costs. Note that external economies are quite different from economies of scale: The individual firm has no control over external economies.

Most economists seem to regard increasing-cost industries as being the most frequently encountered of the three types. Decreasing-cost industries are the most unusual situation, although quite young industries may fall into this category. Later in this chapter, we present estimates of the shape of the long-run supply curve in various industries.

THE ALLOCATION PROCESS: SHORT AND LONG RUN

At this point, it is instructive to describe the process by which a perfectly competitive economy—an economy composed of perfectly competitive industries

—would allocate resources. In Chapter 1, we noted that the allocation of resources among alternative uses is one of the major functions of an economic system. Equipped with the concepts of this and previous chapters, we can now go much farther than we could in Chapter 1 in describing how a perfectly competitive economy goes about shifting resources in accord with changes in consumer demand.

To be specific, suppose that a change occurs in tastes, with the result that consumers are more favorably disposed toward corn and less favorably disposed toward potatoes than in the past. What will happen in the short run? The increase in the demand for corn increases the price of corn, and results in some increase in the output of corn. However, the output of corn cannot be increased very substantially because the capacity of the industry cannot be expanded in the short run. Similarly, the fall in the demand for potatoes reduces the price of potatoes, and results in some reduction in the output of potatoes. But the output of potatoes will not be curtailed greatly because firms will continue to produce as long as they can cover variable costs.

The change in the relative prices of corn and potatoes tells producers that a reallocation of resources is called for. Because of the increase in the price of corn and the decrease in the price of potatoes, corn producers are earning economic profits and potato producers are showing economic losses. This will trigger a redeployment of resources. If some variable inputs in the production of potatoes can be used as effectively in the production of corn, these variable inputs may be withdrawn from potato production and switched to corn production. Even if there are no variable inputs that are used in both corn and potato production, adjustment can occur in various interrelated markets, with the result that corn production gains resources and potato production loses resources.

When short-run equilibrium is attained in both the corn and potato industries, the reallocation of resources is not yet complete since there has not been enough time for producers to build new capacity or liquidate old capacity. In particular, neither industry is operating at minimum average cost. The corn producers are operating at greater than the output level where average cost is a minimum; and the potato producers are operating at less than the output level where average cost is a minimum.

What will happen in the long run? The shift in consumer demand from potatoes to corn will result in greater adjustments in production and smaller adjustments in price than in the short run. In the long run, existing firms can leave potato production and new firms can enter corn production. Because of short-run economic losses in potato production, some potato land and related equipment will be allowed to run down, and some firms engaged in potato production will be liquidated. As firms leave potato production, the supply curve shifts to the left, causing the price to rise above its short-run level. The transfer of resources out of potato production will stop when the price has increased, and costs have decreased, to the point where losses are avoided.

While potato production is losing resources, corn production is gaining them. The short-run economic profits in corn production will result in the entry of new firms. The increased demand for inputs will raise input prices and cost curves in corn production, and the price of corn will be depressed by the movement to the right of the supply curve because of the entry of new firms. Entry ceases when economic profits are no longer being earned. At that point, when long-run equilibrium is achieved, there will be more firms and more resources used in the corn industry than in the short run.

Finally, long-run equilibrium is established in both industries, and the reallocation of resources is complete. It is important to note that this reallocation can affect industries other than corn and potatoes. If potato land and equipment can be easily adapted to the production of corn, which seems unlikely, potato producers can simply change to the production of corn. If not, the resources used in potato production are converted to some use other than corn, and the resources that enter corn production come from some use other than potato production. The full repercussions can be analyzed by general equilibrium analysis, which is discussed in Chapter 14.

THE PATH TO EQUILIBRIUM AND THE COBWEB THEOREM

A great deal of attention has been devoted in this chapter to the equilibrium levels of price and output. However, disequilibrium, rather than equilibrium, has to be the usual state of most real-life markets. Demand curves are constantly shifting in response to changes in tastes and incomes, among other things. Supply curves are constantly shifting in response to changes in technology and resource limitations, among other things. Thus the equilibrium levels of prices are constantly changing, and actual prices differ from them. We must recognize the importance of disequilibrium but it would be a mistake to conclude from this that theories based on equilibrium prices are of no use. On the contrary, equilibrium theories help us to predict the direction of change of price and output. With careful study one can sometimes say a good deal about the way in which price and output are likely to move.

To illustrate how actual price may converge on the equilibrium price, consider one of the simplest dynamic models[7] in economics, the cobweb model or theorem.[8] Suppose that the amount supplied of a commodity, say hogs, is a function of price in the *previous* period. This might be the case because it takes one period to raise a hog. On the other hand, suppose that the amount demanded of the commodity is a function of price in the *present* period. Finally,

---

7. Dynamic models indicate the movement over a period of time of economic variables and the way in which such variables move from one equilibrium to another (or one disequilibrium to another).

8. The name *cobweb* is derived from the appearance of diagrams like Figure 8.14.

Fig.
8.14 THE COBWEB THEOREM / *According to the cobweb theorem, the amount
supplied depends on price in the previous period. If* OQ_1 *is supplied in the
first period, the price will be* OP_1, *which means that the quantity supplied
will be* OQ_2 *in the second period.*

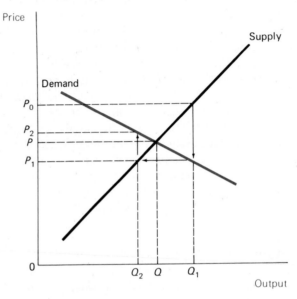

suppose that the demand and supply curves are as shown in Figure 8.14 and
OP_0 was the price in the previous period.

Under these assumptions, the amount supplied in the first period will be
OQ_1. But given that OQ_1 is supplied, the demand curve shows that the price
will be OP_1 in the first period (since this is the price at which OQ_1 units of output will be demanded). With this price in the first period, the supply curve
shows that the amount supplied in the second period will be OQ_2. And with
OQ_2 as the amount supplied in the second period, the demand curve shows that
the price in the second period will be OP_2. This process will go on and on, with
price and output each moving in a cycle. In one period, price is above the equilibrium level, with the result that the quantity supplied in the next period is
above the equilibrium level. Because quantity is then above the equilibrium
level, price will be below the equilibrium level. And so on.

In the case described in Figure 8.14, the process converges. The actual
price and output move closer and closer to the equilibrium levels, OP and OQ.
This is because the supply curve is steeper than the demand curve. If the slopes
of the demand and supply curves are equal (in absolute value), the cycles of
price and output continue undiminished. If the demand curve is steeper than
the supply curve, the amplitude of the cycles increases over time.

Although the cobweb model is extremely simple and mechanical, it may be of use in explaining why the prices and outputs of some commodities have shown pronounced cyclical movements. Jan Tinbergen of the Netherlands, a Nobel laureate, has suggested that this model may be relevant in explaining the patterns of hog prices. Clearly, however, the cobweb theorem is a very simple model that captures only a limited amount of the richness of the real world.

Example 8.2

ANALYZING NEW YORK'S SHORTAGE OF RENTAL HOUSING

Because New York City imposes ceilings on rents, there is a shortage of apartments. (Recall our discussion in Chapter 2.) According to econometric studies, the price elasticity of demand for rental housing in American cities is 1.0 and the price elasticity of supply of rental housing is 0.5 in the long run. If these elasticities are valid in New York City, and if its government pushes the level of rent down to a point that is 1 percent below its equilibrium value, how big will be the difference between the quantity demanded and the quantity supplied, as a percentage of the equilibrium quantity of rental housing?

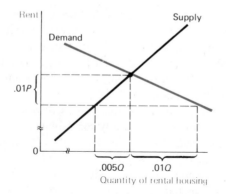

SOLUTION

Suppose that the equilibrium rent and quantity are P and Q, respectively. If the rent is reduced by 1 percent, the quantity demanded will increase by 1 percent, which means it will increase by $.01Q$ (see the graph). At the same time, the quantity supplied will fall by .5 percent, which means it will fall by $.005Q$. Thus the difference between the quantity supplied and the quantity demanded will equal $.01Q + .005Q$, or $.015Q$. In other words, it will equal 1.5 percent of the equilibrium quantity.*

* Of course, the level of rent in New York City may differ by more or less than 1 percent from the equilibrium level, but whatever the percentage may be, one can use this method to determine the percentage difference between the quantity demanded and quantity supplied. For further discussion, see F. deLeeuw and N. Ekanem, "The Supply of Rental Housing," *American Economic Review,* December 1971; and E. Hanushek and J. Quigley, "What Is the Price Elasticity of Housing Demand?," *Review of Economics and Statistics,* August 1980.

ESTIMATES OF PRICE ELASTICITY OF SUPPLY

Previous sections of this chapter have dealt at length with the role of demand curves and supply curves, both short-run and long-run, in the determination of price. Chapter 5 presented the results of various empirical studies of the demand curve for selected commodities. In this section we present the results of various empirical studies of the supply curve for selected commodities. The econometric techniques used to estimate the supply curve are much like those used to estimate the demand curve, which were discussed in Chapter 5.

To illustrate the kind of studies that have been carried out, consider the investigation sponsored by the Environmental Protection Agency of the elasticity of supply of construction services in the United States.[9] Studies made for EPA estimated that a 1 percent increase in the price of construction leads to an increase of 6.5 percent in the supply of construction services. EPA was extremely interested in the price elasticity of supply of construction services because it wanted to know how much construction prices must rise in order to bring forth the extra construction services required to build the treatment plants and other equipment needed to meet new environmental protection standards.

Of course, there is a considerable difference between short-run and long-run elasticities of supply. Turning to agriculture, Marc Nerlove and William Addison have estimated short-run and long-run elasticities of supply for a number of vegetables produced for fresh market in the United States. The short-run elasticity is defined to be the elasticity over one production period. The results are shown in Table 8.3.[10] Note that the short-run elasticities are considerably lower than the long-run elasticities, as would be expected. For example, the short-run elasticity of supply for cabbage is estimated to be 0.36, whereas the long-run elasticity is estimated to be 1.2. According to these estimates the long-run elasticity of supply is greater for cucumbers, green peas, and spinach than for the other commodities. Although these estimates are based on quite sophisticated techniques, Nerlove and Addison caution that they are tentative and presented mainly for purposes of illustration.

AGRICULTURAL PRICES AND OUTPUT: AN APPLICATION

Perhaps the most important sector of the American economy that contains industries that are reasonably close to perfect competition is agriculture.

---

9. See *The Economics of Clean Water—1973*, Environmental Protection Agency (Washington, D.C.: U.S. Government Printing Office, 1973).

10. M. Nerlove and W. Addison, "Statistical Estimation of Long-Run Elasticities of Supply and Demand," *Journal of Farm Economics*, November 1958.

Table ESTIMATED PRICE ELASTICITIES OF SUPPLY
8.3

| | Price elasticity | |
Commodity	Short run	Long run
Green lima beans	0.10	1.70
Green snap beans	0.15	∞*
Cabbage	0.36	1.20
Carrots	0.14	1.00
Cucumbers	0.29	2.20
Lettuce	0.03	0.16
Onions	0.34	1.00
Green peas	0.31	4.40
Green peppers	0.07	0.26
Tomatoes	0.16	0.90
Watermelons	0.23	0.48
Beets	0.13	1.00
Cantaloupes	0.02	0.04
Cauliflower	0.14	1.10
Celery	0.14	0.95
Eggplant	0.16	0.34
Kale (Va. only)	0.20	0.23
Spinach	0.20	4.70
Shallots (La. only)	0.12	0.31

* According to Nerlove and Addison, this estimate holds only for a limited range of output.

SOURCE: M. Nerlove and W. Addison, op. cit.

Farming is still our most important single industry, although it includes a much smaller percentage of our people than it once did. One of the most important points to note about American agriculture is that agricultural prices generally fell, relative to other prices, from World War I to the early 1970s. That is, if we correct for changes in the general price level resulting from overall inflation, there was a declining trend in farm prices. Another important fact is that farm incomes vary between good times and bad to a much greater extent than nonfarm incomes, whereas farm output is much more stable than industrial output.

The theory presented in this and previous chapters is useful in explaining the reasons for these characteristics of American agriculture. Figure 8.15 shows the demand and supply curves for farm products at various points in time. Since we know from Chapter 5 that the demand for food does not grow very rapidly in this country, we would expect the demand curve to shift relatively slowly to the right, from D in the first period to D_1 in the second period to D_2 in the third period. On the other hand, because of very great technologi-

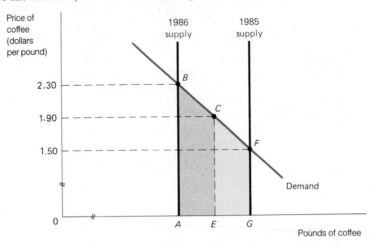
Fig.
8.15
SHIFTS IN DEMAND AND SUPPLY: AGRICULTURE / *Agricultural prices have fallen (relative to other prices) because the demand curve has shifted slowly to the right, whereas the supply curve has shifted rapidly to the right.*

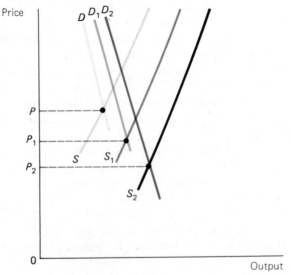

in 1986? (Assume that storage costs are zero.) (b) As they bought more and more 1985 coffee for sale in 1986, what would happen to the price of coffee in 1985? What would happen to the 1986 price? (c) At what point would it no longer be profitable for speculators to buy more coffee in 1985 for sale in 1986? (d) If speculators bought *EG* pounds in 1985 and sold them in 1986, would society gain? (e) If speculators had forecasted a poor coffee crop in 1986, and bought large amounts of coffee in 1985 for sale in 1986, would society have gained by their actions if the 1986 coffee crop turned out to be larger than that in 1985?

SOLUTION

(a) Since the 1985 price was $1.50 per pound and the 1986 price was $2.30 per pound, they would have made $2.30 − $1.50 = $0.80. (b) As they bought more and more coffee in 1985, the price of coffee would have risen then. As they sold more and more coffee in 1986, the price of coffee would have fallen then. (c) If they took *EG* pounds off the market in 1985, the remaining supply would be *OE* pounds, and the price would be $1.90 per pound, as shown in the graph. When these *EG*(= *AE*) pounds are added to the 1986 supply, it would mean that the total supply would be *OE* pounds (the same as in 1985), and the 1986 price would be $1.90 per pound. Since the price would be the same in 1986 as in 1985, there would be no profit in buying more coffee in 1985 for sale in 1986. (d) If we use the area under the demand curve as a measure of the value to society of an additional amount of output (recall Chapter 4), the value of the additional *AE* pounds in 1986 equals shaded area *ABCE* in the graph, and the value of the *EG*(= *AE*) pounds given up in 1985 equals shaded area *ECFG*. Since the former area exceeds the latter, society would gain, at least by this criterion. (e) No. They would have withdrawn coffee from use in 1985 (when relative to 1986 it was scarce) and made it available in 1986 (when relative to 1985 it was plentiful.)*

* For further discussion, see "Coffee Price Boom Stirs Fear in Brazil," *New York Times,* February 17, 1986.

cal improvements in agriculture, the supply curve has been shifting relatively rapidly to the right, from *S* in the first period to S_1 in the second period to S_2 in the third period. The consequence is that agricultural prices fell (relative to other prices) from *OP* to OP_1 to OP_2.

It is also easy to see why farm incomes are so unstable. We know from Chapter 5 that the demand curve for basic farm products is relatively inelastic. Also, the supply curve for basic farm products is relatively inelastic in the short run. Since both the demand curve and the supply curve are inelastic, a small shift (to the right or left) in either curve, or both, results in a large change in price. To illustrate, consider Figure 8.16. In panel A, the demand and supply curves are much less elastic than in panel B, with the result that a small shift in the demand curve results in a much bigger change in price in panel A than in panel B.

Although agricultural prices have generally fallen (relative to industrial prices) over the past sixty years, this trend was reversed sharply in 1973 and 1974, when farm prices rose at an astonishing rate. Due to poor harvests in other countries and the devaluation of the dollar, as well as trade with the Communist world, there was a marked upward shift to the right of the demand curve for American farm products. As would be predicted by our theory, farm

Fig. RELATIONSHIP BETWEEN ELASTICITY OF SUPPLY AND DEMAND AND
8.16 INSTABILITY OF PRICE / *Because the demand and supply curves are much
less elastic in panel A than in panel B, a small shift in the demand curve
(from* D *to* D₁*) results in a much bigger change in price in panel A than in
panel B.*

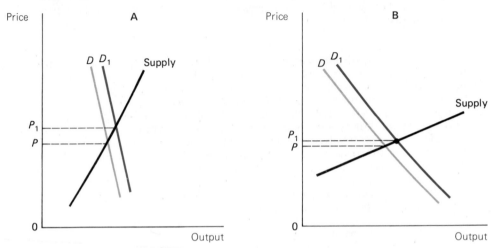

prices rose rapidly in response to this shift in the demand curve. For example,
the price of wheat rose from under $2 to over $5 per bushel. Anyone who wit-
nessed the proceedings would have been quick to agree that farm prices behaved in accord with our model.

Government Subsidy Programs

Another important fact about American agriculture that must be added to
this picture is government intervention and aid. Both Figures 8.15 and 8.16 are
based on the supposition that agricultural markets are free. For about half of
all farm products, the government has established price support programs of
one sort or another. These programs vary in many respects, but the general
idea behind them is that the federal government has tried to increase farm
prices in various ways. For products where such programs exist, the perfectly
competitive model is clearly an inappropriate device to predict price and output. But, as we shall see in this section, the basic elements of the theory remain
useful in analyzing the effects of these programs.

More specifically, the programs in operation until 1973 can be described
in terms of Figure 8.17. A support price, OP', was set which was above the equilibrium price, OP, with the consequence that output equaled OQ_1, consumers
bought OQ_2, and the rest (which equaled $OQ_1 - OQ_2$) had to be purchased by
the government. The imposition of the support price meant, of course, that

Fig.   EFFECT OF PRICE SUPPORT / *Before 1973, a support price, OP′, was set*
8.17   *which was above the equilibrium price, OP. Thus output equaled* OQ_1;
        consumers bought OQ_2; *and the government bought the rest (which*
        equaled $OQ_1 - OQ_2$).

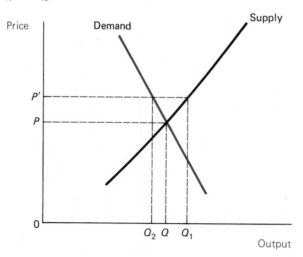

farmers received more for their crop than they otherwise would have, and the difference in their receipts was $OP′ \times OQ_1 - OP \times OQ$.

To cut down on the amount that the government had to purchase (and store or dispose of), production controls were imposed as well. These controls often took the form of quotas on the acreage used to grow the product. With such controls, the situation is shown in Figure 8.18, where OQ_3 is the total quota—in terms of output—for all farms. Because of the imposition of the production control, the government's expenditures were reduced from $OP′ \times (OQ_1 - OQ_2)$ in Figure 8.17 to $OP′ (OQ_3 - OQ_2)$ in Figure 8.18.

In 1973, an alternative plan, proposed earlier by President Harry Truman's Secretary of Agriculture, Charles Brannan, and President Dwight Eisenhower's Secretary, Ezra Taft Benson, was adopted. According to this plan, which is illustrated in Figure 8.19, farmers are still guaranteed a "target" price of $OP′$, but rather than allow the amount the government buys (which equals $OQ_3 - OQ_2$) to waste in storage, they sell this amount at whatever consumers will pay for it. Or, what amounts to the same thing, the government lets the competitive market alone, with the result that an output of OQ_3 is produced and sold at a price of OP_2; then the government issues subsidy checks to farmers to cover the difference between the price they received and the target price, $OP′$.

Clearly, the cost to the government under the Brannan plan is $(OP′ - OP_2) \times OQ_3$. An important question is: Will the cost to the Treasury be greater than under the support plan shown in Figure 8.18? The answer de-

Fig. 8.18 EFFECT OF PRICE SUPPORT AND PRODUCTION CONTROL / *If* OQ₃ *is the total production quota, and* OP' *is the support price, the government has to purchase an amount of the commodity equaling* (OQ₃ − OQ₂).

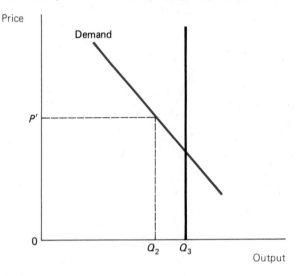

pends on the elasticity of demand. If demand is inelastic, it will be greater; if demand is elastic, it will be smaller. To prove this, recall that the cost under the Brannan plan would be $(OP' - OP_2)OQ_3$, and the cost in Figure 8.18 would be $OP'(OQ_3 - OQ_2)$. Thus the former cost would be less than the latter if

Fig. 8.19 EFFECT OF THE BRANNAN PLAN / *According to the Brannan Plan, farmers sell their output at price* OP₂, *and receive subsidy checks to cover the difference between the price they receive and the target price,* OP'.

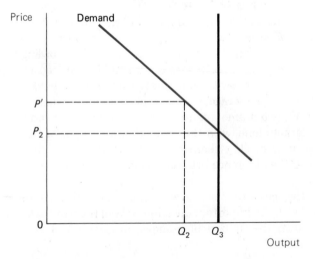

$OP_2 \times OQ_3 > OP' \times OQ_2$. But since $OP_2 \times OQ_3$ is the revenue at price OP_2 and $OP' \times OQ_2$ is the revenue at price OP', the former will be more than the latter only if the price elasticity of demand exceeds 1. (Recall the discussion on p. 27.)

Since the demand for agricultural products is generally inelastic, this means that the Brannan plan will cost the Treasury more than the support plan in Figure 8.18, if the market price is less than the target price. But this is not a necessarily overwhelming argument against the Brannan plan. For one thing, the market price may be above the target price, in which case the Brannan plan will cost the Treasury nothing. For another, the Brannan plan has the advantage that the market price is closer to the true social cost of producing agricultural products. More will be said about the economic advantages and disadvantages of various types of agricultural price support programs in Chapter 14, when we continue this discussion of agricultural subsidies.

SUMMARY

1. Perfect competition is defined by four conditions: No participant in the market can influence price; output must be homogeneous; resources must be mobile; and there must be perfect knowledge.

2. In the market period, where the quantity supplied is fixed, the price of a product is demand-determined. In the short run, the firm maximizes profit or minimizes losses by producing the output at which marginal cost equals price. However, if market price is less than the firm's average variable costs at all levels of output, the firm will minimize losses by discontinuing production. The firm's short-run supply curve is the same as its marginal cost curve, as long as price exceeds average variable cost.

3. The short-run price of a product is determined by the interaction between the demand and supply sides of the market. As a rough approximation, the industry's short-run supply curve can be regarded as the horizontal summation of the short-run supply curves of the individual firms. However, this is not the case if the supply of inputs to the industry is not perfectly elastic.

4. The short-run equilibrium price level is the price at which the quantity demanded and the quantity supplied in the short run are equal. At the equilibrium price, price will equal marginal cost for all firms that choose to produce, rather than shut down their plants.

5. In the long run, firms can change their plant size and leave or enter the industry. The long-run equilibrium position of the firm is at the point at which its long-run average costs equal price. Moreover, firms must be operating at the minimum point on their long-run average cost curves.

6. Industries can be divided into three types: constant cost, increasing cost, and decreasing cost. Constant-cost industries have horizontal long-run supply curves; increasing-cost industries have positively sloped long-run supply curves; and decreasing-cost industries have negatively sloped long-run supply curves. Increasing-cost industries are generally regarded as being the most numerous of the three types.

7. Having presented this basic theory, we described the way in which resources are allocated in a perfectly competitive economy. Then we discussed the process by which actual price may converge on the equilibrium price, using as an illustration the cobweb model.

8. Finally, we used the theory to explain some of the characteristics of American agriculture and to analyze government subsidy programs.

========= QUESTIONS/PROBLEMS =========

1) In the period between the first and second world wars, the cotton textile industry was sometimes described as being closer to perfect competition than any other manufacturing industry in the United States. Considerable excess capacity existed in the cotton textile industry from about 1924 to 1936. Evidence of this overcapacity is presented in the table below, which shows that the profit rate in cotton textiles was considerably below that in other manufacturing. For example, during 1924–28 and 1933–36, textile profits averaged less than 4 percent of the firms' capitalization, whereas profits as a percentage of capitalization in all manufacturing averaged 8 percent. Also, profit rates in cotton textiles were higher in the South than in the North, due to the fact that the prices of many inputs—like labor and raw cotton—were lower in the South.

| | Profits as a percentage of capitalization | |
Period	*Cotton textiles*	*All manufacturing*
1919–23	15.3	11.0
1924–28	4.7	11.0
1933–36	2.4	4.3

(a) Was the industry in long-run equilibrium? (b) What sorts of changes were required to make the industry approach long-run equilibrium? (c) In fact, did these changes occur—as our theory would predict?

2) "In long-run equilibrium, every firm in a competitive industry earns zero profit. Thus, if the price falls, all of these firms will be unable to stay in business." Evaluate this statement.

3) Richard Webster is a Nebraska farmer who produces corn on 1,000 acres of land, 500 of which are rented and 500 of which are owned. In an interview reported in the *New York Times*, he estimated that his costs per acre for corn produced in 1980 on his rented land were as follows:

Fertilizer	$ 41.84
Herbicides	2.76
Insecticides	5.50
Fuel	18.00
Seed	16.50
Electricity	15.00
Cost of services of plant and equipment	85.46
Labor	15.00
Insurance	10.00
Land rent	110.00
Total	$320.06

(a) Does this mean that the average cost of producing corn is $320.06? Why or why not? (b) On each acre of land that he owns, Mr. Webster does not have to pay a rent of $110, included above. Does this mean that the cost of using his own land is less than that of using rented land? (c) If each acre of land yields 120 bushels of corn, and if the price of a bushel of corn were expected to be 80 cents, should Mr. Webster produce any corn? (d) If the price were expected to be $1.50, should he produce any corn?

4) According to some firms in the paper industry, price controls during the early 1970s resulted in price being below average variable cost. What do you think that these firms did? If you had been a consultant to these firms, what advice would you have given them?

5) According to a 1978 study by Neil Ericsson and Peter Morgan, the supply curve for shale oil was as shown below.

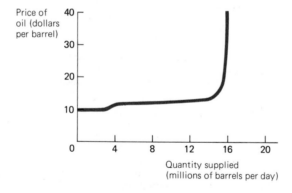

Quantity supplied
(millions of barrels per day)

Two problems in producing shale oil are that the producer must dispose of the spent shale and that air pollution may occur. This supply curve assumes that the disposal of spent shale costs $5 per ton, and that federal air pollution standards are applied. (a) If the disposal of spent shale costs $10 per ton, would you expect the quantity supplied to be more or less than 16 million barrels per day if the price of oil is $40 per barrel? (b) Colorado air pollution standards are stricter than federal standards. If the Colorado standards are applied, would you expect the quantity supplied to be more or less than 16 million barrels per day if the price of oil is $40 per barrel? (c) Since no commercial-scale shale oil plants had been built, the above supply curve was based on engineering estimates. Do you think that this supply curve is very accurate? Why or why not? (d) A shale oil plant is estimated to cost over $1 billion. Would an investment in such a plant be risky? Why or why not? Would this influence the position and shape of the supply curve?

6) Explain how it is possible for an industry to be a constant-cost industry even though each firm in the industry has increasing marginal costs.

7) A perfectly competitive firm has the following total cost function:

Total output (dollars)	Total cost (dollars)
0	20
1	30
2	42
3	55
4	69
5	84
6	100
7	117

How much will the firm produce if the price is (a) $13, (b) $14, (c) $15, (d) $16, or (e) $17?

8) If the textile industry is a constant-cost industry, and the demand curve for textiles shifts upward, what are the steps by which a competitive market insures an increased amount of textiles. What happens if the government will not allow textile prices to rise?

9) An economist estimates that, in the short run, the quantity of men's socks supplied at each price is as follows:

Price (dollars per pair)	Quantity supplied per year (millions of pairs)
1	5
2	6
3	7
4	8

Calculate the arc elasticity of supply when the price is between $3 and $4 per pair. (Review Chapter 2 if you do not recall the definition of the arc elasticity of supply.)

10) Suppose that there are 100 firms producing the good in Question 7, and that each firm has the total cost function shown there. If input prices remain constant (regardless of industry output), draw the industry supply curve.

11) According to D. Suits and S. Koizumi, the supply function for onions in the United States is $\log q = 0.134 + .0123\, t + 0.324 \log P - 0.512 \log C$, where q is the quantity supplied in a particular year, t is the year (less 1924), P is the price last season, and C is the cost index last season. Suppose that price is estimated by one forecaster to be 10 cents this season, whereas another says that it will be 11 cents. Holding other factors constant, how much difference will this make in forecasting the quantity supplied next season?

12) As pointed out in Example 8.2, studies indicate that the price elasticity of demand for rental housing in American cities is 1.0 and that the price elasticity of supply of rental housing is 0.5 in the long run. (a) Suppose that a particular city's government decides that the level of rent should be pushed up in order to bring about a 2 percent increase in the supply of rental housing. How big an increase in the rent is required? (b) What will be the effect on the total amount of rental housing that is demanded?

Price and Output under Pure Monopoly

PURE MONOPOLY

Most Americans are familiar with the word *monopoly*. On rainy afternoons, children in the United States often play a game called Monopoly in which they try hard to become the sole owners of related pieces of property. (According to the rules of the game, the amount that a player can get from the other players is greater if he is the sole owner of related pieces of property.) Whether or not you have ever played this game, the concept of a monopoly is probably familiar: A monopoly is a situation where there is a single source of supply. And whether you live in the United States or Canada or Australia or the United Kingdom, you have probably encountered some firms that are monopolies, or close to it. Electric companies, telephone companies, and water companies often are examples.

Monopoly

In microeconomics, pure monopoly, like perfect competition, is a useful model. The conditions defining pure monopoly are easy to state: There must exist one, and only one, seller in a market. Pure monopoly, like perfect competition, does not correspond more than approximately to conditions in real industries. But, as we have noted several times before, a model must be judged by its predictive ability, not the "realism" of its assumptions. The theory of pure monopoly has proved to be a very useful analytical device. Pure monopoly and perfect competition are opposites in the following sense: The firm in a perfectly competitive market has so many rivals that competition becomes impersonal in the extreme; the firm under pure monopoly has no rivals at all. Under pure monopoly, one firm is the sole supplier. There is no competition.

Having said this, it is important to add that the policies adopted by a pure monopolist are affected by certain indirect and potential forms of competition. Clearly, the monopolist is not completely insulated from the effects of actions taken in the rest of the economy. All commodities are rivals for the consumer's favor, as we saw in Chapter 3. Clearly this rivalry occurs among different products, as well as among the producers of a given commodity. For example, meat competes in this sense with butter, eggs, and even men's suits. Of course, the extent of the competition from other products depends on the extent to which other products are substitutes for the monopolist's product. For example, even if a firm somehow could obtain a monopoly on the supply of steel in a particular market, it would still face considerable competition from producers of aluminum, plastics, and other materials that are reasonably good substitutes for steel.

In addition, the threat of potential competition also acts as a brake on the policies of the monopolist. The monopolist often can maintain its monopoly position only if it does not extract as much short-run profit as possible. If it sets prices above a certain point, other firms may enter its market and try to break its monopoly. If entry can occur, the monopolist must take this possibility into account. Failure to do so may make it an ex-monopolist.

Reasons for Monopoly

Why do monopolies arise? There are many reasons, but four seem particularly important. First, a single firm may control the entire supply of a basic input that is required to manufacture a given product. The example that is cited repeatedly to illustrate this situation is the pre-World War II aluminum industry. Bauxite is an input used to produce aluminum; and for some time, practically every source of bauxite in the United States was controlled by the Aluminum Company of America (Alcoa). For this reason (and others), Alcoa was, for a long time, the sole producer of aluminum in the United States.

Second, a firm may become a monopolist because the average cost of producing the product reaches a minimum at an output rate that is big enough to satisfy the entire market at a price that is profitable. In a situation of this sort, if there is more than one firm producing the product, each must be producing at a higher-than-minimum level of average cost. Each may be inclined to cut the price to increase its output rate and reduce its average costs. The result is likely to be economic

Natural monopoly

warfare—and the survival of a single victor, the monopolist. Cases in which costs behave in this fashion are called *natural monopolies.* When an industry is a natural monopoly, the public often insists that its behavior be regulated by the government.

Third, a firm may acquire a monopoly over the production of a good by having patents on the product or on certain basic processes that are used in its production. The patent laws of the United States permit an inventor to get the exclusive right to make a certain product or to use a particular process. (The patent is in force for seventeen years.) Patents can be very important in keeping competitors out. For example, Alcoa held important patents on basic production processes used to make aluminum. However, it is often possible to "invent around" another company's patents. That is, although a firm cannot use a product or process on which another firm has a patent (without the latter's permission), it may be able to develop a closely related product or process and obtain a patent on it.

Fourth, a firm may become a monopolist because it is awarded a market franchise by a government agency. The firm is granted the exclusive privilege to produce a given good or service in a particular area. In exchange for this right, the firm agrees to allow the government to regulate certain aspects of its behavior and operations. For example, as we shall see in a later section, the government may set limits on the firm's price. Regardless of the form of regulation, the important point is that the monopoly has been created by the government.

The Monopolist's Demand Curve

Since the monopolist is the only firm producing a product, it is obvious that the monopolist's demand curve is precisely the same as the market demand curve for the product. Consequently, the factors determining the shape of the monopolist's demand curve are the same factors that determine the shape of the demand curve for the product. As we saw in Chapter 5 these factors are the prices of other related products (substitutes and complements), incomes, and tastes. However, it should be noted that the monopolist sometimes can affect the prices of related products, as well as consumer tastes. To influence consumer tastes, monopolists often make considerable expenditures on advertising, the purpose being, of course, to shift the demand curve to the right.

Since the monopolist's demand curve is negatively sloped (because the demand curve for a product is negatively sloped, save for a few cases of little significance), average and marginal revenue are not the same. This is quite different from the case of perfect competition where average and marginal revenue were equal. To illustrate the situation faced by a monopolist, consider the hypothetical case in Table 9.1. The price at which each quantity (shown in column 1) can be sold is shown in column 2. The total revenue, the product of the

Table DEMAND AND REVENUE OF MONOPOLIST
9.1

Quantity sold	Price (dollars)	Total revenue (dollars)	Marginal revenue* (dollars)
3	100.00	300.00	—
8	80.00	640.00	68.00 (= $^{340}\!/_5$)
15	74.00	1,110.00	67.14 (= $^{470}\!/_7$)
21	70.00	1,470.00	60.00 (= $^{360}\!/_6$)
26	67.50	1,755.00	57.00 (= $^{285}\!/_5$)
30	65.50	1,965.00	52.50 (= $^{210}\!/_4$)
33	62.00	2,046.00	27.00 (= $^{81}\!/_3$)
35	60.00	2,100.00	27.00 (= $^{54}\!/_2$)

* These figures pertain to the interval between the indicated quantity of output and one unit less than the indicated quantity of output.

first two columns, is shown in column 3. Obviously, the average revenue corresponding to each output is the price corresponding to that output.

Marginal revenue is of great importance to the profit-maximizing firm. How can we estimate marginal revenue from the figures in Table 9.1? Marginal revenue between q and $(q-1)$ units of output is defined as $R(q) - R(q-1)$, where $R(q)$ is the total revenue when the output equals q. The problem in Table 9.1 is that the data are not provided for each level of output; we only have data for $q = 3$, 8, 15, and so on. To cope with this problem, we assume that $R(q)$ is approximately a linear function of q between 3 and 8, 8 and 15, 15 and 21, and so on. If this is the case, the marginal revenue is ($640 - $300) ÷ 5 at an output of between 7 and 8, ($1,110 - $640) ÷ 7 at an output of between 14 and 15, and so forth. The results are shown in the last column of Table 9.1.

The Monopolist's Costs

Although a firm is a monopolist in the product market, it may be a perfect competitor in the market for inputs, in which case it buys so small a proportion of the total supply of each input that it cannot affect input prices. If this is the case, there is no need to dwell further on the monopolist's costs, since the theory in Chapter 7 will apply without modification.

In many cases, however, the monopolist is not a perfect competitor in the input markets, because it buys a large proportion of certain specialized resources that have little use other than to produce the commodity in question. In a case of this sort, the price that the firm has to pay for this input depends on how much it buys. The more the firm wants of this resource, the more it will generally have to pay. Cases of this sort are discussed at some length in

Table 9.2 COSTS OF MONOPOLIST

Output	Total variable cost (dollars)	Fixed cost (dollars)	Total cost (dollars)	Marginal cost* (dollars)
0	0	500	500	—
3	110	500	610	36.67 (= $^{110}/_3$)
8	240	500	740	26.00 (= $^{130}/_5$)
15	390	500	890	21.43 (= $^{150}/_7$)
21	560	500	1,060	28.33 (= $^{170}/_6$)
26	750	500	1,250	38.00 (= $^{190}/_5$)
30	960	500	1,460	52.50 (= $^{210}/_4$)
33	1,190	500	1,690	76.67 (= $^{230}/_3$)
35	1,440	500	1,940	125.00 (= $^{250}/_2$)

* These figures pertain to the interval between the indicated quantity of output and one unit less than the indicated quantity of output.

Chapter 13. In the present chapter we assume that the firm is a perfect competitor in the market for inputs.

Table 9.2 shows the costs of our hypothetical monopolist. Column 1 shows various output rates, column 2 shows the total variable cost at each output rate, and column 3 shows the firm's fixed costs. Finally, column 4 shows the firm's total cost at each output rate, and column 5 shows the firm's marginal costs.

SHORT-RUN EQUILIBRIUM PRICE AND OUTPUT

The monopolist, if unregulated and free to maximize profits, will, of course, choose the price and output at which the difference between total revenue and total cost is largest. For example, combining the data from Tables 9.1 and 9.2 into Table 9.3, we find that our hypothetical monopolist will choose an output

Table 9.3 COST, REVENUE, AND PROFIT OF MONOPOLIST

Output	Total revenue (dollars)	Total cost (dollars)	Total profit (dollars)
3	300	610	−310
8	640	740	−100
15	1,110	890	220
21	1,470	1,060	410
26	1,755	1,250	505
30	1,965	1,460	505
33	2,046	1,690	356
35	2,100	1,940	160

Fig. **TOTAL REVENUE, TOTAL COST, AND TOTAL PROFIT OF MONOPOLIST** / *To*
9.1 *maximize profit, the monopolist will choose an output rate of 26 or 30*
units per period and a price of $65.50 or $67.50.

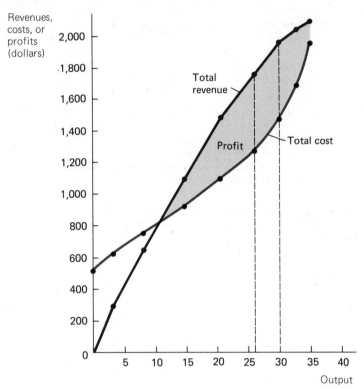

rate of either 26 or 30 units per time period and a price of $65.50 or $67.50. Figure 9.1 shows the situation graphically.

Note that either of these optimal output rates is less than the output rate where price equals marginal cost. Under perfect competition, the profit-maximizing output was the one at which price equals marginal cost; indeed, this fact was used to derive the firm's supply curve. It is obvious from Tables 9.1 and 9.2 that this result is not true for pure monopoly.

Under monopoly, the firm will maximize profit if it sets its output rate at the point at which marginal cost equals marginal revenue. Table 9.4 and Figure 9.2 show that this is true in this example. It is easy to prove that this is generally a necessary condition for profit maximization. At any output rate at which marginal revenue exceeds marginal cost, profit can be increased by increasing output, since the extra revenue will exceed the extra cost. Thus profit will not be a maximum when marginal revenue exceeds marginal cost. At any output rate at which marginal cost exceeds marginal revenue, profit can be increased by reducing output, since the decrease in cost will exceed the decrease

Table MARGINAL COST AND MARGINAL REVENUE OF MONOPOLIST
9.4

Output	Marginal cost* (dollars)	Marginal revenue* (dollars)	Total profit (dollars)
3	36.7	—	−310
8	26.0	68.0	−100
15	21.4	67.1	220
21	28.3	60.0	310
26	38.0	57.0	505
30	52.5	52.5	505
33	76.7	27.0	356
35	125.0	27.0	160

* These figures pertain to the interval between the indicated quantity of
output and one unit less than the indicated quantity of output.

Fig. MARGINAL COST AND MARGINAL REVENUE OF MONOPOLIST / *At the*
9.2 *monopolist's profit-maximizing output (26 or 30 units), marginal cost
equals marginal revenue.*

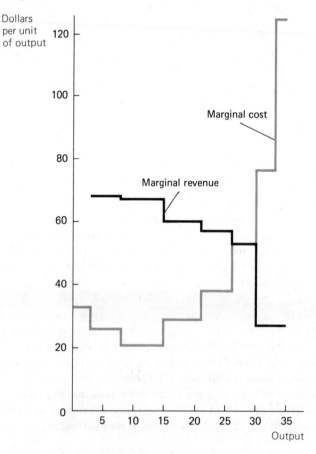

Fig.   EQUILIBRIUM POSITION OF MONOPOLIST / *In equilibrium, the monopolist*
9.3   *produces* OQ *units of output and sets a price of* OP.

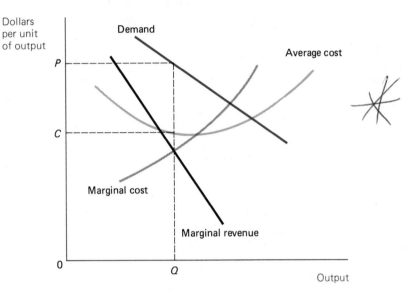

in revenue. Thus profit will not be a maximum when marginal cost exceeds
marginal revenue. Since profit is not a maximum when marginal revenue exceeds marginal cost or when marginal cost exceeds marginal revenue, it must
be a maximum only when marginal revenue equals marginal cost.

Using this result, it is also simple to represent graphically the short-run
equilibrium of the monopolist. Figure 9.3 shows the demand curve, the marginal revenue curve, the marginal cost curve, and the average total cost curve
faced by the firm. Short-run equilibrium will occur at the output, OQ, where
the marginal cost curve intersects the marginal revenue curve. If the monopolist produces OQ units, the demand curve shows that it must set a price of OP.
Moreover, since the average cost curve shows that average costs are OC at an
output of OQ units, the profit per unit of output is $(OP - OC)$, and the firm's
total profit is $OQ[OP - OC]$.

In this case, the monopolist earns a profit, but this need not always be the
case. It does not follow that a firm that holds a monopoly over the production
of a particular product must make a profit. The demand curve for the product
may be such that, even when the firm produces at the point at which marginal
revenue equals marginal cost, average cost exceeds price. For example, even if
one could somehow obtain a monopoly on the sale of cigar-store Indians, it
might not be a profitable business to enter. Indeed, in the short run, a monopolist may not be able to cover its variable costs, in which case it will discontinue production.

Example 9.1

ECONOMICS OF THE POST OFFICE

Postal service, which since 1845 has been largely a government monopoly in the United States, has been the object of continual controversy. Suppose that the short-run demand and cost curves of the Philadelphia post office are as follows:

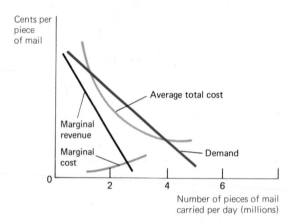

(a) Does the post office appear to be a natural monopoly, as some claim? (b) If the post office is a natural monopoly, must it be operated under government ownership? (c) If the Philadelphia post office wants to carry as many pieces of mail as it can without incurring a short-run deficit, how many should it carry per day? (d) The available evidence indicates that average revenue (per piece of mail) has exceeded average total cost and marginal cost for first-class mail, but not for third-class mail. Which type of mail is likely to attract private competitors? (e) What advantages might accrue if the post office were to face increased private competition?

SOLUTION

(a) One cannot tell, because the answer depends on the long-run (not the short-run) average cost curve. A firm is a natural monopolist if its long-run average cost reaches a minimum at an output rate that is big enough to satisfy the market at a price that is profitable. (b) Many natural monopolies—for example, telephone companies and electric-power producers—are privately owned, so it is by no means clear that government ownership is implied. (c) 4 million pieces, since this is the point where the average total cost curve intersects the demand curve. (d) First-class mail, because it earns a profit. With respect to parcels, there is already considerable competition (from United Parcel Service, in particular). (e) More competition might prod the post office to increase its own efficiency.*

---

* For further discussion, see M. Baratz, "Cost Behavior and Pricing Policy in the Post Office," *Land Economics*, November 1962.

Fig.   MORE THAN ONE OUTPUT LEVEL CORRESPONDING TO A GIVEN PRICE / A
9.4   *price of* OP *can result in an output of* OQ_0 *or* OQ_1, *depending on whether
the demand curve is* D_0 *or* D_1.

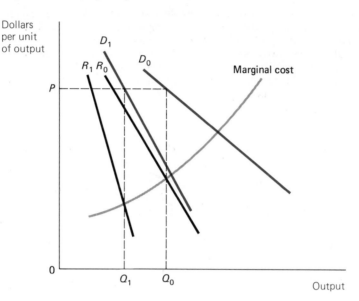

In perfect competition, one can define a unique relationship between the
price of the product and the amount supplied. This is the industry's supply
curve, which we discussed on pp. 229–31 of Chapter 8. In monopoly, there is no
such unique relationship between the product's price and the amount supplied. At first, this is likely to strike the reader as being extremely strange; indeed, one can be pardoned for questioning whether it really is so. The rest of
this section is aimed at convincing the reader that it is true.

Figure 9.4 shows the marginal cost curve of the monopolist. It is assumed
that the demand curve shifts from D_0 to D_1. When the demand curve is D_0, the
firm produces OQ_0 units (since the marginal cost curve intersects the marginal
revenue curve, R_0, at OQ_0) and the price must be OP. When the demand curve
is D_1, the firm produces OQ_1 units (since the marginal cost curve intersects the
new marginal revenue curve, R_1, at OQ_1) and the price must be OP. This result
shows that there is no unique relationship between price and quantity. A price
of OP can result in an output of OQ_0 or OQ_1. Thus a particular price can result
in a wide variety of output levels, depending on the shape and level of the demand curve.

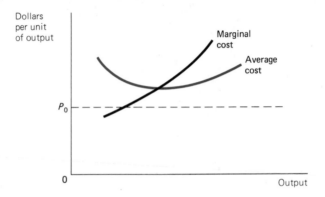
LONG-RUN EQUILIBRIUM PRICE AND OUTPUT

In contrast to perfect competition, the long-run equilibrium of a monopolistic industry is not marked by the absence of economic profits or losses. If a monopolist earns a short-run economic profit, it will not be confronted in the long run with competitors, unless the industry is no longer a monopoly. (The entrance of additional firms into the industry is, of course, not compatible with the existence of monopoly.) Thus the long-run equilibrium of an industry under monopoly may be characterized by economic profits.

On the other hand, if the monopolist incurs a short-run economic loss, it will be forced to look for other, more profitable uses for its resources. One possibility is that its existing plant is not optimal and that it can earn economic profits if it alters the scale and characteristics of its plant appropriately. If this is the case, it will make these alterations in the long run and remain in the in-

pear on the scene? (c) A large number of major lawsuits have alleged predatory behavior. For example, the government alleged that IBM's 360 line of computers was priced in a predatory fashion. To help solve the difficult problem of determining when predatory pricing takes place, Phillip Areeda and Donald Turner of Harvard University have proposed that it be illegal for a dominant firm to set its price below both its average and marginal costs. What problems can you see in this rule?

SOLUTION

(a) Whether the monopolist is well advised to set this price depends on the likelihood that the rival will be driven out of business. Given the monopolist's larger output, it will lose more money than the rival. However, the monopolist may have larger financial resources and may be in a better position to withstand such losses. (b) No. However, if it manages to impose heavy losses on its rival, this may teach other potential entrants the lesson that it does not pay to challenge the monopolist. (c) If the entrant has to enter on a large scale (because of economies of scale or for some other reason), the post-entry price is likely to fall below the pre-entry level (because of the increase in supply). Thus, even if the monopolist does not set its price below its average and marginal costs, a potential entrant may be discouraged from entering because, if it enters (and if the monopolist maintains its output), price is likely to fall below the entrant's average cost, resulting in losses for the entrant. In this way, the monopolist may be able to deter entry without appearing to violate the Areeda-Turner rule. Another problem is that the monopolist may choose its plant size with a view toward allowing it flexibility in responding to new entry by expanding output and reducing the price, while not violating this rule. For reasons of this sort, the Areeda-Turner rule has received considerable criticism. Nonetheless, this rule has been used (or at least considered) by many courts.*

* For further discussion, see P. Areeda and D. Turner, "Predatory Pricing and Related Practices Under Section 2 of the Sherman Act," *Harvard Law Review,* 1975; and G. Hay, "A Confused Lawyer's Guide to the Predatory Pricing Literature," reprinted in E. Mansfield, *Microeconomics: Selected Readings,* 5th ed.

dustry. However, if there is no scale of plant that will enable the monopolist to avoid economic losses, it will leave the industry in the long run.

Returning to the case in which the monopolist earns short-run profits, it must decide in the long run whether it can make even larger profits by altering its plant. For example, assume that the monopolist's demand curve, marginal revenue curve, long-run average cost curve, and long-run marginal cost curve are as shown in Figure 9.5. Suppose that the firm currently has a plant corresponding to short-run average cost curve, A_0A_0', and short-run marginal cost curve, M_0M_0'. In the short run, it will produce OQ_0 units and set a price of OP_0. Since short-run average cost is OB, the firm's short-run profits will be $OQ_0[OP_0 - OB]$.

However, the firm can adjust its plant in the long run so as to make bigger profits than $OQ_0[OP_0 - OB]$. It is easy to show that the monopolist will maximize profit in the long run when it produces the output at which long-run

Fig.   LONG-RUN EQUILIBRIUM FOR MONOPOLIST / *In the long run, the*
9.5   *monopolist will produce the output,* OQ_1, *at which long-run marginal cost*
        equals long-run marginal revenue.

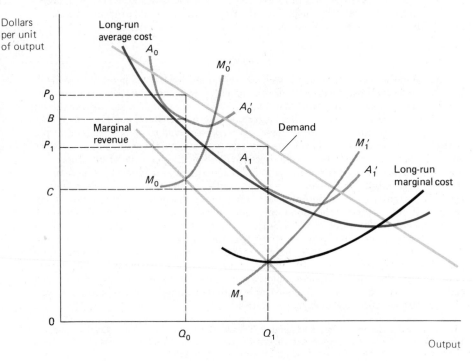

marginal cost equals long-run marginal revenue. The reasoning behind this
rule is precisely the same as that given in the section before last. Thus the firm
will produce OQ_1 units in the long run, since this is the point at which the
long-run marginal cost curve intersects the marginal revenue curve. The long-
run average cost will be OC, the price will be OP_1, and total profit will be
$OQ_1[OP_1 - OC]$. The resulting plant will have short-run average and marginal
cost curves of A_1A_1' and M_1M_1', respectively.

COMPARISON OF MONOPOLY WITH PERFECT
COMPETITION

It is important to note the differences between the long-run equilibrium of a
monopoly and a perfectly competitive industry. Suppose that we could perform an experiment in which an industry was first operated under conditions
of perfect competition and then under conditions of monopoly. Assuming that
the demand curve for the industry's product and the industry's cost curves

would be the same in either case,[1] what would be the difference in the long-run equilibrium?

First, under perfect competition, each firm operates at the point at which both long-run and short-run average costs are a minimum. However, under monopoly, although the plant that is used will produce the monopolist's long-run equilibrium output at minimum average cost, it is not the plant that will produce the product at the lowest possible average cost. In general, if the monopolist expanded its long-run equilibrium output, it could utilize a plant with lower average costs. This is clearly shown by Figure 9.6, which compares the long-run equilibrium of a firm under perfect competition and monopoly. The monopolist produces OQ_M units of output, which is less than the output corresponding to the minimum point on the long-run average cost curve. Consequently, society's resources tend to be used more effectively in perfectly competitive industries than in monopolized industries.[2] More will be said about this in Chapter 14.

Second, the output of a perfectly competitive industry tends to be greater and price tends to be lower than under monopoly. The perfectly competitive firm operates at the point at which price equals marginal cost, whereas the monopolist operates at a point at which price exceeds marginal cost. Under various circumstances, as we shall see in Chapter 14, price is a good indicator of

Fig. 9.6 COMPARISON OF LONG-RUN EQUILIBRIA / *In contrast to perfect competition, the long-run equilibrium output under monopoly* (OQ_M) *is less than the output corresponding to the minimum point on the long-run average cost curve.*

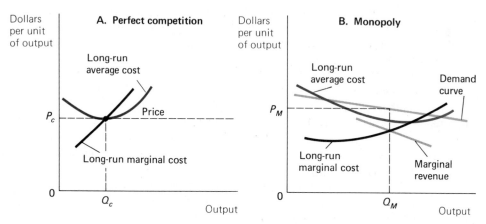

1. However, the cost and demand curves need not be the same, as we noted above.

2. In multiplant monopoly the monopolist operates fewer plants than would a competitive industry.

Fig.   COMPARISON OF PRICE AND OUTPUT: PERFECT COMPETITION VERSUS
9.7   MONOPOLY / *The monopoly price (OP₁) is higher than the competitive
         price (OM), and the monopoly output (OQ₁) is less than the competitive
         output (OQ₀).*

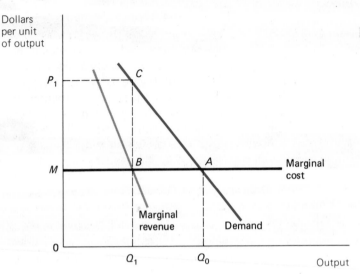

the marginal social value of the good. Consequently, under these conditions, a monopoly produces at a point at which the marginal social value of the good exceeds the good's marginal social cost. In a static sense, society would be better off if more resources were devoted to the production of the good, and if the marginal social value of the product were set equal to the marginal social cost of the product—as it is in perfect competition. Again, more will be said on this score in Chapter 14.

Assuming that the demand curve for the product is linear and that the marginal cost is constant, we compare the equilibrium price and output in monopoly and perfect competition in Figure 9.7. The monopoly price is OP_1 and the competitive price is OM; the monopoly output is OQ_1 and the competitive output is OQ_0. It is assumed, of course, that the marginal cost curve is the long-run supply curve in perfect competition. Under these very special assumptions, the monopoly output will be exactly one-half the competitive output, the reason being that the marginal revenue curve cuts in half any horizontal line from the vertical axis to the demand curve. In general, of course, the ratio of the monopoly to the competitive output could be more or less than one-half, depending on the shape of the demand and cost curves.

Using the concept of consumer's surplus described in Chapter 4, some economists believe that the welfare loss to society due to monopoly, rather than perfect competition, can be measured by the so-called welfare triangle, *ABC,* in Figure 9.7. Basically, the idea is that the value to society of the extra output resulting from perfect competition is equal to $Q_1 CA Q_0$, whereas the cost to society of the extra output is equal to $Q_1 BA Q_0$. Thus the net loss due to the smaller output under monopoly is equal to ABC. One important limitation of this kind of measure is that it assumes that one can simply add up the utilities gained and lost by various members of society. No attention is paid to the effects of monopoly on the distribution of income.

About thirty years ago, Arnold Harberger of the University of Chicago estimated the area of the welfare triangle in each manufacturing industry, based on the assumption that marginal cost is constant (as in Figure 9.7) and that the price elasticity of demand is about 1. The results suggested that the misallocation of resources due to monopoly was quite small. Specifically, he found that the elimination of this resource misallocation would result in an increase in consumer welfare of about .1 percent. These conclusions have been challenged on several counts. For example, as Harvey Leibenstein and others have pointed out, Harberger's results do not recognize that monopolies may be less inclined to minimize costs than competitive firms. Further, as Gordon Tullock has pointed out, Harberger's results ignore the social waste which arises because firms use scarce resources in their attempts to obtain monopoly power.[3]

BILATERAL MONOPOLY

Bilateral monopoly occurs when a monopolistic seller is confronted with only a single buyer. In other words, it is a case where the market is composed of a
Bilateral monopoly
single buyer and a single seller. For example, if all tin plate were produced by a single firm and if only a single firm used tin plate, this would be a case of bilateral monopoly. Clearly, there are few cases of this sort, except perhaps in the labor markets. The market for labor may be dominated, particularly in small areas, by a single firm and a single union. For example, in a small coal town in Appalachia, a single union may include all, or practically all, coal miners, and a single firm may be the only employer of coal miners.[4]

Suppose that the seller's marginal cost curve is as shown in Figure 9.8. The buyer's demand curve is also shown in Figure 9.8; this curve shows the

3. See A. Harberger, "Monopoly and Resource Allocation," and H. Leibenstein, "Allocative Efficiency vs. X-Efficiency," both reprinted in E. Mansfield, *Microeconomics: Selected Readings*, 5th ed. (New York: Norton, 1985); and G. Tullock, "The Welfare Costs of Monopoly and Theft," *Western Economic Journal*, June 1967. Also, see A Bergson, "On Monopoly Welfare Losses," *American Economic Review*, December 1973.

4. However, even here there are problems in applying the theory. As pointed out in Chapter 13, the assumption that labor unions can be represented in this way implies a very special kind of motivation on the part of unions.

Fig.
9.8 BILATERAL MONOPOLY / *The buyer would like to pay a price of* OP₁ *and buy* OQ₁ *units of output. The seller would like to charge a price of* OP₀ *and supply* OQ₀ *units of the good.*

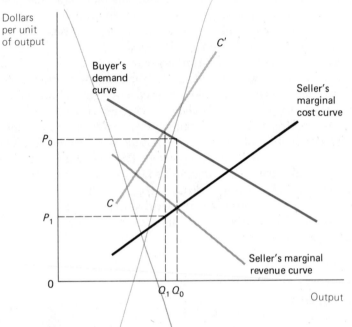

number of units of output demanded by the buyer at each price, given that the price is determined outside the control of the buyer. Under these conditions, the seller would like to set a price that will maximize its profits. Taking the buyer's demand curve as given, the seller's marginal revenue curve is as shown in Figure 9.8; and it would like to operate at the point at which its marginal revenue curve intersects its marginal cost curve. Thus it would like to charge a price of *OP₀* and supply *OQ₀* units of the good.

Turning to the buyer, what price would it like to pay and how many units of output would it like to buy? The buyer views the seller's marginal cost curve as a supply curve. Given a certain price, determined outside the control of the seller, we know that this curve shows how much the seller will supply.[5] Like the seller, the buyer would like to maximize its profits. The buyer's profits will be maximized when the curve showing the buyer's marginal expenditure on the good intersects the buyer's demand curve. The marginal expenditure on

5. On p. 267 we showed that a monopoly has no supply curve. The seller's marginal cost curve is a supply curve only under the condition that the monopolist is constrained to sell at fixed prices outside its control. In other words, the monopolist is assumed to be stripped of its monopoly power. Similarly, in the preceding paragraph, the monopsonist (that is, the sole buyer) is assumed to be stripped of its monopsony power. These assumptions are made to obtain a range within which the outcome is likely to be.

the good when between x and $(x-1)$ units are bought is $R(x) - R(x-1)$, where $R(x)$ is the total amount spent by the buyer on x units. The marginal expenditure on the good is shown by the CC' curve in Figure 9.8. Thus the buyer would like to operate at the point at which the CC' curve intersects the buyer's demand curve, which means that it would like to pay a price of OP_1 and buy OQ_1 units of output.

The price and output that will result in a situation of this sort is indeterminate. It seems likely that the price will lie somewhere between OP_0 and OP_1 and that output will lie somewhere between OQ_0 and OQ_1, but we cannot make any more specific predictions. A theory based on profit maximization is unable to yield a more specific prediction. Other factors, like bargaining power and negotiating skill and public opinion, are likely to play an important role in determining the nature of the final outcome.

PRICE DISCRIMINATION

Price discrimination occurs when the same commodity is sold at more than one price. For example, an operation to cure a particular form of cancer may be "sold" to a rich person for $5,000 and to a poor person for $1,000.

Price discrimination
Even if the commodities are not precisely the same, price discrimination is said to occur if very similar products are sold at prices that are in different ratios to marginal costs. For example, if a firm sells ballpoint pens with a label (cost of label: 1 cent) saying "Super Deluxe" in rich neighborhoods for $2 and sells the same ballpoint pens without this label in poor neighborhoods for $1, this is discrimination. Note that the mere fact that differences in price exist among similar goods is not evidence of discrimination. Only if these differences do not reflect cost differences is there evidence of this sort.

Under what conditions will a monopolist be able and willing to engage in price discrimination? The necessary conditions are that buyers fall into classes with considerable differences in the price elasticity of demand for the product, and that these classes can be identified and segregated at moderate cost. Also, it is important that buyers be unable to transfer the commodity easily from one class to another, since otherwise it would be possible for persons to make money by buying the commodity from the low-price classes and selling it to the high-price classes, thus making it difficult to maintain the price differentials between classes. The differences between classes of buyers in the price elasticity of demand may be due to differences between classes in income level, differences between classes in tastes, or differences between classes in the availability of substitutes. For example, the price elasticity of demand for a certain good may be lower for the rich than for the poor.

If a monopolist practices discrimination of this sort, it must decide two questions: How much output should it allocate to each class of buyer, and what price should it charge each class of buyer? To avoid unnecessary complications, let us assume that there are only two classes of buyers. Also, for the moment, assume that the monopolist has already decided on its total output, and consequently that the only real question is how it should be allocated between the two classes. In each class, there is a demand curve showing how many units of output would be bought by buyers in this class at various prices. In each class, there is also a marginal revenue curve that can be derived from the demand curve.

Given these marginal revenue curves, the monopolist will maximize its profits by allocating the total output between the two classes in such a way that marginal revenue in one class is equal to marginal revenue in the other class. The reason for this is clear. For example, if marginal revenue in the first class is $5 and marginal revenue in the second class is $3, the allocation is not optimal, since profits can be increased by allocating one less unit of output to the second class and one more unit of output to the first class. Only if the two marginal revenues are equal is the allocation optimal. And if the marginal revenues in the two classes are equal, the ratio of the price in the first class to the price in the second class will equal

$$\left(1 - \frac{1}{n_2}\right) \div \left(1 - \frac{1}{n_1}\right)$$

where n_1 is the elasticity of demand in the first class and n_2 is the elasticity of demand in the second class. Thus it will not pay to discriminate if the two elasticities are equal. Moreover, if discrimination does pay, the price will be lower in the class in which demand is more elastic.

Next consider the more realistic case where the monopolist must also decide on its total output. In this case, the monopolist must look at its costs, as well as demand, in the two classes. It can be shown that it will choose the output where the marginal cost of the monopolist's entire output is equal to the common value of the marginal revenue in the two classes. To see this, consider Figure 9.9, which shows D_1, the demand curve in class 1; D_2, the demand curve in class 2; R_1, the marginal revenue curve in class 1; R_2, the marginal revenue curve in class 2; and the firm's marginal cost curve. The monopolist begins to determine its total output by summing horizontally over the two marginal revenue curves, R_1 and R_2. The curve representing the horizontal summation of the two marginal revenue curves is Z. This curve shows, for each level of marginal revenue, the total output that is needed if marginal revenue in each class is to be maintained at this level. The optimal output is shown by the point where the Z curve intersects the marginal cost curve, since marginal cost must be equal to the common value of marginal revenue in each class. If this were not the case, profits could be increased by expanding output (if marginal cost were less than marginal revenue) or by contracting output (if marginal cost were greater than marginal revenue). Thus the firm will produce an output of OQ units and sell OQ_1 units in the class 1 market and OQ_2 units in the class 2 market. Price will be OP_1 in the class 1 market and OP_2 in the class 2 market.

Fig.
9.9

PRICE DISCRIMINATION: THIRD DEGREE / *To maximize profit, the firm will produce a total output of* OQ *units, and set a price of* OP$_1$ *in the class 1 market and a price of* OP$_2$ *in the class 2 market.*

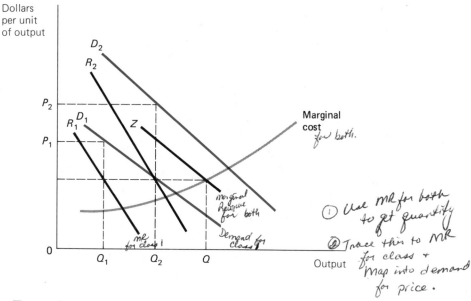

Other Types of Price Discrimination

Price discrimination can take a number of forms. The type discussed in the previous section is often called *third-degree price discrimination.* (This expression was coined by A. C. Pigou, the English economist.)[6] Besides third-degree price discrimination, there are also first-degree and second-degree price discrimination. In *discrimination of the first degree,* the monopolist is aware of the maximum amount that each and every consumer will pay for each amount of the commodity. Since it is assumed that the product cannot be resold, the monopolist can charge each consumer a different price. And since the monopolist is assumed to be a profit-maximizer, it will establish prices so as to extract from each consumer the full value of his or her consumer's surplus.

First-degree price discrimination

To illustrate this case, suppose that each consumer buys only 1 unit of the commodity. In this very simple case, the monopolist will establish a price for each consumer that is so high that the consumer is on the verge of refusing to buy the commodity. In the more realistic case, where each consumer can buy more than 1 unit of the commodity, it is assumed that the monopolist knows each consumer's demand curve for the commodity and that it adjusts its offer accordingly. For example, suppose that the maximum amount that a particular consumer would pay for 20 units of the commodity is $50 and that 20 units

---

6. A.C. Pigou, *The Economics of Welfare,* 4th ed. (London: Macmillan, 1950).

Fig. PRICE DISCRIMINATION: SECOND DEGREE / *The company charges a*
9.10 *different price* (OP$_0$, OP$_1$, *or* OP$_2$) *depending on how much the consumer purchases, thus increasing its revenue and profits.*

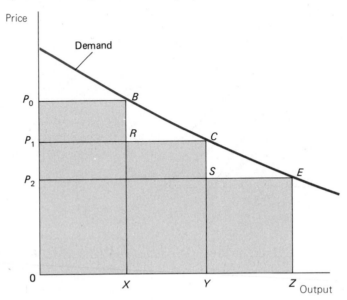

is the profit-maximizing amount for the monopolist to sell to this consumer. Then the monopolist will make an all-or-nothing offer of 20 units of the commodity for $50.

First-degree price discrimination is a limiting case that could occur only in the few cases when a monopolist has a small number of buyers and when it is able to guess the maximum prices they are willing to accept. *Second-degree price discrimination* is an intermediate case. In second-degree

Second-degree price discrimination

price discrimination, the monopolist takes part, but not all, of the buyers' consumers' surpluses. For example, consider the case of a gas company. Suppose that each of its consumers has the demand curve shown in Figure 9.10. The company charges a high price, OP_0, if the consumer purchases less than OX units of gas per month. For any amount beyond OX units per month, the company charges a medium price, OP_1. For purchases beyond OY, the company charges an even lower price, OP_2. Consequently, the company's total revenues from each consumer are equal to the shaded area in Figure 9.10, since the consumer will purchase OX units at a price of OP_0, $(OY - OX)$ units at a price of OP_1, and $(OZ - OY)$ units at a price of OP_2.[7]

---

7. Of course, this assumes for simplicity that each consumer purchases OZ units. Also, other simplifying assumptions (which need not concern us here) are made as well in this and the next paragraph.

It is obvious that the gas company, by charging different prices for various amounts of the commodity, is able to increase its revenue and profits considerably. After all, if it were permitted to charge only one price and if it wanted to sell OZ units, it would have to charge a price of OP_2. Thus the firm's total revenue would equal only the rectangle, OP_2EZ, which is considerably less than the shaded area in Figure 9.10. By charging different prices, the monopolist is able to take part of the consumers' surplus. According to some authorities, the schedules of rates charged by many public utilities—gas, water, electricity, and others—can be viewed as a type of second-degree price discrimination.[8]

Discrimination and the Existence of the Industry

Economists generally regard price discrimination as a socially inefficient way of pricing a commodity, for reasons discussed in Chapter 14. It should be recognized, however, that a good or service sometimes cannot be produced without discrimination. For example, consider the case in Figure 9.11, where there are two types of consumers, their demand curves being D_0D_0' and D_1D_1'. Adding the two demand curves, we find that the total demand for the commodity is D_0UV. As shown in Figure 9.11, no output exists at which price is greater than or equal to average total cost if price discrimination is not practiced.

Fig. 9.11   DISCRIMINATION NECESSARY FOR EXISTENCE OF INDUSTRY / *With price discrimination, an output of* OQ_2 *can be sold at an average price of* OP_2, *which is greater than average total costs.*

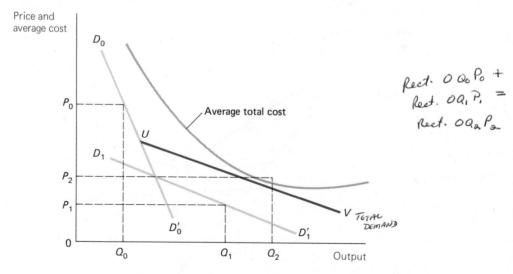

Rect. OQ_0P_0 +
Rect. OQ_1P_1 =
Rect. OQ_2P_2

8. Ralph Davidson, *Price Determination in Selling Gas and Electricity* (Baltimore: Johns Hopkins University Press, 1955); and C. Cicchetti and J. Jurewitz, *Studies in Electric Utility Regulation* (Cambridge, Mass.: Ballinger, 1975).

However, with price discrimination, an output of OQ_0 can be sold at a price of OP_0 to one type of consumer; an output of OQ_1 can be sold at a price of OP_1 to the second type of consumer; and the total output (which equals OQ_2) brings an average price of OP_2, which is greater than average total costs.

PUBLIC REGULATION OF MONOPOLY

State regulatory commissions often have substantial power over the prices charged by public utilities like gas and electric companies. As pointed out earlier in this chapter, these public utilities often are natural monopolies. Consider the firm whose demand curve, marginal revenue curve, average cost curve, and marginal cost curve are shown in Figure 9.12. Without regulation, the firm would charge a price of OP_0 and it would produce OQ_0 units of the commodity. By setting a maximum price of OP_1, the commission can make the monopolist increase output, thus making price and output correspond more closely to what they would be if the industry were organized competitively. For instance, if the commission imposes a maximum price of OP_1, the firm's demand curve becomes P_1BD', its marginal revenue curve becomes P_1BCR', its optimum output becomes OQ_1, and it will charge the maximum price of OP_1. By establishing the maximum price, the commission helps consumers who pay

Fig. **REGULATION OF MONOPOLY: MAXIMUM PRICE** / *By setting a maximum*
9.12 *price of* OP$_1$, *a regulatory commission can make the monopolist increase output to* OQ$_1$.

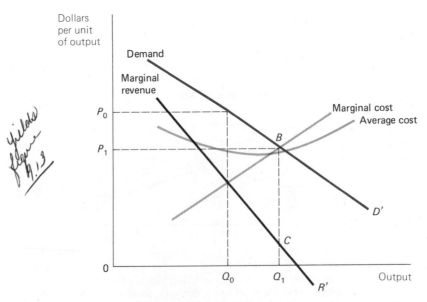

Fig. REGULATION OF MONOPOLY: FAIR RATE OF RETURN / *The regulated price is*
9.13 OP_2, *where the demand curve intersects the average total cost curve which includes what the commission regards as a fair profit per unit of output.*

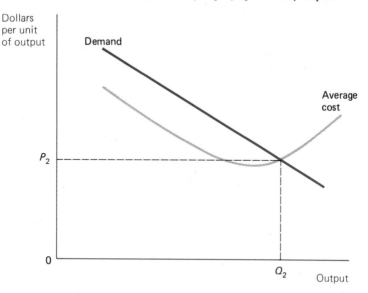

a lower price for more of the good. By the same token, the commission deprives the monopolist of some of its monopoly power.

Commissions often set the price—or the maximum price—at the level at which it equals average total cost, including a "fair" rate of return on the company's investment. For example, in Figure 9.13, the price would be established by the commission at OP_2, where the demand curve intersects the average total cost curve. The latter curve includes what the commission regards as a fair profit per unit of output. Needless to say, there has been considerable controversy over what constitutes a fair rate of return. There has also been a good deal of controversy over what should be included in the company's investment on which the fair rate of return is to be earned.

The regulatory commissions also govern the extent to which price discrimination is used by the public utilities. Intricate systems of price discrimination exist in the rate structures of the electric and gas companies, the telephone companies, and so forth. Although some types of discrimination are prohibited, other types can be practiced if they are "reasonable." For example, a company may be permitted to charge a lower rate for a service where it must meet stiff competition. It should be noted that rate discrimination raises important questions of equity and of redistribution of income, as well as questions regarding economic efficiency. Particularly in transportation, some of the most nettlesome problems of rate regulation are concerned with questions of discrimination.

CASE STUDIES

De Beers: A Case Study of Unregulated Monopoly

According to the *New York Times,* The Central Selling Organization, controlled by De Beers Consolidated Mines Ltd., is "probably the world's most successful monopoly."[9] De Beers, founded in 1880 by Cecil Rhodes in South Africa, controlled over 99 percent of world diamond production until about 1900. At present the firm mines only about 15 percent of the world's diamonds, but it still controls the sales of over 80 percent of the gem-quality diamonds through its Central Selling Organization, which markets the output of other major producing countries like Zaire, the Soviet Union, Botswana, Namibia, and Australia, as well as its own production.

No one doubts that De Beers controls the price of diamonds. Buyers are offered small boxes of assorted diamonds at a price set by De Beers on a "take it all or leave it" basis. Those that choose not to buy may have to wait some time before getting another opportunity. If the demand for diamonds falls, as it did during the early 1980s (when inflation slowed and diamonds as an investment lost much of their sparkle), De Beers stands ready to buy diamonds to support the price. Between 1979 and 1984, its stockpile of diamonds increased from about $360 million to about $2 billion.

Besides limiting the quantity supplied, De Beers also works hard and cleverly to push the demand curve for diamonds to the right. An important part of its sales campaign has been to link diamonds and romance. (According to its fifty-year-old slogan, "A Diamond Is Forever.") Of course, this has also been helpful in keeping diamonds, once sold, off the market. A good that is drenched with lasting sentiment is less likely to be sold when times get tough. De Beers's policies have paid off in very substantial profits, but the consumer has paid higher prices than if the diamond market were competitive.

The Michigan Telephone Industry: A Case Study of Regulation

The previous section described a case of unregulated monopoly. To illustrate the case of regulated monopoly, we turn to the telephone industry in Michigan. The two groups that have played a key role in the regulation of the telephone industry in Michigan are one firm, Michigan Bell (a subsidiary of Ameritech[10]), and one commission, the Public Service Commission in Michi-

---

9. *New York Times,* September 7, 1986, p. 4F.

10. Ameritech (American Information Technologies Corporation) is one of seven regional holding companies resulting from the breakup of the American Telephone and Telegraph Company (AT&T). In 1982, a district court ordered AT&T to divest itself of the exchange telecommunications, exchange access, and Yellow Pages of its 22 wholly-owned Bell operating telephone companies, one of which was Michigan Bell. This decision arose out of an antitrust case brought by the U.S. Department of Justice against AT&T.

gan.[11] Although Michigan Bell is not the only telephone company in the state, it is the dominant firm. The commission, which is composed of three members appointed by the governor, has had authority over the telephone industry for about fifty years.

A general-rate case has been the common sort of regulatory "contest" in the Michigan telephone industry. Such cases have been initiated by the firms and have been based on company claims that earnings are deficient and a higher price level is required. It is generally assumed, though not proved, that demand is inelastic and that higher prices will mean greater revenues. The industry usually has received less than it asked for. Moreover, commission decisions have lagged behind the industry's revenue requests. However, it should be recognized that the fact that the commission has not approved all Bell requests does not mean that the company has been constrained much by the commission. The company may ask for more than it thinks it will get.

Nothing in public utility controls is more conventional, more securely established in regulatory methods, than the idea of a "reasonable return on the value of a firm's existing plant."[12] This is what the commission has been interested in establishing. Yet there are a host of questions, some obvious to the most naïve schoolchild, others difficult for a trained engineer or accountant to understand, concerning what is a "reasonable return" and what is "the value of a firm's existing plant." The original cost or historical cost of the plant is the measure on which most commissions base their estimates of the value of the plant; but some allow firms to use replacement-cost valuations instead. In the early 1980s, regulated firms often sought a rate of return of about 10 to 15 percent; commissions in recent years have approved rates of return of about 6 to 10 percent.[13] There are lots of detailed and difficult questions in each case of this sort that provide employment for a great many lawyers, accountants, engineers, and economists.

Regulation and Deregulation in Railroads and Trucking

Considerable controversy has centered on the regulatory process, with many observers feeling that the commissions are lax and that they tend to be captured by the industries they are supposed to regulate. Also, in some cases, regulation, although effective, seems to have had unfortunate consequences. For example, according to many experts, the Interstate Commerce Commis-

---

11. See C. E. Troxel, "Telephone Regulation in Michigan," in W. G. Shepherd and T. Gies, *Utility Regulation* (New York: Random House, 1966). Also, see M. Irwin, "The Telephone Industry," in W. Adams, *The Structure of American Industry,* 5th ed. (New York: Macmillan, 1977).

12. Ibid., p. 162.

13. See W. Shepherd and C. Wilcox, *Public Policies Toward Business,* 6th ed (Homewood, Ill.: Irwin, 1979); and W. Shepherd, *Public Policies Toward Business: Readings and Cases* (Homewood, Ill.: Irwin, 1979).

sion has set prices of various modes of transportation so as to prevent low-cost firms or industries from taking business away from high-cost firms or industries. In particular, railroads have often been prevented from lowering prices and taking long-distance trucking business away from the trucks. The result has been an inefficient use of the nation's resources. According to Ann Friedlander, the social cost may have been as large as $500 million a year.[14]

In 1980, a trucking deregulation law, which called for full implementation by 1984, was passed by Congress. It encouraged free entry and exit in the trucking industry, and enabled truckers to have more independence in setting prices, choosing routes, and determining the sorts of cargo they convey. Moreover, this law was only one part of a much larger movement toward deregulation in the U.S. transportation sector. Another law was passed in 1980 that reduced the amount of regulation in railroads. (And as described in detail in the cross-chapter case at the end of Part 4, there was a series of steps toward airline deregulation in the late 1970s and early 1980s.) Economists hoped that these reforms would increase efficiency and benefit the public. According to the railroads, rail freight rates, adjusted for inflation, fell 4.9 percent between 1980 and the end of 1986 because of the intense competition that now exists. It will take many years before a definitive study can be made of how well deregulation has worked out, both from the point of view of these industries and of the general public. But there can be no doubt that the movement toward deregulation was one of the most notable changes in the American economy in past decades.[15]

SUMMARY

1. Pure monopoly exists when there is one, and only one, seller in a market. Monopolies arise because a single firm controls the entire supply of a basic input, because a firm has a patent on the product or on certain basic processes, because the average cost of producing the product reaches a minimum at an output rate that is big enough to satisfy the entire market at a price that is profitable, because the firm is awarded a franchise, or for other reasons.

2. The demand curve facing the monopolist is the demand for the product. The cost conditions facing a monopolist may be no different from those facing a perfectly competitive firm, if the monopolist is a perfect competitor in the input markets.

---

14. For example, see Ann Friedlander, *The Dilemma of Freight Transport Regulation* (Washington, D.C.: Brookings Institution, 1969), p. 65.

15. According to some reports, there appears to have been an increase since 1980 in the number of interstate carriers in the trucking industry and a decrease in prices, which is what would have been expected. For further discussion of the effects of the deregulation of railroads and trucking, see Example 14.1; and A. Friedlander and R. Spady, *Freight Transport Regulation* (Cambridge, Mass.: MIT Press, 1981).

3. Under monopoly, the firm will maximize profit if it sets its output rate at the point where marginal cost equals marginal revenue. It does not follow that a firm that holds a monopoly over the production of a particular product must make a profit. If the monopolist cannot cover its variable costs, it will shut down, even in the short run.

4. There are a number of important differences between the long-run equilibrium of a monopoly and of a perfectly competitive industry. Under perfect competition, each firm operates at the point where both long-run and short-run average costs are at a minimum; under monopoly, if the monopolist expanded its long-run equilibrium output, it could utilize a plant with lower average costs. The output of a perfectly competitive industry tends to be greater and price tends to be lower than under monopoly. The perfectly competitive firm operates at the point where price equals marginal cost, whereas the monopolist operates at a point where price exceeds marginal cost. Some economists measure the loss in economic welfare due to monopoly by the welfare triangle.

5. Bilateral monopoly occurs when a monopolistic seller confronts a monopsonistic buyer. The price and output that will result in this situation is indeterminate.

6. Price discrimination occurs when the same commodity is sold at more than one price, or when similar products are sold at prices that are in different ratios to marginal costs. A monopolist will be able and willing to practice price discrimination if various classes of buyers with different elasticities of demand can be identified and segregated, and if the commodity cannot be transferred easily from one class to another.

7. There are three types of price discrimination, and we have discussed the monopolist's behavior in each case. Economists generally regard price discrimination as a socially inefficient way of pricing a commodity, but it is sometimes true that, without discrimination, a commodity cannot be produced at all.

8. Regulatory commissions frequently have the power to set the prices charged by public utilities like gas or electric companies. They often set the price—or the maximum price—at the level at which it equals average total cost, including a "fair" rate of return on the company's investment. There has been considerable controversy over what constitutes a fair rate of return, and over what should be included in the company's investment.

▰▰▰▰▰▰▰▰▰▰▰ QUESTIONS/PROBLEMS ▰▰▰▰▰▰▰▰▰▰▰

1) One of the longest and most expensive antitrust cases in history began in 1969, when the government charged that IBM "has attempted to monopolize and has monopolized . . . interstate trade and commerce in general purpose computers in violation of Section 2 of the Sherman Act." According to IBM's economists, its share of revenue from the sale of electronic data processing products and services in the United States was as follows:

1952	90.1%
1961	56.4
1968	54.0
1972	40.7

(a) Based on these figures, was IBM a monopolist? (b) Even if IBM did not have 100 percent of the market, could it have run afoul of the antitrust laws? (c) If a firm has a very large share of the market, does this mean that it should be prosecuted under the antitrust laws? (d) How should one define a market for these purposes? (e) Whereas IBM argued for a broad definition of the computer industry (including special purpose process control, message switching, and military computers and computer leasing and service activities), the government argued for a narrow definition (general purpose electronic digital computer systems). Why?

2) According to John McGee, "Standard Oil did not use predatory price discrimination to drive out competing refiners . . . Standard discriminated in price, but it did so to maximize profits given the elasticities of demand of markets in which it sold." Describe how you would test this conclusion against historical evidence. Also, indicate how you would go about determining whether such discrimination was good or bad.

3) A monopolist has the following total cost function and demand curve:

Price	Output	Total cost
(dollars)	(units)	(dollars)
8	5	20
7	6	21
6	7	22
5	8	23
4	9	24
3	10	30

What price should it charge?

4) Monopolists sometimes are said to be less interested in maximizing profit than perfectly competitive firms. Why might this be the case, and what nonprofit goals might a monopolist be interested in achieving?

5) The Errata Book Company is a monopolist that sells in two markets. The marginal revenue curve in the first market is

$$MR_1 = 20 - 2Q_1$$

where MR_1 is the marginal revenue in the first market and Q_1 is the number of books sold per day in the first market. The marginal revenue curve in the second market is

$$MR_2 = 15 - 3Q_2$$

where MR_2 is the marginal revenue in the second market and Q_2 is the number of books sold per day in the second market. If the marginal cost of a book is $6, how many books should the Errata Book Company sell in each market?

6) A. C. Harberger, in his study cited in footnote 3, assumed that the price elasticity of demand was unity everywhere. Will a rational monopolist operate at a point where the price elasticity of demand is unity? Can one be sure that monopoly gains are not included in the cost items reported by accountants?

7) Authors customarily receive a royalty that is a fixed percentage of the price of the book. For this reason, economists have pointed out that an author has an interest in a book's price being lower than the price which maximizes the publisher's profits. Prove that this is true.

8) "Regulatory commissions tend to be captured by the industries they are supposed to regulate. They have little or no effect on price." Do you agree? Why or why not? What sorts of analyses can you devise to test these propositions?

9) Suppose that you are the owner of a metals-producing firm that is an unregulated monopoly. After considerable experimentation and research, you find that your marginal cost curve can be approximated by a straight line, $MC = 60 + 2Q$, where MC is marginal cost (in dollars) and Q is your output. Moreover, suppose that the demand curve for your product is $P = 100 - Q$, where P is the product price and Q is your output. If you want to maximize profit, what output should you choose?

10) In Question 3, suppose that the monopolist's total fixed cost increases by $1. What effect will this have on the answer to Question 3?

11) Suppose that you are hired as a consultant to a firm producing ball bearings. This firm is a monopolist which sells in two distinct markets, one of which is completely sealed off from the other. The demand curve for the firm's output in the one market is $P_1 = 160 - 8Q_1$, where P_1 is the price of the product and Q_1 is the amount sold in the first market. The demand curve for the firm's output in the second market is $P_2 = 80 - 2Q_2$, where P_2 is the price of the product and Q_2 is the amount sold in the second market. The firm's marginal cost curve is $5 + Q$, where Q is the firm's entire output (destined for either market). The firm asks you to suggest what its pricing policy should be. How many units of output should it sell in the second market? How many units of output should it sell in the first market? What prices should it charge?

12) Prostatix, Inc., a pharmaceutical manufacturer, is a monopolist. Its president says that its price at its profit-maximizing output is triple its marginal cost. What is the price elasticity of demand of its product?

Monopolistic Competition and Advertising

MONOPOLISTIC COMPETITION

Bergdorf Goodman has a monopoly on the sale of its dresses. However, other firms like Macy's and Altman's sell roughly similar dresses. Each firm has a monopoly over the sale of its own product, but the various brands are close substitutes. This is a case of *product differentiation*. In other words, there is no single, homogeneous commodity called a dress; instead, each **Product** seller differentiates its product from that of the next seller. This, **differentiation** of course, is a prevalent case in the modern economy. Each seller tries to make its product a little different, by altering the physical makeup of the product, the services it offers, and other such variables. Other differences—which may be spurious—are based on brand name, image-making, advertising claims, and so forth. In this way, each seller has some amount of monopoly power, but it usually is small, because the products of other firms are very similar.

Monopolistic competition is a market structure that has elements of both monopoly and perfect competition. Under monopolistic competition, there is a large number of firms producing and selling goods that are close substitutes,

Monopolistic competition

but that are not completely homogeneous from one seller to another. For example, retail trade is often cited as an industry with many of the characteristics of monopolistic competition. Edward Chamberlin[1] of Harvard University pioneered in the development of the theory of monopolistic competition. While his theory has met with considerable criticism, it was a famous and noteworthy attempt to develop a model to handle the important middle ground between perfect competition and monopoly.[2] We start this chapter with a brief description of Chamberlin's theory, after which we take up the closely related topic of advertising.

To begin with, let's consider Chamberlin's concept of a product group. In perfect competition, the firms included in an industry are easy to determine, because they all produce the same product. But if there is product differentiation, it is no longer easy to define an industry, since each firm produces a somewhat different product. Nevertheless, Chamberlin believes that it is useful to group together firms producing similar products and call them a *product group*.

Product group

For example, we can formulate a product group called ladies' dresses. Of course, the process by which we combine firms into product groups is bound to be somewhat arbitrary, since there is no way to decide how close a pair of substitutes must be in order to be included in the same product group. However, Chamberlin asserts that meaningful product groups can be formulated.

The assumptions underlying Chamberlin's theory are as follows: First, he assumes that the product, which is differentiated, is produced by a large number of firms, with each firm's product being a fairly close substitute for the products of the other firms in the product group. Second, he assumes that the number of firms in the product group is sufficiently large so that each firm expects its actions to go unheeded by its rivals and to be unimpeded by any retaliatory measures on their part. Third, he assumes that both demand and cost curves are the same for all of the firms in the group. This, of course, is a very restrictive assumption since, if the products are dissimilar, one would ordinarily expect their demand and cost curves to be dissimilar, too.

DEMAND CURVES UNDER MONOPOLISTIC COMPETITION

Two kinds of demand curves play an important role in the theory of monopolistic competition. On the one hand, there is a demand curve that shows how

---

1. E. Chamberlin, *The Theory of Monopolistic Competition* (Cambridge, Mass.: Harvard University Press, 1933). Another very important work of the same period was J. Robinson, *The Economics of Imperfect Competition* (New York: Macmillan, 1933).

2. Perfect competition and pure monopoly are two polar extremes. There is an extremely large number of firms in a perfectly competitive industry, but only one firm in a pure monopoly. Obviously, many industries in the real world fall between these two extremes.

Fig.   THE TWO DEMAND CURVES UNDER MONOPOLISTIC COMPETITION / *The* dd′
10.1   *demand curve assumes that other firms maintain their prices; the* DD′
       demand curve assumes that all firms raise or lower their prices by the
       same amount as this firm.

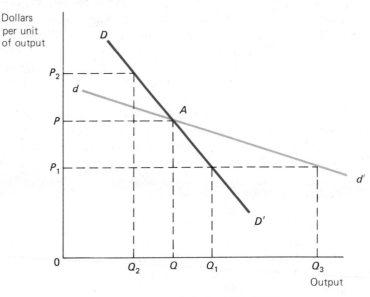

much the firm will sell if it varies its price from the going level and if other
firms maintain their existing prices. As an example of this de-
dd′ *demand*   mand curve, consider the situation in Figure 10.1. The firm is
curve   currently in equilibrium at the point *A*, with price *OP* and output
                   OQ. If the firm reduces its price and if other firms maintain their
prices, the firm can expect a considerable increase in sales, since it will be able
to attract buyers away from other firms in the group (and increase sales to existing customers). If the firm increases its price and if other firms maintain
their prices, the firm can expect a considerable decrease in sales, since it will
lose business to other firms in the group (because buyers will switch alle-
giance). Thus, assuming that each firm expects its actions to go unheeded by
its rivals, each believes its demand curve to be quite elastic. This demand curve
is shown as *dd′* in Figure 10.1.

       There is another important type of demand curve, based on the supposi-
tion that *all* firms raise or lower their prices by the same amount as this firm.
                   This demand curve is shown as *DD′* in Figure 10.1. Thus, if this
DD′ *demand*   firm reduces its price to *OP₁* and all other firms reduce their
curve   prices to *OP₁* as well, this firm will sell *OQ₁* units of output. Simi-
                   larly, if this firm increases its price to *OP₂* and all other firms in-
crease their price to *OP₂* as well, this firm will sell *OQ₂* units of output. Of

course, this second type of demand curve, DD', is less elastic than the first type, dd', since price reductions by this firm will expand its sales by a greater amount if other firms do not meet the price reduction, and price increases by this firm will decrease its sales by a greater amount if other firms do not meet the price increase. For example, if other firms do not meet the price reduction, this firm's sales will increase to OQ_3, rather than OQ_1, if it reduces its price to OP_1.

EQUILIBRIUM PRICE AND OUTPUT IN THE SHORT RUN

In discussing the pricing behavior of firms under monopolistic competition, it simplifies matters to assume that the firms have already decided on the characteristics of product and extent of selling expenses that are most profitable. (Later on in this chapter we shall deal with the ways in which firms determine how much to spend on advertising.) It is also convenient to analyze the behavior of an industry in terms of a "representative firm." Since the demand and cost curves of each firm are assumed to be identical, it is legitimate to think in terms of a representative firm.

To see how the equilibrium price and output of each firm in the group is determined in the short run, consider the situation in Figure 10.2. The market

Fig. INITIAL CHANGE OF PRICE AND OUTPUT / *The firm changes its price from*
10.2 OP_0 *to* OP_1, *but sells* OQ_2, *not* OQ_1, *units of output.*

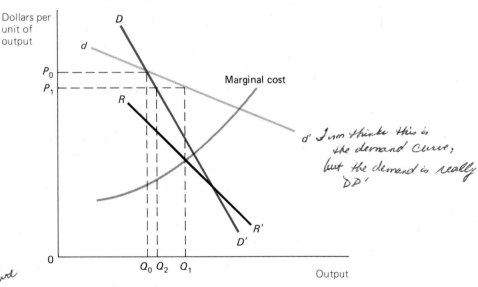

price is OP_0 and the firm is producing and selling OQ_0 units. Suppose that the firm believes that any alteration in its price will not be matched by its rivals in the group, and that it tries to act as a monopolist. Then dd' is the relevant demand curve, RR' is the relevant marginal revenue curve, and the firm will decide to produce and sell an output of OQ_1, since this is the output at which its marginal cost curve intersects its marginal revenue curve, RR'. The price charged by the firm will change to OP_1.

This new price would boost the firm's profits, if the firm were correct in believing that the price charged by other firms in the group would remain constant. However, since all of the firms in the group are confronted with the same situation and since they all make the assumption that the other firms will not change price, they all do the same thing. Thus every firm changes its price to OP_1, and DD'—not dd'—becomes the relevant demand curve. This means that OQ_2, not OQ_1, units of output are sold by each firm at the new price, OP_1.

The results are shown in Figure 10.3. Because all firms are now charging a price of OP_1, the dd' demand curve has now moved down until it intersects the DD' demand curve at OP_1. Clearly, the new dd' demand curve must intersect the DD' demand curve at OP_1, since the new dd' demand curve shows how much the firm will sell at various prices if other firms' prices remain constant at OP_1, not OP_0. Thus, at the point on the dd' demand curve corresponding to a

Fig. SITUATION AFTER INITIAL CHANGE OF PRICE AND OUTPUT / *The firm*
10.3 *changes its price from* OP$_1$ *to* OP$_2$, *but sells* OQ$_4$, *not* OQ$_3$, *units of output.*

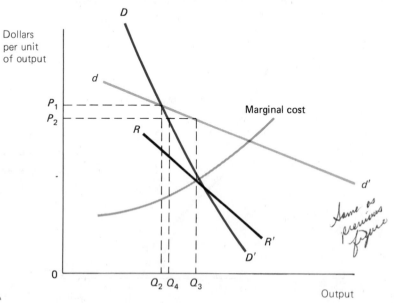

Fig. SHORT-RUN EQUILIBRIUM / *In short-run equilibrium, the firm's price and*
10.4 *output are* OP$_5$ *and* OQ$_5$, *respectively.*

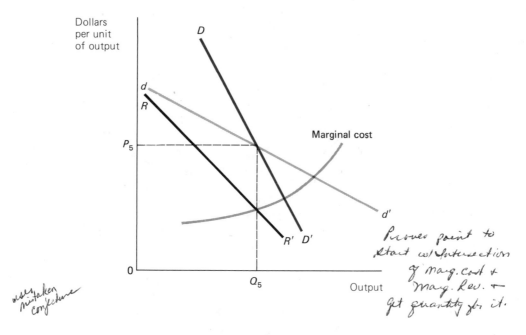

price of OP_1, all firms are charging a price of OP_1, and the firm's sales must correspond to the point on the DD' demand curve corresponding to OP_1.

Again, the firm acts as a monopolist and attempts to maximize profits on the basis of the new dd' demand curve. It sets a price of OP_2 and expects to produce and sell OQ_3 units of output. But since this change in price seems profitable for all firms, they all take the same action, with the result that the DD' demand curve, not the new dd' demand curve, is the relevant one. Consequently, each firm produces OQ_4, not OQ_3, units of output. Again the dd' demand curve shifts to intersect the DD' demand curve at the new price, OP_2. And the process goes on.

This process continues until a point is reached where the firm has no reason to change its price. In the short run, an equilibrium will be reached when the situation is like that in Figure 10.4. That is, the short-run equilibrium price and output of each firm are OP_5 and OQ_5, respectively. It can easily be verified that the firm has no incentive to change its price from OP_5. Since marginal revenue based on the dd' demand curve and a going price of OP_5 equals marginal cost at an output of OQ_5, the firm believes that it is maximizing profits by maintaining its price at OP_5. Of course, the representative firm may not earn profits in short-run equilibrium. But as long as OP_5 exceeds the firm's average variable costs, the firm will continue to produce in the short run.

Fig.   Long-Run Equilibrium / *In long-run equilibrium, the firm's price and*
10.5   *output are OP and OQ, respectively.*

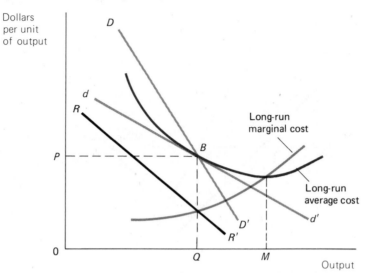

EQUILIBRIUM PRICE AND OUTPUT IN THE LONG RUN

As in perfect competition, firms in the long run are able to change the scale of
their plant and to leave or enter the industry. The long-run equilibrium price
and output of the representative firm are shown in Figure 10.5; the equilibrium
price is *OP* and the equilibrium output is *OQ*. Since there is free entry and exit
in a monopolistic competitive industry, the long-run equilibrium is a situation
in which all firms in the industry, although they are maximizing profits, have
zero economic profits. This, of course, is similar to the long-run equilibrium in
a perfectly competitive industry. Note that the cost curves in Figure 10.5 are
long-run cost curves, not the short-run cost curves shown in Figure 10.4. The
long-run equilibrium position is the point where (1) the long-run average cost
curve is tangent to the *dd'* demand curve, and where (2) the *DD'* demand curve
intersects the *dd'* demand curve and the long-run average cost curve at the
tangency point. (The marginal revenue curve is *RR'*.)

How is this long-run equilibrium position reached? The adjustments that
take place can be described in terms of changes in the *dd'* demand curve and in
the *DD'* demand curve. The *DD'* demand curve shifts in response to the entry
of new firms and the exit of old firms. Increases in the number of firms in the
industry shift the *DD'* demand curve facing the representative firm to the left,
because the market (which is relatively fixed) must be divided among more
firms. Reductions in the number of firms shift the *DD'* demand curve facing
the representative firm to the right, because the market must be divided

Fig. 10.6 MOVEMENT TOWARD LONG-RUN EQUILIBRIUM / *If D_1D_1' is the DD' demand curve, and OP_0 is the price, economic profits exist, and entry occurs, with the result that the DD' demand curve shifts to D_2D_2'.*

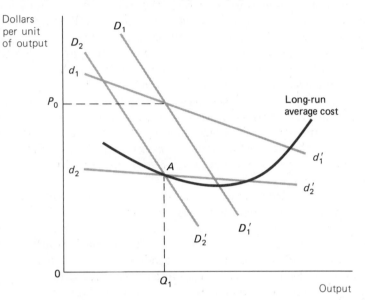

among fewer firms. As a result of entry and exit, the *DD'* demand curve is pushed toward the equilibrium position, where it intersects the *dd'* demand curve at the point at which the *dd'* demand curve is tangent to the long-run average cost curve.

Consider Figure 10.6, where D_1D_1' is the initial *DD'* demand curve. This firm (and the others in the group) is making an economic profit since the current price is OP_0. Thus, it follows that entry is encouraged and the *DD'* demand curve shifts to the left. Simultaneously, the *dd'* demand curve also moves to the left from d_1d_1'. As entry continues, the *DD'* demand curve may shift to D_2D_2'. If so, one might think that point *A* would be a long-run equilibrium position, since the *DD'* demand curve, D_2D_2', intersects the long-run average cost curve at point *A*. However, this is not the case, since the *dd'* demand curve, d_2d_2', lies above the long-run average cost curve for a range of outputs above OQ_1. Thus each firm believes that it is profitable to expand.

Only when at last the situation in Figure 10.5 is reached will a long-run equilibrium be established. At point *B* in Figure 10.5, the *DD'* demand curve intersects the long-run average cost curve, with the result that there is no incentive for entry or exit, since economic profits are nonexistent. Moreover, at point *B*, the *dd'* demand curve is always below the long-run average cost curve, except at point *B* where the two curves intersect. Thus the firm has no incentive to change its price or output, since any such change appears to be unprofitable.

EXCESS CAPACITY

A famous and controversial conclusion of the theory of monopolistic competition is that a firm under this form of market organization will tend to operate with excess capacity. In other words, it is alleged that the firm will construct a plant smaller than the minimum-cost size of plant and operate it at less than the minimum-cost rate of output. Why? Because, as shown in Figure 10.5 (p. 294), the long-run average cost curve must be tangent in long-run equilibrium to the *dd'* demand curve. Thus, since the *dd'* demand curve is downward sloping, the long-run average cost curve must also be downward sloping at the long-run equilibrium output rate. Consequently, the firm's output must be less than *OM,* the output rate at which long-run average cost is minimized, since the long-run average cost curve slopes downward only at outputs less than *OM*.

Since each firm builds a smaller than minimum-cost plant and produces a smaller than minimum-cost output, more firms can exist under these circumstances than if there were no excess capacity. Thus, there is likely to be some "overcrowding" of the industry. It is difficult to know whether particular industries in the real world that are close to the monopolistic competitive model are in fact overcrowded in this sense, but, on the basis of relatively casual empiricism, it is sometimes asserted that a number of cases of this sort exist. For example, in the case of gas stations and grocery stores, both of which bear some resemblance to monopolistic competition, it is sometimes asserted that there are too many firms.

COMPARISONS WITH PERFECT COMPETITION AND MONOPOLY

Frequently, attempts are made to compare the long-run equilibria that result from various market organizations. If we suppose that an industry were monopolistically competitive, rather than purely competitive or purely monopolistic, what difference would it make in the long-run behavior of the industry? It is difficult to interpret this question in a meaningful way, let alone answer it, since the output of the industry would be heterogeneous in one case and homogeneous in the other, and since the cost curves of the industry would probably vary with its organization. Nevertheless, many economists seem to believe that differences of the following kinds can be expected.

First, the firm under monopolistic competition is likely to produce less, and set a higher price, than under perfect competition. The demand curve confronting the monopolistic competitor is not perfectly elastic, as it is in perfect competition. Since marginal revenue is less than price in monopolistic competition, the firm will produce less than the amount at which price equals marginal cost, the consequence being that it will produce less than under perfect competition. However, the difference may not be very great, since the demand curve facing the firm under monopolistic competition may be very close to perfectly elastic.

Second, relative to pure monopoly, monopolistically competitive firms are likely to have lower profits, greater output, and lower prices. The firms in a product group might obtain economic profits if they were to collude and behave as a monopolist. For example, in Figure 10.5, the DD' demand curve is above the long-run average cost curve for outputs less than OQ. Of course, the increase in profits resulting from the monopoly would make the producers better off, but consumers would be worse off because of higher prices and a smaller output of goods.

Third, as noted in the previous section, firms in monopolistic competition may be somewhat inefficient because they tend to operate with excess capacity. Of course, inefficiencies of this sort would not be expected under perfect competition. However, these inefficiencies may not be very great, since the demand curve confronting the monopolistically competitive firm is likely to be highly elastic; and the more elastic it is, the less excess capacity the firm will have.

A good deal of effort has been devoted by economists to determine the effects on social welfare of monopolistic competition. On the one hand, some economists are impressed by the apparent waste in monopolistic competition. They think it results in too many firms, too many brands, too much selling effort, and too much spurious product differentiation. On the other hand, if the differences among products are real and are understood by consumers, the greater variety of alternatives available under monopolistic competition may be worth a great deal to consumers.[3]

CRITICISMS OF THE THEORY OF MONOPOLISTIC COMPETITION

According to some social philosophers (mostly very young or very old), life begins at forty. Chamberlin's theory of monopolistic competition celebrated

---

3. Progress has been made in this area in recent years. For example, several papers have shown that the introduction of new products under monopolistic competition in general does not result in an equilibrium where the socially optimal product mix is offered. See K. Lancaster, "Socially Optimal Product Differentiation," *American Economic Review,* September 1975; H. Leland, "Quality Choices and Competition," *American Economic Review,* March 1977; A. Dixit and J. Stiglitz, "Monopolistic Competition and Optimum Product Diversity," *American Economic Review,* June 1977; F. M. Scherer, "The Welfare Economics of Product Variety: An Application to the Ready-to-Eat Cereals Industry," *Journal of Industrial Economics,* 1979; and M. Spence, "Product Selection, Fixed Costs, and Monopolistic Competition," *Review of Economic Studies,* June 1976.

its fortieth birthday some years ago, but there is still a good deal of argument concerning its significance. A number of important criticisms have been made of the theory. For example, Chicago's George Stigler and others have argued that the definition of the group of firms included in the product group is extremely ambiguous. It may contain only one firm or all of the firms in the economy. Moreover, in Stigler's view, the concept of the group is not salvaged by the assumption that each firm neglects the effects of its decisions on other firms in the group, and that each firm has essentially the same demand and cost curves.

Indeed, according to Stigler, the firms in the group must be selling homogeneous commodities if the assumption of similar demand and cost curves for all firms in the group is to be at all realistic. But if the commodities are homogeneous, there is no reason why firms should have downward-sloping demand curves. If one loosens the assumption that the demand and cost curves are the same for all firms, other criticisms can be made of the analysis. Stigler states that "in the general case we cannot make a single statement about economic events in the world we sought to analyze . . . [although] many such statements are made by Chamberlin."[4]

In addition, a number of economists have questioned the conclusion that undesirable excess capacity will be present under monopolistic competition. For example, Princeton's Avinash Dixit and Joseph Stiglitz, Columbia's Kelvin Lancaster, and Harvard's Michael Spence have argued that, because of the consumer's taste for variety, it is not socially optimal to operate plants at the minimum-average-cost output.[5]

Still other economists claim that there are relatively few markets in the real world where the model of monopolistic competition is really relevant. There certainly is a great deal to be said for this view, since the assumptions underlying the theory are quite stringent.

In conclusion, it must be granted that these criticisms have a considerable amount of merit. Although there was a good deal of enthusiasm for the theory soon after its development, the passage of time seems to have pushed it farther and farther from the center of the stage. However, it remains a standard part of many courses in microeconomic theory, perhaps partly in the hope that it will lead to more adequate models of the middle ground between perfect competition and pure monopoly. Incipient economic theorists take note.

ADVERTISING EXPENDITURES: A SIMPLE MODEL

Industries with the characteristics of monopolistic competition spend very large amounts on advertising. Newspapers, which account for about 30 per-

---

4. G. Stigler, *Five Lectures on Economic Problems* (London: Longmans Green, 1949), pp. 18–19.

5. See the references in footnote 3.

cent of total advertising expenditure in the United States, are full of advertisements by food stores, clothing stores, and other retailers. How much should a profit-maximizing firm spend on advertising? This is a very important question, and one that has occupied the attention of many economists in the half-century since Chamberlin's work. In this section, we derive a simple rule that helps to answer this question.

For a particular firm, suppose that the quantity that it sells of its product is a function of the product's price and the level of the firm's advertising expenditure for the product. In particular, assume that there are diminishing marginal returns to advertising expenditures, which means that beyond some point successive increments of advertising outlays will yield smaller and smaller increases in additional sales. (Table 10.1 shows an illustrative case where successive increments of $100,000 in advertising outlays result in smaller and smaller increases in quantity sold. For example, the quantity sold increases by 2.0 million units when advertising expenditures rise from $800,000 to $900,000, but by only 1.5 million units when they rise from $900,000 to $1 million.)

Table 10.1 RELATIONSHIP BETWEEN ADVERTISING EXPENDITURES AND THE QUANTITY SOLD OF THE FIRM'S PRODUCT

Advertising expenditures (millions of dollars)	Quantity sold of product (millions of units)
0.8	5.0
0.9	7.0
1.0	8.5
1.1	9.5
1.2	10.0

We assume too that neither price nor the marginal cost of producing an extra unit of the product will be altered by small changes in advertising expenditures. Letting P be the price of a unit of the product and MC be the marginal cost of production, the firm receives a gross profit of $(P - MC)$ from each additional unit of the product that it makes and sells. Why is this the *gross* profit of making and selling an additional unit of output? Because it takes no account of whatever additional advertising expenditures were required to sell this extra unit of output. To obtain the *net* profit, the firm must deduct these additional advertising outlays from the gross profit.

To maximize its total net profits, a firm must set its advertising expenditures at the level where an extra dollar of advertising results in extra gross profit equal to the extra dollar of advertising cost. Unless this is the case, the firm's total net profits can be increased by changing its advertising outlays. If an extra dollar of advertising results in more than a dollar increase in gross profit, the extra dollar should be spent on advertising (since this will raise total net profits). If an extra dollar (as well as the last dollar) of advertising results in less than a dollar increase in gross profit, advertising outlays should be cut.[6] Thus, if ΔQ is the number of extra units of output sold due to an extra dollar of advertising, the firm should set its advertising expenditures so that

$$\Delta Q(P - MC) = 1,$$ [10.1]

because the right-hand side of this equation equals the extra dollar of advertising cost and the left-hand side equals the extra gross profit due to this advertising dollar.

Multiplying both sides of Equation 10.1 by $P \div (P - MC)$, we obtain

$$P\Delta Q = \frac{P}{P - MC}.$$ [10.2]

Since the firm is maximizing profit, it is producing an output where marginal cost (MC) equals marginal revenue (MR). Thus, we can substitute MR for MC in Equation 10.2, the result being

$$P\Delta Q = \frac{P}{P - MR}.$$ [10.3]

Using Equation 5.4, it can be shown that the right-hand side of Equation 10.3 equals η, the price elasticity of demand for the firm's product.[7] The left-hand side of Equation 10.3 is the *marginal revenue from an extra dollar of advertising* (since it equals the price times the extra number of units sold due to an extra dollar of advertising). Consequently, to maximize profit, the firm should set its advertising expenditure so that

Marginal revenue from an extra dollar of advertising

Marginal revenue from an extra dollar of advertising $= \eta$.   [10.4]

This rule, derived by Harvard's Robert Dorfman and Michigan's Peter Steiner,[8] is interesting and useful. To illustrate its use, consider the Terratech Corporation, which knows that the price elasticity of demand for its product equals 1.5. If this firm maximizes profit, the rule in Equation 10.4 says that it

---

6. For simplicity, we assume here that the gross profit due to an extra dollar spent on advertising is essentially equal to the gross profit due to the last dollar spent. This is an innocuous assumption.

7. According to Equation 5.4, $MR = P\left[1 - \frac{1}{\eta}\right]$. Thus, $1 - \frac{1}{\eta} = MR/P$, and $\frac{1}{\eta} = 1 - MR/P$, which means that

$$\eta = \frac{1}{1 - MR/P} = \frac{P}{P - MR},$$

which is the right-hand side of Equation 10.3.

8. R. Dorfman and P. Steiner, "Optimal Advertising and Optimal Quality," *American Economic Review*, December 1954.

must set the marginal revenue from an extra dollar of advertising equal to 1.5. Suppose that Terratech's managers believe that an extra $100,000 of advertising would increase the firm's sales by $180,000, which implies that the marginal revenue from an extra dollar of advertising is about $180,000 ÷ $100,000, or 1.8, rather than 1.5. Because the marginal revenue exceeds the price elasticity, Terratech will increase its profit if it does more advertising.[9] To maximize profit, it should increase its advertising up to the point where the marginal revenue from an extra dollar of advertising falls to 1.5, the value of the price elasticity of demand. (Since diminishing returns are assumed, marginal revenue falls as advertising increases.)

OPTIMAL ADVERTISING EXPENDITURES: A GRAPHICAL ANALYSIS

Going a step further, we can use a simple graphical technique to see how much a firm, if it maximizes profit, will spend on advertising. Take the case of the Miller Electronics Company. Suppose that curve F in Figure 10.7 shows the relationship between the price elasticity of demand of this firm's product and

Fig. 10.7 OPTIMAL ADVERTISING EXPENDITURE / *The firm's optimal advertising expenditure is* OV *if the marginal revenue curve is* G *(or* OW *if the marginal revenue curve is* G'*).*

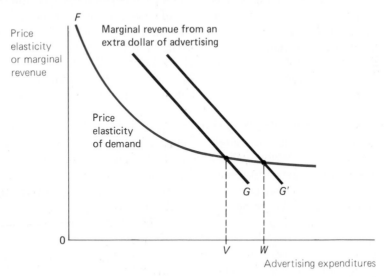

---

9. Had Terratech's managers believed that the marginal revenue from an extra dollar of advertising was *less* than the price elasticity of demand, a *reduction* in the firm's advertising expenditures would increase profit.

the amount it spends on advertising. With little or no advertising, this firm's product would be regarded by consumers as similar to a host of other products; hence, its price elasticity of demand would be very high. However, because appropriate advertising can induce consumers to attach importance to this product's distinguishing features, increases in advertising expenditure reduce its price elasticity considerably.[10] At each level of advertising expenditure, the G curve shows the marginal revenue from an extra dollar of advertising. Since the F curve intersects the G curve when Miller's advertising expenditure is OV dollars, this, based on Equation 10.4, is Miller's optimal level of advertising expenditure.

Clearly, a firm's optimal advertising expenditure depends on the position and shape of its G curve and its F curve. For example, suppose Miller's G curve shifts rightward to G', as shown in Figure 10.7. Such a shift might occur if the firm or its advertising agency found ways to increase the effectiveness of its advertisements. The result would be an increase in the optimal level of the firm's advertising expenditures (to OW dollars in Figure 10.7).

THE SOCIAL VALUE OF ADVERTISING

Thus far, we have considered advertising from the point of view of the firm, rather than of society as a whole. From society's point of view, there are obvious disadvantages stemming from certain kinds of advertising. To begin with, although private groups like the National Advertising Review Board and government agencies like the Federal Trade Commission try to stamp out blatantly deceptive advertising, some advertising misleads, rather than informs, consumers. Many consumers are properly skeptical about advertising claims, but the rest may be duped into making purchasing decisions that are far from optimal from their own point of view (but fine from the advertiser's perspective).

In addition, advertising may tend to augment the advertiser's monopoly power and may permit the advertiser more latitude to raise its price and profits. According to William Comanor and Thomas Wilson, the higher the ratio of advertising expenditures to sales in an industry, the higher the industry's profit rates.[11] If advertising makes customers recognize certain brands and if it encourages them to be loyal to these brands, sellers may have more power to raise prices without losing sales to competitors. In many retail establishments, advertised brands are priced higher than lesser-known brands. Advertising encourages customers to think that advertised brands are better than other brands, even though they may be essentially the same.

---

10. In some cases, the price elasticity of demand is directly, not inversely, related to the amount spent on advertising. More is said below on this score.

11. W. Comanor and T. Wilson, *Advertising and Monopoly Power* (Cambridge, Mass.: Harvard University Press, 1974).

On the other hand, there also are advantages of advertising from a consumer's point of view. Both George Stigler[12] and Phillip Nelson[13] have employed the theory of information to analyze the value of advertising. As they have pointed out, it is costly and time-consuming for consumers to find the best price for a product they want to buy. For example, it may cost a consumer $12 worth of time and travel expense to locate the store that offers a saving of $10 on the price of an item. If so, it is not worthwhile for the consumer to try to locate this store. On the other hand, if advertising (of various stores' prices) enables all consumers to identify and get to the lowest-price seller of this item at an additional cost of only $2, the identification of this lowest-price store is worthwhile—and the consumer will be better off as a result of this advertising.

Also, if advertising is successful in enlarging the market for a firm's product, and if this product's average cost falls as more of it is produced, then the saving in production costs may more than offset the advertising cost. A case in point is the retailing of eyeglasses. (See Example 10.1.) Apparently, significant economies of scale can be realized by achieving a relatively large sales volume in an eyeglass retailing firm, but it is difficult to achieve that volume if sellers are constrained by bans on advertising and other restrictive provisions sometimes found in optometrists' codes of ethics.

In contrast to the view that advertising promotes monopoly power, both Stigler and Nelson conclude that advertising tends to increase the price elasticity of demand for products. According to their findings, the demand for goods that are not widely advertised tends to be price inelastic. The greater the advertising effort, the more price elastic the demand for a good becomes. And the more elastic the demand for a good, the more competitive is the market for that good—and frequently the lower is the price.

Based on the foregoing discussion, it is clear that advertising has a variety of social effects, some positive, some negative. To the extent that it provides trustworthy information to consumers about product quality and other matters, its effects may be positive, but if it is grossly misleading, they may be negative. To the extent that it enables consumers to shop around for lower prices more efficiently and at lower cost, its effects tend to be positive, but if it is used to increase the advertiser's monopoly power, they may be negative.

Because advertising is of so many kinds, it really is impossible to generalize about whether or not it is socially beneficial. The answer depends on the nature of the advertising and the circumstances under which it takes place.[14] Advertising by retail stores, which informs consumers of the price and availa-

---

12. G. Stigler, "The Economics of Information," *Journal of Political Economy,* June 1961.

13. P. Nelson, "The Economic Consequences of Advertising," *Journal of Business,* April 1975.

14. For some recent studies concerning advertising and its effects, see the papers by T. Bresnahan, R. Higgins and F. McChesney, Y. Kotowitz and F. Mathewson, and K. Leffler and R. Sauer in P. Ippolito and D. Scheffman (eds.), *Empirical Approaches to Consumer Protection Economics* (Washington, D.C.: Federal Trade Commission, 1986).

bility of goods, is more likely to be socially beneficial than radio commercials consisting of mindless ditties. Advertising aimed at professional purchasers of equipment is more likely to be socially beneficial than television commercials that feature lots of movie stars and sports heroes but few facts.

Example 10.1

ADVERTISING, SPECTACLES, AND THE FTC

The theory of monopolistic competition emphasizes the significance of selling expenses, including advertising. The market for eyeglasses in large cities has many of the characteristics of monopolistic competition, there being a large number of sellers of eyeglasses, each one's product being slightly different from the others. Some states have banned advertising of prices by sellers of eyeglasses. The following table shows the average price of eyeglasses in these states, as well as in states with no advertising restrictions:

	Average price	
Nature of state law	*Eyeglasses*	*Eyeglasses and eye examinations*
Ban on advertising	$33.04	$40.96
No ban on advertising	26.34	37.10

(a) Since advertising is a selling expense which requires the use of resources, is it reasonable to expect that a firm's costs would be lower if it didn't have to advertise? (b) If advertising increases costs, why did the price of eyeglasses tend to be lower in states with no ban on advertising? (c) In 1978, the Federal Trade Commission (FTC) declared restrictions on eyeglass advertising to be illegal. Why did the FTC take this action?

SOLUTION

(a) Yes. Since advertising must be paid for, it increases a firm's costs. (b) In the markets studied, it appears that advertising improved the consumer's knowledge of the prices and services being offered by various sellers of eyeglasses. Without advertising, the cost to consumers of obtaining such knowledge is relatively high. Armed with such information, consumers were in a better position to seek out relatively low prices, and sellers were more likely to offer them. (Also, see p. 303.) (c) Because the FTC felt that such restrictions impaired the effectiveness of the competitive process. In particular, as shown in the above table, consumers seem to pay higher prices when such restrictions exist. In fact, there tended to be a drop in eyeglass prices after this FTC ruling.*

* For further discussion, see L. Benham, "The Effect of Advertising on the Price of Eyeglasses," *The Journal of Law and Economics*, October 1972.

SUMMARY

1. Under monopolistic competition, there is a large number of firms producing and selling goods that are close substitutes, but that are not completely homogeneous from one seller to another. Each seller tries to make its product a little different, by altering the physical makeup of the product, the services it offers, and other such variables.

2. In the theory of monopolistic competition, there are two kinds of demand curves. On the one hand, there is the dd' demand curve, which shows how much the firm will sell if it varies its price from the going level and if other firms maintain their existing prices. On the other hand, there is the DD' demand curve, which shows how much the firm will sell if all firms raise or lower their prices by the same amount as this firm.

3. In the short run, equilibrium price and output occur when marginal revenue based on the dd' demand curve equals marginal cost at the existing output, while the dd' demand curve intersects the DD' demand curve at the existing price (and output).

4. In the long run, firms, as in perfect competition, are able to change the scale of their plant and to leave or enter the industry. The long-run equilibrium position is the point at which (1) the long-run average cost curve is tangent to the dd' demand curve, and (2) the DD' demand curve intersects the dd' demand curve and the long-run average cost curve at the tangency point.

5. A famous, and controversial, conclusion of the theory of monopolistic competition is that firms under this form of market organization will tend to operate with excess capacity.

6. Under monopolistic competition, as well as other market structures like oligopoly, advertising outlays can be substantial. To maximize profit, a firm should set its advertising expenditures at the level where the marginal revenue from an extra dollar of advertising equals the price elasticity of demand for its product. If the marginal revenue is greater than the price elasticity, the firm should increase its advertising expenditures; if the marginal revenue is less that the price elasticity, it should decrease its advertising expenditures.

7. Whether or not advertising is socially beneficial depends on the nature of the advertising and the circumstances under which it takes place. From society's point of view, there are obvious disadvantages in advertising that mis-

leads, rather than informs, consumers, and in advertising that augments the advertiser's monopoly power. On the other hand, advertising that enables sellers to take advantage of economies of scale in production, as well as advertising that allows customers to shop around for lower prices more efficiently, can be socially beneficial.

QUESTIONS/PROBLEMS

1) Suppose that dress shops are a monopolistic-competitive industry, and that each dress shop's *dd'* demand curve, *DD'* demand curve, and long-run average cost curve are shown below.

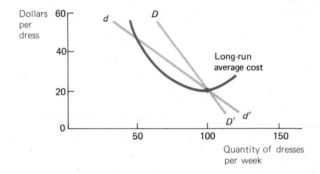

(a) If each dress shop earns no economic profit, what is its price and output? (b) Is each dress shop in long-run equilibrium under these circumstances? (c) Does the individual dress shop believe it is possible to earn positive economic profits under these circumstances? (d) If some dress shops leave the industry, will this shift the *DD'* demand curve to the left? (e) Will the long-run average cost curve of the individual dress shop be increasing, decreasing, or horizontal at the long-run equilibrium point?

2) Explain in detail why you believe that each of the following industries can or cannot be represented by the theory of monopolistic competition: (a) copper, (b) outboard motors, (c) airlines, (d) cement. To answer this question, what characteristics of each industry should you look at? Why?

3) According to a survey conducted by the Conference Board, many firms determine the total amount they spend on advertising by multiplying their anticipated sales by some historical percentage. For example, the marketing vice-president of a consumer products firm said, "Our [advertising] budget is generally established as a percentage of our targeted sales goal. Each product line is considered on its own, and different percentage factors are used for them." These percentages remain relatively constant from year to year and are based on past performance. Is this procedure in accord with the theory of monopolistic competition? If not, how can it be reconciled with this theory (if at all)?

4) For a particular monopolistically competitive firm, the *DD'* demand curve intersects the *dd'* demand curve at a price of $10. Can the price of the firm's product be in equilibrium now at $12? Why or why not?

5) Describe in detail the social advantages and disadvantages of advertising. If a particular advertising campaign is profitable to the advertiser, does this mean that it is socially desirable? Why or why not?

6) Under what circumstances are increases in advertising likely to reduce a product's price elasticity of demand? Under what circumstances are they likely to increase it?

7) The situation facing a particular monopolistically competitive firm is the following:

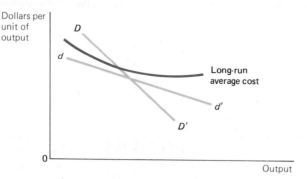

Is this situation a long-run equilibrium? Will entry occur in the industry? Will exit occur in the industry?

8) Would you expect that increases in advertising expenditures will increase a monopolistically competitive firm's sales, regardless of the size of these expenditures? Would you expect advertising to be subject to the law of diminishing marginal returns? Why or why not?

9) According to some economists, there are too many gas stations and grocery stores. Is this in keeping with the theory of monopolisitic competition? Suppose that you were given the job of determining whether there were too many gas stations in your town or city. How would you go about testing this hypothesis? What kinds of data would you need? How would you go about getting these data? (And what does "too many" mean?)

10) The Sonora Software Company estimates that the price elasticity of demand for its product is 2.0 and that an extra $100,000 in advertising expenditure would increase its sales by $150,000. Is this firm maximizing profit? Why or why not? If not, should it increase or reduce its advertising expenditures? Why?

Price and Output under Oligopoly

STRATEGIC BEHAVIOR: CONFLICT AND COOPERATION

Oligopoly is a market structure characterized by a small number of firms and a great deal of interdependence, actual and perceived, among them. Each oligo-

Oligopoly

polist formulates its policies with an eye to their effect on its rivals. Since an oligopoly contains a small number of firms, any change in the firm's price or output influences the sales and profits of competitors. Moreover, since there are only a few firms, each firm must recognize that changes in its own policies are likely to elicit changes in the policies of its competitors as well.

Because of this interdependence, oligopolists face a *strategic* situation, one where the optimal decision of one firm depends on what other firms decide to do, and where there is opportunity for both conflict and cooperation. A good example is the American computer industry, in which a handful of firms, led by the IBM Corporation, account for the bulk of the industry's sales. Each of the major computer firms must take account of the reaction of the others when it formulates its price and output policy, since its policy is likely to affect theirs. Thus, when IBM began an ambitious program in 1986 to increase its sagging earnings, it had to anticipate what the reactions of other firms, like

Digital Equipment and Hewlett-Packard, would be. Even mighty IBM, with annual sales of $52 billion, had to pay careful attention to the reaction of its smaller rivals, since its optimal strategy depended in part on how they were likely to respond.

Oligopoly is a common market structure in the United States. The automobile industry is dominated by three domestic firms—General Motors, Ford, and Chrysler—and a handful of foreign producers. Many parts of the electrical equipment industry are dominated by General Electric and Westinghouse. The aerospace industry has been dominated by Boeing, General Dynamics, Lockheed, McDonnell Douglas, United Technologies, and a few others. And these are only some highly visible examples. Not all oligopolists are large firms. If two grocery stores exist in an isolated community, they are oligopolists, too; the fact that they are small firms does not change this situation.

There are many reasons for oligopoly, one being economies of scale. In some industries, low costs cannot be achieved unless a firm is producing an output equal to a substantial percentage of the total available market, with the consequence that the number of firms will tend to be rather small. In addition, there may be economies of scale in sales promotion as well as in production, and this too may promote oligopoly. Further, there may be barriers that make it very difficult to enter the industry. (A variety of such barriers are discussed later in this chapter.) Finally, of course, the number of firms in an industry may decrease in response to the desire to weaken competitive pressures.

THE COURNOT MODEL

To begin with, we consider a theory put forth by Augustin Cournot[1] about a hundred and fifty years ago. Although this theory is too simple to capture much of the richness of the oligopolistic situation, it has attracted considerable attention and is still cited. Cournot considers the case in which there are two sellers, that is, the case of duopoly; but his model can easily be generalized to include the case of three or more sellers. To describe his model, it is convenient to assume that the two firms, firm I and firm II, produce the same product, have the same cost functions, and are perfectly aware of the demand curve for their product, which is supposed to be linear. More specifically, Cournot discusses the case of two firms selling spring water, with the cost of production being zero for each firm.

Duopoly

Turning to behavioral assumptions, both firms are supposed to maximize profits. Each assumes that, regardless of what output it produces, the other will hold its output constant at the existing level. Taking the other firm's output level as given, each firm chooses its own output level to maximize profit.

---

1. A. Cournot, *Recherches sur les Principes Mathématiques de la Théorie des Riches,* translated by Nathaniel Bacon (New York: Macmillan, 1897). He first published his model in 1838.

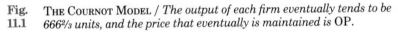

Fig.
11.1
THE COURNOT MODEL / *The output of each firm eventually tends to be*
666⅔ units, and the price that eventually is maintained is OP.

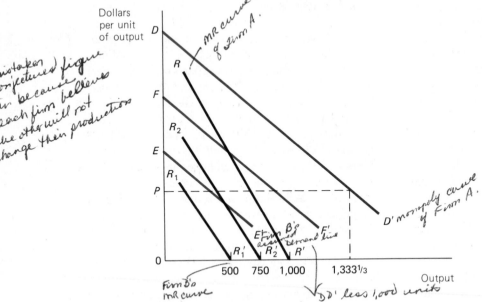

mistaken figure/Conjectured figure in because each firm believes the other will not change their production

Suppose that firm I is the first to act. It sells the monopoly output, 1,000 units,
according to the situation in Figure 11.1. It chooses this output level because it
assumes that firm II will continue to produce nothing. If this is the case, firm
I's marginal revenue (RR') equals its marginal cost (which is zero) at 1,000
units if the demand curve for the product is DD'.

Now it is firm II's turn to act. Contrary to firm I's expectation, firm II is
seriously considering changing its current output level, which is zero. Taking
firm I's output level (of 1,000) as given, firm II believes that the demand curve
for its product is the total market demand curve less 1,000, or EE' in Figure
11.1. Thus firm II chooses an output level of 500, where the marginal revenue,
R_1R_1', based on the demand curve EE' equals its marginal cost, which is zero.

The spotlight now moves back to firm I, which is assumed to have the
next move. Again, firm I assumes that firm II has chosen an output level that
will be maintained regardless of what it, firm I, does. Consequently, firm I believes that the demand curve for its product is the total demand curve less 500,
or FF' in Figure 11.1. Thus firm I chooses an output level of 750, where marginal revenue (R_2R_2') based on the demand curve FF' equals the firm's marginal cost, which is zero.

This process goes on indefinitely, each firm taking the other firm's output
as given and choosing the output that maximizes its own profits. Firm I's output is 1,000, then 750, then 22,000 ÷ 32, . . . [2] Firm II's output is zero, then 500,

2. How do we get 22,000/32? It can be shown that firm I will produce $C/2$, $3C/8$, $11C/32$, $\cdots$,
where C is the competitive output (2,000 in this case). Try to prove this as an exercise.

then $20{,}000 \div 32, \ldots$ [3] Ultimately, it can be shown that the output of each firm tends to $666\frac{2}{3}$.[4] Thus the price that eventually is maintained is OP. If price were set equal to marginal cost, it would equal zero and the industry's output would be 2,000. This is the perfectly competitive solution. Thus the equilibrium output under duopoly in the Cournot model is $\frac{2}{3}$ of the competitive output. Since the monopoly output would be 1,000, it is $\frac{4}{3}$ of the monopoly output.[5]

The Cournot model makes the unrealistic assumption that a firm continually makes the mistake of assuming that its rivals will not alter their output in response to the firm's own changes in output. But despite the fact that it is difficult to accept the way in which the duopolists are visualized as approaching the Cournot equilibrium, the equilibrium itself (which in Figure 11.1 is that each firm produces $666\frac{2}{3}$ units) is regarded as a valuable concept by many economists. This equilibrium has the property that each firm's choice of output is the profit-maximizing choice, given its expectations concerning the other firm's behavior, and that each firm's expectations concerning the other firm's behavior are confirmed by its actual behavior. (Later in this chapter, we shall see that this sort of equilibrium is also called a Nash equilibrium.)

---

3. It can be shown that firm II will produce 0, $C/4$, $5C/16$, $\cdots$, where C is the competitive output (2,000 in this case). Prove this as an exercise. See footnote 2.

4. Firm I's output in the limit can be represented as

$$C[1 - (\tfrac{1}{2} + \tfrac{1}{8} + \tfrac{1}{32} + \cdots)] = C[1 - \tfrac{1}{2}(1 + \tfrac{1}{4} + (\tfrac{1}{4})^2 + \cdots)],$$

which equals

$$C\left[1 - \frac{1}{2}\left(\frac{1}{1 - \tfrac{1}{4}}\right)\right] = C(1 - \tfrac{2}{3}) = \frac{C}{3}.$$

Firm II's output in the limit can be represented as

$$C(\tfrac{1}{4} + \tfrac{1}{16} + \tfrac{1}{64} + \cdots),$$

which equals

$$\tfrac{1}{4}C[1 + \tfrac{1}{4} + (\tfrac{1}{4})^2 + \cdots] = \frac{1}{4}C\left(\frac{1}{1 - \tfrac{1}{4}}\right) = \frac{C}{3}.$$

C is the competitive output.

5. Another way to describe the Cournot model is as follows: There is a demand curve for the industry's product, $p = f(q_1 + q_2)$, where q_1 is the output of firm I, q_2 is the output of firm II, and p is the price of the product. The total cost function of firm I is $C_1(q_1)$ and the total cost function of firm II is $C_2(q_2)$. Thus the profit of firm I is

$$\pi_1 = q_1 f(q_1 + q_2) - C_1(q_1),$$

and the profit of firm II is

$$\pi_2 = q_2 f(q_1 + q_2) - C_2(q_2).$$

If each firm takes the other firm's output as given and maximizes profit

$$\frac{\partial \pi_1}{\partial q_1} = f(q_1 + q_2) + q_1 \frac{\partial f(q_1 + q_2)}{\partial q_1} - \frac{\partial C_1}{\partial q_1} = 0$$

$$\frac{\partial \pi_2}{\partial q_2} = f(q_1 + q_2) + q_2 \frac{\partial f(q_1 + q_2)}{\partial q_2} - \frac{\partial C_2}{\partial q_2} = 0.$$

Solving these two equations simultaneously, we obtain the equilibrium q_1 and q_2, which in turn tells us what the equilibrium value of p will be.

THE KINKED DEMAND CURVE

Another early oligopoly model was due to Paul Sweezy, who in 1939 advanced a theory to explain the rigidity of prices in oligopolistic markets.[6] At that time, there was a widespread feeling that prices in such markets tended to be rigid. A classic example occurred in the steel industry. From 1901 to 1916, the price of steel rails remained at $28 a ton, and from 1922 to 1933, it remained at $43 a ton. Of course, this was an extreme example, but it illustrates the basic point, which was that prices in oligopolistic industries commonly remained unchanged for fairly long periods.[7]

To explain this price rigidity, Sweezy asserted that, if an oligopolist cuts its price, it can be pretty sure that its rivals will meet the reduction. On the other hand, if an oligopolist increases its price, it is likely to find that its rivals will not change their prices. In such a case, the demand curve for the oligopolist's product would be much more elastic for price increases than for price decreases.

Figure 11.2 shows the situation, the oligopolist's demand curve being represented by $D_1 V D_1'$ and the current price being OP_0. Because of the "kink" in the demand curve, the marginal revenue curve is not continuous: It consists of two segments RA and BR'. Given that the firm's marginal cost curve is M, marginal revenue does not equal marginal cost at any level of output. But it can be shown that OQ_0 is the most profitable output of the firm.[8] Moreover, OQ_0 remains the most profitable output—and OP_0 the most profitable price—even if the marginal cost curve changes considerably. For example, it remains the most profitable output if the marginal cost curve shifts to G or H. Also, OQ_0 remains the most profitable output—and OP_0 the most profitable price—for some changes in demand, as long as the kink remains at the same price level. Thus, under these circumstances, one might expect price to be quite rigid.

Soon after Sweezy's theory first appeared, it was regarded by some economists as a general theory of oligopoly. However, subsequent research has cast doubt on its general usefulness. For example, George Stigler found that in seven oligopolistic industries there was little indication that an increase in

---

6. P. Sweezy, "Demand under Conditions of Oligopoly," *Journal of Political Economy,* August 1939.

7. For an early reference, see H. Purdy, M. Lindahl, and W. Carter, *Corporate Concentration and Public Policy* (Englewood Cliffs, N.J.: Prentice-Hall, 1950).

8. To see that OQ_0 is the most profitable output, note that, if output is pushed above OQ_0, the increase in revenue (given by the marginal revenue curve) is less than the increase in cost (given by the marginal cost curve). On the other hand, if output falls below OQ_0, the loss in revenue (given by the marginal revenue curve) is greater than the reduction in cost (given by the marginal cost curve). Since profit decreases when output is pushed above, or falls below, OQ_0, it must be maximized when output equals OQ_0.

Fig. 11.2 THE SWEEZY MODEL / *Because of the "kink" in the demand curve,* OP₀ *remains the most profitable price even if the marginal cost curves change considerably (for example, from M to G or H).*

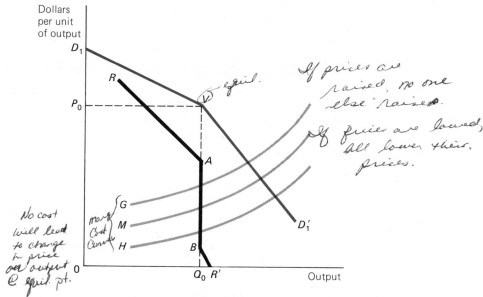

(handwritten annotations on figure:)
If prices are raised, no one else raises.
If prices are lowered, all lower their prices.
No cost will lead to change in price or output @ equil. pt.

price by one firm would not be matched, in general, by other firms.[9] Thus, in these industries at least, there seemed to be little evidence for the existence of a kink in the demand curve. Moreover, although this theory may be useful under some circumstances in explaining why price tends to remain at a certain level (OP_0 in Figure 11.2), it is of no use in explaining why this level, rather than another, currently prevails. For example, it simply takes as given that the current price is OP_0 in Figure 11.2; it does not explain why the current price is OP_0. Thus this theory is an incomplete model of oligopolistic pricing.[10]

COLLUSION AND CARTELS

Both the Cournot model and the Sweezy model assume that oligopolists do not collude. However, conditions in oligopolistic industries tend to promote collu-

---

9. G. Stigler, "The Kinky Oligopoly Demand Curve and Rigid Prices," *Journal of Political Economy,* 1947. Also see W. Primeaux, Jr., and W. Smith, "Pricing Patterns and the Kinky Demand Curve," *Journal of Law and Economics,* April 1976; and J. Simon, "A Further Test of the Kinky Oligopoly Demand Curve," *American Economic Review,* December 1969.

10. For some relevant recent discussions, see Dennis Carlton, "The Rigidity of Prices," *American Economic Review,* September 1986.

sion, since the number of firms is small and the firms recognize their interdependence. The advantages to the firms of collusion seem obvious: increased profits, decreased uncertainty, and a better opportunity to prevent entry. However, collusive arrangements are often hard to maintain, since once a collusive agreement is made, any of the firms can increase its profits by cheating on the agreement. Moreover, collusive arrangements generally are illegal, at least in the United States.

Cartel

When a collusive arrangement is made openly and formally, it is called a *cartel.* In many countries in Europe, cartels have been common and legally acceptable. In the United States, most collusive agreements, whether secret or open cartels, were declared illegal by the Sherman Antitrust Act, which dates back to 1890. However, this does not mean that such agreements do not exist. For example, there was widespread collusion among American electrical equipment manufacturers during the 1950s.[11] Moreover, trade associations and professional organizations may sometimes perform functions somewhat similar to a cartel. In addition, some types of cartels have the official sanction of the United States government.[12]

Suppose that a cartel is established to set a uniform price for a particular (homogeneous) product. What price will it charge? To begin with, the cartel must estimate the marginal cost curve for the cartel as a whole. If input prices do not increase as the cartel expands, this marginal cost curve is the horizontal sum of the marginal cost curves of the individual firms. Suppose that the resulting marginal cost curve for the cartel is as shown in Figure 11.3. If the demand curve for the industry's product and the relevant marginal revenue curve are as shown there, the output that maximizes the total profit of the cartel members is OQ_0. Thus, if it maximizes cartel profits, the cartel will choose a price of OP_0. This, of course, is the monopoly price.

Another important task of a cartel is to distribute the industry's total sales among the firms belonging to the cartel. If the aim of the cartel is to maximize cartel profits, it will allocate sales to firms in such a way that the marginal cost of all firms is equal. Otherwise the cartel could make more

---

11. In early 1960 the Department of Justice charged that a large number of companies and individuals in the electrical equipment industry were guilty of fixing prices and dividing up the market for circuit breakers, switchgears, and other important products. Most of the defendants were found guilty; the companies, including General Electric and Westinghouse, received fines; and some of the guilty executives were sent to prison. The price-fixing agreements were reached in various ways. Many of the meetings occurred at conventions of the National Electric Manufacturers Association and other trade groups. Some agreements were made through telephone calls and written memoranda transmitted from one sales executive to another. Efforts were made to keep the meetings and agreements secret. For example, codes were used, and the participants at meetings sometimes disguised their records and did not use their companies' names when registering at hotels. The executives recognized that these agreements were illegal.

12. For example, airlines flying transatlantic routes have been members of the International Air Transport Association, which can agree on uniform prices for transatlantic flights.

Fig.
11.3 PRICE AND OUTPUT DETERMINATION BY A CARTEL / *The cartel chooses a price of* OP_0 *and an output of* OQ_0.

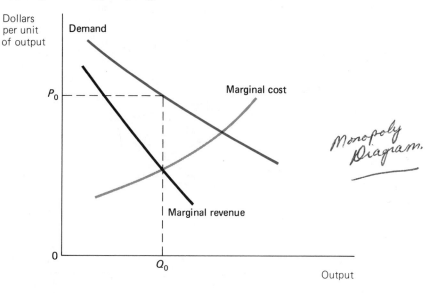

money by reallocating output among firms so as to reduce the cost of producing the cartel's total output. For example, if the marginal cost at firm I was higher than at firm II, the cartel can increase its total profits by transferring some production from firm I to firm II.

However, this allocation of output—sometimes called the ideal allocation by economists—is unlikely to occur, since allocation decisions are the result of negotiation between firms with varying interests and varying capabilities. This is a political process in which various firms have different amounts of influence. Those with the most influence and the shrewdest negotiators are likely to receive the largest sales quotas, even though this increases total cartel costs. Moreover, high-cost firms are likely to receive larger sales quotas than cost minimization would dictate, since they would be unwilling to accept the small quotas dictated by cost minimization. In practice, there is some evidence that sales are often distributed in accord with a firm's level of sales in the past, or the extent of its productive capacity. Also, a cartel sometimes divides a market geographically, with some firms being given certain regions or countries and other firms being given other regions or countries.

The Instability of Cartels

We have already noted that collusive agreements tend to break down. Of course, the difficulty in keeping a cartel from breaking down increases with the number of firms in the cartel. To see why firms are tempted to leave the cartel,

Fig.
11.4   THE INSTABILITY OF CARTELS / *If it leaves the cartel, the firm's profit*
equals $OQ_1 \times BP_1$, *which is higher than if it adheres to the price and sales*
quota established by the cartel.

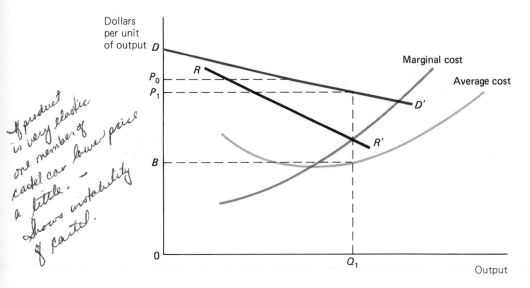

*If product
is very elastic
one member of
cartel can lower price
a little. —
shows instability
of cartel.*

consider the case of the firm in Figure 11.4. If this firm were to leave the cartel, it would be faced with a demand curve of DD' as long as the other firms in the cartel maintain a price of OP_0. This demand curve is very elastic; the firm is able to expand its sales considerably by small reductions in price. Even if the firm were not to leave the cartel, but if it were to grant secret price concessions, the same sort of demand curve would be present.

Under these circumstances the firm's maximum profit if it leaves the cartel or secretly lowers price will be attained if it sells an output of OQ_1, at a price of OP_1, since this is the output at which marginal cost equals marginal revenue. (RR' is the firm's marginal revenue curve.) This price would result in a profit of $OQ_1 \times BP_1$, which is higher than if the firm conforms to the price and sales quota dictated by the cartel. A firm that breaks away from a cartel—or secretly cheats—can increase its profits as long as other firms do not do the same thing and as long as the cartel does not punish it in some way. But if all firms do this, the cartel breaks down.

Consequently, as long as a cartel is not maintained by legal provisions, there is a constant threat to its existence. Its members have an incentive to cheat, and once a few do so, others may follow. Price concessions made secretly by a few "chiselers" or openly by a few malcontents cut into the sales of cooperative members of the cartel who are induced to match them. Thus the ranks of the unfaithful are expanded; and ultimately the cartel may break down completely.

THE OPEC OIL CARTEL: AN APPLICATION

To illustrate the nature and behavior of a cartel, consider the Organization of Petroleum Exporting Countries (OPEC) cartel. This cartel first hit the headlines in late 1973 when its Arab members precipitated a crisis in the United States by announcing a cutback in oil exports to us. Then it attracted further attention by taking a series of actions resulting in very large increases in the price of crude oil. For example, the price of Saudi Arabian crude oil (delivered to the United States East Coast) jumped from $4 in 1973 to over $10 in early 1974. Again in 1979, in the wake of the Iranian revolution, OPEC raised the price enormously, to over $30 a barrel.

What is OPEC, and how has it functioned? OPEC consists of thirteen major oil-producing countries, including Saudi Arabia, Iran, Venezuela, Libya, and Nigeria. The OPEC countries imposed an excise tax of so many cents per barrel on each barrel of oil produced in their countries. These taxes were well publicized and, like any excise tax, they were treated as a cost of production by any of the international oil companies operating in these countries. Thus, by increasing these taxes, the OPEC countries raised the price of crude oil, since no company could afford to sell oil for less than its production costs plus the tax. According to the model discussed on pp. 313–15, one would expect the OPEC cartel to have pushed the crude oil price up toward the monopoly level, since this would have increased their tax revenues. In fact, this seems to have been exactly what occurred. Experts estimate that hundreds of billions of dollars were transferred by this means from oil consumers to OPEC.

However, OPEC's economic power seemed to wane in the mid-1980s. By 1983, a decade after the first of its huge price increases, OPEC seemed to be experiencing problems in maintaining the price of oil, and in 1984 to 1986, the price fell until it was below $15 per barrel. To a considerable extent, the downward pressure on price was due to a continuing shift away from the use of oil. For example, while national output in the United States increased at a 5 percent annual rate in the first three quarters of 1983, oil consumption dropped nearly 2.5 percent. Because of conservation of oil and competition from other fuels (due partly to the great increases in the oil price in earlier years), there was a reduction in the quantity of oil demanded. In addition, non-OPEC oil production (in Mexico and the North Sea, for example) has soared, thus putting additional pressure on OPEC. And individual members of OPEC, like Iran, demanded that the organization's total output be reduced to boost prices, but refused to cut their own production because of the desire to meet major domestic objectives. For all these reasons, OPEC in the mid-1980s seemed to be only a shadow of its former self.[13]

---

13. For further discussion of OPEC, see J. Griffin and H. Steele, *Energy Economics and Policy,* 2d ed. (New York: Academic Press, 1985).

THE THEORY OF GAMES

As we have seen in previous sections, a basic feature of oligopoly is that each firm must take account of its rivals' reactions to its own actions. For this reason an oligopolistic firm cannot tell what effect a change in its output will have on the price of its product and on its profits, unless it can guess how its rivals will respond to this change in its output. Thus oligopolistic behavior has some of the characteristics of a game. One of the most interesting developments in the theory of oligopoly in recent decades has been the appearance and elaboration of the theory of games, which has enriched oligopoly theory considerably.[14] In this section, we provide a basic description of the objectives and concepts of game theory, as well as a very simple example of a two-person game.

Game theory attempts to study decision-making in situations where there is a mixture of conflict and cooperation as in oligopoly. A *game* is a competitive situation where two or more persons pursue their own interests and no person can dictate the outcome. For example, poker is a game, and so is a situation in which two firms are engaged in competitive advertising campaigns. A game is described in terms of the players, the rules of the game, the payoffs of the game, and the information conditions that exist during the game. These elements, common to all conflict situations, are the fundamental characteristics of a game.

Game

More specifically, a player, which may be a single person or an organization, is a decision-making unit. Each player has a certain amount of resources; the *rules of the game* describe how these resources can be used. For example, the rules of poker indicate how bets can be made and which hands are better than other hands. A *strategy* is a complete specification of what a player will do under each contingency in the playing of the game. For example, a corporation president might tell his subordinates how he wants an advertising campaign to start, and what should be done at subsequent points in time in response to various actions of competing firms.

Strategy

The game's outcome clearly depends on the strategies used by each player. A player's *payoff* varies from game to game: It is win, lose, or draw in checkers, and various sums of money in poker. For simplicity this section deals only with *two-person games,* games with only two players. The relevant features of a two-person game can be shown by constructing a *payoff matrix.* To illustrate, suppose that two firms are about to stage rival advertising campaigns and that each firm has a choice of strategies. Firm I can choose strategy *A* or *B,* and firm II can choose strategy 1 or 2. The payoff, expressed in terms of profits for each firm, is shown in

Payoff matrix

14. A seminal work on game theory was J. von Neumann and O. Morgenstern, *Theory of Games and Economic Behavior* (Princeton, N.J.: Princeton University Press, 1944).

Table **Payoff Matrix: Advertising Campaigns**
11.1

Possible strategies for firm I	*Possible strategies for Firm II*	
	1	*2*
A	Firm I's profit: $2 million Firm II's profit: $3 million	Firm I's profit: $1 million Firm II's profit: $2 million
B	Firm I's profit: $3 million Firm II's profit: $2 million	Firm I's profit: $2 million Firm II's profit: $1 million

Table 11.1 for each combination of strategies. For example, if firm I adopts strategy *A* and firm II adopts strategy 2, firm I makes a profit of $1 million, and firm II makes a profit of $2 million.

In this game, there is a *dominant strategy* for each player. Regardless of whether firm II adopts strategy 1 or 2, firm I will make more profit if it chooses strategy *B* rather than *A*. Thus strategy *B* is firm I's dominant strategy. Similarily, regardless of whether firm I adopts strategy *A* or *B*, firm II will make more profit if it chooses strategy 1 rather than 2. Thus strategy 1 is firm II's dominant strategy. The solution to this game is quite simple. Firm I chooses strategy *B,* and firm II chooses strategy 1. Firm I's profit equals $3 million, and firm II's profit equals $2 million. This is the best that either player—that is, either firm—can do.[15]

Dominant strategy

THE PRISONER'S DILEMMA

Having described the basic features of a game, we turn our attention to an important type of game, known as the prisoner's dilemma, which has proved of use in oligopoly theory, as well as in many other areas of economics and behavioral science. Consider a situation where two persons, John Dillinger and Dutch Schultz, are arrested after committing a crime. The police lock each person in a separate room and offer each one the following deal: "If you confess, while your partner does not confess, you will get a 2-year jail term, while he will get 12 years." Each person knows that if they both confess, each will get 10 years (not 12 years because they cooperated with the police). If neither confesses, each will get only 3 years because the evidence against them is weak.

Both Dillinger and Schultz have two possible strategies: to confess or not to confess. The four possible outcomes, depending on which strategy each

---

15. Dominant strategies often do not exist, since one player's optimal strategy often depends on what the other player does. As indicated in more detail in the next section, economists often use the concept of a Nash equilibrium, which does not require that dominant strategies exist. A pair of strategies is a Nash equilibrium if each player's strategy is optimal, given the strategy chosen by the other player.

Table PAYOFF MATRIX: DILLINGER AND SCHULTZ
11.2

| *Possible strategies for John Dillinger* | *Possible strategies for Schultz* | |
	Confess	*Do not confess*
Confess	Both get 10-year jail terms.	Dillinger gets 2 years; Schultz gets 12 years.
Do not confess	Dillinger gets 12 years; Schultz gets 2 years.	Both get 3-year jail terms.

person chooses, are shown in the payoff matrix in Table 11.2. What strategy will Schultz choose? If Dillinger does not confess, the better strategy for Schultz is to confess, since Schultz will serve less time (2 years) than if he does not confess (3 years). If Dillinger confesses, the better strategy for Schultz is to confess, since Schultz will serve less time (10 years) than if he does not confess (12 years). Thus, Schultz will confess, since regardless of which strategy Dillinger adopts, Schultz is better off to confess than not to confess.

Similarly, Dillinger too will confess since, regardless of which strategy Schultz adopts, Dillinger is better off to confess than not to confess. To see this, note that, if Schultz does not confess, the better strategy for Dillinger is to confess, since Dillinger will serve less time (2 years) than if he does not confess (3 years). Also, if Schultz confesses, the better strategy for Dillinger is to confess, since Dillinger will serve less time (10 years) than if he does not confess (12 years).

Thus, in this situation it appears that both Dillinger and Schultz will confess. This is the *Nash equilibrium*[16] for this game. A Nash equilibrium is a situation where each player's strategy is optimal, given the strat-

Nash equilibrium

egies chosen by the other players. (As pointed out earlier, the equilibrium in the Cournot model is a Nash equilibrium because each firm is maximizing profit, given the decision of the other firm.) Given the other person's decision, both Dillinger and Schultz are pursuing their own best interests by confessing—and neither regrets his own decision to confess. But it is important to recognize that each is doing worse than if neither of them confessed. If they could trust each other not to confess, or if they were able to communicate with one another (and thus if each could assure himself that the other would not confess), each could serve 3 years rather than 10 years. However, because there is no way for them to coordinate their decisions, they serve the longer prison term.

---

16. It is named after John F. Nash, a Princeton mathematician. Some games may have more than one Nash equilibrium, and some have no Nash equilibrium of the sort described here. However, for the sort of games considered presently, there will always exist a Nash equilibrium in mixed strategies. (A mixed strategy is one where a probability is attached to each strategy, which is played with this probability.)

CHEATING ON A CARTEL AGREEMENT

The type of game discussed in the previous section—the so-called *prisoner's dilemma*—is useful in analyzing oligopoly behavior. For example, it can help to indicate the circumstances under which firms will tend to cheat (that is, secretly cut price) on a cartel agreement. As we stressed earlier in this chapter, there frequently is a temptation for cartel members to cheat in this way.

Suppose that the only two producers of lasers—Ambler, Inc. and the Elysian Company—form a cartel. Each firm has two possible strategies: to stick by the cartel agreement or to cheat. There are four possible outcomes, depending on which strategy each firm pursues. They are shown in Table 11.3.

Table 11.3 PAYOFF MATRIX: AMBLER AND ELYSIAN

| *Possible strategies for Ambler* | *Possible strategies for Elysian* | |
	Stick by agreement	*Cheat*
Stick by agreement	Ambler's profit: $4 million Elysian's profit: $4 million	Ambler's profit: $1 million Elysian's profit: $5 million
Cheat	Ambler's profit: $5 million Elysian's profit: $1 million	Ambler's profit: $3 million Elysian's profit: $3 million

What should Ambler do? If Elysian sticks by the agreement, it appears that the better strategy for Ambler is to cheat, since Ambler's profits will be greater than if it sticks by the agreement. If Elysian cheats, the better strategy for Ambler seems to be to cheat as well, since Ambler's profits will be higher than if it sticks by the agreement. Thus, it appears that *Ambler will choose the strategy of cheating, since regardless of which strategy Elysian adopts, Ambler seems better off by cheating than by sticking by the agreement.*

What should Elysian do? If Ambler sticks by the agreement, the better strategy for Elysian seems to be to cheat, since Elysian's profits will be greater than if it sticks by the agreement. If Ambler cheats, the better strategy for Elysian appears to be to cheat as well, since Elysian's profits will be higher than if it sticks by the agreement. Thus, it seems that *Elysian will choose the strategy of cheating, since, regardless of which strategy Ambler adopts, Elysian is better off by cheating than by sticking by the agreement.*

Consequently, in this situation it appears that both firms will cheat. Like the game in Table 11.2 involving John Dillinger and Dutch Schultz, this is an example of the prisoner's dilemma. Recall that, because neither Dillinger nor Schultz could trust the other not to confess, both wound up serving more time in jail (10 years versus 3 years) than if they had trusted each other. Similarly, Ambler and Elysian, because they do not trust each other to stick by their agreement, wind up with lower profits than if they both were to stick by the agreement ($3 million versus $4 million).

REPEATED PRISONER'S DILEMMA AND "TIT FOR TAT"

At this point it is essential to recognize that there is an important difference between the situation facing Ambler and Elysian and that facing Dillinger and Schultz. In the case of Dillinger and Schultz, if this was the only crime they performed together and if they did not intend to work together again, it may have been reasonable for each of them to assume that they would play this game only once. But for Ambler and Elysian, such an assumption would not be reasonable. At every point in time, each of these firms must decide whether it will cheat or not. Since they are continually dealing with customers, they must continually decide whether or not to secretly cut price.

Because Ambler and Elysian play this game repeatedly, the analysis in the previous section may not be correct. To see this, suppose that Ambler refuses to cheat the first time it must make such a decision and that it continues to stick by the agreement so long as Elysian does so. But if Elysian fails even once to cooperate, Ambler will revert forever to the safe policy of cheating. If Elysian adopts the same sort of policy, then each can reap profits of $4 million. If either one cheats, it will raise its profit to $5 million for a brief period of time, but subsequently its profit will fall permanently to $3 million. Thus, it will not be in the interest of either firm to cheat.

It is important to recognize that Ambler and Elysian can achieve this outcome even if they do not collude or make any binding agreements. If each presumes that the other will have the intelligence to maintain the monopoly price, their presumptions will tend to be correct. As David Hume, the eighteenth-century British economist, put it over 200 years ago,

I learn to do a service to another, without bearing him any real kindness; because I foresee that he will return my service, in expectation of another of the same kind, and in order to maintain the same correspondence of good offices with me or with others. And accordingly, after I have served him, and he is in possession of the advantage arising from my action, he is induced to perform his part, as foreseeing the consequences of his refusal.[17]

According to Robert Axelrod of the University of Michigan, a good strategy for each player is *"tit for tat,"* which means that each player should do on

---

17. J. Friedman, *Game Theory with Applications to Economics* (New York: Oxford University Press, 1986), p. 70. Of course, this assumes that each firm can quickly detect whether the other firm is cheating. In fact, this may not be so easy. In some cases, trade associations have been authorized to collect detailed information concerning each firm's transactions. In this way, an attempt has been made to detect cheating quickly. Of course, the quicker cheating is detected, the less profitable it tends to be.

this round whatever the other player did on the previous round. If Ambler
pursues a "tit-for-tat" strategy, it should abide by the agreement
Tit for tat   on the first round. If Elysian also abides by it, Ambler should
continue to do so, but once Elysian cheats, Ambler should retali-
ate by cheating as well. Robert Axelrod's experimental results, based on a
computer analysis of the results of various strategies, suggest that this is a very
effective approach.[18]

In accord with Axelrod's findings, some cartels seem to have adopted
"tit-for-tat" strategies in the past. For example, the cartel that set the price of
railroad freight in the United States in the 1880s (prior to the Sherman Antitrust Act) retaliated against member firms that cut price to increase their
market shares. When such cheating occurred, the other members of the cartel
would cut their own price as well, thus inflicting economic damage on the price
cutters.[19]

PRICE LEADERSHIP

Another model of oligopolistic behavior is based on the supposition that one of
the firms in the industry is the price leader. This form of behavior seems to be
quite common in oligopolistic industries, where one or a few firms apparently
set the price and the rest follow their lead. Examples of industries that have
been characterized by price leadership, according to various studies, are steel,
nonferrous alloys, agricultural implements, and retail groceries. Two forms of
price leadership are discussed in this section, the dominant-firm model and
the barometric-firm model.

The *dominant-firm* model applies to industries in which there is a single
large dominant firm in the industry and a number of small firms. It is assumed
that the dominant firm sets the price for the industry, but that it lets the small
firms sell all they want at that price. Whatever amount the small firms do not
supply at that price is supplied by the dominant firm. If this model holds, it is
easy to derive the price that the dominant firm will set if it maximizes profits.
Since each small firm takes the price as given, it produces the output at which
price equals marginal cost. Thus a supply curve for all small firms combined
can be drawn by summing horizontally the marginal cost curves of the small
firms. This supply curve is labeled S in Figure 11.5. The demand curve for the
dominant firm can be derived by subtracting the amount supplied by the small
firms at each price from the total amount demanded at that price. Consequently, if D is the demand curve for the industry's product, the demand curve

18. R. Axelrod, *The Evolution of Cooperation* (New York: Basic Books, 1984).

19. R. Porter, "A Study of Cartel Stability," *Bell Journal of Economics,* Autumn 1983.

Fig. THE DOMINANT-FIRM MODEL / *The dominant firm sets a price of* OP_1,
11.5 *and supplies* OQ_1 *units of the product. Total industry output is* OD_1.

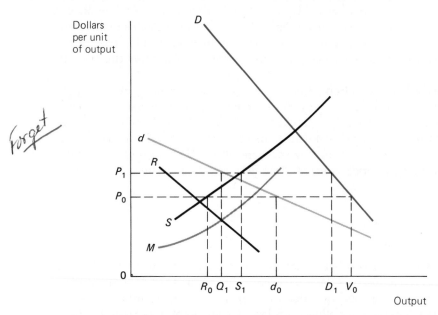

for the output of the dominant firm, d, can be determined by finding the horizontal difference at each price between the D curve and the S curve.

To illustrate the derivation of d, suppose that the dominant firm sets a
price of OP_0. The S curve shows that the small firms will supply OR_0, and the D
curve shows that the total amount demanded will be OV_0. Thus the amount to
be supplied by the dominant firm is $OV_0 - OR_0$, which is the quantity on the d
curve at price OP_0. In other words, Od_0 is set equal to $OV_0 - OR_0$. The process
by which the other points on the d curve are determined is exactly the same;
this procedure is repeated at various price levels.

Given the demand curve for the output of the dominant firm, d, and the
dominant firm's marginal cost curve, M, it is a simple matter to determine the
price and output that will maximize the profits of the dominant firm. The
dominant firm's marginal revenue curve, R, can be derived from the dominant
firm's demand curve, d, in the usual way. The optimal output for the dominant
firm is the output, OQ_1, where its marginal cost equals its marginal revenue.
This output will be achieved if the dominant firm sets a price of OP_1. The
total industry output will be OD_1, and the small firms will supply
$OS_1 (= OD_1 - OQ_1)$.

The *barometric-firm* model applies to another form of price leadership in
which one firm usually is the first to make changes in price that are generally
accepted by other firms in the industry. The barometric firm may not be the
largest, or most powerful firm. Instead it is a reasonably accurate interpreter of

changes in basic cost and demand conditions in the industry as a whole. According to empirical studies, barometric price leadership frequently occurs as a response to a period of violent price fluctuation and cutthroat competition in an industry, during which many firms suffer and greater stability is widely sought. The gasoline market in Ohio is often cited as an example of barometric price leadership. Standard Oil of Ohio has generally initiated price changes which have been accepted, wholly or in part, by other producers. Studies suggest that Standard Oil of Ohio has acted as a barometer of market conditions, lowering the list price when market conditions have been depressed, and raising it successfully only when demand and cost conditions permit.[20]

THE LONG RUN AND BARRIERS TO ENTRY

So far we have been concerned primarily with oligopolistic behavior in the short run. In the long run it may be possible for entry or exit of firms to occur. We are already familiar, of course, with the in-migration and out-migration of firms from our discussions of other market structures in Chapters 8 to 10. However, the importance of entry of new firms—and the exit of old firms—in modifying the structure of an industry should be noted once more. In particular, an oligopolistic industry may not be oligopolistic for long if every Tom, Dick, and Harry can enter.

Whether or not the industry remains oligopolistic in the face of relatively easy entry depends on the size of the market for the product relative to the optimum size of firm. Above-average profits will attract new firms. If the market is small relative to the optimum size of firm in this industry, the number of firms will remain sufficiently small so that the industry will still be an oligopoly. If the market is large relative to the optimum size of the firm, the number of firms will grow sufficiently large so that the industry will no longer be an oligopoly.

Ease of entry also tends to erode collusive agreements. We saw in Figure 11.4 that existing firms are tempted continually to "cheat" on a collusive agreement, since they can attract business from their rivals by lowering prices. The situation is similar for entrants. They, too, are faced by a relatively elastic demand curve as long as existing firms adhere to collusive agreements to maintain price at its existing level. As long as profits exist in the industry, firms will be tempted to enter and take business away from the collusive group by lowering the price a bit. Once entry of this sort occurs, it becomes more and more difficult to keep a cartel together.

Since it may not be possible to maintain an oligopoly for long if firms can enter the industry, it is important that we discuss the various kinds of barriers

---

20. See F. M. Scherer, *Industrial Market Structure and Economic Performance*, 2d ed. (Chicago: Rand McNally, 1980).

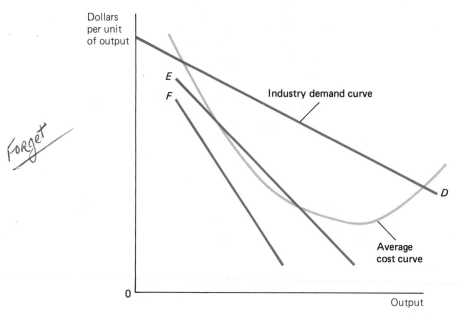

Forget

to entry. The first barrier to entry, already noted, is smallness of the market relative to the optimum size of firm. For example, suppose that the industry demand curve is *D* in Figure 11.6. Thus, if the industry is composed of two identical duopolists producing a homogeneous product, each firm faces a demand curve of *E*, which is half of *D* at each price. On the other hand, if the industry is composed of three identical oligopolists producing a homogeneous product, each firm faces a demand curve of *F*, which is one-third of *D* at each price. If the average cost curve of a firm in this industry is as shown in Figure 11.6, only two firms can exist in this industry; once there are two firms, there is an effective barrier to entry.

Another barrier to entry is the requirement in some industries that a firm build and maintain a large, complicated, and expensive plant. It is difficult to obtain the funds required to build a modern automobile or steel plant, which may cost hundreds of millions of dollars. Also, skilled personnel must be acquired, distribution channels must be established, and various types of productive and repair facilities must be set up. Of course, it is not impossible for newcomers to obtain the necessary capital, even if it is very large, but the scale of the undertaking is likely to discourage some potential entrants.

Still another barrier to entry is the unavailability of natural resources. This factor is often cited in the case of nickel, sulfur, diamonds, and bauxite. A further barrier to entry is the existence of important patents. The holder of these patents, which may relate to the product itself or key processes by which the product is made, may license only a few firms to produce the product. Moreover, the firms in an industry may allow one another to use their patents but refuse to permit any outsider to use them. Finally, the government is sometimes responsible for other important barriers to entry. For example, taxicabs and buses must obtain franchises, and local licensing laws may be used to limit the number of plumbers, barbers, and so on.

In some oligopolistic industries it is sometimes asserted that firms set price so as to bar entry. This is called *limit pricing*. A limit price is a price that discourages or prevents entry. Firms that practice limit pricing give up short-run profits in order to earn larger longer-term profits. The limit price must lie somewhere below the price that would maximize profits if entry were impossible regardless of price. The exact

Limit pricing

Example 11.1

ENTRY AND EXIT IN THE BEER INDUSTRY

In 1980, the top five firms—Anheuser-Busch, Miller, Pabst, Schlitz (now part of Stroh's), and Coors—accounted for about three-quarters of all beer produced in the United States. (a) Is the beer industry an oligopoly? (b) Since World War II, have many new firms built breweries in the United States? (c) About how much does it cost to build a new brewery? (d) In the 1960s, the long-run average cost of producing beer was at a minimum when a firm produced about 2 million barrels per year. In the late 1970s, it was at a minimum when a firm's output was about 18 million barrels per year. Can you guess why this change occurred? (e) Do you think that this change in the long-run average cost curve resulted in the decrease shown below in the number of firms in the brewing industry?

Year	Number of firms	Year	Number of firms
1963	171	1972	108
1967	125	1976	49

SOLUTION

(a) Yes. (b) No. Only about five have done so. (c) In the late 1970s, it cost about $70 million to build a new brewery. Also, an entrant generally must invest heavily in advertising and other selling expenses. (d) This shift in the long-run average cost curve occurred as a consequence of technological change. For example, on the closing line, 900 cans could be moved per minute in 1965, whereas about 1,500 cans per minute could be moved in the late 1970s. (e) Certainly, this shift in the long-run average cost curve was one of the factors responsible for the decrease in the number of firms. Because breweries had to get so much bigger, fewer of them were required.*

* For further discussion, see K. Elzinga, "The Beer Industry," in W. Adams (ed.), *The Structure of American Industry* (New York: Macmillan, 1982); and W. Lynk, "Interpreting Rising Concentration: The Case of Beer," *Journal of Business*, January 1984.

level of the limit price will depend on how difficult it is to enter the industry. Of course, the firms already in the industry must agree, at least within certain bounds, concerning the advisability and proper level of a limit price.

GAME THEORY AND THE DETERRENCE OF ENTRY

To see more clearly how oligopolists try to deter entry, it is useful once again to apply game theory. Consider a single oligopolist, the Martin Company, which faces the threat of entry by the Newton Company. Table 11.4 shows the profits of each firm, depending on whether or not Newton enters the market and on whether or not Martin resists Newton's entry (for example, by cutting price and increasing output).[21]

Table 11.4 PAYOFF MATRIX, BEFORE MARTIN MAKES CREDIBLE ITS THREAT TO RESIST

Possible strategies for Martin Company	*Possible strategies for Newton Company*	
	Enter	*Do not enter*
Resist entry	Martin's profit: $2 million	Martin's profit: $12 million
	Newton's profit: $5 million	Newton's profit: $8 million
Do not resist entry	Martin's profit: $3 million	Martin's profit: $12 million
	Newton's profit: $11 million	Newton's profit: $8 million

In this game, the first move is up to Newton, which must decide whether or not to enter. If it enters, Martin must decide whether or not to resist. Based on the payoff matrix in Table 11.4, Martin will not resist because its profits will be $1 million less (that is, $2 million rather than $3 million) if it resists than if it does not resist. Knowing this, Newton will enter because its profits will be $3 million higher (that is, $11 million rather than $8 million) if it enters than if it does not enter. Of course, Martin may well threaten to resist, but given the nature of the payoff matrix in Table 11.4, this threat is not credible because resistance would lower Martin's profits.

What can Martin do to deter Newton's entry into the market? It can alter the payoff matrix. For example, suppose that it builds excess production capacity and establishes marketing and product development programs that increase its profits if it chooses to resist Newton's entry. After adopting these measures, Martin's profits if it resists are $1 million higher than if it does not resist (that is, $4 million rather than $3 million), since the new payoff matrix is as shown in Table 11.5. Thus, Martin's threat to resist becomes credible, and

---

21. If Newton does not enter the market, there is no difference between Martin's resisting and not resisting, so the profit figures are the same, regardless of which strategy Martin is assumed to adopt.

Table 11.5 PAYOFF MATRIX, AFTER MARTIN MAKES CREDIBLE ITS THREAT TO RESIST

Possible strategies for Martin Company	Possible strategies for Newton Company	
	Enter	Do not enter
Resist entry	Martin's profit: $4 million	Martin's profit: $12 million
	Newton's profit: $5 million	Newton's profit: $8 million
Do not resist entry	Martin's profit: $3 million	Martin's profit: $12 million
	Newton's profit: $11 million	Newton's profit: $8 million

Newton will not enter because its profits will be $3 million lower (that is, $5 million rather than $8 million) if it enters than if it does not enter.

CONTESTABLE MARKETS

Having discussed barriers to entry and the ways in which oligopolists try to deter entry, we turn to the theory of contestable markets, developed in the 1980s. Entry and exit of firms play a particularly important role in this theory.

Contestable market

A contestable market is one in which "entry is absolutely free, and exit is absolutely costless."[22] In other words, firms can enter and leave the market readily. For example, if the government permits, the owner of a commercial jet aircraft can use it to fly passengers on a particular route, then devote it to other uses. The essence of contestable markets is that they are vulnerable to hit-and-run entry. "Even a very transient profit opportunity need not be neglected by a potential entrant, for he can go in, and before prices change, collect his gains and then depart without cost, should the climate grow hostile."[23]

Despite the fact that a contestable market contains only a few firms (or perhaps only one), it will perform much like a competitive market. Economic profit will tend to be zero. If it is positive, a new entrant can enter the market, produce the same output (at the same cost) as a firm already in the market, undercut the existing firm's price slightly, and make a profit. Entrants will do this if economic profit is positive, and the price will be pushed down to the point where economic profit is zero. In other words, if they like, entrants can hit and run.

The firms in a contestable market, like those under competition, will produce at minimum cost. If they produce at more than minimum cost, firms

---

22. W. Baumol, "Contestable Markets: An Uprising in the Theory of Industry Structure," *American Economic Review,* March 1982, p. 3. Also see W. Baumol, S. Panzar, and R. Willig, *Contestable Markets and the Theory of Industry Structures* (San Diego: Harcourt Brace Jovanovich, 1982).

23. Ibid., p. 4. For criticism of this theory, see W. Shepherd, "Competition versus Contestability," *American Economic Review,* 1984.

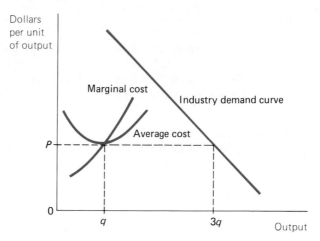

will enter the industry, produce at lower costs than the existing firms, undercut the existing firms' price, and make a profit. Thus, costs will be pushed
down to the minimum level. Also, in an oligopoly, price cannot exceed marginal cost. If existing firms are charging a price in excess of marginal cost, it is
profitable for an entrant to undercut the price of the existing firms. Thus, for
an equilibrium to occur, price cannot exceed marginal cost.

To illustrate the workings of a contestable market, suppose that an industry contains three firms, each with the marginal and average cost curves
shown in Figure 11.7. If each firm produces Oq units of output, and charges a
price of OP, total output will be 3 times Oq, and all three firms will earn zero
economic profit. Although they could attempt to collude and push up the price,
they do not do so because they know that new firms would enter the market
very quickly and undercut their price. Given that entrants could sell the product at a price of OP, each firm maximizes its profit by producing Oq units of
output and selling it at that price.

The theory of contestable markets has provoked considerable controversy. Its critics charge that it is based on extremely unrealistic assumptions
concerning entry and exit. (In reality, of course, entry is not free and exit is not
costless.) However, as stressed in Chapter 1, models based on simplified
assumptions can be very useful. At this point, it is too early to tell how important this relatively new theory will turn out to be, but there can be no question
that it has had a noteworthy impact on many economists' views concerning oligopoly.

NONPRICE COMPETITION

In many oligopolistic industries, firms tend to use advertising and variation in product characteristics, more than price, as competitive weapons. They seem to view price-cutting as a dangerous tactic, since it can start a price war that may have grave consequences. On the other hand, advertising and product variation are viewed as less risky ways of wooing customers away from competitors.

When a firm advertises, it attempts to shift the demand curve for its product to the right. An effective advertising campaign will make it possible for a firm to sell more at the same price. Firms use advertising to differentiate their product from those of their competitors. In this way customers may be induced to stick with a particular brand name, even though the products of all firms in the industry are much the same. For example, various brands of cigarettes are quite similar, although not identical. The cigarette industry has spent over $200 million a year on advertising to impress their brand names, and whatever differences exist among brands, on the consumer.[24]

Sometimes advertising expenditures only have the effect of raising the costs of the entire industry, since one firm's advertising campaign causes other firms to increase their advertising. The total market for the industry's product may not increase in response to the increased advertising, and the effects on the sales of individual firms may be small, since the effects of the advertising may cancel out. However, once every firm has increased its advertising expenditures, no single firm can reduce them to their former size without losing sales. Thus the cost curves—including both production and selling costs—of the firms in the industry are pushed upward.[25]

Frequently a firm varies the characteristics of its product as well as advertises in order to differentiate its product from those of its competitors. Like advertising, one purpose of varying the firm's product is to manipulate the firm's demand curve. Of course, changes in product, like other competitive tactics, often result in retaliatory moves by competitors. Successful changes in product design or product quality tend to be imitated by competitors, although with a lag of varying length. The costs of competition through style and quality of product can be very great. For example, the automobile industry has been

---

24. Other industries that spend very heavily on advertising are department stores, retail food stores, drugs and medicines, and beer. See L. Telser, "Advertising and Cigarettes," *Journal of Business,* 1963; and W. Comanor and T. Wilson, *Advertising and Market Power* (Cambridge, Mass.: Harvard University Press, 1974).

25. To see why an individual firm may spend a large amount on advertising even though its profits might have been higher with a smaller advertising budget, recall the prisoner's dilemma. If each firm believes that its profits will fall if its rival spends more on advertising, it may feel that a large advertising budget is in its own interest, although its profits, as well as those of its rival, would be greater if both it and its rival agreed to spend less on advertising.

engaged for many years in intense competition of this sort; the cost of model changes during the 1950s was approximately $5 billion per year.[26]

EFFECTS OF OLIGOPOLY

This chapter has taken up some of the oligopoly models that economists have constructed. Since there is no agreement that any of these models is an adequate general representation of oligopolistic behavior, it is difficult to estimate the effects of an oligopolistic market structure on price, output, and profits. Nevertheless, a few things can be said.

First, the models we have discussed usually indicate that price will be higher than under perfect competition. The difference between the oligopoly price and the perfectly competitive price will depend, of course, on the number of firms in the industry and the ease of entry. The larger the number of firms and the easier it is to enter the industry, the closer the oligopoly price will be to the perfectly competitive level.

Second, if the demand curve is the same under oligopoly as under perfect competition, it also follows that output will be less under oligopoly than under perfect competition. However, it is not always reasonable to assume that the demand curve is the same under oligopoly as under perfect competition, since the large expenditures for advertising and product variation that are incurred by some oligopolies may tend to shift the demand curve to the right. Consequently in some cases both price and output may tend to be higher under oligopoly than under perfect competition.

Third, we have already noted that oligopolistic industries tend to spend large amounts on advertising and product variation. The use of some resources for these purposes is certainly worthwhile, since advertising provides buyers with information, and product variation allows greater freedom of choice. Whether or not oligopolies spend too much for these purposes is by no means obvious. However, there is a widespread feeling among economists, based largely on empirical studies (and hunch), that in some oligopolistic industries such expenditures have been expanded beyond the levels that are socially optimal.[27]

Fourth, one would expect on the basis of the models presented in this chapter that the profits earned by oligopolists should be higher, on the average, than the profits earned by perfectly competitive firms. About forty years

---

26. F. Fisher, Z. Griliches, and C. Kaysen, "The Cost of Automobile Model Changes since 1949," *Journal of Political Economy*, October 1962. For more recent data, see L. White, *The Automobile Industry Since 1945* (Cambridge, Mass.: Harvard University Press, 1971).

27. Note that we are not talking here about expenditures on relatively fundamental research and development, when we talk about product variation. A great deal of existing product variation is based on relatively superficial differences among products.

ago, a seminal study by Berkeley's Joe Bain found that firms in industries in which the largest few firms had a high proportion of total sales tended to have higher rates of return than firms in industries in which the largest few firms had a small proportion of total sales. However, there has been considerable disagreement over the interpretation of such evidence. According to some economists, these results are due in considerable part to the largest firms' superior efficiency in oligopolistic industries.[28]

---

28. See J. Bain, "Relation of Profit Rate to Industry Concentration: American Manufacturing, 1936–1940," *Quarterly Journal of Economics,* August 1951; H. Demsetz, "Industry Structure, Market Rivalry, and Public Policy," *Journal of Law and Economics,* April 1973; L. Weiss, "The Concentration-Profits Relationship and Antitrust," in H. Goldschmid, H. M. Mann, and J. F. Weston, *Industrial Concentration: The New Learning* (Boston: Little, Brown, 1974); and J. Kwoka, "The Effect of Market Share Distribution on Industry Performance," *Review of Economics and Statistics,* February 1979.

Example 11.2

THE BRAVE NEW WORLD OF ROBOTICS

The industrial robot is one of the most important technological innovations of this century. In 1985, about fifty American firms produced robots, with the following six firms accounting for about 70 percent of total sales:

	Sales (millions of dollars)		*Sales* (millions of dollars)
GMF Robotics	180	ASEA	39
Cincinnati Milacron	59	GCA	35
Westinghouse	45	DeVilbiss	33

(a) Is the robotics industry an oligopoly? (b) In 1980, the top six firms in the robotics industry accounted for over 94 percent of total sales. Between 1980 and 1985, did robot sales become more concentrated in the hands of a few firms? (c) Robotics firms devoted about 17 percent of their sales to research and development in 1983. Is nonprice competition important in this industry? (d) During 1979–82, the robotics industry experienced substantial losses, although its sales increased at a relatively rapid rate. Why did firms stay in this industry in the face of these losses?

SOLUTION

(a) Yes. (b) No. There was a reduction in the share of total sales accounted for by the top six firms (from 94 percent in 1980 to 70 percent in 1985), due in part to the emergence and growth of new entrants. (c) Yes. Firms invest heavily in new technology in order to improve their products and introduce features their rivals cannot match. (d) Because they felt that their losses were only temporary.*

* For further discussion, see E. Mansfield, "Firm Growth, Innovation, and R and D in Robotics: Japan and the United States", Symposium on Research and Development, Industrial Change, and Economic Policy, University of Karlstad, Sweden, 1987.

SUMMARY

1. Oligopoly is characterized by a small number of firms and a great deal of interdependence, actual and perceived, among them. A good example of an oligopoly is the American computer industry, where a small number of firms accounts for the bulk of the industry's capacity.

2. Oligopolistic industries may be marked by independent action or collusion. An early model based on the supposition that firms act independently is the Cournot model. Another is Sweezy's model based on the kinked demand curve. The equilibrium in the Cournot model (often called a Nash equilibrium) has the property that each firm's behavior maximizes its profits, given its expectations concerning its rivals' behavior, and that each firm's expectations in this regard are confirmed by their actual behavior.

3. Conditions in oligopolistic industries tend to promote collusion, since the number of firms is small and firms recognize their interdependence. The advantages to be derived by the firms from collusion seem obvious: increased profits, decreased uncertainty, and a better opportunity to control the entry of new firms. However, collusive arrangements are often hard to maintain, since once a collusive agreement is made, any of the firms can increase its profits by "cheating" on the agreement. Also, such arrangements are illegal in the United States. An interesting example of collusion is the OPEC cartel, which has played so important a role in the oil markets of the 1970s and 1980s.

4. An interesting development of recent decades has been the theory of games, which has enriched oligopoly theory considerably. In this chapter, game theoretic models have been presented to analyze firms' choices of advertising strategies, the incentives for cartel members to cheat, and the ways in which oligopolists try to deter entry. Particular attention has been devoted to a type of game called the prisoner's dilemma.

5. In the 1980s, an interesting development was the theory of contestable markets, which assumed that entry is absolutely free and exit is absolutely costless. According to this theory, oligopolists will behave much like perfectly competitive firms, because of the threat of entry into their market.

6. Another model of oligopolistic behavior is based on the supposition that one of the firms in the industry is a price leader, either because it is a dominant firm or a barometric firm. Still other models assume that oligopolists use limit pricing.

7. The effects of oligopoly are difficult to predict, but most models suggest that price and profits will tend to be higher than under perfect competition. Also, oligopolists engage in nonprice competition, perhaps excessively in some cases from the point of view of social welfare.

APPENDIX / COST-PLUS PRICING

Empirical studies have often suggested that cost-plus pricing is used by many oligopolists. There are two basic steps in this approach to pricing. First, the firm estimates the cost per unit of output of the product. Since this cost will generally vary with output, the firm must base this computation on some assumed output level. Usually, firms seem to use for this purpose some percentage, generally between two-thirds and three-quarters, of capacity. Second, the firm adds a *markup* (generally put in the form of a percentage) to the estimated average cost. This markup is meant to include certain costs that cannot be allocated to any specific product and to provide a return on the firm's investment. The size of the markup depends on the rate of profit that the firm believes it can earn. Some firms have set up a *target return* figure that they hope to earn, which determines the markup. For example, General Electric at times has established a target rate of return of 20 percent.

There is considerable controversy over the extent to which cost-plus pricing is compatible with profit maximization. At first glance, it seems extremely unlikely that this form of pricing can result in the maximization of profits. Indeed, this pricing technique seems naïve, since it takes no account, explicitly at least, of the extent or elasticity of demand or of the size of marginal, rather than average, costs. Nevertheless, some economists believe that cost-plus pricing may result in firms, under oligopolistic circumstances, coming close to maximum profits. They argue that cost-plus pricing is used to "stabilize" competition and lessen uncertainty. Moreover, if marginal cost is really what is being marked up, and if the elasticity of demand remains relatively constant, cost-plus pricing could result in something approaching profit maximization.

To see this, recall from Equation 5.4 that

$$MR = P\left[1 - \frac{1}{\eta}\right]$$

where MR is the firm's marginal revenue, P is its price, and η is the price elasticity of demand of its product. Solving this equation for P, and recognizing that marginal revenue will be equal to marginal cost if the firm is maximizing profit, we get

$$P = MC\left[\frac{1}{1 - \frac{1}{\eta}}\right] = MC\left[1 + \frac{\frac{1}{\eta}}{1 - \frac{1}{\eta}}\right] \qquad [11.1]$$

Thus, if marginal cost (rather than average cost) is what is being marked up, and if the markup (in absolute terms) equals $MC\left[(1/\eta) \div (1-1/\eta)\right]$, the firm can obtain the profit-maximizing price in this way.

Unquestionably, many firms do compute prices on the basis of some sort of cost-plus pricing procedure. However, a model of this sort is incomplete unless (as in Equation 11.1) it specifies more precisely the determinants of the size of the markup. Although firms may construct these markups to yield a certain target rate of return, it is clear that these markups frequently do not prevail, since the firm's actual rates of return frequently vary considerably from the target rates of return. The simple cost-plus pricing model is silent on this score.

QUESTIONS/PROBLEMS

1) Suppose that a computer manufacturer's perceived demand curve is DVD', its marginal revenue curve is RAR', and its marginal cost curve is MM' in panel A below:*

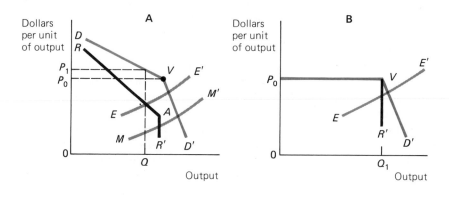

*In both panels of the graph, only parts of the marginal revenue curve are shown, but these parts are sufficient for present purposes.

Suppose further that, because of a jump in material prices, the firm's costs increase sharply, with the result that the marginal cost curve rises from MM' to EE'. (a) An economist says that, because the firm's demand curve is kinked, this will not increase its price. Is he correct? (b) Fearful that the cost increase will result in a price hike, the government specifies that the firm's price must not exceed OP_0. What effect does this have on the firm's demand curve? Marginal revenue curve? Output?

2) Suppose that two firms are producers of spring water, which can be obtained at zero cost. The marginal revenue curve for their combined output is

$$MR = 10 - 2Q$$

where MR is marginal revenue and Q is the number of gallons per hour of spring water sold by both together. If the two producers collude to maximize their total profits, how much will be their combined output? Why?

3) Suppose that a cartel is formed by three firms. Their total cost functions are as follows:

	Total Cost		
Units of output	Firm 1	Firm 2	Firm 3
0	20	25	15
1	25	35	22
2	35	50	32
3	50	80	47
4	80	120	77
5	120	160	117

If the cartel decides to produce 11 units of output, how should the output be distributed among the three firms, if they want to minimize cost?

4) Describe how advertising expenses can be an important barrier to entry in some industries. What are some industries where this is the case? Describe how large research and development expenses can be an important barrier to entry. What are some industries where this is the case?

5) A firm estimates its average total cost to be $10 per unit of output when it produces 10,000 units, which it regards as 80 percent of capacity. Its goal is to earn 20 percent on its total investment, which is $250,000. If it were sure that it could sell 10,000 units, what price should it set to achieve this goal? Can it be sure of selling 10,000 units if it sets this price?

6) Suppose the pay-off matrix is as given below. What strategy will firm I choose? What strategy will firm II choose?

Possible strategies for firm I	Possible strategies for firm II		
	1	2	3
	(Profits for firm I, or losses for firm II, in millions of dollars)		
A	10	9	11
B	8	7	10

7) In the previous question, the game is a zero-sum game; that is, the amount that one player wins is exactly equal to the amount that the other player loses. Is this realistic in the case of duopoly? Why or why not?

8) According to the Senate Subcommittee on Antitrust and Monopoly, there has been a long history of international cartels that have controlled the price and output of quinine. What do you think the effects of the cartels have been? Do you think that such cartels should be broken up? If so, how can individual governments go about doing this?

9) Suppose that you are on the board of directors of a firm which is the dominant firm in the industry. That is, it lets all of the other firms, which are much smaller, sell all they want at the existing price. In other words, the smaller firms act as

perfect competitors. Your firm, on the other hand, sets the price, which the other firms accept. The demand curve for your industry's product is $P = 300 - Q$, where P is the product's price (in dollars per unit) and Q is the total quantity demanded. The total amount supplied by the other firms is equal to Q_r, where $Q_r = 49\,P$. If your firm's marginal cost curve is $2.96\,Q_b$, where Q_b is the output of your firm, at what output level should you operate to maximize profit? What price should you charge? How much will the industry as a whole produce at this price? (Q, Q_b, and Q_r are expressed in millions of units.)

10) In the United States agreements to fix prices and restrict output are illegal. Section 1 of the Sherman Antitrust Act says, "Every contract, combination . . . , or conspiracy in restraint of trade or commerce among the several states, or with foreign nations, is hereby declared to be illegal." (a) Does this mean that oligopoly is illegal? (b) Is any formal agreement among firms necessary to constitute an unlawful conspiracy? (c) For decades, the Big Three of the cigarette industry—American Tobacco, Liggett and Myers, and Reynolds—followed a pattern of setting the same price. Even at the pit of the Great Depression, the other two firms matched a price increase by Reynolds. Also, they behaved in such a way as to make it likely that each would pay much the same price for tobacco. Can such parallel action be used in court as convincing circumstantial evidence of illegal collusion? (d) Is mere recognition of mutual interdependence and parallel behavior by a group of firms sufficient to make conspiracy charges against them stick?

11) There has been considerable criticism of the historically high price of milk in New York City. In 1986, Farmland Dairies, a New Jersey milk producer, began selling milk on Staten Island, one of New York City's five boroughs. Its low price drove down the retail price of milk by 40 cents per gallon. New York state law dictated that each milk producer like Farmland must get a license to sell milk, borough by borough. Existing dairies in New York City argued that the entry of Farmland into other parts of the city would not benefit consumers because it costs a great deal to distribute milk there. Further, they said that New York jobs should not go to New Jersey. In January 1987, a Federal judge ruled in favor of Farmland, saying that a state decision barring its expansion of sales in New York was unconstitutional. Evaluate in detail the above arguments of the existing New York dairies.

THE DEREGULATION OF AIR TRANSPORTATION

One of the most startling economic developments of the late 1970s was the deregulation of air transportation. This development illustrates very effectively the ways in which microeconomic analysis can be used in formulating—and reforming—public policy. Much of the initial impetus toward deregulation came from economic theorists who used simple microeconomic models to point out the disadvantages and problems in existing regulatory policies. Some of the principal public officials who presided over and guided the process of deregulation were economists who contributed to the construction of these models.

To begin with, we must describe the nature of the industry prior to deregulation. During the mid-1970s, ten major trunk airlines (such as Eastern, TWA, American, and United) provided more than 90 percent of scheduled airline service in the United States. Because there were no huge economies of scale, smaller airlines like Northwest and Continental operated profitably next to giants like TWA. Nonetheless, profits tended to be low; between 1960 and 1975 they topped 10 percent in only five of the fifteen years.

The Civil Aeronautics Board was established in 1938 to promote the growth of aviation and to administer the subsidy that the federal government paid the industry for its air mail service. In addition, the CAB regulated the prices charged by the interstate scheduled airlines as well as entry into the industry. However, unlike some of the cases described in Chapter 9, this was not because the industry is a natural monopoly; on the contrary, it can support a number of firms of efficient size. Beginning in the 1950s, academic economists published a variety of criticisms of CAB regulation. Much of the criticism centered on the CAB's entry policies. Between 1938 and 1977, the CAB permitted no entry into markets that already had two or more carriers. Even in markets with no nonstop service or where there was only one carrier, there was little new entry. As we have seen in Chapters 8 to 11, entrants are important in promoting competition, reducing prices, and stimulating efficiency; thus, this policy had obvious disadvantages.

Academic economists also fired some salvoes at the CAB's pricing policies, which prevented price competition but encouraged scheduling competition. In other words, the airlines, not being able to compete through lower prices, tried to lure travelers away from their rivals through more flights, more planes, and more frills like in-flight gourmet meals. (Like the oligopolists described on pp. 331–32, they engaged in nonprice competition.) According to

Fig.
1 EFFECTS OF CAB REGULATION ON PRICE AND COSTS / *The CAB established*
a price of OP₁. *The airline's long-run average cost curve was pushed*
upward (because of frills and more flights), as shown in panel A.

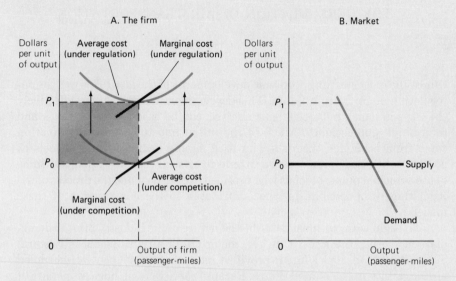

some critics, this resulted in an upward spiral of fare increases because the increased profits from each fare raise were soon dissipated through more scheduling and service competition. Many experts argued that, if price competition
were allowed, fares would tend to drop as travelers opted for reduced prices
rather than more service.

To understand the situation, it is useful to consult Figure 1, which shows
(in the right-hand panel) the demand and supply curves for airline transportation. (For simplicity, the supply curve is assumed to be horizontal.) If competition prevailed, the equilibrium price would be OP_0. However, the CAB
established a price of OP_1. If each firm's costs were the same under regulation
as under competition, it would make a profit under the price set by the CAB. In
particular, if its long-run average cost curve (under competition) was as shown
in the left-hand panel of Figure 1, it would make a profit equal to the shaded
area shown there.

However, this was not an equilibrium position because each airline could
make still a larger profit if it could lure travelers away from its rivals. (Why?
Because the price established by the CAB exceeded the airline's marginal cost,
as shown in the left-hand panel of Figure 1.) Thus, since each airline could not
attract customers by lowering its price, it scheduled more frequent flights and
gave travelers more frills, the result being that the airline's long-run average
cost curve was pushed upward (because the larger number of flights and the
frills obviously cost money). Eventually an equilibrium was reached when the
airline's long-run average cost curve was pushed to the upper position shown

in the left-hand panel in Figure 1. At this position, each airline was no longer making economic profits, and there was no longer an incentive for each airline to add further flights or frills because marginal cost equaled price.

Clearly, airline fares were considerably higher than they would have been under competition. According to the General Accounting Office (a federal government agency), airline fares would have been 20 to 50 percent lower in the absence of CAB regulation. This conclusion was born out by a comparison of the fare between Los Angeles and San Francisco and that between Washington and Boston. While the distance was the same, the fare was almost twice as high on the Washington-Boston route (which was regulated by the CAB) than on the Los Angeles–San Francisco route (which was unregulated because it was intrastate). Further, influential studies by economists like George Douglas of the University of North Carolina and James Miller, subsequently head of the Office of Management and Budget, suggested that many consumers would gladly trade off the more frequent flights and frills for substantially lower air fares.

In 1975, hearings were held by a subcommittee of the U.S. Senate Judiciary Committee, the purpose being to present and reshape the economic evidence and arguments in ways that the executive branch and Congress could understand, and to make the case for flexible pricing and easier entry. Important too was the appointment of Alfred Kahn, a Cornell economist, as chairman of the CAB. During the late 1970s, the CAB carried out extensive policy reforms. Airlines were allowed to institute discount fares. For example, American Airlines began to offer the Super-Saver fare (which was 30 percent below economy fare) in the New York–San Francisco and New York–Los Angeles markets. Also, entry restrictions were relaxed.

During 1977 and 1978, the first years in which the deep discount fares were allowed, average airfares increased by considerably less than the Consumer Price Index. Indeed, average airfares actually decreased from 1977 to 1978, even though all consumer prices went up by 8 percent. Thus regulatory reform was resulting in lower airfares, as the academic economists had predicted. At the same time, the airlines were benefiting too. Because the price elasticity of demand for air travel is about 1.3 (according to the CAB's Bureau of Economics),[1] the reduced prices meant a substantial increase in passengers. The general economic upturn also boosted the number of air passengers and the amount of air freight. The result, as shown in Table 1, was that the airlines' profits were much higher in 1978 than in 1977.

Faced with fares going down and profits going up, the Congress was enthusiastic about the steps toward deregulation. In 1978, it passed legislation that phased out various powers of the CAB. The power to regulate routes ter-

---

1. See G. Douglas and J. Miller, *Economic Regulation of Domestic Air Transport* (Washington, D.C.: Brookings, 1974), p. 177.

Table OPERATING PROFIT OF U.S. TRUNK AIRLINES
1

Month	1978	Dollar increase over 1977
		(thousands of dollars)
March	137,760	87,951
April	93,096	39,641
May	112,189	67,168
June	172,121	59,367
July	217,324	48,735
August	263,653	72,691
September	136,475	103,041

SOURCE: E. Bailey, "Deregulation and Regulatory Reform of U.S. Air-Transportation Policy," in B. Mitchell and P. Kleindorfer, *Regulated Industries and Public Enterprise* (Lexington, Mass.: Lexington, 1980).

minated at the end of 1981, and the power to regulate rates terminated at the end of 1982. Moreover, the airlines were given much more freedom with regard to pricing and entry even before these powers of the CAB were completely phased out.

In the 1980s, deregulation became more controversial, for at least three reasons. First, the airlines experienced losses. After large operating profits in 1978 and more modest ones in 1979, the trunk carriers incurred substantial operating losses in 1980 to 1983, due to higher fuel prices, the recession, and price wars, particularly on the long hauls. By early 1986, some airlines like Eastern continued to lose money. Second, some people complained that deregulation resulted in poorer service to medium and small towns. Third, the airline industry became much more concentrated, as a number of firms merged. Texas Air took over Eastern (among others) in 1986; and Northwest acquired Republic. Many observers are worried that the industry is becoming dominated by a few giants.

Nonetheless, there is no indication that the clock will be turned back. On the contrary, advocates of deregulation point out that it has increased the industry's efficiency by raising the number of passengers per plane, encouraging the carriers to get more productivity out of their employees, and improving the match between types of equipment and types of market. Further, it has offered the consumer a much greater variety of combinations of price and service quality. As predicted by microeconomic theory, deregulation has resulted in many economic advantages, although not all of its effects have been beneficial.[2]

2. See A. Kahn, "The Airline Industry: Is It Time to Reregulate?," National Economic Research Associates, 1982; E. Bailey, "Deregulation and Regulatory Reform of U.S. Air-Transporta-

ANALYTICAL QUESTIONS

1) During every year from 1968 to 1977, the trunk airlines were less profitable than the average manufacturing firm. Based on this fact, a government official argued that, if permitted, firms would leave the industry, rather than enter it. Is this correct? Why or why not?

2) Between 1979 and 1981, eleven airlines, such as People Express and Southwest Airlines, began providing interstate air service. They tended to offer no-frills low-price transportation. Adding these firms to the existing trunk airlines, there were over twenty airlines. Doesn't this mean that the market for air transportation was close to perfect competition? Why or why not?

3) During 1981, the average cost of carrying a passenger on a 200-mile flight was estimated to be $24 on Southwest Airlines, compared with $58 on United Airlines. What sorts of factors could be responsible for this considerable difference?

4) Bailey, Graham, and Kaplan,[3] having compared wages paid by the major airlines with wages for similar jobs in other industries, concluded that "wages in the airline industry appear to be substantially higher, even for jobs where no industry-specific skills are required." Why would regulation (of the sort practiced by the CAB) be expected to contribute to this result?

5) A lawyer argues that air transportation between New York and Los Angeles is a natural monopoly. Do you agree? What sorts of evidence would you use to support your position?

6) Some economists argue that, despite the few firms competing on most airline routes, the airlines will, for the most part, be unable to earn more than zero economic profit. Doesn't this conflict with the theory of oligopoly? If not, why not?

tion Policy," in B. Mitchell and P. Kleindorfer, eds., *Regulated Industries and Public Enterprise* (Lexington, Mass.: Heath, 1980); S. Breyer, *Regulation and Its Reform* (Cambridge, Mass.: Harvard University Press, 1982); and Douglas and Miller, *Economic Regulation.*

3. E. Bailey, D. Graham, and D. Kaplan, *Deregulating the Airlines* (Cambridge, Mass.: MIT Press, 1985).

Markets for Inputs

Price and Employment of Inputs under Perfect Competition

INCOMES: DISTRIBUTION AND INEQUALITY

No one needs to be convinced that income is an interesting topic. Both a struggling member of the working class and a dowager whose labor is confined to endorsing dividend checks recognize the significance of income. Moreover, no one has to be intimately acquainted with government statistics to know that there are enormous differences in the amounts of money that people make. For example, a stroll through midtown Manhattan will provide plenty of evidence of abject poverty and great affluence existing almost side by side.

Why do these differences in income exist? Why is it that one person receives so much more income than another? As we pointed out in Chapter 1, a person's income depends partly on the quantity of resources owned. Some people own lots of land; others own none. Some people have unusual skills and talents; others do not. Some people own equipment and factories; others own little beyond their clothes (and even their clothes may not be completely paid for).

But the quantity of resources a person owns is by no means the only determinant of income. The other important determinant is the price received for the services of each type of resource. For example, if a man is a landowner with 100 acres of land, he will receive $10,000 per year if the price he obtains from the farmers who work his land is $100 per acre (annually); however, if the price goes down to $50 per acre, he will receive only $5,000 per year. Similarly, a laborer's income will obviously depend on the price received for the services performed.

Thus, to understand why differences in income exist, we must understand why the prices of the services of each type of resource are what they are. We must ask questions like: Why is the wage rate for physicians frequently in the neighborhood of $100 an hour while the wage rate for secretaries is often about $7 an hour? Why is the wage rate for mathematicians so much higher than it was several decades ago? Why is it that land of one kind yields a higher financial return than land of another kind?

In other words, we must try to understand the determinants of input prices. In a free-enterprise economy, input prices are important determinants of the incomes of consumers. In the typical household, the breadwinner sells his or her services to a firm; the wage that the worker receives is an input price from the viewpoint of the firm. Wages are a cost to the firm but to the worker they are an important determinant of income, which (as we saw in Chapter 3) helps to determine the worker's choice of consumers' goods. The distribution of income among individuals in the economy is determined to a considerable extent by the configuration of input prices.

PRICE AND EMPLOYMENT OF INPUTS

The previous four chapters were concerned with the analysis of the pricing and output of consumers' goods. We turn now to the determinants of the price and employment of inputs, which will be the topic of the present chapter as well as Chapter 13. This chapter assumes that there is perfect competition in both commodity and input markets; the next chapter relaxes these assumptions.

At the outset, two points should be noted. First, a good deal of the theory presented in the previous four chapters is applicable to inputs as well as commodities; for example, the price of inputs as well as commodities is determined by the interaction of supply and demand. However, the demand for inputs differs in important respects from the demand for commodities, and the supply of inputs differs in important respects from the supply of commodities. These differences stem largely from the fact that inputs are demanded by firms, not consumers; and that some important inputs, like labor, are supplied by consumers, not firms.

Second, in the nineteenth century it was customary for economists to classify inputs into three categories: land, labor, and capital. The theory of input pricing was therefore a theory of the distribution of income among land-owners, wage earners, and capitalists, three important economic and social classes. (The incomes of these classes were rent, wages, and profits, respectively.) A disadvantage of this simple classification of inputs is that each category contains such an enormous amount of variation. For example, labor includes the services of a Nobel Prize–winning biochemist and the services of a secretary whose typing is strictly hunt-and-peck. In this chapter we shall seldom use this tripartite classification;[1] instead we shall present our results in general terms so that the user of the model can classify inputs to fit any particular problem.

PROFIT MAXIMIZATION AND INPUT EMPLOYMENT

Fortunately, we do not have to start from scratch in constructing a model of input pricing and utilization under perfect competition. We learned a great deal that is relevant and useful in Chapters 7 and 8 when we analyzed the firm's decisions concerning input combinations and output level. A moment's reflection should convince you that, when we determined how much the firm would produce and the input combination it would use to produce this output, we in effect determined how much of each input the firm would demand under various sets of circumstances. This, of course, is an important beginning.

To make sure that the implications of our findings in Chapter 7 are clear, we shall review a few of these findings. In particular, recall the way in which a firm combines inputs in order to minimize costs. We showed that the firm will pick a combination of inputs where the ratio of each input's marginal product to its price is equal. That is, it will set

$$\frac{MP_x}{P_x} = \frac{MP_y}{P_y} = \quad \cdot \quad \cdot \quad \cdot = \frac{MP_z}{P_z} \qquad [12.1]$$

where MP_x is the marginal product of input x, P_x is the price of input x, MP_y is the marginal product of input y, P_y is the price of input y, and so on. If Equation 12.1 does not hold, the firm can always reduce costs by changing the utilization of certain inputs. For example, if the marginal product of a unit of input x is 2 units of output, the price of a unit of input x is \$1, the marginal product of a unit of input y is 6 units of output, and the price of a unit of input y is \$2, the firm can reduce its costs by using 1 unit less of input x—which reduces output by 2 units and cost by \$1—and by using $\frac{1}{3}$ unit more of input y—which increases output by 2 units and cost by \$0.67. This substitution of input y for input x has no effect on output but reduces the cost by \$0.33.

---

1. Toward the end of the nineteenth century, a fourth "factor of production"—or type of input —was recognized: entrepreneurship. Then profits were viewed as the return to the entrepreneur, and interest was viewed as the return to the owner of capital.

Going a step further, it can be shown that, if a firm minimizes cost, each of the ratios in Equation 12.1 equals the reciprocal of the firm's marginal cost. In other words,

$$\frac{P_x}{MP_x} = \frac{P_y}{MP_y} = \cdot \quad \cdot \quad \cdot = \frac{P_z}{MP_z} = MC \qquad [12.2]$$

where MC is its marginal cost. To prove this, consider input x. What is the cost of producing an extra unit of output if this extra unit of output is achieved by increasing the utilization of input x, while holding constant the utilization of other inputs? Since an extra unit of input x results in MP_x extra units of output, $(1/MP_x)$ units of input x will result in 1 unit of extra output. Since $(1/MP_x)$ units of input x will cost $(1/MP_x)P_x$, $P_x \div MP_x$ equals marginal cost. This same type of reasoning can be used for any input, not just input x, with the consequence that Equation 12.2 holds.

As an illustration, suppose that there are only two inputs, input x and input y. Suppose that the marginal product of a unit of input x is 2 units of output, the price of a unit of input x is \$1, the marginal product of a unit of input y is 4 units of output, and the price of a unit of input y is \$2. The extra cost of producing an extra unit of output, if the extra production occurs by increasing the use of input x, is \$0.50, since an extra $\frac{1}{2}$ unit of input x—at \$1 a unit—will result in an extra unit of output. Similarly, the extra cost of producing an extra unit of output, if the extra production comes about by increasing the use of input y, is \$0.50, since an extra $\frac{1}{4}$ unit of input y—at \$2 a unit—will result in an extra unit of output. Thus the ratio of the price of each input to its marginal product equals marginal cost, which is \$0.50.

Going another step, the firm, if it maximizes profit, must be operating at a point at which marginal cost equals marginal revenue. Thus it follows that

$$\frac{P_x}{MP_x} = \frac{P_y}{MP_y} = \cdot \quad \cdot \quad \cdot = \frac{P_z}{MP_z} = MR \qquad [12.3]$$

where MR is the firm's marginal revenue. Rearranging terms,

$$MP_x \cdot MR = P_x \qquad [12.4a]$$
$$MP_y \cdot MR = P_y \qquad [12.4b]$$
$$\cdot$$
$$\cdot$$
$$\cdot$$
$$MP_z \cdot MR = P_z. \qquad [12.4c]$$

Thus we conclude that the profit-maximizing firm employs each input in an amount such that the input's marginal product multiplied by the firm's marginal revenue equals the input's price. This result, as we shall see in the following section, provides the basis for the firm's demand curve for an input.

THE FIRM'S DEMAND CURVE: THE CASE OF ONE VARIABLE INPUT

Our first step in analyzing the demand for an input is to consider the demand curve of an individual firm for an input, assuming that this input is the only variable input in the firm's production process. In other words, the quantities of all other inputs are fixed. This assumption is relaxed in the next section. The demand curve of a firm for this input—call it input x—shows the quantity of input x that the firm will demand at each possible price of input x. Assuming that the firm maximizes its profits, it will demand that amount of input x at which the value of the extra output produced by an extra unit of input x is equal to the price of input x. This is the meaning of Equation 12.4a.

Value of the marginal product

To make this more concrete, suppose that we know the firm's production function, from which we deduce that the marginal product of input x (at each level of utilization of input x) is as shown in Table 12.1. Suppose that the price of the product is \$3. Since the product market is perfectly competitive, the marginal revenue is also \$3. The value to the firm of the extra output resulting from its increasing its utilization of input x by 1 unit is shown in the last column of Table 12.1. This is called the *value of the marginal product* of input x, and equals $MP_x \cdot P$, where P is the price of the product. Since $P = MR$ in perfect competition, the value of the marginal product is the left-hand side of Equation 12.4a.

How many units of input x should the firm use if input x costs \$10 a unit? A 1-unit increase in the utilization of input x adds to the firm's revenues the amount shown in the last column of Table 12.1, and it adds \$10 to the firm's costs. (Since the input markets are perfectly competitive, the firm cannot influence the price of any input.) Thus the firm should increase its utilization of

Table 12.1 VALUE OF MARGINAL PRODUCT OF INPUT x

Quantity of x	Marginal product*	Value of marginal product* (dollars)
3	8	24
4	7	21
5	6	18
6	5	15
7	4	12
8	3	9
9	2	6

* The figures pertain to the interval between the indicated quantity of input x and one unit less than the indicated quantity of input x.

input x as long as the increase in revenues exceeds the increase in costs; in other words, as long as the figure in the last column of Table 12.1 exceeds $10. For example, if the firm is using 5 units of input x, the use of an extra unit will increase revenues by $15 and increase costs by $10; consequently, the extra unit should be used. What about adding still another unit? If the firm is using 6 units of input x, the use of an extra unit will increase revenue by $12 and increase costs by $10; thus it too should be added. Increases in the utilization of input x are profitable up to 7 units; beyond this point, an extra unit of input x increases costs more than revenues. Thus the firm should use 7 units of input x.

The optimal number of units of input x is the number at which the value of the marginal product of input x equals the price of input x. This, of course, is just another way of stating the result in Equation 12.4a, since under these circumstances the value of the marginal product of input x is equal to the left-hand side of the equation and the price of input x is the right-hand side of the equation.[2]

If the firm demands the optimal amount of input x at each price of input x, its demand schedule for input x must be the value-of-marginal-product schedule in the last column of Table 12.1. For example, if the price of input x is between $6 and $9, the firm will demand 8 units of input x; if the price of input x is between $9 and $12, the firm will demand 7 units of input x. Thus the firm's demand curve for input x is the value-of-marginal-product curve, which shows the value of input x's marginal product at each quantity of input x used. This curve will slope downward and to the right, because it is proportional to the curve showing the input's marginal productivity.

THE FIRM'S DEMAND CURVE: THE CASE OF SEVERAL VARIABLE INPUTS

Suppose now that the firm uses a number of inputs that can be varied in quantity and input x is only one of them. Under these circumstances, the firm's demand curve for input x is no longer the value-of-marginal-product curve. This is because a change in the price of input x will result in a change in the quantities of the other variable inputs used, and these changes in the quantities of the other variable inputs used will affect the quantity of input x used.

As an example, suppose that the price of input x is initially $10 and the

---

2. This assumes that the quantity of the input can be varied continuously, which is often the case. However, it is not the case in Table 12.1. Since only integer values can be used, according to Table 12.1, this rule must be changed somewhat here. In this case, the optimal number of units of input x is the largest integer at which the value of the marginal product of input x is greater than or equal to the price of input x.

Fig.
12.1 DEMAND CURVE OF THE FIRM FOR INPUT x / *Points* A *and* B *are on the firm's demand curve for input* x. (V$_1$ *and* V$_2$ *are value-of-marginal-product curves.*)

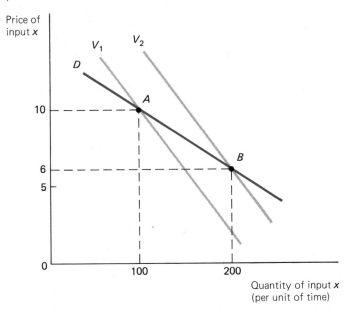

quantity of input x used is 100 units. Holding constant the use of other inputs, suppose that the value-of-marginal-product curve is V_1 in Figure 12.1. If none of the other inputs were variable, this would be the demand curve for input x. In fact, however, a number of other inputs are variable. Suppose that the price of input x falls to \$6. What will happen to the quantity of input x demanded by the firm? Since the value of its marginal product exceeds its new price, the firm will tend to expand its use. But the increase in its use will shift the value-of-marginal-product curves of other inputs. For example, if another variable input is complementary to input x, its value-of-marginal-product curve will shift to the right. These shifts in the value-of-marginal-product curves of other variable inputs will result in changes in the amounts used of them. And the changes in the amounts used of other inputs will in turn shift the value-of-marginal-product curve of input x.

When all of these effects have occurred, the firm will be on another value-of-marginal-product curve for input x, say V_2 in Figure 12.1. And the amount demanded of input x will be such that the value of its marginal product will be equal to its new price. Thus the firm will demand 200 units of input x. Points A and B are both on the firm's demand curve for input x. Other points can be determined in a similar fashion; the complete demand curve is D. It can be shown that all demand curves of this type slope down and to the right, as would be expected.

THE MARKET DEMAND CURVE

When we derived a market demand curve for a commodity in Chapter 5, we summed horizontally over the demand curves of individual consumers of the commodity. At first glance it may seem that we can derive the market demand curve for an input by simply summing horizontally over the demand curves of individual firms for the input. Although this would provide a first approximation, it would not yield the correct result because it neglects the effect of changes in the input price on the product price.

Each firm's demand curve for the input is based on the supposition that the firm's decisions cannot affect the price of its output. For example, in Table 12.1, the firm assumes that the price of its product will be $3, regardless of how it alters its utilization of input x in response to changes in the price of input x. This is a perfectly reasonable assumption for the firm to make, because it is only a very small portion of the industry. But this is not the situation underlying the market demand curve. The market demand curve shows the total amount of the input demanded at various possible prices of the input. Thus it shows the effect of changes in input price on the utilization of the input *when all firms in the industry respond at the same time.*

Suppose that the price of input x decreases substantially. This will result in increased utilization of input x by all firms in the industry and in increased output by all members of the industry. Although the increased output by any single firm cannot affect the price of the industry's product, the combined expansion of output by all firms results in a decrease in the price of the product. This decrease in the price of the product shifts each firm's value-of-marginal-product curve, and consequently it shifts each firm's demand curve for input x.

To derive the market demand curve for input x, suppose that its initial price is $8 and that each firm in the market is in equilibrium, with its demand curve for input x being d in Figure 12.2. Each firm uses Oq units of input x. Multiplying Oq by the number of firms in the market we get OQ, the total amount taken off the market at a price of $8. Thus A is a point on the market demand curve.

Suppose that the price of input x falls to $6. Each firm will increase its use of input x and increase output, with the consequence that the price of the product will fall and the individual firm demand curves for input x will shift toward e. When all adjustments have been made, each firm will be using Or units of input x. This is less than the Os units that each would have used if it had remained on the demand curve, d. Multiplying Or by the number of firms in the market, we get OR, the total amount taken off the market at a price of $6. Thus B is another point on the market demand curve. Other points on the market demand curve can be obtained in similar fashion; the complete market demand curve for input x is D.

Fig. Derivation of Market Demand Curve for Input x / *If the price of input*
12.2 x *is $8, each firm uses* Oq *units, and* OQ *units is the total amount taken off the market. The market demand curve for input* x *is* D.

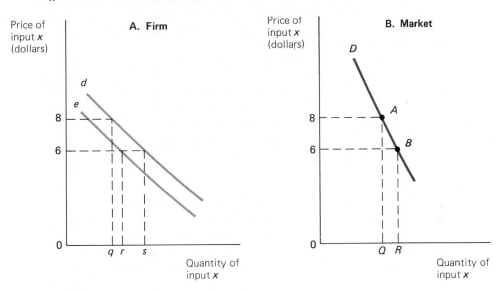

DETERMINANTS OF THE PRICE ELASTICITY OF DEMAND FOR AN INPUT

In Chapter 5 we pointed out that, in the case of commodities, the price elasticity of market demand varies enormously, the quantity demanded of some commodities being very sensitive to price changes, and the quantity demanded of other commodities being quite insensitive to price changes. This is true of inputs as well. The quantity demanded of some inputs is very sensitive to price changes, whereas the quantity demanded of other inputs is not at all sensitive to price changes. Why is this the case? What determines whether the price elasticity of demand for a particular input will be high or low? Several rules are important.

1. The more easily other inputs can be substituted for a certain input, say input *x*, the more price elastic is the demand for input *x*. This certainly makes sense. If the technologies of the firms using input *x* allow these firms to substitute other inputs readily for input *x*, a small increase in the price of input *x* may result in a substantial decrease in its use. But if these firms cannot substitute other inputs readily for input *x*, a large increase in the price of input *x* may result in only a small decrease in its use.

2. The larger the price elasticity of demand for the product that input *x*

helps to produce, the larger the price elasticity of demand for input x. This, too, seems clear enough. The demand for an input is prompted by the demand for the product it produces; in other words, the demand for an input is a *derived demand*. The greater the price elasticity of demand of the product, the more sensitive is the output of the commodity to changes in its price that occur in response to changes in the price of input x.

3. The greater the price elasticity of supply of other inputs, the greater is the price elasticity of demand for input x. The supply curve for an input is the relationship between the amount of the input that is supplied and the input's price. The price elasticity of supply of an input is the percentage increase in the quantity supplied of the input resulting from a 1 percent increase in the price of the input. Thus, if small increases in price bring forth large increases in the quantity of other inputs supplied, this will mean that the demand for input x will be more price elastic than if large increases in price are required to bring forth small increases in the quantity supplied of other inputs.

4. The price elasticity of demand for an input is likely to be greater in the long run than in the short run. The reasoning here is like that underlying the similar proposition in Chapter 5 concerning the demand for commodities. Basically, the point is that it takes time to adjust fully to a price change. For example, if the price of skilled labor increases, it may not be possible for many plants to reduce very greatly the quantity of skilled labor demanded in the short run, since their plants are built to use fairly rigidly defined amounts of this input. But in the long run, firms can build new plants to reduce their utilization of skilled labor.[3]

THE MARKET SUPPLY CURVE

Under perfect competition, the supply of an input to an individual firm is infinitely elastic. In other words, the firm can buy all it wants without influencing the price of the input. When we consider the market supply curve, which is the relationship between the price of the input and the total amount of the input supplied in the entire market, it is often untrue that the supply is infinitely elastic. In many cases, the total amount of the input supplied in the entire market will increase only if the price of the input is increased. Indeed, in some cases it is alleged that the market supply curve is perfectly inelastic, that is, the

---

3. Another proposition that is frequently advanced is that the demand for an input will be less elastic if the payments to this input are a small, rather than a large, proportion of the total cost of the product. There is good deal of truth in this proposition, but it does not always hold. See M. Brofenbrenner, "Note on the Elasticity of Derived Demand," *Oxford Economic Papers*, October 1961, as well as the accompanying note by J. Hicks.

For a useful study of the price elasticity of demand for labor, see K. Clark and R. Freeman, "How Elastic is the Demand for Labor?" *Review of Economics and Statistics*, November 1980.

total amount of the input supplied in the entire market is fixed and unresponsive to the price of the input.

There is, of course, no contradiction between the assertion that the supply of an input *to an individual firm* is perfectly elastic under perfect competition and the assertion that the *market* supply curve may not be perfectly elastic under perfect competition. For example, arable land might be available to any one farmer in as great an amount as he could possibly use at a given price; yet the aggregate amount of arable land available to all farmers may increase little with increases in the price per acre. The situation is similar to the sale of commodities: We saw in Chapter 8 that any firm under perfect competition believes that it can sell all it wants at the existing price; yet the total amount of a commodity sold in a given market can usually be increased only by reducing price.

There is sometimes a tendency to underestimate the extent to which the market supply of an input will be increased in response to an increase in the price of the input. For example, it is sometimes argued that the nation is provided with a certain amount of land and mineral resources, and that there is no way to change these amounts. For this reason, it is assumed that their market supply is perfectly inelastic, the available supply being completely unresponsive to price. But this can be quite wrong. For present purposes, what is important is the amount of land and mineral resources that is used, not the amount in existence. A large increase in price generally will increase the amount of these resources in use. This will occur because a higher price will result in more exploration for resources, in the reopening of high-cost mines and farms, and in the irrigation and upgrading of poorer land.

The Market Supply Curve: The Backward-Bending Case

Most inputs are *intermediate goods,* goods that are bought from other business firms. For example, an important input in the electric power industry is coal, which is bought from the coal industry. The supply curve for inputs of this kind is already familiar, and there is no need to discuss once again the determinants of the nature and shape of the market supply curve in these cases.

However, not all inputs are supplied by business firms. One of the most significant inputs—labor—is provided by individuals. (In addition, individuals provide other inputs like savings.) When individuals supply an input like labor, they are supplying something that they themselves can use, since the time that they do not work can be used for leisure activities. Thus sellers of these inputs want to keep some of them for themselves. And the amount of these inputs that is supplied to firms depends on the quantities of these inputs that are produced and the quantities that the suppliers want to keep for themselves.

In Chapter 8, we saw that the market supply curve for inputs supplied by business firms will generally slope upward and to the right. In other words

Fig.   BACKWARD-BENDING SUPPLY CURVE / *If the supply curve is*
12.3   *backward-bending, increases in price (beyond some point) result in*
        smaller amounts of the input being supplied.

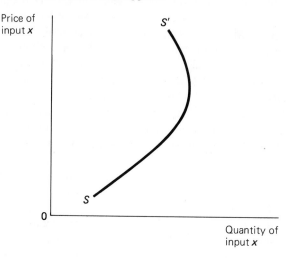

Backward-
bending supply
curve

higher prices generally are required to bring forth an increased supply. An interesting feature of the market supply function for inputs supplied by individuals is that it, unlike the supply function for inputs supplied by business firms, may be *backward-bending*. That is, increases in price may result in smaller amounts of the input being supplied. An example of a backward-bending supply curve is *SS'* in Figure 12.3.

To see how such a case can occur, consider the labor time supplied by a single worker, Bill Jones. Jones has twenty-four hours a day to allocate between work and leisure. To him leisure time is a commodity he desires, and its price is the hourly wage rate—the amount of money he gives up to enjoy an hour of leisure time. What will be the effect of an increase in the wage rate on the amount of leisure time that Jones will demand? Clearly, this is a problem of consumer choice, since the question can be restated: What is the effect of an increase in the price of leisure time on the quantity of leisure time that Jones demands? The theoretical tools discussed in Chapter 4 can help us to answer this question.

As we learned in Chapter 4, we can divide the effect of the price increase into two parts: the substitution effect and the income effect. The substitution effect is the effect of the increase in the cost of leisure relative to other commodities. Since other consumer goods will become relatively less expensive, the substitution effect will result in his reducing his leisure time and increasing his purchase of other consumer goods. Thus the substitution effect will result in his increasing the amount of labor time he puts forth.

Example 12.1

THE SUPPLY CURVE FOR PHYSICIANS' SERVICES

Martin Feldstein estimated that physicians have a backward-bending supply curve for labor. He found that the price elasticity of supply of physicians' services was about −0.91.

  (a) Draw a graph where hours per week devoted to leisure are plotted along the horizontal axis, and income derived from working is plotted along the vertical axis. Letting leisure be one good and income derived from working be the other, construct an individual physician's budget line and indifference curves. (b) Using the graph constructed in (a), show how the physician's desired amount of leisure is influenced by a decrease in his or her wage rate, if his or her supply curve for labor is backward-bending. (c) The American Medical Association has argued that any legislation that reduces the fees that physicians can charge will cut the supply of physicians' services. Does this appear to be true?

SOLUTION

  (a) Such a graph is shown in panel A below. The budget line here is *CD*. To derive this budget line, note that a physician who devoted every hour in the week to leisure would receive no income from working. That there are 168 hours in a week explains why the budget line passes through point *D*. If the physician devotes no time to leisure, the amount of income received from working is *OC* (which equals 168*W*, where *W* is the physician's hourly wage rate). This explains why the budget line passes through point *C*. Note that the slope of the budget line equals −1 times the physician's hourly wage rate, because every extra hour devoted to leisure reduces the amount of income received from working by an amount equal to the hourly wage rate. Panel A also shows the physician's indifference curves. Given these indifference curves and the budget line, the physician will maximize utility by choosing *OX* hours of leisure and by obtaining *OY* dollars of income from working.

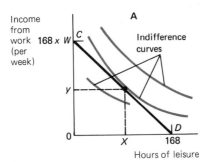
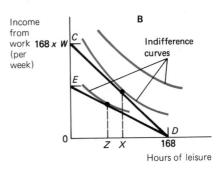

  (b) A decrease in the physician's hourly wage rate reduces the amount that he or she can earn if no time is devoted to leisure from *OC* to *OE* in panel B. Thus the budget line is no longer *CD*, but *ED*, and the physician will maximize utility by choosing *OZ* rather than *OX* hours of leisure. Since he or she is in the backward-bending portion of the supply curve, *OZ* is less than *OX*. (c) If the price elasticity of supply for physicians' services is negative, this does not appear to be true.*

* For further discussion, see M. Feldstein, "The Rising Price of Physicians' Services," *Review of Economics and Statistics,* May 1970.

In addition, there is an income effect, which is quite different from the income effect in the case of the purchase of most consumer products. In the first place, the income effect here works in the opposite direction from the income effect in the case of the purchase of the typical consumer product. As we saw in Chapter 4, the income effect of a price increase of a good is generally to reduce the consumption of the good, since the price increase reduces the consumer's real purchasing power. But this is not the case here. An increase in the price of his leisure time due to an increase in his wage makes Jones more affluent and better able to afford the things he wants, including leisure. Thus the income effect of an increase in the price of leisure is likely to be an increase in the demand for leisure.

The income effect in this case differs from the income effect for most consumer products in another important respect: It is likely to be much stronger than for most consumer products. In general, the consumer spends only a small percentage of his budget on the product in question, with the result that an increase in its price has only a small impact on his real income. However, in the case of leisure, an increase in its price will almost certainly have a great effect on his real income, since most of his income is likely to stem from the sale of his labor. (Remember that the price of leisure time is equal to the wage rate.) Thus an increase in the price of leisure time is likely to have a great effect on Jones's income and on his consumption pattern.

The income effect may offset the substitution effect, with the result that an increase in the wage rate may reduce the supply of labor. In other words, an increase in the price of leisure time may increase the quantity demanded of leisure time. Of course, institutional constraints often prevent workers from choosing their own working hours; for example, the 40-hour week is commonly worked in industry. But the typical, or average, work week responds to the shape of the supply curve for labor. Thus, in the United States, as workers have become more affluent the average work week has tended to decrease. For example, the average work week in 1850 was almost 70 hours, as contrasted with about 40 hours at present.

DETERMINATION OF PRICE AND EMPLOYMENT OF AN INPUT

The market demand and supply curves for an input determine the input's equilibrium price. The price of the input will tend in equilibrium to the level at which the quantity of the input demanded equals the quantity of the input supplied. Thus, in Figure 12.4, the equilibrium price of the input is OP_0. If the price were higher than OP_0, the quantity supplied would exceed the quantity demanded, and there would be downward pressure on the price. If the price were lower than OP_0, the quantity supplied would fall short of the quantity demanded, and there would be upward pressure on the price.

Fig. 12.4 DETERMINATION OF EQUILIBRIUM PRICE AND QUANTITY / *The equilibrium price is* OP_0, *and the equilibrium quantity is* OQ_0.

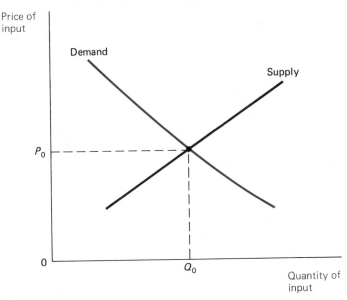

The equilibrium amount of the input that is employed is also given by the intersection of the market demand and supply curves. For example, in Figure 12.4, OQ_0 units of the input will be employed in equilibrium. In equilibrium the value of the marginal product of an input will be equal in each and every place where the input is used. In all uses the value of the marginal product of an input will equal the price of the input—and the price of the input will, of course, be the same to all firms under perfect competition.

The Market for Engineers: An Application

At this point, it is advisable to pause for a moment and illustrate how the theory we have been discussing has been put to use. During much of the period since World War II, top government policy-makers have been concerned with the adequacy of the national supply of engineers. During the 1950s and early 1960s, there was a widespread fear among government officials and senior scientists that a serious shortage of engineers existed in the United States. Then during the late 1960s and early 1970s, there was a feeling that too many engineers were being turned out by the nation's colleges and universities. Both during the period of apparent shortage and that of apparent surplus, questions were repeatedly raised by knowledgeable people concerning the workings of the market for engineers. In particular, it was asked whether the sort of model

Fig.   ESTIMATED RELATIONSHIP BETWEEN NUMBER OF PEOPLE GOING INTO
12.5   ENGINEERING AND THE LEVEL OF ENGINEERING SALARIES, UNITED STATES /
*An increase in starting engineering salaries results in a substantial
increase in freshman engineering enrollment, as well as an increase in the
number of engineers graduating from college.*

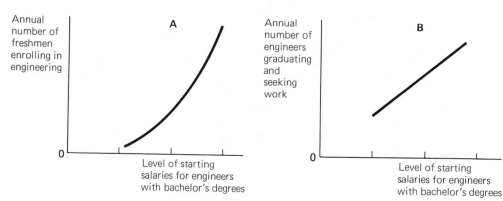

described in previous sections of this chapter really explained the quantity of
engineers graduated in a particular period and the level of their salaries.

To help answer this question, Richard Freeman of Harvard University
gathered detailed data concerning the annual number of freshmen enrolling in
engineering, the annual number of engineers graduating and seeking work,
and the annual level of starting salaries of engineers (with a bachelor's degree).[4] Based on careful statistical analysis, he estimated the supply and demand curves for engineers during this period. In the case of the supply curve,
he divided the analysis into two parts. First, he estimated the effect of the level
of engineering starting salaries on the number of freshmen enrolling in engineering. Holding other factors (like the total number of freshmen in all fields
and the previous levels of salaries and enrollments) constant, he found that
the relationship between the number of freshmen enrolling in engineering and
the level of engineering starting salaries was as shown in panel A of Figure 12.5.
Specifically, a 1 percent increase in starting salaries results in a 2.9 percent
increase in freshman enrollment in engineering.

Next, taking the freshman enrollment in engineering as given, he estimated the effect of the level of engineering starting salaries on the number of
engineers graduating four years later and seeking work. Holding the freshman
enrollment (and other factors) constant, he found that the relationship between the number of engineers graduating (and seeking work) and the level of

---

4. Richard B. Freeman, *The Market for College-Trained Manpower* (Cambridge, Mass.: Harvard University Press, 1971).

starting salaries[5] was as shown in panel B of Figure 12.5. Specifically, a 1 percent increase in starting salaries results in about a 1 percent increase in the number of graduate engineers. In other words, more students switched to engineering or stayed in engineering when engineering salaries were relatively high than when they were relatively low. But as one would expect, the quantitative impact of salaries was smaller here than on freshman enrollment in engineering.

Together, the two panels of Figure 12.5 provide some interesting insights concerning the supply curve for engineers in the United States. To government policy-makers, information of this sort is of great importance. For example, if national goals seem to require a certain number of engineers, the information such as that in Figure 12.5 can be used to indicate the level of starting salaries that, in the absence of other measures, would be required to call them forth. Further, Freeman's results shed valuable light on the extent to which the theory presented in previous sections can explain the workings of the market for engineers. He concludes that "traditional market forces—shifts in supply and demand—explain changes in engineering starting salaries, though with a lag due to sluggish adjustment to unexpected supply conditions."[6]

THE CONCEPT OF RENT

Earlier in this chapter we stated that there is sometimes a tendency to underestimate the extent to which the market supply of an input will be increased in response to an increase in the price of the input. Nevertheless, some inputs, like certain types of land, may be in relatively fixed supply. Suppose that the supply of an input is completely fixed: Increases in its price will not increase its supply and decreases in its price will not decrease its supply. Following the terminology of the classical economists of the nineteenth century,

Rent

the price of such an input is rent. This use of the word *rent* is quite different from everyday usage, according to which *rent* is the price of using an apartment or a car or some other object owned by someone else.

If the supply of an input is fixed, its supply curve is a vertical line, as shown in Figure 12.6. Thus the price of this input, that is, its rent, is determined entirely by the demand curve for the input. For example, if the demand curve is D, the rent is OP; if the demand curve is D_0, the rent is OP_0. Since the

---

5. Starting salaries here refer to a couple of years before graduation.

6. Freeman, *The Market,* p. 72. In panel B of Figure 12.5, the annual number of engineers graduating and seeking work is estimated holding constant the number of freshmen enrolled in engineering four years earlier.

Fig.   AN INPUT IN COMPLETELY FIXED SUPPLY / *The price of an input in fixed*
12.6   *supply is called a rent. If the demand curve is* D, *the rent is* OP.

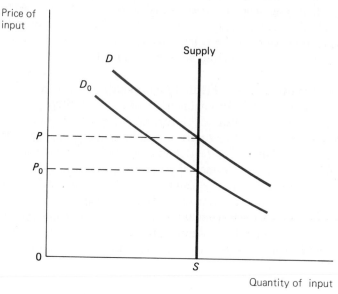

supply of the input is fixed, the price of the input can be lowered without influencing the amount of the input that is supplied. Thus a rent is a payment
above the minimum necessary to attract this amount of the input.[7]

In recent years, there has been a tendency among economists to extend
the use of the word *rent* to encompass all payments to inputs that are above
the minimum required to make these inputs available to the industry or to the
economy. To a great extent these payments are costs to individual firms, since
these firms must make such payments in order to attract and keep these
inputs, which are useful to other firms in the industry. But, if the inputs have
no use in other industries, these payments are not costs to the industry as a
whole (or to the economy as a whole) because the inputs would be available to
the industry whether or not these payments are made.

Why is it important to know whether or not a certain payment for inputs
is a rent? Because a reduction of the payment will not influence the availability and use of the inputs if the payment is a rent; whereas, if it is not a rent, a
reduction of the payment is likely to change the allocation of resources. For example, if the government imposes a tax on rents, there will be no effect on the
supply of resources to the economy.

---

7. Note that whether rent is or is not price-determined depends on whether we are looking at the
matter from the point of view of a firm, a small industry, a large industry, or the whole economy. Although a payment to an input that is in fixed supply to the whole society or a large
industry may be a rent from the point of view of the society or the industry, it may appear to
be a price-determining cost to an individual small firm or a small industry.

Quasi-Rents

The payment to any input in temporarily fixed supply is called a quasi-rent. In previous chapters, we have seen that many inputs are in fixed supply to a firm in the short run. For example, a firm's plant cannot be changed appreciably. In the short run, fixed inputs cannot be withdrawn from their current use and transferred to a use where the returns are higher. Also, fixed inputs cannot be supplemented with other similar inputs in the short run. Thus the payments to the fixed inputs are determined differently from the payments to the variable inputs. Whereas inputs that are variable in quantity are free to move where the returns are highest, fixed inputs are stuck where they are, at least in the short run. Consequently, firms must pay the variable inputs as much as they can earn in alternative uses, and the fixed inputs receive whatever is left over.

Quasi-rent   The return to the fixed inputs is a *quasi-rent*. It is a residual. To understand its nature, it is useful to consider the diagram in Figure 12.7, which shows a firm's short-run cost curves. Suppose that the price is OP_0, with the result that the firm will produce OQ_0 units and its total variable costs will be $OGBQ_0$ (since OG equals its average variable cost). This area, $OGBQ_0$, represents the amount that the firm must pay in order to attract and keep the amount of variable inputs corresponding to an output of OQ_0. It cannot pay less and expect to keep them. The fixed inputs get the residual, which is GP_0CB. This is the quasi-rent.

Fig. Quasi-Rent / *A quasi-rent is the payment to any input in temporarily*
12.7 *fixed supply. The amount received by the fixed inputs, which equals*
  GP_0CB, *is a quasi-rent.*

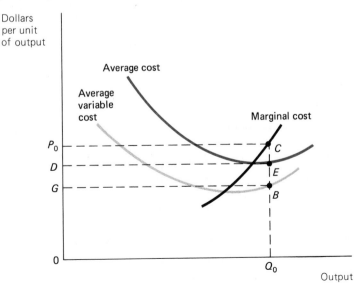

Example 12.2

EFFECTS OF AN INFLOW OF IMMIGRANTS

During recent years, there has been a substantial inflow of immigrants from Asia, Mexico, Cuba, and other areas to the United States. Suppose that the economy is competitive (with constant returns to scale) and that the value-of-marginal-product curve for labor is as shown below.

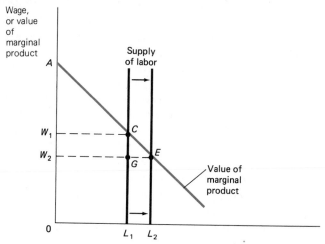

(a) If immigration results in an increase from OL_1 to OL_2 in the supply of labor, what is the effect on the equilibrium wage? (b) What is the effect on the total amount of wages received by nonimmigrant U.S. labor? (c) What is the effect on the total income of U.S. owners of capital (and other nonlabor resources)? Assume that all capital (and other nonlabor resources) is owned by Americans other than the immigrants. (d) Taking account of the effects of the immigration on both the wages received by nonimmigrant U.S. labor and the income of owners of capital (and other nonlabor resources), is there a net benefit to Americans other than the immigrants? If so, how big is it?

The short-run average total cost curve includes both the average variable costs and the average fixed costs. To determine the average fixed costs, we see what the returns on the firm's fixed assets would be if the rate of return were equal to that available elsewhere in the economy. Thus, since the firm's average total cost curve is as shown in Figure 12.7, the total fixed costs of the firm are equal to *GDEB*. Consequently, this amount of the quasi-rent is not pure economic profit; only DP_0CE is economic profit. Needless to say, quasi-rent need not be greater than total fixed costs. Firms with pure economic losses do not have quasi-rents that are large enough to cover total fixed costs.

SOLUTION

(a) The equilibrium wage will drop from OW_1 to OW_2. Before the immigration, the intersection of the demand and supply curves for labor was at point C; after the shift in the supply curve for labor, it is at point E. (b) The quantity of nonimmigrant U.S. labor is OL_1. Since the wage rate was OW_1 before the immigration, nonimmigrant U.S. labor received total wages amounting to OW_1 times OL_1, which equals area OW_1CL_1. After the immigration, nonimmigrant U.S. labor received total wages amounting to OW_2 times OL_1, which equals area OW_2GL_1. Thus the immigration reduced the total wages of nonimmigrant U.S. labor by an amount equal to area W_2W_1CG. (c) The value of the total output produced by n workers is the sum of the values of the marginal products of the first, second, . . . , and n^{th} workers.* Thus, since OL_1 workers were hired before the immigration, the value of the total output at that time equaled the sum of the values of the marginal products of the OL_1 workers—which amounts to area $OACL_1$. Since wages equaled area OW_1CL_1, owners of capital (and other nonlabor resources) received an amount equal to W_1AC (the difference between area $OACL_1$ and area OW_1CL_1). After the immigration, the value of the total output produced by the OL_2 workers is the sum of the values of their marginal products, which equals $OAEL_2$. Subtracting total wages, owners of capital (and other nonlabor resources) received an amount equal to area W_2AE (the difference between area $OAEL_2$ and area OW_2EL_2). Thus owners of capital (and other nonlabor resources) received an increase in income amounting to the area W_2W_1CE (the difference between area W_2AE and area W_1AC). (d) The increase in the total income of U.S. owners of capital and other nonlabor resources (area W_2W_1CE) exceeds the loss to nonimmigrant U.S. labor (area W_2W_1CG), the difference equaling triangle CGE.†

* To see this, let the value of total output be $V(n)$ when n workers are hired. Since the value of the marginal product of the first worker is $V(1) - V(0)$, the value of the marginal product of the second worker is $V(2) - V(1)$, . . . , and the value of the marginal product of the nth worker is $V(n) - V(n-1)$, it follows that the sum of the values of the marginal products of the n workers equals

$$[V(1) - V(0)] + [V(2) - V(1)] + \ldots + [V(n) - V(n-1)].$$

Since $V(1), V(2), \ldots V(n-1)$ appear with both positive and negative signs, they cancel out; and since $V(0) = 0$, this sum must equal $V(n)$.

† For further discussion, see B. Chiswick, "Immigrants and Immigration Policy," in W. Fellner, ed., *Contemporary Economic Problems* (Washington, D.C.: American Enterprise Institute, 1978).

QUALITATIVE DIFFERENCES IN INPUTS

In previous sections we have dealt with inputs that have been assumed to be homogeneous. In this section, we take account of the fact that inputs may differ in productive capacity. For example, some carpenters may be more skillful than others. Suppose that there are two types of carpenters: skilled and unskilled. Then the firm, if it maximizes profit, should hire each type of carpenter up to the point at which

$$MP_s \cdot MR = P_s \qquad [12.5a]$$

$$MP_u \cdot MR = P_u \qquad [12.5b]$$

where MP_s is the marginal product of skilled carpenters, MP_u is the marginal product of unskilled carpenters, P_s is the wage rate for skilled carpenters, P_u is the wage rate for unskilled carpenters, and MR is marginal revenue. This follows directly from Equations 12.4a to 12.4c. Equations 12.5a and 12.5b show that the differential in wages between skilled and unskilled carpenters will equal the differential in their marginal products, that is,

$$P_s \div P_u = MP_s \div MP_u.$$

Suppose that we can no longer divide workers into two groups, since each worker differs from the next in the value of his or her output. Then the difference in wages paid to workers will equal the difference in the total value of their output. For example, suppose that Joe (together with the appropriate tools and materials) produces output worth $1,000 per month and Bill (with the same tools and materials) produces output worth $900 per month. In equilibrium, Joe will earn $100 more per month than Bill. If the difference in wages were less than $100, Bill's employer would find it profitable to replace Bill with Joe, since this would increase the value of output by $100 and cost less than $100. If the difference were more than $100, Joe's employer would find it profitable to replace Joe with Bill; although this would reduce the value of output by $100, it would reduce costs by more than $100.

This kind of analysis has been applied repeatedly to explain differences in land rents. According to the classical discussions of this subject, only the better tracts of land will be used at a given point in time; the less productive lands will not be in use because they are not sufficiently productive to earn a profit. The least productive lands in use earn neither a profit nor a loss; consequently their price is zero, since no one would be willing to pay more for them. The rent of any other tract of land in use will equal the difference between its value yield and the value yield of this zero-priced *marginal land,* when the area of the plot is held constant. Thus the tracts of land (that are worked) will rent at a variety of levels, but after subtracting rental costs they will earn an equal net profit for those who work them.

Wage Differentials among Labor of Similar Quality

In previous sections we pointed out that variable inputs will be transferred from one use to another in response to differences in the return they can yield. Thus labor will move from uses in which its wages are low to uses in which its wages are high. This migration from low-wage uses to high-wage uses tends to equalize the wage level for labor of comparable quality, but it does not

Example 12.3

THE EFFECTS OF MINIMUM-WAGE LAWS

Congress has passed round after round of minimum-wage legislation. The minimum wage, which was only 25 cents per hour in 1938, was $3.35 in 1987. Suppose that a minimum wage, OP_m, is instituted in a competitive labor market, with the demand and supply curves for labor as follows:

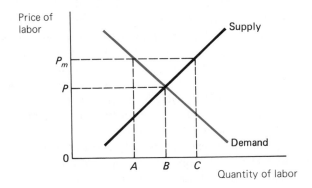

(a) Will the minimum wage affect the level of employment? If so, how big will its effect be? (b) How may employers (and workers) get around the minimum wage? (c) Are certain types of workers affected more than others by the minimum wage? If so, which types are affected most?

SOLUTION

(a) Yes. The minimum wage will cause employment to fall from OB to OA workers; thus AB workers will be laid off. Note that this is less than the excess supply of workers (the difference between the quantity of workers supplied and the quantity demanded), which equals AC. The excess supply of workers is the total number that would like to work at the minimum wage, but cannot do so. (b) Sometimes employers can provide less in-kind benefits, such as meals, or employees are willing to pay for items that normally would be the responsibility of the employer. In this way, the *net* amount paid by the employer is below the minimum wage, although the wage appears to be above it. (c) Unskilled workers and occupations are affected much more than skilled workers and occupations, because only in unskilled labor markets does the minimum wage exceed the equilibrium wage. There is a strong effect on teen-agers, particularly black teen-agers. One study indicated that the unemployment rate for black teen-agers increases about 1.8 percentage points for each percentage point rise in the ratio of the minimum wage to the average hourly earnings of production workers in private nonagricultural employment.*

* For further discussion, see C. Brown, C. Gilroy, and A. Kohen, "The Effect of the Minimum Wage on Employment and Unemployment," *Journal of Economic Literature,* June 1982; and F. Welch, *Minimum Wages: Issues and Evidence* (Washington, D.C.: American Enterprise Institute, 1978).

eliminate all wage differentials among such labor. Even if all workers were identical, even to their fingerprints (a criminal's paradise), some wage differentials would still be required to offset differences in the characteristics of various occupations and areas.[8]

For example, some occupations require large investments in training, while other occupations require a much smaller investment in training. Consider John Sharp, a physicist who spends about eight years in undergraduate and graduate education. During each year of his training, he incurs direct expenses for items like books and tuition, and he loses the income that he could make if he were to work rather than go to school. Clearly, if his net remuneration is to be as high in physics as in other jobs he might take, he must make a greater wage when he gets through than a comparable person whose job requires no training beyond high school; the difference in wages must be at least sufficient to compensate for his investment in extra training.

Similarly, members of some occupations incur larger occupational expenses than others. For example, a psychologist may have to buy testing materials and subscribe to expensive journals. In order for net compensation to be equalized, such workers must be paid more than others. Also, some jobs are more unstable than others. For example, some types of workers may be subject to frequent layoffs and have little job security, whereas others may be assured stable and secure employment. If the former jobs are to be as attractive as the latter, they must pay more than the latter.

In addition, there are other differences among jobs that must be offset by wage differentials if the net remuneration is to be equalized. For instance, there are differences among regions and communities in the cost of living. (Living costs generally are lower in small towns than in big cities.) Also, some jobs are more prestigious than others, with the result that people would be willing to accept them even though they paid less than others. (However, the high-paying jobs frequently tend to be the more prestigious ones.)

THE ELASTICITY OF SUBSTITUTION AND THE DISTRIBUTION OF INCOME

The *elasticity of substitution* measures the extent to which the capital-labor ratio changes in response to changes in the ratio of the price of capital to the price of labor. More precisely, the elasticity of substitution equals

Elasticity of substitution

$$S = -\left(\frac{\Delta(X_K/X_L)}{X_K/X_L} \div \frac{\Delta(P_K/P_L)}{P_K/P_L} \right) \qquad [12.6]$$

where X_K is the quantity of capital employed, X_L the quantity of

---

8. In addition, of course, such wage differentials may arise because of less than perfect mobility of inputs and frictions of various kinds.

labor employed, P_K the price of capital, and P_L the price of labor. The level of output is held constant.

The elasticity of substitution is an important determinant of how a change in the price of labor or in the price of capital will alter the share of total income going to labor or capital. Since capital's total income is $X_K P_K$ and labor's total income is $X_L P_L$, the ratio of capital's share of total income to labor's share is

$$X_K P_K \div X_L P_L \quad \text{or} \quad \frac{X_K}{X_L} \times \frac{P_K}{P_L}.$$

Suppose that P_K/P_L decreases by 1 percent. Then, if $S > 1$, this decrease in the price of capital relative to the price of labor results in a more than 1 percent increase in the capital-labor ratio. If $S = 1$, it results in a 1 percent increase in the capital-labor ratio. If $S < 1$, it results in less than a 1 percent increase in the capital-labor ratio.

Given the value of S, one can determine the effect of a change in the price of labor or in the price of capital on the ratio of capital's total income to labor's total income. For example, suppose that the price of labor increases relative to the price of capital. If $S < 1$, the relative increase in X_K/X_L is less than the relative decrease in P_K/P_L, with the result that $X_K/X_L \times P_K/P_L$ must decrease. If $S = 1$, the relative increase in X_K/X_L is just equal to the relative decrease in P_K/P_L, with the result that $X_K/X_L \times P_K/P_L$ does not change. If $S > 1$, the relative increase in X_K/X_L is greater than the relative decrease in P_K/P_L, with the result that $X_K/X_L \times P_K/P_L$ must increase. Thus, when the price of labor increases relative to that of capital, if $S < 1$, the ratio of capital's share to labor's share will decrease; if $S = 1$, it will stay the same; and if $S > 1$, it will increase.

According to many observers, the share of income going to labor and capital has been relatively constant in the United States. Over the past seventy-five years, labor has received about 70 to 85 percent of the total real income; the exact number varies with the definition of labor income that is used. Some economists have tried to explain this phenomenon by asserting that the aggregate production function exhibits an elasticity of substitution of 1. (If, for example, the appropriate production function were the Cobb-Douglas function discussed in Chapter 6, the elasticity of substitution would be 1.) Three points should be noted in this regard. First, not all observers are impressed by the constancy of shares. Second, technological change as well as the elasticity of substitution influences the ratio of capital's share to labor's share. Third, we have relatively little evidence concerning the value of the elasticity of substitution.[9]

---

9. For a survey of empirical studies of the elasticity of substitution, see M. Nerlove, "Recent Empirical Studies of the CES and Related Production Functions," in M. Brown, *The Theory and Empirical Analysis of Production* (New York: National Bureau of Economic Research, 1967); E. Berndt, "Reconciling Alternative Estimates of the Elasticity of Substitution," *Review of Economics and Statistics,* February 1976; and C. Paraskevopoulos, "Alternative Estimates of the Elasticity of Substitution," *Review of Economics and Statistics,* August 1979.

THE SHORTAGE OF NURSES: ANOTHER APPLICATION

On July 2, 1987, the front page of the *New York Times* trumpeted: "Sudden Nurse Shortage Threatens Hospital Care." During the past thirty years, there have been repeated complaints of a shortage of professional nurses. According to Donald Yett of the University of Southern California,

In recent years, 10 to 20 percent of all budgeted positions for hospital registered nurses . . . have been reported vacant . . . Reported hospital vacancies were higher for general duty nurses than for directors, supervisors, and head nurses . . . Nursing and hospital leaders agree that teaching and supervisory positions should be filled by college-trained nurses, but the existing supply is not sufficient. Consequently, many of these positions have been filled by nurses who otherwise would have been assigned to general duty, an area in which, as a result, the shortage appears to be concentrated.[10]

There are many reasons for the persistence of this shortage—and these reasons have changed over time. One of the factors that has been involved is illustrated by the following simple model devised by Stanford's Nobel laureate Kenneth Arrow and William Capron.[11] According to many authorities, the demand curve for nurses has shifted to the right in the past thirty years, as population and demand for hospital care have increased. In particular, suppose that the demand curve for nurses shifted from D_1 to D_2 in Figure 12.8. Under these circumstances, the wage for nurses that would bring supply and demand into balance is OP_2. But as Arrow and Capron point out, it will take time for the wage to move from OP_1 to OP_2. During the transition period—the period when the wage is moving from OP_1 to OP_2—the organizations hiring nurses will experience a "shortage" in the sense that they will not be able to hire as many nurses as they would like at the going wage. For example, when the wage is OP_3, they would like to hire OQ_3 nurses, but they will be able to hire only OQ_2 nurses.

A shortage of this sort can persist for a number of years if the demand curve continues to shift to the right (as it seemed to for nurses during this pe-

---

10. D. Yett, "The Chronic Shortage of Nurses," in Herbert Klarman, ed., *Empirical Studies in Health Economics* (Baltimore: Johns Hopkins University Press, 1970). See also his *An Economic Analysis of the Nurse Shortage* (Lexington, Mass.: Lexington Books, 1975). I am indebted to Donald Yett for comments on this section.

11. K. Arrow and W. Capron, "Dynamic Shortages and Price Rises: The Engineer-Scientist Case," *Quarterly Journal of Economics,* May 1959. This paper had a considerable influence in clarifying issues and helping to guide policy regarding the market for scientists and engineers. The fact that the model was designed to deal with the market for scientists and engineers in the late 1950s does not mean, of course, that it is not applicable to nurses (or other groups).

Fig. 12.8 SHORTAGE OF NURSES / *If the demand curve shifts from* D₁ *to* D₂, *it takes time for the wage to move from* OP₁ *to* P₂. *When the wage is* OP₃, *there will be a shortage of nurses.*

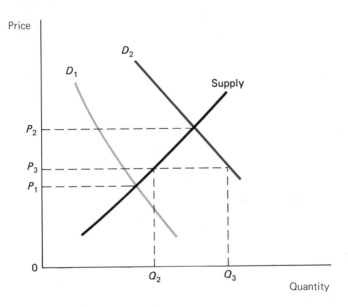

riod) and if the wage rate tends to be "sticky" and to increase slowly in response to the excess demand. Among the reasons why the wage may be sticky is "the prevalence of long-term contracts, the influence of the heterogeneity of the market in slowing the diffusion of information, and the dominance of a relatively small number of [employers]."[12] Such a shortage will be over when the necessary wage increases occur. For example, when the wage rate increases to OP_2 in Figure 12.8, the quantity demanded equals the quantity supplied.

This model sheds useful light on the nurse shortage, a problem which has commanded the attention of the Congress, the Department of Health and Human Services; and other groups. But according to Donald Yett, this is not the whole story. He points out that the labor market for nurses is not perfectly competitive, and that the imperfections in the labor market may also have been responsible for the apparent shortage. (The discussion of the price and employment of inputs under imperfect competition is reserved for the next chapter.) Nonetheless, the simple concepts put forward in this example can take us a substantial way toward understanding at least part of this complex problem.

---

12. Ibid., p. 303.

SUMMARY

1. In a free-enterprise economy, input prices are an important determinant of any consumer's income. Our first step in analyzing the demand for an input is to consider the demand curve of an individual firm. If there is only one variable input, the firm's demand curve is the same as the value-of-marginal-product schedule. If there is more than one variable input, the situation is somewhat more complicated.

2. The market demand curve for the input can be derived from the demand curves of the individual firms in the market; however, it cannot be derived by simply taking their horizontal sum.

3. Under perfect competition, the supply of an input to an individual firm is infinitely elastic. However, when we consider the market supply curve, which is the relationship between the price of the input and the amount of the input supplied in the entire market, it is often not true that supply is infinitely elastic.

4. Many inputs are supplied by business firms, and the factors influencing their supply have been discussed in previous chapters. But other inputs—notably labor—are supplied by individuals, not business firms. For inputs supplied by individuals, the supply curve may be backward bending; that is, increases in input price may result in a smaller supply of the input, at least over some range of variation of input price.

5. Given the market demand and supply curves for an input, the price of the input will tend in equilibrium to the level at which the quantity of the input demanded equals the quantity of the input supplied. The equilibrium amount of the input that is utilized is also given by the intersection of the market demand and supply curves. To illustrate how these concepts can be used to help solve important problems of public policy, we described how economists have used these concepts to analyze the market for engineers and the shortage of nurses.

6. The payment to an input that is completely fixed in supply is called a rent; and the payment to an input in temporarily fixed supply is a quasi-rent.

7. Wage differentials are due to qualitative differences among inputs, as well as differences among jobs in training required, occupational expenses, security, and other factors.

8. The elasticity of substitution, which measures the extent to which the capital-labor ratio changes in response to changes in the ratio of the price of capital to the price of labor, is an important determinant of how a change in the price of labor or capital affects the share of total income going to labor or capital.

═══════════════ QUESTIONS/PROBLEMS ═══════════════

1) Suppose that a negative income tax is enacted. If a family's income level is as shown in the first column of the table below, the amount that it will receive from the government is given in the second column, and the family's total income (including the cash payment from the government) is given in the third column. Thus, if a fam-

Family income	Government's cash payment to family	Family's total income (including payment by government)
$ 0	$4,500	$4,500
1,000	4,000	5,000
2,000	3,500	5,500
3,000	3,000	6,000
4,000	2,500	6,500
5,000	2,000	7,000
6,000	1,500	7,500
7,000	1,000	8,000
8,000	500	8,500
9,000	0	9,000

ily's income is $2,000, it will receive $3,500 from the government (this being its *negative* tax payment), and its total income (including the cash payment from the government) is $5,500. (a) In the absence of a negative income tax, suppose that the relationship between a worker's after-tax income and his number of hours of leisure would be the straight line *EF* in the graph on p. 374. If he devoted no time at all to leisure, he would earn an income of *OE*. If he devoted no time at all to work (and 8,760 hours[13] to leisure), he would earn a zero income. As pointed out in Example 12.1, the slope of line *EF* equals −1 times the worker's (after-tax) hourly wage rate, because every extra hour devoted to leisure reduces the amount of income received from working by an amount equal to the after-tax hourly wage rate. What point on line *EF* will the worker choose? How many hours of work per year will he do? (b) How many hours of work will he do if the government establishes a minimal annual income of $4,500 per year? (c) If the negative income tax in the table above is adopted, how many hours per year will he work? (d) Will all workers devote more time to work under the negative income tax than under the guaranteed annual income?

───

13. The number of hours in a year equals 365 times 24, or 8,760.

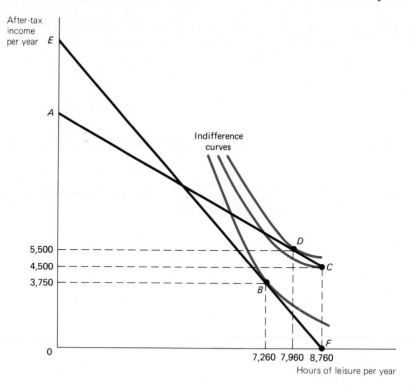

2) According to 1981 Nobel laureate James Tobin, "When there are only a few people left in the population whose capacities are confined to garbage-collecting, it will be a high-paid calling. The same is true of domestic service and all kinds of menial work." Do you agree? Using the concepts presented in this chapter, explain why you agree or disagree.

3) A biotechnology firm uses labor and capital. The price of a unit of labor is $5 and the price of a unit of capital is $6. The marginal product of a unit of labor is the same as the marginal product of a unit of capital. Is this firm (which is a perfect competitor) maximizing its profit? Explain.

4) Describe how the cobweb model (described in Chapter 8) can be applied to the market for engineers. (In fact, this model has been used by some economists to represent the workings of this market.)

5) A perfectly competitive firm can hire labor at $30 per day. The firm's production function is as follows:

Number of days of labor	Number of units of output
0	0
1	8
2	15
3	21
4	26
5	30

If each unit of output sells for $5, how many days of labor should the firm hire?

6) A firm sells its product for $10 per unit. It produces 100 units per month, and its average variable cost is $5. What is its quasi-rent? If its average fixed cost is $4, does its quasi-rent equal its economic profit?

7) Suppose that the ratio of the price of capital to the price of labor decreases by 1 percent in 1988, with the result that the capital-labor ratio increases by 0.5 percent. What is the elasticity of substitution? If the elasticity of substitution remains at this value, and if the ratio of the price of capital to the price of labor decreases by 1 percent again in 1989, will the ratio of capital's total income to labor's total income rise in 1989? Or will it fall? Explain.

8) William Moran, a (hypothetical) bricklayer who suffers from a disability, is $\frac{1}{4}$ as productive as the typical bricklayer; that is, his marginal product is $\frac{1}{4}$ of that of the typical bricklayer. If the going wage for typical bricklayers is 3 times the minimum wage, will Mr. Moran find work? Explain.

9) Using the conventional supply and demand apparatus, show why nonwhite labor receives lower wages than white labor, if racial discrimination exists in a society. What would happen to nonwhite wages, white wages, and total output if discrimination were to cease?

10) Using the concepts presented in this chapter, describe the effect on the market for unskilled labor if the existing minimum wage was abolished.

11) (Advanced) Suppose that a chemical firm's production function is $Q = L^8 K^2$, where Q is output, L is the amount of labor used, and K is the amount of capital used. If the firm takes the product price and the input prices as given, show that total wages paid by the firm will equal 80 percent of its revenues.

Price and Employment of
Inputs under
Imperfect Competition

INTRODUCTION

In some parts of the economy, perfect competition is clearly not the best
model. In this chapter, we continue our discussion of the determinants of the
price and employment of inputs, but we relax the assumption that there is
perfect competition. More specifically, this chapter is divided into three parts.
In the first part, we consider the case in which there is perfect competition in
the market for the input, but imperfect competition (that is, monopoly,
oligopoly, or monopolistic competition) in the relevant product markets. In
other words, we allow some of the firms that are potential buyers of the input
to have some monopoly power in the sale of their products. In the second part,
we take up the case in which there is only a single buyer of an input. In the
third part, we discuss an important and highly visible form of market imper-
fection in the market for labor—the labor union.[1]

---

1. Of course, this is only a brief introduction to the economics of collective bargaining; readers
   with a particular interest in this field should take a specialized course in labor economics.
   The material presented here is chosen and viewed from the vantage point of microeconomic
   theory.

PROFIT MAXIMIZATION AND INPUT EMPLOYMENT: IMPERFECT COMPETITION IN THE PRODUCT MARKET

In the previous chapter we showed that a firm, if it maximizes profit, will employ inputs in such a way that each input's marginal product multiplied by the firm's marginal revenue will equal the price of the input. Put in symbols, this condition for profit maximization is

$$MP_x \cdot MR = P_x \qquad\qquad [13.1a]$$

$$MP_y \cdot MR = P_y \qquad\qquad [13.1b]$$

$$\vdots$$

$$MP_z \cdot MR = P_z \qquad\qquad [13.1c]$$

where MP_x is the marginal product of input x, MP_y is the marginal product of input y, MP_z is the marginal product of input z, P_x is the price of input x, P_y is the price of input y, P_z is the price of input z, and MR is the marginal revenue of the firm's output.

Suppose that the firm is a monopolist or an oligopolist or a monopolistic competitor, rather than a perfect competitor as assumed in the previous chapter. Will the firm still employ inputs in the way described by Equations 13.1a, 13.1b, · · ·, 13.1c if it maximizes profit? The answer is yes. As long as the market for the input is perfectly competitive and the firm cannot influence the price of the input by its purchases, it must conform to Equations 13.1a, 13.1b, · · ·, 13.1c if it maximizes profit. It is a simple matter to prove to yourself that this is the case: Merely turn back to pp. 347–48 of Chapter 12 and work through the derivation of the conditions in Equations 12.4a, 12.4b, · · ·, 12.4c. Nowhere in that derivation is it assumed that the firm's product is sold in a perfectly competitive market. Thus the results hold whether the firm is a perfect competitor or an imperfect competitor in the product market.

The Firm's Demand Curve: The Case of One Variable Input

Equations 13.1a, 13.1b, · · ·, 13.1c are the basis for the theory of input demand under imperfect competition in the product market (just as they are under perfect competition in the product market). As in the previous chapter our first step in analyzing the demand for an input is to consider the demand of an individual firm for an input, assuming that this input is the only variable input in the firm's production process. In other words, the quantities of all other inputs are fixed. This assumption is relaxed in the next section. In the section after next, we discuss the market demand for the input and the determination of input price and employment.

Suppose that the only variable input is input x. The demand curve of a firm for this input shows the quantity of input x that the firm will take at var-

Table 13.1 MARGINAL REVENUE PRODUCT OF INPUT *x*

Quantity of x	Marginal product of x*	Total output	Price of good (dollars)	Total revenue (dollars)	Marginal revenue product of x* (dollars)
3	10	33	20.00	660.00	—
4	9	42	19.50	819.00	159.00
5	8	50	19.00	950.00	131.00
6	7	57	18.50	1,054.50	104.50
7	6	63	18.00	1,134.00	79.50
8	5	68	17.50	1,190.00	56.00
9	4	72	17.00	1,224.00	34.00

* These figures pertain to the interval between the indicated amount of input *x* and one unit less than the indicated amount of input *x*.

ious possible prices of input *x*. Assuming that the firm maximizes its profits, it will take that amount of input *x* at which the value of the extra output produced by an extra unit of input *x* is equal to the price of a unit of input *x*. This is the meaning of Equation 13.1a.

To be more specific, suppose that the marginal product of input *x* at various levels of utilization of input *x* is that shown in Table 13.1; the total amount of output that can be derived from each number of units of input *x* is shown in the third column of Table 13.1. Because the firm is an imperfect competitor, the price of its product will vary with the amount it sells; the fourth column of Table 13.1 provides the price that corresponds to each output in the third column. Multiplying the output in the third column by the price in the fourth column, we get the total revenue corresponding to each number of units of input *x* used; this is shown in column 5.

Finally, in column 6 of Table 13.1 we show the increase in total revenue that stems from the use of each additional unit of input *x*. For example, the fifth unit of input *x* (that is, going from 4 units to 5 units of input *x*) increases the firm's total revenue by $131. Similarly, the seventh unit of input *x* (that is, going from 6 units to 7 units of input *x*) increases the firm's total revenue by $79.50. The increase in total revenue due to the use of an additional unit of input *x* is called the *marginal revenue product* of input *x*, which explains the heading of column 6. The marginal revenue product of input *x* is equal to the marginal physical product of input *x* times the firm's marginal revenue.[2] Thus it is equal to the left-hand side of Equation 13.1a.

Marginal revenue product

---

2. It is easy to prove that the marginal revenue product (*MRP*) is the product of the marginal product (*MP*) and marginal revenue (*MR*). By definition,

$$MRP = \frac{\Delta R}{\Delta I}$$

If the firm maximizes profit it sets the marginal revenue product of input x equal to the price of input x. This is the meaning of Equation 13.1a. Thus the firm's demand schedule for input x must be the marginal-revenue-product schedule in column 6 of Table 13.1. For example, suppose that the price of input x is $56. Then according to Equation 13.1a the firm will set the marginal revenue product of input x equal to $56, which means that it will demand 8 units of input x. Or suppose that the price of input x is $34. Then the firm will set the marginal revenue product of input x equal to $34, which means that it will demand 9 units of input x. Thus the number of units of input x that the firm will demand at any price is given by the marginal-revenue-product curve, which shows the marginal revenue product of input x at various quantities of input x used. This curve is shown in Figure 13.1.

Two points should be noted concerning the marginal-revenue-product curve. First, it will slope downward and to the right (as a demand curve should for an input) for two reasons: the input's marginal product will decrease as more of it is used, and the firm's marginal revenue will decrease as its output

Fig. 13.1   MARGINAL-REVENUE-PRODUCT CURVE FOR INPUT x / *The marginal revenue product of input* x *is the increase in total revenue due to the use of an additional unit of input* x. *The data come from the last column of Table 13.1.*

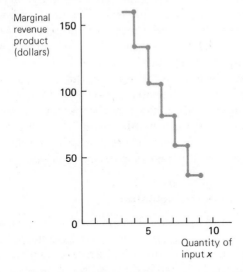

where ΔR is the change in total revenue and ΔI is the change in the quantity of the input. Since $MR = \Delta R \div \Delta Q$, where ΔQ is the change in output, it follows that

$$MRP = \frac{MR\Delta Q}{\Delta I}.$$

But since $MP = \Delta Q \div \Delta I$, it also follows that $MRP = MR \times MP$, which is what we set out to prove.

increases. Since the marginal revenue product is the product of the input's marginal product and the firm's marginal revenue, it will decrease for both reasons as more of the input is used. Second, the value-of-marginal-product schedule in the previous chapter can be regarded as a special case of the marginal-revenue-product schedule. If marginal revenue is equal to price (as it is in perfect competition), the marginal-revenue-product schedule becomes precisely the same as the value-of-marginal-product schedule.

The Firm's Demand Curve: The Case of Several Variable Inputs

Suppose that the firm uses a number of inputs that can be varied in quantity, with input x being only one of them. As in the case of perfect competition, the firm's demand curve for input x is no longer its marginal-revenue-product curve. This is because a change in the price of input x will result in changes in the quantities used of other variable inputs, and these changes in the quantities used of other inputs will affect the quantity used of input x.

For example, suppose that the price of input x is initially $5 and that 80 units of input x are used at this price. Holding constant the use of other inputs, the marginal-revenue-product curve is assumed to be M_1 in Figure 13.2. This would be the demand curve for input x if the other inputs were not variable. Suppose that the price of input x falls to $4. Since the marginal revenue product of input x exceeds its new price, the firm will tend to increase its use of input x. But this will shift the marginal-revenue-product curves of other variable inputs, which in turn will change the amount used of them, which in turn will shift the marginal-revenue-product curve of input x.

When all of these effects have taken place, the firm will be on another marginal-revenue-product curve for input x, say M_2 in Figure 13.2. Since the amount demanded of input x will be such that the marginal revenue product of input x will equal its new price, the firm will demand 120 units. Points U and V are both on the firm's demand curve for input x. Other points can be determined in similar fashion; the complete demand curve is D.

The Market Demand Curve and Input Price

The previous sections derived the demand curve of an individual firm for an input. The next step is to combine the demand curves of the individual firms in the market (for the input) into a single market demand curve for the input. This step can be accomplished in different ways, depending on whether the firms are all monopolists or whether some are oligopolists or monopolistic competitors. If all firms are monopolists in their product markets, the market demand curve for the input would simply be the horizontal summation of the demand curves of the individual firms.

On the other hand, if some of the firms are oligopolists or monopolistic competitors, one cannot simply sum (horizontally) the demand curves of the

Fig. 13.2 FIRM'S DEMAND CURVE FOR INPUT *x* / *Points* U *and* V *are on the firm's demand curve for input* x. *(*M₁ *and* M₂ *are marginal-revenue-product curves.)*

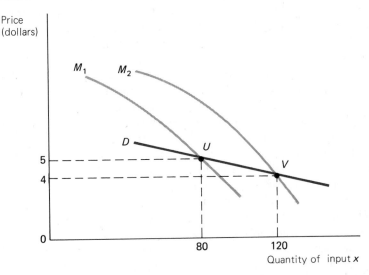

individual firms to derive the market demand curve. This will not work for the same reason that it would not work in the case of perfect competition (discussed in the previous chapter): A change in the price of the input will affect both the output of the individual firm and the outputs of its competitors. Because of the change in its competitors' outputs, the demand curve for its own product will change, and this in turn will change its demand curve for the input. In a case of this sort, the market demand curve for the input can be determined only by finding at each price the amount of the input that will maximize the profits of each firm in the market, and by summing these amounts over all firms in the market.

Given the market demand curve for the input, the equilibrium price of the input will be the price at which this demand curve intersects the input's market supply curve. Moreover, the total amount of the input that will be used in equilibrium in this market is also determined in the usual way by the intersection of this demand curve and this supply curve. The nature and determinants of an input's market supply curve, discussed in the previous chapter, need not be altered by the existence of imperfect competition in the product market.

MONOPSONY

Up to this point we have assumed that there is perfect competition in the input market. Now we change this assumption. We begin by considering the case of

Monopsony

monopsony. *Monopsony* is a situation in which there is a single buyer. For example, a group of small firms may be set up to provide tooling, supplies, or materials for a single large manufacturing firm, and because this large firm is the only one of its type in the area and its requirements are highly specialized, this large firm may be the only buyer for the product of the small firms. This is a case of monopsony.

Note the difference between monopsony and monopoly: Monopsony is a case of a single buyer; monopoly is a case of a single seller. Other market situations that could also be studied are oligopsony (where there are a few buyers) and monopsonistic competition (where there are many buyers but the inputs are not homogeneous and some buyers prefer some sellers' inputs to other sellers' inputs). However, it is sufficient for present purposes to limit our attention to monopsony.

Monopsony can occur for various reasons. In some cases, a particular type of input is much more productive in one kind of use than in others. For example, some land that is rich in iron ore may be much more profitably devoted to iron mining than to any other use. Or a person with certain specialized skills may be much more profitably employed using these skills than working at other jobs. If there is only one firm that rents such land or hires such labor, the result is a monopsonistic situation.

The classic case of monopsony is the company town in which a single firm is the sole buyer of labor services. Many "mill towns" and "mining towns" have been dominated by a single firm. As long as workers are unable or unwilling to move elsewhere to work, this firm is a monopsonist. If the mobility of labor can be increased, the monopsony can be broken, at least partially. However, the difficulties in increasing the mobility of labor should not be underestimated: Workers become emotionally attached to a particular area and to their friends and family located there; they often are ignorant of opportunities elsewhere; and they sometimes lack the money and skills that are required to move.

Input Supply Curves and Marginal Expenditure Curves

The supply curve of the input facing the monopsonist is the market supply curve: This is the key feature of monopsony. The reason why the monopsonist faces the market supply curve of the input is that the monopsonist is the entire market for the input: It is the sole buyer. Since the market supply curve of an input is generally upward sloping, as we saw in the previous chapter, this means that the supply curve for the input that the monopsonist faces is upward sloping. In other words, the monopsonist is forced to increase the price of the input if it wishes to use more of it, and it can reduce the input's price if it chooses to use less of it.

The contrast between this situation and the situation under perfect competition in the input market should be noted. In the case of perfect competi-

Table **Marginal Expenditure for Input** x
13.2

Quantity of x	Price of x (dollars)	Total cost of x (dollars)	Marginal expenditure for x* (dollars)
8	10.00	80.00	—
9	10.50	94.50	14.50
10	11.00	110.00	15.50
11	11.50	126.50	16.50
12	12.00	144.00	17.50
13	12.50	162.50	18.50
14	13.00	182.00	19.50

* Each figure pertains to the interval between the indicated amount of input x and one unit less than the indicated amount of input x.

tion in the input market, each firm buys only a very small proportion of the total supply of any input, the consequence being that each firm faces a perfectly elastic supply curve for the input. In other words, each firm can buy all it wants of an input without affecting the input's price.

The situation under monopsony is illustrated by the case in Table 13.2. Suppose that a firm is a monopsonist with respect to input x. Suppose that the market supply schedule for input x is that shown in columns 1 and 2. For example, 8 units of input x will be supplied if the price of input x is $10.00; 9 units of input x will be supplied if the price of input x is $10.50; and so forth. Column 3 shows the total cost to the firm of buying the quantities of input x in column 1. For example, the total cost of 8 units of input x is $80.00; and the total cost of 9 units of input x is $94.50. Of course, column 3 is simply the product of the figures in column 1 and column 2.

Column 4 shows the additional cost to the firm of increasing its utilization of input x by one unit. This is called the *marginal expenditure* for input x. For

Marginal expenditure for an input

example, the marginal expenditure for the ninth unit of input x is $14.50; and the marginal expenditure for the tenth unit of input x is $15.50. When the market supply curve for the input is upward sloping, the marginal expenditure for the input will be greater than the input price. The reason for this is simple. Suppose, for example, that the firm in Table 13.2 increases its use of input x from 8 units to 9 units. If it did not have to increase the price of input x in order to expand the supply of the input, it would have to pay only the price, $10, of another unit. But because the supply curve *is* upward sloping, the firm *will* have to increase the price of input x in order to increase the supply. *Moreover, this will mean paying all 9 units the higher price, not just paying more for the ninth unit.* Consequently, the marginal expenditure will exceed the input's price.

Fig.
13.3
SUPPLY CURVE AND MARGINAL EXPENDITURE CURVE FOR INPUT *x* / *The marginal expenditure curve,* EE′, *lies above the supply curve,* SS′. *The data come from Table 13.2.*

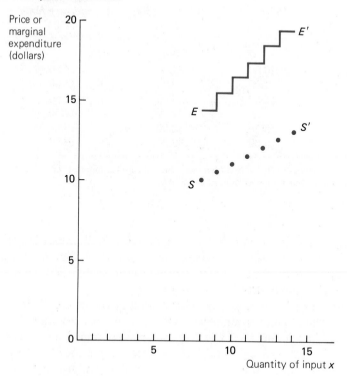

Figure 13.3 shows input *x*'s supply curve, *SS′*. If the input is bought by a single buyer, the monopsonist's marginal expenditure curve, which shows the marginal expenditure for the input at various quantities used of the input, is *EE′*. Since the supply curve is upward sloping, the marginal expenditure curve lies above it.

Price and Employment: A Single Variable Input

Suppose that there is only one variable input. If the monopsonist maximizes profit, it will purchase larger amounts of the input as long as the extra revenues derived from the additional quantity of input are at least as large as the extra cost of the additional quantity of input. When this is no longer the case, the monopsonist will no longer increase its employment of the input. Indeed, if the extra revenues derived from an additional quantity of input are less than the extra cost of the additional quantity of input, the monopsonist will cut back its employment of the input.

Table OPTIMAL EMPLOYMENT OF INPUT *x:* MONOPSONY
13.3

Quantity of input x used by monopsonist	Price of x (dollars)	Marginal revenue product of x* (dollars)	Marginal expenditure for input x* (dollars)
5	9	40	—
6	10	38	15
7	11	35	17
8	12	30	19
9	13	24	21
10	14	18	23
11	15	10	25
12	16	2	27

* These figures pertain to the interval between the indicated amount of input *x* and one unit less than the indicated amount of input *x*.

More specifically, consider the case in Table 13.3. Column 3 shows the marginal revenue product of the input, that is, the additional revenue derived from an additional unit of the input. For example, the addition of the sixth unit of the input results in $38 of additional revenue. Column 4 shows the marginal expenditure for the input, that is, the additional cost of an additional unit of the input. For example, the addition of the sixth unit of the input results in $15 of additional costs.

Clearly, the monopsonist, if it maximizes profit, will employ additional units of the input as long as the marginal revenue product of the input exceeds the marginal expenditure. When the marginal revenue product no longer exceeds the marginal expenditure, it will stop adding further units of the input. Thus, in Table 13.3, the monopsonist will employ 9 units of the input. Also, in Figure 13.4, if the marginal-revenue-product curve is DD' and the marginal expenditure curve is EE', the firm will hire OQ units of the input.

Note the difference between the condition for profit maximization under monopsony and the condition for profit maximization when there is perfect competition in the input market. Under perfect competition in the input markets, we saw in the previous chapter and in Equation 13.1a of this chapter that the firm must set

$$MP_x \cdot MR = P_x. \tag{13.2}$$

However, if the firm is a monopsonist, it must set

$$MP_x \cdot MR = ME_x \tag{13.3}$$

where ME_x is the marginal expenditure for input *x*.

The difference between Equation 13.2 and 13.3 lies in the quantities on the right-hand side: P_x in one case and ME_x in the other. Since ME_x is greater

Fig. 13.4 OPTIMAL EMPLOYMENT OF INPUT *x*: MONOPSONY / *The monopsonist sets a price of* OP *and hires* OQ *units of the input. Under perfect competition, the price would be* OP₁.

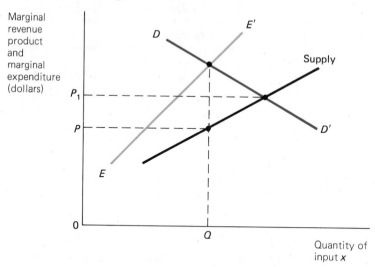

than P_x if the input's supply curve is upward sloping (see p. 383) and since the marginal·revenue product of input *x* (which equals $MP_x \cdot MR$) decreases as more of input *x* is used, it follows that less of input *x* is used if Equation 13.3 is met than if Equation 13.2 is met. Thus the monopsonist will employ less of the input than would be used if the input market were perfectly competitive.

The monopsonist sets the input's price at the level at which the quantity it demands—the quantity at which marginal revenue product equals marginal expenditure—will be supplied. Thus, in Table 13.3, it sets a price of $13. And in Figure 13.4 it sets a price of *OP*, if the supply curve for input *x* is as shown there. Note that the price set by the monopsonist is lower than would be set in a competitive market for the input. For example, in Figure 13.4, if *DD′* were the demand curve for the input in a competitive market, the equilibrium price of the input would be OP_1 rather than *OP*.

Price and Employment: Several Variable Inputs

The previous section dealt with the case where the monopsonist uses only one variable input. It is easy to generalize our results to the case in which it uses more than one variable input. For example, suppose that there are a number of variable inputs: input *x*, input *y* · · ·, input *z*. For each of these inputs, it will pay the monopsonist to increase its use of the input only as long as the extra revenue derived from the additional quantity of input is at least as large as the extra cost of the additional quantity of input. Thus the monopsonist will increase its use of each input as long as the marginal revenue product of the input exceeds its marginal expenditure for the input. The firm will stop increasing its use of each input when the input's marginal revenue product equals the marginal expenditure for the input.

Thus, since an input's marginal revenue product equals its marginal product times the firm's marginal revenue, it follows that the monopsonist will hire inputs so that

$$MP_x \cdot MR = ME_x \qquad\qquad\qquad [13.4a]$$

$$MP_y \cdot MR = ME_y \qquad\qquad\qquad [13.4b]$$

$$\vdots$$

$$MP_z \cdot MR = ME_z \qquad\qquad\qquad [13.4c]$$

where ME_x is the marginal expenditure for input x, ME_y is the marginal expenditure for input y, and ME_z is the marginal expenditure for input z.

These equations are the basic conditions for profit maximization under monopsony. Note that Equations 13.1a · · · 13.1c can be regarded as a special case of Equations 13.4a · · · 13.4c. If the markets for the inputs are perfectly competitive, the marginal expenditure for each input is simply equal to the price of each input, since a firm can buy all it wants of each input without affecting its price. Thus, Equations 13.1a · · · 13.1c are special cases of Equations 13.4a · · · 13.4c that hold under perfect competition in the input markets.

It is often stated that a monopsonist will hire inputs so that

$$\frac{MP_x}{ME_x} = \frac{MP_y}{ME_y} = \cdot \quad \cdot \quad \cdot = \frac{MP_z}{ME_z}. \qquad\qquad [13.5]$$

To see that Equation 13.5 follows from Equations 13.4a, 13.4b, · · ·, 13.4c, note that Equations 13.4a, 13.4b, · · ·, 13.4c imply

$$MP_x \div ME_x = \frac{1}{MR}$$

$$MP_y \div ME_y = \frac{1}{MR}$$

$$\vdots$$

$$MP_z \div ME_z = \frac{1}{MR}.$$

Thus Equations 13.4a, 13.4b, · · ·, 13.4c imply that Equation 13.5 is true. Note also that Equation 13.5 is equivalent to the standard condition for cost minimization under perfect competition,

$$\frac{MP_x}{P_x} = \frac{MP_y}{P_y} = \dots = \frac{MP_z}{P_z},$$

Example 13.1

EFFECTS OF MINIMUM-WAGE LAWS UNDER MONOPSONY

In Example 12.3, we examined the effects of a minimum wage when a labor market is perfectly competitive. Now let's test its effects when a labor market is monopsonistic. In the absence of a minimum wage, suppose that the supply curve for labor, the marginal-revenue-product curve for labor, and the marginal expenditure curve for labor are as shown below.

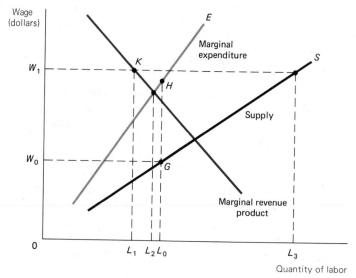

if there is perfect competition in the input markets. This follows from the fact, noted previously, that the marginal expenditure for an input equals its price under perfect competition.

Baseball: A Case Study

Before leaving the subject of monopsony, sports fans (and others) may be interested to note that the labor market in professional baseball has had many monopsonistic characteristics. There has been a tight set of rules governing contractual arrangements between players and teams. Until the mid-1970s, once a player signed his first contract, the club could renew his contract for the following year at a price that the club could set (as long as it was not less than about 75 percent of his current salary). Another stipulation was that the team had exclusive rights to the use of the player's services. He could not play baseball for anyone else without the team's consent.

Consequently, once a player had signed his first contract in organized

(a) If the minimum wage is set at OW_0, how much labor will the monopsonist hire? Will there be unemployment? If so, how much? (b) If the minimum wage is set at OW_1, how much labor will the monopsonist hire? Will there be unemployment? If so, how much? (c) Under monopsony, does a minimum wage reduce employment? (d) Do you think that most low-wage labor markets are monopsonistic?

SOLUTION

(a) If the minimum wage is set at OW_0, the effective supply curve of labor to the monopsonist is W_0GS. Thus the marginal expenditure curve is W_0GHE. The monopsonist will hire OL_0 units of labor, since this is the point where the marginal expenditure curve (W_0GHE) intersects the marginal-revenue-product curve. There is no unemployment perceived. (b) If the minimum wage is set at OW_1, the effective supply curve of labor to the monopsonist is W_1K. Since this effective supply curve is horizontal, it is also the marginal expenditure curve, which means that the monopsonist will hire OL_1 units of labor. Since OL_3 units of labor will be supplied at this wage, there will be ($OL_3 - OL_1$) units of labor trying to find jobs but not succeeding. (c) A minimum wage of OW_0 will increase, not decrease, employment. Without the minimum wage, employment would be OL_2; with it, employment is OL_0. However, if the minimum wage is high enough (OW_1, for example), it will reduce employment. A minimum wage of OW_1 would result in employment of OL_1, which is less than OL_2, the level of employment without a minimum wage. (d) No. One study of 1,774 labor markets found that the four largest employers employed at least half of the unskilled and semi-skilled workers in less than 4 percent of the labor markets.[*]

[*] See C. Brown, C. Gilroy, and A. Kohen, "The Effect of the Minimum Wage on Employment and Unemployment," *Journal of Economic Literature*, June 1982; and F. Welch, *Minimum Wages: Issues and Evidence* (Washington, D.C.: American Enterprise Institute, 1978).

baseball, he was no longer able to sell his services in any way he chose. He could not move freely from one team to another. He could, of course, drop out of organized baseball and take up some other occupation. But if he stayed in organized baseball, he had to do what the team with his contract said. If the team assigned his contract to another team, the player had to work for the assignee team. No other team in organized baseball could hire him.

Given these rules, one would expect, on the basis of the analysis in the previous four sections, that baseball players would receive less than they would if the labor market for baseball players were perfectly competitive. It may seem hard to believe that baseball stars making very large salaries were being exploited—in the sense that their salaries were less than they would have received in a free labor market. But leading labor economists like Simon Rottenberg of the University of Massachusetts reached this conclusion after careful study of the market for baseball players.

According to some observers, the situation could be represented (in simplified form) by Figure 13.5, which shows the club owners' demand curve for

Fig.
13.5 THE MARKET FOR BASEBALL PLAYERS: A SIMPLE MONOPSONY MODEL /
The club owners hire OU *players and pay a wage of* OX *thousands of dollars per year, which is below the competitive wage of* OY *thousands of dollars per year.*

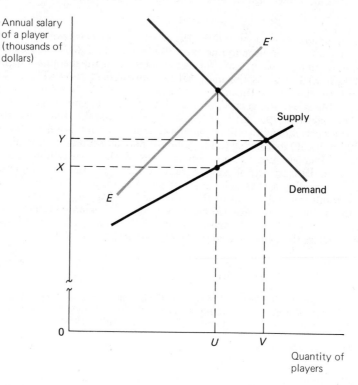

baseball players and the supply curve for baseball players. Assuming that the club owners did not compete among themselves for players, but acted as a monopsonist, they would hire players up to the point where the marginal expenditure curve (*EE'*) intersected the demand curve. That is, they would hire *OU* players and pay a wage of *OX* thousands of dollars per year. On the other hand, if the market for players was competitive, the club owners would hire *OV* players and pay a wage of *OY* thousands of dollars per year. In this highly simplified situation, it is clear that the wage was lower in the former case than in the latter.[3]

A number of reasons were given for the restrictive rules built into con-

---

3. The material in this section is based largely on S. Rottenberg, "The Baseball Players' Labor Market," *Journal of Political Economy*, June 1956; and D. North and R. Miller, *The Economics of Public Issues* (New York: Harper and Row, 1973). Note that Figure 13.5 is highly simplified. For one thing, it assumes that the players do not band together to try to counteract the monopsony power of the club owners. In fact, the players have formed an association and have carried out strikes on occasion. Thus there is a strong element of bilateral monopoly, discussed in Chapter 9. For further discussion, see R. Noll and B. Okner, *The Economics*

tracts for professional athletes. For example, it was frequently asserted that they were necessary to maintain a relatively equal distribution of playing talent among the various teams. Without these rules, it was claimed that the wealthier clubs would buy up most of the best players, with the result that games would be uneven and attendance would drop. This argument was challenged by many observers. According to Rottenberg and others, a free market for players would produce better results: "It appears that free markets would give as good aggregate results as any other kind of market for industries, like the baseball industry, in which all firms must be nearly equal if each is to prosper. On welfare criteria, . . . the free market is superior to the others, for in such a market each worker receives the full value of his services and exploitation does not occur."[4]

In the mid-1970s, after protracted legal battles, the rules governing the hiring of baseball players were changed. Players were allowed to declare themselves free agents, and other teams were allowed to bid for their services. These and other such changes (some of which were factors in the baseball strike of 1981) meant a reduction in the monopsonistic power of the baseball clubs.

LABOR UNIONS

One of the most important inputs is, of course, labor, and an important feature of the labor market is the existence of unions. About one in six nonfarm workers in the United States belongs to a union. The four largest unions are the Teamsters, the National Education Association, the Food and Commercial Workers, and the Auto Workers. Until the 1930s, there was strong opposition to unions, but since the passage of the Wagner Act in 1935, most manufacturing industries have become unionized. In the remainder of this chapter, we discuss briefly the ways in which unions can try to increase wages, the nature of union objectives, tactical considerations in collective bargaining, and the economic effects of unions.

For the moment, let us suppose that a union wants to increase the wage rate paid its members. How might it go about accomplishing this objective? First, the union might try to shift the supply curve of labor to the left. For example, it might shift the supply curve from S to S_0 in Figure 13.6, with the result that the price of labor will rise from OP to OP_0. To cause this shift in the supply curve, the union might restrict entry into the union, or it might not let

---

of Professional Baseball (Washington, D.C.: Brookings Institution, 1973); J. Quirk and M. El Hodiri, "Model of a Professional Sports League," *Journal of Political Economy,* December 1971; and G. Scully, "Pay and Performance in Major League Baseball," *American Economic Review,* December 1974. I am indebted to Edward D. Mansfield for sharing his extensive knowledge of this subject with me, and for doing his best to keep me from error.

4. S. Rottenberg, ibid.

Fig. 13.6 SHIFT IN SUPPLY CURVE FOR LABOR / *If the union shifts the supply curve from S to S_0, the price of labor will rise from OP to OP_0.*

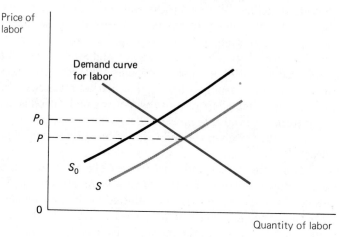

nonunion workers obtain jobs, or it might restrict the labor supply in other ways.

Second, the union might try to get the employers to pay a higher wage, while allowing some of the supply of labor forthcoming at this higher wage to find no opportunity for work. For example, in Figure 13.7, the union might

Fig. 13.7 INCREASE IN PRICE OF LABOR / *If the union gets employers to raise the price of labor from OP to OP_0, not all of the available supply of labor will find jobs. While the quantity of labor supplied will be OQ_1, the quantity demanded will be OQ_0.*

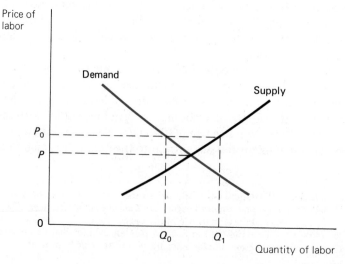

Fig.   SHIFT IN DEMAND CURVE FOR LABOR / *If the union can shift the demand*
13.8   *curve from* D *to* D$_1$, *the price of labor will increase from* OP *to* OP$_1$.

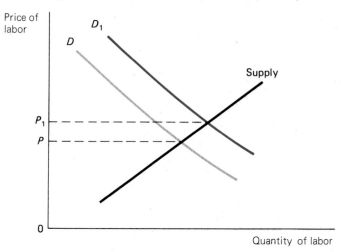

exert pressure on the employers to get them to raise the price of labor from OP
to OP_0. At OP_0, not all of the available supply of labor can find jobs, because
the quantity of labor supplied is OQ_1, while the amount of labor demanded is
OQ_0. The effect is the same as in Figure 13.6, but in this case the union does not
limit the supply directly: It lets the higher wage reduce the opportunity for
work.

Third, the union might try to shift the demand for labor upward and to
the right. For example, in Figure 13.8 it might shift the demand curve from D
to D_1, with the result that the price of labor will increase from OP to OP_1. To
cause this shift in the demand curve for labor, the union might help the employers advertise their products; it might help them to be more efficient and
better able to compete against other industries; or it might try to get Congress
to pass legislation to protect the employers from foreign competition. Also, it
might try to force employers to hire more workers than are needed for particular jobs.

Collective Bargaining and Bilateral Monopoly

In the previous section, we described various ways in which unions might
influence the price of labor. But this does not tell us what the price of labor will
be. Can we predict the equilibrium wage level in a unionized labor market? For
simplicity, suppose that the union is confronted by a single group representing
the employers. For example, the Steel Workers might be confronted by a single group representing the steel firms. To some extent, the union can be viewed
as a labor monopoly in a case of this sort, and the process of wage negotiation

Fig.
13.9

BILATERAL MONOPOLY IN THE LABOR MARKET / *The employers want to set a wage rate of* OX. *The union wants to set a wage rate of* OY.

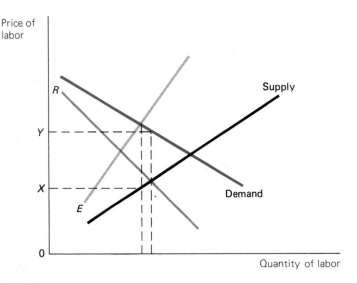

can be viewed as a case of bilateral monopoly, the union on the one side, management on the other.

Figure 13.9 shows the demand curve for labor and the union's supply curve for labor.[5] If R is the marginal revenue curve corresponding to this demand curve, and E is the curve showing the firms' marginal expenditure for labor, it will be recalled from Chapter 9 that, according to the theory of bilateral monopoly, the employers will want to set a wage rate of OX and the union will want to set a wage rate of OY. Since the wage that will result in such a situation is indeterminate, we cannot go any further toward predicting the wage level. The result depends on the relative bargaining power and negotiating skill of the two parties. For example, the industry may feel that it is not in a position to withstand a strike, while the workers may feel that they can easily weather a strike. The result also depends on public opinion and political action. For example, some government unions, like the letter carriers, have obtained wage increases through congressional influence, and some strikes result in government intervention to try to protect vital public services.

Note an important problem in applying the theory of bilateral monopoly to this situation: The theory assumes that the union wants to maximize the difference between the total wages that are paid to (employed) workers and the amount of money required to bring this amount of labor onto the market if each unit of labor were paid only the price necessary to induce it to work. It is

---

5. See footnote 5, Chapter 9, (p. 274).

by no means obvious that this is what unions are trying to do. Indeed, a number of other assumptions concerning the objectives of unions are equally plausible, as we shall see in the next section.

The Nature of Union Objectives

What are the objectives of unions? This is a difficult matter to settle, since unions, like firms, have diverse goals that are not easy to encapsulate and measure. Indeed, the problem is even more difficult for unions than for firms, because there is less agreement that any relatively simple objective like profits is a reasonable first approximation. Nevertheless, it is worthwhile discussing the implications of some simple hypotheses concerning union motivation that have been put forth. Three possible union objectives that are often considered are: (1) The union wants to keep its members fully employed; (2) the union wants to maximize the aggregate income of its members; and (3) the union wants to maximize the wage rate subject to the condition that a certain minimum number of its members be employed. All three hypotheses concerning union motivation have a certain amount of plausibility. It is easy to show, however, that they lead to quite different conclusions regarding union behavior.

Suppose that the demand curve for labor that faces the union is as shown in Figure 13.10. If the union has objective 1 and if it contains OM_1 members, it will have to accept a wage of OP_1, since this is the highest wage that will enable all of its members to find work.

But suppose that it has objective 2. Then it will choose OP_2, since this is the wage that maximizes the total wage bill of the union. To prove this, note that the wage bill is the union's total revenue from its product, labor; and that consequently the wage bill is maximized when the union's marginal revenue is zero. Using the techniques described in Chapter 5, one can derive the union's marginal revenue curve from the demand curve; the result is RR'. Since this marginal revenue curve intersects the horizontal axis at OM_2, the union's wage bill is maximized when OM_2 workers are employed, which means that the wage must be OP_2. Note that, if the union has objective 2, it must be prepared to see a great many of its members out of work.[6]

On the other hand, suppose that the union has objective 3. Specifically, suppose that it wants to maximize the wage rate subject to the condition that OM_3 of its members are employed, these members being perhaps those with considerable seniority. If this is its objective, it will choose a wage of OP_3, since this is the highest wage at which the employment level is at least OM_3.

It is clear that the wage desired by the union—and the supply of labor—will vary considerably, depending on which of these objectives is pursued.

---

6. And there is the difficult question of which members should be unemployed and which members should work.

Fig. 13.10 THREE TYPES OF UNION BEHAVIOR / *If the union wants to keep its members fully employed, it will have to accept a wage of* OP$_1$. *If it wants to maximize the aggregate income of its members, it will choose* OP$_2$.

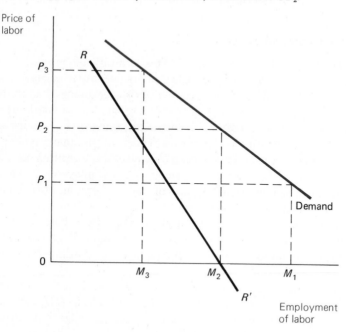

After all, OP_1, OP_2, and OP_3 are quite different wage levels, and OM_1, OM_2, and OM_3 are quite different labor supplies. Moreover, it is also perfectly clear that the three objectives stated above are only three possibilities out of a very large number. For example, the union leadership obviously has as one objective the maintenance of its own position in the union.[7]

TACTICAL CONSIDERATIONS IN COLLECTIVE BARGAINING

The wage demands made by unions depend on tactical considerations, as well as on the union's basic objectives. The initial asking figure put forth by the union is likely to be higher than the union's real expectations. The difference between the initial asking figure and the union's real expectation is governed by what the union regards as the best tactics. In most cases the union refrains from making the difference so large that the initial asking figure seems ridicu-

---

7. For an excellent discussion of this topic, see J. Dunlop, *Wage Determination Under Trade Unions,* Reprints of Economic Classics (New York: Augustus M. Kelley, 1966). This section is based largely on Dunlop's book.

Example 13.2

ECONOMIC EFFECTS OF UNIONS

Suppose that the economy can be divided into a unionized sector and a nonunion sector. The demand curve for labor in the union sector is D_u, the demand curve for labor in the nonunion sector is D_n, and the demand curve for labor in both sectors combined is D_c. The supply curve for labor in the economy as a whole is shown below.

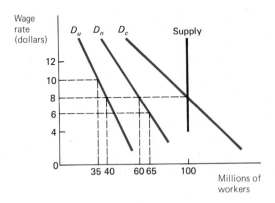

(a) Before the entry of the union, what will be the wage rate? (b) If the union raises the wage rate to $10 in the unionized sector, how many workers will the union sector lay off? (c) If all of these workers get jobs in the nonunion sector, what will be the effect on the wage rate in the nonunion sector? (d) Unions sometimes engage in featherbedding, which requires employers to hire more workers than they would otherwise. For example, railroads often have been required to hire more operating employees per train than they deemed necessary (or profitable). In the short run, such practices often increase the employment of union members. Does this effect persist in the long run as well?

SOLUTION

(a) $8, since this is where the combined curve, D_c, intersects the supply curve. (b) Its employment will fall from 40 million to 35 million, so 5 million will be laid off. (c) The wage rate in the nonunion sector will have to fall to $6 if an additional 5 million workers are to be hired there. (d) In the long run, the effect is unpredictable since the increase in the labor costs may accelerate types of substitution that the union cannot block. For example, new technologies utilizing fewer or other types of labor may be developed more quickly, or the product (made more expensive by featherbedding) may lose some of its markets to competing products or to imports.*

* For further discussion, see A. Rees, "The Effects of Unions on Resource Allocation," *Journal of Law and Economics,* October 1963; and his *The Economics of Work and Pay,* 2d ed. (New York: Harper & Row, 1979).

lously large. On the other hand, the union often considers it unwise to make the difference so small that there is little room for compromise.

The union's basic demand, the one for which it fundamentally is striving, is likely to be influenced considerably by what other unions are obtaining for their memberships. If other unions are getting increases of 60 cents an hour, the union may feel that it must do at least this well in order to show the membership that it can produce for them. Thus wage negotiations in a few major industries like automobiles and steel may set a pattern for other industries. Also, the union's basic wage demands will depend on the size of the industry's profits (its "ability to pay"), the mood and militancy of the membership, and the extent of the union's nonwage demands (work rules, pensions, union shop, etc.).

The employer tries, of course, to pay only what it must for what it regards to be the optimal number of employees. Like the union, it is influenced by tactical considerations in bargaining with the union concerning wages. For example, it may adopt a hard bargaining position when it thinks the union is in a relatively weak position, or an easy bargaining position when it wants to maintain a friendly group of union officials in office. It may adopt a hard bargaining position when it thinks that the union needs to be "put in its place," or an easy bargaining position when it wants to persuade the union to reduce its nonwage demands.

Given the basic objectives of the union and the employer in a particular case, the wage level that actually is negotiated is determined by the relative bargaining strength of the two parties and by their relative skill at negotiation. The strength of the employer depends on its ability to withstand a strike and to keep its head above water. The strength of the union depends on the extent of its membership, its ability to keep out nonunion workers and to enlist the support of other unions, and the size of its financial reserves.

EFFECTS OF UNIONS ON WAGES

Given the apparent importance of labor unions in the American economy, it may seem that we should be able to describe the effects of unions on wages with relative ease. Unfortunately, we are not able to do so. Although a considerable amount of research has been carried out, there is a great deal of uncertainty concerning the effects of unions. Of course, if unions provide labor with a relative bargaining advantage—or counterbalance monopsonistic pressures by employers—it would seem that the wage rate should be higher with unions than without them. But it is very difficult to isolate and measure this effect.

Empirical studies of the effect of unions on wages have generally been based on comparisons of wage increases in unionized industries with those in nonunion industries. Using such methods, H. G. Lewis concluded that unions increased wages by about 15 percent during the 1950s.[8] Similarly, Weiss found that "unions that organize entire jurisdictions seemed to raise earnings by 7 to 8 percent for craftsmen and 6 to 8 percent for operatives, compared with poorly organized industries."[9] More recent studies, by Richard Freeman, James Medoff, Albert Rees, and others,[10] come to broadly similar conclusions. However, the results vary considerably from industry to industry and from time period to time period. Moreover, comparisons of this sort are difficult to interpret because increases in union wages may prompt increases in nonunion wages, with the result that the difference in wage increases between union and nonunion fields underestimates the effect of unions on wages.

Besides influencing the general wage level, unions may influence the size of wage differentials among firms, jobs, and regions. With respect to wage differentials among firms or regions, it seems quite likely that unionization will reduce such differentials, particularly if industry-wide bargaining develops. However, if some firms or regions become unionized and others do not, differentials may increase. With respect to wage differentials among occupations, the available evidence seems to suggest that unions have tended to reduce wage differentials between high-paid and low-paid occupations. This is probably due in part to the tendency of unions to seek larger percentage increases for the least skilled workers.

SUMMARY

1. If there is imperfect competition in product markets but perfect competition in the market for an input, a firm will use an input in such a way that the marginal revenue product of the input equals the price of the input. Thus, if there is only one variable input, the firm's demand curve for the input is the same as the marginal-revenue-product curve. If there are several variable inputs, the firm's demand curve for an input is no longer the same as the marginal-revenue-product curve, since a change in the price of one input will result in changes in the quantity used of other inputs.

2. The market demand curve for an input can be derived by finding at each price the amount of the input that will maximize the profits of each firm

8. H. G. Lewis, *Unionism and Relative Wages in the United States* (Chicago: University of Chicago Press, 1963).

9. L. Weiss, "Concentration and Labor Earnings," *American Economic Review,* March 1966.

10. R. Freeman and J. Medoff, "The Two Faces of Unionism," *The Public Interest,* Fall 1979; A. Rees, *The Economics of Work and Pay,* New York: Harper & Row, 1973; and H. G. Lewis, "Union Relative Wage Effects: A Survey of Macro Estimates," *Journal of Labor Economics,* 1983.

in the market, and by summing these amounts over all firms in the market. The equilibrium price of the input is given by the intersection of the market demand and supply curves for the input.

3. Monopsony is a situation in which there is a single buyer. The supply curve of the input facing the monopsonist is the market supply curve. If the monopsonist maximizes profit, it sets the marginal expenditure for the input equal to the marginal revenue product of the input.

4. The monopsonist will employ less of the input than would be used if the input market were perfectly competitive. Also, the monopsonist will set a lower price for the input than if the input market were perfectly competitive. The market for baseball players has had some monopsonistic aspects.

5. An important feature of the market for labor is the existence of labor unions. To some extent, unions can be viewed as labor monopolies. However, it is difficult to know what the objectives of the union are. Under certain circumstances the union might want to keep its members fully employed. Under other circumstances, a union might want to maximize the aggregate income of its members. And these two objectives are only two possibilities out of a very large number.

6. The wage demands made by unions depend on tactical considerations, as well as the union's basic objectives. The initial asking figure put forth by the union is likely to be higher than the union's real expectations.

7. The wage that actually results from collective bargaining is indeterminate: It is likely to depend on the relative bargaining strength and negotiating skill of the two parties, as well as on public opinion and other factors.

8. If unions provide labor with a relative bargaining advantage—or counterbalance monopsonistic pressures by employers—it would seem that the wage rate should be higher with unions than without them. Empirical studies seem to indicate such an effect, but they are subject to many limitations.

QUESTIONS/PROBLEMS

1) Studies by John Landon and Robert Baird indicate that, when other factors are held equal, the level of teachers' salaries in a school district depends on the number of other school districts in the county containing the district in question. (a) If there are a relatively large number of other districts in the county containing a particular school district, would you expect the salary level of teachers in this district to be relatively high or relatively low? Why? (b) Suppose that teachers could move costlessly to school districts outside the county. Would this influence your answer to

question (a)? (c) In recent years, there has been a tendency for large metropolitan school districts to decentralize into a number of autonomous districts, each of which makes its own hiring and firing decisions. What effect, if any, do you think that such decentralization will have on teachers' salaries? (d) What are some of the arguments put forth by those who favor such decentralization?

2) An input is said to be "exploited" when it receives less than the value of its marginal product. Is labor exploited under (a) perfect competition, (b) unions, (c) monopsony?

3) Suppose that a firm's demand curve for its product is as follows:

Output	Price of good (dollars)
23	5.00
32	4.00
40	3.50
47	3.00
53	2.00

Also, suppose that the marginal product and total product of labor (the only variable input) is

Amount of labor	Marginal product of labor	Total output
2	10	23
3	9	32
4	8	40
5	7	47
6	6	53

(Note that the figures regarding marginal product pertain to the interval between the indicated amount of labor and one unit less than the indicated amount of labor.) Given these data, how much labor should the firm employ if labor costs $12 a unit?

4) According to Albert Rees, there is evidence that agreements sometimes exist "among employers not to raise wages individually or not to hire away each other's employees. ... Except in the unusual case of professional sports, however, these agreements must be very difficult to enforce." Using the concepts presented in this chapter, analyze the effects on wages and employment of such agreements. Also, indicate some of the reasons why they may be difficult to enforce.

5) Suppose that the market supply schedule for input Y is as follows:

Quantity of Y	Price of Y (dollars)
10	1
11	2
12	3

Plot the marginal expenditure curve for Y in the relevant range. (Assume that input Y must be used in integer amounts.)

6) If the market supply curve for an input is a horizontal line, will the marginal expenditure curve for this input differ from the market supply curve? Explain.

7) A craft union is formed, which forces employers to hire only union members. The union membership is restricted by high initiation fees and a variety of other devices. What are the effects on the demand curve, supply curve, and price of labor?

8) What would be the effect of a union on a monopsonistic labor market? Would it necessarily lead to unemployment?

9) According to Allan Carter and F. Ray Marshall, former President Carter's Secretary of Labor, the impact of unionism on wage levels of organized workers is most noticeable during periods of recession. Why?

10) Several hundred colleges and universities belong to the National Collegiate Athletic Association (NCAA), which investigates and enforces the rules pertaining to over twenty sports. The NCAA rules prohibit bidding for college athletes in an open manner, and the NCAA regulates the number of student athletes, as well as the prices, wages, and conditions under which colleges can hire them. Is the NCAA a monopsonist? Why or why not? Do colleges tend to cheat on the NCAA rules? If so, how?

SEX DISCRIMINATION AND COMPARABLE WORTH

In 1986, most adult American women (two-thirds of those between the ages of 25 and 54) worked outside the home. One reason why more women enter the labor force today than in the early twentieth century (when only about 20 percent of adult American women worked outside the home) is that household management requires less time than it did then. Technological advances have resulted in a variety of labor-saving devices in the home. In addition, the decline in the birth rate has provided women with more time for work, while the demand for women's services has increased as physical strength has become less important in many jobs and the service sectors of the economy have grown. Also, prevailing attitudes toward the proper role of women have changed.

Despite the tremendous growth in the participation of women in the labor force, women's earnings tend to be considerably lower than men's. Among workers between the ages of 20 and 24, the percentage gap in earnings averages about 15 percent; among workers between 45 and 54, it averages about 40 percent. (See Table 1.) This pay differential can be attributed to many factors. For example, as the Council of Economic Advisers pointed out in the 1987 Annual Report, the "average employed man has more work experience, fewer interruptions in that work experience, and longer tenure with his current employer than does his female counterpart of a comparable age."[1] Economet-

Table 1 EARNINGS OF FEMALES AS A PERCENTAGE OF EARNINGS OF MALES, 1979, 1982, AND 1985

| | *Age of workers (years)* | | | |
Year	*20–24*	*25–34*	*35–44*	*45–54*
1979	77	68	58	57
1982	82	72	61	60
1985	86	75	63	60

Source: *Economic Report of the President* (Washington, D.C.: U.S. Government Printing Office, 1987), p. 222.

1. *Economic Report of the President* (Washington, D.C.: U.S. Government Printing Office, 1987), p. 220.

ric evidence suggests that these factors explain some but not all of the earnings gap. It is not always clear which way the causality runs, either; to some extent, low earnings may encourage interrupted work lives, since the opportunity cost of leaving the work force is low.

Although Congress has passed laws, such as the Equal Pay Act of 1964, that prohibit discrimination against women, many observers believe that this pay differential is due partly to discrimination. If there were only one employer of a particular type of labor, it is easy to see how discrimination of this sort might occur. Even if men and women are equally productive, this monopsonist can increase its profits if it separates the labor supply into two groups —men and women—and if it pays different wages to each group. To see this, recall from Equation 13.4 that a monopsonist will maximize profit by setting each input's marginal revenue product equal to the marginal expenditure on the input. Suppose that, as shown in Figure 1, the supply curve for labor is less elastic for women than for men because women have fewer opportunities other than this type of work. Thus, the marginal expenditure curves are E_M for men and E_W for women. If the marginal revenue product of both men and women equals OX, the wage will be OP_M for men and OP_W for women. Clearly, men are paid more than women even though their marginal revenue product is the same.

But this model assumes that labor markets are monopsonies, which, as pointed out in Example 13.1, is seldom the case. If labor markets are competitive and if men and women are hired for the same jobs, there are limitations on the extent to which firms can discriminate. Suppose, for example, that male

Fig. 1   SEX DISCRIMINATION UNDER MONOPSONY / *The monopsonist pays women a lower wage (OP_W) than men (OP_M).*

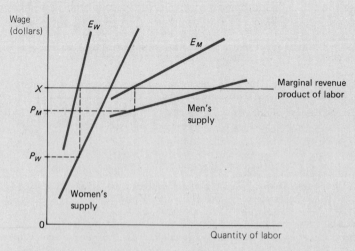

lawyers earn $50,000 and (equally talented and productive) female lawyers earn $40,000. Under these circumstances, an employer can make $10,000 (that is, $50,000 − $40,000) by hiring a female lawyer rather than a male. As more and more employers respond in this way to the profit motive, the wage of female lawyers will be bid up and the wage of male lawyers will decline until the wage differential between them tends to disappear.

However, it is important to recognize that discrimination of this sort can be due to the preferences of consumers, not employers. For example, the clients of some law firms may not trust female lawyers as much as males. Also, other employees of law firms (including male lawyers) may prefer not to work with female lawyers. If prejudice and discriminatory attitudes are sufficiently widespread, and if people are willing to absorb significant costs rather than change their attitudes, women will be paid less than men, even for equivalent performance.

A striking fact about female employment is that women tend to be found in a relatively small cluster of occupations. In 1986, women constituted 94 percent of registered nurses, 98 percent of secretaries, and 85 percent of waiters and waitresses in the United States. Some believe that these jobs are underpaid because they tend to be filled by women, and to eliminate what they regard as a major inequity, they argue for "equal pay for work of comparable worth." The idea is to compare the worth of one occupation with that of another occupation, and to press for equal wage rates for them if they are judged to be of equal worth. Thus, if a nurse does work that is of equal worth to that of a stevedore, nurses should get the same wage as stevedores.

How do the proponents of "comparable worth" propose to measure the worth of an occupation? A common answer is to use a job evaluation point system. In 1983, a federal court found the state of Washington guilty of discrimination because it paid male-dominated occupations more than "comparable" female-dominated occupations. To determine what occupations were comparable, every state job was evaluated in terms of "accountability," "knowledge and skills," "mental demands," and "working conditions." A committee decided how many points to give each occupation on each of these criteria, and two occupations were regarded of comparable worth if they got the same total number of points.

This decision, which said that Washington should raise women's wages and grant restitution for past injuries to them (cost to the state: $600 million), has caused an enormous amount of controversy. Many economists have criticized the idea that an occupation's wage rate should be determined in this way by "comparable worth." Nonetheless, in 1984, one of the presidential candidates declared his support for this concept. Other politicians have espoused it as well. Whether or not this concept should be employed more widely in the public and private sectors of the economy is a lively issue.

ANALYTICAL QUESTIONS

1) How can one determine how many points to give a particular occupation with regard to "mental demands"? Are the four criteria given above the only ones that could be used? How can one determine the proper weights to apply to various criteria? Is a point system of this sort largely arbitrary?

2) According to the point system described above, the value of each occupation can be determined from its characteristics alone. But the marginal revenue product of workers in a particular occupation decreases as more and more of them are hired. Can one legitimately determine the value of an occupation to society without specifying how many people are in this occupation?

3) Suppose that the doctrine of "comparable worth" is accepted by Boston's municipal government and that a study concludes that the value of a typist's job is comparable to that of an electrician, the result being that the wage of typists is raised from $6 to $9 an hour. Will this result in more and better applicants for the city's typing jobs?

4) If skilled typists not working for Boston's municipal government can displace the typists currently working there, is such a displacement likely to occur (under the conditions described in question 3)? Will the increase in the wage rate be of benefit to the typists currently working there in the short run? In the long run?

5) The doctrine of comparable worth has received more serious attention and has been put into effect more often in government agencies than in business firms. (A majority of state governments have studied the idea, and some have begun to apply it.) Why would such a scheme be more likely to encounter resistance among firms than government agencies?

6) Is adoption of the idea of "comparable worth" the only way that women can improve their access to high-paid jobs? If not, what are some other important ways? According to Chicago's Gary Becker, "Changes in the earnings and occupations of women in this country are much more closely related to changes in their productivity than to government action."[2] Do you agree?

---

2. *Business Week,* April 27, 1987, p. 18.

Welfare Economics, General Equilibrium, and Political Economy

Welfare Economics and
General Equilibrium Analysis

OPTIMAL RESOURCE USE

At the beginning of this book, we made the claim that microeconomics is of use in clarifying public-policy issues. Having made this claim, we hastened to add that microeconomics alone is seldom able to provide a clear-cut solution to such issues, but that, in combination with other relevant disciplines, it frequently can provide useful ways of structuring and analyzing these issues. The purpose of this chapter is to provide an introduction to welfare economics, the branch of microeconomics that is concerned with the nature of the policy recommendations that economists can make.

To prevent confusion, note that welfare economics is not concerned with the various government "welfare" programs you read about in the newspapers. Instead, welfare economics covers a much broader set of questions; its primary concern is with policy issues concerning the allocation of resources. In other words, it deals mainly with questions concerning the optimal allocation of inputs among industries and the optimal distribution of commodities among consumers.

At the beginning of this book we also said that microeconomics is concerned with the economic behavior of individual decision-making units like consumers, resource owners, and firms. At first glance one might interpret this statement to mean that microeconomics views the behavior of such individual units and the workings of individual markets in isolation, with each unit or market being considered separately. Such an interpretation would be quite wrong. Microeconomics is also concerned in an important way with how these units and these markets fit together. Indeed, some of the intellectually most exciting, and practically most significant, aspects of microeconomics deal with the interrelations among individual units and among various markets.

In previous chapters we looked in detail at the behavior of individual decision-making units and the workings of individual markets. Now we must show how economists have attempted to form an integrated model of the economy as a whole. This clearly is an important task: Every schoolchild knows that it is important not to get so engrossed in the trees that one loses sight of the forest.

PARTIAL EQUILIBRIUM ANALYSIS VERSUS GENERAL EQUILIBRIUM ANALYSIS

As stressed in the last section, our analysis in previous chapters has focused on a single market, viewed in isolation. According to the models we have used, the price and quantity in each such market are determined by supply and demand curves, and these supply and demand curves are drawn on the assumption that other prices are given. Each market is regarded as independent and self-contained for all practical purposes. In particular, it is assumed that changes in price in this market do not have significant repercussions on the prices existing in other markets.

But this assumption in reality may be seriously wrong. No market can adjust to a change in conditions without there being a change in other markets, and in some cases the change in other markets may be substantial. For example, suppose that a shift to the left occurs in the demand for pork. In previous chapters, it was assumed that when the price and output of pork changed in response to this change in conditions, the prices of other products would remain fixed. However, the market for pork is not sealed off from the markets for lamb, beef, and other meats.[1] (For that matter, it is not completely sealed off from the markets for other food products or from the markets for other less similar products, like washing machines and autos.) Thus the market for pork cannot adjust without disturbing the equilibrium of other markets *and without having these disturbances feed back on itself.*

---

1. Quantitative evidence on this point was presented in Table 5.4, where the cross elasticity of demand for beef with respect to the price of pork was given.

An analysis that assumes that changes in price can occur without causing significant changes in price in other markets is called a *partial equilibrium analysis*. This is the kind of analysis we carried out in previous

Partial equilibrium analysis

chapters. An analysis that takes account of the interrelationships among prices is called a *general equilibrium analysis*. Both kinds of analysis are very useful, each being valuable in its own way. Partial equilibrium analysis is perfectly adequate in cases in which the effect of a change in market conditions in one market has *little* repercussion on prices in other markets. For example, in studying the effects of a

General equilibrium analysis

proposed excise tax on the production of a certain commodity, the assumption that prices of other commodities are fixed may be a good approximation to the truth. However, if the effects of a change in market conditions in one market result in *important* repercussions on other prices, a general equilibrium analysis may be required.

INPUT-OUTPUT ANALYSIS

Léon Walras,[2] a nineteenth-century French economist, was the first to construct a model of the general equilibrium of a perfectly competitive economy. His model has been modified in subsequent years but the general formulation remains much the same. Vilfredo Pareto[3] was another great nineteenth-century figure in the development of this field. In the period since these men did their pioneering work, many improvements and extensions have been made in general equilibrium analysis, some of which have been cited in previous sections. In more recent years, a dominant figure in general equilibrium analysis has been Wassily Leontief,[4] a Nobel laureate and the father of input-output analysis.

Input-output analysis puts general equilibrium analysis in a form that is operationally useful to governments and firms faced with a variety of important practical problems. An important feature of input-output analysis is its emphasis on the interdependence of the economy. Each industry uses the outputs of other industries as its inputs, and its own output may be used as an input by the same industries whose output it uses. Recognizing this interdependence, input-output analysis attempts to determine the amount that each industry must produce in order that a specified amount of various final goods can be consumed. It has been applied to help predict production requirements

2. L. Walras, *Elements of Pure Economics,* translated by W. Jaffé (London: Allen & Unwin, 1954). It originally appeared in French in 1874.

3. V. Pareto, *Cours d'Economie Politique* (F. Rouge, 1897).

4. W. Leontief, *The Structure of the American Economy* (New York: Oxford University Press, 1951).

to meet estimated demands; for example, it has been applied by economic planners to estimate capacity requirements in various industries.

To put general equilibrium analysis in a form that is operationally useful, input-output analysis makes a number of simplifying assumptions. To begin with, it uses as variables the *total* quantity of a particular good demanded or supplied, rather than the quantity demanded by a particular consumer or the quantity supplied by a particular firm. This reduces enormously the number of variables and the number of equations that are included. Also, it is assumed that consumer demand for all commodities is given. This assumption, together with the assumption (discussed in the following paragraph) that inputs are used in fixed proportions, means that demand theory does not play an impor-

---

Example 14.1

THE DEREGULATION OF RAILROADS AND TRUCKS

During the 1980s, steps were taken toward the deregulation of both the railroad and trucking industries. In 1981, Ann Friedlander and Richard Spady of Massachusetts Institute of Technology published a study attempting to forecast the effects of the deregulation of both industries. Before deregulation, they found that the demand curve for rail services for bulk commodities in the South and West was as shown below.

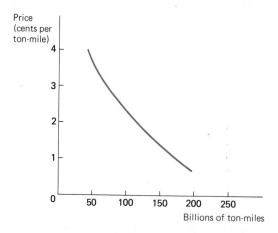

(a) If deregulation would result in a cut in the price of rail service from 2 cents to 1 cent per ton-mile, what would be the effect on the number of ton-miles carried by the railroads in the South and West, based on the above graph? (b) Can the market for rail service adjust to deregulation without disturbing the equilibrium in the market for trucking service? (c) Will the disturbances in the market for trucking service

tant part in input-output analysis.[5] Input-output analysis attempts to find out what can be produced, and the amount of each input and intermediate good that must be employed to produce a given output. The question is viewed as being largely a matter of technology.

Finally, it is assumed that inputs are used in fixed proportions in producing any product and that there are constant returns to scale. This is a key as-

---

5. Strictly speaking, this is true only in Leontief's open model, which is all that is described here. In his closed model, at least some attention must be given to the determinants of demand. See W. Leontief, *Input-Output Economics* (New York: Oxford University Press, 1966); and H. Chenery and P. Clark, *Interindustry Economics* (New York: Wiley, 1959).

(due to railroad deregulation of this sort) have an impact on the market for rail services? (d) In trying to estimate the effects on each industry of the simultaneous deregulation of them both, what are the advantages of general equilibrium analysis over partial equilibrium analysis? (e) Friedlander and Spady estimate that, when all the reverberations of deregulation from one market to the other (and vice versa) have worked themselves out, the price of some (but by no means all) types of rail service are likely to rise. Does this mean that deregulation would not be a success?

SOLUTION

(a) The number of ton-miles carried by the railroads would increase from about 120 billion to about 180 billion. (b) No. The lower price of railroad services will push the demand curve for trucking services to the left since railroad and trucking services are substitutes. Consequently, the price of trucking services is likely to fall. (c) Yes. The fall in the price of trucking services described in the answer to part (b) is likely to shift the demand curve for railroad services to the left, thus causing a change in the price and quantity of rail service. (d) Since the demand for rail service depends on the price of truck service, a change in the price of truck service due to deregulation will have an effect on the demand curve for rail service. Similarly, the demand for truck service depends on the price of rail service. Further, each industry's costs depend on the way in which traffic is divided between them. When both the prices of rail service and of truck service change due to deregulation, it is very hazardous to carry out a partial equilibrium analysis of either the market for rail service or the market for truck service, since such an analysis disregards many of the interdependencies between the two markets. In fact, Friedlander and Spady carried out a general equilibrium analysis. (e) No. In these cases, the price before deregulation was below marginal cost, which means that railroads were losing money on these services. The test of the success of deregulation is whether economic efficiency and equity are promoted, not the direction in which particular prices move.*

---

* See A. Friedlander and R. Spady, *Freight Transport Regulation* (Cambridge, Mass.: MIT Press, 1981).

sumption of Leontief's input-output system. For example, in the production of steel, Leontief would assume that, for every ton of steel produced, a certain amount of iron ore, a certain amount of coke, a certain amount of fuel, and so on would be required. The amount of each input required per unit of output is assumed to be the same, regardless of the level of output. For example, if a certain amount of iron ore is required to produce 1 million tons of steel, it is assumed that 10 times that amount is required to produce 10 million tons of steel.[6]

A Simple Input-Output Model

Anyone with a rudimentary understanding of the solution of simultaneous linear equations can quickly grasp the essentials of input-output analysis. For example, suppose that the economy consists of only three industries: coal, chemicals, and electric power. Suppose that each industry uses the products of the other industries in the proportions shown in Table 14.1. For instance, the second column of Table 14.1 states that every dollar's worth of coal requires 20 cents worth of electric power, 10 cents worth of coal, and 70 cents worth of labor.[7]

Suppose that this economy has set consumption targets of $100 million of electric power, $30 million of coal, and $40 million of chemicals. Input-output analysis is concerned with the question: How much will have to be produced by each industry in order to meet these targets? To begin to solve this problem, consider the case of coal. If electric power output is E, chemical output is C, and coal output is X (E, C, and X are measured in millions of dollars), it follows from Table 14.1 that

$$X = .4E + .1X + .2C + 30 \qquad [14.1]$$

if the target is met. Why? Because an amount of coal equal in value to $.4E$ must be produced to meet the needs of the electric power industry, an amount of coal equal in value to $.1X$ must be produced to meet the needs of the coal industry, an amount of coal equal in value to $.2C$ must be produced to meet the needs of the chemical industry, and an amount of coal equal in value to 30 must be produced for consumption. Thus the total output of coal must be equal to the sum of these four terms, as shown in Equation 14.1.

---

6. In Chapter 6, we said that the proportion in which inputs are combined can generally be altered. This, of course, is a direct contradiction of the assumption of fixed proportions in input-output analysis. But it often takes a fair amount of time for changes to be made and they are often gradual, with the result that Leontief's assumption of fixed proportions may work reasonably well in the short run despite this fact.

7. In some cases, outputs and inputs are measured in physical units rather than dollars. For example, coal output and coal input might be measured in tons per year, and labor input might be measured in hours per year. Clearly, one can carry out the analysis in either way.

If we construct similar equations for electric power output and chemical output, we find that

$$E = .2E + .2X + .2C + 100 \qquad [14.2]$$

$$C = .2E + .1C + 40 \qquad [14.3]$$

if the targets are to be met. For example, Equation 14.3 must hold because chemical output must equal the amount needed by the electric power industry $(.2E)$ plus the amount needed by the chemical industry itself $(.1C)$ plus 40 for consumption.

Equations 14.1 to 14.3 are three simultaneous linear equations in three variables, X, E, and C. It is a simple matter to solve for these unknowns; the solution is $X = 131$, $E = 178$, and $C = 84$. This provides the answer to our question: \$131 million of coal, \$178 million of electric power, and \$84 million of chemicals must be produced if the consumption targets are to be met. Also, we can find out how much labor will be required to meet these targets, since (according to Table 14.1) the total value of labor required equals

$$.2E + .7X + .5C.$$

Substituting the 131, 178, and 84 for X, E, and C, respectively, we find that \$169 million of labor are required. If this is within the available labor supply, the solution is feasible; otherwise the targets must be scaled downward.

This simple example illustrates the fundamentals of input-output analysis. It also suggests why the assumption that inputs are used in fixed proportions is so convenient. Without this assumption, the input-output table in Table 14.1 would not hold for each output level of the industries; instead the numbers in the table would vary depending on how much of each commodity was produced. The added complexity that would arise if this assumption were relaxed is obvious. Even with this assumption, the computational difficulties and problems of estimation involved in obtaining solutions to large input-output models can be substantial. Although a model involving 450 industries has been constructed for the United States, usually far fewer industries are included in such models.

Table 14.1   AMOUNT OF EACH INPUT USED PER DOLLAR OF OUTPUT

	Type of output		
Type of input	Electric power (dollars)	Coal (dollars)	Chemicals (dollars)
Electric power	0.2	0.2	0.2
Coal	0.4	0.1	0.2
Chemicals	0.2	0.0	0.1
Labor	0.2	0.7	0.5
Total	1.0	1.0	1.0

RESOURCE ALLOCATION AND THE EDGEWORTH BOX DIAGRAM

We now turn our attention to a somewhat different, but related, topic. In previous chapters, we have stated repeatedly that microeconomics is concerned with the way in which resources should be allocated. Once we consider more than a single market, it becomes possible to consider many interesting questions concerning the optimal allocation of resources. The rest of this chapter is devoted to a discussion of some of these questions.

In the simple models that we shall take up, the Edgeworth box diagram finds extensive use. The Edgeworth box diagram shows the interaction between two economic activities when the total amount of commodities consumed or inputs used by these activities is fixed in quantity. To see how the Edgeworth box diagram is constructed, and how it should be interpreted, see Figure 14.1. We assume that there are two goods, food and medicine, and two consumers, Tom and Harry. The total amount of food that they have is OF and the total amount of medicine that they have is OM.

The amount of food that Tom has is measured horizontally from the origin at O. The amount of medicine that Tom has is measured vertically from O. Thus any point in the box diagram indicates a certain amount of food and a certain amount of medicine consumed by Tom. For example, the point, P, in-

Fig. 14.1   Edgeworth Box Diagram / *Point* P *indicates that Tom consumes* OR *of food and* OS *of medicine, while Harry consumes* (OF − OR) *of food and* (OM − OS) *of medicine.*

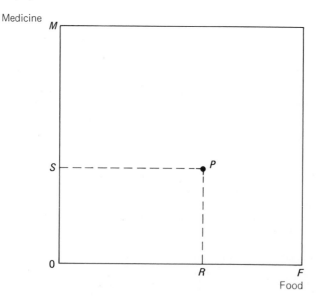

dicates that Tom consumes OR of food and OS of medicine. The amount of food that Harry consumes is measured by the horizontal distance to the left of the upper right-hand corner of the box diagram. And the amount of medicine that Harry consumes is measured by the vertical distance downward from the upper right-hand corner of the box diagram. Thus every point in the diagram indicates an amount of food and medicine consumed by Harry. For example, the point P indicates that Harry consumes $(OF - OR)$ of food and $(OM - OS)$ of medicine.

The important points to remember about the Edgeworth box diagram are that its length and width represent the total amounts of the two commodities that both consumers together have, and that each point in the box represents an allocation of the total supplies of the two goods between the two consumers.

The Edgeworth box diagram can be used for production problems, as well as consumption problems. For example, suppose that there are two industries, industry A and industry B, and that there are two inputs, labor and capital. Suppose that the total amount of labor available to the two industries is OL and the total amount of capital available to the two industries is OK. Figure 14.2 shows the relevant Edgeworth box diagram, the height of which equals the total amount of labor, OL, and the width of which equals the total amount of capital, OK.

Any point in the box represents an allocation of this total supply of labor

Fig. 14.2   EDGEWORTH BOX DIAGRAM: PRODUCTION / *Point* Q *indicates that industry A has* OU *of labor and* OV *of capital, while industry* B *receives* (OL − OU) *of labor and (OK − OV) of capital.*

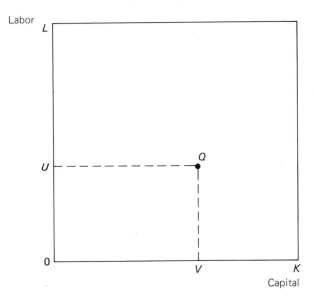

and total supply of capital between the two industries. The amount of labor allocated to industry A is represented by the vertical distance upward from the origin, and the amount of capital allocated to industry A is represented by the horizontal distance to the right of the origin. For example, point Q indicates that industry A has OU of labor and OV of capital. The amount of labor allocated to industry B is represented by the distance downward from the upper right-hand corner of the box diagram, and the amount of capital allocated to industry B is represented by the distance leftward from the upper right-hand corner of the box diagram. Thus point Q indicates that industry B receives $(OL - OU)$ of labor and $(OK - OV)$ of capital.

EXCHANGE

Let's return now from production to consumption, and discuss the process of exchange. To begin with, consider an economy of the simplest sort. There are only two consumers, Tom and Harry, and only two commodities, food and medicine. There is no production; the only economic problem is the allocation of a given amount of food and medicine between the two consumers. If it helps, you may regard Tom and Harry as two shipwrecked sailors marooned on a desert island with a certain amount of food and medicine that they rescued from their ship.

The amount of food and medicine brought by Tom to the island is indicated in the Edgeworth box diagram in Figure 14.3: He arrives with OH units of food and OI units of medicine. The amount of food and medicine brought by Harry to the island is also indicated in Figure 14.3: He arrives with $(OF - OH)$ units of food and $(OM - OI)$ units of medicine. The total amount of food brought to the island by both men is OF, and the total amount of medicine brought to the island by both men is OM.

If the two men are free to trade with one another, what sort of trading will take place? What can be said about the optimal allocation of the commodities between the two men? To find out, we must insert the indifference curves of Tom and Harry into the Edgeworth box diagram in Figure 14.3. Three of Tom's indifference curves are T_1, T_2, and T_3. The highest indifference curve is T_3; the lowest is T_1. Three of Harry's indifference curves are H_1, H_2, and H_3. The highest indifference curve is H_3; the lowest is H_1. In general, Tom's satisfaction is increased as we move from points close to the origin to points close to the upper right-hand corner of the box. Conversely, Harry's satisfaction is increased as we move from points close to the upper right-hand corner of the box to points close to the origin.

Given the initial allocation of food and medicine, we find that Tom is on indifference curve T_2 and Harry is on indifference curve H_1. At this point, Tom's marginal rate of substitution of food for medicine is much higher than Harry's, as shown by a comparison of the slope of T_2 with the slope of H_1 at

Fig.   EXCHANGE / *Points* P_0, P_1, *and* P_2 *are on the contract curve, which*
14.3   *includes all points where the marginal rates of substitution are the same
          for both consumers.*

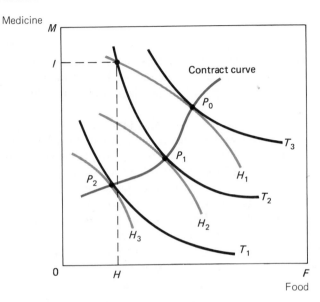

this point. Thus, if both men are free to trade, Tom will trade some medicine to
Harry in exchange for some food. The exact point to which they will move
cannot be predicted, however. If Tom is the more astute bargainer, he may get
Harry to accept the allocation at point P_0, where Harry is no better off than
before (since he is still on indifference curve H_1) but Tom is better off (since he
has moved to indifference curve T_3). On the other hand, if Harry is the better
negotiator, he may be able to get Tom to accept the allocation at point P_1,
where Tom is no better off than before (since he is still on indifference curve
T_2) but Harry is better off (since he has moved to indifference curve H_2). The
ultimate point of equilibrium is very likely to be between P_0 and P_1.

One thing is certain. If the object is to make the men as well off as possible, the optimal allocation of the commodities is one in which the marginal
rate of substitution of food for medicine will be the same for both men. Otherwise one man can be made better off without making the other worse off. In
other words, the optimal allocation is a point at which Tom's indifference
curve is tangent to Harry's. The locus of points at which such a
Contract curve: tangency occurs is called the *contract curve*. This curve, shown in
exhange   Figure 14.3, includes all points, like P_0, P_1, and P_2, where the
                          marginal rates of substitution are equal for both consumers. The
contract curve is an optimal set of points in the sense that, if the consumers
are at a point *off* the contract curve, it is always preferable for them to move to

a point *on* the contract curve, since one or both can gain from the move while neither incurs a loss.

PRODUCTION

In the previous section we discussed the case in which consumers exchange quantities of commodities, when there is no production. In this section and the next, we take up a simple case in which there is production but no consumption.

Consider a simple economy in which only two goods are being produced, the production sector of the economy being composed of a food industry and a medicine industry. Suppose that there are two inputs, labor and capital, and that the total amount of labor to be allocated between the two industries is OL and the total amount of capital to be allocated between the two industries is OK. Suppose that the initial allocation of labor and capital is that represented by point Z in the Edgeworth box diagram in Figure 14.4. That is, the food industry has OA units of labor and OB units of capital, and the medicine industry has $(OL - OA)$ units of labor and $(OK - OB)$ units of capital.

On the basis of the production functions for food and medicine one can insert isoquants for both food production and medicine production in Figure 14.4. Three isoquants for food production are F_1, F_2, and F_3. The isoquant per-

Fig.   PRODUCTION / *Points U and V are on the contract curve, which includes*
14.4   *all points where the marginal rates of technical substitution between the*
       inputs are the same for both industries.

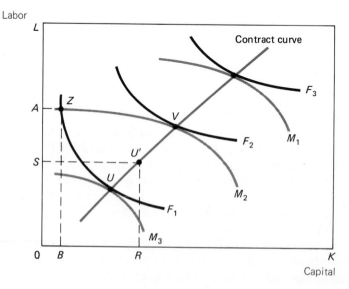

Example 14.2

THE ALLOCATION OF FISSIONABLE MATERIAL

During the early 1950s, a key U.S. defense problem was how to allocate fissionable material between our tactical and strategic forces. There were a fixed total number of aircraft (OA) and a fixed supply of fissionable materials (OM) in the short run. Every point in the Edgeworth box diagram shown below indicates an allocation of fissionable material and airplanes to the tactical and strategic forces. For example, point P represents a case where our strategic forces get OU units of aircraft and OV units of fissionable material, and our tactical forces get ($OA - OU$) units of aircraft and ($OM - OV$) units of fissionable material. Within limits, it was possible to substitute airplanes for fissionable material and vice versa. For example, fewer aircraft would be required to destroy a certain number of targets if atomic weapons, rather than conventional weapons, were used. Curve T_1 contains combinations of aircraft and fissionable material that result in equal effectiveness of the tactical forces. Curve T_0 also contains combinations that result in equal effectiveness of the tactical forces—but at a lower level than curve T_1. Curve S_2 contains combinations of aircraft and fissionable material that result in equal effectiveness of the strategic forces. Curve S_3 also contains combinations that result in equal effectiveness of the strategic forces—but at a higher level than curve S_2. The allocation at that time was represented by point W. Was this an optimal choice?

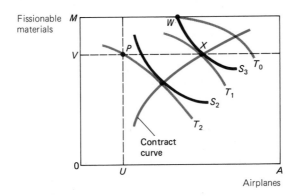

SOLUTION

No, because point W is not on the contract curve. The Defense Department could increase the effectiveness of either the tactical or strategic forces without reducing the effectiveness of the other by moving to a point on the contract curve. For example, point X results in the same effectiveness of our strategic forces as point W, since both points are on curve S_3. But point X results in more effectiveness of our tactical forces than point W. In fact, this simple kind of economic analysis was used to help solve this important policy problem.*

* For further discussion, see S. Enke, "Using Costs to Select Weapons," *American Economic Review*, May 1965; and "Some Economic Aspects of Fissionable Materials," *Quarterly Journal of Economics*, May 1964.

taining to the highest output level is F_3; the isoquant pertaining to the lowest output is F_1. Three isoquants for medicine production are M_1, M_2, and M_3. The isoquant pertaining to the highest output level is M_3; the isoquant pertaining to the lowest output level is M_1.

What will be the optimal allocation of inputs between the two industries? At the original allocation at point Z, the marginal rate of technical substitution of capital for labor in producing food is higher than in producing medicine. This is indicated by the fact that the slope of F_1 is steeper than the slope of M_2 at point Z. The fact that the marginal rates of technical substitution are unequal means that the inputs are not being allocated efficiently. For example, suppose that at point Z the food industry can substitute 2 units of labor for 1 unit of capital without changing its output level, while the medicine industry must substitute 1 unit of labor for 2 units of capital to maintain its output level. In this case if the medicine industry uses more labor and less capital and if the food industry uses less labor and more capital, it will be possible for one industry to expand its output without any reduction in the other industry's output. Specifically, it is possible to move to point U, where the output of food is the same as at Z but the output of medicine is at the level corresponding to M_3. It is also possible to move to point V, where the output of medicine is the same as at Z but the output of food is at the level corresponding to F_2. Or it is possible to move to a point between U and V.

Regardless of which point is chosen, production should occur at a point at which the marginal rate of technical substitution between inputs is the same for all producers, if the allocation of inputs is to be efficient in the sense that an increase in the output of one commodity can be achieved only by reducing the output of the other commodity. Thus the optimal allocation of inputs will lie somewhere along the locus of points where the marginal rates of technical substitution are equal—and consequently where a food isoquant is tangent to a medicine isoquant. This locus of points, like the analogous set in the previous section, is called the *contract curve,* and is shown in Figure 14.4.

Contract curve: production   This curve is an optimal set of points in the sense that, if producers are at a point *off* the contract curve and if society is interested in producing as much as possible of each good, it is always socially desirable for them to move to a point *on* the contract curve, since output in one industry or the other can be increased without a reduction in the other's output.

Note that this analysis of production is entirely analogous to the analysis of exchange in the previous section. The total amounts of the two inputs determine the dimensions of the Edgeworth box in this section; the analogous quantities in the previous section are the total amounts of the two commodities. The isoquant maps play an analogous role to the indifference maps in the previous section.

NECESSARY CONDITIONS FOR OPTIMAL RESOURCE ALLOCATION

In the previous three sections, we took up a case where there were only two consumers and two goods. Now let's consider the more realistic case where there are more than two consumers and more than two goods. Fundamentally, there are three necessary conditions for optimal resource allocation. The first pertains to the optimal allocation of commodities among consumers. It states that *the marginal rate of substitution between any two commodities must be the same for any two consumers*. The proof that this condition is necessary to maximize consumer satisfaction is quite simple. All that needs to be noted is that, if the marginal rates of substitution were unequal, both consumers could benefit by trading. For example, suppose that the first consumer regards an additional unit of product A as having the same utility as 2 extra units of product B, whereas the second consumer regards an additional unit of product A as having the same utility as 3 extra units of product B. Then, if the first consumer trades 1 unit of product A for 2.5 units of product B from the second consumer, both consumers are better off.

This condition implies that commodities should be distributed in such a way that consumers are on their contract curve, since the contract curve is composed of points where the marginal rates of substitution are equal for the consumers. In the case of only two commodities and two consumers, we showed in the section before last that this condition must be met if consumer satisfaction is to be maximized. We are now stating the more general proposition that this condition must also be met in the more realistic case in which there are more than two commodities and two consumers.

The second condition pertains to the optimal allocation of inputs among producers. It states that *the marginal rate of technical substitution between any two inputs must be the same for any pair of producers*. If this condition does not hold, it is possible to increase total production merely by reallocating inputs among producers. For example, suppose that, for the first producer, the marginal product of input 1 is twice that of input 2, whereas for the second producer the marginal product of input 1 is 3 times that of input 2. Then, if the first producer gives 1 unit of input 1 to the second producer in exchange for 2.5 units of input 2, both firms can expand their output.

To see this, suppose that the marginal product of input 1 is M_1 for the first producer and M_2 for the second producer. Then the output of the first producer is reduced by M_1 units because of its loss of the unit of input 1, but it is increased by $2.5 \times M_1/2$ units because of its gain of the 2.5 units of input 2, with the consequence that, on balance, its output increases by $M_1/4$ units because of the trade. Similarly, the output of the second producer is increased by M_2 units because of its gain of the 1 unit of input 1, but it is decreased by

$2.5 \times M_2/3$ units because of its loss of the 2.5 units of input 2, with the consequence that, on balance, its output increases by $M_2/6$ units because of the trade.

This condition implies that inputs should be allocated so that producers are on their contract curve, since the contract curve is made up of points at which the marginal rates of technical substitution are equal for producers. In the case of only two inputs and two producers, we showed in the previous section that this condition must be met if the output of each producer is maximized, holding constant the output of the other producer. We are now stating the more general proposition that this condition must also be met in the more realistic case in which there are more than two inputs and two producers.

The third condition pertains to both the optimal allocation of inputs among industries and the optimal allocation of commodities among consumers. It states that *the marginal rate of substitution between any two commodities must be the same as the marginal rate of product transformation between these two commodities for any producer.* The product transformation

Product transformation curve

curve shows the maximum amount of one good that can be produced, given various output levels of another good. For example, PP' in Figure 14.5 is a product transformation curve showing the maximum amount of good X that can be produced, given various output levels for good Y. The marginal rate of product transformation is the negative of the slope of the product transformation curve; it

Fig. 14.5   PRODUCT TRANSFORMATION CURVE AND INDIFFERENCE CURVES / *To maximize consumer satisfaction, production must take place at point* T.

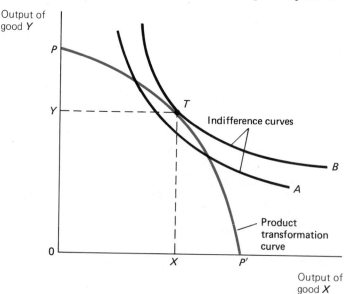

shows the number of units of good Y that society must give up in order to get an additional unit of good X.

Suppose that curves A and B in Figure 14.5 represent the indifference curves of a consumer who, for simplicity, is assumed to be the only consumer in the economy. To maximize the consumer's satisfaction, production must take place at point T, where the output of good X is OX and the output of good Y is OY. Clearly, T is the point on the product transformation curve that is on the consumer's highest indifference curve. Since the product transformation curve is tangent to the indifference curve at point T, it follows that the marginal rate of product transformation equals the marginal rate of substitution at point T. Thus the marginal rate of product transformation equals the marginal rate of substitution if consumer satisfaction is maximized. This result will hold for any number of consumers, not just for one.

AGRICULTURAL PRICE SUPPORTS: AN APPLICATION

We can use these three conditions for optimal resource allocation to analyze many interesting questions, such as the choice among alternative agricultural price support schemes. From Chapter 8 it will be recalled that in the past such schemes have commonly specified that each farm can produce a certain quota, represented by OX in panel A of Figure 14.6. The total quota for the entire industry is OY in panel B of Figure 14.6. Also, a support price has frequently been set by the government, which is OP in this case. Since the demand curve for the product is as shown in panel B of Figure 14.6, consumers will purchase OQ_1 units of the product, and the government will buy $(OY - OQ_1)$ units of the product. This is in contrast to the situation that would prevail if there were no quotas and price supports; under these circumstances, price would be OP_1 and the total output of the product would be OQ_2. The purpose of the quotas and price supports is to increase the income of farmers.

Unfortunately, this type of support scheme leads to inefficiencies of various kinds in the use of resources. First, because the marginal cost at OX will certainly vary from farm to farm, the industry's total output will be produced inefficiently. That is, the total cost of producing the total output could be decreased by reducing the output of farms with high marginal cost at OX and increasing the output of farms with low marginal cost at OX. Since the industry's total output is being produced inefficiently, it is clear that the second condition in the previous section is being violated. Second, part of the industry's output is unnecessary, and is taken off the market by the government. Third, since price is above marginal cost for this product (see panel A of Figure 14.6), the third condition in the previous section is also violated, if the price of other goods equal marginal cost (as they would in a perfectly competitive economy). The reasoning underlying this statement is explained in some de-

Fig.
14.6　AGRICULTURAL PRICE SUPPORTS / *If* OP *is the support price, and* OX *is the quota for each farm, the industry's total output will be produced inefficiently. Consumers will buy* OQ_1 *units of the product, and the government will buy* $(OY − OQ_1)$ *units.*

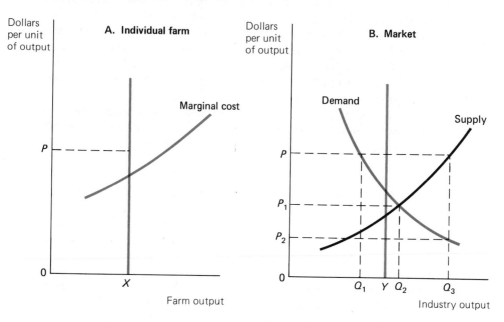

On the right: A. Individual farm — Dollars per unit of output; Marginal cost curve; P; X; Farm output. B. Market — Dollars per unit of output; Demand; Supply; P, P_1, P_2; Q_1, Y, Q_2, Q_3; Industry output.

tail in the section after next. For the moment, it is sufficient to accept it on faith.

On the other hand, suppose that the government adopts a different sort of scheme, one closer to that adopted in 1973. Suppose that the government guarantees each farmer a price of *OP*, with the result that the industry produces OQ_3 units of the product. But then suppose that it lets the free market alone, with the result that the OQ_3 units of the agricultural product command a price of only OP_2 in the market and the government pays each farmer $(OP − OP_2)$ per unit. The first type of inefficiency would be eliminated because each farmer would set marginal cost equal to *OP*, with the result that the marginal cost for each farm would be the same. The second type of inefficiency would be eliminated because the government no longer would take part of the industry's output off the market. The third type of inefficiency remains, since the price to consumers would be less than marginal cost.[8]

However, this does not mean that this scheme is necessarily an improvement. For instance (as noted earlier in this chapter), any choice among policies must take into account their effects on the income distribution. This kind of

---

8. See G. Stigler, *The Theory of Price* (New York: Macmillan, 1966), pp. 187–90.

plan would result in a different distribution of benefits and costs among consumers and farmers. For example, the abandonment of the quota system would hurt farmers who possess quotas. These aspects of the choice may outweigh all others in many people's minds. (Congressmen in particular may be sensitive to the question of whose ox is gored.) More will be said on this score in the next section.

INTERPERSONAL COMPARISONS OF UTILITY AND PARETO EFFICIENCY

Having described the three necessary sets of conditions for optimal resource allocation, we must recognize that more than one pattern of resource allocation will satisfy these conditions. In other words, these conditions do not determine a single best pattern of resource allocation. Instead, they result in many patterns of resource allocation, and which one is regarded as best depends on what one regards as an optimal distribution of income.

The choice of an optimal income distribution must be made on ethical, not purely scientific grounds. *There is no scientifically meaningful way to compare the utility levels of various individuals.* The reader will recall that in our previous discussion of utility and demand theory in Chapters 3 and 4 we were not required to make any such interpersonal comparisons. This was fortunate, and intentional. There is no way that one can state scientifically that a piece of Aunt Mary's apple pie will bring you more satisfaction than it will me, or that your headache is worse than mine. This is because there is no scale on which we can measure pleasure or pain in such a way that interpersonal comparisons can be made validly.

Because we cannot make interpersonal comparisons of utility, we cannot tell whether one distribution of income is better than another. For example, suppose you receive twice as much income as I do. Economics cannot tell us whether this is a better distribution of income than if I receive twice as much income as you do. This is a value judgment, pure and simple. However, most problems of public policy involve changes in the distribution of income. For example, even a decision to increase the production of numerically controlled machine tools and to reduce the production of conventional machine tools may mean that certain stockholders and workers will gain, while others will lose (since some machine tool firms specialize more heavily than others in the production of numerically controlled tools). Because it is so difficult to evaluate the effects of such a decision on the distribution of income, it is correspondingly difficult to come to any conclusion as to whether or not such a decision is good or bad.

Faced with this problem, economists have adopted a number of approaches, all of which have important difficulties. Some economists simply have paid no attention to the effects of proposed policies on the income distribution. Others have taken the existing income distribution as optimal, while still others have asserted that income distributions exhibiting less inequality of income are preferable to those exhibiting more inequality of income. Purists have argued that we really cannot be sure a change is for the better unless it hurts no member of society. Others have suggested that we must accept the judgment of Congress (or the public as a whole) as to what is an optimal distribution of income.[9]

Despite these disagreements, practically all economists accept the proposition that a change that harms no one and improves the lot of some people (in their own eyes) is an improvement. This criterion, put forth by

Pareto criterion

Vilfredo Pareto at about the turn of the century and often called the *Pareto criterion*,[10] evades the question of income distribution. If a change benefits one group of people and harms another group, this criterion is not applicable. Nonetheless, this criterion is by no means useless, as we shall see below, and most economists would agree that all changes that satisfy this criterion should be carried out. That is,

Pareto-efficient

they believe that society should make any change that harms no one and improves the lot of some people. If all such changes are carried out—and thus no opportunity to make such changes remains—the situation is termed *Pareto-optimal* or *Pareto-efficient*. On pp. 421–23 we described and discussed three conditions for a Pareto-optimal allocation of resources.

PERFECT COMPETITION AND ECONOMIC EFFICIENCY

One of the most important, and most fundamental, findings of microeconomics is that a perfectly competitive economy satisfies the three conditions for welfare maximization set forth on pp. 421–23. The argument for competition can be made in various ways. For example, some people favor competition simply because it prevents the undue concentration of power and the exploitation of consumers. But to the economic theorist, the basic argument for a perfectly competitive economy is the fact that such an economy satisfies these conditions. In this section we prove that this is indeed a fact. In the next two sections, we discuss how prices can be used in planned economies and by regulated industries to achieve the same kinds of results.

The first condition for welfare maximization is that the marginal rate of substitution between any pair of commodities must be the same for all con-

---

9. One contribution to this literature that has received considerable attention is J. Rawls, *A Theory of Justice* (Cambridge, Mass.: Harvard University Press, 1971). Rawls argues that "all social values . . . are to be distributed equally unless an unequal distribution . . . is to everyone's advantage." Needless to say, this proposition has aroused much controversy.

10. V. Pareto, *Manuel d'Economie Politique* (1909).

sumers. To see that this condition is met under perfect competition, we must recall from Chapter 4 that under perfect competition consumers choose their purchases so that the marginal rate of substitution between any pair of commodities is equal to the ratio of the prices of the pair of commodities. Since prices, and thus price ratios, are the same for all buyers under perfect competition, it follows that the marginal rate of substitution between any pair of commodities must be the same for all consumers. For example, if every consumer can buy bread at 50 cents a loaf and butter at $1 a pound, each one will arrange his or her purchases so that the marginal rate of substitution of butter for bread is 2. Thus the marginal rate of substitution will be the same for all consumers: 2 for everyone.

The second condition for welfare maximization is that the marginal rate of technical substitution between any pair of inputs must be the same for all producers. To see that this condition is met under perfect competition, we must recall from Chapter 7 that, under perfect competition, producers will choose the quantity of each input so that the marginal rate of technical substitution between any pair of inputs is equal to the ratio of the prices of the pair of inputs. Since input prices, and thus price ratios, are the same for all producers under perfect competition, it follows that the marginal rate of technical substitution must be the same for all producers. For example, if every producer can buy labor services at $4 an hour and machine tool services at $8 an hour, each one will arrange the quantity of its inputs so that the marginal rate of technical substitution of machine tool services for labor is 2. Thus the marginal rate of technical substitution will be the same for all producers: 2 for each of them.

The third condition for welfare maximization is that the marginal rate of product transformation must equal the marginal rate of substitution for each pair of goods. The proof that this condition is met under perfect competition is somewhat lengthier than in the case of the other conditions. To begin with, we must note that the marginal rate of product transformation is the number of units of good A that must be given up to produce an additional unit of good B. The additional cost of producing the extra unit of good B is, of course, the marginal cost of good B. To see how many units of good A must be given up to get this extra unit of good B, we must divide the marginal cost of good B by the marginal cost of good A. This will tell us how many extra units of good A cost as much as one extra unit of good B. Thus the marginal rate of product transformation under perfect competition equals the ratio of the marginal cost of good B to the marginal cost of good A.

From Chapter 8 it will be recalled that price equals marginal cost under perfect competition. Consequently, the ratio of the marginal cost of good B to the marginal cost of good A equals the ratio of the price of good B to the price of good A under perfect competition. Coupled with the result of the previous paragraph, this means that the marginal rate of product transformation is equal to the ratio of the price of good B to the price of good A under perfect competition. But, as we noted in connection with our discussion of the first condition, the marginal rate of substitution is equal to the ratio of the price of good B to the price of good A under perfect competition. Consequently, it follows that the marginal rate of product transformation equals the marginal rate of substitution for any pair of products under perfect competition.

Referring back to our earlier discussion of agricultural price supports in this chapter, it is obvious now why these price supports violate the third condition for optimality. Since the price of the agricultural good does not equal marginal cost (see Figure 14.6), the third condition must be violated if the prices of other goods equal marginal cost. For example, take some other good with marginal cost, MC_x, and price, P_x. The marginal rate of product transformation between this good and the agricultural product is $MC_A \div MC_x$, where MC_A is the marginal cost of the agricultural good. Moreover, if consumers maximize satisfaction, the marginal rate of substitution between the two goods is $P_A \div P_x$, where P_A is the price of the agricultural product. However, since $P_x = MC_x$ and $MC_A \neq P_A$, it follows that the marginal rate of substitution does not equal the marginal rate of product transformation.

Returning to the original topic of this section, we find that all three conditions for optimal resource allocation are satisfied under perfect competition. This is one of the principal reasons why economists are so enamoured of perfect competition and so wary of monopoly. If a formerly competitive economy is restructured so that some industries become monopolies, these conditions for optimal resource allocation are no longer met. As we know from Chapter 9, each monopolist produces less than the perfectly competitive industry that it replaces would have produced. Thus too few resources are devoted to the industries that are monopolized, and too many resources are devoted to the industries that remain perfectly competitive. This is one of the economist's chief charges against monopoly. It wastes resources because its actions result in an overallocation of resources to competitive industries and an underallocation of resources to monopolistic industries. Society is then less well off.[11]

ECONOMIC PLANNING AND MARGINAL COST PRICING

The previous section showed that the three conditions for optimal resource allocation are satisfied under perfect competition. Economists interested in the functioning of planned, or socialist, economies have argued that a price system could be used in a similar way to increase social welfare in such econo-

---

11. In evaluating this result and judging its practical relevance, it is important to note that it stems from a very simple model that ignores such things as technological change and other dynamic considerations, risk and uncertainty, and externalities. The reader should be very careful to note the qualifications and assumptions that must be made. Sometimes the argument for perfect competition is made without full recognition of these qualifications.

mies. According to economists like Abba Lerner,[12] rational economic organization could be achieved in a socialist economy that is decentralized, as well as under perfect competition. For example, the government might try to solve the system of equations that is solved automatically in a perfectly competitive economy, and obtain the prices that would prevail under perfect competition. Then the government might publish this price list, together with instructions for consumers to maximize their satisfaction and for producers to maximize profit. (Of course, the wording of the instructions to consumers might be a bit less heavy-handed than "Maximize your satisfaction!")

An important advantage claimed for planning and control of this sort is that the government does not have to become involved in the intricate and detailed business of setting production targets for each plant. It need only compute the proper set of prices. As long as plant managers maximize "profits," the proper production levels will be chosen by them. Thus decentralized decision-making, rather than detailed centralized direction, could be used, with the result that administrative costs and bureaucratic disadvantages might be reduced.

The prices that the government would publish, like those prevailing in a perfectly competitive economy, would equal marginal cost. Many economists have recommended that government-owned enterprises in basically capitalist economies also adopt *marginal cost pricing,* that is, that they set price equal to marginal cost. For example, Harold Hotelling argued that this should be the case.[13] Taking the case of a bridge where the marginal cost (the extra cost involved in allowing an additional vehicle to cross) is zero, he argued that the socially optimal price for crossing the bridge is zero, and that its cost should be defrayed by general taxation. If a toll is charged, the conditions for optimal resource allocation are violated.

Marginal cost pricing

Marginal cost pricing has fascinated economists during the more than forty years that have elapsed since Hotelling's article.[14] But there are a number of important problems in the actual application of this idea. One of the most important is that, if (as is frequently the case in public utilities) the firm's average costs decrease with increases in its scale of output, it follows from the discussion in Chapter 7 that marginal cost must be less than average cost, with

12. A. Lerner, *The Economics of Control* (New York: Macmillan, 1944).

13. See H. Hotelling, "The General Welfare in Relation to Problems of Taxation and of Railway and Utility Rates," *Econometrica,* July 1938.

14. For example, see J. Nelson, *Marginal Cost Pricing in Practice* (Englewood Cliffs, N.J.: Prentice-Hall, 1964); N. Ruggles, "Recent Developments in Marginal Cost Pricing," *Review of Economic Studies,* 1949–50; W. Vickrey, "Some Implications of Marginal Cost Pricing for Public Utilities," reprinted in Mansfield, *Microeconomics: Selected Readings,* 5th ed.; and R. Turvey, "Practical Problems of Marginal-Cost Pricing in Public Enterprise," in A. Phillips and O. Williamson, eds., *Prices: Issues in Theory, Practice, and Public Policy* (Philadelphia: University of Pennsylvania Press, 1968).

the consequence that the firm will not cover its costs if price is set equal to marginal cost. This means that marginal cost pricing must be accompanied by some form of subsidy if the firm is to stay in operation. However, the collection of the funds required for the payment of the subsidy may also violate the conditions for optimal resource allocation. Moreover, this subsidy means that there is a change in the income distribution favoring users of the firm's output and penalizing nonusers of its output. Whether or not marginal cost pricing results in improved economic welfare depends on how one views this change in the income distribution.

Marginal Cost Pricing: A Case Study

During the mid-fifties, Électricité de France, the French nationalized electricity industry, introduced marginal cost pricing for its high-tension service. The ultimate goal of the new pricing scheme was that the price paid for a kilowatt-hour of electricity at a given time of day in a given season of the year in a given region was to approximate the cost of an additional kilowatt-hour at this time in this season in this region.

Of course, a great many simplifications had to be made in computing the new price schedule. First, consider price differences at various times of day. In the winter, the day is divided into three periods: the peak daytime hour, the other daytime hours, and the night. In the summer, it is divided into two periods: day and night. A consumer in a given region must pay a different price for kilowatt-hours in each period, with the differences reflecting differences in marginal costs. Next, consider price differences among regions. To estimate the marginal costs in each region, a pattern of movements of electricity from generating stations to consumption areas is derived that meets estimated demands at minimum total cost given present capacity. The marginal costs corresponding to this pattern are used to determine prices in various regions.

Finally, consider price differences among seasons. Differences among seasons in demand curves, as well as differences in hydroelectric reservoir levels and river flows, are responsible for these differences in price. The seasonal differences in demand are assumed by the industry to be like those observed in the past. Average snow and rainfall levels in each season can be used in the calculations. Since water tends to be less abundant in the winter, peak demands for electricity have to be satisfied by using less efficient thermal plants than have to be used in the summer. Also, demand for electricity tends to be higher in the winter. Both of these factors clearly influence the level of the marginal cost of electricity.

What has the new pricing scheme achieved? According to Berkeley's Thomas Marschak, who made a careful study of the French experience, Électricité de France's marginal cost pricing had a number of important beneficial results. In his view, a clear improvement over the [old] pricing scheme is very plausibly claimed. Preliminary observation suggests that a leveling of consumption between the daytime and the nighttime periods may be expected. One immediate result is a reduction by 5 percent in the capacity required to meet peak demands . . . Another is a substantial saving of imported (American) coal in winter, since the flattening of peaks eliminates the need for some of the inefficient thermal output previously required.[15]

EXTERNAL ECONOMIES AND DISECONOMIES

Up to this point, we have generally assumed implicitly that there is no difference between private and social benefits, or between private and social costs. For example, costs to producers have been assumed to be costs to society, and costs to society have been assumed to be costs to producers; benefits to producers have been assumed to be benefits to society, and benefits to society have been assumed to be benefits to producers. In fact, however, there are many instances in which these assumptions do not hold. Instead, producers sometimes confer benefits on other members of the economy but are unable to obtain payment for these benefits, and they sometimes act in such a way as to harm others without having to pay the full costs. In these cases, the pursuit of private gain will not promote the social welfare. The purpose of this section is to describe how differences between private and social returns are likely to arise and the ways in which these differences influence our results. The following sections apply this theory to two areas of the modern economy.

It is convenient, and customary, to classify these divergences into four types. First, there are *external economies of production.* An external economy occurs when an action taken by an economic unit results in uncompensated benefits to others; when such benefits are due to an increase in a firm's production, they are called external economies of production. The firm may benefit others directly. For example, it may train workers that eventually go to work for other firms that do not have to pay the training costs. Or the firm may benefit other firms indirectly because its increased output may make it more economical for firms outside the industry to provide services to other firms in the industry. For example, a great expansion in an aircraft firm may make it possible for aluminum producers to take advantage of economies of scale, with the result that other metal fabricating firms can also get cheaper aluminum. In either case, there is a difference between private and social returns; the gains to society are greater than the gains to the firm.

External economies of production

Second, there are *external economies of consumption,* which occur when an action taken by a consumer, rather than a producer, results in an uncom-

---

15. T. Marschak, "Capital Budgeting and Pricing in the French Nationalized Industries," *Journal of Business,* January 1960, p. 151.

*External
economies of
consumption*

pensated benefit to others. For example, if I maintain my house and lawn, this benefits my neighbors as well as myself. If I educate my children and make them more responsible citizens, this too benefits my neighbors as well as myself. The list of external economies from consumption could easily be extended, but the idea should be clear at this point.

Third, there are *external diseconomies of production*. An external diseconomy occurs when an action taken by an economic unit results in uncompensated costs to others; when such costs are due to increases in a

*External
diseconomies
of production*

firm's production, they are called external diseconomies of production. For example, a firm may pollute a stream by pumping out waste materials, or it may pollute the air with smoke or materials. Such actions result in costs to others; for instance, Chesapeake Bay's oyster beds and Long Island's clam beds continually are being threatened by water pollution. However, the private costs do not reflect the full social costs, since the firms and cities responsible for the pollution are not charged for their contribution to poorer quality water and their harm to industries dependent on good water. There are many cases of external diseconomies of production, such as traffic congestion and the defacement of scenery.

Fourth, there are *external diseconomies of consumption,* which occur when an action taken by a consumer results in an uncompensated cost to

*External
diseconomies
of consumption*

others. Some external diseconomies of consumption can be fairly subtle. For example, Mrs. White may be trying hard to keep up with the social leader in town, Mrs. Brown. If Mrs. Brown obtains a new mink coat, this may make Mrs. White worse off, since she may become dissatisfied with her old mink coat. Similarly, a family that feels that a three-year-old Ford is perfectly adequate may become dissatisfied with it after moving to a community where everyone drives a new Cadillac.

The foregoing are some of the most important cases where social and private costs and benefits differ. At first glance, these cases may not seem very important. But when all of these types of external economies and diseconomies are considered, their aggregate significance can be substantial. For example, the fact that environmental pollution of various kinds resulting from industrial output is important has been stressed repeatedly in the United States in recent years. The importance of various types of external economies of production is undeniable, and the fact that consumer tastes and well-being are determined by the tastes and well-being of other members of society is obvious as well.

How do these external economies and diseconomies alter the optimality of the allocation of resources under perfect competition? If a man takes an action that contributes to society's welfare but which results in no payment for him, he is certainly likely to take this action less frequently than would be socially optimal. The same holds true for firms. Thus, if the production of a certain good, say beryllium, is responsible for external economies, less than the socially optimum amount of beryllium is likely to be produced under perfect competition, since the producers are unlikely to increase output simply because it reduces the costs of other companies. By the same token if a man takes an action that results in costs that he is not forced to pay, he is likely to take this action more frequently than is socially desirable. The same holds true for firms. Thus, if the production of a certain good is responsible for external diseconomies, more of this good is likely to be produced under perfect competition than is socially optimal.[16]

Public Policy toward Basic Research: An Application

To illustrate how the theory of external economies and diseconomies, together with the other principles discussed in this chapter, can be used to throw light on problems of public policy, consider the nature of social policy toward basic research. One of the most fundamental questions in this area is: Why should the government support basic research? Why not rely on private enterprise to support sufficient basic research?

To answer this question, it is important to recognize that basic scientific research is likely to generate substantial external economies. Important additions to fundamental knowledge often have an impact on a great many fields. If a firm produces an important scientific breakthrough, it generally cannot hope to capture the full value of the new knowledge it creates. It cannot go into the full range of activities in which the knowledge has use, and it is seldom able to capture through patent rights the full social value of the new knowledge. Indeed, fundamental discoveries, such as natural laws, cannot be patented at all.

Because of these external economies, there is likely to be a divergence between the private and social benefits from basic research, with the result that a perfectly competitive economy would be expected to devote fewer resources to basic research than is socially optimal. Consequently, there seems to be a good case on purely economic grounds for the government (or some other agency not motivated by profit) to support basic research. As pointed out in the 1987 report of the Council of Economic Advisers,

The Federal Government has an important role in funding basic scientific research. Such research can contribute to technological advance in the longer term. However, its benefits are often too diffuse and difficult to profit from for it to be undertaken by private business.[17]

---

16. This section is based partly on the treatment in W. Baumol, *Economic Theory and Operations Analysis*, 3d ed. (Englewood Cliffs, N.J.: Prentice-Hall, 1972), pp. 392–95 and 399–404.

17. Economic Report of the President (Washington, D.C.: U.S. Government Printing Office, 1987), p. 49.

Based on similar considerations, there is a strong argument for government support of fundamental research to extend the technological underpinnings of broad industrial areas. For example, the National Advisory Committee on Aeronautics carried out research and development concerning wind tunnels, aircraft fuels, aircraft design, and other fundamental matters regarding aviation. No individual firm had much incentive to do such work because it could appropriate only a small share of the benefits. But because the benefits to the economy as a whole were substantial, the government intervened to finance work of this sort. The simple principles of welfare economics help to indicate why such a policy was justified.

OPTIMAL POLLUTION CONTROL

In recent years, the American public has become much more concerned about environmental pollution. External diseconomies result in considerable air and water pollution. When firms (and governments and households) dispose of their wastes by pumping them into the air and water, this often means that others must incur costs to put the environment back into a usable condition. Thus the polluters tend to pay less than the full social costs of using the environment in this way, with the result that they engage in an undesirably high level of pollution. Given that this is the case, an important question facing policy makers is: What is the optimal level of pollution control? In other words, how much pollution ought we to allow an industry to discharge?

Figure 14.7 shows the total social cost of each level of discharge of an industry's wastes, holding constant the industry's output. Clearly, the more untreated waste the industry dumps into the environment, the greater the total

Fig. 14.7   COST OF POLLUTION / *The cost of pollution increases as larger quantities of pollutants are emitted.*

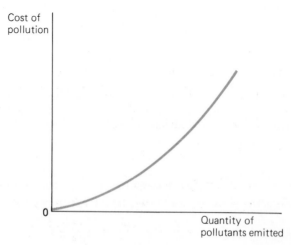

Fig.
14.8
COST OF POLLUTION CONTROL / *The cost of pollution control decreases as larger quantities of pollutants are emitted.*

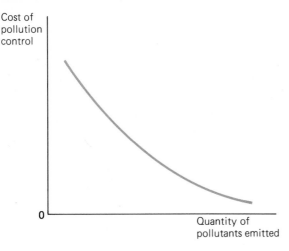

costs. Figure 14.8 shows the costs of pollution control at each level of discharge of the industry's wastes. Clearly, the more the industry cuts down on the amount of wastes it discharges, the higher are its costs of pollution control. Figure 14.9 shows the sum of these two costs—the cost of pollution and the cost of pollution control—at each level of discharge of the industry's wastes.

Fig.
14.9
SUM OF POLLUTION COST AND COST OF POLLUTION CONTROL / *From the point of view of society as a whole, the optimal level of pollution in this industry is OR.*

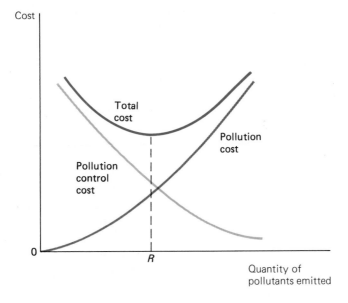

Example 14.3

EXTERNAL DISECONOMIES ON THE HIGHWAYS

Each morning, thousands of motorists travel the route from Philadelphia's western suburbs to the central business district where they work or shop. Suppose that the full cost of this auto trip—including both the money costs (of fuel, oil, tire wear, and so on) and *the value of the driver's (and passengers') time*—is measured along the vertical axis of the graph below, and that the number of vehicles attempting this trip between 7 a.m. and 8 a.m. on a particular day is measured along the horizontal axis. The relationship between the full cost of this trip to a motorist and the number of vehicles attempting this trip is CC'. The demand curve shows at each price of this trip (including both money and time costs) the number of vehicles that will set out on this route.

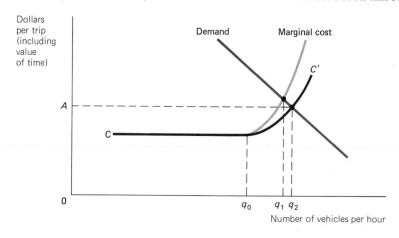

From the point of view of society as a whole, the industry should reduce its discharge of pollution to the point where the sum of these two costs—the cost of pollution and the cost of pollution control—is a minimum. Specifically, the optimal level of pollution in the industry is OR in Figure 14.9. Why is this the optimum level? Because if the industry discharges *less* than this amount of pollution, a one-unit increase in pollution will reduce the cost of pollution control by more than it will increase the cost of pollution, whereas if the industry discharges *more* than this amount of pollution, a one-unit reduction in pollution will reduce the cost of pollution by more than it will increase the cost of pollution control.

To make this more evident, Figure 14.10 shows the marginal cost of an extra unit of discharge of waste, at each level of discharge of the industry's wastes: This is designated by AA'. Figure 14.10 also shows the marginal cost of reducing the industry's discharge of waste by one unit: This is designated by BB'. The socially optimal level of pollution for the industry is at the point where the two curves intersect. At this point, the cost of an extra unit of pollution is just equal to the cost of reducing pollution by an extra unit. Regard-

(a) If more than Oq_0 vehicles attempt this trip, the cost of the trip increases as more and more vehicles per hour set out on this route. Why? Is this due to external diseconomies? (b) How many autos per hour will travel along this route? (c) Is this the socially optimal number? (d) What measures might be taken to push the actual number closer to the optimal number?

SOLUTION

(a) If more than Oq_0 vehicles per hour travel this route, the highway becomes congested. Traffic becomes tied up, it takes longer to make the trip, and the full cost (including time) increases. As more and more vehicles travel this route, the congestion gets worse. Each extra vehicle, by delaying other vehicles taking this route, is responsible for external diseconomies. (b) Oq_2 vehicles per hour. If less than Oq_2 vehicles per hour travel this route, the full cost of the trip (indicated by the CC' curve) is less than the value of the trip to the motorist (indicated by the demand curve), and more vehicles will make the trip. If more than Oq_2 vehicles per hour travel this route, the full cost of the trip exceeds the value of the trip to the motorist, and less vehicles will make the trip. (c) No. The socially optimal number is Oq_1 vehicles per hour. If more than Oq_0 vehicles per hour travel this route, the marginal cost to society of an extra vehicle's traveling this route (shown by the colored line in the graph) exceeds the cost to the motorist driving this extra vehicle because the extra vehicle delays other motorists. Up to Oq_1 vehicles per hour, the marginal cost to society of an extra vehicle (shown by the colored line) is less than the marginal benefit (shown by the demand curve), and society gains if more vehicles per hour take this route. But above Oq_1 vehicles per hour, this is no longer true. (d) Some economists have suggested that a tax be imposed on motorists that travel congested highways.* In this way, the private costs would be brought closer to the true social costs. Tolls can be used, at least under some circumstances.

* See A. Walters, "The Theory and Measurement of Private and Social Cost of Highway Congestion," *Econometrica*, October 1961.

Fig.
14.10   MARGINAL COST OF POLLUTION AND MARGINAL COST OF POLLUTION
CONTROL / *At the socially optimal level of pollution,* OR, *the cost of an extra unit of pollution is equal to the cost of reducing pollution by an extra unit.*

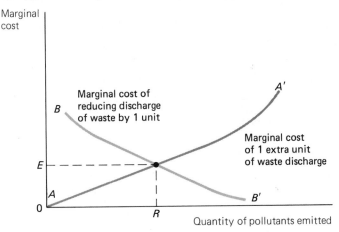

less of whether we look at Figure 14.9 or 14.10, the answer is the same: OR is the socially optimal level of pollution.

It is important to note that the optimal level of pollution is generally not zero. Despite the fact that some observers seem to believe that zero is the optimal level, our analysis shows clearly that this simply is not true. Why isn't it true? Because beyond some point, the cost of reducing pollution exceeds the benefits. In Figures 14.9 and 14.10, this point is reached at a pollution level of OR.[18]

Direct Regulation and Effluent Fees

Left to its own devices, the industry in Figure 14.10 will not reduce its pollution level to OR, because it does not pay all of the social costs of its pollution. This, as we have seen, is the heart of the problem. How can the government establish incentives that will lead to the optimal amount of pollution control? One way is by direct regulation. For example, the government may decree that this industry is to limit its pollution to OR units. Direct regulation of this sort is relied on in many sectors of the American economy, but most economists seem to prefer the use of effluent fees.

An *effluent fee* is a fee that a polluter must pay to the government for discharging waste. The idea behind the imposition of effluent fees is that they can bring the private cost of waste disposal closer to the true social costs. For example, in Figure 14.10, an effluent fee of OE per unit of pollution discharge might be charged. If so, the marginal cost of an additional unit of pollution discharge to the industry is OE, with the result that it will cut back its pollution to the socially optimal level, OR units. Why? Because it will be profitable to cut back pollution so long as the marginal cost of reducing pollution by a unit is less than OE—and, as you can see from Figure 14.10, this is the case so long as the pollution discharge exceeds OR. Thus, to maximize their profits, the firms in the industry will reduce pollution to OR units.[19]

Effluent fee

Economists tend to favor effluent fees over direct regulation for at least two reasons. First, it obviously is socially desirable to use the cheapest way to achieve any given reduction in pollution. A system of effluent fees is more likely to accomplish this result than direct regulation. To see why this is the

---

18. For further discussion, see A. Freeman, R. Haveman, and A. Kneese, *The Economics of Environmental Policy* (New York: Wiley, 1973).

19. Another way for the government to intervene is to establish tax credits for firms that introduce pollution-control equipment. Such subsidies may not be very effective, since it still may be cheaper for the firms to continue polluting. Also, they may not be very efficient, since pollution-control equipment may not be the most economical means of reducing some kinds of pollution. Further, they are frequently attacked on the grounds that they are not equitable. Nonetheless, such subsidies are sometimes used.

case, consider a particular polluter. Faced with an effluent fee—that is, a price it must pay for each unit of waste it discharges—the polluter will find it profitable to reduce its discharge of waste to the point where the cost of reducing waste discharges by one unit equals the effluent fee. (Recall our discussion in the previous paragraph.)

It follows that, since the effluent fee is the same for all polluters, the cost of reducing waste discharges by one extra unit is then the same for all polluters. But if this is so, the total cost of achieving the resulting decrease in pollution must be a minimum. To see this, suppose that the cost of reducing waste discharges by an additional unit is *not* the same for all polluters. Then there is a cheaper way to reduce pollution to its existing level—by getting polluters whose cost of reducing waste discharges by an additional unit is low to reduce their waste disposal by an additional unit, and by allowing polluters whose cost of reducing waste discharges by an additional unit is high to increase their pollution commensurately.

Second, economists tend to favor effluent fees because this approach requires far less information in the hands of the relevant government agencies than does direct regulation. After all, when effluent fees are used, all the government has to do is meter the amount of pollution a firm or household produces (which admittedly is sometimes not easy) and charge accordingly. It is left to the firms and households to figure out the most ingenious and effective ways to cut down on their pollution and save on effluent fees.

Effluent fees have proven useful in practice as well as attractive in theory. For example, in West Germany's Ruhr Valley, a highly industrialized area with limited water supplies, effluent fees are used to help maintain the quality of the local rivers. The results have been highly successful. But this does not mean, of course, that direct regulation is not useful too. Some ways of disposing of certain types of waste are so dangerous that the only sensible thing to do is to ban them. Also, it sometimes is not feasible to impose effluent fees—for example, in cases where it is very difficult to meter the amount of pollutants emitted by various firms and households. In practice, public policy in the United States has tended to stress the regulatory approach.

PROPERTY RIGHTS AND COASE'S THEOREM

Under certain circumstances, a perfectly competitive economy will allocate resources optimally, even in the face of seemingly important external benefits or costs. For example, consider a firm that pollutes a stream by pumping out waste materials. Suppose that the downstream water users have well-defined property rights to water of a specified quality level, which means that they can sue the firm for damages if it passes water on to them that is below this quality level. In such a case, the firm can be required to pay for the pollution costs it imposes on others. Or consider a firm that upgrades the water in a stream, thus benefiting downstream water users. If this firm raises the water quality above the legally required level, it can seek compensation from the water users if property rights of this sort are well defined.

If the costs of negotiating are not too large, the parties responsible for an external benefit or cost can negotiate with the parties affected by this externality. For example, if downstream water users are entitled to water of a particular quality, a firm may purchase from them the right to pollute the stream to a certain extent. Or the downstream users may purchase from the firm the right to water of better quality than they would otherwise be entitled to. In this way, the externality is brought into the calculations of the interested parties. Thus there is no divergence between social and private costs because a firm or individual that harms others must pay for this right, and a firm or individual that benefits others receives compensation.

According to Ronald Coase of the University of Chicago, a competitive economy will allocate resources efficiently, even in the face of seemingly important external effects, if it is possible to carry out such negotiations at little or no cost. In the course of these negotiations, the relevant parties will be led to take proper account of the effects of their actions on others. For example, if downstream water users are endowed with a property right to obtain water of a particular quality, a firm that wants to pollute a stream will be led to offer compensation to them, and, pursuing its own interest, it will not find it worthwhile to pollute beyond the socially optimal point. Moreover, Coase has shown that, *regardless of which party is endowed with the relevant property rights,* the outcome will be the same. That is, regardless of whether the downstream users are endowed with the right to obtain water of a particular quality or the firm is endowed with the right to emit a certain amount of pollutants into the stream, the parties will be led to buy or sell these rights so that the socially optimal amount of pollution results.[20]

This theorem, often referred to as Coase's theorem, is of considerable interest and importance. However, it is important to recognize that it assumes that the costs of negotiating and contracting by the interested parties are relatively small. For example, it assumes that the downstream water users can get together with the polluting firm and that they can negotiate effectively without prohibitive expense. In fact, however, when there are more than a relatively small number of interested parties, the costs of such negotiations may be so high that they are not feasible. Indeed, even if the costs are moderate, negotiations of this sort may not be practical. If the number of interested parties is large, it may not be possible to get the unanimity required to make the negotiations effective. And if the the number of interested parties is small, the fact

---

20. R. Coase, "The Problem of Social Cost," *Journal of Law and Economics,* October 1960, reprinted in Mansfield, *Microeconomics: Selected Readings.*

that mutually advantageous deals are possible does not mean that they will necessarily be consummated.

Nonetheless, Coase's theorem suggests that the assignment of well-defined property rights might help to promote economic efficiency. For example, to get around the difficulties caused by external diseconomies arising from waste disposal, society might find it useful to try to establish more unambiguous property rights for individuals and firms with respect to environmental quality. Then, assuming that the relevant negotiations are feasible, the interested parties in a particular area might try to negotiate to determine how much pollution will occur. Note that if these negotiations are to be effective, property rights must be exchangeable, as well as unambiguous. That is, it must be possible for a person (or firm) to buy or sell his or her property rights of this sort.

PUBLIC GOODS

Earlier in the chapter, we learned that under the specified conditions, a perfectly competitive economy results in an optimal allocation of resources. Two assumptions, among others, were made there. First, it was assumed that the exclusion principle operates. That is, whether or not a person consumes a good depends on whether or not he or she pays the price. Those who pay for the good can consume it, while those who do not pay cannot consume it. Second, it was assumed that the benefits from a good flow to a particular consumer. Thus the consumption of a particular good is rival, in the sense that, if one person consumes a particular good, someone else cannot consume it too. For example, if one person drinks an entire bottle of beer, another person cannot drink the same bottle of beer as well. (Tavern owners and publicans the world over will pale at the thought that anything else might be true!)

But not all goods have both of these characteristics. Indeed, many very important goods, like the quality of the environment and national security, do not have them. Goods that do not have the second characteristic

Public goods   —rivalry in consumption—are called *public goods*. Such goods can be enjoyed by one person without reducing the enjoyment they give others. Consider an uncrowded bridge. If Mr. Smith crosses the bridge, this does not interfere with Mr. Jones's crossing it. Thus the use of this bridge is a public good.

It is important to note that the market mechanism will not work properly for a public good, even if it has the first characteristic—that is, even if it conforms to the exclusion principle. For example, in the case of the uncrowded bridge, it is perfectly feasible to charge a fee for crossing the bridge, and to prevent people who do not pay from crossing it. Nonetheless, it would be inefficient to do so. Why? Because excluding those who do not pay reduces their satisfaction and does not increase the satisfaction of others. Thus, although the market mechanism can be applied, it is not optimal to do so.[21]

Public goods will not be provided in the right amounts by the market mechanism. The market mechanism operates on the principle that those who do not pay for a good cannot consume it. However, as we have just seen, this principle is inefficient for public goods. Moreover, it frequently is impossible to prevent people from consuming a public good whether or not they pay for it. For example, there is no way to prevent someone from benefiting from national defense, regardless of whether or not he or she helps pay for it. Thus, in many cases, the market mechanism simply is not applicable.

THE OPTIMAL QUANTITY OF A PUBLIC GOOD

If resources are to be allocated efficiently, how much should be produced of a public good? In this section, we analyze this question from the point of view of partial equilibrium analysis. Suppose for simplicity that there are only two consumers, the Adams family and the Brown family. Suppose that D_A is the Adams family's demand curve for a good, D_B is the Brown family's demand curve for the same good, and the supply curve for the good is as shown in Figure 14.11.

Fig.   DETERMINATION OF OPTIMAL OUTPUT: PRIVATE GOOD AND PUBLIC GOOD /
14.11   *For a private good, the optimal output is* OQ *in panel* A. *For a public good,*
         the optimal output is OR *in panel* B.

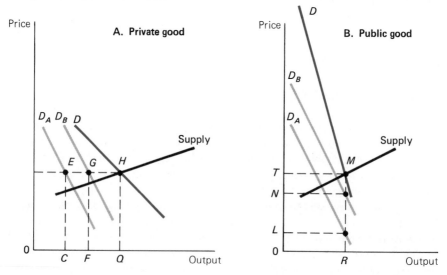

The left-hand panel of Figure 14.11 shows the optimal output of this good, assuming that it is a *private* good produced under perfect competition. Summing horizontally the demand curves of the two consumers, we obtain the market demand curve for the good, *D*. The optimal output is *OQ*, where this market demand curve intersects the market supply curve. Why is this optimal? Because at this output, the marginal benefit each consumer would obtain from an extra unit of the good equals its marginal cost. Assuming that the marginal benefit can be measured by the maximum amount that each family will pay for the extra unit, the marginal benefit for the Adams family would be *CE*, and the marginal benefit for the Brown family would be *FG*. The marginal cost of the extra unit is *QH* at an output of *OQ*. (Recall from Chapter 8 that the supply curve shows the marginal cost at each level of output.) Since *CE = FG = QH*, it follows that the marginal benefit to each consumer equals the marginal cost.

If, on the other hand, the good is a *public* good, the optimal output is shown in the right-hand panel of Figure 14.11. In this case, the market demand curve is obtained by summing the individual demand curves[22] *vertically,* not horizontally. This fundamental difference stems from the fact that both consumers consume the *total* amount of the good, and that the combined price paid by the two consumers is the sum of the prices paid by each one. The optimal output of the good is now *OR*, and the total price (the sum of the prices paid by each consumer) is *OT*.

To see why *OR* is the optimal output, recall (from p. 272 of Chapter 9) that the optimal output is the one where marginal social benefit equals marginal social cost. Next, note that the marginal social benefit from an extra unit of output of a public good is obtained by adding vertically the distances under every consumer's demand curve. This is because all consumers share entirely in the consumption of whatever quantity of the good is available, and because the marginal social benefit is the sum of the marginal benefits to each consumer. (Also, if an extra unit of the good is worth to an individual the maximum amount that he or she is willing to pay for it, the marginal benefit to each consumer is the distance under his or her demand curve.) Thus, if output is *OR*, the marginal social benefit from an extra unit of output is the vertical sum of *OL* and *ON*, which equals *OT*. Since the marginal social cost of an extra unit of output is *RM* (as in the case of a private good), and since the optimal output is where marginal social benefit equals marginal social cost, it follows that *OR* must be the optimal output, since marginal social benefit (*OT*) and marginal social cost (*RM*) are equal at this output.

This analysis is illuminating. For example, Figure 14.11 shows the important fact that, whereas economic efficiency requires that each consumer's

---

22. These demand curves are sometimes called pseudo-demand curves or willingness-to-pay curves. See R. and N. Dorfman, *Economics of the Environment,* 2d ed. (New York: Norton, 1977).

marginal benefit equal marginal cost for a private good, it requires that the *sum* of the marginal benefits of all consumers equals marginal cost for a public good. But despite its good points, this kind of analysis can take us only so far. For one thing, the demand curves in Figure 14.11 will not be revealed voluntarily if citizens believe that the amount they pay will be related to the preference they reveal. Consumers will find it worthwhile to be *free riders.* In other words, when consumers feel that the total output of the good will not be affected significantly by the action of any single person, they are likely to make no contribution to supporting the good, although they will use whatever output of the good is forthcoming.[23]

THE PROVISION OF PUBLIC GOODS

If the number of people in a society is quite small, it may be worthwhile for people acting individually to provide some quantity of public goods. For example, consider a case where there are two families on an island that is infested with poisonous snakes. The reduction of the number of such snakes is a public good, if there is no way of preventing the snakes from moving from one family's land to the other's, and if providing enhanced protection against the snakes for one family automatically provides it for the other family at no additional cost. Under these conditions, one of the families may well deem it worthwhile to engage in some activities to kill the snakes, even though this benefits the other family as well. Thus, when numbers are small, it is a mistake to say that no public goods will be produced unless the government does so. However, this does not mean that the proper amount of public goods will be produced, which brings us to the next point.

Even if there are few people in the society, there is a tendency for the provision of a public good to be too small, if its provision is left entirely up to the people acting individually in their own self-interest. To see why, suppose that a family lives alone for some time on the island cited above, and then is joined by a family that formerly lived alone on another island. Once the second family arrives, the first family will reduce its efforts to kill poisonous snakes because it will count on the other family to do some such work. Similarly, the other family will do less work of this sort than when it lived alone on the other island, for the same reasons. Both will cut back too much on their efforts because, whereas each family pays the full cost of devoting its time to this activity, it receives only part of the benefits, some of which accrue to the other family. Thus less will be produced of this public good than is socially optimal.

---

23. In addition, a partial equilibrium analysis of this problem has obvious limitations. For a general equilibrium analysis, see P. Samuelson, "Diagrammatic Exposition of a Theory of Public Expenditure," *Review of Economics and Statistics,* November, 1955, reprinted in E. Mansfield, *Microeconomics: Selected Readings,* 5th ed.

Example 14.4

ECONOMICS OF A LIGHTHOUSE

A lighthouse warns fishing boats away from a treacherous rock. Different levels of service can be provided by the lighthouse, resulting in different probabilities that a boat will be warned of its nearness to the rock. For example, the more powerful the beacon or signal emitted by the lighthouse, the higher the probability that a boat will receive the warning. The marginal cost of attaining various probabilities that a boat will be warned is as shown in the graph below. There are three boats in the area, owned by Captains Amos, Barnaby, and Columbus. The price that each captain is willing to pay for each level of service (that is, each probability that a boat will be warned) is shown by the individual demand curves in the graph below.

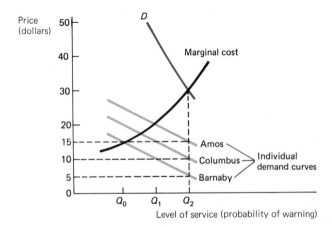

(a) Is the service provided by the lighthouse a private or public good? (b) What is the optimal level of service? That is, what should be the probability that a boat will be warned? (c) How much should each captain pay for this service? (d) Is it impossible for a lighthouse to be privately owned and operated?

SOLUTION

(a) It is a public good because, if the service is provided for any fishing boat, it is available to all other boats at no extra cost. (b) To obtain the market demand curve for the service, we must sum the three individual demand curves vertically, the result being D. The optimal level of service is at the point where the marginal cost curve intersects the D curve; that is, the optimal level of service is OQ_2. (c) Barnaby should pay $5, Columbus should pay $10, and Amos should pay $15. (d) No. In England lighthouses were private for many years. They assessed the shipowners at the docks. Ordinarily only one ship was in sight of the lighthouse at a particular point in time. The light would not be shown if the ship (which was identified by its flag) had not paid.*

* For further discussion, see N. Singer, *Public Microeconomics* (Little, Brown, 1976); and R. Coase, "The Lighthouse in Economics," *Journal of Law and Economics*, October 1974.

If there are few people in the society, there is a tendency for those who have the biggest interest in the outcome, or the biggest share of the resources, to provide a disproportionately large share of the amount of a public good that is supplied. For example, suppose that the first family in the previous paragraph owns 90 percent of the land (and other resources) on the island, and the second family owns 10 percent. Then the first family will recognize that whatever attempts are made to control the snake nuisance will rest largely on its shoulders, and it will act almost as if it were by itself on the island. On the other hand, the second family, recognizing that the first family has an incentive to do an effective job of this sort, is likely to reduce its efforts to a minimal level. Consequently, the first family is likely to do more than 90 percent of the snake-control work, and the second family is likely to do less than 10 percent.

The larger the number of people in the society, the farther it will fall short of producing an optimal amount of a public good. Thus, in large societies like the United States, the government intervenes in an attempt to assure the proper amount of public goods. There is general agreement that the government must provide public goods like national defense, and the provision of such goods unquestionably accounts for a significant portion of the government's expenditure. In democratic societies, the ballot box is used to determine the amount spent on various public goods. Each person votes for candidates that represent (often imperfectly) the set of public expenditures and taxes that is closest to his or her own preferences.[24]

SUMMARY

1. Previous chapters have been concerned with partial equilibrium analysis, which assumes that changes in price can occur in whatever market is being studied without causing significant changes in price in other markets, which in turn affect the market being studied. An analysis that takes account of the interrelationships among prices in various markets is called a general equilibrium analysis.

2. Input-output analysis attempts to make the general equilibrium model empirically useful. It assumes that inputs are used in fixed proportions in producing any product, that there are constant returns to scale, and that consumer demand for all commodities is given. An important feature of input-output analysis is its emphasis on the interdependence of the economy. Input-output analysis involves the solution of a number of simultaneous linear equations.

---

24. To a considerable extent, this section is based on M. Olson, *The Logic of Collective Choice*, rev. ed. (New York: Shocken, 1971). Also, see M. Olson and R. Zeckhauser, "An Economic Theory of Alliances," *The Review of Economics and Statistics*, August 1966.

3. Welfare economics is concerned with the nature of the policy recommendations that economists can make. An important limitation of welfare economics is that there is no scientifically meaningful way to compare the utility levels of different individuals, with the result that we cannot tell whether one distribution of income is better than another.

4. Putting aside the question of income distribution, there are three conditions for a Pareto-optimal allocation of resources: (1) The marginal rate of substitution between any two commodities must be the same for any two consumers; (2) the marginal rate of technical substitution between any two inputs must be the same for any pair of producers; and (3) the marginal rate of substitution between any two commodities must be the same as the marginal rate of transformation between these two commodities for any producer.

5. One of the most fundamental findings of microeconomics is that a perfectly competitive economy satisfies these three sets of conditions for welfare maximization. To the economic theorist, this is one of the basic arguments for a perfectly competitive economy. Economists interested in the functioning of planned, or socialist, economies have argued that a price system could be used in a similar way to increase welfare in such economies. The prices that would be set would equal marginal cost.

6. If social costs differ from private costs and/or social benefits differ from private benefits, perfect competition will not lead to an optimal allocation of resources. If the production of a certain good is responsible for external economies, less than the socially optimum amount of this good is likely to be produced under perfect competition. If the production of a certain good is responsible for external diseconomies, more of this good is likely to be produced under perfect competition than is socially optimal. To a large extent, undesirably high levels of pollution are due to external diseconomies in waste disposal.

7. A public good can be enjoyed by one person without reducing the enjoyment it gives others. Even if the market mechanism can be applied to a public good, it is inefficient to do so, because the market mechanism cannot function except by excluding those who will not pay; but excluding them reduces their satisfaction and does not increase the satisfaction of others.

8. Whereas economic efficiency requires that each consumer's marginal benefit equal marginal cost for a private good, it requires that the sum of the marginal benefits of all consumers equal marginal cost for a public good. An important problem is to get people to reveal their true preferences since, if they can avoid paying, they can often get the benefits from public goods anyway.

9. If the number of people in a society is quite small, it may be worthwhile for people acting individually to provide some quantity of public goods. However, there is a tendency for the provision of a public good to be too small; the larger the number of people in the society, the farther it will fall short of providing an optimal amount of a public good. Thus the government tends to intervene in an attempt to assure the proper amount of such goods.

━━━━━━━━ QUESTIONS/PROBLEMS ━━━━━━━━

1) Suppose that the following table shows the amount of each type of input used per dollar of output:

| | *Output* | | |
Type of input	*Electric power* (dollars)	*Coal* (dollars)	*Chemicals* (dollars)
Electric power	0.1	0.3	0.0
Coal	0.5	0.1	0.0
Chemicals	0.2	0.0	0.9
Labor	0.2	0.6	0.1
Total	1.0	1.0	1.0

Express the value of electric power output as a function of the value of coal output and the value of chemical output.

2) According to Milton Friedman, significant external economies are gained from the education of children: "The gain from the education of a child accrues not only to the child or its parents but also to other members of the society." Moreover, "It is not feasible to identify the particular individuals (or families) benefited and so to charge for the services rendered." What kind of government action is justified by these considerations?

3) Suppose that two consumers, after swapping goods back and forth, have arrived at a point on the contract curve. In other words, neither can be made better off without making the other worse off. Does this mean that neither of them can find a point *off* the contract curve which is preferable to the point at which they have arrived? If it does not mean this, why do economists claim that points on the contract curve are to be preferred?

4) In 1986, Congress passed a bill making business entertainment expenses partly, but not wholly, tax deductible. (Previously they had been completely deductible.) What segments of the population did this hurt? What segments did it help? Is there any way to tell whether, on balance, it was good or bad for society?

5) A small private jet lands at Kennedy Airport in New York at the busiest time of day. It pays a nominal landing fee. What divergences may exist between the private and social costs of this plane's landing there at that time? What policies might help to eliminate such divergences?

6) Welfare economics is concerned largely with the determination of ways to satisfy human wants as best we can. But is this really a sensible goal? For example, suppose that people want the wrong things. Is it still sensible to try to satisfy these wants as completely as possible? Shouldn't welfare economics be concerned, too, with how wants are created?

7) Suppose that the market for videocasette recorders is in disequilibrium; that is, the actual price does not equal the equilibrium price. If all industries in the economy are perfectly competitive (including videocassette recorders), will the necessary conditions for optimal resource allocation be met?

8) In judging various social mechanisms and policies, welfare economics tends to emphasize the outcomes of these mechanisms and policies, as measured by the extent to which various human wants are satisfied. But shouldn't welfare economics be concerned with *means* as well as *ends*? For example, suppose that a particular policy resulted in an ideal allocation of resources, but that it was achieved by trickery or coercion. Doesn't this matter?

9) Suppose that there are only three citizens of a (very small) nation and that the amount of national defense each would demand (at various prices) is as follows:

Price of a unit of national defense (dollars)	Citizen A	Citizen B	Citizen C
	(number of units demanded)		
1	10	8	12
2	9	7	9
3	8	6	7
4	7	5	5

If the marginal cost of a unit of national defense is $9, what is the optimal amount of national defense for this nation?

EFFECTS OF QUOTAS ON STEEL IMPORTS INTO THE UNITED STATES

During the 1980s, the system of free trade that helped to bring about the economic prosperity of the 1960s and 1970s came under increasing attack. The recession of 1981–82 resulted in serious unemployment in many nations of the world. With over 20 million people out of work in 1983 in the United States and Western Europe alone, a growing number of businessmen, labor leaders, and politicians raised their voices to demand protectionist barriers against foreign competition. Nowhere was there more concern over foreign competition than in the American steel industry, which rolled up an impressive record of losses in the early 1980s. (For example, Bethlehem Steel Corporation lost about $1.5 billion in 1982.) Faced with great difficulties in competing with Japanese and other foreign steelmakers, American steel firms pleaded with the government to set quotas limiting the quantity of steel that could be imported into the United States, and their petitions were heard. In September 1984 the U.S. government announced a plan to tighten the coverage of restraints on imports of foreign steel. Between 1984 and 1987, steel imports fell from about 26 percent to 23 percent of the American market.

An enormous amount of controversy resulted among economists and others. Traditionally, most economists have argued against quotas of this sort on the grounds that they reduce trade, raise prices, protect domestic industry at the expense of consumers, and reduce the standard of living of the nation as a whole. To estimate the effects of such a quota, the staff of the Federal Trade Commission (FTC) carried out a detailed economic study,[1] which is useful in demonstrating how microeconomic theory can contribute to the analysis of major public policies. To begin with, the FTC economists estimated the demand curve for steel in the United States and the supply curve for U.S.-produced steel, both shown in Figure 1. The supply curve for foreign-produced steel was a horizontal line at $311. Thus, adding horizontally the supply curve for U.S. steel and the supply curve for foreign steel, we get the supply curve of all steel in the United States, which is *SGW*. Since this supply curve intersects the demand curve at point *A,* the equilibrium price is $311 per ton and the equilibrium quantity is 91.7 million tons of steel. The U.S. steel industry supplies 78.1 million tons, and foreigners supply 13.6 million tons.

---

1. Federal Trade Commission, *Staff Report on the United States Steel Industry and Its International Rivals,* November 1977.

Fig. 1

EFFECTS OF A STEEL IMPORT QUOTA / *U.S. steel producers gain $868.5 million per year from the quota, while U.S. consumers lose $1,003.75 million per year. Thus consumers lose more than producers gain.*

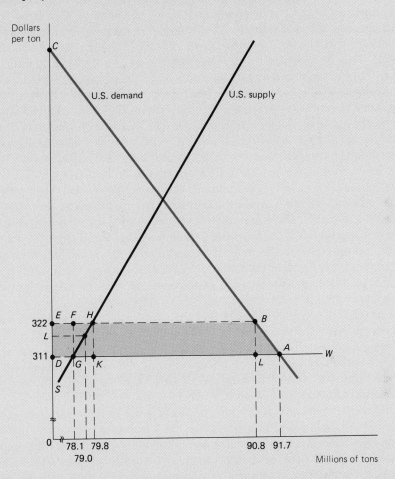

What is the effect if the U.S. government imposes a quota which limits imports to 11 million tons? In other words, what would happen if American steel imports could not exceed 11 million tons? The demand and supply curves show that, if the price is $322, American demand will exceed American supply by 11 million tons. Thus, once the quota is imposed, the price will rise to $322, since this is the price that will reduce our imports to the amount of the quota. Consequently, the equilibrium will be at point *B*, where price is $322 per ton and the equilibrium quantity is 90.8 million tons of steel. The U.S. steel industry supplies 79.8 million tons, and foreigners supply 11 million tons.

Who gains and who loses from this quota? American consumers lose an amount equal to the shaded area in Figure 1. Before the imposition of the quota, consumer's surplus in the United States equals the area under the demand curve above the price of $311 (that is, it equals the area of triangle DCA). After the imposition of the quota, consumer's surplus in the United States equals the area under the demand curve above the price of $322 (that is, it equals the area of triangle ECB). The reduction in consumer's surplus due to the imposition of the quota is area DCA minus ECB, or area $DEBA$ (which is shaded). This area equals $\frac{1}{2}(322 - 311) \cdot (90.8 + 91.7) = 1,003.75$ millions of dollars. Thus consumers stand to lose about $1 billion per year from the quota.

American steel producers gain from the quota, their gain being of two types. First, they are able to sell the 78.1 million tons that they would have sold without the quota at a higher price ($322 rather than $311). The extra profit equals the area of rectangle $DEFG$, or $(322 - 311)(78.1) = 859.1$ millions of dollars. Second, they are able to sell 79.8, rather than 78.1 million tons. Their profit from the extra 1.7 million tons equals the area of triangle GFH, or $\frac{1}{2}(322 - 311)(79.8 - 78.1) = 9.4$ millions of dollars. (Why is this their profit? Because the supply curve shows the industry's marginal cost at each level of output. For example, the marginal cost of the 79-millionth ton of U.S.-produced steel equals OL. Thus the profit earned from the 79-millionth ton equals its price minus OL, or $322 - OL$. If we add up the difference between price and marginal cost for all of the extra 1.7 million tons, we get the area of triangle GFH.) Adding the two types of gain, American steel producers increase their profits by $859.1 + 9.4 = 868.5$ millions of dollars per year.

Part of U.S. consumers' losses find their way into the pockets of foreign steelmakers. After the imposition of the quota, U.S. consumers buy 11 million tons of foreign steel products, which cost $322 - 311 = 11$ dollars per ton more than before the imposition of the quota. Thus $11 \times 11 = 121$ millions of dollars per year (the area of rectangle $KHBL$) of U.S. consumers' losses are transferred to foreign steelmakers.[2]

In addition, part of U.S. consumers' losses is due to their consuming 90.8 rather than 91.7 million tons of steel products. The loss in consumer's surplus arising from their forgoing the consumption of these 0.9 million tons equals the area of triangle LBA, or $\frac{1}{2}(322 - 311)(91.7 - 90.8) = 5.0$ millions of dollars. As we know from Chapter 4, the area of this triangle equals the consumer's surplus from the consumption of these 0.9 million tons.

Finally, part of U.S. consumers' losses is due to the fact that more costly U.S. steel is being substituted for less costly foreign steel. After the quota is introduced, U.S. steel firms produce 79.8 million tons, in contrast to 78.1 million tons before the imposition of the quota. The extra $79.8 - 78.1 = 1.7$ million tons could be obtained more cheaply from foreign producers. The total extra amount that U.S. consumers pay for this 1.7 million tons equals the area of tri-

---

2. This assumes that foreign exporters would be called upon to monitor exports to comply with the quota. Alternatively, with restrictive licensing of domestic importers, the importers extract this profit. According to the FTC economists, the former assumption is more likely.

angle *GHK,* or ½(322 − 311) (79.8 − 78.1) = 9.4 millions of dollars. (Why is this the correct measure? Because the extra amount paid for each ton is the difference between the marginal cost of producing it in the United States and the cost of obtaining it from abroad. For example, for the 79-millionth ton produced in the United States this difference equals *OL* − $311, since its marginal cost equals *OL* and the cost of obtaining it from abroad is $311. Thus, if we sum up the differences for all 1.7 million extra tons, the total extra amount that consumers pay for this reason equals the area of triangle *GHK.*)

To sum up, this analysis indicates that U.S. steel producers gain $868.5 million per year from the quota, while U.S. consumers lose $1,003.75 million per year. Thus consumers lose more than producers gain. Part of the difference goes to foreign producers; the rest is due to lower consumption of steel products and the substitution of high-cost U.S. steel for cheaper foreign steel.[3]

ANALYTICAL QUESTIONS

1) This analysis looks at how all U.S. consumers and all U.S. steel producers are affected by the import quotas. It what ways are the results clouded by the fact that we cannot make interpersonal comparisons of utility?

2) According to the Congressional Budget Office, if imports of steel are limited to 15 percent of the U.S. market, the cost to consumers would be about $178,000 for each American steel job created (or saved). Relative to the quotas, under what circumstances would both consumers and steelworkers be better off if the former paid the latter not to work?

3) Can the transfer of income from consumers to steelworkers due to the import quotas be defended on the grounds that it helps the poor? (Hint: In 1983, the average wage of steelworkers was about 75 percent higher than that of all American workers in manufacturing.)

4) Proponents of quotas often argue that quotas provide the protected industry with the time and resources to modernize, thus enabling it to become competitive internationally. According to the National Academy of Engineering, the average cost of producing steel is appreciably higher in the United States than in Japan, due partly to the fact that total hourly compensation paid to steelworkers in the United States as been about 40 percent higher than in Japan. What measures can American steel producers take to offset this competitive disadvantage?

5) What pressure groups have favored steel import quotas? Why have government officials adopted these quotas?

---

3. For further discussion, see W. Cline, "U.S. Trade and Industrial Policy: The Experience of Textiles, Steel, and Automobiles," in P. Krugman (ed .), *Strategic Trade Policy and the New International Economics* (Cambridge, Mass.: MIT Press, 1986), and National Academy of Engineering, *The Competitive Status of the U.S. Steel Industry,* (Washington, D.C.: National Academy Press, 1985).

Glossary of Terms

Alternative cost The value of what particular resources could have produced had they been used in the best alternative way; also designated as opportunity cost.

Arc elasticity of demand If P_1 and Q_1 are the first values of price and quantity demanded, and P_2 and Q_2 are the second set, the arc elasticity equals $-(Q_1 - Q_2)$ $(P_1 + P_2) \div (P_1 - P_2)(Q_1 + Q_2)$.

Average cost Total cost divided by output. It is also called average total cost.

Average fixed cost Total fixed cost divided by output.

Average product Total output divided by the quantity of input.

Average variable cost Total variable cost divided by output.

Barometric firm A firm that usually initiates price changes that are generally accepted by other firms in an oligopolistic industry. It is a reasonably accurate interpreter of basic changes in cost and demand conditions in the industry as a whole.

Bilateral monopoly A form of market structure occurring when a monopolistic seller is confronted with a single buyer.

Break-even chart A chart showing how both total revenue and total cost vary with changes in the total number of units of a product that is sold. The break-even point is the minimum number that must be sold to avoid loss.

Budget line A line showing all combinations of quantities of good X and good Y the consumer can buy. Its slope equals -1 times the price of good X divided by the price of good Y.

Capital Equipment, buildings, inventories, raw materials, and other nonhuman producible resources that contribute to the production, marketing, and distribution of goods and services.

Capitalism A type of economic system that depends on the price system to answer the basic economic questions: What is produced? How is it produced? Who gets how much? What should be the rate of economic growth?

Cardinal utility Utility that is measurable in a cardinal sense, like a person's weight or height (which means that the difference between two utilities, i.e., marginal utility, is meaningful). This is in contrast to ordinal utility, which is measurable in only an ordinal sense.

Cartel A form of market structure where there is an open and formal agreement among firms to collude.

Cobb-Douglas production function A production function where $Q = AL^{\alpha_1}K^{\alpha_2}M^{\alpha_3}$. In this equation, Q is the output rate, L is the quantity of labor, K is the quantity of capital, M is the quantity of raw materials, and A, α_1, α_2, and α_3 are constants.

Cobweb theorem A simple dynamic model of price and output where the quantity supplied depends on price in the previous period, and the quantity demanded depends on price in the current period.

Collusion Agreements by firms with others in their industry with regard to price, output, and other matters.

Complements If goods X and Y are complements, the quantity demanded of X is inversely related to the price of Y.

Constant-cost industry An industry with a horizontal long-run supply curve; its expansion does not result in an increase or decrease in input prices.

Constant returns to scale If the quantities of all inputs are increased by the same percentage, and if as a result output increases by the same percentage, there are constant returns to scale.

Consumer's surplus The maximum amount that the consumer would pay for a particular good or service less the amount that he or she actually pays for it.

Contestable market A market in which entry is absolutely free and exit is absolutely costless. The essence of contestable markets is that they are vulnerable to hit-and-run entry.

Contract curve The locus of points where the marginal rates of substitution are the same for both consumers (in exchange between consumers) or the locus of points where the marginal rates of technical substitution are the same for both producers (in exchange between producers).

Cross elasticity of demand The percentage change in the quantity of good X resulting from a 1 percent change in the price of good Y.

Decreasing-cost industry An industry with a negatively sloped long-run supply curve; its expansion results in a decrease in its average cost.

Decreasing returns to scale If the quantities of all inputs are increased by the same percentage, and if as a result output increases by less than this percentage, there are decreasing returns to scale.

Demand curve A curve showing the amount of a product demanded at each price.

Dominant firm In an oligopolistic industry, a single large firm that sets the price, but lets the small firms in the industry sell all they want at that price.

Dominant strategy A strategy that is best for a player regardless of what the other player's strategy may be.

Duopoly A form of market structure where there are two sellers. The Cournot model, among others, is concerned with duopoly.

Economic profit The difference between a firm's revenues and its costs, where the latter include the returns that could be gotten from the most lucrative alternative use of the firm's resources.

Economic region of production The input combinations where isoquants are negatively sloped. No profit-maximizing firm will operate at a point where the isoquant has a positive slope, since the marginal product of one or the other input must be negative if this is so.

Economic resource A scarce resource, which commands a nonzero price.

Elasticity of substitution Minus 1 times the relative change in the capital-labor ratio divided by the relative change in the ratio of the price of capital to the price of labor.

Engel curve The relationship between the equilibrium quantity purchased of a good and the consumer's level of income. It was named after Ernst Engel, a nineteenth-century German statistician.

Equilibrium A situation where there is no tendency for change. For example, an equilibrium price is a price that can be maintained.

Excess capacity The difference between the minimum-cost output and the actual output in long-run equilibrium. A famous and controversial conclusion of the theory of monopolistic competition is that firms under this form of market structure will tend to operate with excess capacity.

Expansion path The locus of points where the isoquants corresponding to various outputs are tangent to the isocost curves. (No inputs are fixed.)

Explicit costs The ordinary expenses of the firm that accountants include, such as payroll costs and payments for raw materials.

External diseconomy An uncompensated cost to one person or firm resulting from the consumption or output of another person or firm.

External economy An uncompensated benefit to one person or firm resulting from the consumption or output of another person or firm.

Fixed cost The total cost per period of time of the fixed inputs.

Fixed input A resource used in the production process (such as plant and equipment) whose quantity cannot be changed during the period under consideration.

Free resource A resource that is so abundant that it can be had for a zero price.

General equilibrium analysis An analysis that (in contrast to a partial equilibrium analysis) takes account of the interrelationships among various markets and prices.

Giffen's paradox A situation where the quantity demanded of a good is directly related to its price. This occurs when the substitution effect of a price change is not strong enough to offset an inferior good's income effect.

Implicit costs The alternative costs of using the resources owned by the firm's owner, such as his or her time and capital.

Income-consumption curve A curve connecting points representing equilibrium market baskets corresponding to all possible levels of the consumer's money income. Curves of this sort can be used to derive Engel curves.

Income effect The change in the quantity demanded of good X due entirely to a change in the consumer's level of satisfaction, all prices being held constant.

Income elasticity of demand The percentage change in quantity demanded resulting from a 1 percent change in consumer income, when prices are held constant.

Increasing-cost industry An industry with a positively sloped long-run supply curve; its expansion results in an increase in input prices.

Increasing returns to scale If the quantities of all inputs are increased by the same percentage, and if as a result output increases by more than this percentage, there are increasing returns to scale.

Indifference curve The locus of points representing market baskets among which the consumer is indifferent.

Inferior good A good where the income effect is such that increases in real income result in decreases in the quantity demanded.

Innovation An invention, when applied for the first time, is called an innovation.

Input Any resource used in the production process.

Interest rate The premium received by the lender one year hence if he or she lends a dollar for a year. If the interest rate equals r, he or she receives $(1 + r)$ dollars a year hence.

Intermediate good A good that is used to produce other goods and services.

Investment The process of creating new capital assets.

Isocost curve A curve showing the combinations of inputs that can be obtained for a fixed total outlay.

Isoprofit curve A curve showing all input combinations that can produce a given level of profit.

Isoquant A curve showing all possible (efficient) combinations of inputs that are capable of producing a certain quantity of output.

Isorevenue line A line showing all combinations of outputs of two commodities that result in the same total revenue.

Kinked demand curve A demand curve facing an oligopolist where there is a kink at the existing price, demand being more elastic for price increases than for price decreases.

Labor Human effort, physical or mental, used to produce goods and services.

Land Natural resources, including both minerals and plots of ground, used to produce goods and services.

Law of diminishing marginal returns According to this law, if equal increments of an input are added (and if the quantities of other inputs are held constant), the resulting increments of product will decrease beyond some point; that is, the marginal product of the input will diminish.

Law of diminishing marginal utility According to this law, as a person consumes more and more of a given commodity (the consumption of other commodities being held constant), the marginal utility of the commodity eventually will tend to decline.

Limit pricing A form of pricing in oligopolistic industries where price is set so as to bar entry. A limit price is one that discourages or prevents entry.

Long run The period of time in which all inputs are variable. The firm can change completely the resources it uses in the long run.

Marginal cost The addition to total cost resulting from the addition of the last unit of output.

Marginal cost pricing A pricing rule whereby firms or government-owned enterprises set price equal to marginal cost.

Marginal expenditure curve A curve showing the additional cost to the firm of increasing its utilization of input X by one unit.

Marginal product The addition to total output due to the addition of the last unit of an input (when the quantity of other inputs is held constant).

Marginal rate of product transformation The negative of the slope of the product transformation curve.

Marginal rate of substitution The number of units of good Y that must be given up if the consumer, after receiving an extra unit of good X, is to maintain a constant level of satisfaction.

Marginal revenue The addition to total revenue due to selling one more unit of the product.

Marginal revenue product The increase in total revenue due to the use of an additional unit of input X. It equals the marginal product of input X times the firm's marginal revenue.

Marginal utility The additional satisfaction (that is, utility) derived from an additional unit of a commodity (when the levels of consumption of all other commodities are held constant).

Market A group of firms and individuals in touch with each other in order to buy or sell some good.

Market demand curve A curve that shows the relationship between a product's price and the quantity of it demanded in the entire market.

Market demand schedule A table that shows the relationship between a product's price and the quantity of it demanded in the entire market.

Market period A period of time during which the quantity that is supplied of a good is fixed.

Market structure Four general types of market structure are perfect competition, monopoly, monopolistic competition, and oligopoly. The structure of a market depends on the number of buyers and of sellers, as well as the extent of product differentiation and other factors.

Market supply curve A curve that shows the relationship between a product's price and the amount supplied of the product in the entire market.

Market supply schedule A table showing the quantity of a good that would be supplied at various prices.

Markup A percentage (or absolute) amount added to a product's estimated average cost to obtain its price; this amount is meant to include costs that cannot be allocated to any specific product and to provide a return on the firm's investment.

Microeconomics The part of economics dealing with the economic behavior of individual units such as consumers, firms, and resource owners (in contrast to macroeconomics, which deals with the behavior of economic aggregates like gross national product).

Model A theory based on assumptions that simplify and abstract from reality, from which predictions or conclusions about the real world are deduced.

Money income Income of the consumer measured in actual dollar amounts per period of time.

Monopolistic competition A market structure where there are many sellers of differentiated products, where entry is easy, and where there is no collusion among sellers.

Monopoly A market structure where there is only one seller of a product. Public utilities often are examples.

Monopsony A market structure where there is only a single buyer. A firm that hires all the labor in a company town is an example.

Multiplant monopoly A monopolist that owns and operates more than one plant, and that must determine the output of each of its plants.

Nash equilibrium An equilibrium in game theory where, given that every other player's strategy is what it is, each player has no reason to change his or her own strategy.

Natural monopoly An industry where the average cost of production reaches a minimum at an output rate large enough to satisfy the entire market; thus, competition cannot be sustained and one firm becomes the monopolist.

Nonprice competition Rivalry among firms based on the use of advertising and other marketing weapons, as well as on the variation in product characteristics due to research and development and styling changes.

Normal goods Goods that experience increases in quantity demanded in response to increases in the consumer's real income.

Oligopoly A market structure where there are only a few sellers of products that can be identical or differentiated. Examples are the markets for computers or petroleum.

Oligopsony A market structure where there are few buyers.

Opportunity cost The value of what particular resources could have produced if they had been used in the best alternative way; also designated as alternative cost.

Optimal input combination The combination of inputs that maximizes social welfare (optimal from society's point of view) or the combination that maximizes profit (optimal from a profit-maximizing firm's point of view).

Ordinal utility Utility that is measurable in an ordinal sense, which means that a consumer can only rank various market baskets with respect to the satisfaction they give him or her.

Pareto criterion A criterion to determine whether a particular change improves social welfare; according to this criterion, a change that harms no one and improves the lot of some people (in their own eyes) is an improvement.

Pareto-efficient A situation where all changes that harm no one and improve the well-being of some people have already been carried out; also called Pareto-optimal.

Pareto-optimal A situation where all changes that harm no one and improve the well-being of some people have already been carried out; also called Pareto-efficient.

Partial equilibrium analysis An analysis assuming (in contrast to a general equilibrium analysis) that changes in price in a particular market can occur without causing significant changes in price in other markets.

Partnership A form of business organization in which two or more persons agree to conduct and own a business, with each party contributing some proportion of the capital and/or labor and receiving some proportion of the profit or loss.

Patent An exclusive right to one's invention, including the right to prevent others from using it.

Pecuniary benefits Benefits arising because of changes in relative prices that come about as the economy adjusts to a project (as distinguished from real benefits, which augment society's welfare).

Perfect competition A market structure where there are many sellers of identical products, where no one buyer or seller has control over price, where entry is easy, and where resources can switch readily from one use to another. Examples having many of the characteristics of perfectly competitive markets include many agricultural markets.

Predatory pricing The practice of setting price below costs in order to drive a rival firm out of business.

Price ceiling A government-imposed maximum for the price of a particular good. For example, New York City's rent controls impose a ceiling on rents.

Price-consumption curve A curve connecting the various equilibrium points corresponding to market baskets chosen by the consumer at various prices of a commodity.

Price discrimination The practice whereby one buyer is charged more than another buyer for the same product.

Price elastic The demand for a product if its price elasticity of demand exceeds 1.

Price elasticity of demand The percentage change in quantity demanded resulting from a 1 percent change in price (by convention, always expressed as a positive number).

Price elasticity of supply The percentage change in quantity supplied resulting from a 1 percent change in price.

Price floor A government-imposed minimum for the price of a particular good. For example, federal farm programs impose floors for the prices of wheat and corn.

Price inelastic The demand for a product if its price elasticity of demand is less than 1.

Price leader A firm in an oligopolistic industry that sets a price that other firms are willing to follow.

Price system A system whereby each good and service has a price, and which in a purely capitalistic economy carries out the basic functions of an economic system (determining what will be produced, how it will be produced, how much of it each person will get, and what the nation's growth of per capita output will be).

Prisoner's dilemma A situation in which two persons (or firms) would both do better to cooperate than not to cooperate, but where each feels it is in his or her interests not to do so; thus, each fares worse than if they cooperated.

Private cost The expense incurred by the individual user to obtain the use of a resource.

Product transformation curve A curve showing the various combinations or quantities of two products that can be produced with a given amount of resources.

Production function The relationship between the quantities of various inputs used per period of time and the maximum amount of output that can be produced per period of time.

Profit The difference between a firm's revenue and its costs.

Proprietorship A firm owned by an individual.

Public good A good or service that can be consumed by one person without reducing the amount of it that others can consume. It often is impossible to prevent citizens from consuming public goods whether they pay for them or not.

Quasi-rent A payment to an input in temporarily fixed supply. For example, in the short run, a firm's plant cannot be altered, and the payments to this and other fixed inputs are quasi-rents.

Real benefits Benefits that augment society's welfare (as distinguished from pecuniary benefits, which arise because of changes in relative prices that come about as the economy adjusts to a project).

Rent The return paid to an input that is fixed in supply.

Ridge lines Lines (on a graph with capital on one axis and labor on the other axis) between which are included all input combinations that would be chosen by a profit-maximizing firm.

Saving When a consumer refrains from consuming part of the goods he or she has, this is saving.

Second-degree price discrimination A monopolist charges a different price, depending on how much the consumer purchases, thus increasing its revenue and profit.

Selling expenses The expenses of advertising and distributing a product and of trying to convince potential customers that they should buy it.

Short run A period of time in which some of the firm's inputs (generally its plant and equipment) are fixed in quantity.

Social cost The cost to society of producing a given commodity or taking a particular action. This cost may not equal the private cost.

Substitutes If goods X and Y are substitutes, the quantity demanded of X is directly related to the price of Y.

Substitution effect The change in the quantity demanded of a good resulting from a price change when the level of satisfaction of the consumer is held constant.

Supply curve A curve that shows how much of a product will be supplied at each level of the product's price.

Target return A desired rate of return that a firm hopes to achieve by means of cost-plus pricing.

Technological change New ways of producing existing products, new designs enabling the production of new products, and new techniques of organization, marketing, and management.

Technology Society's pool of knowledge regarding how goods and services can be produced from a given amount of resources.

Third-degree price discrimination A situation where a monopolist sells a good in more than one market, where the good cannot be transferred from one market and resold to another, and where the monopolist can set different prices in different markets.

Tit for tat A strategy in game theory where each player does on this round what the other player did on the previous round.

Total cost The sum of a firm's total fixed cost and total variable cost.

Total cost function Relationship between a firm's total cost and its output.

Total fixed cost A firm's total expenditure on fixed inputs per period of time.

Total revenue A firm's total dollar sales volume per period of time.

Total utility A number representing the level of satisfaction that a consumer derives from a particular market basket.

Total variable cost A firm's total expenditure on variable inputs per period of time.

Transaction cost The cost of bringing buyers and sellers together, of contracting, and of obtaining information concerning the market.

Unitary elasticity A price elasticity of demand equal to 1.

Utility A number that represents the level of satisfaction that the consumer derives from a particular market basket is the utility attached by the consumer to this market basket.

Value of marginal product The marginal product of an input (i.e., the extra output resulting from an extra unit of the input) multiplied by the product's price.

Variable cost The total cost per period of time of the variable inputs.

Variable input A resource used in the production process whose quantity can be changed during the particular period under consideration.

Brief Answers to Odd-Numbered Questions and Problems

Chapter 1

1) (a) The amount of cigarettes bootlegged into a particular state depends on this state's tax rate relative to that of its neighboring states. If a state's tax rate is much higher than that of its neighbors, bootleggers can make money by bringing cigarettes into this state. Also, the amount bootlegged into a particular state depends on the cost of transporting the cigarettes. The higher the cost per mile of transporting a truckload of cigarettes, the smaller the distance it is profitable to take them. (b) No. Florida's loss from tax evasion is over 15 percent of that in all states, which is disproportionately large. Thus, its tax rate would be expected to be higher than that of neighboring states (which in fact is true). (c) Since its loss from tax evasion increased (while that in other states decreased) during 1975–79, one would expect that its tax increased relative to that in neighboring states. In fact, it increased its tax by 3 cents per pack. (d) Yes. The cost of transporting the cigarettes increased.

3) No, because most of the disagreements stem from differences in ethical and political views.

5) No. This is the so-called fallacy of composition.

7) Yes, because the latter statements reflect the value judgments of the economist.

9) The most important test of a model is how well it predicts. Another is whether its assumptions are logically consistent. Another important consideration is the range of phenomena to which the model applies.

Chapter 2

1) (a) According to the economic consultant's demand curve, about 60,000 tickets will be purchased if the price of a ticket is $400; about 70,000 will be purchased if the price is $200. Thus the arc elasticity of demand is

$$\frac{-(70,000 - 60,000)}{(70,000 + 60,000)/2} \div \frac{(200 - 400)}{(200 + 400)/2} = 0.23.$$

This is quite different from Verleger's finding (that the price elasticity is 0.67). (b) Such an increase in price would reduce the *quantity of tickets demanded,* but it would *not* shift the demand curve. In other words, there would be a *movement along* the demand curve from a point corresponding to the old price to a point corresponding to the new price, but no *shift* in the demand curve.   (c) Yes, it may shift it to the left, because fewer people will travel between these two cities for vacations and recreation, and because business travel may also be curtailed.   (d) No, but it does affect the supply curve, which is shifted to the left.

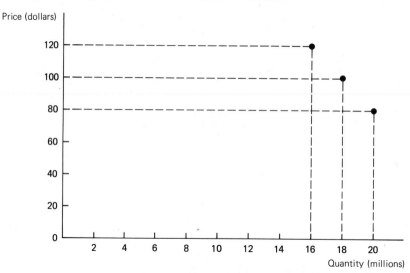

3)

(a) $\eta = -\dfrac{(20 - 18)}{(20 + 18)/2} \div \dfrac{(80 - 100)}{(80 + 100)/2} = 0.47$

(b) $\eta = -\dfrac{(18 - 16)}{(18 + 16)/2} \div \dfrac{(100 - 120)}{(100 + 120)/2} = 0.65$

5) $100.   Excess demand.   Excess supply.

7) With the excise tax, the supply curve is

Price (dollars)	Quantity supplied (millions)
100	14
120	16
140	18
160	19

Thus the equilibrium price of a bicycle is $120, since at this price the quantity supplied equals the quantity demanded. If the government sets a price ceiling of $100, there will be a shortage of 4 million bicycles per year, since the quantity demanded will equal 18 million while the quantity supplied will equal 14 million.

9) Since the quantity supplied (Q_S) must equal the quantity demanded (Q_D), we have two equations to be solved simultaneously:

$$120 - 3Q_D = 5Q_S$$
$$Q_D = Q_S.$$

Letting quantity equal Q, it follows that

$$120 - 3Q = 5Q$$
$$120 = 8Q$$
$$15 = Q.$$

Since $P = 5Q$, it follows that $P = 75$. Thus the equilibrium price is 75 cents and the equilibrium quantity is 15 million pounds per year.

11) From Question 9,

$$P = 120 - 3Q_D$$

or

$$3Q_D = 120 - P$$

$$Q_D = 40 - 1/3\ P.$$

Also, $Q_S = 1/5\ P$. Thus, if $P = 80$, $Q_D = 40 - 80/3 = 13\frac{1}{3}$, and $Q_S = 80/5 = 16$. Consequently, $Q_S - Q_D = 16 - 13\frac{1}{3} = 2\frac{2}{3}$, which means that the resulting surplus equals $2\frac{2}{3}$ million pounds per year. To reduce this surplus, the government could attempt to reduce the amount of cantaloupes produced by farmers or expand the demand for cantaloupes.

Chapter 3

1) He should set the ratio of the marginal utility of good X to its price equal to the ratio of the marginal utility of good Y to its price. If he buys 5 units of good X and 1 unit of good Y, the total amount spent is $1,000, and this condition is met, since for each good this ratio equals 1 util ÷ $10.

3) $1,000, since the budget line intersects the vertical axis at 20. $Q_A = 20 - 0.5Q_B$, where Q_A is the quantity consumed of good A and Q_B is the quantity consumed of good B. $- 0.5$.   It must be $1,000 ÷ 40, or $25.   0.5.

5) 1.   It does not vary at all, at least in this range.   No.

7) Martin will be better off and will consume less bread. Because the $50 gift enables him, despite the price increase, to buy as much bread (and the other good) as he did before the price increase, the new budget line (after the price increase and gift) goes through point A, which corresponds to the old market basket Martin purchased. (See the figure on p. A-12.) The new equilibrium market basket (point B) is on a higher indifference curve than point A, and contains less bread than point A.

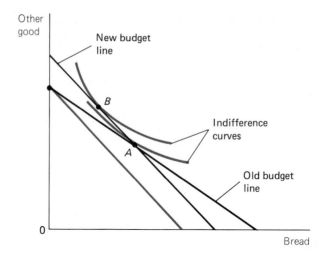

9) No.   Los Angeles, because the price of a pear divided by the price of an apple is higher in Los Angeles.

Chapter 4

1) (a) According to the diagram, a decrease in the price of good X from P_1 to P_2 results in an increase (from OA to OB) in the amount not spent on good X but spent on all other goods. This means that the consumer's expenditure on good X must have declined with a decrease in price, which implies that the consumer's demand for good X is price inelastic. (Recall p. 27.)   (b) If this price-consumption curve were downward sloping, a decrease in the price of good X would result in a decrease in the amount not spent on good X. Thus, the consumer's expenditure on good X must have increased with a decrease in price, which implies that the consumer's demand for good X is price elastic. (Recall p. 27.)

3) (a) The loss is the area under the demand curve from 5 to 10 trips, which equals $6 + $4 + $3 + $2 + $1, or $16.   (b) Once a family buys the permit, a trip to the lake is free. Thus, if it buys the permit, it will make 10 trips per year, as shown by the demand curve. The maximum amount that each family would pay for these 10 trips is the area under the demand curve from zero to 10 trips, which is $20 + $16 + $12 + $10 + $8 + $6 + $4 + $3 + $2 + $1, or $82. Since this maximum amount exceeds $75, each family would find it worthwhile to buy the permit.
(c) The calculations assume that these indifference curves are parallel. That is, if we measure the number of trips along the horizontal axis and the amount of money for all other goods along the vertical axis, the vertical distance between any two indifference curves is assumed to be the same regardless of where along the horizontal axis one measures this distance.

5) (a) Yes.   (b) If all consumers are maximizing utility (and if the optimal point is a tangency point, not a corner solution), the marginal rate of substitution of telephone calls for newspapers must equal the price of a telephone call divided by the price of a newspaper.   (c) Yes, it equals $25 \div 25$, or 1.

7) Both part (b) and part (c) are true.

9) The budget line is $Q_c + 0.5Q_p = 100$. This line is tangent to an indifference curve when $Q_p = 100$.

Chapter 5

1) (a) A 1 percent increase in the price of electricity would cut electricity consumption by 1.2 percent, because the price elasticity of demand is 1.2. A 6 percent increase in the price of natural gas would raise electricity consumption by about 1.2 percent, because the cross elasticity of demand is 0.2. Thus, if the price of natural gas were to increase by about 6 percent, this would offset the effect of the increase in electricity's price.   (b) Based on the data in the table given on p. 134, a 10 percent increase in income seems to result in about a 1 percent increase in electricity consumption. Thus the income elasticity seems to be about 0.1, not 0.2, as reported by Chapman, Tyrell, and Mount. This discrepancy could be due to the fact that the inhabitants of this suburb regard electricity to be more of a necessity than do all Americans.   (c) Both would be expected to be lower in the short run because consumers have less time to adapt to changes in income or price. In fact, Chapman, Tyrell, and Mount found both to be about 0.02 in the short run.

3) (a) There are a considerable number of important substitutes, notably plastics, aluminum, and concrete. For example, buildings and bridges formerly requiring structural steel can now use prestressed concrete.   (b) No, because the demand curve for the output of a single firm (Bethlehem) is not the same as the demand curve for the output of the steel industry as a whole. In general, we would expect the demand curve for the output of a single firm to be more price elastic than the industry's demand curve, because the output of other firms in the industry can be substituted for the output of the firm in question.   (c) If the demand for a firm's product is inelastic, this means that its price elasticity of demand, η, is less than 1. Based on Equation 5.4, it follows that, if η is less than 1, the firm's marginal revenue must be *negative*. Since marginal revenue is the change in total revenue attributable to the increase of one unit to sales, it follows that a *reduction* in the amount produced and sold by the firm would *increase* total revenue (because price would be raised enough to more than offset the smaller number of units sold). In a case of this sort, the firm could increase its profit by reducing its output (and raising its price). Why? Because profit equals total revenue minus total cost, and a reduction in output would increase total revenue and reduce total cost (since it would cost less to produce fewer units). Consequently, a reduction in output would increase profit, which means that the firm is not currently maximizing its profit.   (d) The cross elasticity of demand is positive because Bethlehem's steel and imported Japanese steel are substitutes.

5) Holding his income constant, the total amount he spends on Geritol is constant too; that is,

$$PQ = I$$

where P is the price of Geritol, Q is the quantity demanded by the consumer, and I is his income. Thus

$$Q = \frac{I}{P}.$$

Since I is held constant, this demand curve is a rectangular hyperbola, and the price elasticity of demand equals 1.　　Since $Q = I/P$, it follows that a 1 percent increase in I will result in a 1 percent increase in Q, when P is held constant. Thus the income elasticity of demand equals 1.　　Since Q does not depend on the price of any other good, the cross elasticity of demand equals zero.

7) Substitutes have a positive cross elasticity of demand. Thus cases (b) and (e) are likely to have a positive cross elasticity of demand.

9) It would indicate the extent to which fare increases would decrease subway travel. For example, if demand is price inelastic, fare increases would increase total revenue. Obviously this is an important fact.

11) Other factors—notably the general level of prices and incomes and the quality of the students—have not been held constant. Holding these factors—and the tuition rates at other universities—constant, it is almost surely untrue that large increases in tuition at this university would not cut down on the number of students demanding admission to the university.

13) The Engel curve shows the relationship between money income and the amount consumed of a particular commodity. If this relationship is a straight line through the origin, it follows that the amount consumed of this commodity is *proportional* to the consumer's money income. Thus a 1 percent increase in the consumer's money income results in a 1 percent increase in the amount consumed of this commodity. Consequently, the income elasticity of demand for this commodity equals 1.

Chapter 6

1) The complete table is

Number of units of variable input	Total output	Marginal product	Average product
3	90	Unknown	30
4	110	20	$27\frac{1}{2}$
5	130	20	26
6	135	5	$22\frac{1}{2}$
7	$136\frac{1}{2}$	$1\frac{1}{2}$	$19\frac{1}{2}$

3) Because of the law of diminishing marginal returns, the marginal product begins to decline at some point. If the marginal product exceeds the average product at that point, the marginal product can fall to some extent without reducing the average product. Only when it falls below the average product will the average product begin to decrease. The marginal product can continue to fall without reducing the total product. Only when it falls below zero will the total product begin to decrease.

5) 1.04 percent.

7) Yes.

9) (a) Yes, since it seems to reduce the amount of grain and protein that must be used to produce 150 pounds of pork. However, this assumes that it has no negative effect on the quality of the pork and that it does not increase the amount of other

inputs that must be used.   (b) At each quantity of protein, curve B is steeper than curve A. In other words, the absolute value of its slope is greater. Thus the marginal rate of technical substitution of protein for grain is greater when Aureomycin is added than when it is not (when the quantity of protein is held constant).

Chapter 7

1) (a) The marginal cost is the extra cost of an additional flight in 1989. The fuel, wages, and other extra costs are included.   (b) No, because some of these costs would be incurred regardless of whether the extra flight occurred.   (c) There probably will be additional costs to raise safety levels.

3) The table is as follows:

Total fixed cost (dollars)	Total variable cost (dollars)	Average fixed cost (dollars)	Average variable cost (dollars)
50	0	—	—
50	20	50	20
50	50	25	25
50	70	$16\frac{2}{3}$	$23\frac{1}{3}$
50	85	$12\frac{1}{2}$	$21\frac{1}{4}$
50	100	10	20
50	110	$8\frac{1}{3}$	$18\frac{1}{3}$
50	115	$7\frac{1}{7}$	$16\frac{3}{7}$

Each value of marginal cost would increase by 50 percent.

5) (a) Its fixed cost equaled $182.1 million, because, when $Q = 0$, $C = 182.1$, according to the equation.   (b) If U.S. Steel produced 10 million tons of steel, $Q = 10$. Thus $C = 182.1 + 55.73 (10) = 739.4$. This is total cost, not total variable cost. To obtain total variable cost, we subtract the fixed cost, 182.1, from 739.4, the result being $557.3 million. Since 10 million tons were produced, average variable cost was $557.3 million divided by 10 million, or $55.73 per ton.   (c) If output increased by 1 ton, the equation indicates that total cost increased by $55.73. Thus, marginal cost was $55.73 per ton.   (d) No. Beyond some point, as output increased, marginal cost was bound to increase, because of the law of diminishing marginal returns. (See p. 000 for further discussion of this point.)   (e) This equation is not appropriate for present conditions, because it is based on the input prices and technology of the 1930s, not those of today.   (f) No, because it is based on input prices and technology in the United States in the 1930s, not on those in Japan now.

7) (a) No, since no information is given concerning the way in which cost varies with output when capacity is held constant.   (b) The steam reforming process using natural gas, since its cost is lowest.   (c) Yes, because costs tend to fall as the scale of a plant increases.   (d) Yes, the function shifted downward. In the early 1960s, it was not possible to produce ammonia for $16 a ton, as is evident from the graph.

9) 1,000 copies sold.

Chapter 8

1) (a) No.   (b) Firms had to leave the textile industry, so that eventually the profit rate in cotton textiles would increase to the point where it approximated the profit rate in other industries. Also, the industry had to become more concentrated in the South, the exit rate being higher in the North than in the South. (c) Yes.

3) (a) No. This is the cost per acre, not the cost per bushel of corn produced.   (b) If Mr. Webster could rent the land that he owns for $110 per acre, the alternative cost of using an acre of land he owns is $110. Thus, based on the concept of alternative cost, the cost of using his own land is the same as that of using rented land.   (c) If each acre of land yields 120 bushels of corn, the cost per bushel of corn of fertilizers, herbicides, insecticides, fuel, seed, electricity, and labor equals ($41.84 + 2.76 + 5.50 + 18.00 + 16.50 + 15.00 + 15.00) ÷ 120, or 95.5 cents. Assuming that these inputs (and no others) are variable, average variable cost is 95.5 cents per bushel. Since the price of 80 cents is less than average variable cost, he should not produce any corn (unless, of course, he can somehow reduce his average variable cost by altering his output or by taking some other measures).   (d) Since the price of $1.50 per bushel exceeds the average variable cost of 95.5 cents per bushel, he should produce corn, even though the price is less than average total cost.

5) (a) Less. The supply curve will be to the left of the one shown on p. 255. (b) Less. The supply curve will be to the left of the one shown on p. 255.   (c) There commonly are substantial errors in estimates of this sort, if they are based on no actual operating experience. Many unanticipated problems can arise in operating new types of plants.   (d) Because of the uncertainties cited in part (c), such an investment would clearly be risky. Thus less shale oil is likely to be produced than under riskless conditions.

7) The firm's marginal cost curve is

Output	Marginal cost (dollars)
0 to 1	10
1 to 2	12
2 to 3	13
3 to 4	14
4 to 5	15
5 to 6	16
6 to 7	17

(a) If the price is $13, the firm will produce 2 or 3 units.   (b) 3 or 4 units. (c) 4 or 5 units.   (d) 5 or 6 units.   (e) 6 or 7 units.

9) $$\eta_s = \frac{(8-7)}{(8+7)/2} \div \frac{(4-3)}{(4+3)/2} = 0.47.$$

11) A difference of about 3.24 percent.

Chapter 9

1) (a) In the early 1950s, IBM seems to have been close to a monopoly, since it sold over 90 percent of the electronic data processing products and services in the United States. But during the 1960s and 1970s, its share of the market fell to about 50 percent and then to about 40 percent, according to its economists. Based on these data, they argued that IBM was not a monopolist.   (b) Yes. If a firm has a large share (say 60 percent or more) of the market, and if there is evidence that the firm's dominant position resulted from its own policies (and particularly if some form of abuse can be shown), past experience indicates that it may be challenged under Section 2 of the Sherman Act.   (c) Not necessarily. If the firm's large market share has been achieved by its own "superior skill, foresight, and industry," this can be an effective defense. (In fact, this was one of IBM's defenses.) The firm may argue that, if it were broken up, this would result in a slower rate of innovation and less efficiency.   (d) One of the most important considerations is the cross elasticity of demand among products. One wants to include products that are closely substitutable (i.e., that have high cross elasticities of demand).   (e) The narrower the definition of the market, the larger IBM's share is likely to be. Based on the government's definition, IBM's market share exceeded those shown in the table on p. 286. Clearly, it was consistent with the government's case to show that IBM's market share was high. (Nonetheless, in 1981, the Justice Department ended the case on the grounds that it was "without merit.")

3) The monopolist's total revenue, total cost, and total profit at each level of output are as follows:

Output	Total revenue (dollars)	Total cost (dollars)	Total profit (dollars)
5	40	20	20
6	42	21	21
7	42	22	20
8	40	23	17
9	36	24	12
10	30	30	0

Thus the optimal output is 6, which means that price should be $7.

5) If we follow the procedure described on pp. 275–76, the first step is to sum the two marginal revenue curves horizontally. To do so, we first express Q_1 and Q_2 as functions of MR_1 and MR_2. From the equations in Question 5 (p. 286), it follows that

$$Q_1 = 10 - \tfrac{1}{2} MR_1 \qquad\qquad\qquad\text{[B.1]}$$

$$Q_2 = 5 - \tfrac{1}{3} MR_2. \qquad\qquad\qquad\text{[B.2]}$$

Then setting $MR_1 = MR_2 = MR$, we find the value of $(Q_1 + Q_2)$ of each value of MR, with the result,

$$Q_1 + Q_2 = (10 - \tfrac{1}{2} MR) + (5 - \tfrac{1}{3} MR) = 15 - \tfrac{5}{6} MR.$$

Turning this equation around,

$$MR = 18 - \tfrac{6}{5} (Q_1 + Q_2),$$

which corresponds to the Z curve in Figure 9.9. Since the marginal cost curve is a horizontal line at $6, the Z curve intersects the marginal cost curve when

$$18 - \tfrac{6}{5}(Q_1 + Q_2) = 6,$$

or when $(Q_1 + Q_2) = 10$. When $MR_1 = MR_2 = \$6$, it follows from Equations B.1 and B.2 that $Q_1 = 7$ and $Q_2 = 3$. Thus the Errata Book Company should sell 7 books per day in the first market and 3 books per day in the second market. (Of course, in this elementary case, the answer can be obtained simply by setting MR_1 and MR_2 in Equations B.1 and B.2 equal to $6.)

7) Since the author's royalty is a fixed percentage of the price of the book, the total royalties per year earned by the author are proportional to the total revenue per year from the book. Consequently, the author would like to maximize total revenue, since this maximizes his or her royalties. To maximize total revenue, marginal revenue should be set equal to zero. On the other hand, the publisher would like to maximize profit, which means that marginal revenue should be set equal to marginal cost. Thus the author would like to set marginal revenue equal to a lower value than would the publisher. Holding constant the price elasticity of demand, marginal revenue decreases as price is lowered. Thus the author tends to prefer a lower price than does the publisher.

9)   Marginal revenue $= 100 - 2Q$.
            Marginal cost $= 60 + 2Q$.
            Consequently, $100 - 2Q = 60 + 2Q$
            $$40 = 4Q$$
            $$10 = Q.$$

That is, you should choose an output of 10 units.

11) $MR_1 = 160 - 16Q_1$
         $MR_2 = 80 - 4Q_2$
         $MC = 5 + (Q_1 + Q_2)$.
         Therefore $160 - 16Q_1 = 5 + Q_1 + Q_2$
         $80 - 4Q_2 = 5 + Q_1 + Q_2$.
         Or $155 - 17Q_1 = Q_2$
         $75 - 5Q_2 = Q_1$.
         Thus $155 - 17[75 - 5Q_2] = Q_2$
         $155 - 1275 + 85Q_2 = Q_2$
         $84Q_2 = 1120$
         $Q_2 = 13\tfrac{1}{3}$.

It should sell $13\tfrac{1}{3}$ units in the second market, and the price in this market should be $53\tfrac{1}{3}$.

$$Q_1 = 75 - 5Q_2$$
$$= 75 - 5(1120/84)$$
$$= 75 - \frac{5600}{84}$$
$$= 75 - 66\tfrac{2}{3}$$
$$= 8\tfrac{1}{3}.$$

It should sell $8\tfrac{1}{3}$ units in the first market, and the price in this market should be $93\tfrac{1}{3}$.

Chapter 10

1) (a) Price is $20, and output is 100 dresses per week, because this is the point where the *dd'* and *DD'* demand curves intersect the long-run average cost curve. Thus no economic profits are being earned.　　(b) No, because the *dd'* demand curve is not tangent to the long-run average cost curve. Since the *dd'* demand curve lies above the long-run average cost curve, when output per week is between 50 and 100 dresses, each shop believes that it can earn economic profits by reducing its output rate. (c) As pointed out in the previous sentence, the individual dress shop believes that it can earn positive economic profits if it reduces its output rate to between 50 and 100 dresses per week.　　(d) No, the exit of some firms will shift the *DD'* demand curve to the right.　　(e)Average cost will be decreasing. This is always the case (at least to some extent) in monopolistically competitive firms in long-run equilibrium.

3) The theory of monopolistic competition says that firms will choose the level of their advertising expenses so as to maximize their profit. To the extent that they can estimate the effects of variation in advertising costs on their profits, firms often do try to set their advertising budgets so as to maximize their profits. But some firms find it so difficult to estimate the effects of variation in their advertising expenses on their profit levels that they feel the best they can do is to formulate their advertising budgets by taking a relatively fixed percentage of sales. If such firms could obtain more and better information concerning the effects of variation in their advertising expense on their profits, they probably would not adhere to this policy. But given their ignorance, they feel that this policy is about as likely as any other to maximize their profits.

5) For the social advantages and disadvantages of advertising, see pp. 302–4. No. Although a particular advertising campaign may increase the firm's profits, it may do so by deceiving consumers.

7) No.　　Exit will occur, because at every output average cost exceeds price (based on the *dd'* demand curve).

9) Yes. It is quite in keeping with the excess capacity theorem.

Chapter 11

1) (a) No. As shown in panel A in Question 1, the new marginal cost curve (*EE'*) intersects the marginal revenue curve at an output of OQ, which means that the profit-maximizing price is OP_1, not OP_0. Thus, if the firm maximizes profit, it will increase its price to OP_1.　　(b) Its demand curve now is P_0VD', as shown in panel B in Question 1. In contrast to the situation before Congress acted, the firm now cannot sell anything at a price exceeding OP_0. Its marginal revenue curve now is P_0VR'. Since its demand curve is horizontal for outputs less than OQ_1, so is its marginal revenue curve. Its output now is OQ_1, since this is the output where the marginal revenue curve (P_0VR') intersects the new marginal cost curve (*EE'*).

3) They should set the marginal cost at one firm equal to the marginal cost at each other firm. If firm 1 produces 4 units, firm 2 produces 3 units, and firm 3 produces 4 units, the marginal cost at each firm equals $30. Thus this seems to be the optimal distribution of output.

5) $15. No.

7) No. In duopoly, there frequently are strategies where one firm's gains are not entirely at the expense of the other firm.

9) Since $Q = 300 - P$, and the demand for the firm's output is $Q - Q_r$, it follows that the firm's demand curve is

$$Q_b = Q - Q_r = (300 - P) - 49P$$
$$= 300 - 50P,$$

or

$$P = 6 - 0.02\, Q_b.$$

Thus the firm's marginal revenue curve is $MR = 6 - 0.04\, Q_b$. And since its marginal cost curve is $2.96Q_b$

$$6 - 0.04Q_b = 2.96\, Q_b$$
$$Q_b = 2.$$

That is, your output level should be 2 million units.

Since $P = 6 - 0.02\, Q_b$, and $Q_b = 2$, it follows that $P = 6 - 0.02\,(2) = 5.96$.

That is, the price should be $5.96 per unit.

Since $Q = 300 - P$, and $P = 5.96$, it follows that $Q = 300 - 5.96 = 294.04$.

That is, the industry output is 294.04 million units.

11) Whether or not it costs a great deal to distribute milk in other parts of New York, the competition from Farmland is likely to reduce prices, thus benefiting consumers. New York consumers should be able to buy goods (including milk) produced by workers outside New York.

Chapter 12

1) (a) Point B. 1,500 hours per year.   (b) None.   (c) The relation between income and leisure is now AC. Thus, he will choose point D, and work $8,760 - 7,960 = 800$ hours per year.   (d) No. It depends on the specific provisions of the negative income tax and on a worker's preferences (as reflected in the indifference curves).

3) No. It should set the marginal product of labor divided by $5 equal to the marginal product of capital divided by $6.

5) The value of the marginal product is shown on the next page.

Number of days of labor	Output	Marginal product	Value of marginal product (dollars)
0	0		40
		8	
1	8		35
		7	
2	15		30
		6	
3	21		25
		5	
4	26		20
		4	
5	30		

Thus, if the daily wage of labor is $30, the firm should hire 2 or 3 days of labor.

7) 0.5. The ratio of capital's total income to labor's total income will decrease, since the elasticity of substitution is less than 1.

9) Where discrimination exists, nonwhite labor is not allowed to compete with white labor. There are thus two quite different labor markets, one for whites, one for nonwhites. The demand curve for nonwhite labor reflects the fact that nonwhites are not allowed to enter many of the more productive jobs. Because of the differing positions of the demand (and supply) curves, the equilibrium wage for nonwhites is lower than for whites. Without discrimination, nonwhites and whites would compete in the same labor market, and it is likely that nonwhite wages would be higher than under discrimination, the white wage would be somewhat lower, and total output would rise.

11) The wage, P_L, will equal the price of the product, P, times the marginal product of labor, which equals

$$\frac{\delta Q}{\delta L} = 0.8L^{-.2}K^2 = \frac{0.8Q}{L}.$$

Thus $P_L = \frac{0.8Q}{L} \cdot P$, which means that

$$\frac{P_L L}{PQ} = 0.8.$$

Since $P_L \cdot L$ equals the total wages paid by the firm and PQ equals its revenues, this completes the proof.

Chapter 13

1) (a) Based on the theory of monopsony, one might expect school districts that are the only buyers of teachers' services in a particular area to pay less than those that must compete with other school districts in the area.   (b) If teachers could move costlessly to school districts outside the county, a school district that was the sole buyer of teacher's services within a county would have much less monopsonistic power, and would be less able to pay lower salaries than is now the case.   (c) It will probably tend to increase teachers' salaries, because there will be more competition among school districts for teachers.   (d) One major argument is that decentralization allows educational curricula to be tailored more closely to the differences among communities in preferences.

3) 3 or 4 units of labor, because labor's marginal revenue product is $12 when between 3 and 4 units of labor are used. To see this, note that total revenue is $128 when 3 units of labor are used, and $140 when 4 units of labor are used.

5)

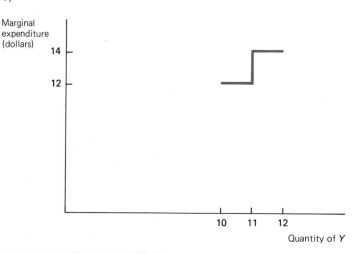

7) The supply curve for labor is shifted to the left, with the result that the price of labor will increase. There may be no effect on the demand curve for labor, unless employers are forced to hire more labor than they otherwise would have.

9) Because union contracts tend to introduce rigidity in wage structures.

Chapter 14

1) $E = 0.1E + 0.3X +$ final consumption of electric power, where E is output of electric power and X is output of coal.

3) No.   Because, if the two consumers arrive at any point off the contract curve, they can find a superior point on the contract curve, in the sense that one of them can be made better off without making the other worse off.

5) The plane's landing at that time may delay large commercial jets and impose substantial costs (in terms of delay and inconvenience) on the passengers carried by these commercial aircraft. Increases in the landing fees paid by small private aircraft could help to eliminate such divergences.

7) No.

9) 7 units of national defense.

Brief Answers to Analytical Questions in Cross-Chapter Cases

Part Two: National Dental Insurance and the Demand for Dental Care

1) No. No.

2) Yes, because the price elasticity of demand for dental services seems to be higher among high-income than lower-income people.

3) No. Yes.

4) Probably because it is more of a luxury item since it tends to be cosmetic rather than necessary to prevent pain or disease.

Part Three: Optimal Lot Size and Japanese Manufacturing Methods

1) Yes, it reduced the amount of labor time required to set up a press.

2) $5 \times \$100,000 = \$500,000$.

3) 5,000 parts. Because the cost of financing the inventory and the amount of space required to hold the inventory increase as the inventory gets bigger.

4) $5,000 \times \$2 = \$10,000$. $\$500,000 + \$10,000 = \$510,000$.

5) No. The optimal lot size equals $\sqrt{\dfrac{2(\$100,000)50,000}{\$2}} = \sqrt{5 \text{ billion}} = 70,711$.

6) This question is important because firms would like to know whether they should be concerned about relatively small departures from the optimal lot size or whether, so long as the lot size is reasonably close to the optimum, costs are not much higher than if the optimum lot size is adopted. To answer this question, a firm can use the first equation in footnote 1 on p. 217 to determine the total costs if various lot sizes (near the optimum) are used, and compare these costs with the cost with the optimal lot size.

7) How much American firms should invest depends on how much extra profit they will make per year if they reduce their setup costs to the Japanese level. Clearly, beyond some point, it will not pay them to increase further their investment to achieve this goal.

Part Four: The Deregulation of Air Transportation

1) No, because regulation created an environment in which costs were pushed up, as indicated in Figure 1 on p. 340. With deregulation, costs might have been expected to decrease, and low-cost potential entrants might have found entry profitable. Also, deregulation resulted in more price competition, which entrants might have considered to be in their interest.

2) No, because not all airlines flew all routes, and because, if perfect competition prevails, the number of firms is greater than twenty.

3) Southwest used preprinted tickets (and cash register receipts as boarding passes), and it provided no food. Its pilots flew more hours per month, and fewer flight attendants were employed per flight than on United. Also, its aircraft were operated more hours per day than United's.

4) The airlines sometimes did not resist the unions' wage demands very strongly, since they believed that the Civil Aeronautics Board would allow them to raise their prices enough to offset the wage increase.

5) No. There is a considerable number of airlines competing on this route, and no indication that average costs would be lower if only one airline flew this route.

6) No. It is in accord with the theory of contestable markets.

Part Five: Sex Discrimination and Comparable Worth

1) It is very difficult to determine how many points to give a specific occupation with regard to "mental demands" or to determine the proper weights to apply to various criteria. Moreover, these four criteria are not the only ones that could be used. Such a point system seems largely arbitrary.

2) No.

3) Yes.

4) Yes. Yes. Not if they are displaced by other typists.

5) Because firms have to keep their costs down in order to be competitive with their rivals.

6) No. Efforts should be continued to reduce barriers to entry by women into high-paid occupations like law and medicine. Changes in productivity, due to education and other factors, certainly are important.

Part Six: Effects of Quotas on Steel Imports into the United States

1) There is no entirely satisfactory way to compare the losses of the losers (such as consumers) with the gains of the gainers (such as steel producers).

2) Consumers could pay up to $178,000 to each steelworker who would lose his or her job if the quotas were abandoned, and still be better off than under the quotas. If a steelworker earns less than $178,000, he or she would be better off as well. (Of course, parties other than consumers and steelworkers are involved.)

3) No.

4) They might try to introduce more modern equipment and to keep a tight lid on wage increases.

5) Steel producers and their employees, as well as regions dependent on the steel industry, have favored these quotas.

INDEX